Discourse and Knowledge

Most of our knowledge is acquired by discourse, and our ability to produce and understand discourse is impossible without the activation of massive amounts of knowledge of the world. Both "discourse" and "knowledge" are fundamental concepts of the humanities and social sciences, but they are often treated separately. Based on a theory of natural knowledge, the book deals with the cognitive processes, social distribution, cultural differences and the linguistic and discursive "management" of knowledge in interaction and communication in epistemic communities. The first book to adopt a multidisciplinary approach to studying the relationship between the two concepts, *Discourse and Knowledge* introduces the new field of epistemic discourse analysis. Using a wide range of examples to illustrate the theory, it is essential reading for both students and academics interested in epistemology, linguistics, discourse analysis, cognitive and social psychology, and the social sciences.

TEUN A. VAN DIJK was professor at the University of Amsterdam until 2004 and then at the Universitat Pompeu Fabra, Barcelona, until his retirement in 2014. For details of his previous publications, visit his website www.discourses.org.

Discourse and Knowledge

A Sociocognitive Approach

Teun A. van Dijk

CAMBRIDGE
UNIVERSITY PRESS

CAMBRIDGE
UNIVERSITY PRESS

University Printing House, Cambridge CB2 8BS, United Kingdom

Cambridge University Press is part of the University of Cambridge.

It furthers the University's mission by disseminating knowledge in the pursuit of education, learning and research at the highest international levels of excellence.

www.cambridge.org
Information on this title: www.cambridge.org/9781107416550

© Teun A. van Dijk 2014

First published 2014

Printed in the United Kingdom by Clays, St Ives plc

A catalogue record for this publication is available from the British Library

Library of Congress Cataloguing in Publication data
Dijk, Teun A. van, 1943–
Discourse and knowledge : a sociocognitive approach / Teun A. van Dijk.
    pages   cm
Includes bibliographical references and index.
ISBN 978-1-107-07124-7 (hardback) – ISBN 978-1-107-41655-0 (paperback)
1. Knowledge, Sociology of.   2. Discourse analysis.   I. Title.
HM651.D55 2014
306.4′2–dc23
2014004089

ISBN 978-1-107-07124-7 Hardback
ISBN 978-1-107-41655-0 Paperback

Contents

List of figures   *page* vi
List of tables   vii
Acknowledgment   viii

1   Introduction   1

2   Elements of a theory of natural knowledge   14

3   Discourse, knowledge and cognition   45

4   Discourse, knowledge and social cognition   90

5   Discourse, knowledge and society   139

6   Discourse, knowledge and culture   167

7   Language, discourse and knowledge   222

8   Conclusions   310

References   329
Index   395

Figures

4.1 System of social beliefs *page* 96
4.2 System of social beliefs, and the integrated position of
   social representations 105
7.1 Schema of the structure of the information sources controlling
   knowledge management in the current communicative event 267

Tables

7.1 Schema of the knowledge–discourse interface in past and
    current research   *page* 223
7.2 Types of knowledge, representation and their social basis   225
7.3 Epistemic structures in discourse semantics   304

Acknowledgment

Part of the research for this book has been made possible by a grant from the Spanish Ministry of Economy and Competitiveness (MINECO) for project No. FFI2008-00070 *Epistemic Strategies in Discourse, Interaction and Communication.*

1 Introduction

1.1 Aims

Just after Christmas in 2011, the British newspaper the *Daily Telegraph* published the following routine news article on asylum seekers:

01 **Taxpayer funding £100,000 a day for failed asylum seekers**
02 **The taxpayer is spending more than £100,000 a day to house**
03 **failed asylum seekers who have no right to be in the country.**
04 By Tom Whitehead, Home Affairs Editor
05 8:00AM GMT 26 Dec 2011
06 The Home Office spent almost £40 million last year supporting
07 so-called "hard cases" – asylum seekers who have had their claims
08 rejected but cannot leave for one reason or another.
09 It is usually because of unsafe conditions in their home country, a
10 medical condition or they have launched a judicial review on a legal
11 point in their case.
12 But in the meantime the taxpayer must fund their accommodation
13 and living allowances.
14 And the cost of the asylum system is growing after separate figures
15 showed the number of asylum seekers who are still awaiting a deci-
16 sion and need accommodation increased in 2011.
17 Sir Andrew Green, chairman of Migration Watch UK, said: "This is
18 a measure of the lengths to which people will go to stay in Britain.
19 "But in the end, if their cases fail they must leave or the credibility
20 of the whole system is completely undermined."
21 Under what is known as Section 4 support, asylum seekers who
22 have had their claim for shelter rejected but cannot currently return
23 home are given accommodation and living support. In the 12 months
24 up to September 2011, a total of 4,430 people were awarded such
25 support – the equivalent of 12 a day.
26 Some of those will have since left the country but others may be
27 here indefinitely if their particular circumstances do not change.

28   Over the period, the Home Office spent £38.2 million on Section 4
29   support or £104,658 a day.
30   To be eligible for such support, a failed asylum seeker must be des-
31   titute and satisfy one of the following requirements.
32   They [are] taking all reasonable steps to leave the UK, cannot leave
33   because of a physical impediment to travel or for some other medical
34   reason, cannot leave the UK because, in the Secretary of State's opin-
35   ion, no viable route of return is currently available or have applied for
36   a judicial review of their asylum application and been given permis-
37   sion to proceed with it.
38   As well as accommodation, recipients are given a payment card,
39   worth £35.39 per person a week, which is used to buy food and essen-
40   tial toiletries.
41   However, they cannot use the payment card to obtain cash from a
42   cash point or car fuel.
43   It emerged in May that the public are paying more than £1 million
44   a month to "bribe" illegal immigrants and failed asylum seekers to
45   go home.
46   Up to £74 million has been spent in the past five years on a volun-
47   tary return scheme for those who have no right to remain in the UK.
48   The programme offers packages worth up to £2,000 of "in kind" sup-
49   port, such as help setting up home or a business, in return for them not
50   fighting removal.
51   Destitute asylum seekers whose cases are still being considered
52   and who are not detained are also given support.
53   Some 2,406 applicants were given such support in the first nine
54   months of 2011 suggesting the annual total will be higher than the
55   2,551 awarded it throughout the whole of 2010.

Copyright Telegraph Media Group Limited 2011

For readers to understand this news report, they need to have and activate a vast amount of 'knowledge of the world.' Among many other things, they need to know what asylum seekers and taxpayers are, what Home Office is referred to by the definite expression *the Home Office* (line 6) and which country by the expression *the country* (line 3), although the country has not been mentioned before in the article. The reader should also know that whereas there is only one Home Office and one country referred to, the definite expression *the tax-payer*, the first word in both the main headline and the sub-headline, is not referring to one taxpayer, but to all of them. And once they have understood what or who such expressions refer to, readers must also be able to understand that asylum seekers are people who can make claims, may be sent back to their country, and, especially in this article, that they allegedly cost a lot of money to 'the taxpayer.' More specifically, apart from their general or generic knowledge of the world, readers are also assumed by the journalist to know about more concrete situations, such as the fact that there are asylum seekers in the UK in the first place.

Besides all this presupposed *old* knowledge, the *news* report is also about *new* knowledge, that is, knowledge the journalist assumes the readers did not yet have. It is precisely one of the functions of news reports to provide information so that readers can *update* their knowledge about current events in the world in general and their own country in particular. This new(s) knowledge is summarized in the complex headline, namely that the (British) taxpayers pay £100,000 a day for failed asylum seekers, and then further detailed in the rest of the article.

This book is about these and many other ways language users manage knowledge in text and talk. It deals with the kind of general, sociocultural knowledge journalists or readers, among many other language users, must have in order to be able to write or read and understand a news report, to engage in a conversation, to teach a class or to participate in professional meetings as well as in many other genres of discourse.

Before we are even able to study such specific uses of knowledge in the production or reception of news articles, conversations or textbooks, we shall start in the next chapter with the more fundamental issue of the very definition of knowledge as some kind of belief, and how it can be distinguished from other beliefs. Thus, whereas some information in the *Telegraph* article may be about facts as communicated by reliable sources, other information may be more speculative, for instance that asylum seekers may stay indefinitely in the country. In that case, we usually call such beliefs *opinions* and not *knowledge*.

On the other hand, beginning with the headline, the news report is replete with numbers, which seem to provide objective information from reliable official sources that may increase the credibility of the journalist and the newspaper. Notions such as objectivity, reliability, credibility are all related to knowledge, knowledge sources and people who know, and hence also need further analysis.

Similarly, we may want to inquire *why* specific information is spread (or not) in public discourse and why precisely the *negative* information that asylum seekers cost the taxpayer a lot of money is focused on in the article. Indeed, does the newspaper always mention for any public expenditure that it is a heavy burden for the taxpayers? Also, there are many other relevant facts about asylum seekers that are *not* mentioned or detailed in the article, such as daily discrimination and other hardships they suffer in 'the country.' At least for some readers, such daily repeated negative beliefs, especially about ethnically different Others, may be called stereotypes, prejudices and ideologies. Thus, we need to address the classical question of the differences between knowledge and these other forms of socially shared beliefs.

The capacity to spread negative information about specific outgroups among hundreds of thousands of readers is a very important power resource of the mass media, so that we also need to pay attention to the relation between knowledge and power: who has more, and who has less knowledge, defined as a symbolic resource, and what types of knowledge are being acquired, sold or otherwise provided by the mass media, elite groups and other powerful groups and organizations (Van Dijk, 2008b, 2011a).

We have mentioned above that for readers to be able to understand this news article, they need to activate and apply vast amounts of knowledge of the world. Such understanding is usually studied in terms of mental representations and processes of language users involved as participants in communicative situations. Within the framework of the cognitive psychology of discourse, we therefore need to review what is known today about the nature and organization of knowledge in memory and how it is acquired, stored, activated and applied during discourse processing.

A crucial aspect of this use of knowledge in discourse is the establishment of local and global coherence, one of the fundamental properties of all text and talk. More generally, if speakers and writers assume that recipients share general sociocultural knowledge with them, they need not express such knowledge in discourse in the first place, and may assume that the recipients will make the necessary inferences from such knowledge, for instance to establish coherence. In this sense, discourses are like icebergs of which usually only the new information is 'visible' and explicitly expressed, but the vast amounts of known or inferable information remains largely 'invisible' or implicit.

If news reports presuppose vast amounts of knowledge among the readers, a more social psychological approach would ask how such knowledge is spread and acquired, and what the role of newspapers is in processes we may call 'knowledge distribution,' 'social information processing,' or simply 'public communication.'

The sociology of knowledge and discourse may then focus on such notions as epistemic communities in order to make explicit how various kinds of knowledge are shared by different groups in society. Similarly, apart from studying the role of the mass media in society, such a sociology of knowledge may also examine what other epistemic organizations or institutions, such as schools, universities, laboratories or academies are involved in the (re)production, regulation and legitimation of socially shared knowledge. For instance, in the article on asylum seekers, the journalist refers to the ministry as a reliable source of information, and readers of the *Telegraph* may in turn cite the newspaper as a reliable source of their knowledge and opinions about asylum seekers.

In the framework of journalism and media studies one might ask whether the information as brought by the *Telegraph* is being conveyed in the same way by other newspapers in the UK. Thus, it is likely that the 'same' events may give rise to different, more or less *biased* or *truthful versions* of 'reality.'

More broadly ethnographic or anthropological research may be needed to investigate how knowledge is defined, acquired and communicated in other cultures. Indeed, what in one period or culture is called, used or presupposed as knowledge, may be seen as mere opinion, prejudice or superstition in another time or culture. As is the case for different newspapers in the same country – and in the same culture – we see that also across cultures and history knowledge may be *relative*, that is, relative to the members and the criteria of different epistemic communities.

Finally, we observed that 'old' or 'known' knowledge is expressed in the news report by definite expressions, marked by the definite article *the*, which, however, also may be used generically, e.g., when referring to all taxpayers.

Moreover, discourse may mark as 'evidentials' *how* the journalist got his information, in this case by quoting several people, and whether or not the information is quite certain or less certain, as is the case for the use of the modal verb *may* in line 26. A more linguistic approach to knowledge thus examines the many ways old and new knowledge or *Common Ground* is implied, presupposed, signaled, and expressed in intonation (such as the special stress on new, focused information), in syntax (such as known information often expressed first in the sentence), in definite articles and pronouns (expressing known information), as evidentials (referring to knowledge sources), as well as many aspects of semantics, such as levels, degrees, precision and other aspects of descriptions. If people acquire knowledge largely by text or talk, such a more linguistic approach needs to detail the grammatical aspects of such communication. Other approaches in the field of discourse studies may then examine the many kinds of structure involved in the communication of knowledge by news articles, textbooks, argumentation or storytelling, among other formats and genres.

These and many other aspects of the study of knowledge and its relation to discourse define the object of investigation of a multidisciplinary field we may call **discourse epistemics**, as we also speak of discourse semantics or discourse pragmatics. This field of discourse epistemics is especially interesting on the one hand because most of human knowledge is acquired and shaped by discourse, and on the other hand because language use, in general, and the production and understanding of discourse, in particular, are impossible without the activation of massive amounts of knowledge of the world. These alone are excellent reasons to examine the many complex relations between discourse and knowledge.

There are many thousands of books on knowledge, in many disciplines, and many hundreds of books on discourse, but despite the many interesting relationships between the two notions, there is no single monograph that systematically studies these relationships. This book is intended to do just that.

1.2   The multidisciplinary study of knowledge

Especially for students of language and discourse, we may need to recall that knowledge is one of the fundamental objects of study in the humanities and social sciences. The respective chapters of this book will therefore briefly review how knowledge is studied in various disciplines, but will do so especially from a discourse analytical perspective. After this brief introduction, relevant references will then be provided in these next chapters.

Epistemology. Since Antiquity, epistemology has debated the fundamental nature of knowledge, and how it may be distinguished from mere belief or opinion. Traditionally, knowledge was defined as *justified true beliefs*, and much of the philosophy of knowledge has thus been concerned with making explicit what criteria, standards or methods are being used to justify beliefs as knowledge. In the news report on asylum seekers, the journalist does this by mentioning reliable, official sources, and citing 'objective' numbers.

In this book, instead of focusing on abstract philosophical notions such as absolute 'truth,' we shall rather focus on the more pragmatic conditions and empirical criteria being used in different periods, social situations and cultures in the justification, acquisition, presupposition, expression, communication and circulation of beliefs as knowledge. In that sense, knowledge is defined *relative* to knowers and communities of knowers who deal with knowledge 'for all practical purposes': *epistemic communities*. In the same way as linguists speak of 'natural languages' – e.g., in order to distinguish them from formal or machine languages – we shall thus talk about *natural knowledge* as the object of discourse epistemics and as shared by language users as members of epistemic communities.

Although much if not most knowledge is acquired by interpersonal and public text and talk, even the more empirical (cognitive, social, cultural) approaches in epistemology have largely ignored the role of language and discourse in the acquisition, diffusion and justification of knowledge. One major motivation of this book is to provide such a multidisciplinary discourse analytical approach to knowledge.

Psychology. On the other hand, psychology, including the study of Artificial Intelligence (AI), has taken a very active and fruitful interest in the mental representations and processes involved in the activation and use of knowledge in the (simulation of the) production and reception of discourse. If readers of the

Telegraph are assumed to know what asylum seekers are, a cognitive approach to knowledge would need to make explicit how such knowledge is acquired, stored and organized, and where in memory, the mind or the brain this happens. For instance, given the crucial role of the perception of, and the relations with, other groups for our daily interaction and discourse as group members, and the fact that we are members of many social groups, it is plausible that we have developed a special group schema that features categories representing the main social characteristics of groups. When comprehending a news article on asylum seekers, readers activate such a schema in order to construe their own interpretation of the article, that is, the subjective mental representation of the current events the article is about.

In other words, generic knowledge thus serves primarily to construe what are called *mental models*, that is, subjective event representations involved in the production and comprehension of discourse such as news reports or stories, and more generally to engage in everyday social interaction. We thus distinguish between generic, socially shared knowledge, on the one hand, and personal knowledge about specific events, on the other – although there may also be socially shared knowledge about specific events (such as 9/11) and personal generic knowledge (about our personal routines or people we know). Thus, the news report in the *Telegraph* is an expression of the subjective mental model of the recent events regarding asylum seekers as it is construed and expressed by the journalist, and the readers each construe their own personal interpretation, their own mental model, of the events as referred to by the news report.

As yet, little is known about the **neuropsychological** properties of knowledge as it is stored in the brain, but we shall see that some recent proposals emphasize the multimodal nature of knowledge as it is associated with visual, auditory, sensorimotor or emotional regions and processing in the brain. Although it may be asked whether such a multimodal characterization is also relevant for abstract, conceptual knowledge (indeed, what brain regions would be involved in our knowledge of taxpayers or immigration, in that case?), it is likely that such multimodality defines the concrete personal experiences as they are represented in mental models. Readers may have seen asylum seekers, if only on TV, and some may have various emotions when reading the article – e.g., anger at paying taxes to finance their stay in the country. This also suggests that mental models not only represent subjective knowledge of specific events, but that such knowledge may be related to current personal opinions or emotions, based on attitudes or prejudices about asylum seekers shared by specific groups, which in turn may be grounded in racist (or anti-racist) ideologies.

Social Psychology. Although one would expect differently, given their domain of study relating individuals and society, we shall see that most of social psychology has paid scant attention to knowledge. Rather it has focused on attitudes, public opinion and persuasion, and hardly on the ways knowledge is communicated and shared among members of epistemic communities. Yet, this is no doubt the discipline that should deal with the relations between different kinds of social cognition, such as the relations between knowledge, attitudes, ideologies, norms and values and how they influence the interaction and hence the discourse among people as group members. Thus, we already suggested that, depending on their own attitudes and ideologies, at least some readers of the article in the *Telegraph* may associate the selective negative information about asylum seekers as a typical example of the reproduction of stereotypes and prejudices about immigrants and not as unbiased communication of objective knowledge.

Sociology. The sociology of knowledge is interested, among many other things, in the way the knowledge of the readers of the *Telegraph* is specific to a social group, class or community, an *epistemic community* that may be different from that of the readers of a tabloid newspaper, or readers in another country. Similarly, a sociological account of knowledge deals with the prestige of the press as an institution and as a reliable source of information and similar social conditions for the justification of knowledge. The discursive reproduction of knowledge, thus involves many social groups and 'epistemic professions' (teachers, professors, journalists, etc.) and social institutions. The very *power* of these groups and institutions also tells us something about the power of their knowledge and how they control the 'official' knowledge of epistemic communities and societies.

Whereas the study of the production of knowledge by groups, organizations and institutions such as mass media, schools, universities and laboratories is the classical domain of a macrosociological approach, the uses of *knowledge in conversation* represent an increasingly important topic of the study of the microlevel of society. Thus, speakers may have more or less access, authority or superiority, as well as other epistemic relations to the facts and among each other, and thus may be more or less entitled to express or convey knowledge to recipients in talk. Thus, an eyewitness of a car accident generally has more epistemic rights to tell a story about that than other participants who did not have this direct access to the events.

Anthropology. Anthropology has often defined culture in terms of the shared knowledge of its members, and hence specifically examines the way knowledge – and knowledge criteria – may differ from one country or society to the next. In this sense, the notion of epistemic community is both a social and a cultural notion we need to deal with in this study. Thus, not only social psychologists but also anthropologists may be interested in studying the cultural assumptions of journalists about people from other countries and cultures, as they no doubt also influence the article in the *Telegraph*. More generally and critically, they may ask what kinds of knowledge and knowledge criteria dominate in the world, and why it is that speakers of ethnic minorities or developing countries are often found by 'our' journalists to be less reliable sources of information than professional, white, Western, middle-class male sources in the north-west of the world.

Communication Studies. The study of knowledge as we need and acquire it by reading the *Daily Telegraph* more specifically is within the scope of the study of communication studies, traditionally focusing on how information is spread in society by the mass media, on the role of the press and of journalists in this process and on the actual effects of news reporting on the (knowledge of the) readers. Yet, also in this discipline, the role of knowledge in the processing of media messages, as well as the role of the media in the (re)production of knowledge in society, has received relatively little attention. Our more general study of the relations between discourse and knowledge is also intended as contribution to the study of communication, as is also emphasized by our choice of a news article as the example in this chapter and as the standard way many people acquire new knowledge about the world.

Organization Studies. There has been a new and vast interest in knowledge in the field of organization studies since the 1990s, often in terms of *knowledge management* as a competitive strategy, to enhance innovation and organizational learning and in general to improve the organization. Unfortunately, there is no space in this monograph to review and integrate the massive current literature on this topic (but see Chapter 5 for some references).

Linguistics, Semiotics, Discourse Studies. And finally, as already indicated above, linguistics, semiotics and discourse studies focus on the structures and strategies of multimodal text and talk and the ways knowledge is presupposed, expressed, formulated, organized and managed in language use, communication and interaction. This may happen at the level of the sentence, such as the well-known distribution between old and new information in sentence topics and focus, how knowledge sources are indexed by evidentials or how the quality of knowledge is expressed by modalities. But it is also relevant at the level of whole discourses, still ignored by most formal linguistics, such as the way old and new knowledge is managed in, for instance, conversations, news reports, textbooks, interrogations and parliamentary debates, among hundreds of discourse genres and communicative events and practices.

Thus, as we have seen above, **conversation analysis** has more recently begun to explore which speakers may express what kind of knowledge to what kind of recipients, and how entitlements, responsibility, imbalances and norms influence such talk. For instance, in conversations, mothers are supposed to have more knowledge of their own children than strangers, and hence are *entitled* to tell stories about them, and divulge details that other interlocutors cannot or should not express. In many forms of conversation, especially also of professionals, knowledge and its expression may thus also need to be *negotiated* among participants.

The study of discourse has become increasingly *multimodal*. Discourse is not only oral and verbal, but as written text also features relevant variations of typography (as in the bold and broad headline of the article on asylum seekers), images (in the article on asylum seekers the picture of an agent of the border police), music and other sounds, as well as many types of 'embodied' signs, such as gestures, facework, body position in spoken interaction, as studied in the **semiotics** of discourse. This means that knowledge may be acquired, presupposed and expressed also in these many multimodal forms, as they may directly influence the formation of the multimodal mental models language users construe when they understand text and talk.

1.3   The study of discourse

In the same way we summarized above various approaches to the study of knowledge for students of discourse, we also briefly need to say something on discourse studies for students of knowledge, although contemporary discourse studies are widely practiced and known in most of the humanities and social sciences.

It is important to stress at the outset that *discourse analysis* is not a method but a cross-discipline in which a large variety of qualitative and quantitative methods are being used – besides the usual methods of grammatical or linguistic analysis. Hence, we prefer the term *Discourse Studies* for this cross-discipline that increasingly merged with concurrent and initially largely independent other studies of text and talk in the 1960s and 1970s. We may summarize these different approaches as follows:

- After the earlier studies of folklore, myths and storytelling, the **ethnography of speaking** focused more generally on culturally situated and variable communicative events in different societies.
- **Text and discourse grammars** emphasized that both linguistic competence as well as actual language use is not limited to (knowledge of) isolated sentence structures, but has a much broader, textual or discursive scope, as is the case for the account of semantic coherence, narrative and argumentative structures, as well as many other 'global' structures of different **genres** of text and talk.
- Rejecting the more abstract structural approach of macrosociology, **ethnomethodology** and, more generally, **microsociology** focused on interaction as the basis of the social order, more specifically studying the details of informal and institutional conversation. Thus, **Conversation Analysis** became a

widely influential, and partly independent, approach in the general field of discourse studies.

- Unlike psycholinguistics, more closely related to dominant sentence linguistics, **cognitive and educational psychology** soon broadened its scope from the mental processing of words and sentences to the experimental study of text production and comprehension. It thus was able to explain for the first time how language users (despite their limited working memory) are able to strategically produce, understand and store and recall complex discourse, establish local and global coherence and activate and apply knowledge in the construction of mental models that represent the subjective interpretation of discourse.

After these initial developments, mostly between 1964 and 1974, Discourse Studies later spread to or merged with studies of text and talk in sociolinguistics, pragmatics, discursive psychology and communication studies. Of the social sciences, only political science has been quite impervious to this general discursive turn.

The methods of Discourse Studies range from the earlier ethnographic, grammatical and experimental studies of the structures and processing of text and talk, to contemporary approaches as multimodal semiotic studies, computer simulation and the automatic analysis of vast text corpora, as well as participant observation, or any other method of the social sciences. *Critical Discourse Studies* more specifically focuses on the role of discourse in the social reproduction of power abuse, for instance in sexist or racist discourse.

Despite various attempts towards a broad, multidisciplinary integration, for instance in my own earlier work on racism, ideology and context, there remains a regrettable gap in discourse studies between asocial cognitive (often experimental) approaches on the one hand, and (often anticognitivist) social approaches, especially in conversation and interaction studies, on the other hand.

Relevant for this book is the fact that despite the fundamental role of knowledge in discourse, discourse studies outside of cognitive psychology have paid very little attention to the role of knowledge at all levels of text and talk, especially beyond the information structure of sentences. This book is a first integrated attempt to remedy this lack of discourse epistemics in Discourse Studies.

1.4   The study of discourse and knowledge

In the brief summary of the study of knowledge in the humanities and the social sciences we already found that, with the exception of cognitive psychology, research on the relations between knowledge and discourse is as yet quite limited. Philosophy, sociology and anthropology have extensively paid attention to knowledge, but have generally ignored the specific role of discourse in the study of the way knowledge is acquired, expressed or justified. Cognitive psychology has extensively shown, mostly through laboratory experiments, that knowledge plays a fundamental role in discourse production and comprehension, but has paid scant attention to the socially shared nature of knowledge. In social psychology there has been interest in lay epistemics and social representations, but the dominant paradigms have been more interested in opinions, attitudes or prejudice rather than in epistemic communities or knowledge-based interaction of group members. In linguistics the study of knowledge is limited to a few properties of sentences, such as the dynamics of information structure (topic–focus articulation), evidentials, modalities and presupposition, while often disregarding the fundamental role of knowledge in the semantics of discourse, for instance in the study of coherence, storytelling, argumentation, descriptions, explanations, definitions and the study of many genres.

We see that we need a general, multidisciplinary framework in the humanities and the social sciences that allows an integrated study of the ways knowledge is acquired, presupposed, expressed, communicated and justified in various genres of talk and text, and in the communicative situations of epistemic communities, societies and cultures. This book will attempt to elaborate such a framework by reviewing and discussing the literature on knowledge in epistemology, psychology, sociology and anthropology, and by focusing especially on the role of discourse in various ways knowledge is 'managed' by language users and epistemic communities.

It goes without saying that a single monograph cannot possibly review the thousands of studies on knowledge in the humanities and social sciences. For each discipline, thus, we shall largely limit our review to research that is specifically relevant for the construction of a multidisciplinary framework that can account for the fundamental properties of the knowledge–discourse interface.

1.5   The triangulation of discourse, cognition and society

The broader theoretical framework of this multidisciplinary study, as well as of my earlier work on racism, ideology and context, consists in a triangulation of discourse, cognition and society. Discourse is thus defined as a form of social interaction in society and at the same time as the expression and reproduction of social cognition. Local and global social structures condition discourse but they do so through the cognitive mediation of the socially shared knowledge, ideologies and personal mental models of social members as they subjectively define communicative events as context models.

We are thus able to account both for the social, political and cultural aspects of discourse and for the subjective ways individual social actors produce and reproduce social representations as well as social structure. As we have done before for the study of ideology, this integration of a structural and an inter-actional approach to knowledge and discourse may be seen as one of the ways the notorious macro–micro gap can be bridged in the social sciences.

2   Elements of a theory of natural knowledge

2.1   Introduction

Eleven years ago, on March 8, 2003, Tony Blair, then Prime Minister of Great Britain, introduced and then defended a motion in the House of Commons urging the Members of Parliament to, among other things,

> (1) support(s) the decision of Her Majesty's Government that the United Kingdom should use all means necessary to ensure the disarmament of Iraq's weapons of mass destruction; offers wholehearted support to the men and women of Her Majesty's Armed Forces now on duty in the Middle East.

After a debate of many hours, with the support of the Conservative Opposition, but against the position of many Labour and Liberal Members of Parliament (MPs), and defying huge public protests, British parliament voted to go to war against Iraq – as did the conservative governments in the USA and Spain, led by George W. Bush and José María Aznar, respectively. Defending his motion, and according to the official record in Hansard, Blair argued:

> (2) It is that, with history, we know what happened. We can look back and say, "There's the time; that was the moment; that's when we should have acted."

After a decade, we now know the consequences of that parliamentary decision and the ensuing war. Using his very words, we now also know "with history" that what Tony Blair in his motion presupposed to be true, namely that Iraq had weapons of mass destruction (WMDs) – a main reason to go to war, as the motion suggests – turned out to be false. Does this mean that Tony Blair lied in his motion? Or was he simply mistaken and ill-informed by the security services of the UK and the USA?

In his speech, Blair often claims that he knows something that is relevant for his motion and his policy. Here is a long passage that rhetorically emphasizes what he claims to know:

> (3) Let me tell the House what I know. I know that there are some countries, or groups within countries, that are proliferating and trading in weapons of

mass destruction – especially nuclear weapons technology. I know that there are companies, individuals, and some former scientists on nuclear weapons programmes, who are selling their equipment or expertise. I know that there are several countries – mostly dictatorships with highly repressive regimes – that are desperately trying to acquire chemical weapons, biological weapons or, in particular, nuclear weapons capability. Some of those countries are now a short time away from having a serviceable nuclear weapon. This activity is not diminishing. It is increasing.

We all know that there are terrorist groups now operating in most major countries. Just in the past two years, around twenty different nations have suffered serious terrorist outrages. Thousands of people – quite apart from 11 September – have died in them. The purpose of that terrorism is not just in the violent act; it is in producing terror. It sets out to inflame, to divide, and to produce consequences of a calamitous nature. Round the world, it now poisons the chances of political progress – in the Middle East, in Kashmir, in Chechnya and in Africa. The removal of the Taliban – yes – dealt it a blow. But it has not gone away.

We see that in parliamentary debates and many other genres of political discourse, as well as in everyday conversations, language users routinely presuppose many things to be the case, and sometimes explicitly claim to *know* these to be the case, as did Tony Blair in his speech. As critical analysts, and "with history," we now also know that Tony Blair did not really *know* that there were WMDs in Iraq, but at most strongly *believed* that they were there, and that what he implied and purported to be knowledge was hardly justified by irrefutable evidence.

As a preparation for the next chapters, this chapter offers a theoretical discussion of these fundamental concepts of knowledge and belief as they also appear in discourse and decision making. When do language users correctly presuppose or explicitly claim that they *know* something, and not merely *believe* something to be the case?

This is not the place to present a detailed analysis of Tony Blair's speech and the Iraq debate in the UK parliament, but we shall occasionally use this example in this chapter to illustrate some of our theoretical notions. For detail on the Iraq debate, see my books on context, Van Dijk (2008a, 2009a); for knowledge in parliamentary debates, see Van Dijk (2003, 2004c, 2006a, 2012).

2.1.1   *Natural, relative and contextual knowledge*

Although this chapter is informed by insights in contemporary epistemology, the philosophy of mind and the philosophy of language, a single chapter cannot do justice to the complexity of the ideas currently being discussed in the many directions of research in these fields of philosophy. Our general conception will be in line with developments in epistemology and the philosophy of mind towards a more 'natural' theory of knowledge, for instance by integrating notions from cognitive psychology (e.g., as recommended by Quine, 1969; see also Brown and Gerken, 2012; Goldman, 1986, 1993; Kornblith, 1994, 2002), on the one hand, and from the social sciences, on the other (see, e.g., Fuller, 2002; Goldman, 1999; Haddock *et al.*, 2010; Jovchelovitch, 2007; Schmitt, 1994; Stehr and Meja, 2005). We shall come back to this interface of discourse, knowledge, cognition, society and culture in the next chapters.

As is the case for the history of linguistics, which developed from normative grammar to an empirical study of natural language, and then since the 1960s from more formal sentence grammars to a study of real, situated language use, discourse and interaction, we are interested in an analysis of *natural knowledge*, that is, knowledge as it is being used by *real people in real situations and in real epistemic communities*, as we have seen in the speech of Tony Blair. This also means that instead of a more abstract notion of knowledge defined in terms of (absolutely) 'true' beliefs, the study of natural knowledge tends to be more *relativistic* and *contextual* (see, e.g., DeRose, 2009; García-Carpintero and Kölbel, 2008; Preyer and Peter, 2005; see also Stalnaker, 1999, 2008).

Indeed, Blair and many others would claim that their decision to go to war was based on the kind of relative or contextual knowledge on WMDs and terrorists as expressed in example (3) above – knowledge contested by others and later revealed to be mere belief.

2.1.2   A discourse analytical perspective

As is the case in the other chapters of this book, this chapter deals with knowledge *from the perspective of the study of discourse*. This is also why we started this book, as well as this chapter, on epistemology, with concrete discourses as examples of the sociopolitical uses and manifestations of knowledge and belief. This means, first of all, that we focus on properties of knowledge that are relevant for a multidisciplinary theory of discourse. Secondly, we repeatedly emphasize also that epistemology needs prominently to account for knowledge and beliefs as they are acquired, expressed and reproduced by naturally occurring text and talk, and not (only) as expressed in short, invented, sentences without co-text and context. Indeed, as we shall see, beyond observation and experience, discourse is the major source of human knowledge as well as one of its major verification criteria.

Our approach to knowledge is not only contextual but also co-textual and interactional, as is the case for the other sciences of language and discourse today (for recent introductions and handbooks, see, e.g., Gee and Handford,

2012; Schiffrin *et al.*, 2013; Van Dijk, 2007, 2011b). In fact, a discourse ana-lytical approach to epistemology should even be broader, namely also inter-textual and semiotic (see Kockelman, 2006; Van Leeuwen, 2005). Knowledge expressed in text and talk also depends on other, related discourses – as Tony Blair's speech and his knowledge claims are based on reports from the secret services. Knowledge is not only presupposed and expressed in conversation or printed text, but also in a variety of multimodal discourses, as we typically know them from the Internet as well as face-to-face conversation, including images, sounds, gestures and so on.

Indeed, to prove the existence of WMDs in Iraq, the then US Secretary of State, Colin Powell, in his speech for the Security Council, a month earlier, on February 5, 2003, used slides, aerial photographs and other visual means (showing a vial of anthrax) to sustain the purported truth of his own public speech, which also significantly emphasized purported knowledge by using the explicit formula "we know," as did Tony Blair:

> (4) We have firsthand descriptions of biological weapons factories on wheels and on rails. We know what the fermenters look like. We know what the tanks, pumps, compressors and other parts look like.

Again, also this 'knowledge' about WMD on trailers later turned out to be misguided at best, if not fabricated in order to strengthen the case for a war against Iraq.

Crucial for a discourse approach to knowledge, also in epistemology, is to study the triangular relations between knowledge, its expression or pre-supposition in discourse, and how both are in turn related to the world. For instance, both discourse and knowledge are often defined in *representational* or *intentional* terms (Searle, 1983). They both *represent* events or situations in the world they are *about*, where discourse is *indirectly intentional* because the mental representations involved in its production and comprehension are intentional. Thus, Blair's beliefs and his speech are both *about* Iraq, Saddam Hussein and the WMDs, but his speech presupposes that he had his beliefs first, and only then expressed them in his speech.

As already mentioned above, within our broader triangular (discourse–cognition–society) approach to discourse and knowledge, in this chapter *cog-nition* also plays a central and mediating role. And as we shall see in more detail in the next chapter, in epistemology, too, natural knowledge should be accounted for in terms of specific types of *mental representations* (such as epi-sodic models) of members of epistemic communities engaged in discourse or other forms of situated interaction. Indeed, typical of a sociocognitive theory is a plea for the presently inadequate or missing integration of cognitive and interactional approaches to discourse (see, e.g., the special issue of *Discourse Studies* dedicated to this debate: Van Dijk, 2006b).

Against this more general background, we summarize some elements of a simple theory of knowledge as it will be used to explore the relations between discourse and knowledge in the rest of this book. We are of course indebted to theories of knowledge as they have been developed in epistemology – also in the sense of how *not* to study knowledge in a more naturalist paradigm. However, a full-scale review of even the most prominent contemporary approaches to knowledge is far beyond the scope of this book. This means that we shall choose some basic notions without entering into the many contemporary debates about such concepts (see, among many other books, e.g., Audi, 2010; Bernecker and Dretske, 2000; Greco and Sosa, 1999; Lehrer, 1990; Steup and Sosa, 2005).

2.1.3   *Propositional vs. operational knowledge*

To further reduce the scope of this chapter, we shall deal only with what has been called *declarative knowledge* (knowledge-*that*), and not with *operational knowledge* or *ability* (knowledge-*how-to*, such as 'knowing how to' ride a bike) (Ryle, 1949: Ch. 2). Note, though, that there are types of knowledge that seem to have both aspects, such as knowing how to give a speech in parliament, as Blair did, for instance, because such ability-knowledge has been largely taught, communicated or acquired by discourse. Also, we are aware that ignoring practical knowledge in favor of declarative knowledge may imply a gender bias if much women's knowledge is of a more practical nature (Tanesini, 1999).

This chapter and this book will also ignore knowledge as acquaintance or identification (knowledge-*who-or-what*, knowledge *of*), such as my knowing a person or a city, even when such knowledge may be associated with (or even be a summary of) a large amount of 'propositional' knowledge. Indeed, in languages such as French and Spanish, such knowledge is described by another verb (*connaître, conocer* vs. *savoir, saber*, respectively, as is also the case for German *kennen* vs. *wissen*). The same is true for several other uses of knowledge (e.g., knowing one's place) that cannot be reduced to the kind of declarative or representational knowledge we intend to focus on in this book.

2.2   Basic conditions and functions of knowledge

In order to better understand fundamental notions such as knowledge and belief, it makes sense to inquire into their *practical functions* in the everyday lives of human beings. Such fundamental questions have (partial) answers not only in an empirical inquiry into the uses of knowledge in human information processing and in contemporary society, but also in the study of the evolution of humans, their minds and their adaptation to their natural and social environments (Hahlweg and Hooker, 1989; Munz, 1993; Popper, 1972; Ruse, 1986).

Crucial for the survival and reproduction of an organism and a species is their adequate *adaptation* to their specific environment. Such adaptation not only takes place, rather slowly, in the evolution of the species, but also in the daily *interaction* with elements in the environment in the various situations in which the organism is involved during its lifetime. For human beings this means that they need to be able to *adequately* interact with their *natural environment*, as well as with other humans in their *social environment*. Thus, Tony Blair in his speech emphasizes that his purported knowledge about the WMDs in Iraq, as part of the political and military environment as he defines it, is crucial for the security and the peaceful survival of the UK and the world:

> (5) Because the outcome of this issue will now determine more than the fate of the Iraqi regime and more than the future of the Iraqi people who have been brutalised by Saddam for so long, important though those issues are. It will determine the way in which Britain and the world confront the central security threat of the 21st century, the development of the United Nations, the relationship between Europe and the United States, the relations within the European Union and the way in which the United States engages with the rest of the world. So it could hardly be more important. It will determine the pattern of international politics for the next generation.

Such interaction with the environment presupposes at least three fundamental mechanisms of social agents:

(i) reliable *perception* of what is the case and what goes in the environment (including the body and mind of the social agent) as it is *relevantly (re) construed* by the agents

(ii) a *mental representation* that stores these construed perceptions in memory for current and later use in cognition, action, interaction and discourse

(iii) *language use and discourse* to communicate such knowledge to other members of epistemic communities, as well as to obtain knowledge from others.

These mental representations of the environment we call *beliefs* (Price, 1969). Animals also must have some kind of representation of their environment (Allen and Bekoff, 1997; Gallistel, 1992). However, we focus only on human beings – who not only have beliefs about their environment, but – unlike animals – are also *conscious* of many of these beliefs and can explicitly express and communicate them in natural language.

It is not only crucial that human beings develop beliefs about themselves and their (external) environment, but also that these beliefs be more or less *correct* in the sense that they optimally *correspond* to what is actually the case. Our health, well-being, survival and daily interaction depend on correct beliefs about the natural and social environment (including ourselves).

Hence, in order to be able to consistently form correct beliefs, instead of interaction based on trial and error, human beings both individually and collectively develop basic *criteria*, *standards* or *methods* that enhance the correctness of their beliefs. Such criteria may, for instance, prescribe detailed, repeated and independent observation by several people, in different situations, on the one hand, as well as communication about experiences, and ways to relate beliefs to other beliefs, for instance by inference in everyday argumentation or formal proof, on the other.

Knowledge criteria may be summarized by three keywords: Perception/ Experience, Discourse and Thought/Reasoning. Thus, most of Blair's speech is dedicated to what he sees as the criteria that sustain his purported knowledge about WMDs and the threat of Saddam Hussein, such as previous events (Saddam's earlier use of such weapons against the Kurdish population), reports of the weapons inspection teams of the UN, declarations of Saddam's son-in-law.

Beliefs that can be trusted as correct representations of the environment come to function as beliefs with a special status and role: *knowledge*. Although this is true for individual human beings and their interaction with their environment, thus defining *personal knowledge*, especially fundamental are the beliefs that are communicatively *shared* and *accepted* by a community: *social knowledge*. This is also why Blair consistently aims to defend his knowledge claims by referring to earlier UN declarations and the international consensus.

Given the role of knowledge about the environment as a basic condition of the adaptation and survival of the species, on the one hand, and the success of individual action and interaction, on the other, we may further assume that the basic formats and mechanisms for the acquisition, representation and uses of knowledge for any organism or group have been genetically encoded, improved and phylogenetically reproduced in the most relevant way for each species. Although many of our personal experiences, as well as most of our socially shared generic knowledge, are acquired by each person and each group, we are born with genetically preprogrammed mental devices, schemas and elementary knowledge formats that allow us to learn a natural language, interact and communicate, on the one hand, and to perceive, analyze and represent our natural and social environment, on the other.

Accounts of human knowledge, its acquisition, uses and adaptation, as well as its neurological implementation in the brain and its discursive communication and reproduction in society, are built on that fundamental presupposition (Gazzaniga, 1998; Plotkin, 1997, 2007). Thus, we shall argue below and in the next chapter that the basic format of human experience and perception of the environment, and hence of the specific knowledge of situations and events, is *mental models* and their generalization and abstraction as generic knowledge, on the one hand, and their expression and reproduction in discourse, on the other.

2.3   Steps towards a theory of natural knowledge

2.3.1   *A preliminary definition of knowledge*

This chapter and the rest of the book defines **social knowledge as the shared beliefs of an epistemic community, justified by contextually, historically and culturally variable (epistemic) criteria of reliability**. This implies that a community may use, presuppose and define knowledge as 'true belief' what members of another community or period may deem to be 'mere' or 'false' belief, ideology, prejudice or superstition. In other words, natural knowledge is *relative*, that is, relative to the epistemic criteria of an epistemic community. **Personal knowledge** may then be defined as the justified beliefs of individual members acquired by applying the epistemic criteria of their community to their personal experiences and inferences.

With respect to the kind of knowledge Tony Blair claimed to have, he would assert that he used the criteria of various epistemic communities (e.g., those of politicians, those of parliament, or those of the UK), such as evidence gathered by experts as well as historical precedent, and so on. On the other hand, many people, including experts, did not believe that there was solid evidence that there were still WMDs in Iraq, so that there was no general consensus as would be required of socially shared knowledge of the whole epistemic community, but only different opinions. In other words, when Blair repeatedly claims "we all know," this is either a means to hide a lie, or a rhetorical hyperbole to enhance mere belief.

2.3.2   *Discourse*

Especially relevant for our discussion is that, besides and beyond reliable perception and experience as sources and criteria of knowledge, *discourse* plays a crucial role, especially in the social reproduction of knowledge. Most of what we know about the world – beyond our experiences and immediately perceived environment – is acquired by, or derived from, text and talk of parents, caregivers, teachers, friends, the mass media, textbooks and the Internet, among many other genres and forms of communication. This is by definition true of most historical knowledge as well as for generic knowledge accumulated on the basis of the shared experiences of the members of an epistemic community.

Examining the claims of both Blair and his opponents, we see that virtually all their arguments sustaining their claims are based on (contradictory) discursive evidence, such as reports of experts, historical texts, declarations of Iraqis, and so on. Indeed, since no reliable observers had actually seen and documented the presence of WMDs, the evidence as used was discursive and, in that sense, indirect. This is mostly the case in everyday life for all knowledge of events beyond our direct personal experiences and observations.

Compared to perception and inference/reasoning as sources for criteria of knowledge, epistemology has paid scant attention to this crucial role of discourse in the acquisition and justification of knowledge. There is one area of epistemology that does pay attention to discourse, namely the study of the role of testimony as a major (but not always reliable) source of social knowledge and justification (Audi, 1997; Coady, 1992; Fricker, 2006; Goldman, 1999; Reynolds, 2002). Note, though, that unlike all other disciplines in the humanities and social sciences, epistemology uses the specific notion of testimony (or 'hearsay') instead of more general notions such as discourse, text and talk.

On the relations between knowledge and discourse, especially relevant for epistemology is a study of argumentation as an expression of reasoning and one of the major ways reliable inferences can be derived from given knowledge and shown to others (Goldman, 1999). Yet, many discourses in our everyday lives are hardly argumentative. We learn more about the world from news reports than from editorials or opinion articles, which function especially to learn about the *opinions* of others. More broadly, then, we need to examine in detail the relevant genres of discourse and the ways they presuppose, imply, convey and produce old or new knowledge.

2.3.3   Context

Discourse and knowledge are not only both intentional as representations of states of affairs, but also *contextual*. Whereas we assume that knowledge is relative to epistemic communities and their criteria, as well as to specific situations of perception and experience, all discourse is produced and understood in specific communicative situations. The 'same' discourse may be true in one situation, false or otherwise (non) satisfied in another, if only because of the variable interpretation of its deictic (indexical) expressions. Thus, when Blair gave his speech in 2003, his arguments may well have been 'true' for him and others, whereas it later appeared that his beliefs were incorrect.

More generally, discourses are more or less pragmatically *appropriate* in each communicative situation, as defined by the parameters of that situation, such as the Setting, Participants (and their identity, role or relationship), current social Action, Goals and the shared Knowledge (Common Ground) of the participants. In the next chapter we shall show that such communicative situations are not very complex objective social or environmental configurations but are subjectively summarized and defined by the participants in terms of rather simple dynamic *context models* (Van Dijk, 2008a, 2009a). These are specific instances of more general mental models defining and controlling everyday experiences. This also means that the reliability of discourse as a source of knowledge depends on its context. For instance, what an expert asserts in a mass-media interview may be considered true in that informal, public context, but deemed to be false in an academic context.

Although Tony Blair's speech may have been false, it was pragmatically appropriate if he honestly believed his beliefs were correct, and moreover pronounced on that date, and in parliament, as Prime Minister and before MPs, assuming the then current knowledge of all participants and with the aim of seeking parliamentary support for the decision of his government to go to war in Iraq. These are the key conditions defining the communicative situation *as he subjectively defined it* in the context model that controlled his speech (for details, see Van Dijk, 2008a, 2009a; for the old sociological notion "defining the situation," see also Thomas, 1928/1966).

Especially interesting for this chapter and this book is that context models have a special knowledge device, or K-device, that dynamically establishes, at each point of the discourse, what speakers or writers know or believe about the various kinds of knowledge of the recipients, and adapts their text or talk to such shared knowledge or *Common Ground*. Thus, Blair may assume that what he claims to be evidence and arguments as presented in his speech will sequentially change the knowledge (and opinions) of the recipients, and hence their reasons to support his motion.

As we indicated before, contemporary epistemology also features a contextualist approach. Yet, such contextualism hardly provides a systematic analysis of such contexts, but rather defines as context what it cannot handle in the semantics, such as the use of vague or scalar terms (such as "large"), speaker meanings, indexicals or situationally variable epistemic criteria (see DeRose, 2009; Preyer and Peter, 2005).

2.3.4   Mental models

A cognitive approach to knowledge and its criteria needs a theoretical notion that accounts for the way people mentally construe and represent states of affairs, and especially the specific situations, events and actions of their direct or indirect (discursively mediated) daily experiences. As we shall see in more detail in the next chapter (also for references), cognitive psychology introduced the notion of a *mental model* to describe and explain such subjective representations as they discretely define the past, present and future experiences of everyday life.

Mental models are not mental 'copies' of events, but human beings actively *construe* such events on the basis of perception, experience, old models and generic, sociocultural knowledge.

Mental models are assumed to be stored in *episodic memory*, part of long-term memory (LTM), and with the Self as the central actor–experiencer (see, e.g., Brown, 1991; Brueckner and Ebbs, 2012; Ismael, 2007; Neisser, 1993, 1997; Schacter, 1999).

It is in this way that social agents mentally organize the ongoing, permanent 'stream of consciousness' of their daily life, by segmenting it into sequences of mental models representing discrete episodes, separated and individuated by changes in the model: different location, time unit, participant structure, goals, activity and so on (Newtson and Engquist, 1976; Shipley and Zacks, 2008; Van Voorst, 1988; Zacks and Swallow, 2007; Zacks *et al.*, 2001).

2.3.4.1 Mental models as knowledge

Mental models defined as subjective mental constructions and representations of (experiences of) situations are also useful as concepts in a natural epistemology because they define the everyday experiences of members of epistemic communities. That is, knowledge of a specific situation or event is represented by a mental model that meets socially shared K-criteria, e.g., of reliable perception, inference or discourse. Instead of speaking of *true* beliefs, as is common in traditional definitions of knowledge in epistemology, models that reliably represent, or correspond to, a state of affairs will be called *correct*.

If such personal event knowledge is communicatively shared in the epistemic community, it may become *social* knowledge if it meets the epistemic criteria of the community. If generalized over several situations, mental models may become *generic* knowledge by abstracting from the spatiotemporal and other unique properties of a situation or experience (see also McHugh, 1968).

On the other hand, personal models may feature unique emotions and opinions that do not meet the K-criteria of the community and are not generally shared, and hence are considered to be personal beliefs or *opinions*.

Since human beings have been experiencing and representing events and situations of their natural and social environments for many thousands of years (Plotkin, 1997), it is likely that they have developed a genetically based *schema* that strategically allows them to do so fast and efficiently in their everyday lives, consisting of such categories as spatiotemporal Setting, Participants, Action/Event, Goals, etc. This schema organizes not only the structure of mental models of situations but even the semantic representations of the clauses or sentences that describe such situations in everyday text and talk, traditionally represented as propositions on the one hand, or the structures of specific discourse genres, on the other. Indeed, mental models of specific events and personal experiences are the typical cognitive basis of stories and news reports.

Consciousness and the daily experience of Self and the social and natural environment involves filling in or adapting the model schema with the memorized or perceived data of the current situation. We do this when we wake up in the morning or after having lost consciousness: we activate, perceive, infer or are told who we are, where we are, what time or day it is, what we are doing now (what the state of our body is), what we want to do (plans), what we have done before (memories), etc. That is, models are embodied and multimodal, and involve vision, audition, touch and awareness of our bodies (Barsalou, 2008; Glenberg, 1999; Varela *et al.*, 1991). Obviously, there are many other, especially neurological, aspects of models as forms of consciousness, but these will not be discussed here (for debate, see Platchias, 2011; Searle, 1993, 2002; Velmans and Schneider, 2007).

The direct, multimodal experience involved in the perception of the environment, which may be defined as the partial cause of the mental model of an event, constitutes only an initial, basic, largely pre-conscious and non-conceptual part of the process of the construction of the mental model that defines our conscious understanding of events (see, e.g., Audi, 2010: Chs. 2 and 3; Raftopoulos, 2009).

Epistemically, self-knowledge from personal experiences, as described here, is usually considered to be reliable in normal circumstances – e.g., if all our senses and interpretations function by normal standards – and hence admissible as evidence in court. In high-stake contexts, criteria may be stricter, e.g., the use of independent witnesses, the use of 'objective' measuring instruments (cameras, recorders, etc.), especially since eyewitness testimony is not always reliable (Loftus, 1996; Thompson, 1998b).

Reliability is assumed to hold for thoughts, feelings or emotions to which others do not have access, like being afraid or having a headache (Brueckner and Ebbs, 2012; Gertler, 2003). We may see the experience model as the relevant context of these ongoing thoughts, that is, what psychologists have called 'ruminating' mental activity (Wyer, 1996).

With the notion of a mental model not only psychology but also epistemology has a fundamental theoretical instrument to account for the structures of knowledge and the reliable construction and representation of specific situations and events of the environment. At the same time, the notion of mental model will prove to be useful to account for the production and comprehension of discourse – and of discourse as a criterion for the formation of knowledge.

2.3.4.2 *Mental models and discourse*

As we shall see in more detail in the next chapter, the *intentional* role of mental models for the production and comprehension of discourse is that language users are able to relate discourse and its meaning to what it is *about* or what it *represents*. However, based on socioculturally shared generic knowledge, models are much more detailed than the discourses that express and convey them, because recipients are able to derive any missing information by making inferences from their generic knowledge shared with the speaker or writer. That is, for pragmatic reasons, discourses are incomplete when compared to their underlying situation models. Many properties of discourse, such as their local and global coherence, are thus defined relative to the mental models of the participants about the situation the discourse refers to.

Above we saw that representations of the communicative situation also take the forms of subjective mental models, context models, which control the situational appropriateness of discourse. In other words, mental models provide the basis of both the (extensional, referential) semantics and the pragmatics of discourse.

Epistemology is concerned about discourse (in epistemology often called testimony) as a reliable source of knowledge, and how knowledge can be transmitted to other people (see, e.g., Adler, 1996; Audi, 1997; Coady, 1992; Fricker, 2006; Goldman, 1999; Lackey, 1999; Matilal and Chakrabarti, 1994; Reynolds, 2002).

Since many forms of discourse, such as news reports and stories, are interpreted by language users as mental models representing specific events, such discourses function epistemically as indirect evidence of such events if specific contextual conditions are satisfied – such as credibility and other properties of speakers/authors, and the reliability of their own epistemic criteria or 'methods' (perception, experience, discourse, inference).

Since there is often less evidence about the reliability of speakers or their sources, indirect evidence about events as told by others (hearsay) is typically found less reliable than direct personal experience shared by several eyewitnesses, in high-stake contexts such as court proceedings. In the contexts of everyday life, however, credible evidence as based on what reliable speakers have said or written is typically assumed to be a valid source of knowledge, as we also know from one of the normative conversational postulates that requires that in general people are assumed to 'tell the truth' (see, Grice, 1989).

Taking Tony Blair's speech again as an example, the complex state of affairs he talks about, namely the alleged presence of WMDs in Iraq, the threat to world peace and the military action to be taken against Saddam Hussein, is subjectively represented in his own mental model. All MPs as participants in the debate have their own mental model of the current situation – featuring not only their knowledge and beliefs about Iraq, Saddam Hussein, WMDs, present military action, but also opinions about whether such action is legitimate or efficient and emotions related to the risks of war. Thus, it is not the situation in Iraq itself that is the direct cause or reason for Blair's speech, but his beliefs as represented in his personal mental model of the situation. And those who disagree with him do so on the basis of their own mental model.

2.3.5   Generic knowledge and discourse

Much of our historical and generic knowledge is not based on personal experience and hence not on personal mental models, nor on the experiences and discursively mediated models of others, but on expository text and talk. Such generic knowledge is itself construed by the generalization and abstraction of shared mental models, by inferences from discourses about such models (e.g., stories or news reports), or by inferences and reasoning on the basis of previous generic knowledge and the discourses expressing it.

Pedagogical parent–child discourse, lessons, textbooks, the mass media and many other types of public expository discourse typically convey such generic knowledge as it has been accumulated and reproduced in the epistemic community and its institutions – as we shall see in more detail in Chapter 5 on the sociology of knowledge.

Note that the mental models of Blair and the MPs about the situation in Iraq, and hence their speeches based on them, are construed not only on the basis of evidence about specific facts derived from a variety of discourses, as well as from their earlier personal experiences (old models), but as instantiations (applications) of tacit generic knowledge about parliament, policies, war, military, WMDs, and a host of other concepts. Most of this general knowledge is not asserted in their speeches but presupposed as shared generic knowledge of the epistemic community, and hence as part of the Common Ground of the ongoing debate, and as indexed in the context models of all participants.

Socially shared generic knowledge as collective knowledge has become the basis as well as the touchstone of all knowledge. When we talk about knowledge in general, we often refer to socially shared knowledge rather than to the subjective knowledge of personal experience, as represented in mental models. Even our personal knowledge derived from personal experiences is normatively construed on the basis of the criteria of socially acquired and shared knowledge – which allows us to talk understandably about and share such knowledge with others. This is also one of the reasons for the development of a more social epistemology (Cohen and Wartofsky, 1983; Corlett, 1996; Fuller, 1988; Goldman, 1999; Haddock *et al.*, 2010; Schmitt, 1994; Searle, 1995). *Thus, we see that socially shared knowledge is both a condition and a consequence of all public discourse.*

In the next chapter we shall deal with the representation of such generic knowledge in conceptual 'semantic' memory, and how it is used and acquired in the production and comprehension of discourse. Relevant for this chapter is again that much, if not most, socially shared knowledge is based on various forms of contextually situated text and talk.

More generally, discourse may be taken as the source of knowledge produced by *reasoning* and debate and as the basis for any *inferences* of knowledge

collectively produced in a community, as is the case for epistemology itself –
hardly prone to get its premises from observations or experiments other than
those of text, talk or thought. It is this kind of knowledge as 'justified acceptance,' produced by reasons or argument, that Lehrer (2000) calls *discursive
knowledge*. Since knowledge thus produced must be *coherent* with the existing
knowledge system, this position also implies a so-called 'coherentist' approach
to knowledge.

At the intersection of discourse, cognition and society, we thus arrive at the
kernel of a theory of natural knowledge. In the following chapters we then
need to examine in much more detail exactly how such knowledge is mentally
organized, how it is used and expressed in discourse, and how it is socially
communicated, distributed, accepted and used by epistemic communities in
different cultures.

2.4   Some properties of natural knowledge

After the very general account of the nature and functions of knowledge and
some of its relations to discourse presented above, we now need to examine
in more detail some of its properties. We do so with a brief discussion of
some of the classical concepts as they have been used in the study of knowledge in epistemology and as they have been used above and in the next
chapters.

2.4.1   Beliefs

Classical approaches in epistemology define knowledge as a special kind of
belief – namely as *justified true belief*. Hence we need to discuss in some detail
this notion of belief as it is being discussed in philosophy – and leave a discussion of its psychological properties for the next chapter.

The definition of knowledge as a type of belief is consistent with at least
some everyday uses of the terms, in the sense that when we state that we
know something, it is usually implied that we also believe it (hence the
assumed validity of $Kp \rightarrow Bp$ in an epistemic logic). Indeed, it is strange to
say that one knows something without believing it – unless in special definitions of knowledge that involve full acceptance (see, e.g., Cohen, 1992;
Lehrer, 1990).

However, in most everyday uses of the terms, the concepts of 'belief' and
'believing' are used to refer to subjective or tentative thought or talk about the
world, that is, when we are insecure about what is the case, when our beliefs
may not be shared by others or when we give an opinion. In that sense, natural
knowledge is stronger than (mere) belief, namely belief of which one is sure,
according to the K-criteria of the relevant epistemic community.

The problem with the definition of knowledge in terms of beliefs is also that the technical concept of belief itself is not well defined but usually taken for granted as a mental state or propositional attitude (for discussion, see, e.g., Williams, 2000). Rather than dealing with the detailed cognitive structures and functions of actual beliefs of real people, most studies in classical epistemology deal with normative questions of justification and truth, that is, with the nature of the relations between beliefs and the world, and by what criteria we are warranted to describe beliefs as knowledge (Goldman, 1986, 1993).

The detailed analysis of beliefs tends to be left to a more general philosophy of mind (but see, e.g., Crimmins, 1992). Summarizing a vast number of debates in various branches of philosophy, beliefs are traditionally described and analyzed in the following terms, where we shall sometimes formulate our own perspective (for detail see, among many other studies, Armstrong, 1973, 2004; Brandom, 1994; Carnap, 1956; Cohen, 1992; Crimmins, 1992; Davidson, 1984; Dennett, 1987; Dretske, 1981, 2000; Perner, 1991; Putnam, 1975; Quine, 1960; Ryle, 1949; Searle, 1983, 1992, 1998; Stalnaker, 1999, 2008):

- Together with desires, wishes, hopes, doubts, fears, regrets and other 'mental states,' beliefs are traditionally described as *propositional attitudes*, that is, as mental 'stances' towards some state of affairs.
- Beliefs are traditionally represented by a *proposition*, as is typically expressed in English by a dependent *that*-clause. This proposition is taken as the 'content' of the belief (see, e.g., Anderson and Owens, 1990; Cresswell, 1985; Richard, 1990). We have seen above that we prefer a more complete and more complex mental representation of beliefs in terms of *mental models* – and reserve propositions for the representation of semantic structures of clauses of natural language.
- We distinguish between beliefs as *mental representations* (however described) and the ways these may be *expressed in text or talk* (or other semiotic systems), a distinction that seems sometimes blurred in traditional discussions of beliefs as represented in example sentences.
- Unlike hopes and wishes, beliefs that are taken by the speaker to be correct, and hence represent personal knowledge, tend not to be explicitly indexed by prefatory clauses such as *I believe that* – which are generally reserved for the expression of personal *opinions*.
- People not only have beliefs representing a situation in a real or fictitious world, but also *about themselves* and their mental states. In that sense, hopes, wishes and similar propositional attitudes might be defined as reflexive mental models (of our own mental states) about mental models (representing a states of affairs), that is, as *meta-models* (see also Perner, 1991). Such a position also relates to the debate whether or not people have direct and

reliable *access* to their own knowledge and other beliefs (self-knowledge or a special device to evaluate their own beliefs; see Brueckner and Ebbs, 2012; Carruthers, 2009; Coliva, 2012; Gertler, 2003).

- As is the case for knowledge, beliefs are also generally formed or *construed* on the basis of personal experience and perception, by the interpretation of discourse and social interaction, and by inference from other beliefs in the agent's belief system.
- Beliefs are *intentional* in the sense that they are *about* something, usually a state of affairs (real or possible event or situation in a real or fictitious world, see Kockelman, 2006), as it is represented in the content of the belief (Searle, 1983). Some philosophers define beliefs in non-representational ways, e.g., in terms of causes or disposition of action.
- Beliefs as intentional objects, or rather their contents (as propositions), unlike other propositional attitudes, are traditionally qualified as *true* or *false* (or as *correct* or *incorrect*), depending on whether or not they *correspond to* events, situations or facts – or are made true by any other 'truthmaker' in the world – or whether or not they can be derived/inferred from other beliefs (among a vast number of studies and objections to classical and modern 'correspondence theories' of truth, see, e.g., Alston, 1996; Armstrong, 2004; Blackburn and Simmons, 1999; Englebretsen, 2006; Wright, 1993). As indicated above, however, *we reserve the notions of truth and falsity for language use or discourse, and correctness as a property of beliefs as mental representations* (see below).
- Other propositional attitudes, such as hopes or fears, are not usually assigned truth values, but may be satisfied in other ways, e.g., they can be realized, complied with, or obeyed, among other ways their contents are related to the world, depending on their 'direction of fit.' Thus, beliefs are assumed to *'fit' the world* they represent, whereas with hopes or desires the world is expected to fit (actions carried out, events occur) the representation of the respective mental states (Boisvert and Ludwig, 2006; Searle, 1983, 1998).
- Belief contents (whether represented as propositions or not) can be *expressed*, *communicated* and *shared*. Thus, under specific further conditions, different people or a whole group or community may share the 'same' belief.
- Sharing the 'same' belief presupposes that we should distinguish between belief *types* and belief *tokens* – the latter being beliefs that are being held by a specific person at a specific moment – which may similarly be expressed by sentence types or sentence tokens (uttered by a language user in a specific context)(see below).
- Beliefs may be *activated* (now being processed – depending on the cognitive theory – e.g., in short-term memory [STM]) or *non-activated* (see next chapter).

- Beliefs may be *explicit* or *implicit (tacit, virtual)* where implicit beliefs become part of the belief system only after being derived from other beliefs (see Crimmins, 1992; Manfredi, 1993).
- Depending on what states of affairs they are about, beliefs may be *specific* or *generic*, that is, refer to unique specific events or occurrences (particulars), or to properties, categories, schemas or prototypes of possible worlds, situations, events, persons or objects in general.
- Beliefs may vary in *strength*: We may be *more or less certain* about what we believe. Such variation is usually expressed in variable modalities of sentences (as expressed in English by such expressions as *I guess, maybe, perhaps, likely, surely*, to be studied in Chapter 7).
- Beliefs are *variable*. What we are sure about today, we may be less sure about tomorrow, and doubt or completely reject later.
- Similarly, we may more or less *accept* beliefs, depending on the strength of the *evidence* we have for doing so.
- The expression of beliefs in uttered sentences of natural languages in a specific communicative context is *indexical*, that is, it may vary according to the time, place and participants of the context. The same sentence type uttered by another speaker at another time or in another place may thus express a different belief and hence be true (or satisfied) in one situation and false in another (see, e.g., Blome-Tillmann, 2008; Davis, 2004; Perry, 1993; Preyer and Peter, 2007). Note that in our theory of context, sentences and discourses are produced and interpreted contextually even when contextual parameters (such as those of Time, Place or Speaker) are not explicitly expressed (remain 'unarticulated') in the utterance at all (see the debate on minimalist semantics, e.g., in Cappelen and Lepore, 2005).
- As is the case for many beliefs, knowledge is also explicitly indexed (*I know that …*) only in specific situations. Instead of asserting *I know that p*, language users simply assert *p* (which also has given rise to so-called 'deflationary' approaches to knowledge; see, e.g., Strawson, 1950). Indeed, the explicit use of *I know that* often indexes doubt about such knowledge (see the discussion in Hazlett, 2009). Typically, politicians who state *We all know that...* usually express a belief that is not generally known at all, as was the case for Tony Blair and his 'knowledge' about WMDs in Iraq.
- Although the precise mental format or 'language' of beliefs is still unknown, generic beliefs are assumed to be *organized* in belief systems, from which they may be inferred, as well as internally *structured* by distinct components that allow the construction of an infinite number of new beliefs.
- The system of beliefs is *dynamic and productive*. This also allows the construction of 'mere thoughts' or 'virtual beliefs' that are not asserted (hoped, wished, etc.) or about (represent) any real or possible states of affairs or worlds at all (Perry, 1993).

2.4.2   Truth, correctness and correspondence

As we have seen above, knowledge is traditionally defined as justified *true* belief. Indeed, not only in epistemology, but more generally in philosophy, truth plays a crucial role (Blackburn and Simmons, 1999; Davidson, 1984, 2005; Dummett, 1978; Horwich, 1990; Kirkham, 1992).

Interestingly, although knowledge is also crucial in language use, linguistics and discourse studies have paid much less attention to the notion of truth. In fact, it was especially in the philosophy of language and in the study of speech acts, for instance in the definition of assertions, that truth began to play a role in language (Austin, 1950; Searle, 1969; Strawson, 1950). Outside of philosophy, discourse and language use are seldom described in terms of truth or truthfulness, except, indirectly, in the characterization of fictional discourse, as well as in the study of specific sentence or clause types, such as counterfactuals (see, e.g., Ferguson and Sanford, 2008; Nieuwland, 2013; Nieuwland and Martin, 2012). Rather, the focus in these disciplines is on syntactic, semantic, narrative or argumentative *structures* or conversational *strategies*.

The concept of truth is so fuzzy that in this chapter we will avoid defining it (see also the reluctance expressed by Davidson, 1996). It is not surprising, therefore, that the last decades have witnessed various directions of research in epistemology to develop 'deflationary' or 'minimalist' theories of truth so as to avoid the problems of the classical 'robust' theories concerned with presenting a general theory of truth. Current debates feature older misgivings about truth, such as expressed in the famous debate between Austin (1950) and Strawson (1950) about truth and facts, a debate that is also relevant for the analysis of discourse (see, e.g., the debates in Blackburn and Simmons, 1999).

In our framework, as stated above, the notion of truth is limited to language use or discourse and is not predicated of beliefs. Only statements (actual discourse), in assertive contexts, may be (said to be) true or false. Hence, in our framework it is more appropriate to qualify 'true' or 'false' beliefs as *(in)correct* (Ryle, 1971: 37), namely if they refer to *existing situations, states of affairs* or *facts* in the real world or in its fictional extensions (Armstrong, 1997; Searle, 1995; see below).

2.4.3   Relative relativism

Besides the well-known philosophical problems of the definition of truth, there is another issue that is quite fundamental for a theory of natural knowledge. Truth in a philosophical definition usually refers to the 'absolute' or 'universal' truth of beliefs, independent of social actors, language users or social contexts.

In everyday life, however, knowledge is not defined in terms of absolute truth but in terms of the knowledge criteria of an epistemic community and its members, making knowledge essentially *relative*. Thus, in the Middle Ages, the belief that the earth was flat *was used and presupposed as generally shared knowledge* and not as subjective belief, although this belief is false (or rather: incorrect) in our own, contemporary epistemic community, and by our own knowledge standards.

Contrary to many philosophical approaches to knowledge and ethics, the relativism of natural knowledge in everyday life is no problem because a consequent concept of *relativism is itself relative* – as it should be. That is, relativism is defined for and across epistemic communities and contexts, but *within such communities and contexts knowledge is **not** relative* but described, used and presupposed as justified, correct belief, and hence often described in terms of 'truth,' 'facts' and so on (for relativism, see, e.g., García-Carpintero and Kölbel, 2008; Kirk, 1999; Rorty, 1991; see also below). Obviously, for an epistemological theory that only recognizes absolute, universal truth and knowledge, any relativism is heresy (see, e.g., Goldman, 1999). In such a framework, the 'true' knowledge as recognized and accepted by a community should be defined as socially shared belief, whether or not the community itself defines and uses such beliefs as knowledge. The latter criterion (the actual uses of beliefs as knowledge in a community) is rather characteristic of a pragmatic approach to knowledge (see, e.g., Rorty, 1991).

2.4.4   Justification and reliability

Above we mentioned that the three conditions by which knowledge is acquired may be summarized by the notions Perception/Experience, Discourse and Inference/Memory from prior knowledge. These are also the three basic social criteria or standards for the acceptance and *justification* of beliefs as knowledge (Alston, 2005; Goldman, 1992, 1999, 2002; Sosa, 1994). More specifically, we are normatively entitled to assume or say that we know something if such knowledge is derived from *reliable* experiences and perception, *reliable* discourse (based on reliable experiences of others) or *reliable* (valid) inferences from given knowledge. The actual cognitive processes involved in such acquisition and justification will be studied in more detail in the next chapter.

The application of the norm of *reliability*, and hence the actual processes or discourses of justification, may vary in different situations, periods or epistemic communities (Dretske, 1981). It is typically stricter in high-stake scientific or legal contexts than in most informal everyday situations, and different in contemporary science compared to science 500 or even 100 years ago. It is in this normative and practical way that beliefs are reproduced, shared and certified as knowledge in epistemic communities (Alston, 1993; Blackburn, 1985; Cohen, 1987; Ziman, 1991).

Strictly speaking, most justification criteria or methods for the acquisition of knowledge may be defined in terms of *inferences*: inferences (interpretations) of perceptions and direct bodily experiences, inferences from discourse, and inferences from given specific and general knowledge (for the cognitive nature of inferences, see the next chapter; for philosophical approaches, see Kornblith, 1993; Lerner, 1960). Yet, in order to avoid an infinite regress of such inferences, it is often assumed that at least some beliefs need no further justification, as is the case, for instance, for feelings of pain or visual perception in everyday discourse, or a priori assumptions (axioms, etc.) in formal discourse – a position known as foundationalism in epistemology.

The empirical relevance of justification criteria (standards, methods) for knowledge also shows in variously expressed evidentials in different languages (Aikhenvald, 2004; Chafe and Nichols, 1986). Thus, we may supply evidence for statements by referring to our personal experiences, especially what we have seen, heard or felt, or to what we have read or heard from others (and their experiences), or by providing an argument – that is, by making explicit inferences of already accepted knowledge. In some languages, such evidentials may or must be expressed by different verb morphemes, for instance indexing events as facts while seen with one's own eyes. We shall deal with such evidentials in Chapter 7.

Often the justification of knowledge is absent or implicit in everyday discourse. In conversation we usually supply evidence only when there may be doubts about our knowledge or if recipients show curiosity about how we know. On the other hand, the norms of scholarly discourse, variable across disciplines, require evidence in the usual way, that is, in terms of reliable observation, reliable sources (references to other studies) and inference (proof, argumentation). News reports do not always provide (reliable) sources, although journalistic practices are also controlled by such a norm, as we shall see in Chapter 5.

The methods of justification are socioculturally normative. Epistemology may thus be defined as a normative discipline when it formulates the appropriate ways to construe knowledge in general. Indeed, following such methods may be seen as an intellectual virtue of those people (or groups) who search for the 'truth' (see, e.g., Goldman, 1999; Greco, 2010; Steup, 2001; Zagzebski, 1996).

Alternatively, epistemology may be seen as part of the empirical study of knowledge and contribute to our insight into how different cultures, societies, groups or communities actually define and produce knowledge by their own epistemic standards. This more descriptive approach is closer to our project of a natural epistemology.

2.4.5   *Propositions and models*

We have seen above that traditional approaches to knowledge and beliefs tend to be formulated in terms of *propositions*, variously (and vaguely) understood as statements, meanings or contents of sentences, meanings of *that*-clauses, among other conceptions, and usually in terms of entities that may be *true* or *false* (see the discussion in, e.g., King, 2007; Salmon and Soames, 1988; Sayre, 1997). In more formal terms, propositions are often defined as sets of possible worlds, namely those worlds in which they are true, for instance in the semantics of modal expressions (see, e.g., Blackburn *et al.*, 2006; Hughes and Cresswell, 1968).

Although the use of propositions to represent knowledge has the advantage of a large history in philosophy and logic (Nuchelmans, 1973), and more easily allows for more formal accounts, it also has several disadvantages (Goldman, 1986: 15–16; Ryle, 1971: Ch. 2).

The first problem with the use of propositions is their traditional definition as entities that can be *true* or *false*, thus confounding propositions as mental representations with their expression in sentences when uttered as assertions in specific contexts, that is, with *statements* (Austin, 1950). Obviously, if relevant at all, propositions as meanings are also expressed in other speech acts, such as promises, questions or accusations that do not have traditional truth values but whose relation to the world may be 'satisfied' in other ways. For the same reasons, it is not useful to define the 'content' of beliefs, hopes or wishes in terms of propositions or to use the very term of *propositional attitude* to denote these subjective mental states.

If propositions are sentence 'meanings' or the 'semantic content' of sentences, and if such sentences have deictic expressions, then when expressed in sentences uttered at different moments, in different places or by different speakers, the 'same' proposition (as a type and not as a token) could sometimes be true and sometimes false. This is another reason why truth values, where relevant, need to be associated with uttered sentences (statements) in specific contexts, where the deictic expressions can thus be interpreted, and not with propositions. Hence the need to complete the account of discourse meaning and interpretation not only in terms of 'semantic' situation models (which are more complex than propositions) but also with 'pragmatic' context models that account for the (sometimes implicit) indexical meanings of discourse (see next chapter for detail).

Again, it is important to distinguish between beliefs and knowledge and their structures as *mental representations*, on the one hand, and the *meanings of sentences or discourse that express such knowledge*, on the other (see, e.g., Searle, 1971, 1983). Knowledge and beliefs (as mental models) may be expressed in, and be required or presupposed in the production or understanding of the meanings of sentences or discourse, but they are not equivalent to these meanings (provisionally represented as propositions as long as we have no other format for the explicit representation of meaning).

Crucial for the theory of this book is that knowledge and beliefs can be communicated and *shared* among language users as members of a community, and hence are not restricted to contexts of specific discourses or language users. Hence they must also represent *decontextualized types* of information (for propositions as types, see, e.g., Hanks, 2011; Soames, 2010; see also Anderson, 1980; Bezuidenhout and Cutting, 2002; as well as the other papers in the special issue of *Journal of Pragmatics*, 34(4), 2002). Perry (1993) distinguishes between propositions and 'belief states' that can be shared and hence are described as 'universal,' whereas the 'same' propositions (as a type), when thought or expressed by different persons (as tokens), may sometimes become true and sometimes false. Thus, in his speech, Tony Blair states:

> (6) The inspectors probed.

This statement, made in this speech on this occasion, expresses a specific proposition about specific inspectors, referred to with a definite expression, co-referring with similar expressions in the co-text, and hence already identified in the mental model of Blair and the MPs, and is about a specific action in the past, as expressed by the past tense of the verb. Yet this specific information is, as such, merely indexed in the sentence, but not actually expressed, and only present in the mental models of Blair and the MPs in that situation. This is, of course, as it should be because it allows vast amounts of different information, as represented in specific mental models of specific language users in specific contexts, to be expressed by the more 'abstract,' 'incomplete' or 'vague' propositions or meanings expressed in the sentences of natural languages. We see that if we want to talk about knowledge and beliefs and their expression in discourse it is analytically useful to distinguish between

  (i) the communication situation as defined by the context model of the speaker
 (ii) the speech act (assertion) made in that situation
(iii) the sentence expressed in order to make that assertion
 (iv) the (general) proposition or sentence meaning expressed by the sentence
  (v) the (specific) proposition or speaker-meaning expressed by the utterance in that situation
 (vi) the specific mental model of the speaker about the specific events talked about.

In this case, we may probably eliminate (v) because the specific meanings of specific propositions (e.g., as referring to specific people, actions, times and places) are precisely supplied by the information in the situation models (vi) and context models (i). On the other hand, it may be relevant to add another level of representation, namely that of the *co-text*, which is able to identify referents and specify meanings that are not supplied by the sentence and sentence meaning in isolation.

The assertion in example (6) is made by the expression of a very simple sentence, expressing a simple proposition type consisting of a tensed predicate (*probed*) and a specific argument or constant (*the inspectors*) – more or less in the traditional format, enriched by time indicators. However, many sentences and propositions in natural language, and especially in institutional discourse, may be very complex, such as the following in Tony Blair's speech:

> (7) So we constructed this framework: that Saddam should be given a specified time to fulfil all six tests to show full co-operation; and that, if he did so, the inspectors could then set out a forward work programme that would extend over a period of time to make sure that disarmament happened.

Of course, this complex sentence expresses a very complex proposition or specific structure of propositions, but the traditional proposition format would even then hardly be able to represent the initial discourse connective *So*, the indexical pronoun *we*, the cataphoric demonstrative *this*, the colon ':', the expression *that* introducing a specifying dependent clause, the modal auxiliary of obligation *should*, and so on, and so on. In other words, we need formats vastly more 'expressive' to represent all the relevant information in the underlying semantic and pragmatic models as expressed or indexed by this complex sentence as uttered in this communicative situation in order to make this assertion.

It is therefore not surprising that in *formal approaches* to language and discourse the traditional propositional format of predicate logic is extended or substituted in many ways – which are outside of the scope of this chapter and this book (see, e.g., Davis and Gillon, 2004; Groenendijk *et al.*, 1987; Kadmon, 2001; Kamp and Partee, 2004; Kamp and Reyle, 1993; Levelt and Barnas, 2008). Within his program of developing dynamic logic, van Benthem has also focused on the logic of information and interaction, emphasizing that logic should deal not only with the products of knowledge but also with the dynamic aspects of interaction and information exchange (see, e.g., Van Benthem, 2011).

Whereas this is true for the meanings of sentences and discourses, similar developments have taken place for knowledge representations in mind and brain (for representation formats, see the discussion in Goldman, 1986: Ch. 11; Haugeland, 1998; Markman, 1999; Sowa, 2000; Van Harmelen *et al.*, 2008).

2.4.6   Facts

If knowledge is defined as correct belief, and a correct belief is defined as a belief that corresponds to a fact (or another 'truthmaker') in the real world, we also need a more explicit metaphysics of *facts* – as well as other concepts used to refer to what is the case in the real world. We may use the notion 'fact' because of its widespread use in ordinary discourse, e.g., in order to have a referent of a true statement or an entity that makes a belief correct.

However, as is the case for many of the notions discussed here, that of 'fact' is also both vague and complex. One problem is its seemingly circular nature: facts that make beliefs correct and statements true are usually construed by these very beliefs and described by these very statements. If that is so, the identity of facts seems to depend on statements or how we describe the beliefs about them, and we thus have no independent way to define facts as real-world correlates of correct beliefs. Also, this would be inconsistent with the common practice of describing the *same* fact with different words or sentences. So, facts must be defined independently of how they are believed or described – but the problem remains that we have no mind-independent access to them (one of the problems of a correspondence theory of truth).

Another problem is the *delimitation* of *discrete* facts and whether there are minimal or basic facts. We may have a very complex mental model or discourse about facts at different levels of generality or specificity, as is the case of Tony Blair's mental model of the situation in Iraq, the UK and the world. We may then 'analyze' such a fact in increasingly small component facts, but the question is where to stop. Indeed, quite concretely, in the speech and mental model about Iraq, when exactly is Saddam Hussein defined to have complied with a UN resolution – as is the case especially for verbs defining continuous actions? And conversely, we can always combine facts into bigger ones, and thus construe the Macro Fact of the universe. Tony Blair seems to do something similar when he defines the situation in Iraq and WMDs as part of world peace.

Cognitive studies show that we usually identify, name and process objects and events at specific, 'natural' intermediate levels (we more commonly think and talk about a dog, rather than as an animal and rather than as a poodle; see e.g., Rosch, 1975, 1978; Rosch and Lloyd, 1978) – so that here, too, formal epistemological problems do not seem to hinder a more natural approach to knowledge as based on loosely identified and delimited facts in the real world.

Again, we see that facts appear to depend on the way we are cognitively able to construe or analyze events or situations in the world and at various levels. But if facts depend on beliefs, then it makes no sense to define the correctness of beliefs as mental models in terms of facts because there is no independent way to define such facts.

To resolve this problem, we may distinguish between different kinds of fact. Following Searle (1995), thus, there are observer-dependent and observer-independent facts. Facts are defined as observer-independent if their existence in no way depends on the existence of human beings or their observations or language.

As soon as we observe, understand, represent or talk 'about' such natural facts, we mentally or linguistically project and identify, delimit, categorize, define and hence construe such 'natural' facts. Yet, even then, the naïve realism of natural knowledge and discourse takes such facts as independent of the mind. Thus, facts of nature are said to be *discovered*, not construed (but see constructionist approaches to science, e.g., Knorr Cetina, 1999; Latour and Woolgar, 1986; see Chapter 5).

Social facts, such as (the use of) money, books, marriages, hospitals, car accidents and so on, are observer-dependent, not only because of the involvement of human beings, but also because they have been categorized, defined or instituted as such by human beings and their institutions.

Note that the observer-(in)dependence of facts says something about their *ontology*, not about their *epistemology*. As a shorthand, one may speak of natural and social facts.

Secondly, still following Searle (1995), within an *epistemological* perspective, both natural and social facts may be experienced, defined and described *objectively* or *subjectively*. Our body (blood pressure, emotions, etc.) may objectively react to natural facts. On the other hand, we may have a subjective experience (opinion, emotion) of, and subjectively speak about, the natural fact of a sunset or a headache as well as of the social fact of a terrorist attack or a divorce. However, social facts may be found to be 'objective' in everyday life in a way that is hardly different from natural facts, as is the case for a car accident as compared to an earthquake. Such is generally the case for (the use of) money, the streets, cities or pollution. Ontologically, these are observer-dependent facts, but they may be *experienced* in everyday life as facts that are the basis of *objective social knowledge* (see also Popper, 1972).

This distinction is also relevant for the definition of ideology as opposed to objective knowledge (Van Dijk, 1998). Objective social knowledge is shared, accepted and used in a community as a whole, whereas subjective social beliefs are personal or shared by ideological groups. In other words, in epistemic communities the *existence* of objective social facts is taken for granted, although our personal or shared beliefs about them may not be.

We shall later see how these distinctions also influence *discourse*. For instance, shared objective social knowledge may be presupposed as such in discourse, and need not be presented as terms of beliefs (*I believe that, probably*, etc.). Important also is that we now understand how people may think about and describe the *same* objective social fact (such as a terrorist attack) in different discourses, for instance because they may also have different beliefs (opinions) or perspectives about it. We here touch upon one of the crucial aspects of the relations between discourse, knowledge and beliefs.

2.4.7   Some more ontology

We have seen that knowledge and beliefs are about actual or possible facts in the real or imagined worlds. We also have informally introduced some of the furniture of this world (such as states of affairs and facts, consisting of situations, events, actions, persons, objects and their properties and relations) so as to have some specific correlates for thought and talk. For this study, the ontology is very simple, and without much definition. For discourse, the ontology is again derivative: we assume that we can talk about anything we can think about, although such discourse is not always contextually appropriate.

Traditionally, ontology in philosophy postulates the existence of, for instance, states of affairs, consisting of particulars (or individuals), properties and relations, and maybe time, sets, etc. (Armstrong, 1997, 2004). However, we may need a more specific and maybe more articulated ontology as a basis for a natural epistemology.

So, what kinds of things do we have in the real world about which we talk and think?

First of all, as we have seen above, beliefs and discourse are about *situations*, because we mostly do not think of facts as part of the (real) world, but as existing or happening in specific spatiotemporally defined fragments or parts of worlds, namely situations (Barwise and Perry, 1999). The concept of a situation has also been chosen as the real-world correlate of the concept of situation model in our own theory of discourse processing (Van Dijk and Kintsch, 1983), and has been widely adopted in the psychology of discourse, as we shall see in the next chapter (Zwaan and Radvansky, 1998).

As we have done above for mental models, situations may then be analyzed in terms of, for instance (see, e.g., Radvansky and Zacks, 2011; Shipley and Zacks, 2008):

(i)   settings (specific combinations of space and time fragments)
(ii) animate or inanimate participants (individual, particular things, people, etc.)
(iii) properties of or relations between participants
(iv) states and/or dynamic events (defined as changes of states) or courses of events. More specifically, events may be actions when they have people as participants that make the event happen.

Finally, we probably will not be able to avoid at least some abstract entities in our world, such as sets, classes and numbers. Yet the ontology of abstract entities in a real world is not clear, and might have to be reduced to the reality of thought of real people in the world.

Some of these entities are seen and experienced as *basic*, and hence do not consist of other entities, whereas others may be *compound* or *complex*.

Again, compositionality should be defined in the practical terms of a natural epistemology, for instance as prototypes, not in naturalist physical or biological terms, depending on the epistemic domain and community. If needed, we shall later introduce other types of entity, for instance for the semantics of discourse.

2.4.7.1 Imagined worlds, situations and events and the problem of intentionality

Facts are defined as existing states of affairs in the real world. But we not only think and talk about the real world but also imagine and talk about counterfactual, wished-for, fictional or other 'possible' worlds and their situations, as we also do in the formal terms of modal logic (Hughes and Cresswell, 1968) and the semantics of counterfactuals (Ichikawa and Jarvis, 2012).

People reading a novel or watching a movie may know or believe events to happen or people to exist in the imagined world of these discourses. This means that the aboutness or intentionality of knowledge and discourse should also include imagined worlds, situations, individuals and their properties or relations (see Crane, 2009; Searle, 1993). The truth of discourses and correctness of beliefs about such alternative worlds or situations is quite naturally asserted in such cases, as it is for discourse and beliefs about the 'real' world defined in terms of our everyday experiences, that is as the shared *Lebenswelt* or *Lifeworld* (Schutz, 1962).

The problem is that these alternative worlds have no real existence outside the discourse or beliefs of human beings. As imagined worlds and situations they only exist as mental representations such as mental models. Whereas fictional or counterfactual discourse may express such mental models as if they were mental models of the real world, the mental models representing imagined situations do not seem to be *about* anything else but themselves. How do we account for this issue in our framework?

We have seen above that specific propositional attitudes, such as hopes and wishes, may be represented as higher-level mental models (representing a speaker or thinker's specific mental state) about mental models (the 'content' of these hopes and wishes) about some (future) situation or event in the world. In the same way, we may represent counterfactual, imagined or fictional events as construed mental models in the same way as we do for the representation of real situations, which are also (re)construed by thinkers and language users. However, the fictional situations and events are the intentional objects of higher-level *mental (meta-)models* reflexively self-representing language users as *imagining* these situations and events (see McGinn, 2009) – much in the same way as we do for hopes and wishes, and as is the case for lies and errors (for this kind of introspective metacognition and mindreading, see Carruthers, 2009; Nichols and Stich, 2003).

Note also that counterfactual or fictional discourse may well be about the imagined actions or properties of 'real' people, as is the case for plans and lies, thus mixing real and imagined worlds in construed situation models that resemble models of real events even more closely. For the dynamic and productive cognitive systems that produce beliefs, knowledge, hopes and imaginings, the genetically preprogrammed processes of model construction are probably the same in all cases, only (more or less) monitored by a self-reflective meta-model that should (but does not always) keep us aware of the 'mode' of reality we are dealing with in each case.

Indeed, models of fictional events, as represented in fantasies and movies, may appear so real that people sometimes have a hard time distinguishing them from representation of real events – and producing real emotions such as happiness and fear. Apart from the control of the reflexive meta-model ('I am now imagining things'), the construction of the models of real and fictional events is most likely to be the same mental process (see the work on reality monitoring, for instance Johnson, 2007; Johnson and Raye, 2000). Similarly, we are able to construe possible future events on the basis of our earlier experiences – for which the same brain region is also used (Schacter *et al.*, 2007).

Neuropsychological studies, e.g., using Event-Relation-Potential (ERP/ N400) (brain scans of neuronal activity) methodology, suggest that if counterfactual discourse is plausible, language users have no problem understanding (at least plausible) 'counterfactually true' sentences in discourse even when referring to facts that are historically false (see, e.g., Nieuwland, 2013; Nieuwland and Martin, 2012). These results also suggest that construing mental models of counterfactual worlds and events is not fundamentally different from construing models of 'real' events – and so is the understanding of discourse on real events and the discourse on counterfactual or fictional events (see also Byrne, 2002; Gerrig and Prentice, 1991; Roese, 1997).

2.4.8   *Final remarks on the epistemology of knowledge*

Following our earlier disclaimer, the few remarks on the general properties of knowledge are only a very elementary summary of some basic ideas in epistemology, partly reformulated in our own theoretical framework. The details and sophistication of current epistemological debate are beyond the scope of this chapter and this book, and largely irrelevant for a more empirical approach to natural knowledge as it is dealt with in the next chapters.

Many of the theoretical issues briefly mentioned above have given rise to a large number of theories, positions and debates traditionally referred to with many *–isms* in epistemology, such as such as realism, skepticism, foundationalism, mentalism, internalism, externalism, reliabilism, and many more, defining the many ways truth or knowledge are produced and justified (there are hundreds of books and thousands of articles on these topics; for a selection of relevant articles and references, as well as current debate, see, e.g., Sosa *et al.*, 2008; Steup and Sosa, 2005). Within these many debates, as we have seen, our approach combines:

- *naturalism* (dealing with real knowledge of real language users)
- *relativism* (correctness of belief depends on the criteria of different epistemic communities)
- *contextualism* (correctness of belief depends on observational or communicative situations)
- *cognitivism* (belief and knowledge should be analyzed and represented in terms of mental representations and studied in the framework of the cognitive sciences).

More specifically, we have taken a more *discourse analytical perspective* that stresses that knowledge and belief should be studied by detailed analysis of text and talk, and with the awareness that most knowledge is acquired and socially reproduced by situated discourse. We shall later see that the converse also holds, namely that in order to study discourse we also need detailed epistemic analysis, presupposing philosophical, psychological, sociological and anthropologic insights about knowledge.

2.5 Summarizing the definition of natural knowledge

Given the conceptual considerations mentioned above about knowledge and belief, we now must take stock and summarize what we mean by (human) knowledge in our multidisciplinary theory of the relations between knowledge and discourse:

1. Knowledge is the result of socially situated (conscious or unconscious) mental processes or *thought* of human beings implemented in the brain.
2. Knowledge is *intentional*, i.e., *about* or *representing situations* or *states of affairs* in real or imagined worlds.
3. Knowledge is a mental representation, e.g., a model, representing *facts* (existing states of affairs) in real (external) or fictitious (internal, imagined) worlds.
4. Knowledge is not true belief, but *correct belief*. Correct belief may be expressed in *true sentences uttered in speech acts of assertions.*
5. Knowledge is correct belief *justified* or *warranted* by socially accepted *criteria* of (knowledge) *communities*. Criteria define what sources or methods of belief acquisition count as *reliable* (credible, etc.) enough to warrant

beliefs to count as knowledge in a knowledge community. Insufficiently warranted beliefs, e.g., about possible or probable states of affairs in the real world, are simply called beliefs.

6. Knowledge may be *personal, interpersonal* or *social.* The evaluation of personal knowledge also involves the application of socially relevant knowledge criteria.

7. Personal knowledge is warranted belief acquired in events of *personal experience* and represented in *mental models* in episodic memory.

8. Knowledge of fictional (hoped, wished, etc.) events and situations is represented in meta-models reflexively representing the specific mental activity dominating the construed mental models of fictional events.

9. *Interpersonal knowledge* is represented in the mental models of the participants of joint experience, or inferred from participant discourse about (inter)personal experiences.

10. Social, public or sociocultural knowledge is *distributed, shared* and *represented* in the general 'semantic' (social) memory (part of LTM) of members of an epistemic community.

11. Social knowledge is *acquired, changed* and *confirmed* by mental processes involving generalization, abstraction and decontextualization of mental models of experience, on the one hand, and communication of general knowledge, on the other.

12. Knowledge is acquired, expressed, presupposed and reproduced by natural language defined as socially situated discourse, interaction and communication. This is the second crucial function and condition of knowledge for humankind.

13. Knowledge is not represented in terms of *propositions* but as mental models and generic knowledge structures (scripts, conceptual relations, etc.), which may be expressed and communicated by sentences in situated discourse with meanings represented as proposition types contextualized by context models.

14. As we shall see later, social knowledge is *legitimated* as official knowledge by the prevalent knowledge institutions of society or the knowledge community: academies, universities, laboratories, the quality press, the courts, the administration and the government.

These are merely the general features of the theory of knowledge. The next chapters will deal with the details of the cognitive, sociocognitive, social, cultural and linguistic aspects involved in these general statements, for instance with the kind of mental states, processes, representations or models, on the one hand, and with the social distribution, communication and evaluation of knowledge in various communities and societies, on the other.

3   Discourse, knowledge and cognition

3.1   Introduction

The introduction of a large entry on racism in *Wikipedia*, "the Free Encyclopedia,"
on the Internet (version March 2013) runs as follows:

01   Racism is usually defined as views, practices and actions reflecting
02   the belief that humanity is divided into distinct biological groups
03   called races and that members of a certain race share certain
04   attributes which make that group as a whole less desirable, more
05   desirable, inferior or superior.
06   The exact definition of racism is controversial both because there
07   is little scholarly agreement about the meaning of the concept "race,"
08   and because there is also little agreement about what does and doesn't
09   constitute discrimination. Critics argue that the term is applied differ-
10   entially, with a focus on such prejudices by whites, and defining mere
11   observations of racial differences as racism. Some definitions would
12   have it that any assumption that a person's behavior would be influ-
13   enced by their racial categorization is racist, regardless of whether the
14   action is intentionally harmful or pejorative. Other definitions only
15   include consciously malignant forms of discrimination. Among the
16   questions about how to define racism are the question of whether to
17   include forms of discrimination that are unintentional, such as making
18   assumptions about preferences or abilities of others based on racial
19   stereotypes, whether to include symbolic or institutionalized forms of
20   discrimination such as the circulation of ethnic stereotypes through
21   the media, and whether to include the socio-political dynamics of
22   social stratification that sometimes have a racial component. Some
23   definitions of racism also include discriminatory behaviors and beliefs
24   based on cultural, national, ethnic, caste, or religious stereotypes.
25   Racism and racial discrimination are often used to describe discrim-
26   ination on an ethnic or cultural basis, independent of whether these
27   differences are described as racial. According to the United Nations

28   convention, there is no distinction between the terms racial discrim-
29   ination and ethnic discrimination, and superiority based on racial
30   differentiation is scientifically false, morally condemnable, socially
31   unjust and dangerous, and that there is no justification for racial dis-
32   crimination, in theory or in practice, anywhere.
33   In politics, racism is commonly located on the far right, along with
34   nativism and xenophobia. In history, racism has been a major part of
35   the political and ideological underpinning of genocides such as The
36   Holocaust, but also in colonial contexts such as the rubber booms in
37   South America and the Congo, and in the European conquest of the
38   Americas and colonization of Africa, Asia and Australia. It was also
39   a driving force behind the transatlantic slave trade, and behind states
40   based on racial segregation such as the USA in the nineteenth and
41   early twentieth centuries and South Africa under apartheid. Practices
42   and ideologies of racism are universally condemned by the United
43   Nations in the Declaration of Human Rights.

Wikipedia, like all encyclopedias, offers current academic knowledge of the world for a general public. Thus, the entry on racism, after the introduction cited above, provides information on several usages of the term *racism*, as well as various definitions (e.g., legal and sociological ones), a typology of various sorts of racism, ethnic conflict, as well as information on racist ideologies, academic racism, the history of racism, antiracism, and final references, notes and suggestions for further reading.

The format and style of this entry is academic rather than popular, but otherwise quite accessible for most educated readers, as is the aim of the *Wikipedia* Encyclopedia.

Although an encyclopedia item in principle does not presuppose any knowledge of the concept or phenomena covered in the item, those who search for such knowledge are usually not ignorant about it, especially when the term or the phenomenon is often dealt with in everyday discourse and the mass media. Thus, most people who search for this item usually have some basic knowledge (or misconceptions) about what racism is, but only want to know more about it, or what the current scientific literature says about it.

Interesting for this book and this chapter, then, is how exactly such general or generic *knowledge of the world*, such as our knowledge about racism, is acquired, organized and used, and especially how it is expressed and reproduced in discourse. We approach this topic through a more detailed study, already begun in the previous chapter, of how such generic knowledge influences the ways language users employ and form mental models of events in the world as well as of the communicative situation itself. This theory is part of a general theory of discourse processing, which is summarized here as a necessary framework for the understanding of the role of knowledge in discourse production and comprehension.

Before presenting a detailed review of empirical research on the role of knowledge in discourse processing, we present our own current theory so as to be able to critically formulate the results of earlier research from the perspective of our own general framework of this book and this chapter. The theory presented here further develops the theory of strategic discourse processing presented in Van Dijk and Kintsch (1983), which itself was partly inspired by my earlier work on text grammar (Van Dijk, 1972, 1977) and by Kintsch (1974), and later modified by Kintsch (1988).

3.2   Towards a new theory of discourse processing

Compared to earlier theories of discourse processing and the role of knowledge in discourse production and comprehension, our current theory features (or emphasizes the need for) the following components:

- **Theory of context**. As we already suggested in the previous chapter, discourse is produced and understood under the control of context, defined as the subjective 'definition of the communicative situation,' as it is represented by participants in dynamic **context models**. This cognitive theory of context is part of a multidisciplinary theory of the relations between discourse and context (Van Dijk, 2008a, 2009a). Its relevance here lies in the fact that context models regulate the shared knowledge of language users by means of a specific knowledge device (K-device) defining the *Common Ground* of the participants (Clark, 1996).
- **Natural discourse processing**. As is the case for a theory of natural knowledge as presented in this book, the cognitive theory of discourse also should be based on a theory of natural discourse as it is being used in everyday communication and interaction (for an introduction, see Schiffrin *et al.*, 2013; Van Dijk, 1985, 2007, 2011b; see also the criticism in psychology itself and a plea for a more ecologically valid study of cognition and discourse processing, e.g., by Neisser, 1978, 1982, 1997; Neisser and Hyman, 2000; Van Oostendorp and Zwaan, 1994; and many others). This means that many of the results of experiments done with artificial discourse examples in the laboratory, and as reviewed below, may need to be revised when dealing with natural discourse in natural communicative situations.
- **Multimodal discourse processing**. One of the shortcomings of previous theories of discourse and discourse processing was their limitation to spoken and written text and talk, ignoring the embodied, multimodal nature of experiences in general (Barsalou, 2003, 2008) and of interaction, communication

and discourse in particular. These experiences also feature gaze, touch, gestures and other body movements (Catt and Eicher-Catt, 2010; Givry and Roth, 2006; Glenberg, 1999; Zwaan, 1999, 2009) as they also define various **genres** of discourse (Bhatia, 1993; Goldman and Bisanz, 2002; Zwaan, 1994). These developments in psychology should also integrate the semiotic and multimodal analysis of text and talk in current discourse studies (see, e.g., Van Leeuwen, 2005).

- **The neuropsychology of discourse**. Relevant for this chapter are the developments in the neuropsychology of discourse in the last decade (of a plethora of studies, see, e.g., Gernsbacher and Robertson, 2005; Gillett, 2003; Mason and Just, 2004; Sherratt, 2007; Stemmer, 1999; Zwaan and Taylor, 2006). This research at the same time provides more detailed insight into the neuropsychological basis of discourse disorders in, e.g., semantic dementia, Alzheimer's Disease, aphasia, schizophrenia and brain injury (see, among many other studies, e.g., Bartels-Tobin and Hinckley, 2005; Beeman and Chiarello, 1997; Brownell and Friedman, 2001; Brownell and Joanette, 1990; Caspari and Parkinson, 2000; Chapman *et al.*, 1998; Dijkstra *et al.*, 2004). It is to be hoped that in this framework more insight can be acquired into the brain mechanisms underlying the role of mental models and generic knowledge in the production and comprehension of discourse.

- **Evolutionary insights**. In the same way as a study of the brain may reveal insights into the mental processes of discourse production and comprehension and the role of knowledge, progress in theories of the evolution of language and knowledge may provide insight into the basic, genetic structures of mental models and their relations to the structures of, e.g., narratives and sentences (see, e.g., Bickerton, 1995; Christiansen and Kirby, 2003; Deacon, 1997; Jackendoff, 2003; Lieberman, 1987; Tomasello, 2008). The same is true for an evolutionary account of knowledge, as we have seen in the previous chapter (see, e.g., Greenberg and Tobach, 1990; Plotkin, 1993, 1997, 2007; Rescher, 1990; Wuketits, 1990).

- **The new cognitive theory of knowledge**. As we shall see in more detail below, the cognitive theory of knowledge itself has gone beyond earlier accounts in terms of conceptual frameworks, prototypes, scripts or schemas, and has explored a neuropsychologically grounded multimodal approach (Barsalou, 2003, 2008).

In sum, the cognitive theory of discourse and knowledge processing should (i) be better grounded neurologically, (ii) be more ecologically valid through studying natural and multimodal discourse in natural communicative situations, (iii) account for context and (iv) be inspired by evolutionary insights into adaptive developments and the genetic programming of language, discourse and knowledge.

3.3   Mental models

3.3.1   *Modeling experience*

The cognitive theory of discourse and knowledge processing summarized here is based on assumptions about the ways language users as human beings represent their natural, social and communicative environments in terms of *multimodal mental models*. These models define and control our everyday perception and interaction in general and the production and comprehension of discourse in particular.

Due to our processing and memory limitations the vast multimodal (e.g., visual, auditory, sensorimotor) complexity of the scenes, situations, events, actions, persons and objects of the environment cannot and need not be fully processed, stored or reproduced. Hence it needs to be reduced and organized in terms of structurally less complex representations that define the *situationally relevant* information of our daily experiences: *experience models*. These models at the same time are the cognitive foundation of our discourse and communication about such experiences, as is the case in everyday storytelling.

The generalization and abstraction of similar models produces, bottom-up, *generic knowledge* about the world, and this knowledge in turn is used, topdown, in the construction of new models of experience. This means that understanding the situations of our natural and social environment is not merely a form of copying properties of the environment, but an active, *constructive* process of model building, updating and abstraction. This also allows that – and explains why – we are able to form mental models of imagined, fictional or counterfactual situations. We already observed in the previous chapter that empirical research shows that language users have no problem understanding plausible but historically false consequences of counterfactual conditional sentences: once they construe a counterfactual mental model for a discourse, the (rest of the) discourse is perfectly well understood even if the events referred to are false (Nieuwland, 2013; Nieuwland and Martin, 2012).

Whereas the neurology and cognitive psychology of the processes of object perception are now relatively well understood, we know less about the processing of more complex information, e.g., about the *scenes*, *situations*, *events* and *actions* that define our everyday social lives. Especially relevant for us is the processing of *events* and *actions*, of which discourse is only a very specific but crucially relevant case. Thus, events involve changes of objects or scenes, occurring in time, and hence usually with specifically marked and noticeable beginnings and ends, often causally related to other events as their preceding causes or following consequences. Events and actions are perceived, construed, represented and memorized as parts or constituents of sequences of events or actions that jointly may define more comprehensive, higher-level events or actions in complex (macro) hierarchies (Van Dijk, 1980). Large events such as storms, earthquakes or economic crises consist of complex sequences of component events (for details on event and action perception, see e.g., Shipley and Zacks, 2008; Tversky *et al.*, 2008; Zacks and Sargent, 2009).

Similarly, our everyday life consists of a long sequence of activities that are segmented in units of variable length and complexity that are meaningful and relevant for the participants. Such segments are marked by transitions and changes (of time, location, participants, activity, etc.), and defined by more or less conscious intentions and goals that may be planned as well as recalled as such. The result of this strategic, constructive processing of the situations and events of our environment are mental models stored in episodic memory (EM) (part of long-term memory (LTM)).

3.3.2   The structures and functions of mental models

Since human beings have been processing their natural and social environments for thousands of years, it is likely they have developed genetically preprogrammed mechanisms for the fast and relevant analysis and representation of situations and events in terms of mental models (Ackermann and Tauber, 1990; Ehrlich *et al.*, 1993; Garnham, 1987; Gentner and Stevens, 1983; Johnson-Laird, 1983; Johnson-Laird *et al.*, 1996; Van Dijk and Kintsch, 1983).

These mental models control interaction with the natural environment, as well as with other human beings, and at the same time enable communication and discourse about present, past and future situation and events – a human ability unique among primates. They are also the experiential basis for the formation of generic knowledge about the world.

Since fast analysis of the relevant aspects of the situations and events of the environment is crucial for survival as well as for everyday social interaction and communication, *model structures must be relatively simple* so as to be processed in terms of the limitations of short-term memory (STM) (working memory) (to be further discussed below). Thus we will see that some of the schematic categories of mental models, such as Setting (Place, Time), Participants (and their identity, role and relations), Event/Action and Goals, are also ubiquitous in language in discourse.

After their construction or updating in working memory, mental models are *stored in episodic memory*, the part of memory where our personal experiences are represented. Recalling a previous experience consists in activating an old mental model of such an experience. Mental models may be combined in larger, hierarchically more complex models, as is the case for our models of making a train trip as part of a vacation. As we shall see below, the higher-level, more global parts of these mental models (as well as emotionally salient information) tend to be more easily accessible and hence better recalled later – and are used more often in, for instance, storytelling or news reporting, which again makes them more accessible, as we know from episodes of autobiographical memory (Bauer, 2007; Bluck, 2003; Conway, 1990; King, 2000; Neisser and Fivush, 1994; Rubin, 1986; Thompson, 1998a; Tulving, 2002; see also below). We shall come back to the role of memory in discourse and knowledge processing below.

As we have surmised in the previous chapter, models not only represent and construe external information from the environment, but also *internal, embodied and mental, information*, such as desires, wishes, hopes, emotions and opinions, which may be combined with the representation of external events. Indeed, the embodied nature of events crucially also involves representing one's own body and mind and their current states.

Repeated experiences as represented in mental models tend to be *abstracted from and generalized into generic knowledge*, which is *instantiated*, top-down, together with information from old mental models (previous experiences) and the current environment during the construction of new mental models.

Although co-produced by the instantiation of socially shared generic knowledge, *mental models are personal and unique*, because of the unique personal episodic memory (life experiences, old models) of each person, and the unique contextual properties of each moment of perception, understanding and representation (time, place, event, goals, etc.).

Since mental models are personal, they centrally feature a category of Self (Neisser and Fivush, 1994), representing not only the unique, embodied and 'performed' nature of mental models and currently construed roles, but also that such experiences are influenced by the personal experiences of autobiographical memory as they contribute to a trans-situational personal identities.

3.3.3   Situation models of discourse

We not only construe models of situations we observe or experience, but also of situations we read or hear about in text or talk. Indeed, as we have seen before, beyond our personal experiences, situation models construed from discourse are a major means of obtaining knowledge about the world, as is the case for storytelling in everyday conversation and news reports about world events.

Whereas earlier theories of discourse processing, until the 1980s, were limited to mental representations of local and global meanings, the fundamental intentional dimension of discourse also requires a representation of the objects, persons, events or actions a discourse is *about: situation models* (see, e.g., Johnson-Laird, 1983; Rickheit and Habel, 1999; Van Dijk and Kintsch, 1983;

Wyer, 2004; Zwaan and Radvansky, 1998; taking part of their inspiration from earlier work on the application of formal model theories, see, e.g., Chang and Keisler, 1973; Kopperman, 1972, in the study of meaning and discourse, Van Dijk, 1977).

Situation models for discourse have the same general properties as models of personal experience. They are ongoingly activated or construed, during the various grammatical and other processes of discourse production and comprehension in working memory, stored in episodic memory, and subjectively represent the objects, persons, events and actions a discourse is about.

Situation models account for what was traditionally described as speaker and recipient meaning, including the presuppositions and implications that remain implicit in discourse because they can be derived from the explicit information of discourse, the communicative situation (see below), as well instantiations of generic knowledge. That is, the situation model of a speaker is much more detailed than the meanings actually expressed in the sentences or turns of discourse. It features many of the 'bridging inferences' derived from generic knowledge that remain implicit in discourse (see, e.g., Graesser and Bower, 1990; Graesser *et al.*, 2003), as well as fragments of the earlier, personal experiences of the recipient as represented in old mental models of episodic memory.

Since the situation models of speaker and recipient may be different, partial understanding or misunderstanding of discourse is common, although the socially shared generic meaning and mutual knowledge of the participants guarantee that in most situations understanding is adequate.

Situation models have many fundamental *functions* for the processing of discourse. First of all, they are the starting point for all semantic processing of text and talk: the personal experiences, specific knowledge, opinions or emotions language users want to express or communicate in the first place.

Secondly, situation models define local and global *coherence*. Sequences of sentences or turns not only exhibit various kinds of functional meaning relations (such as generalizations and specifications), but also express temporal or causal relations between events or actions represented in the situation model (Van Dijk, 1977). This means that discourse coherence is relative: a discourse is coherent-for-recipients if recipients are able to construe a mental model for it.

Besides this local, sequential coherence, discourse features overall coherence as described in terms of its semantic macrostructures at higher levels, defining the gist or upshot of text or talk, and based on the higher levels of the mental models of the participants (Van Dijk, 1980). Given the limitations of STM, such overall meanings or discourse topics are crucial for all complex information processing. Instead of keeping activated all information of a sequence of preceding sentences, both speakers and recipients only need to maintain available or immediately accessible the locally relevant discourse topic as defined in the situation model. As such a topic may remain implicit, strategies of discourse production and comprehension make use of many ways to express or signal such topics by means of headlines, introductions and summaries, as we also observed for the text of the *Wikipedia* entry about racism. These not only strategically pre-define overall topics but also serve to pre-activate the generic knowledge needed to understand the (rest of the) discourse.

Whereas we focus here specifically on discourse structures, the structure of situation models might also be mapped onto at least some aspects of the structures of clause and sentence meanings, such as their case structure reflecting the underlying participation structure represented in a mental model (Fillmore, 1968).

It is not surprising, therefore, that at all levels of language use and discourse, from the propositional structure of clause meaning to the overall structure of stories or other genres, we find the same kinds of structures, both in discourse itself and in its mental representations in episodic memory. Once stored and organized as such by similar fundamental, multimodal categories, these episodic experiences will function to prepare future ones (Schacter *et al.*, 2007). They also serve to derive more generic conceptual knowledge that may again be instantiated when construing new models of new experiences and discourse. We shall see below that the same applies to modeling the communicative situation in context models.

Mental models are crucial for discourse and knowledge production because they are both the starting point and the intended results of discourse: language users generally do not communicate for its own sake but in order to transmit personal experiences and specific knowledge they have in turn acquired from other sources (including discourse), as represented in mental models. Thus, recipients seldom memorize the exact wording or even the local meanings of discourse, but rather the mental model they have construed during their understanding, including possible 'false recalls' of meanings that were never expressed in the discourse in the first place (among many studies, see Albrecht and O'Brien, 1993; Blanc *et al.*, 2008; Guéraud *et al.*, 2005; Morrow *et al.*, 1989; Van Oostendorp, 1996; Van Oostendorp and Goldman, 1999).

In other words, discourses and the models they express and convey are the primary means of the reproduction of knowledge in society, both in everyday interaction and in much public discourse.

Besides these and many other crucial functions of mental models in discourse processing, they also explain various forms of multimodality, such as cross-modal influences between text, picture and gestures. Indeed, after some delay, language users may no longer remember whether they have read, heard or seen a news item about an event, unless some properties of the discourse itself were salient, as may be the case in poetry, advertising or some conversations.

3.3.4   Context models

As we have seen before, discourse is controlled not only by underlying situation models that are the basis of its semantics, but also by models that represent the *communicative situation itself: context models* (Van Dijk, 2008a, 2009a). If all our daily experiences are represented in mental models, this is also the case for our specific experiences of verbal interaction and communication.

Context models are just like any other model of experience, but they subjectively represent the ongoing definition of the *communicative* situation by the participants and as occasioned by the *affordances* of the situation (Clancey, 1997; Gibson, 1986). As is the case for all models of experience, they feature the standard categories of event representation, but tailored to the specifics of the communicative situation: Setting (Time, Place) of ongoing text and talk, the Participants in the interaction or communication, with special communicative roles, such as various kinds of speakers or recipients, social identities and relationships, and a central category of communicative (inter) action, such as speech acts and conversational activities and their intentions and goals.

More specifically, context models represent the parameters of the communicative situation that at each moment are *relevant* for speaker and/or recipients. Hence they also provide a more cognitively embedded theory of relevance than more philosophical and formal approaches to relevance (see, e.g., Carston and Uchida, 1998; Rouchota and Jucker, 1998; Sperber and Wilson, 1995).

Crucial for the discussion in this chapter and book is that context models also feature a *knowledge device (K-device)* that regulates the complex management of *Common Ground* shared by the participants. Since most discourse and communication, before other social functions, convey knowledge, it is crucial that both speakers and recipients keep track of the information they have already shared and what new information in now being conveyed by text and talk. As we shall see in more detail below, the K-device of the speaker is the mechanism that ongoingly 'calculates' the Common Ground of the participants, and hence what knowledge need not be (fully) expressed and asserted but what may be merely indexed or presupposed.

Like all mental models (Zwaan and Radvansky, 1998), context models are *multimodal* and defined by the ongoing visual, auditory, tactile, proxemic and emotional properties of the communicative situation, not only of talk or text (and its layout, pictures or schemas) itself, but also featuring or expressing the embodied representations of gestures, facework, handshakes, touching or distance of the participants.

Contexts are not fixed but *dynamic*. They are ongoingly adapted to the communicative circumstances. Each moment of the context model is at least temporally and epistemically different from preceding ones. Also the social identities and communicative roles of the participants, their opinions and emotions, as well as their intentions and goals may change during a conversation. Each word, sentence or turn may be shaped by the observed effects on the recipients as these are understood and modeled by the speaker.

Context models are partly *pre-planned* for many communicative activities or genres, even before their detailed meanings or mental models, let alone their precise grammatical realization. Thus, a scholar engaged in academic writing in general, and of an online encyclopedia in particular, already has a large part of the context model in place before starting to write such an entry or before giving a lecture. A reader searching the Internet usually already has a plan to read about racism and even to search specifically for such knowledge in *Wikipedia*, and hence construes, activates or updates the partial context model that will control the process of searching and reading. Indeed, for most situations in everyday life, we engage in routine interaction and communication for which we already have partial context models as 'pragmatic plans.' What may be different are the place or time of communication or the identity of the interlocutors, but when having a conversation with friends or colleagues on the job, buying something in a shop, or visiting the doctor, among many other conversational activities, much of the context model is already construed before starting the conversation, given our general, sociocultural shared knowledge of such situations, or our own, personal knowledge of such situations derived from earlier context models.

The main function of context models is to make sure that the current discourse fits the conditions of the communicative situation. Thus, whereas situation models define the *semantic meaningfulness* of a discourse, context models define their *pragmatic appropriateness* (Austin, 1962; Grice, 1989; Levinson, 1983; Searle, 1969; Verschueren *et al.*, 1994). They thus provide the cognitive basis for the appropriateness conditions of speech acts, on the one hand, and of many other interactional dimensions of talk and text, such as politeness, on the other. Besides the intentions, wishes and beliefs of the speakers defining different speech acts, their social position, status, roles and power and their relations to the recipients define various forms of self-presentation, deference or persuasion.

In the case of our example of the *Wikipedia* entry on racism, it is obvious that the parameters of its production context are crucially influential for its style and contents. An item written for another medium, at another time, by other authors, with a different aim, different knowledge and different readers would be very different. The knowledge conveyed, and as signaled by its footnotes and references, is academic, the authors are no doubt academics, and they are addressing the general public using the Internet. No doubt, not only the knowledge, but also the opinions, attitudes and ideologies of the authors influence an entry on a socially sensitive phenomenon such as racism and especially its overt form of racist conduct and discrimination. Thus, we assume that the item has been composed by authors who more or less consciously have a specific definition of the communicative situation, a context model, such as the production of an item for *Wikipedia* – including a representation of the assumed previous knowledge of the recipients, for instance about various forms of discrimination.

Thus, in the *Wikipedia* Racism item, as is quite common in academic discourse, the identities of the authors are not expressed indexically, for instance by such pronouns as *we* or by recounting personal experiences. Rather, passive constructions (such as *Racism is usually defined as*, line 1), implicitly refer to definitions by other authors, often cited in the footnotes. The same is true for the expression of general contemporary knowledge (e.g., as expressed by the use of the present tense and the continuously updated nature of *Wikipedia*). Although different concepts of racism are mentioned, its association with colonialism, the slave trade and the history of Europe and the United States, as well as the political far right, suggests a socially critical stance about racism (*universally condemned*, line 42) that no doubt would be formulated in a different way by authors of the extreme right, at another moment of history, in another medium and for a different audience (see also Van Dijk, 1984a, 1987, 1991, 1993, 1998, 2009b).

The encyclopedic or academic context model not only controls what can and should be said in an entry report, but also *how* such should be done, that is, the register or style associated with this genre and for this encyclopedia, as is the case for the rather formal lexical items, as in the following sentence (lines 19–22):

> whether to include symbolic or institutionalized forms of discrimination such as the circulation of ethnic stereotypes through the media, and whether to include the socio-political dynamics of social stratification that sometimes have a racial component

as well as the overall organization and format of the entry, such as its headline, byline, the initial summarizing fragment cited above, its footnotes and references, and so on. In another communicative situation, for instance talking to friends in a bar, speaking on television or the radio, or speaking for students, discourse on racism would be very different. What the different authors or speakers know about racism may well be more or less the same, but the context model and hence the discourse controlled by it may be very different. Hence, different genres, different types of communication, different participants give rise to different context models and hence different discourses. Thus, for a psychological theory of discourse, context models are a crucial component to account for the ways language users produce and understand discourse and how they manage their knowledge during discourse production.

Context models are not only implicit, but may be partly expressed or indexed by *deictic expressions and other indexicals*. Current speech acts may be expressed in performatives, emotions and opinions expressed by lexical expressions, intonation, gestures or facework, and parameters of the communicative situation may be referred to by indexical expressions. These include first and second person personal pronouns, verb tenses and spatial and temporal adverbs, among many other expressions that reflexively offer insight into the ways speakers define themselves, the recipients, the relationship of power and the ongoing interaction and its intention and purposes (Brown and Gilman, 1960; Koven, 2009).

Finally, context models control not only *how* discourse should be shaped in order to be appropriate in the current communicative situation, but also *what* information of the 'semantic' situation model is currently appropriate. Moreover, the K-device of the context model regulates what knowledge should be presupposed, recalled or asserted.

If context models are impaired or have become (partly) inaccessible, as may be the case for Alzheimer's patients or people with brain lesions, it may be expected that some of the pragmatic aspects of discourse may also be affected. This may result in inappropriate discourse, interaction and communication, e.g., lacking or erroneous deictic expressions, politeness formulas, repetition of (or questions about) already communicated information, inability to perform the specific discourse genre, as well as a general lack of interactional goals (Asp and de Villiers, 2010).

Context models provide a more explicit basis not only for the pragmatics of discourse but also for *sociolinguistics*. Its theory holds that it is not the 'objective' social characteristics (age, social class, gender, ethnicity, occupation, etc.) of the speaker that directly influence the structures and variations of text or talk, as is held in most sociolinguistic theories (see, e.g., Ammon *et al.*, 2006; Coulmas, 1998; Labov, 1972a, 1972b; Meyerhoff and Schleef, 2010), even in those focusing on contextual cues, such as Gumperz (1982a, 1982b), or on discourse structures beyond phonological variations, such as Macaulay, (2004, 2005). Rather, it is the currently relevant, subjective definition of such identities of the participants, as represented in their context models, which influences the selection of situationally appropriate variations of discourse. Social structure cannot directly influence discourse structure but needs to do so through the cognitive mediation of mental models.

Psycholinguistics and the *psychology of discourse processing* have also until now generally ignored the central role of context models. This is not surprising because most of these studies are based on laboratory experiments and not on a study of real communicative situations in everyday life. Hence such experiments are carried out with very limited variations of context, such as the age, knowledge or gender of participants in their role as experimental subjects, in which such variations are only accounted for as independent variables, but not in terms of the subjective context models of participants (see the discussion in, e.g., Koriat and Goldsmith, 1994).

3.3.5   Discourse processing

Under the ongoing control of 'semantic' situation models and 'pragmatic' context models, language users engage in the local, sequential and global production and comprehension of the actual words, clauses, sentences, sequences of sentences, paragraphs and turns of text and talk.

Language users thus strategically project situation models of events on the simplified propositional structures of sentence meanings. Causal and temporal relations between events in a model control locally coherent sequences of sentences, and higher-level global model structures govern the macrosemantics of discourse, e.g., as expressed in headlines, titles or summaries (Van Dijk, 1980; Van Dijk and Kintsch, 1983), which in discourse comprehension function as strategic markers for the derivation of overall topics or themes (Schwarz and Flammer, 1981).

Similarly, overall model structures of events may be mapped onto overall schematic structures such as those of narrative (Labov and Waletzky, 1967; Trabasso and van den Broek, 1985) or news schemas (Van Dijk, 1988b). As we have seen for the *Wikipedia* entry, the same is true for the production of a scholarly article, starting with Summary (Title + Abstract), Introduction, Theoretical Framework, Method, Data and Analysis – depending on the discipline – often explicitly expressed as conventional categories in the text itself (see, e.g., Goldman and Bisanz, 2002: Otero *et al.*, 2002).

On the other hand, as we have seen, context models control deictic expressions, speech acts, politeness markers and many other properties of discourse. Yet, as is the case for the actual control of semantic representations by underlying situation models, so the details of the control of grammatical structures by context models still need to complement the classical theories of sentence production in psycholinguistics (see, e.g., Levelt, 1989).

In general, we know more about discourse comprehension strategies, because they are more easily accessed by using text and talk as given input in laboratory experiments. Discourse production, as suggested, is controlled by underlying situation and context models and generic knowledge as well as knowledge of the rules of language and discourse, which are more difficult to give and control as input in experiments (for discourse production, see De Beaugrande 1984; Freedle, 1977; Graesser *et al.*, 2003; Zammuner, 1981; as well as references given below). Even more difficult is to assess the cognitive processes involved in actual conversation.

Details of discourse processing are beyond the scope of this chapter (see Kintsch, 1998; McNamara and Magliano, 2009; Van Dijk and Kintsch, 1983; as well as the chapters in Graesser *et al.*, 2003). Below and in the last chapter, we shall focus on the ways discourse expresses knowledge structures.

3.3.6   *Producing and understanding expository discourse*

We have seen that producing or comprehending discourse starts and finishes with the contextually controlled partial expression, construction or updating of (multimodal) situation models represented in episodic memory and mediated by semantic representations. This is true for processing discourse about specific situations, actions or events, as is the case for most everyday stories as well as for news reports.

Although much of this – except the modal nature of models – is standard theory, it has not always been recognized that this hypothesis may not apply to other discourse genres, such as expository discourse (Britton and Black, 1985), many of whose generic propositions directly map from or onto knowledge structures – traditionally located in semantic memory (see below), without intermediate 'semantic' situation models of specific events (yet *all* discourse is produced under the influence of context models, of course).

Thus, the *Wikipedia* item on racism barely reports knowledge about specific events, beyond variable opinions of different scholars, as referred to in the text, footnotes and references. That is, such expository discourse offers more abstract and generic information about the phenomenon, the history, the concept or the terms used to describe racism. As we have seen, only the context model of the authors about the communicative situation of writing for *Wikipedia* is specific. The text itself is thus a direct expression of the generic knowledge construed by the author(s), in general again on the basis of the (expository) discourse of other authors, e.g., as referred to in the footnotes. In the same way as mental models (together with context models defining genres) may define the semantics of discourse, we may assume that underlying knowledge structures also do so – as we shall see in more detail below.

3.3.7   *The organization of the generic knowledge of the Racism entry in Wikipedia*

In light of what has been remarked above about the organization of generic knowledge in memory, let us briefly examine whether and how knowledge about racism is organized and expressed in the *Wikipedia* entry.

First of all, as explained above, discourse not only expresses underlying mental models and generic knowledge, but is controlled by context models subjectively defining the communicative situation. The author(s) of the *Wikipedia* entry thus know that they are writing a specific entry for the Internet, and hence for a potentially very large audience. The 'same' knowledge would be differently expressed in a textbook, a lecture, an opinion article or in a conversation among friends.

Yet, the *Wikipedia* entry is like a chapter in a textbook, with footnotes and references, and in its overall organization and formal style. It also contextually marks from where its knowledge is derived, as indexed by such passive expressions as *"racism is usually defined"* (line 1), *"the exact definition of racism is controversial"* (line 6), *"critics argue that"* (line 9) and *"there is little scholarly agreement"* (line 7), explicitly or implicitly referring to the current literature.

As we have seen before, much knowledge, especially generic and abstract knowledge, is acquired through discourse, in this case, other academic discourse. Indeed, at its highest level, the text does not so much summarize what racism is, but how different scholars have dealt with it, and hence exhibits a well-known academic form of intertextual, and hence contextual (source), nature. This also means that it does not exhibit one integrated knowledge system of the author(s), but fragments of knowledge systems of different authors.

The semantic structure of the *Wikipedia* text exhibits complex conceptual structures that do not simply fit one of the usual conceptual formats (such as *A isa B*, or *A is composed of B, C*). It explicitly mentions various definitions that exhibit different knowledge structures. Also, the entry not only describes what racism is, that is knowledge, but also expresses an attitude, attributed to the United Nations, namely that the prejudice of racial superiority underlying racism is false and wrong. The highest summary definition, described as "usual" may be seen as the consensual one, that is, as socioculturally shared in the scholarly community, namely that racism consists of specific views, practices and actions, which are then specified, in summary, more or less as follows:

RACISM <Different definitions>
General definition: Racism = <**views** (prejudices, ideologies), **practices, actions**>
Views = <races exist; members of races have attributes; some races are superior>
Evaluation by United Nations: racial superiority <morally wrong, unjust and false>
Actions = According to definitions: {institutionalized racism: media circulate stereotypes; speaking of racial behavior, whether or not conscious and intentional, forms of discrimination}

Practices = [**history, politics, geography**]
History <colonization, apartheid, segregation, slave trade>
Politics <far right, xenophobia>
Geography <countries: South Africa, USA, etc.>
Correction of definition: Racism = not only 'racial' but also 'ethnic'
Moral: Racism is condemned by United Nations

We see that the epistemic structure of the concept of racism integrates, first of all, many other specific concepts of the same knowledge domain about society, namely about groups and group relations, such as discrimination, prejudices and ideologies. Then it specifies some of these forms of social cognition, such as (i) views about the existence and superiority of races, (ii) what social actions (e.g., of institutions) are considered forms of racist discrimination and (iii) what practices in the past and in what countries were based on racist prejudices. Finally, the definition also presupposes a misunderstanding of many readers by correcting that racism is not only racial but also ethnic.

Ignoring many details of the actual discursive formulation of this item (a full discourse analysis would take dozens of pages), the question is whether we are able to derive a *schematic form* of this kind of abstract, generic knowledge, at least for the domain of social relations of power abuse among groups (which would also characterize sexism and other forms of domination). Thus, abstracting even further, we see that racism is implicitly defined as a morally wrong system of group domination consisting of different forms of discriminatory action or practices of the dominant (mostly white) groups (especially on the right) and countries, and based on specific ideologies and attitudes about racial or ethnic specificity and superiority, historically causing specific systems of domination (such as colonialism, the slave trade, apartheid and segregation).

We see that the knowledge structure on racism is dominated by higher-level notions such as groups and group relations, social cognitions (e.g., prejudices, attitudes and ideologies), history (of racist systems), geography (of racist countries), as well as international institutions (such as the United Nations).

Although such an informal summary of the definition comes closer to a schematic structure, we would still need to apply further abstraction, which would involve basic knowledge categories such as human groups, group relations, domination, and ideas (views, attitudes, prejudices, ideologies) and a moral evaluation.

Notice that although this summary and the rest of the (long) article provides a summary of much of the current knowledge on racism as it is reported in the literature, it still tends to favor a more traditional view of racism as (i) prevalent in the past and on the extreme right and as (ii) focusing on explicit and blatant forms of prejudice and discrimination. Indeed, most forms of everyday racism today are no longer based on views of racial superiority (but on cultural identities differences) and certainly not only on the extreme right and not only in the past.

Linguistically, the common academic use of nominalizations (views, actions, practices) also leaves initially implicit who exactly has these views and who engages in such actions and practices, even when later 'whites,' and countries with groups of European descent are mentioned.

In other words, despite the concrete examples of historical systems of racist domination, the initial definition is of racism in much more general terms. Indeed, it would also fit a movement of Black Power and views about Black Is Beautiful, better characterized as forms of antiracist counter-power, and not as forms of domination. Indeed, specifically missing is the general characterization of racism as a system of social domination being reproduced by specific racist views and practices.

3.4   The standard cognitive theory of knowledge

Mental models represent the *subjective knowledge* people build of the situations and events of their environment, and as expressed and reproduced in, for instance, everyday stories and news reports. We have seen that such models, whether obtained by observation or by discourse, may be generalized, bottom-up, and thus give rise to generic knowledge, and that such generic knowledge is again instantiated and applied, *top-down*, in the construction of new models defining new experiences. As we have seen for the *Wikipedia* entry, such generic knowledge may also be derived from other discourses, as is the case for the *Wikipedia* entry itself. Especially relevant for this book and this chapter is that most of this generic knowledge, as reproduced in public discourse, is socially shared by the members of epistemic communities.

In the preceding sections we have been quite brief about the very nature of generic knowledge, and only assumed it is stored in semantic memory of LTM, probably modally grounded and applied in the construction of propositions (sentence and text meanings) and mental models. However, as the core of this chapter and as the cognitive basis of this whole study, we need to be more explicit about the units, structures and organization of the knowledge system.

In our very informal analysis of the initial fragment of the *Wikipedia* entry on racism, we have already seen that there does not seem to be a standard format for the organization of knowledge, besides such general conceptual relations as A is a kind of B, A consists of B and C, or A manifests itself as B and C, etc. Thus, what people know about racism has a very different format from what they know about chairs, professors, chocolate or computers.

Strangely, despite the vast number of studies in cognitive psychology, neuropsychology and Artificial Intelligence (AI), we as yet know surprisingly little about the nature of knowledge as a cognitive system or human capacity. Here is a summary of the major theoretical proposals of earlier studies (with only minimal references to some key texts – because the literature on each dimension of the theory is enormous):

- Conceptual knowledge is assumed to be stored in the human memory system, specifically in relatively stable and accessible **long-term memory** as it is neurally implemented and distributed in various regions of the brain, and as distinct from **working memory** (Conway, 1997).
- More specifically, knowledge is stored in what has been called **semantic memory** (a term that is hardly appropriate because it has little to do with the semantics of any language) – as distinct from **episodic memory**. This distinction, however, is not made by all theorists, who may view episodic memory as part of one memory system (Baddeley *et al.*, 2002; Tulving, 1972, 1983).
- The basic units of the knowledge system are **concepts**. Such concepts may be represented as *prototypes* (for instance, representing the main characteristics of phenomena such as racism; Rosch and Lloyd, 1978), *schemas* (representing the structure of a discriminatory act; Minsky, 1975) or *scripts* (e.g., of denouncing racial discrimination to the police; Schank and Abelson, 1977).
- The system of concepts may be hierarchically structured by **categorical** (superordinate or subordinate) **relations** (e.g., racism is a system of domination, as is the case for sexism) (Caramazza and Mahon, 2003; Collins and Quillian, 1972).
- Newer proposals on the structure of knowledge propose that concepts are (partly) grounded in **modal neural networks**. For instance the concept RACISM may be grounded in (i) visual regions of the brain (representing the visual result of perception of color differences between people), (ii) discriminatory actions, (iii) negative opinions and emotions (hate, fear, etc.) (Barsalou, 2003, 2008).
- Concepts are 'syntagmatically' related with other concepts to form (factual or spurious) **beliefs**. Thus, in the *Wikipedia* entry, the concept of 'racism' is associated with beliefs of superiority or priority by white people (Schacter and Scarry, 2000).
- Beliefs are organized in **belief systems**, variously organized by natural or social **domains**, as are our beliefs about nature, animals, human beings, social groups or organizations, politics, education or the mass media. For instance, our knowledge about racism is related to our knowledge about prejudice, groups of people, group relations, group identity, discrimination, power and social inequality, as is also shown in the descriptions of the *Wikipedia* article. Unfortunately, belief systems are less studied in cognitive psychology than in social psychology and the social sciences (Abelson, 1973). In cognitive and neuropsychology, however, there in increasing interest in the neurally

based differences of knowledge domains (see, e.g., Leonard *et al.*, 2009; Shears *et al.*, 2008).

3.5   The role of knowledge in discourse processing: empirical research

On the basis of the theoretical framework summarized in the preceding sections, we are now able to review some of the empirical studies that have been carried out on the role of knowledge in the production and comprehension of discourse. Then, finally, we need to examine the reverse question, namely the role of discourse in the (trans)formation of the knowledge system – and more concretely, how people obtain knowledge, that is, *learn* from text and talk.

As has been recalled above, most psychological studies of the role of knowledge in discourse processing have been carried out in the laboratory and the classroom. This has the obvious advantage of strict(er) control of test materials, subjects, specific tasks to be carried out and measurable or otherwise analyzable results, such as recall, recognition, reading times, priming, problem solving, and so on. The disadvantages are also well known: laboratory situations especially are only approximate simulations of natural communication situations, where language users may be very different (in gender, age, education, reading abilities, motivations, interest, etc.). In communicative situations outside the laboratory, discourse goals may be complex and diffuse, discourse production or comprehension may not be completed, and there are many more genres of discourse being used. In sum, most of the laboratory-based research we review provides only fragmentary and even ad hoc insights into the role of knowledge in discourse processing.

As to the more specific topic of this chapter, perhaps the most defeating limitation of any experimental study is the problem of *how to describe, measure or analyze the knowledge of the experimental subjects* – both before and after reading or hearing a discourse. Even when limited to a special knowledge domain or topic – as is usually the case – such as knowledge about racism, we are only able to assess part of the actual knowledge of the subjects. Some of this knowledge may be shared, and represent social knowledge, but at least some other knowledge may be more idiosyncratic, based on personal experiences or interest, thus also giving rise to different mental models and hence to different processing of discourse. It is hard to tease these different types of knowledge apart and to generalize over groups of subjects about how in general personal and social knowledge have different influence on the production or comprehension of discourse.

In a more explicit and practical way, this issue has been dealt with extensively in research on *knowledge acquisition, knowledge engineering, expert systems*, etc. – in which experts are interviewed so as to assess their specialized knowledge in view of representing such knowledge in computer programs for the automatic performance of specialized tasks. This is a vast and specialized field, however, whose review is outside of the scope of this book. In addition, much of this research is more concerned with the formal representations of such languages in computer programs, whereas we are (here) more interested in the study of knowledge as represented in memory and how it is managed and expressed in text and talk (for detail on knowledge representation in AI and related domains, see, e.g., Van Harmelen *et al.*, 2008).

3.5.1   The role of 'prior knowledge' in discourse comprehension

Most of the empirical studies on knowledge and discourse focus on the role of what is routinely called 'prior knowledge' in discourse comprehension. In general, these studies study independent subject variables, such as the general or specific *domain* or *topic* knowledge of (different) subjects, on the one hand, and the effects of different tasks and text materials on the other.

Given the theory summarized above, it may be expected that, all other things being equal, subjects with more (general or specialized) knowledge are able to construe more detailed situation models of a discourse, because they are able to derive more relevant inferences from their general knowledge. If the (semantic) comprehension of a discourse about specific events, such as a news report or story, is based on a situation model, then this means that such readers have better (more 'deeply,' more completely, more coherently, etc.) understood the text. Such better understanding should show, for instance, in more detailed recall protocols, longer delays of recall, correctly answering questions, especially those that require inferences from explicitly expressed information in the text, and so on.

However, although such is the general prediction for the outcomes of experimental research, there are, as usual, many variations on this pattern of theoretically based expectations and general findings. Indeed, this may happen if, for instance, experts (who by definition know much about a topic) process the text much less carefully and thus may pay less attention to details that cannot be predicted by inferences from their general knowledge.

Although most research on the topic of the role of prior knowledge was only starting to get published after the 'discursive turn' in cognitive psychology in the late 1970s, there was some earlier research on the role of prior knowledge on discourse comprehension. Bartlett's seminal book *Remembering*, reporting research conducted in 1918 (but not published until 1932) on natural discourse comprehension and (serial) recall, showed that comprehension as measured by various delays of recall tends to be gradually adapted to the knowledge of the subjects: a North American indigenous story was thus understood and gradually more and more recalled in terms of the 'Western' sociocultural knowledge of the readers rather than the (indigenous) knowledge (e.g., about ghosts) presupposed by the story. As one of the precursors of the cognitive revolution of the 1960s, Bartlett thus showed not only that understanding is not mere repetition or imitation, but is *(re)construction*, but also that knowledge is represented in *schemas* – one of the distinct theoretical concepts of later cognitive psychology. At the same time, Bartlett thus deals with social psychological and anthropological (intercultural) aspects of knowledge, namely what happens if people of a different epistemic community read and (try to) understand a text. We shall come back to these topics in the next chapters – also because they have barely been addressed in most cognitive psychological work on discourse comprehension.

The theory of context models accounts for this fundamental result by including strategies about the relevant knowledge of the participants in the K-device of context models: readers activate their own knowledge system in order to understand discourse, and so do speakers or writers (as did the indigenous people who shared the story used by Bartlett: "The War of the Ghosts").

Turning to more contemporary (mostly laboratory) research on prior knowledge, we may summarize some results as follows (for review, see, e.g., Mannes and St. George, 1996).

- Waern (1977), in one of the earliest studies on the role of knowledge in discourse comprehension, reproduced the effect already found by Bartlett, namely that readers tend to **assimilate** their comprehension of a text to their existing knowledge (defined as beliefs expressed in statements previously accepted as true).
- Alvermann and associates in the 1980s examined comprehension of counterintuitive science texts after activating students' prior knowledge (misconceptions) with reading activities. They found that, in order to correct prior **misconceptions**, science texts need to explicitly reject such beliefs and show the correct beliefs (Alvermann and Hague, 1989; Alvermann and Hynd, 1989). Hence, again we see that unless prior knowledge is explicitly corrected, it tends to influence the way we understand discourse. Only incongruity of earlier beliefs with texts may produce new learning (Kintsch, 1980). Similarly, Kendeou and van den Broek (2007) showed that in actual processing, readers adjust their comprehension when the text explicitly refutes their earlier misconceptions. Lipson (1982) found that readers (in a recognition test) tend to rely on prior knowledge even when it is incorrect. Mannes and St. George (1996) conclude that prior knowledge structure (an outline) that is different from a text to be read stimulates elaborations and better integrated comprehension of text. On the other hand, a consistent outline merely confirms earlier knowledge, but does not lead to the generation of new ideas.

- Many studies show that, in general, level of **expertise** (more prior knowledge) favors discourse comprehension, recall and recognition (Samuelstuen and Bråten, 2005; Spires and Donley, 1998; Valencia and Stallman, 1989). However, specific results depend on the text structures, tasks or questions asked to test comprehension – as we shall review in more detail below (Caillies and Tapiero, 1997; Caillies *et al.*, 2002; Calisir and Gurel, 2003; Callahan and Drum, 1984; Kendeou and van den Broek, 2007). For instance, less knowledgeable students may better comprehend a text when it is better (e.g., hierarchically) organized and when they may reread the text or reread notes, etc. (Haenggi and Perfetti, 1992).
- Fincher-Kiefer (1992) showed that, whereas readers with different **knowledge levels** are all able to make local inferences, only those with higher levels of knowledge are better able to make global inferences.
- It is often found that more **knowledgeable subjects** take more advantage of more implicit texts, whereas subjects with less knowledge benefit more from explicitly coherent texts (Kintsch, 1994; McNamara, 2001; McNamara and Kintsch, 1996; Schnotz, 1993) or more elaborated texts (Kim and van Dusen, 1998). This is especially the case for informative, rather than for persuasive texts (Kamalski *et al.*, 2008). McNamara (2001), examining the role of various levels of knowledge and coherence, found that, under specific conditions, high-knowledge subjects take more advantage of a low-coherent text. O'Reilly and McNamara (2007), on the other hand, show that it is not generally the case that high-knowledge readers benefit from more implicit texts – this appears to be true especially for less skilled high-knowledge readers. Skilled, high-knowledge readers also benefit from more coherent discourse. See also Ozuru *et al.* (2009).
- Kobayashi (2009) showed that students with more **topic knowledge** – and with more (college) education (and hence probably with more overall knowledge) – better understand intertextual relations and intratextual arguments.
- Metusalem *et al.* (2012), using ERP/N400 (brain scan) methodology, although not explicitly using the notion of mental model, showed that sentences in discourse are processed on the basis of general knowledge about the events described, and that such knowledge even facilitates the processing of words that are related to general event knowledge but incoherent in the text.

The (predictable) general conclusion from this experimental research is that subjects with more or better organized prior knowledge (however defined, tested or construed) tend to do better on most aspects of discourse processing: better comprehension, more recall, etc. They especially tend to do better than subjects with less knowledge when texts are more implicit, less coherent, etc., because in that case they can take advantage of their better knowledge to generate more inferences, and hence construe more integrated mental models – representing better discourse comprehension. Low-knowledge subjects generally need more explicit, more coherent and better organized texts in order to (better) comprehend them.

We also see that, although the effect of prior knowledge is pervasive, exactly how subjects understand and recall discourse, such as cohesion, coherence or various kinds of organizers (like summaries), also very obviously depends on text structure. As just suggested, high-knowledge subjects benefit less from better discourse structure than low-knowledge subjects – and may even be less motivated to pay attention to texts that are too explicit, and thus may fail to attend to all (new) information in the text (see also Hidi, 1995).

Incidentally, none of the studies reviewed engages in a detailed theory of knowledge and knowledge representation in memory. Authors only briefly sketch the processes involved in the activation and application of knowledge in comprehension and the production of recall protocols, replies to questions and so on. Hence they can only superficially account for the exact reasons *why* better prior knowledge has the effects it has on comprehension and recall. This is a problem that should more generally be attributed to the short, limited format of experimental articles in psychological journals – which hardly allow the development of detailed theory. In fact, they do not even have a standard section such as 'Theoretical Framework' – which usually is limited to the 'Introduction.' Predictions and hypotheses in that case are often barely more than the result of common sense arguments, based on minor theory fragments, rather than on detailed theory – which usually is relegated to book chapters.

3.6   Knowledge acquisition by discourse

We have often repeated before that most of our personal and especially our socially shared generic knowledge is acquired by text and talk. Obviously, initially, most knowledge is derived from non-verbal, multimodal experiences: vision, audition, touch, (inter)action, etc., as is the case for babies and toddlers. But as soon as children watch TV and go to school, when they are being read stories by their caregivers or are able to talk to their peers, knowledge acquisition soon becomes largely discursive, especially for knowledge about non-observables, such as non-present entities (people, animals, things, countries, etc.), mental objects (beliefs) and all abstract objects (time, numbers, structures, systems, etc.).

For most adults in contemporary information society, practically all new knowledge is thus acquired from mass-media discourse – TV, newspaper, radio, Internet, books, etc. – educational discourse and the many genres of professional discourse, or – indirectly – from the everyday conversations or institutional talk based on these sources. Interestingly, we do not know if there is even any large-scale, longitudinal research of the sources of knowledge of adult citizens. In any case, if we limit knowledge to the socially shared knowledge of epistemic communities, the very necessity of the communication and validation of beliefs as knowledge generally implies that such knowledge is acquired discursively in the first place.

The obvious exception to the pervasive discursive source of knowledge would be the basic beliefs acquired in everyday experiences about fundamental properties of the world that are not typically taught in school or commented on in children's stories, but are nevertheless shared, and hence may be presupposed in public discourse. For instance, we probably have not explicitly learned by talk or text that people (outside of fiction) cannot walk through a wall or fly, as well as about many properties of the physical and biological world: what most things look like, how they feel, what they do or what their functions are.

The detailed consequences of this massive presence of discourse as our main source of knowledge are as yet hardly made explicit in theoretical frameworks about the nature of that knowledge, its organization in memory and its distribution and uses in society. For instance, if language has many expressions referring to abstract and other amodally acquired knowledge, we may not want to abandon the possibility that at least part of our knowledge is represented in memory in some kind of symbolic 'language' that has its own neural grounding and that may also function as the interface that may be the missing link between language use and experience. It surely is remarkable how easily humans are able to 'translate' their sensorimotor experiences, or those of others, into talk or text – or vice versa, understand discourse on such experiences by building models of them.

3.6.1   Learning from text

At least one discipline and direction of research has obviously thought about the discursive basis of knowledge acquisition: psychology and its classical study of 'learning from text,' and its important applications, especially in education. As is the case for most other work in the cognitive psychology of discourse, these studies are also largely experimental and take place in the laboratory and sometimes in classrooms – and very seldom in other, more 'natural' communication situations (for review, see, e.g., Alexander and Jetton, 2003; Goldman, 1997).

This also means that language users as experimental subjects have very different context models from 'real' language users in natural situations, and the same is true of those who conduct the experiments, who have different context models from the authors of the texts that may be used in the experiment. Indeed, the context models of the laboratory are specific, and involve the lab as the Setting, specific time constraints, subjects as Participants, experimental Actions with experimental Goals.

The experimental situation also requires control of the whole process: special materials (often constructed ones), special modes of reading or listening, time limitations, and products (recall protocols, replies to questions, reaction times, etc.) that can be measured or analyzed relatively easily. This means, maybe quite trivially but rather significantly, that it is not feasible (if possible in the first place) to somehow get at all the relevant knowledge of subjects about a domain or topic before and after an experiment, and hence what *new* knowledge has thus been acquired and how it is integrated into previously existing knowledge. This means that in order to control prior knowledge, subjects are usually being questioned about specific prior knowledge of topics or domains or are being taught such knowledge prior to an experiment about the same topic or domain.

There are many other problems and questions related to this kind of experimental research in the laboratory – and even in the classroom. First of all, it is not always (made) clear in the experiments what 'learning' means exactly. Subjects may learn the information provided by a text, as do many students in the classroom or reading a textbook. Learning in that case usually means they are able to reproduce such knowledge, for instance in immediate (or sometimes somewhat delayed) recall or question answering. On the other hand, we may say that we really learn from text and acquire knowledge only if it is retained for a long(er) time (or forever) and can be used in many other situations, for problem solving, deriving inferences, and – indeed – to understand future discourses about the same domain or topic. To test these abilities one would need more complex and often longitudinal experimental designs – which are very hard to carry out. Hence, it makes sense to distinguish between 'learning text' and 'learning from text' (as acquiring knowledge from text).

Indeed, more generally, can we speak of 'learning' (from text or otherwise) if people are able to use newly acquired information in the same situation, but no longer recall it or are able to use it a day or a few days later? Much of the detailed fact knowledge we thus 'learn' at school is later forgotten, although there is evidence of very long-term knowledge learned (such as learning Spanish or math at school) which may still be active (at least in recognition, after more than 50 years (see, e.g., Bahrick, 1984; Bahrick and Hall, 1991). Note, though, that knowledge of language and mathematics is not exactly fact knowledge but close to procedural knowledge, ability, which is retained for longer.

The issue of the nature of learning has implications for the general theory of knowledge, namely the status of knowledge we once had but have now 'forgotten.' The same may be asked for various forms of implicit knowledge, or knowledge that is only retrieved incompletely, or only recognized with given search cues. Again we see that the notion of knowledge is very fuzzy, on the one hand because of the distinction between autobiographical personal knowledge (derived from models in EM) and socially shared knowledge, between declarative knowledge and procedural knowledge, between actively accessible and passively accessible knowledge, between correct and incorrect knowledge, vague and precise knowledge and so on.

Thirdly, the kind of knowledge learned from text in the laboratory is not the kind of everyday knowledge most subjects (usually university students) already have – as members of the epistemic community. Rather, such knowledge must be rather specific or specialized – and is probably not directly relevant in their everyday lives. Hence, after a test such new information may be retained long enough to perform the experimental tasks (recall, answer questions, etc.), but is hardly the kind of knowledge that is acquired more or less permanently.

Finally, even if we are able to assess that experimental subjects have 'learned' specific knowledge from text, e.g., by analyzing protocols, we still have no idea how this new knowledge is stored in the knowledge system, and especially how it is related to other knowledge. If learning is synonymous with the acquisition of relatively permanent knowledge, we need further insight into its *integration* in the conceptual system (see also Kintsch, 1998).

With these caveats in mind about empirical research into the acquisition of knowledge from discourse, let us now briefly summarize the results of some experimental studies. We shall do so by organizing the studies according to the independent variables that influence learning from text – with the important proviso that many, if not most, of the studies do not clearly distinguish between 'text learning' (i.e., learning text contents), often assessed by recall, recognition, question answering and other methods, on the one hand, *and the acquisition of new information derived from text and its integration into the conceptual knowledge system* – as assessed, for instance, by its later use in tasks unrelated to the earlier text from which the new knowledge items were derived. If such use of new knowledge takes places in the same experimental session, it will usually be very difficult to make sure it is not ad hoc (non-integrated) knowledge that may not be used on later occasions. In that case, the knowledge may only exist as part of the episodic context model of a previous task.

Obviously, even in situations of genuine knowledge acquisition, subjects may later forget such knowledge anyway – as is the case for much of what we learned in school or from reading the newspaper. Since much of the new knowledge acquired from school texts is not everyday knowledge, but often (semi) scientific knowledge that is not part of people's prior knowledge, and such new scientific knowledge may be hardly relevant in the lives of people, the tendency will be that most of this new knowledge is no longer or only partly accessible after several months or years.

The conditions of learning from text, experimentally defined as independent variables, may be organized by the following general categories, mostly used in combination in complex designs. For instance, it is quite typical to combine high- or low- prior domain or topic knowledge of subjects with more or less coherent text structures, as we have seen above. Such designs presuppose that the experimental conditions mutually influence each other. Thus, generally, more coherent discourse will enhance understanding, which in turn positively influences learning from text, but this is especially the case for less knowledgeable subjects, who can rely less on their own knowledge to make inferences and hence need the text to do so in more coherent (and usually more explicit) ways. Here is a brief summary of these various conditions – to be specified below in the review of some of the literature:

1. Context conditions
   a. Experimental situation (Time, Place, e.g., laboratory, classroom)
   b. Participant properties and activities
      i. Experimenter (gender, age, etc.; instructions, task formulation, etc.)
      ii. Subject properties and activities (gender, age, etc.; goals; reading ability, prior knowledge, learning strategies, etc.)
      iii. Interaction and collaboration among participants
   c. Experimental activities (e.g., reading, summarizing, paraphrasing, elaborating).
2. Text conditions
   a. Multimodal: with pictures, schemas, maps, etc.
   b. Hypertext, text complexes
   c. Text only
      i. Surface structures
         written vs. spoken
         syntax, lexicon, cohesion
      ii. Semantic structures
         local and global coherence
         more or less explicit text
         more or less elaborated text, etc.

3.6.2   Context conditions: Setting

As we indicated above, most experimental studies **take place** in the *laboratory* and the *classroom*, a situational condition that of course influences the context models of the experimental subjects, and hence their reading and learning, but which is usually taken for granted and not studied as an independent variable in a comparative experimental design involving different experimental settings.

There are various **Time** variables. **Date** and **hour** of the experiments are conditions that are seldom reported, although the **time of day** especially may have some influence on reading and learning (e.g., if they are related to the sleepiness of tiredness of the subjects). **Reading or study times** are standard conditions – and hence nearly always reported – and it seems obvious that when subjects have more (or at least enough) time to read or to listen to text or talk, this will positively influence learning (see, e.g., the early experiments by King in the 1970s (e.g., King, 1973). Generally, having more time facilitates learning because this allows subjects to derive more bridging inferences (for low-coherent discourse – see, e.g., McNamara and Kintsch, 1996), construct local and global coherence and construe more detailed situation models (for stories or other event discourses) or establish connections between text meanings and prior knowledge structures – so as to construe new conceptual structures in memory.

3.6.3   *Participant characteristics*

All discourse processing takes place in a communicative situation, even in the laboratory, and obviously such a situation also involves Participants. Strangely, experimental reports in psychology usually only provide more or less detailed information about the experimental **subjects**, but little or nothing about the **experimenter** or other participants in such a situation, although implicitly the authors of the report (or their assistants) may be assumed to have this role. Generally, no further information is provided, probably because it is assumed that the properties (age, gender, ethnicity, friendliness, etc.) of the experimenter do not measurably influence reading or learning, although such is no doubt the case in natural settings (as we know, for instance, for the role of gender and ethnicity). In educational contexts, however, there is research on the instructional dialogues and self-assessment of teachers (Roskos *et al.*, 2000).

The experimenter is usually implicitly present only through previous **instructions** given to the experimental subjects. For instance, an instruction to summarize a text facilitates learning from expository text (see, e.g., Armbruster *et al.*, 1987; Coleman *et al.*, 1997). More generally, instructional strategies variably influence learning (see, e.g., Kanuka, 2005).

Obviously, as suggested, information about experimental **subjects**, and how they were recruited, is standard in psychological reports, although usually the information provided is only what is experimentally tested as an independent variable, such as occupation (mostly students), age, gender and prior knowledge. Since most subjects are students (from primary school to university), and usually from the same educational group or institution, they may be supposed to have similar social background, education, etc., although such individual differences are seldom described or explicitly studied (see, however, Duek, 2000; Williams, 1991). Let us summarize some of the results that have been found for the role of individual characteristics of the subjects in the process of learning (see also Fox, 2009).

Prior knowledge. Crucial in a study of learning defined as knowledge acquisition, is of course the prior (declarative, conceptual) knowledge of the subjects. Above we have already reviewed the usually positive role of prior knowledge in discourse understanding and recall: subjects who know more about a domain or topic better understand (recall, etc.) texts on such a domain or topic, for instance because they are better able to derive inferences to construe local and global coherence as well as mental models (Britton *et al.*, 1998). These more detailed or better connected semantic representations or models in turn positively influence knowledge acquisition from discourse. Of a large number of studies, see e.g., Armand (2001); Butcher and Kintsch (2003); Kintsch (1994); Lipson (1982); McNamara and Kintsch (1996); Stahl *et al.* (1996); and Wolfe and Mienko (2007).

Boscolo and Mason (2003) found that prior knowledge not only generally facilitates learning but at the same time also enhances interest, which itself is a well-known factor of learning. As reviewed above, several studies relate prior knowledge to the role of more or less coherent discourse, with the common finding that more coherent texts are especially useful for low-knowledge subjects, as we saw above (see, e.g., McNamara and Kintsch, 1996).

Prior knowledge not only pertains to general world knowledge. It obviously also involves knowledge of the language (usually taken for granted in experiments that do not test linguistic abilities) as well as knowledge of genre and the structures of text and talk (Berkenkotter and Huckin, 1995; Goldman and Rakestraw, 2000; Goldman and Varma, 1995). Thus, crucially, language users in general, and hence subjects in the laboratory or the classroom in particular, need to know the differences between, for instance, a story and an expository text – both as to their communicative and interactional functions (part of their context models), and as to their prototypical structures. It is usually found that when subjects know and monitor text structures (as part of their metacognitive and metatextual abilities) this also contributes to better comprehension, recall and learning (see, e.g., Dymock, 1999; Thiede *et al.*, 2003).

Especially interesting are the studies that compare prior knowledge with incompatible information in the text, as we already saw above. What do subjects do: incorrectly understand and represent the text because of their (e.g., mistaken) prior knowledge, or correct their prior knowledge as a consequence of text understanding? It is generally found that in order to change their prior knowledge, subjects need to be told or read that such knowledge was wrong. Thus, it is easier to learn new knowledge than to correct inaccurate old knowledge (see, e.g., Lipson, 1982; Maria and MacGinitie, 1987).

Reading ability. One of the most obvious and powerful conditions influencing discourse comprehension, and hence, indirectly, learning from text is the reading ability of subjects. Traditionally measured in terms of grammar and the lexicon, discourse studies have emphasized the crucial role of the semantic competence of generating inferences, establishing local and global coherence, deriving macrostructures, generating summaries, overall recall and thus the ability to construct a rich and highly connected situation model. It follows that if subjects have difficulty reading and understanding (especially complex) texts, it is plausible they also may have more problems integrating new information in their conceptual system (but for dyslexic children, see Bråten et al., 2010). As we have seen above for prior knowledge, research with subjects with different reading ability (measured by standard tests) finds that less able readers need more explicit/coherent texts in order to understand them (Lipson, 1982; see also Williams, 1991).

Gender. Do women and men differ when learning from text? Although gender is often considered to be one of the relevant variables of learning, studies about knowledge acquisition from text usually do not include gender as one of the independent variables of the design. Thus, Chambers and André (1997) found that gender only makes a difference when mediating prior knowledge, interest and experience. Similarly, Slotte et al. (2001) conclude that there is no gender difference in comprehending (philosophical) texts, but found that women tend to make more notes than men, and this may influence learning. On the other hand, gender and gendered language in the classroom is known to influence interest and motivation and hence learning (see the discussion in Guzzetti, 2001).

Learning goals. One of the crucial parameters of context models are the goals of the participants, represented as the state of affairs to be realized by action. Obviously, the goals of experiments, defined by explicit or implicit tasks and whether self-imposed or imposed by the experimenter, also influence how texts are read and understood. Hence, similar to our notion of context model, Beck et al. (1989) argue that teachers should help students to develop a "model of the situation" that is the target of instruction – including clear content goals, for instance.

Goals of learning from text have been studied since the 1970s (see, e.g., Gagné and Rothkopf, 1975). For later studies of goals as variable conditions of learning, see, e.g., Dee-Lucas and Larkin (1995); Duell (1984); McCrudden and Schraw, (2007); Pfister and Oehl, (2009); Wosnitza and Volet, (2009).

Theoretically, the goals of learners are assumed to be represented in their context models and as such they control text production and comprehension, together with other cognitive properties of participants, such as knowledge and interest (Van Dijk, 2008a, 2009a; see also Hijzen *et al.*, 2006; Rinck and Bower, 2004).

Incidentally, these *pragmatic* goals should be carefully distinguished from the representation of the goals of *represented* participants, for instance in stories, which are represented in the *semantic* situation model of the participants, and which crucially control story comprehension (of many studies, see, e.g., Goldman *et al.*, 1999; Trabasso, 2005).

Interest and motivation. Many studies have emphasized the important role of interest and motivation in learning from text. Usually a distinction is made between the general interest of subjects (in many contexts and for many topics), associated with personality characteristics, intelligence, etc., and local or topical interest (just for the specific text or topic used in the current situation), and between cognitive and emotional interest (Harp and Mayer, 1997; Kintsch, 1980; Renninger *et al.*, 1992; Schiefele, 1999; Wade, 1992).

Incidentally, these studies usually take the notion of interest (about topics or materials or of people) theoretically for granted, as is the case for many properties of the experimental situation in the laboratory. Indeed, if interest is not part of the conceptual knowledge system, nor part of episodic memory of events, but still a property of people's conduct or character, how and where is such a property cognitively stored? If it is a recurrent property of actions, it may have an episodic dimension, but not as a unique part of unique experiences, but as a general, abstract property of 'Self' as the central participant of autobiographical episodes (models). On the other hand, as a situational variable (interest in this particular text or topic), interest would obviously be part of the context model of subjects.

Consistent with the usual expectations, subject interests or interesting materials, tasks or goals, all contribute to enhanced attention, deeper processing, better models and better and well organized knowledge – again interacting, as everywhere in the studies reviewed here, with other variables (see, e.g., Garner *et al.*, 1989). Boscolo and Mason (2003) found that interest increases with knowledge. Chambers and André (1997), in a study of gender differences for text processing about electricity, found that such differences only exist when one excludes level of knowledge, interest and experience. Naceur and Schiefele (2005), discussing various personality characteristics, found that interest not only has a long-term effect on learning but also has an effect that is independent of other learning variables. Sadoski (2001) shows that in order for (expository) texts to be found interesting, they need to be concrete, and only then will they be better recalled and learned.

Interest is usually defined as part of the broader dynamic subject characteristic of **motivation**, another participant characteristic often studied in text processing and learning (of the large literature on the role of motivation in learning from text, see, e.g., Anmarkrud and Bråten, 2009; Carr *et al.*, 1998; and Salili *et al.*, 2001).

3.6.4   Interaction and collaboration

Whereas traditional studies largely investigate how individual subjects process and learn from text, contemporary research increasingly simulates natural discourse processing and learning in natural situations, including the interaction and collaboration between various participants, for instance in the classroom (see, e.g., Cowie and van der Aalsvoort 2000; Goldman, 1997).

Although it is true that in such situations individual participants themselves still need to read, listen and process (multimodal) experimental materials according to the fundamental constraints of individual cognition (memory limitations, representation, storage, retrieval, recall, etc.), the context of 'peer learning' is, of course, quite different from individual learning. Participants jointly engage in experimental activities, cooperate, discuss and mutually help each other in the accomplishment of learning tasks – as is also the case in much natural discourse processing, problem solving and professional interaction (see, e.g., Frederiksen, 1999).

Such forms of **collaborative learning** presuppose not only prior knowledge of the language, rules and structures of talk in interaction, as well as knowledge of the domain or topic the instructional materials are about, but also prior knowledge and application of the general and specific (e.g., educational, experimental) rules and strategies of social interaction in general, and interactional argumentation in particular (see also Lin and Anderson, 2008; Nussbaum, 2008).

Studies of collaborative learning generally find that cooperation facilitates learning. There are several theoretical reasons why this is the case. First of all, explicit reflection and discussion about discourse presupposes or implies enhanced think aloud, attention, repetition and explanation – which in single subject text processing also facilitates learning. Secondly, discussion involves argumentation, and argumentation often implies making inferences from text as well as prior knowledge. Thirdly, joint text processing obviously presupposes a larger, combined knowledge set from which relevant inferences may be derived. Fourthly, memory limitations, both of working memory as well as episodic memory, are less constrained in groups than for individual subjects: what one person overlooks or forgets may be attended to or recalled by one or more others. This is obviously especially the case for amnesic subjects (Duff *et al.*, 2008).

Much experimental research of the last decades has studied such collaborative learning of text and talk, often in educational situations and with educational materials. Arvaja *et al.* (2000) emphasize that the positive results of cooperative learning presuppose shared reflection: if there is no shared, high-level understanding and interactive reasoning then learning in groups barely has advantages. In other words, experiments of collaborative learning require a design in which the nature of the interaction, the materials and the tasks require and enable reasoning and sharing high-level understanding. Chan (2001) also showed that collaborative learning is successful only if the participants go beyond more superficial interaction (rating, ignoring, correcting, etc.) and engage in problem-centered moves: such as problem formulation, recognition and explanations. Chinn *et al.* (2000) focused in more detail on the actual discourse structures of peer learning and found that the structure of arguments (against or in favor of a conclusion) of a discussion provides insight into the way a joint task is accomplished.

As is the case for all discourse processing, in collaborative discourse processing the 'depth' of processing (inferences, explanations, discussions, etc.) is also a valid indicator of memory and learning – whether in the construction of mental models, as is the case for stories, or for the construction of knowledge units. Jeong and Chi (1997, 2007) and Jeong and Lee (2008) show that overall group learning also depends on the various roles or types of participants – for instance whether they are more or less active or reflective, or whether pairs of learners are just 'nominal' or engage in real, cooperative interaction.

Important for our review is not only the collaborative aspects of interactive learning, but also the (usually) **oral nature** of (usually) classroom debate, discussion, teaching and learning. Learning from oral discourse, whether interactive or not, of course poses special conditions on comprehension because of the usual limitations of working memory. Whereas in most forms of learning from (written) text, subjects are able to self-pace their reading speed, can reread what they have read, and so on, in oral discourse processing this is not the case. Moreover, in oral discourse processing attention needs to be focused so as not to miss words or sentence parts. Moreover, spreading activation not only activates relevant knowledge and inferences, but also other, possibly less relevant, associated beliefs that may prevent focusing – which in listening to oral discourse may mean losing part of the input. For detail on the specific role of **discussion** in learning, see, among many other studies, Alvermann *et al.*, (1995); Bennett *et al.*, (2010); Chinn *et al.*, (2000); Goodyear and Zenios, (2007); Pontecorvo, (1987); Wilen, (1990).

3.6.5   Experimental activities and strategies

The activities of the experimental subjects are the heart of the experiment and define what they (must) do, apart from reading text (or listening to talk). Generally these activities are varied so as to obtain different results of understanding and learning (for a study of various activities, see, e.g., Chan *et al.*, 1992). Among many other activities and discourse processing strategies, here are some that have been studied in the literature:

- assimilation (Chan *et al.*, 1992)
- building models of several texts instead of one (Bråten, 2008)
- contrasting target concepts (Hamilton, 1997)
- explanation (Ainsworth and Burcham, 2007; see also Coleman *et al.*, 1997)
- extrapolation (Anderson, 1973; Chan *et al.*, 1992)
- generation of topic headers or topic sentences (Clariana and Marker, 2007; Dee-Lucas and di Vesta, 1980)
- use of hypertext and hyperlinks (Alexander and Jetton, 2003; Azevedo and Jacobson, 2008; Eveland *et al.*, 2004; see several studies in Rouet *et al.*, 1996)
- macro vs. microstrategies (Gallini *et al.*, 1993)
- metacognitive monitoring (Bartholomé and Bromme, 2009; Britton *et al.*, 1998)
- organization (e.g., linking, grouping, etc.) (Castañeda *et al.*, 1987)
- previous training in discourse structures (Armbruster *et al.*, 1987)
- problem solving (Chan *et al.*, 1992)
- repetition (Castañeda *et al.*, 1987)
- retelling (Chan *et al.*, 1992)
- thinking aloud (Chan *et al.*, 1992).

Obviously these required or self-initiated experimental activities and strategies are mutually related. Wherever they facilitate learning, they usually imply the **construction of links**, for instance links between concepts, among propositions (local coherence), between propositions and macropropositions (global coherence), model structures, different modes of representation (pictures and amodal symbols or concepts), between concepts and knowledge domains, between current text (concept, fragment) and other text (e.g., via hyperlinks), and so on. Indeed, learning not only implies the integration of new concepts or new beliefs, but especially also the establishment of links between known concepts and beliefs. Moreover, more links (e.g., coherence, schemas) in discourse and mental models favor more links and hence better integrated general knowledge.

3.6.6   Discourse structures

Finally, both classical and contemporary studies of learning emphasize the prominent role of text structure – and today more generally of multimodal discourse structures – in the acquisition of knowledge. The general finding in many studies is that better organized oral or written discourse, at any level, facilitates understanding and recall, and hence better organized models, and hence more and 'better' knowledge – especially for less knowledgeable, less able, less experienced, etc. subjects.

The consequence of these findings is that in order to improve understanding and learning, participants (experimenters, subjects) may strategically 'add' structure in many ways, for instance by interpolating 'bridging' inferences, organization at higher (macro) levels of meaning, summarizing and conclusions, keywords and topic sentences, organization by schemas, bullets, underlining, colors, etc. Some of these will enhance memory for local structure (such as bullets and underlining), others for global structure (topics, summaries, conclusions, headlines, etc.). Of these, global structures, as for global structures of mental models, are best recalled, while also representing more important or more relevant information – which hence is more likely to be integrated into the knowledge system.

There are potentially a very large number of discourse structures that could be manipulated in experiments: phonological and visual (oral vs. written, picture, etc.) structures, syntactic structures (e.g., word order, sentence complexity, active vs. passive sentences, pronouns), lexicon (easier or more difficult words), propositional structures of meaning, semantic relations between propositions, implicitness vs. explicitness, presuppositions, foregrounding and backgrounding, degree of detail (granularity), types of person, event and action description, levels of description (general vs. specific), conventional schemas (e.g., narrative, argumentative), rhetorical structures (hyperboles, euphemisms), style and register, speech acts, conversational strategies, and so on. Many of these have been used, and some have often been used – for instance coherence (for discussion of various types of organization, see also Alexander and Jetton, 2003; McNamara and O'Reilly, 2002; Vezin, 1980). Here are some examples of experimental studies of various text variables – among a vast number of others – in alphabetical order:

- adjunct questions (Panda and Mohanty, 1981)
- analogy (Glynn and Takahashi, 1998; Iding, 1997)
- argumentation (Lin and Anderson, 2008)
- cause–effect structures (Armand, 2001; Britt *et al.*, 1994; McCrudden *et al.*, 2007)

- chronology, time lines (Davis *et al.*, 1966)
- coherence (Ainsworth and Burcham, 2007; Boscolo and Mason, 2003; McNamara and Kintsch, 1996; McNamara *et al.*, 1996)
- concreteness (Sadoski, 2001)
- detail ('seductive')(Garner *et al.*, 1989)
- diagrams (Ainsworth and Loizou, 2003; Butcher, 2006; Guri-Rozenblit, 1988; McCrudden *et al.*, 2007)
- discussion/debate (oral discourse) (Alvermann *et al.*, 1995; Bennett *et al.*, 2010)
- explicitness vs. implicitness (Franks *et al.*, 1982)
- genre (Dymock, 1999; Wolfe and Mienko, 2007)
- gestures (Cutica and Bucciarelli, 2008)
- hyperlinks (Eveland *et al.*, 2004)
- intertextuality (learning from multiple texts, etc.) (Boyd and Thompson, 2008; Bråten, 2008; Britt *et al.*, 1999; Goldman, 1997; Short, 1992; Strømsø *et al.*, 2008; Voithofer, 2006)
- linear vs. hierarchical organization (Calisir and Gurel, 2003; Calisir *et al.*, 2008)
- maps (Abel and Kulhavy, 1986; Scevak and Moore, 1998; Verdi and Kulhavy, 2002)
- metaphor (Gallini *et al.*, 1995)
- more or less detailed (Thorndyke, 1979)
- narrative vs. expository text (Dymock, 1999; Wake, 2009; Wolfe and Mienko, 2007)
- online discussion (Chen and Looi, 2007)
- oral discourse (for review see Alexander and Jetton, 2003)
- pictures, illustrations (Bartholomé and Bromme, 2009; Carney and Levin, 2002; Iding, 1997; Mayer, 2002; Peeck, 1993; Reid and Beveridge, 1986; Schnotz, 2002)
- problem–solution structure (Armbruster *et al.*, 1987)
- refutation of incorrect prior knowledge (Diakidoy *et al.*, 2003; Lipson,1982; Maria and MacGinitie, 1987)
- 'rhetorical' markers (indicating discourse functions) (Lorch, 1989; Meyer, 1975)
- topic (Thorndyke, 1979)
- visual vs. auditory presentation (Kalyuga *et al.*, 2004).

This series of studies, among many others, conclude that, in general, more detailed, more explicit, multilevel and multimodal structures contribute to better understanding, more detailed, coherent or otherwise connected semantic representations, more detailed and organized mental models and, on that basis, more and better organized knowledge. Such main effects are especially noticeable for less knowledgeable, less able, less interested and less motivated students.

More knowledgeable students often do not need the 'extra' structure (modes, levels, etc.) and may even profit from the positive consequences of self-initiated inferences, elaborations and other comprehension and learning strategies, so that they sometimes do worse on tasks that require attention to detail, as reviewed above. Hence, it should also be emphasized again that *textual* conditions such as text structure only have influence on comprehension and learning through the type of mediating *contextual* conditions: knowledge, ability, strategies, tasks, goals and so on.

3.7   Knowledge and memory

So far, we have taken for granted, without much further analysis, that knowledge is stored in, and activated from semantic memory, instantiated or applied in the construction of specific mental models in episodic memory by means of processes in working memory. It is further assumed that conceptual knowledge is multiply organized by various types of structural mechanism, such as categorical relations, schemas, frames or scripts, as well as grounded in multimodal neural structures of the brain.

This more or less sums up the state of the art, with ongoing debate on the nature of working memory and whether or how all conceptual structure is modal or more abstractly symbolic – since it is difficult to imagine (and harder to prove) that *all* knowledge, and especially its more complex and higher levels, have modal character. Indeed, what would be the modal nature of such concepts as 'democracy,' 'capitalism,' 'philosophy' or indeed of 'racism'? (for debate, see Barsalou, 2003, 2008; Caramazza and Mahon, 2003).

It is beyond the scope of this chapter to review the extensive literature on different kinds of memory beyond what has been briefly mentioned above. So, we shall only briefly summarize current theorizing as it is relevant for the theory of discourse and knowledge processing.

3.7.1   Working memory

Discourse is produced and understood by detailed processing of grammatical and other discourse structures in *working memory* (WM), for instance by strategically decoding phonological, morphological, syntactical and multimodal structures in terms of propositions and coherent proposition sequences. As we have seen, such semantic interpretation and the establishment of coherence, requires the construction of mental models and the instantiation of generic knowledge. WM, however, has only limited capacity, of only a few structural units at each level (Baddeley, 1994; Miller, 1956). The question is then not only how complex discourse and model structures can thus be construed, but especially how these processes can be controlled by overall topics (macrostructures) and pragmatic context models and how exactly (and how much) generic knowledge is instantiated, for instance by deriving inferences needed to construe local and global coherence.

Many of the contemporary approaches to WM are formulated in terms of their agreement with or differences from the classical and continuously updated theory of Allan Baddeley and his associates (Baddeley, 1986, 2007) since his seminal article with Hitch (Baddeley and Hitch, 1974). In this article they proposed a Central Executive and two "slave systems," one for phonological processing ("the phonological loop") and one for visual processing ("the visuo-spatial sketchpad"), recently updated with an "episodic buffer" to temporarily store the information that does not fit into the two "slave systems" and that integrates information from both systems.

However, these proposals are limited to very simple memory tasks and hardly seem to be adequate to account for more complex discourse and knowledge processing. In our terms, a Central Executive, for instance, would need to feature semantic macropropositions to guarantee overall coherence and a context model to dynamically regulate appropriateness, besides controlling the many levels of local (sentence) discourse processing. It especially also would need to control the activation and application of generic knowledge for understanding as well as the contextual nature of knowledge management (Common Ground). We are only beginning to understand how such processing takes place in WM (see also Miyake and Shah, 1999). Indeed, the necessary control structures obviously do not fit the traditionally conceived capacity of WM. Hence we may need to assume a Central Executive or Control System in an extended form of long-term working memory (Ericsson and Kintsch, 1995). Indeed, current theories of WM are unable to account for the processing and control of complex social and communicative environments as well as of discourse and interaction structures at many levels.

Moreover, processing complex information is not only situated – as represented in context models – but also *embodied*. Empathy, mirror neurons and Other Minds are the keywords of the increasing research on this important dimension of Self, interaction and simulation (see, among many book-length studies, Arbib, 2006; Chemero, 2009; Givón, 2005; Goldman, 2006; Neisser, 1993; Semin and Smith, 2008; Shapiro, 2010; Tomasello, 1998, 2008; Varela *et al.*, 1991).

3.7.2   *Episodic memory and personal knowledge*

We have assumed above that mental models are stored in LTM, and more specifically in the part where our autobiographical experiences are represented:

episodic memory (EM) (for detail, see, e.g., Baddeley *et al.*, 2002; Neisser and Fivush, 1994; Rubin, 1986; Tulving, 1983, 2002; Williams *et al.*, 2008).

Although EM is traditionally portrayed in terms of events or experiences we remember about the past, and hence in terms of a kind of mental 'time travel' (Tulving, 2002), it should not be forgotten that these autobiographical experiences were construed in what *then* was the present. In other words, as we have explained above for experience models, mental models are continuously being construed, updated, modified or planned for the past, the present and the future. Hence, they define and control our ongoing experiences (see also Berntsen and Jacobsen, 2008; Botzung *et al.*, 2008; Friedman, 2007). Neuropsychological studies have confirmed that when imagining the future the same brain region is used as when remembering the past (Schacter *et al.*, 2007). Most likely this is also the region in which ongoing, present experience models, and hence context models, are processed.

Producing a story about an event we have experienced (or heard about) involves the activation of a subjective situation model of such an event in EM. This process is controlled by the current context model, whose K-device specifies what information of the situation model should be presupposed, recalled or asserted as new information. The result of that process is then sequentially processed as words and sentences in WM, as mentioned above.

Relevant for our theory is that mental models of specific experiences may be generalized and abstracted from first of all in terms of *personal, autobiographical knowledge* about our life (our family, friends, schools, places where we lived, etc.) (Conway, 1990). This may take place by deleting setting or participant information from mental models. This autobiographical knowledge is crucial for the construction of new experience and to assign coherence and continuity to our experiences as they are organized about the central category of Self. Thus, whereas most of the everyday experiences of our lives (like a breakfast or shopping in the supermarket today) are later no longer accessible, generic personal knowledge (what we usually have for breakfast or where we do our shopping) remains relevant for many situations, and hence tends to be represented as separate knowledge in EM.

In the literature on EM a distinction is often made between 'remembering' and 'knowing' about past events (see, among many studies, e.g., Bodner and Lindsay, 2003; Fivush and Hudson, 1990; Knowlton, 1998; Rajaram, 1993; Tulving, 2002). This distinction is explained by Tulving (2002) in terms of the notion of "autonoetic consciousness," which plays a role when we actively remember concrete details, as when re-activating a mental model with Self, often with memory for visual detail. On the other hand, in the sense of 'knowing,' we only know *that* an event happened, we feel it is 'familiar' but we no longer have access to its details – or in fact whether it happened to us.

Secondly, personal experiences and, especially, the processing of public discourse about events (such as the news) also allow the construction in *semantic memory* (see below) of *generic, socioculturally shared knowledge*, e.g., on immigration or racism, by various forms of decontextualization, abstraction and generalization. Despite the neurally grounded theoretical distinction between episodic memory and semantic memory, the two systems are in permanent interaction (Kompus *et al.*, 2009; Menon *et al.*, 2002). We construe mental models on the basis of our experiences but also with instantiated general knowledge, and vice versa, we use mental models to construe generic knowledge by abstraction and generalization. It is not surprising, therefore, that, after longer delays, autobiographical experiences tend to be increasingly 'recalled' by reconstruction of plausible details with inferences from general knowledge (Barclay, 1993), although also striking details may often be remembered. This is also the result of most studies on recall for stories (not only personal stories), as we have found earlier (Kintsch and van Dijk, 1978), so that the same mechanisms are most probably involved. More generally, autobiographical memory appears to be a mixture of concrete mental models of personal experiences and instantiated knowledge of events, as is the case for scripts – for the obvious reasons that many of our daily experiences are routine and tend to be generalized and hence abstracted from (see, e.g., Hudson and Nelson, 1986).

3.7.3   *Semantic memory and generic social knowledge*

Just like 'working memory,' 'semantic memory' (SM), too, is hardly named adequately, because it has little to do with meaning or reference or with the semantics of any language. Since it is the part of memory that represents our knowledge of the world, a name such as 'epistemic memory' would have been more appropriate – although we have earlier assumed that SM probably also represents group ideologies, norms and values, that is, any form of social cognition, as we shall see in more detail below (Van Dijk 1998).

As we already indicated above, the conceptual knowledge stored in SM is usually viewed as more general and abstract compared to the specific, personal experiences stored in episodic memory. In that comparative sense, it might even be more appropriate to speak of *social memory*, because it is also typically the kind of general or generic knowledge socially shared by members of an epistemic community.

However, not all socially shared knowledge, as it may be presupposed in discourse, is generic or abstract. Knowledge about *the* Second World War, *the* Holocaust or *the* terrorist attack on the World Trade Center on September 11, 2001, are examples in case, and hence typically referred to with a definite article signaling shared knowledge. The structure of such *historical knowledge* is also more like that of a mental model, defined by a spatiotemporal Setting, a Participant structure and Actions or Events. Unlike generic knowledge, this kind of historical event knowledge is also less likely to be used as a basis for inferences, as when a generalization is specified by an exemplar.

It has been indicated earlier that conceptual knowledge is assumed to be variously organized by schemas, scripts, categories, prototypes and domains (see references given above). Such organization allows fast search and retrieval in the vast knowledge store, as well as the automatic activation of parts of schemas once the schema is activated. Thus, if the complex event knowledge about, for instance, terrorist attacks is organized in a script, the various associated other concepts may (at least partly) be activated and sometimes even presupposed – for instance, that there are victims or that buildings have been destroyed. Concepts may be related with higher-level or lower-level *categories*, such that, for instance, racism is organized as a specific 'kind of' social domination.

After their earlier work on scripts, Schank and Abelson (1995) proposed a *narrative* theory of memory, with the argument that our memory is based on experiences and hence on stories (see also Bruner, 2002). This is consistent with a model-based (or experience-based) approach of knowledge acquisition, but excludes all "generic" learning, for instance with expository discourse – as is the case with most texts used in education and science, and is the case for the Racism entry in *Wikipedia*. Obviously, stories are forms of discourse and inter-action. We have no stories in memory, but only mental models of experiences, and general knowledge derived from such models – as well as from expository discourse. Stories are based on such mental models and are further constrained by context models: we tell the 'same' story in a different way in different com-municative situations (Polanyi, 1981; see the other contributions in the debate on Schank and Abelson's view: Wyer, 1995).

Another way to facilitate the use of generic knowledge is to assume that concepts are represented as *prototypes*, as the more representative exemplar of a category (there is massive literature inspired by Rosch, 1978). Thus, some forms of racism, such as discrimination in hiring or housing, would be rec-ognized as (proto)typical, whereas many forms of 'everyday racism,' such as quickly helping black customers in a shop, may only be found racist by black customers (see the discriminatory situations described by black women in Essed, 1991).

Finally, concepts may be organized by larger *domains*, as we also do in politics, media reporting or encyclopedias, for instance the concepts associ-ated with the domains of nature, animals, people, instruments, literature or countries, or with politics, education or health, as is the case for the division of ministries. Obviously, many types of more or less large domains may thus be distinguished, often overlapping or cross-categorized (among many applied studies of the role of knowledge domains, see, e.g., Beghtol, 1998).

The question, however, is in what respect such domains are cognitively real, in the sense of playing a role in easier access, spreading activation, priming or other phenomena that indicate a form of organization. Such organization may also be the result of frequent co-occurrence in public discourse, so that concepts such as 'politician' tend to cluster with concepts such as 'government,' 'elections,' 'voters,' 'parliament' and so on. Conversely, texts with a relatively high number of such related concepts may thus be seen as more coherent, more integrated or more prototypical, as we know from work on Latent Semantic Analysis (LSA; see, e.g., Kintsch *et al.*, 2007). It should be stressed, though, that here we are dealing with *probability* measures (vectors) of discourse coherence: discourse may well be coherent without such frequently co-occurring concepts, and their presence is no guarantee that discourse is coherent. Hence LSA may be a practical diagnostic of discourse coherence but obviously cannot replace structural theories.

We have seen that especially in later studies of knowledge it is assumed that knowledge is not represented in some kind of amodal, abstract representation – as we would do in terms of propositions or schemas – but grounded in the modal nature of the brain, in terms of audition, external experiences and perception such as that of vision, touch, smell, movement or internal experiences such as thoughts and emotions (Barsalou, 2003, 2008). It remains to be seen, however, whether all conceptual knowledge, and especially abstract notions (say notions such as 'democracy' and 'racism'), have such modal grounding, as is also the case at higher levels of organization (indeed, how to modally represent the aggregate concepts of 'furniture,' 'nature' or 'animals'?).

If much knowledge is derived from our experiences, that is, from multimodal experiences, and as such is neurally coded in the brain, and in terms of more abstract symbols or structures, this also has problematic consequences for the *social acquisition and uses of knowledge in discourse*. People may have very different personal experiences with, or have learned about, for instance, animals, cars or furniture. If these experiences are modally different, interaction, communication and discourse, based on *shared* knowledge and *Common Ground* might be hard to account for in such a theory. It is especially this social dimension of knowledge, interaction and communication that probably requires at least *also* a representation in more generic, symbolic terms.

Similarly, concepts are used in very different actions, interactions and discourse, and if they were defined only in terms of their modal grounding, language users would be unable or less able to produce or understand discourses about experiences or properties of a concept that is inconsistent with personal sensory experiences. The same would be true for the account of word meanings. If they are associated with conceptual knowledge, and if such knowledge is (only) modal, then word meanings might also be personally different – which would require a different theory of language and language use.

It seems more plausible, therefore, to associate modality not so much with the knowledge system, but rather with its personally or socially variable *uses*, for instance in the construction of mental models, and hence also with the experience-based *acquisition* of knowledge. What is personal, and may be modally based, are people's personal experiences (or the simulated ones of others), including varying sensorimotor experiences, emotions, and so on. Indeed, what is usually tested in experiments is not so much abstract conceptual knowledge but rather the ways people *apply* such knowledge in more specific, more personal, and hence more modal, embodied experiences, including laboratory tasks.

3.8   Concluding remarks

In this chapter we have developed a theoretical framework of the cognitive aspects of the relations between discourse and knowledge and reviewed some of the relevant literature on this topic. The theory extends dominant theories in cognitive psychology by introducing context models as crucial aspects of the control system for the processing of appropriate discourse, including the role of mutual and shared knowledge.

The classical result of the role of knowledge in discourse processing is that the instantiation of generic knowledge is crucial in the construction of mental models that define discourse understanding. Pragmatic rules of shared knowledge in an epistemic community allow language users to produce discourse that is much less detailed than their mental models, since recipients are able to reconstruct mental models on the basis of inferences from the same socially shared generic knowledge.

Studies on the role of knowledge in discourse processing are typically limited to controlled variables in laboratory or classroom tasks. Within these contextual and ecological limitations, it is generally found that participants with more knowledge better understand discourse – and may show this in many ways, e.g., by replying to questions, better recall and so on. On the other hand, better organized discourse usually produces better knowledge, especially among less competent readers.

A plethora of experimental studies is thus dedicated to examining the processing consequences of different discourse structures (more or less coherent, etc.) or the variation of different tasks or experimental subjects, of which prior knowledge is one variable among many.

We have also seen that whereas the experiments may be ingenious, the theoretical frameworks of these studies are usually very simple. No detailed theory is provided for the nature and the organization of knowledge in memory. Learning text and learning from text may not be carefully distinguished. The details of the processing model in which knowledge is activated and changed are seldom specified, nor is how knowledge is represented in episodic memory and semantic memory. Since no explicit theory of knowledge representation is provided, it is also unclear how new knowledge is acquired and integrated in existing knowledge.

We now have a reasonably explicit theory of the ways generic knowledge is activated, instantiated and applied in the construction of mental models as representations of the understanding of discourse, including the role of inferences for the establishment of local and global coherence. On the other hand, much less is known about the ways generic knowledge is in turn acquired or changed by discourse processing and through the generalization or abstraction of mental models, especially in long-term learning in everyday life.

Similarly, also due to previous linguistic and discourse analytical studies, we are able to vary and study many different kinds of discourse structures and their effect on comprehension, recall and other mental processes. We have much less detailed, systematic and explicit insight into what exactly the 'prior' knowledge is as it is involved – and updated – in discourse processing.

Indeed, perhaps the most prominent lack of insight in the psychology of knowledge is the precise nature and organization of the generic knowledge system. Beyond classical definitions of knowledge in terms of conceptual relations and hierarchies, prototypes, scripts or schemas, and newer neurologically oriented assumptions about the modal nature of knowledge (or at least its acquisition and uses), we basically have no idea exactly about how generic knowledge is organized in the mind and the brain. This also severely limits our insights into its uses and changes in all cognitive tasks and processes, as well as in discourse production and comprehension in particular.

We have assumed that beyond childhood and concrete everyday experiences, knowledge is largely acquired, updated and changed by discourse in a large variety of communicative situations, genres and contextual conditions. Although this is a very plausible hypothesis – when we realize that most of our vast knowledge about the world beyond our daily experiences is derived from the mass media – we have little empirical evidence on how our knowledge is thus construed during our lifetime. Beyond the classical literature on learning in educational contexts, we thus need a much more general research paradigm focused on the way knowledge is acquired from public discourse in various stages of our lives, and how such knowledge is organized in memory.

4   Discourse, knowledge and social cognition

4.1   Introduction

On February 28, 2013, the *New York Times* published the following editorial:

01   **The White House Joins the Fight**
02   President Obama made good on the promise of his second Inaugural
03   Address on Thursday by joining the fight to overturn California's ban
04   on same-sex marriage. Having declared that marriage equality is part
05   of the road "through Seneca Fall and Selma and Stonewall," we can't
06   imagine how he could have sat this one out.
07   The administration's brief to the Supreme Court was a legally
08   and symbolically important repudiation of Proposition 8, the 2008
09   voter referendum that amended California's Constitution to forbid
10   bestowing the title of marriage on a union between two people of
11   the same sex – a right the California Supreme Court had found to
12   be fundamental under the State Constitution.
13   Like the arguments made by the lawyers for those who seek to
14   overturn Proposition 8, and by a group of prominent Republicans earl-
15   ier this week, the government's brief says any law attempting to ban
16   same-sex marriage must be subjected to heightened scrutiny because
17   it singles out a class of Americans, historically subject to discrimin-
18   ation, for unequal treatment.
19   The brief said California's civil unions law provides the rights and
20   protections of marriage, so Proposition 8's denial of the designation
21   of marriage "does not substantially further any important governmen-
22   tal interest."
23   The government made mincemeat of the argument that same-sex
24   couples threaten "traditional" marriage. "Petitioners' central argu-
25   ment is that Proposition 8 advances an interest in responsible procre-
26   ation and child-rearing because only heterosexual couples can produce
27   'unintended pregnances' and because the 'overriding purpose' of
28   marriage is to address that reality by affording a stable institution for

29 procreation and child-rearing," the brief said. "But, as this court has
30 recognized, marriage is far more than a societal means of dealing with
31 unintended pregnancies."
32   Proposition 8, it said, neither promotes opposite-sex parenting nor
33 prevents same-sex parenting. In any case, "the overwhelming expert
34 consensus is that children raised by gay and lesbian parents are as
35 likely to be well adjusted as children raised by heterosexual parents."
36   The legal analysis advanced by the Obama administration leads
37 inexorably to the conclusion that all attempts to ban same-sex mar-
38 riage are inherently unconstitutional. But the administration stopped
39 short of declaring that truth, recognized earlier this week even by the
40 Republicans' brief. In fact, the administration said the court need not
41 consider the constitutionality of marriage bans beyond the context of
42 this particular scheme.
43   We don't know why the administration did not take that step.
44 Perhaps it was to allow Mr. Obama to go on asserting that the issue of
45 same-sex marriage should generally be left up to the states. We hope
46 the justices recognize the broader truth that the Constitution does not
47 tolerate denying gay people the right to wed in any state (*New York*
48 *Times (NYT)*, February 28, 2013)

Newspaper editorials by definition editorialize. They express and communicate
the opinions of the editors on recent issues. These are seldom personal opinions, but opinions that tend to be based on attitudes that are probably widely
shared among the readers. Though contextually addressed to the readers of the
newspaper as primary recipients, editorials are usually indirectly addressed to
powerful institutions, organizations, politicians and other major news actors,
whose policies or actions they seek to support or criticize.

Opinions and attitudes are the classical domain of social psychology. More
recently, they have been studied as forms of social cognition shared by social
groups. They are relevant for study in this chapter because they presuppose and
also convey knowledge, as is the case of the editorial quoted above, which not
only informs readers about the opinion of the *NYT*, but starts with a summary
of the events (Obama's actions) it provides an opinion about, as is typical for
editorials (Van Dijk, 1988a, 1988b, 1989, 1992, 1998). Yet, such a summary
may not only summarize and recall information of events earlier or elsewhere
reported in the newspaper, and hence express shared knowledge, but do so
from its own perspective and in evaluative language that expresses opinions
and attitudes: *Obama made good* (line 2), *the government made mincemeat*
(line 23), etc.

Knowledge and attitudes, together with ideologies, are all forms of socially
shared cognition. Yet, they are also different. As we have seen in the previous

chapter, socially shared knowledge is assumed to be shared by the whole epistemic community, and hence is presupposed in most public discourse. Attitudes and ideologies, on the other hand, are only shared by the members of specific sociopolitical groups, and hence are in need of specific assertion and argumentative and other persuasive discourse when addressed to other group members, as is also clear in the editorial, whose opinions on same-sex marriage obviously are not generally shared in the USA. Indeed, the aim of Proposition 8 in California, defeated by the Supreme Court, precisely shows that many conservative and religious citizens are against this fundamental right of homosexual citizens.

If there is one discipline that specifically should focus on knowledge and its relation to discourse, it is social psychology, given the combined social and cognitive nature of knowledge and the largely discursive nature of its reproduction in society. It is therefore surprising that knowledge hardly takes a prominent position among the many topics of traditional and contemporary social psychology, such as attribution, attitude, prejudice, social identity and intergroup relations, among many others.

There is at present in this discipline not a single monograph and only one edited book – published more than twenty years ago (Bar-Tal and Kruglanski, 1988) – that specifically deals with the sociocognitive study of knowledge. Virtually all standard introductions to social psychology, even those specialized in social cognition, lack the concept of 'knowledge' in their subject index. The same is true for the concept of 'discourse,' for that matter. The third edition of the standard textbook in the field (Fiske and Taylor, 2007) only casually refers to knowledge and discourse. We may conclude that, until today, the discursive reproduction of knowledge is not a hot topic in the mainstream of the field.

With the demise of behaviorism in the 1960s, the cognitive revolution in psychology finally also influenced social psychology, especially in the study of *social cognition*, most prominently so in the USA (Fiske and Taylor, 2007; for a more personal account of this transition, see especially Abelson, 1994). Although social psychology had a longer (European) tradition of cognitively oriented studies (see, e.g., Heider, 1958), this meant that, from the 1980s, many of the classical topics, such as attitudes and attribution, came to be reformulated in terms of memory schemata and information processing that had obvious links with knowledge (Ostrom *et al.*, 1994). However, this usually happened with a predominant individualistic focus and experimental laboratory methods, ignoring the social nature of beliefs and their study in natural contexts. 'Social memory,' thus, usually meant individual memory about other people (see, e.g., Hastie *et al.*, 1984).

No wonder that critical voices in social psychology itself, not only in Europe, soon advocated a more *societal* psychology (Bar-Tal, 2000; Himmelweit and

Gaskell, 1990) and a new focus on *socially shared* cognition (Resnick *et al.*, 1991), and asked what is *social* about social cognition (Nye and Brower, 1996). Thus, despite the dominant paradigm of individualist, experimental laboratory studies in social psychology until today, especially in the USA, there have been many voices that criticized this limitation, and advocated a more social focus as well as more diverse, and also qualitative, methods of inquiry.

In Europe, at least outside the dominant academic influence of the USA, a more sociocognitive perspective continued to flourish, most prominently with *social identity* theory and the study of *intergroup relations*, in a paradigm initiated by Henri Tajfel in the UK, on the one hand, and especially with the study of *social representations* under the influence of Serge Moscovici (1981, 2000) in France, on the other (for a general introduction to these different directions of research, see, e.g., Augoustinos *et al.*, 2006; for integrative proposals for these paradigms, see, e.g., Operario and Fiske, 1999; for more detailed references, see below).

It is no doubt the latter paradigm of social representation research that most explicitly emphasized the relevance of the study of socially shared, common-sense knowledge and its reproduction in society. Yet, although interest in the communication of social representations has always characterized this direction of research, it was soon criticized for a lack of detailed discourse analysis – besides methodological and theoretical flaws as well as conceptual vagueness – by the protagonists of *Discursive (Social)Psychology* (for debate, see, e.g., Breakwell and Canter, 1993). These discursive psychologists also criticized individualistic and experimental attitude and social cognition research in the USA, not least because their own exclusive focus on the study of talk was accompanied by a principled rejection of (the study of) mental representations (Edwards and Potter, 1992).

It is against this much simplified general background of contemporary social psychology that this chapter will examine the nature and role of **knowledge defined as shared, justified and generally accepted ('true') social beliefs and their discursive reproduction in epistemic communities and in society at large**. In other words, it will connect ideas from various directions in social psychology in an integrated perspective that combines the cognitive and the social, and emphasizes the role of discourse in the reproduction of knowledge in society. We thus want to avoid the tendency of reduction and exclusion that characterizes many of the theoretical positions and debates in the discipline – despite various contemporary attempts to build bridges between the different paradigms (for discussion, see Augoustinos *et al.*, 2006).

Not only because they have been studied extensively in social psychology, knowledge will be studied as the basis of other 'widespread' **social beliefs**, such as public opinion, attitudes, stereotypes, social representations and ideologies.

We shall see, by analyzing fragments of the editorial on Obama, that in practice it is not so simple to distinguish between knowledge and opinion.

Social beliefs have a structural basis in terms of the **groups** or **communities** that acquire, share and reproduce them, a topic that also needs to be studied from a sociological perspective in the next chapter. In this chapter, we focus on the **communication** of knowledge and other social beliefs in society. Indeed, social beliefs are not only social because they are socially shared but also because they are socially communicated and acquired, are about socially relevant issues and because they are the basis of all discourse and other social practices (for different uses of the notion of 'social' in social psychology, see, e.g., McGuire, 1986; for a comparison between attitudes and other social beliefs, see also Eagly and Chaiken, 1993; McGuire, 1989). In that sense, social beliefs are also studied as 'widespread beliefs' (Gaskell and Fraser, 1990).

4.2   Social beliefs

4.2.1   Knowledge as social vs. personal belief

One of the central theses of this book is that knowledge is not merely justified *individual* belief, but should rather be analyzed as a type of **shared social belief**. Knowledge is *social* belief in various senses (see also Bar-Tal, 2000):

- **Acquisition**. Both personal and social knowledge is usually *acquired and changed* in social situations, mostly through social interaction and discourse.
- **Distribution**. Knowledge is justified belief *socially shared* among members of (social, cultural) communities.
- **Justification**. Justification criteria or standards that define belief as knowledge are *socioculturally* developed, shared and changed, sometimes by social institutions.
- **Reference/Intentionality**. Social beliefs are generally about *socially relevant* topics or issues.

Specifically interesting for this chapter is the study of the ways such personal experiences and knowledge are **communicated and shared** with others, thus giving rise to interpersonal knowledge and beliefs – which eventually may even become socioculturally shared. For instance, even when also based on socially shared insights, many general ideas and theories are initially personal constructs (see, e.g., Hultman and Horberg, 1998).

The fundamental social nature of knowledge does not exclude *personal knowledge* (see, e.g., Briley and Aaker, 2006; Bukobza, 2008; Phye, 1997; Razmerita *et al.*, 2009), but this personal knowledge is largely based on, or derived from, activated, social knowledge and socioculturally shared knowledge criteria. Personal knowledge may also consist of **personal versions** of social knowledge (Potter, 1996).

In order to be able to interpret personal experiences as personal knowledge, people need to understand their environment, other people and their own thoughts, emotions and body. The very concepts or categories of this basic understanding are socially shared and have been largely acquired in verbal and non-verbal interaction, first with caregivers, family members and peers, and then with other members of the same epistemic community as well as school and the mass media. We have also seen that the vast majority of the daily subjective representations of the *specific* events and situations of the environment as they are stored in mental models in episodic memory are soon no longer accessible, but tend to be combined into higher-level models of major events and periods of our lives, and generalized and abstracted from in terms of *episodic personal knowledge* (Conway, 2007).

4.2.2   The system of social cognition

Knowledge and other socially shared beliefs are represented in long-term memory (LTM) as a system of social cognition whose overall structure at present is still unknown. In order to be able to relate knowledge with other social beliefs, however, we must assume that the system of social cognition is organized in a way that is cognitively and socially functional. Thus, as we have argued before, a social group can only develop specific beliefs such as attitudes, stereotypes and ideologies when they have generic sociocultural knowledge in common with the whole community. Hence social knowledge is fundamental and the basis of all cognition. Similarly, we have seen in the previous chapter that subjective mental models as they are stored in autobiographical episodic memory also need to be based on such generic knowledge. But since individuals are not only members of epistemic communities, but also of social groups, their mental models, and especially their opinions, are also based on other social beliefs. Figure 4.1 thus shows how we represent the system of social cognition and its relationship with personal cognition.

In what follows we summarize what we know about social beliefs in order to be able to relate them to the knowledge system. Since attitudes and social representations have received ample attention in social psychology, we shall deal with them more briefly than with ideologies, which have been generally ignored in the field.

4.2.3   Ideologies

Unlike attitudes, ideologies have hardly been studied in social psychology (but see Aebischer *et al.*, 1992; Augoustinos, 1995; Billig, 1982; Billig *et al.*, 1988;

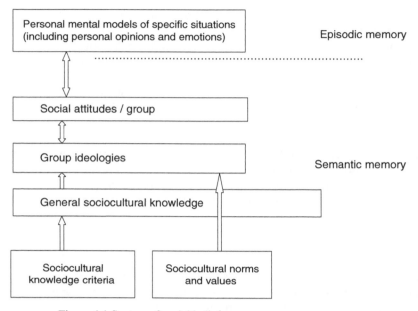

Figure 4.1 System of social beliefs

Scarbrough, 1984, 1990; Tetlock, 1989). Rather, they have been a major topic of research in the history of philosophy, sociology and political science (among a vast number of books on ideology, see, especially the following more general books, Abercrombie *et al.*, 1990; Eagleton, 1991; Larraín, 1979; Thompson, 1984; Van Dijk, 1998).

Especially in political science, ideology has been studied for decades, although so far with little influence in mainstream social psychology (see, e.g., Lau and Sears, 1986). More recent work by Jost and others has stimulated research on ideology and system justification (see, e.g., Jost, 2006; Jost and Banaji, 1994; Jost and Major, 2001; Jost *et al.*, 2008; and especially the recent review by Jost, 2009; see also the domination theory of Sidanius, e.g., Sidanius and Pratto, 1999).

The classical debate on ideology in the social sciences has focused especially on the relations between 'true' knowledge and ideologies defined as 'false consciousness' since Destutt de Tracy invented the notion of 'ideology' – as a science of ideas – more than 200 years ago, and especially since their discussion by Marx and Engels (see especially Mannheim, 1936).

In contrast to the tradition of the negative conception of ideology as misconceived ideas, our notion of ideology is more general and pertains to the basic social beliefs of a group, whether or not these are 'positive' or 'negative' (for detail, see Van Dijk, 1998). Crucial is that ideologies cognitively define the identity, values and goals of a group and provide a basis for its interest. Ideologies may function as a legitimation of domination as well as of the resistance against domination, as is the case for sexism and feminism, capitalism and socialism, militarism and pacifism. Mannheim (1936) called the 'positive' ideologies *utopias*. Contemporary political science also takes a more general view of ideologies as systems of beliefs (Freeden, 1996, 2013), but with the frequent observation that people, even members of groups, have so many different opinions that one can barely speak of coherent belief systems (Converse, 1964).

As an illustration of the relation between knowledge and ideology consider the editorial on Obama cited above. The editorial summarizes and hence recalls shared knowledge about the current debate in the USA on same-sex marriages, but apart from an opinion on Obama's and the current government's policies and actions, it also takes an explicit stance on the issue in its last paragraph:

> We don't know why the administration did not take that step. Perhaps it was to allow Mr. Obama to go on asserting that the issue of same-sex marriage should generally be left up to the states. We hope the justices recognize the broader truth that the Constitution does not tolerate denying gay people the right to wed in any state.

Such an opinion in favor of the civil rights of gay people is not only part of a broadly shared attitude, both in the USA and in Europe as well as some other countries, but is also based on fundamental ideologies of social equality, sexuality and gender. For Obama and his followers, these are 'positive' ideologies, whereas for his conservative opponents these are no doubt negative ideologies.

4.2.4   The social vs. the personal aspects of ideology

Jost and his co-authors propagate a renewed psychological approach to ideology, focusing especially on people's personal preferences, dispositions and character traits as important conditions, e.g., of left vs. right ideological orientation – and hence as an aspect of personal *ideological choice*. Thus, feelings of uncertainty and threat as well as preferences for order, stability and authority are assumed to favor conservative ideological identification, whereas new and different experiences and a preference for change and equality favor progressive ideological identification – as was earlier assumed by Adorno (1950) in his study of the authoritarian personality. The studies of Jost and his colleagues largely deal with the polarization between conservative (right) and progressive (left) in the USA. These are very general (meta)ideological orientations, and not concerned with specific ideologies such as socialism, feminism or pacifism, especially outside the USA (where one can be both 'conservative' and a socialist if one is against neoliberal attacks on the welfare state). Within such an individualist approach to ideology, it is hard to explain how one can be conservative on economic issues and progressive on gender issues, or how ideologies can change historically (as from communist to neoliberal in Russia or from racist to antiracist in South Africa) – without assuming that suddenly the personality of all or most members change in ideological groups.

Our approach focuses on a more social and political definition of ideologies as shared by the members of a group, and not on the personal choices people make in the *acquisition* or *uses* of ideologies as a function of their *personality* and *personal experiences*. These would rather be accounted for in terms of an individual psychology and in terms of mental models. Ideologies have to do with the relations between groups, their goals and norms, with domination and resistance, not with personality. Similarly, philosophers may have specific personal beliefs about socially relevant issues, but they become ideologies only when shared by specific groups in society.

Relevant for this chapter and this book is that ideologies – just like socially shared knowledge – are *largely acquired and reproduced by public discourse*. Although personal experiences may be very relevant in choosing or developing an ideology, we generally become feminists or pacifists because of socially shared beliefs we learn about through communication, e.g., by the media or ideologues of an ideological group.

Individuals may be a member of *several ideological groups*. One may be a socialist, feminist and a pacifist at the same time. This may mean that on specific attitudes, and especially in the mental models of daily experiences and practices, we may find ideological contradictions. Indeed, one may be a feminist but against same-sex marriages – as the current debate in the USA also shows. This shows again that we should distinguish between a collective group ideology and the ways it is being 'applied' by its members in concrete situations. Ideologies *influence* our discourse and social practices as group members but do not *determine* them, because our mental models of social practices are controlled by many social and personal representations, such as our personal experiences. Hence interviews often show very heterogeneous ideological beliefs (Converse, 1964; see also the review by Jost, 2009). They are not about shared group beliefs but about personal uses and hence possible adaptations of such beliefs – as is also the case for the knowledge of the language in a community and its personal uses.

As socially shared basic beliefs, ideologies are about the fundamental issues or concerns of human and social life, such as life, death, class, gender, race, ethnicity, sexuality, the earth, reproduction and survival. Unlike personal opinions (mental models) they must be rather stable so as to serve the identity, goals and interest of a group, as is the case for social movements (see, e.g., Klandermans, 1997; Oberschall, 1993). One does not become a feminist or pacifist overnight.

Because of their goals and interests, ideological groups are typically confronted with other groups – whether dominated or dominant (Jost and Major, 2001; Mény and Lavau, 1991). This is also why ideologies continue to be seen in terms of ideological struggle. Part of the identity of groups and their ideologies is precisely defined in terms of the relation to outgroups and their ideologies (see, e.g., Bar-Tal, 1990, 1998, 2000). Hence, ideologies are typically polarized by a positive self-image of their own group, the ingroup (and its allies), and a negative one, the outgroup(s) (and its allies). It is this polarized structure of ideological systems that is also easily observable in its manifest discourses and social practices.

Thus, many of the aspects of ideologies and ideological groups can be framed within a general theory of intergroup relations and conflict (Billig, 1976; Brewer, 2003; Brown, 2001; Hogg and Abrams, 2001; Stroebe *et al.*, 1988; Tajfel, 1982). Also, earlier general work in social psychology on group beliefs and societal beliefs has shown many properties in common between ideologies and other socially shared beliefs, such as social representations (see, especially Bar-Tal, 1990, 2000). It is therefore strange that such earlier work seldom speaks of ideologies (see, however, Scarbrough, 1990).

Since people are members of various groups, they slowly acquire not only the relevant ideologies of these groups, but also a more general schema for the construction of ideologies (Van Dijk, 1998). Such an *ideological schema* is assumed to form the cognitive basis of ideological group formation and reproduction, and features such categories as:

- identity (who are we, who belongs to us, who is a member of us?)
- action (what do we do, what must we do?)
- goals (why do we do this, why are we together?)
- norms and values (what is good or bad for us, what are we (not) allowed to do?)
- reference groups (who are our allies and enemies?)
- resources (what are the power resources at our disposal – or which we need – to reproduce our group?).

Ideologies need to apply to the activities of many people in many types of situation. This means that they need to be very *general* and *abstract*. Since they are slowly developed, reproduced and accepted by groups of people, they also change very slowly and usually do not specify minor details of everyday actions or changing circumstances, specific topics and so on.

Below we shall see that ideologies are derived from and then control more specific social *attitudes* – thus a racist ideology may be the basis of negative attitudes about immigration or the use of language.

4.2.5   Attitudes

We may be brief about attitudes because they have been the core of traditional social psychology and do not need much introduction and elaboration here. However, since my concept of the notion of attitude is rather different from the dominant and traditional one, let me briefly summarize my own view of attitudes as a form of social belief, partly embodying theory fragments in a more cog- nitivist as well as a more societal social psychology (for standard views, espe- cially also about *attitude change*, see especially Eagly and Chaiken, 1993):

- **Attitudes are social.** Attitudes are socially shared beliefs on important social issues and should be distinguished from permanent or ad hoc personal opinions as represented in mental models (Fraser and Gaskell, 1990; Jaspars and Fraser, 1984).
- **Attitudes are organized by general schemas**, as we have also seen for ideologies, featuring group identities, actions, goals, norms and values, and relations to other groups. The internal structure or organization of an atti- tude was traditionally limited to three major components, the ABC structure: Affect, Behavior and Cognition (Rosenberg and Hovland, 1960), or repre- sented in terms of balance Heider (1946, 1958), or as a more motivational notion of cognitive dissonance by Festinger (1957). The more cognitive approaches to attitudes since the 1980s did pay more attention to their sche- matic organization (see, e.g., Eagly and Chaiken, 1993: Ch. 3), but detailed schematic studies of the structures of attitudes are rare (see, e.g., the papers in the three-volume handbook of Wyer and Srull, 1984; see also Fiske and Taylor, 2007; McGuire, 1989; Ostrom, Skowronski and Nowak, 1994). For a more contemporary approach to the schematic organization of attitudes, see Smith and Queller, 2004.
- **Attitudes are based on socially shared knowledge**. Attitudes are not only based on the ideologies of a group but on the general knowledge of a com- munity – allowing mutual communication and debate in the first place. In order to have a debate or opinions on gay marriages, as is the case in the *NYT* editorial, one needs to *know* what gay marriages are in the first place.
- **Attitudes are often polarized**. A central structural aspect of ideologies is that they are often polarized (Eagly and Chaiken, 1993: 97ff.), with a gen- eral *ingroup–outgroup* dimension emphasizing *Our* good things, and another dimension emphasizing *Their* bad things (Burnstein and Sentis, 1981;

Mackie and Cooper, 1983; Van Dijk, 1998). Yet, attitudes may also be one-sided, for instance emphasizing the negative aspects of an outgroup without emphasizing the positive aspects of the ingroup, or vice versa (see, e.g., Kerlinger, 1984).

- **Some attitudes are script-like**. Structural conceptions of attitudes have been compared to a more dynamic script (Abelson, 1976; Schank and Abelson, 1977), rhetorical dilemmas (Billig, 1989), or narrative (Bruner, 2002; Schank and Abelson, 1995), for instance as we know it from popular stories already studied by Propp (1968): an initial (good) state is violated and our group (and its heroes) wants to reestablish such a state through our struggle against these violators. Note, though, that we distinguish between the *cognitive organization* of attitudes and the conventional, culturally based *discourse structures* of stories.

- **Attitudes are evaluative**. The evaluative dimension (see, e.g., Pratkanis *et al.* 1989) has been generally retained in contemporary definitions of attitudes (see, e.g., Fiske and Taylor, 2007). Note, though, that these are socially shared evaluations based on socially shared norms and values, not personal opinions or emotions (as was typical in traditional approaches). Many conservative attitudes tend to have an overall *negative* orientation. Thus we have attitudes *against* abortion, immigration, euthanasia, but the same is true for attitudes against war and against pollution – which, however, may have to be defined as a positive one in favor of peace and the environment. Conservative attitudes, thus, seem to share a concern to maintain the status quo, existing power relations, etc. – which may precisely attract members with traditional or authoritarian personalities (Jost, 2009).

- **Attitudes vs. practices and discourse**. As is the case for ideologies, attitudes are forms of social cognition as represented in LTM and shared by members of a group. They are distinct from but influence the mental models, and hence the opinions, of individual members about specific events, as they are expressed by discourse and other social practices. Thus, we may have ideological opinions and discourses of individual people, but these are *applications* or *uses* of underlying, socially shared attitudes. (Van Dijk, 1998). The relation between attitudes and discourse is not circular (in the sense of deriving attitudes from discourse that also determine discourse), because underlying attitudes also control other social practices as well as discourse. They are a different kind of structure.

4.2.6   *Public opinion*

The concept of public opinion as a form of social belief is closely related to that of attitudes, but in actual research, both in social psychology and in political science, public opinion rather refers to aggregate personal opinions – usually collected in surveys – on a socially or politically relevant issue and as distributed in society (Himmelweit, 1990). If personal opinions are similar they may be instantiations of socially shared attitudes. In that sense, public opinion is not a type of social belief distinct from others. If they are collective, socially shared beliefs (and not a mere aggregate of personal opinions) then public opinion should rather be called public attitudes – defined as systems of attitudes as distributed in society – as happens in many publications, typically reporting survey research on varied issues of social concern, such as immigration, (among many others see, e.g., Fetzer, 2000).

If we consider the following list of topics studied under the label of 'public attitudes,' we also see that such topics do not fundamentally differ (apart from the methods used to collect such attitudes) from those studied as attitudes – or indeed 'public' opinion, a notion used in thousands of studies – and for social representations, as discussed below:

abortion	advertising	AIDS
capitalism	cloning	communications
community mental health	gay marriages	gays and lesbians
genetics	hydrogen energy	immigration
mentally ill	nanotechnology	nuclear power
organ donation	peace	policing
power plants	smoking	social security
sustainable energy	television	terrorism
unemployment benefits	violence against women	welfare policies
welfare state		

These topics appear to cluster around such general themes as public health and welfare, security and risk, new technologies, energy, war and peace, and social groups, identity and relations (such as homosexuality, gay marriages, etc.). Abstracting even more, these theme clusters all appear to focus on issues that are new for the citizens, and may be interpreted, at least by many, as a threat to what is good or known, including traditional values.

Hence it was proposed to associate attitudes with personal, motivational dynamics, such as the conservative tendency among many people to accept or justify what is known, familiar or the status quo, on the one hand, and the fear of the new and the unexpected, on the other (Jost, 2009). Contrary to such an individualist, motivational account, we suggested interpreting such 'personal' characteristics in terms of individual instances of *group* relations and the persuasive and manipulative discourse powers of the dominant elites defending or promoting dominant attitudes and ideologies (Van Dijk, 2006a). These are prevalent as long as opposition or dissident groups have little or no access to public discourse in order to advocate social changes.

In sum, the topics of public 'opinion' represent attitudes that embody concerns as well as a conception of society or specific groups at risk by new social, political, economic or scientific developments. We briefly mention these issues because they apparently are what many people think about – whether spontaneously because of their own personal experiences (e.g., with welfare or unemployment) or because politicians, researchers or journalists put a topic on the public agenda and want an 'opinion' of the public at large (e.g., about genetics or nanotechnology). These are the shared concerns of various kinds of social belief, as studied in this chapter.

4.2.7   Prejudice, stereotypes

We may also be brief about other social beliefs, such as prejudice and stereotypes, because they may be defined as a special case of attitudes (or social representations) about outgroups – and have been extensively studied in social psychology, both in terms of traditional attitudes, as mental schemas and as intergroup relations as well as social representations (Augoustinos and Reynolds, 2001; Bar-Tal, 1989; Dovidio and Gaertner, 1986; Dovidio *et al.*, 2005; Pickering, 2001; Zanna and Olson, 1994).

One way to define prejudices is to see them as attitudes that consist of generic social beliefs attributing negative properties to social outgroups, organized by a general group schema as we also have found for the structure of ideology (Van Dijk, 1984a, 1998). Given the polarized nature of underlying ideologies, prejudices are also organized in a polarized system, in which Our group (the ingroup) is assigned positive characteristics and Their group (the outgroup) negative ones, following a system of social values that are specifically important for Us. Thus, if in Our group, intelligence is an important value, the outgroup will be represented as being less intelligent than we are and so on. Because of principles of balance and feelings of social justice, the outgroup may be assigned positive characteristics on values that are less important for Us (e.g., musicality or hospitality).

Relevant for our discussion in this chapter is again the relation with knowledge. As we have shown for attitudes, group prejudices also presuppose community knowledge: one can have prejudices about immigrants only if one knows what immigrants are – although in some classic research, people are found to have negative opinions about outgroups (especially people) they do not know – that is, a general xenophobia.

Interestingly, prejudice has often been characterized in terms of a *lack* of detailed knowledge about a group, hence the need for overgeneralizations when confronted with actions by members of an outgroup. In other words, at least for some outgroups, more and more detailed knowledge about them seem to diminish stereotypes and prejudice. Maybe this applies to ethnic outgroups, or peoples abroad, but hardly seems relevant for local minorities or women.

As we have seen before, members of ingroups may sometimes conceive of stereotypes or prejudices as (objective) 'knowledge,' especially if these are widespread and hardly contested – as has been historically the case for prejudices about women and Africans. In that case, such prejudice is not asserted and defended as a socially shared opinion against those who do not share such an attitude, but presupposed and taken for granted as if it were socioculturally shared knowledge *within such an ideological group*. From the perspective of a broader sociocultural community in which such prejudices are not shared and may be contested, they are, of course, treated as what they are, namely sexist or racist prejudices or stereotypes. We see that if the notion of knowledge is relative, so is the notion of prejudice.

Note also that knowing (about) a prejudice or stereotype does not necessarily imply that it is actually adhered to. This is not only the case for adults but also for children, who may learn prejudices and stereotypes – as forms of 'knowledge' – at a very early age, but it remains to be seen whether it makes theoretical or practical sense to speak of prejudiced toddlers. At the same time, such a question presupposes that we know exactly *when* and especially *how* people actively adhere to, accept and share prejudices – and hence are ready to assert them as their own and identify with an ideological group. It seems that this generally happens in periods when independent social and especially political identities are being developed, namely in adolescence and young adulthood (see also Aboud, 1988; Devine, 1989; Holmes, 1995; Quintana and McKown, 2008; Van Ausdale and Feagin, 2001).

4.2.8   Social representations

The notion of social representation (SR) has certainly occupied center stage in many current debates on knowledge and social beliefs in social psychology, especially in Europe and Latin America. Since the current literature on the topic is vast (dozens of monographs and edited books, and thousands of articles – in the summer of 2010, the Web of Science listed more than 500 articles that had the term "social representation" in their title and many more that had the term in their keywords), we are only able to provide a brief summary of some of its main tenets, mostly intended to establish a relation to knowledge and its discursive reproduction in society.

- **SR as popularization of science.** The original notion of SR was defined in terms of the popular recontextualization, acquisition, uses and reproduction of scientific beliefs, e.g., about psychotherapy (Moscovici, 1961) or about madness (Jodelet, 1989), featuring both lay knowledge as well as attitudes as defined above (for general studies of SRs see Breakwell and Canter,

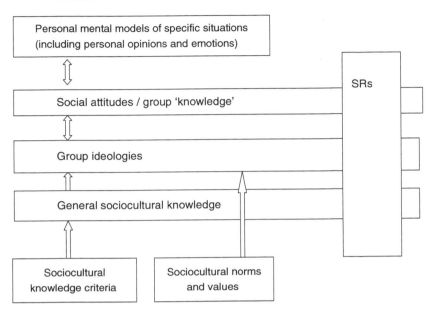

Figure 4.2 System of social beliefs, and the integrated position of social representations

1993; Deaux and Philogène, 2001; Farr and Moscovici, 1984; Jodelet, 1989; Moscovici, 2000; Von Cranach *et al.*, 1992). In that sense, SRs are close to the notion of *commonsense* (Jodelet, 2008; Jovchelovitch, 2007) or implicit theories of everyday life (Wegener and Petty, 1998; Wegner and Vallacher, 1981). In SR studies no explicit distinction is made between knowledge, attitudes and stereotypes and the ways these are expressed in social practices, explanations, discourse and debate – as argued above. If culturally shared, SRs seem to be close to what anthropologists call 'cultural models' (Holland and Quinn, 1987; Shore, 1996; see Chapter 6).

- **SRs and knowledge acquisition**. SRs are assumed to be integrated into the existing knowledge system by a process metaphorically described as 'anchoring.' It is, however, not made explicit what cognitive processes are involved in such knowledge integration.
- **The structure of SR**. There is as yet little insight into the internal structure or organization of SRs – beyond a distinction between central (more permanent) and peripheral (contextually variable) beliefs (Abric, 1994).
- **SRs represent concerns for social issues**. Existing SR research especially deals with such social issues as AIDS and other illnesses, poverty, violence, minorities, gender and so on, which may be summarized as general

macro-themes, such as health, age, reproduction, danger, risk and social structure that reflect basic concerns about the human and social condition.

If SRs are different from what we have defined above as social attitudes, then they might be represented in our design for the architecture of social cognition, cross-cutting other types of social beliefs, as shown in Figure 4.2, modifying Figure 4.1.

4.2.9   Social beliefs and knowledge

We have seen that social beliefs such as ideologies, attitudes, prejudices and social representations are multiply related to socially shared knowledge, and generally presuppose such knowledge or adapt it to the concerns or interests of a group. Although defined for epistemic communities, we may also speak of **specific group knowledge**. Thus, ideological group knowledge need not be biased but may feature knowledge that is not (yet) generally accepted and presupposed in the community. This is, for instance, the case for feminist-based knowledge about gender discrimination (see, e.g., Hotter and Tancred, 1993), ecologically based knowledge about pollution (Johnson and Griffith, 1996; Yearley, 1992) and the knowledge production of social movements in general (Fals-Borda, 1991; Hosseini, 2010)

Finally, the same principle might be extended to any kind of **specialized group knowledge**, including **expert knowledge**. In this case, each specific epistemic community presupposes general world knowledge but develops its own knowledge criteria ('methods') and sometimes very detailed forms of specialized knowledge, as is prototypically the case in science (Ellis, 1989; Musgrave, 1993). Research on social representations as well as on popularization has shown how such specialized knowledge may again influence the formation and changes of commonsense or non-specialized knowledge (Myers, 1990; Purkhardt, 1993).

If we integrate these assumptions into our general architecture of social beliefs, we have several options. We may add (see Figure 4.1) a special box for specialized (scientific) knowledge above general knowledge as the basis for the discourse and social practices among specialists (scientists). In this case, specialists presuppose both general sociocultural knowledge as well as specialized knowledge in their social practices (including discourse). In the same way as other people they may then also have general ideologies and attitudes of a specialized character, as we know from science (Aronowitz, 1988).

Alternatively, we may treat specialists as a group and not as a community, and consider their specialized knowledge, ideologies and attitudes, as well as their norms and values, as part of a special (transversal) social representation. This seems a more attractive proposal because it allows many other 'specialized' groups with more or less independent norms, values, knowledge, ideologies and attitudes – but all based on the same general system of sociocultural knowledge and its underlying criteria.

This may well mean that some of this specialized knowledge (ideologies, etc.) is inconsistent with or critical of general knowledge, for instance if such general knowledge is assumed to be mistaken. This may be routinely the case for scientific representations being critical of mundane knowledge, but is also so for social movements, churches or ideological collectivities (racists, etc.) – obviously for different reasons.

The general interest within SR theory for the propagation of scientific knowledge among the general population would thus consist of an introduction of social beliefs of special (e.g., scientific) SR groups into the general knowledge system of the community, but after the usual transformations into everyday commonsense or 'lay' knowledge (Purkhardt, 1993; see also Kruglanski, 1989).

Unfortunately, this is not only the case for 'true' knowledge, but also for misguided, racist 'knowledge,' as we know from the history of racist science in general, and from that of eugenic ideas in particular (Barkan, 1992; Haghighat, 1988). The same is obviously true for the misguided 'scientific knowledge' about women and the history of the propagation of such beliefs in patriarchal society – as well as for the struggle of (mostly female) scientists and other feminists to counter such forms of ideologically based knowledge legitimating systems of gender domination (Joshi, 2006).

As soon as specialized group knowledge, ideologies and attitudes are being adopted by the general community at large, they become taken for granted and transformed into commonsense beliefs. Examples are not only (at least some) ideas of the feminist movement, but especially also ideas of the ecological movement that have been generally accepted in discourse and routine practices in everyday life, laws, regulations and so on (Agnone, 2007; Sunderlin, 2002; see also SR studies on minority influence Moscovici et al., 1994).

4.2.10 How to distinguish knowledge from opinion – a partial epistemic and doxastic analysis of the editorial in the New York Times

We have assumed above that personal opinions as well as social attitudes and ideologies are based on knowledge. For example, to have an opinion on immigration presupposes one knows (more or less) what immigration is. Yet, as usual with fundamental notions, things are more complicated than that. If a man has been convicted for a proven theft, we may call him a thief, and that is no doubt a statement of knowledge. But if someone steals an idea from us, and we call him a thief, many would see this is our opinion and not as a statement of fact.

An editorial is a genre that expresses the opinion of a journalist, or even expresses an attitude or an ideology of a group of people, as is undoubtedly the case for the editorial on such a notoriously debatable topic as same-sex marriages today in the USA. So, let us examine this editorial somewhat more closely to see whether and how opinion and knowledge are related.

First of all, as we have observed above, the little systematic genre research on newspaper editorials in the world seems to suggest that before they for-mulate an opinion or recommendation, editorials state and repeat an issue, and tend to summarize what has been reported, as known, in news reports of the same day or previous days. This indeed seems to be case in this editorial, because it begins by repeating the news that President Obama has "joined the fight" against the Californian ban of same-sex marriages – no doubt a fact already known by most of the readers. That by doing this Obama "made good on his promise of his second Inaugural Address," however, is harder to categorize as opinion or fact, even when Obama in his address had liter-ally promised to join this fight. No doubt for the *NYT* editor who wrote the editorial, this is not a personal opinion but a way to describe what Obama did, namely 'keep his promise.' So, let's accept this as a subjective way to describe what happened, in the sense that, as yet, no explicit evaluation is being formulated about Obama's keeping his promise, although describing someone as keeping a promise may implicate, pragmatically, that this is a good thing. On the other hand, at the end of the first paragraph the clause, "we can't imagine how he could have sat this one out," as pragmatically indexed by the pronoun *we* is more clearly an opinion about Obama's actions and alternatives. But even then, such an opinion requires some implicit reasoning and inferences, such as: 'in order to be consistent in his policies and earlier declarations about (marriage) equality, Obama hardly had an alternative but to join the fight against the same-sex marriage ban right now.' But even such a subjective reasoning is very close to observing the facts and hence stating a fact by denying a politically viable alternative. Indeed, the statement could have been made by an opponent of Obama.

Just these two relatively simple examples show that the boundary between fact and opinion, and hence between a news report and an editorial, is not as easy to make as the principle of US newspapers (not to mix fact with opinion) seems to suggest. Easier is when the editorial in lines 7–8 states that the brief of the government was "a legally and symbolically important repudiation," because the adjective *important* implies an evaluation (for a linguistic approach to evaluative words, see, especially the work on *appraisal*, e.g., Martin and White, 2005). But again this is not as straightforward as it seems. All mem-bers of the epistemic community may agree that the brief was *important*, in the same way as they may agree that the president is powerful, and hence we are theoretically within the confines of what we defined as knowledge. Yet, as is the case for such adjectives as *large, small, heavy* and *beautiful*, it depends on context. No doubt there are other things that are much more important, and hence someone could claim that the brief, comparatively speaking, was not important at all. On the other hand, the nominalized expression *repudiation*, which seems to denote a fact of what the brief did, and hence expresses shared knowledge of the editor, may very well be rejected by Obama's opponents, namely that the brief did not actually repudiate anything, for instance because its opinions were flawed. Closer to a justified belief, would be, to say that the brief *attempted to repudiate* California's ban on same-sex marriages. These and many other examples have puzzled epistemologists for a long time and have led to various forms of relativism and contextualism, as we have seen in Chapter 2. That is, short of formulating an explicit opinion based on an implicit evaluation, descriptions of states of affairs may be 'true' from the point of view of a speaker, or in a special context or when compared to other situations. And acts or processes may be described as having obtained when their aims are actually and completely realized, but it depends again on the perspective of the observer whether they are or not. Indeed, the Supreme Court may deem that the government's brief did not actually manage to repudiate California's position.

The next paragraphs rather straightforwardly summarize the facts of the debate, and rather unambiguously repeat what is shared knowledge even among the opponents in the debate – a good test to distinguish between knowledge and opinion. But the metaphor "the government made mincemeat" (line 23), as suggested above, may be a lively way to describe that the government successfully refuted the argument of the proponents of Proposition 8 (namely that same-sex marriages threaten traditional marriages), and hence comes close to a mere observation of what was the case. But, as is the case for metaphors, they often are politically hardly innocent (Lakoff, 2004, 2008). Also in this case, the metaphor rhetorically enhances the literal meaning of the literal verb *to refute*, said of arguments, by making an abstract verb very much concrete in terms of the everyday observation of grinding meat to minced meat. But as we saw with the nominalization *repudiation*, that way of describing the counterarguments of the government's brief is no doubt a (positive) evaluation of the correctness of the arguments and the success of its aims, namely to refute those of the opponent – an evaluation Obama's opponent no doubt would reject. Indeed, later in the editorial it says that

> The legal analysis advanced by the Obama administration leads inexorably to the conclusion that all attempts to ban same-sex marriage are inherently unconstitutional,

but that conclusion is that of the editorial, which indeed regrets in the next sentence that Obama "stopped short" of drawing that conclusion, which implicates that he should have done what he did not do, which again is no doubt an opinion on Obama's policy. Similarly, when the editorial in line 43 wonders "We don't know why the administration did not take that step" this is literally a statement about a lack of knowledge, which as an internal self-description should be taken at face value, that is, as self-knowledge, but again the political implicature in this text and context is that, according to the *NYT*, Obama *should* have taken that step, and hence we here have a case of an indirect opinion statement. The final statement of the editorial, by way of evaluative conclusion and as a recommendation to the judges, is an explicit expression of a propositional attitude of hope, but the use of the factive verb *to recognize* implicates that what the judges should recognize is the (moral, political) truth, namely that the Constitution does not tolerate discrimination: "We hope the justices recognize the broader truth that the Constitution does not tolerate denying gay people the right to wed in any state."

We see that even a brief, and far from complete, epistemic and doxastic analysis of an editorial no doubt arrives at the conclusion that the editorial expresses opinions of the newspaper, but that many of its statements of facts are equally biased, and close to opinions. In other words, not surprisingly, and despite epistemological and psychological theorizing, in everyday editorial discourse, no less than everyday conversation, the distinction between statements of facts and statements of opinions are sometimes hard to distinguish. This is especially so because even statements of facts may contextually implicate an opinion and that nearly all descriptions of the social and political environment are made from the perspective of the speaker or writer.

Finally, the personal opinions implicitly expressed in the editorial are part of a mental model of the *NYT* journalist(s) about the debate on Proposition 8, and the debate on same-sex marriages, which instantiates a more general liberal attitude on same-sex marriages, as summarized in the last sentence (on the Constitution). That is, we know what the general attitudes of the *NYT* are and even when not made explicit in the editorial, this contextual knowledge about this attitude allows us to derive the doxastic implicatures. Even more generally, the more fundamental ideology of equal rights shared by the *NYT* would even allow us to predict this very liberal attitude. In other words, the editorial is ideologically consistent.

For this chapter, this brief analysis shows how ideologies, attitudes and (institutional) opinions are related and how in discourse it is sometimes hard to distinguish between biased, relative or contextual knowledge on the one hand, and opinion, on the other – as both define the mental model people have about many events and situations. One often needs a deeper analysis of implicatures, and especially knowledge of the social attitude and ideology shared by the speaker or writer, in order to know what the opinions and what the biased descriptions of facts are. Obviously, more generally in political and other public discourse, this also allows writers to deny that they made any explicit opinion statements. Deniability is an important strategic advantage of contextual implicatures – while judges tend to respect only the 'facts' of explicit statements and ignore the facts of contextual implicatures, as we know from many forms of implicit racist text and talk.

4.3   Social groups and communities

Knowledge and other social beliefs are not mere abstract entities floating in the air, or mere mental representations in isolated minds and brains but 'owned' and shared by concrete human beings who are members of collectivities. Besides the individual focus of cognitive psychology and even of much social psychology, it is crucial to define social beliefs in terms of various kinds of social collectivities, such as groups and communities. We have seen that it is hard to even define social groups without reverting to some kind of social representation shared by its members or by through awareness of being and acting as a member of a group, as we know it from social identities. But the converse is also true: it is hard to define social beliefs without an obvious social basis in terms of groups, communities and whole societies or cultures.

Although some kinds of social knowledge and belief as *systems* are typically defined only at the level of collectivities, as is the case for languages, attitudes and ideologies, a social or societal approach to social beliefs does *not* imply denying the relevance of individual social members in the acquisition, application and uses of such beliefs in actual discourse and other social practices at the microlevel of analysis. Not quite trivially, collectivities only 'exist' in terms of the existence and the interactions of their members. Their collective knowledge and beliefs only exist because they are being acquired, shared and used by members. This in turn presupposes that these members need to have such knowledge, as represented in their mind/brain.

Despite its frequent individualist approaches, and especially in much contemporary social cognition research, social psychology has always also considered this complex dialectic between individuals and social collectivities, as we know especially from the rich tradition of intergroup research founded by Tajfel (1978, 1981) and his associates (see, e.g., Billig, 1976; Brown, 2001; Turner and Giles, 1981; among many other books, see also Brewer, 2003; Stephan and Stephan, 1996).

Relevant for our discussion is the social foundation of knowledge and other social beliefs as being shared by members of groups and other social collectivities. Although the notion of group is quite general, and may even be taken as generic for all kinds of collectivities, we need to make some analytical distinctions between different kinds of collectivities.

Thus, first of all, we speak of **communities** as *sociocultural collectivities* whose members share the same language, religion, knowledge, nationality and/or ethnic identity. People become members of community by birth, socialization, migration and/or by a rather slow process of cultural integration. Thus, we speak of cultural, ethnic, linguistic and epistemic communities. Another example might be a professional community, defined in terms of shared knowledge, education, abilities and types of activities – although a professional *organization* is a group rather than a community.

The popular but vague notion *community of practice* (Lave and Wenger, 1991) is not always a community in our sense, but is often constituted by members who engage in a joint activity and who share one or more goals, and hence is a type of *group* in our terms. They are communities if defined in terms of shared repertoires (including knowledge), norms, values, etc.

Groups – in the strict sense – are collectivities whose members share (in) a specific activity, goal, attitude or ideology, as is the case for socialists, feminists, antiracists or pacifists, on the one hand, or social movements and political action groups, on the other. Thus, a community, such as a national community, may have different kinds of (ideological, etc.) groups. Groups may be more or less organized or institutionalized, e.g., by formal admission procedures, formal membership (card-carrying members), leadership, roles, routines, centers, proselytism.

There are many **types of group**, as defined by different types of members, goals, activities, cohesion, permanence, organization and so on. They range from conversational dyads, parties, teams and other work groups, committees, clubs, social movements, gangs, sects, political parties, fraternities and many more, on the one hand, to large organizations, businesses, churches and nation-states, and so on, on the other. A complete typology would be based on sociological criteria, such as type of organization, leadership, membership management or financing, as well as sociocognitive criteria, such as shared knowledge, attitudes, ideologies, norms and values.

Although hardly a special category of group, but rather a class of groups, **small groups**, such as work teams, have been studied in social psychology not only for their interaction patterns or decision making but also for their production and sharing of knowledge and other beliefs (see, e.g., Devine, 1999; Nye and Brower, 1996). This research is also relevant for broader studies of knowledge management in organizations (Thompson *et al.*, 1999; see further references in Chapter 5).

The sociocognitive criteria are relevant for our discussion here. Thus, we speak of **ideological groups** such as socialists, feminists or pacifists, that is, groups of people who share basic ideological goals, attitudes, norms and/or values as the basis for ideological activities and identification of its members.

We have seen above that although general sociocultural knowledge is assumed to define epistemic communities, within such a community we may also distinguish **epistemic groups**. These may be defined as collectivities of people who share specialized knowledge and who engage in joint activities (e.g., give advice) based on such knowledge, as is the case for think tanks, teams of experts, boards, panels, committees and so on. Like for ideological groups, the specialized knowledge of these epistemic groups presupposes the general sociocultural knowledge of the epistemic community as a whole. In the literature, such epistemic groups are sometimes also called 'epistemic networks' or 'epistemic communities' – which again shows the rather fuzzy boundaries between groups and communities (see, e.g., Haas, 1992; Leydesdorff, 2001; Miller and Fox, 2001; Roth, 2005; Roth and Bourgine, 2005).

Note that although groups are not primarily defined in epistemic terms, such as action groups, social movements, political parties or business organizations, they may well share specific group knowledge, if only about the nature and goals of the group or its specific domain of activities. It is precisely also for that reason that the study of knowledge management has become such a hot topic in the study of organizations (see next chapter for some references).

The definition of knowledge at the level of groups and other collectivities also implies a different account of knowledge than in the psychology of individual minds/brains. Again, we have assumed that one way to account for collective knowledge is to assume such knowledge to be shared and distributed among members, as we shall see below – for instance in the way people of a linguistic community share more or less the same (basic) knowledge of a natural language.

However, collective knowledge of a group may also be analyzed in terms of **joint, accumulated knowledge**, in which each member of the group not only shares general sociocultural knowledge with the whole community, and some specific basic organizational knowledge of the group, but also individual expert knowledge, as is typically the case in many organizations, such as universities, laboratories and business corporations. Such knowledge differences among members of an organization also imply different forms of interaction and communication, and hence complex 'epistemic interaction management' because the specialized knowledge of one member (or group of members) may not be presupposed in the interaction with others (see Canary and McPhee, 2010). Yet, the joint knowledge of the group may be used in joint action such as the production of a scholarly publication, the construction of a bridge or governing a country (for general discussion on collective group knowledge, see, e.g., Back, 2005; Benson and Standing, 2001; Hagemann and Grinstein, 1997; Lewis et al., 2007; Rolin, 2008).

4.4   Sharing social beliefs

The next fundamental issue we need to address and that is at the basis of the relations between discourse and knowledge is the question of how social beliefs get communicated, spread, disseminated or diffused in groups, communities and society in the first place. Indeed, they are only *social* beliefs if they are *shared*, and if they are not innate they can only be shared if they have been spread or distributed among a collectivity of people. And they can only be spread among members of collectivities if this happens during the socialization of new members, as we get to learn our first language and our culture, or by specific forms of interaction and communication later in life (for the notion of 'sharing beliefs,' see, e.g., Bar-Tal, 2000; Echterhoff *et al.*, 2009; Eiser *et al.*, 1998; Lee, 2001; Sperber, 1990).

The obvious answer to the question of sharing is that we acquire social beliefs through processes of 'social learning' and that such acquisition usually takes place through talk and text – and certain forms of non-verbal communication. Such a process presupposes that members are able to *express* knowledge and other social beliefs in (multimodal) discourse and that other members are able to interpret such discourse and thus acquire the social beliefs as expressed in the discourse, as explained in the previous chapter. Indeed, this is the traditional definition of communication in the first place: communication is not primarily defined as form of interaction but as a means to 'transmit' beliefs.

4.4.1   What is sharing beliefs?

Unfortunately, the question of 'sharing' is not that simple. First of all, if we acquire social beliefs (knowledge, attitudes, ideologies, social representations, etc.) through discourse in specific situations or genres of communication, how do we know that what we are acquiring are *social* beliefs in the first place and not just the *personal* knowledge and opinions of a speaker or writer – as would be the normal case in conversation or other genres such as the editorial that serves as the example of this chapter? Thus, if part of our social beliefs, such as sociocultural knowledge, is first acquired from caregivers, how do children know these are 'social' and not just the personal beliefs of their caregivers?

The obvious answer to that question is that children (or other newcomers to a group or community) cannot possibly know that – until they meet other members of the collective and get to know (more or less) the same beliefs. In other words, social beliefs may be acquired by repetition, comparison and abstraction from experiences (mental models) or directly from various forms of expository discourse (e.g., from parents, teachers or other epistemic experts of the community). In this way, members discursively learn both common sense and 'uncommon' sense, what is normal and abnormal, and what is biased or unbiased. Although the cognitive details of this process are not that easy to make explicit, it does not seem to be very mysterious how people derive generic, common beliefs from (limited) sets of discourses or other forms of interaction. Indeed, such is also the way we learn a language, including the words of a language and their relationship to our general knowledge.

Even if we assume that this is more or less how we acquire social beliefs, the question still remains whether such beliefs are strictly the 'same' for each member or not. Thus, it may well be that people by their repeated experiences and discourses with various members of a collectivity are able to compare, generalize and abstract 'common' beliefs, but the execution of these processes themselves is still personal. Moreover, each member has her or his own autobiographical experiences, and grows up or otherwise gets socialized in different groups and communities, so that the resulting 'common' belief systems still are 'personal' at the same time – that is, as *idiosyncratic versions* of the general system.

Thus, if all members have their own versions of social belief systems (knowledge, attitudes, ideologies) – as we also may notice in the individually variable uses of these systems in text, talk and interaction – *there would not exist one 'shared' belief system in the first place.* In a way that might be compared to imperfect genetic copying, so may our social systems be imperfectly transmitted to new members of our group or collectivity.

Fortunately, there seems to be a form of general social or cultural 'self-repair' mechanism for such imperfections: *normalization.* When dealing with many different members, each with their own idiosyncratic version of a social belief system, we learn to disregard the personal versions and establish a more or less abstract common denominator. This is also crucial for many other reasons such as our own discourse with other members: we generally know from experience where our own version of shared knowledge, attitudes or ideologies is different from that of (most) others, or the abstract 'common' beliefs. As is the case for personal or dialectic variants of a language, this means that in order to be understood, we may not presuppose our personal variant to be known to other members who do not know us personally, and may thus tend to accommodate the use of our 'personal' knowledge or other beliefs in a way that is understandable to others.

The same process takes place for each group and community where there may be a shared, common social belief system (which may itself be a variant of a more general system), but again with personal variation.

Whereas for language the procedures of normalization are quite strict, because otherwise we are unable to communicate with (most) other members of the community and because of the normative aspects of linguistic socialization at school, for the other belief systems such normalization may be quite different. Thus, if one has seriously divergent beliefs from the normative ones in a church, sect or party, one may be excommunicated or expelled. But within many social movements, such as feminism or pacifism, there are many internal ideological variations and subgroups: one may be a socialist feminist or a neoliberal pacifist, and so on – and such differences may give rise to heated internal debates and conflict – and still consider oneself and be considered a feminist or pacifist (of course, social movements also have forms of exclusion and marginalization).

4.4.2   Distributed cognition

After dealing with the general notion of *sharing* social belief systems, we briefly need to consider the question whether we thus have at least partly accounted for what is usually called **distributed cognition** (Hutchins, 1995; Salomon, 1997). Are knowing a language, sharing an attitude, a social representation or an ideology forms of distributed cognition in the sense that these social belief systems do not characterize the belief systems of individuals but are only defined at the higher level of collectivities? If we assume that there are no private languages nor private ideologies, only social ones, then the empirical existence of belief systems is as (abstractions from) *individually distributed versions* of the system.

Obviously, there is another, more appropriately called, form of distributed knowledge, namely when a group – such as a team – has different systems of specialized knowledge next to the common knowledge that serves as a basis for communication, interaction and especially *coordination*. As we have seen above, it is in this sense that a group as a whole may have 'more' knowledge than its members if such a **joint belief system** is used in specific forms of interaction, such as building a bridge, executing a research project or writing a report.

Such different knowledge among members need not be limited to expert belief systems and cooperation but also takes place in informal everyday talk among friends. Some participant member may have just read about a new government policy, another participant the latest news about the love life of a friend and so on. In this case, it is the *personal knowledge of participants* that is being shared rather than a form of joint belief system used for the execution of collaborative tasks.

4.4.2.1 Ecological distribution
Besides these more obvious uses of the notion of distributed cognition, the term has been used in a much broader sense, where cognition is not limited to the minds of individuals or even as shared by members of groups or collectivities, but stretches to the environment in various ways.

This 'ecological' conception of distributed cognition would first of all emphasize the *embodiment* of social belief systems, such as the abilities and affordances of our body. Knowledge of a bicycle would not be limited to a schema in semantic memory but would also involve the practical (visual, motor) knowledge and emotions needed to recognize, handle, ride or repair bicycles. Such multimodal abilities and experiences may then be *transduced* as conceptual knowledge about bikes (including our relations with bikes)(see also Barsalou, 2008).

Similarly, distributed cognition may also be represented in objects and symbols, as is the case for religious or political symbols that have a special meaning for a collective, or for collective memories represented in a statue or a silent march. In other words, what traditionally is associated with the mind, such as shared meaning and memory, may more broadly be associated with specific elements of the natural or construed environment or artifacts.

Finally, complex mental operations usually need ways of 'off-loading' part of the tasks of working memory, as we have seen in the previous chapter, e.g., when we use a pen, pencil, paper and/or computer to make calculations and to store and retrieve information. Again, the whole operation of calculating or sending a message may be a specific way of coordinating mental processes with objects, properties or affordances of the environment.

Relevant for our discussion is especially the relation between distributed cognition, knowledge and discourse. Thus, as we have seen, social belief systems exist through being distributed among their members. Secondly, a collective may be defined as having accumulated, joint knowledge, e.g., for the execution of complex tasks. Thirdly, there is an embodied relationship between knowledge and skill – not only for how to 'know' about a bicycle, but also how we know about language and discourse. Fourthly, we see that knowledge and other social beliefs, as well as operations based on them, may be distributed over objects or symbols in the environment. For our theory this is important because shared meanings and the acquisition of knowledge may not be limited to discourse, but may also be 'carried' by images, movies, artifacts and even landscapes.

Note, though, that this is only possible when such external objects are first associated with meanings, memories, knowledge and so on. That is, whatever the role of the external objects, it is still the human mind that is needed to assign meanings, to interpret and to share meanings and knowledge.

4.4.3   Common Ground

Finally, let us also briefly examine again the notion of **Common Ground** as it has been used for language use and communication (most of the bibliography about Common Ground is about social and political common ground).

Whereas social belief systems are defined at the level of shared beliefs of a group or community, Common Ground as usually defined is *context bound*, that is, it defines shared knowledge *in specific communicative situations*, such as two participants in a conversation or other kind of interaction, or the shared knowledge of journalists and their readers. We shall therefore focus more specifically on this notion in Chapter 7.

In such situations there are several types of Common Ground (CG) (Clark, 1996). Thus, first of all, we have as CG the social belief systems mentioned above, including general common knowledge, of which the participants in discourse or communication are members. Thus, participants of a communicative event may have various levels or dimensions of CG, such as:

- the same general language and/or dialect
- interpersonal knowledge (among family members and friends)
- joint participation in the same (communicative) situation
- the same general knowledge system of the epistemic community (local, regional, national, international)
- the same specialized knowledge system (e.g., among professionals)
- the same attitude or social representation about an issue
- the same ideology
- the same norms and values.

Besides such shared beliefs, CG also needs to be defined in specific terms, that is, in terms of *mental models* and their properties. Thus, participants often know each other personally and hence may share personal knowledge. Such knowledge is largely acquired by talk or text, and participants may thus need to know when or whether such information has been shared or not. In other words, participants need to mutually represent each other, including each other's personal or social knowledge, in context models, and they may activate and recall previous context models in order to know whether an old model (previous communication) is known to the recipient. But not only *that* there was earlier interaction, but especially also the specific information (situation model) communicated in such earlier discourse may need to be (partly) activated as CG.

In conversation and other forms of interaction CG is not only based on instantiated general knowledge and beliefs or on specific beliefs shared by previous discourse or the current talk. Mental models of participants may also represent mutual knowledge about observed properties of the communicative, social or physical situation, such as the presence of observed objects and their properties – as well as the (possibly different) observations or perspective of the other participants. Thus, mental models of communicative situations may have embedded mental models of the models of other participants – a well-known case of mutual belief recursion – typically limited in practice by contingent limitations of working memory, time or other conditions.

Obviously, models of the models of other participants are necessarily incomplete or hypothetical – and because they also require quite heavy memory resources, people may have recourse to fast but imperfect strategies to guess the current knowledge of other participants, assuming that if knowledge is presupposed that is in fact lacking, participants will ask for it, if relevant, or if knowledge is asserted that is in fact known, recipients will either say so or ignore such a pragmatic mistake. This typically is the case for knowledge communicated earlier in the same situation or on earlier occasions, or for a different current view or perspective of the current situation (for various accounts of CG, see, among many studies, e.g., Clark, 1996; Clark and Marshall, 1981; Davidson, 2002; Gerrig, 1987; Gibbs, 1987; Horton and Gerrig, 2005; Horton and Keysar, 1996; Keysar, 1997; Keysar and Horton, 1998; Keysar et al., 1998; Keysar et al., 2000; Krauss and Fussell, 1990; Lee, 2001; Planalp and Garvin-Doxas, 1994; Stalnaker, 2002).

Interestingly, few of these studies account for CG or shared and mutual knowledge in terms of situation and context models, which seem the most obvious theoretical construct to describe and explain how various kinds of knowledge and other beliefs may be shared by participants.

When applied to language use and conversation, many of these studies specifically deal with the pragmatic CG constraints on the use of presuppositions, pronouns, definite descriptions and in general on deictic expressions – topics to which we return in Chapter 7.

Again, as is generally the case, the constraints and the strategies will be different for different communicative situations, that is, for different genres. What may be an acceptable strategy in everyday communication may not be so in a textbook, a police interrogation, a trial or a news article. Indeed, different genres may also be defined precisely in terms of their basic contextual mechanisms of CG and knowledge management, as is the case for news, confessions, exams and interrogations.

In other words, our account of CG is in terms of shared social belief systems as well as specific personal mental models, as explained above, and controlled and managed by the context models of the participants – mutually representing the participants, as well as their general and specific knowledge, their identity and their goals.

The question then is *how speakers know about the knowledge of recipients* so that they are able to represent such knowledge in their context model. Again, part of the answer to this question has been provided above, namely:

- The speaker knows or believes that the recipients are members of the *same belief system*, especially that of general, sociocultural knowledge.
- The speaker knows that the recipient has been informed of new knowledge by *another source*, or the speaker has provided this information on an earlier occasion or previously in the same situation.

- The speaker knows that the recipient now participates in the *same interaction situation* or has *participated in an event* from which the shared information may be derived, as based on mutual perception and the affordances of the local environment.

Again, all this information should be accounted for in the current context model that simulates CG and keeps track of the relevant social belief systems, previous experiences and situation models.

Philosophers have also dealt with CG in more formal ways, namely as (various levels of) **mutual knowledge** (Smith, 1982; Sperber and Wilson, 1990; Stalnaker, 2002). Thus, a speaker may assume that a recipient already knows about an event E – and hence will either omit making an assertion about it or will presuppose it. The recipient, listening to such talk, also knows about this speaker knowledge about the knowledge of the recipients – and hence will make an effort to remember what the speaker has told her before. Similarly, the speaker knows about this recipient knowledge about her own knowledge about the knowledge of the recipient, and hence may assume that the recipient will make an effort to remember this (old) shared knowledge. In brief, we here have a well-known case of epistemic recursion or embedding. In actual communication, recursion will usually not go beyond a level of embedding of three or four, due to obvious working memory limitations, and the higher levels become relevant only in moments of conflict, misunderstanding or very delicate forms of politeness or negotiation (see also Lee, 2001).

Research on mirror neurons, theory of mind and simulation further suggests that context models that control discourse and interaction make plausible strategic guesses about what recipients know and want, e.g.,

- because recipients, especially of the same epistemic community, tend to think and interpret situations more or less like the speaker
- because speakers know about everyday routine actions and their intentions and goals
- because of other contextual cues (objects present or absent, etc.), because of earlier discourses or other sources, and because of shared social belief systems (see, e.g., Antonietti *et al.*, 2006; Arbib, 2006; Goldman, 2006; Tomasello, 1998, 2008).

We shall return to the topic of CG and the mutual knowledge of discourse participants and the pragmatics of discourse in Chapter 7.

4.5   Knowledge, communication and distribution in society

Finally, we need to examine the social psychological dimensions of the ways knowledge and other social beliefs are spread or distributed in society. We have argued many times above that this largely happens through discourse. *How* this takes place, that is, through what kind of discourse structures, will be investigated in Chapter 7. In this chapter we focus on the *parameters of the communicative situations* in which knowledge is communicated, such as their settings, participants and goals.

We have seen before that – except in discursive psychology – discourse is not a central notion in social psychology, and I have criticized this situation many times in my earlier work (there are some – few – studies in social cognition that briefly deal with discourse, such as Kraut and Higgins, 1984). A brief look at some major topics of classical and contemporary social psychology is enough to make us wonder how such topics could possibly have been studied in any detail without at least *also* examining the actual text and talk involved in their expression or implementation:

Aggression, attitude change, attribution, beliefs, bias, communication, cooperation, emotion, impression management, interpersonal relationships, interaction, intergroup competition and conflict, persuasion, prejudice, relationships, social identity, social influence, stereotypes.

In sum, if social psychology deals with such general topics as relations among people, the relations between individuals and society, social identity, social cognition and representation, groups and group relations, then language use and discourse is not only the way many of these relationships and cognitions are actually expressed and implemented, but it is also a primary methodological resource for their study. Attitudes, attitude change, prejudice and group schemas, among other sociocognitive phenomena, are also expressed in other social practices, but they are expressed most 'eloquently' in discourse. And only in discourse can they be explained, detailed, argued and accounted for (in social psychology, Augoustinos and her associates have been among the few who have studied social beliefs, such as prejudice and ideologies, in terms of discourse analysis; see, e.g., Augoustinos and Every, 2007; Augoustinos, LeCouteur and Soyland, 2002).

The need for a discourse analytical approach is even more imperative in a study of the communication, distribution or diffusion of knowledge and other socially shared beliefs in society. There are some non-verbal and non-semiotic ways of social belief acquisition and distribution, e.g., through mere perception of the environment and other people, or through mere interaction with other people, especially in early socialization when language use is still limited (Augoustinos *et al.*, 2006: 67ff.). But such implicit social learning needs to be made explicit and normalized: in order to know and to share the social meanings based on such perception and interaction we need discourse (for the structure and acquisition of social knowledge, see, e.g., Holyoak and Gordon, 1984).

Perhaps a (hard to envisage) general research project would need to examine how exactly in real life people acquire most of their knowledge and other social beliefs, whether through discourse and communication or by mere non-verbal and non-semiotic perception and interaction. We shall assume, however, as a working hypothesis, that most new knowledge – acquired after early childhood and especially of the vast world outside of one's daily experiences – is acquired by discourse: everyday conversations, discourse on the job, the mass media (especially TV, radio and the press), the new media (phones), books and the Internet.

Whereas the societal dimension of these communication processes, such as the role of organizations and institutions (e.g., schools and the mass media) will be dealt with in the next chapter on the sociology of knowledge, our focus in this chapter is on the sociocognitive aspects of the discursive acquisition, spreading and reproduction of knowledge and other social beliefs.

More or less in the margin of most communicative approaches to the reproduction of social beliefs in society there are (metaphorical) 'epidemiological' and evolutionary views that see the spread of beliefs in terms of contagion by idea units or *memes* (Lynch, 1996; see also Sperber, 1990). The 'memes' mentioned in this work appear to be very similar to what is traditionally called 'attitudes,' and whereas 'disease' is in the subject index of Lynch's book, discourse and communication are not – so we do not get much insight into the actual processes involved in such contagion.

Our examination of the social psychology of the discursive (re)production of knowledge is articulated along several levels and coordinates. First of all, we follow the usual division in major fields of social psychology where the discursive reproduction of knowledge may be analyzed:

- interpersonal discourse and communication
- intragroup discourse and communication
- intergroup discourse and communication.

Within each of these major fields we then proceed to a systematic analysis of the social situations in which knowledge is typically expressed and communicated.

Interpersonal relationships are of many types, several of which have been prominent areas of research in social psychology, such as interpersonal perception, attraction, aggression, conformity, impression management, interaction, cooperation, persuasion, social influence, disclosure and so on, as shown in contemporary introduction to social psychology (see, e.g., Hewstone *et al.*, 2008).

Some of these topics would fall under the broader topic of communication, as is obviously the case for impression management (Tedeschi, 1981) and especially persuasion (Benoit and Benoit, 2008; O'Keefe, 2002; Perloff, 2003; Petty and Cacioppo, 1981, 1986), traditionally defined in terms of (personal) attitude change. Another relevant topic, less studied in social psychology, is interpersonal knowledge management and communication: what do people tell about themselves, about others and about the world in general?

Interpersonal communication is at the very heart of the most mundane of human interactions, as is the case for everyday informal conversations with family members, friends, colleagues and professionals (see Antos *et al.*, 2008). Yet, despite a vast number of studies in everyday conversation (see, e.g., for introduction, Ten Have, 2007; see also Chapter 7), we have very little idea of *what people actually talk about in informal, everyday talk:*

- Conversation analytical studies in sociology and discourse analysis in general rather analyze *how* conversation is being conducted, but are seldom interested in its 'contents.'
- Similarly, linguistics is mostly interested in the grammar, its acquisition and its social variation. For studies in corpus linguistics we do have vast language data banks with millions of words that allow us to locally study such words in their co-texts, but seldom the overall topics of such text or talk.
- Cognitive psychology is interested in text processing, but hardly studies the contents of talk. Even discourse analytical studies focus more on the structures and strategies of text and talk (Van Dijk, 2007, 2011b) than on their themes or topics (but see Louwerse and van Peer, 2002).

So, we may conclude that it would be an excellent task for social psychology to study empirically what people talk about in various social situations.

In order to limit and manage this vast domain, we first need to focus on different communicative situations as they are represented in the context models of the participants. Thus, interpersonal talk may take place in more or less (in) formal situations among and with family members, friends, colleagues, service providers, professionals and so on, each situation with its own setting, participants with different identities, roles and relations, intentions, goals, knowledge and ongoing actions.

Thus, the review of some studies in the social psychology of interpersonal, intragroup and intergroup communication presented below has the specific aim of finding out how social ideas in general and knowledge in particular is communicated and reproduced among members and social groups.

4.5.1   *Knowledge and topics of informal talk*

Let us start with the basic of all these forms of verbal interaction, namely *informal talk* with family members, friends, etc. in informal (non-institutional) situations and focus on *declarative speech acts* in which knowledge may be communicated.

As is the case for all aspects of appropriate discourse, topics of talk depend on the *communicative situation* as it is interpreted as *context models* by the participants, that is, on the kind of setting, place, time, participants (and their social identity, roles and relations) as well as the goals of the communicative event and the common ground of the participants.

There is empirical social psychological research on topics of (informal) talk, usually as part of the study of interpersonal relations or interpersonal communication. Unfortunately, such studies seldom observe and analyze real informal talk. Many of them are experimental, for instance in the sense that subjects are being asked what they actually or potentially talk about with whom. Although these data may tap some generalized experiences as stored in past context models in episodic memory, we also know that such memories of earlier talk are not necessarily reliable, whereas hypothetical situations are not necessarily realized in real life.

Kellermann and associates have paid extensive attention to the exchange of information in informal talk (Kellermann, 1987). More specifically, they focus on "topical profiling," namely, the emergent, co-occurring and relational defining topics of talk (see, e.g., Kellermann and Palomares, 2004) within a theory of conversation such as (Schank's) Memory Organization Packet. They conclude that a general profile of topics of conversation does not exist and that there is hardly any insight into how topics tend to co-occur in talk. They conclude that the empirical literature on topics of talk is usually limited to small samples, unique participants (e.g., students, children or the elderly) and special settings. Yet they assume that at least some topics must co-occur, if only because of interactional routines. For instance, people typically may engage in greetings and ask about each other's health at the start of everyday conversations. Topics also co-occur because they fulfill various conversational functions or personal needs. Topics of talk typically reflect the type of relationship people have with others, within a range of intimacy that runs from significant others and very close friends to siblings, parents, grandparents, acquaintances, bosses and co-workers and strangers (Kellermann and Palomares, 2004, p. 313). For the same reason, such topics may be more or less appropriate in such situations, as is also defined by our theory of context models, featuring a category of participants and their relationship as conditions for the pragmatic appropriateness of discourse (Van Dijk, 2008a). In their study, Kellermann and associates elicited topics of conversation with thirteen different relational types, asking people to list topics of conversations they had recently had and with whom, where topics were defined in terms of what the participants viewed as such. In 500 reported conversations, they found ninety topics of talk. In other words, people (in these data) often talk about the same topics. The most co-occurring topics were those that went together when "checking in" with people, updating knowledge at the beginning of conversations, or when "checking out" (departing) as usual conversational routines and interactional functions – showing that participants count as topics what the researchers counted as rituals (see also Schegloff and Sacks, 1973). People typically talk about the topics that are central to their lives and reflect the interests of themselves and their conversation partners: activities, relationships, emotions, help-seeking, etc. The authors say they can predict which topics are discussed in what type of relationship more than forty-five percent of the time. Yet topics are not fixed but are dynamic, and are rather chosen strategically in conversation so as to manage the interaction with others.

Though interesting as a systematic study of topics of talk (based on self-reports, not on observed conversations), unfortunately this research does not provide us with much insight into the reproduction of *socially shared knowledge* and other social beliefs in society – other than that people tend to talk on their own everyday lives and interests. There is some 'encyclopedic' talk on beliefs, but such topics do not co-occur with others and hence tend to be isolated. We would need more empirical insight into more societal talk, for instance when people tend to talk about issues and problems in society, for instance as stimulated by viewing a TV program or recent breaking news on a salient topic.

Argyle *et al.* (1988) also studied the relationship between topics and types of conversational partners, assuming that one discloses different things to one's bank manager than to one's doctor. After reviewing earlier studies about what kind of things people typically talk about with whom – such as whom to turn to talk about personal worries (see also Veroff *et al.*, 1981) – they first elicited topics students had recently talked about and then asked eighty Australian students of psychology which of these topics they would talk about with what type of partner. Analysis of variance showed that the type of relationship is by far the largest source (80%) of variance. Topics were grouped into five factors, of which personal events (daily events, books read, TV programs watched) appeared to be most important – besides personal problems (sex, relationships), daily events (accidents), money, politics and religion. High-disclosure topics are generally associated with talks with a romantic partner, siblings, close friends and mothers, and only occasionally with fathers (with whom, however, they would talk with when money, success or politics is involved). Low-disclosure topics generally are associated with talk to doctors, and, less typically, with professors, neighbors or ministers. There was also a gender effect, in the sense that women would talk more with mothers and siblings.

Several studies are about topics in *family dinnertime conversations*, also studied from the perspective of discourse and conversation analysis (see, e.g., Ochs and Capps, 2001; Tannen *et al.*, 2007). In such conversations, participants typically are expected to tell about their experiences of the day, in which case the mother has a mediating role between children and fathers. Abu-Akel

(2002) found that, although many topics are offered in such conversations, only a few are actually taken up. The criterion of uptake is usually the impact a topic proposal has on the recipients. Typically, family topics presuppose a vast amount of accumulated knowledge about previous, shared family experiences.

Caughlin and Petronio (2004), in a more social psychological study of family communication, topic avoidance, secrecy and disclosure, deal with strategies of privacy management. Thus family members may 'own' person-ally private information, or co-own it with other family members, in which case co-owned private information is subject to rules of disclosure to other family members. Although these studies do not tell us much about the details of the topics of everyday family talk, and even less about how social know-ledge is distributed in society, they provide us with insight into some of the settings, participants, pragmatic rules and strategic management of appropri-ate talk in which personal knowledge is being locally shared, for instance in families.

Other experimental and field studies examine what topics are typically *avoided* in interpersonal communication. Caughlin and Afifi (2004) in a study of one hundred couples found that topic avoidance is associated with unsatisfactory relationships, but conclude that such avoidance may also be benign, for instance between parents and their children (see also Caughlin and Golish, 2002). Dailey and Palomares (2004) also stressed the relation between topic avoidance and relationship satisfaction and closeness between people.

4.5.2   Gender differences of topics in informal talk

Gender differences of topics of informal talk, in general, and of storytelling in particular, have been studied – with different methods – in several disciplines, such as discourse and conversation studies, gender studies and sociolinguistics as well as social psychology (see, e.g., Tannen, 1994a).

Bischoping (1993) compares 1990 data with those of a well-known gender-difference study by Henry T. Moore in 1922 and several following studies on the same issue between 1922 and 1990. Moore had used what could be called a "street method": listening to and recording during a month what women and men talk about when walking on Broadway in New York in the evening. He observed that women with women talk about men, clothes, buildings and inter-ior decorating, whereas men with other men tend to talk about business or amusement, and he vaguely attributed these differences to differences in the "original nature" of women and men.

Many studies since then have examined gender differences of topics of talk, but no general quantitative data exist on natural conversations. So Bischoping presented a replication of the 1922 study by Moore by having conversations among women and men observed on various sites on or near the University of Michigan campus. Conversations (261) and their topics were recorded in field notes as close as possible to verbatim, and topics that occurred more than five times were compared to those also used by Moore. Interestingly, she found quite similar gender differences of topics: in 1990, too, 'men' was still a main topic in women's (i.e., female students') conversations, only less frequently than in 1922. Men still talked more about work and money than women in 1990 (43.2% vs. 37.5%), but the differences between men and women are much less dramatic than in 1922 (when they were 56.7% vs. 3.7%). The topic of leisure, nearly exclusively a male topic in 1922, in 1990 had increased significantly for both women and men, but especially for women (from 3.7% to 25.8%). In 1990, work, money and leisure were the most frequent topics for both women and men, but closely followed by the topic of men as discussed by women. Most other studies since 1922 (usually done with students) show smaller gender differences than in 1922, probably also due to social changes during World War II. Where some gender differences may not have changed, it was observed that what did change in the last decades was the very topic of gender differences of discourse.

Haas and Sherman (1982), in a self-report study, found substantial role and gender differences in the popularity of certain topics, although the most frequent topic in each role was the same for both women and men. The other gender is talked about with friends, work with co-workers and family matters with parents, siblings or children. Clark (1988) found that young men and young women have different goals and topics of conversation – where women emphasize feeling-centered topics and men are more interested in the entertainment function of talk.

Martín Rojo and Gómez Esteban (2005) found that men have more problems talking about personal problems than about soccer (and that men who do talk about personal topics are evaluated more positively by women). Similarly, Eggins and Slade (1997) also found that during coffee breaks at work men talk more about work and sports whereas women talk more about personal experiences and 'gossip' more about other people. Note that Cameron (1997) recalls that men may also engage in gossiping, as she found in a study of fraternity boys' talk while watching TV.

Aries and Johnson (1983) questioned parents of students, and found – stereotypically – that women talk more on intimate topics and more in depth than men about personal and family matters. And even more stereotypically, men are found to talk more and more in depth about... sport. In a study of relaxed talk in a university cafeteria Dunbar et al. (1997) concluded that most talk is about personal experiences and relations (of the speaker or other people) – but seldom gives advice or criticizes recipients. But there are also gender differences: women appear to dedicate more conversation time to networking and men more to forms of self-display.

Soler (2004), in a discourse analytical thesis on storytelling by women and men in Colombia in informal interview contexts, found that topics of talk are not fundamentally different, but she did observe some stereotypical differences: whereas women tend to talk more about home and children, men tend to focus more on political and street events as well as sport. Both women and men in the same social situation focus on shared experiences, such as crime and insecurity in the neighborhood.

This finding as well as some of the earlier results reviewed here give us an idea that there may be a gender bias in the reproduction of social beliefs, in the sense that political knowledge is more typically shared and reproduced by men, and other social topics – especially as related to children and home-related issues – rather by women. However, it may be assumed that there will still be considerable variance among different types of women (education, profession, etc.) and especially among the communicative situations. Obviously, it is likely that most professional women on the job will speak much less, if at all, on personal topics.

Riley (2003), in a study of the discourses of professional white men in the UK, found that one major topic is that these men identify themselves in terms of their role as providers – thus implementing a general ideology in their talk as it is controlled by their context models.

4.5.3   Age differences of topics of informal talk

Of course, there are also age differences in topics of talk. Boden and Bielby (1986) recorded conversations among elderly (> 62) people, and found that their talk focuses on time periods in their lives as well as personal experiences in these periods. Thus, the elderly are able to strategically interweave talk about current topics with topics of their past. In one of the few studies of age differences of intentional and incidental memory for topics of talk, Kausler and Hakami (1983) found that, in general, young people (18–23) recall more topics and questions of a conversation, but the elderly (58–86) recognized just as well as the younger ones whether any topic was old or new.

On the other hand, in an old study of children's talk, Dawson (1937) found that children of grades III to VI (i.e., between nine and twelve years old) generally prefer to talk about games, sport, pets, family experiences and trips. Although there are many later studies of the topics children talk about with their caregivers or peers, these will not be reviewed here, because young children do not yet seem to have a prominent *active* role in the wider reproduction of social beliefs – although they obviously are crucial in the acquisition of such beliefs.

4.5.4   Constraints on topics of informal talk

More generally, studies of topics in informal talk should take into account the obvious memory limitations of all storytelling and discourse in general. Given our generally bad episodic memory for details of less significant events, we are able on the one hand to tell stories about the major periods and episodes of our life, and at a rather abstract (macro) level, and on the other hand to talk especially about more recent and salient events (see the literature on autobiographical memory in the previous chapter).

Much everyday storytelling is about mundane events we may no longer remember weeks, months and especially years later. Their analysis, thus, does not seem to contribute much to our insight into the social reproduction of prominent social, political or scientific events. However, the situation models on which such mundane everyday stories are based also construe such experiences in terms of general, socially shared knowledge, attitudes and ideologies. This means that we are able to *infer such social beliefs from such stories*, as is the case for the inferences about socially shared beliefs about gender, class, race, age, profession, politics, health and so on.

Of the studies of topics in informal talk reviewed above, and of the role of gender in topic selection, perhaps the most general conclusion is that people generally prefer to talk about their personal experiences, daily activities and their worries, and that topics – as is the case for other discourse properties – typically vary with the usual parameters of context models: setting, identity, role and relationships between participants, goals and shared knowledge and beliefs. Where children, students, younger or older people, women or men talk on different topics, this reflects first of all differences of daily personal experiences as well as those of their social group, category or class, and secondly the ideologies of their group.

Thus, social knowledge, as well as other shared beliefs, such as attitudes and ideologies, is locally reproduced in informal everyday talk according to the social identities and roles of the participants as well as their personal experiences. However, recall that these experiences need not reflect 'real' events, but may be defined by ideologically based situation models. Thus, in the informal situations of everyday life, in which personal and interpersonal experiences play a prominent role, so too are informal talk, knowledge and ideology closely intertwined. Personal experiences are also talked about by people as members of social groups and categories, and hence conditioned by their socially and ideologically conditioned interests, fields or experiences and attitudes. People tell stories as women or men, young or old, students or professors and so on, and thus frame their personal experiences with knowledge and attitudes about those acquired from talk with other members of the same group.

Although interesting for our insight into the local (re)production of social topics in society, most of these and related studies of informal talk have not been carried out with the aim of studying how social beliefs such as knowledge, attitudes and ideologies are acquired, reproduced and shared in society.

Thus, we may assume that 'basic' knowledge about everyday life (people, objects, the environment) is largely acquired by children in their talk with parents, teachers and friends, by television and children's stories, as well as by their non-verbal personal and interpersonal experiences. But we have much less insight into the gradual discursive acquisition, in everyday talk, of commonsense beliefs about relevant social issues, for instance about work, unemployment, discrimination, diversity, gender and so on. We may assume that much of such knowledge, as well as other social beliefs, is directly or indirectly acquired via the mass media, especially by those people who are not personally involved in such issues.

4.5.5   Knowledge management in interpersonal talk in organizations and institutions

Conversation Analysis has stressed that not all talk with professionals or in organizations or institutions is organizational or institutional talk. Also in a shop, with the doctor, or on the job, at school and other 'societal' sites, there are frequent moments of informal, interpersonal talk, sometimes mixed with 'business talk' (Atkinson, 1992; Lee, 2007; Schegloff, 1992). Theoretically, this is the case as soon as one or more of the participants in the conversation change one parameter of their context models, such as their social identity or role (e.g., from professor to friend) or the goal of the conversation fragment (e.g., when telling a joke or a personal experience among colleagues on the job).

A typology of organizational talk is as complex as the structure of society, and each communicative situation gives rise to different context models controlling different properties of talk for their appropriateness – properties we deal with in Chapter 7 (see Arminen, 2005; Boden, 1994; Drew and Heritage, 1992; McHoul, 2001; Sarangi and Roberts, 1999; Tannen, 1994b). Relevant here are the structures of the communicative situations, such as the settings, the types of participant identities, roles and relations, the goals of the interaction and the types of knowledge of the participant, and especially the situations in which social beliefs are being (re)produced. More generally, this specific field has also been the object of various approaches (e.g., veristic vs. constructivist) to the study of the transfer of knowledge in groups, for instance in social epistemology (see, e.g., Goldman, 2002; Jacobson, 2007; Schmitt, 1994).

Thus, in doctor–patient interaction, patients tell about personal health problems with the aim of informing the doctor about them and hoping that the doctor can solve such problems on the basis of that information. Conversely, doctors may respond with medical advice or prescriptions or with new information about tests that have been done (among a vast number of studies, see, e.g., Cassell, 1985; Chenail and Morris, 1995; Fisher and Todd, 1983; West, 1984).

As sites for the reproduction of social knowledge, these institutional occasions may be relevant (beyond professional interpersonal interaction, medical expertise and ideology), especially if doctors are able to generalize over personal health problems, for instance in case of a new epidemic, or if doctors are thus able to inform their patients of new drugs or treatments – known from colleagues, drug companies or specialized literature – as was the case, for instance, with AIDS or Mad Cow disease. In other words, we here have one of the – possibly limited – interfaces between scientific discourse and knowledge, on the one hand, and general, commonsense knowledge, on the other, as it is the special object of social representation research. Since doctor–patient interaction is primarily interpersonal, its scope of diffusion is limited compared to information about epidemics, new drugs and treatments through the mass media.

There are many types of client–professional interaction that have similar characteristics: clients with a personal problem consult professionals and thus inform professionals about the incidence, nature, frequency or other properties of such problems (see, e.g., Natti et al., 2006). And conversely, professionals communicate (applied) professional knowledge to clients, directly, indirectly or implicitly in concrete advice, recommendations or prescriptions of various kinds (Prosser and Walley, 2006). Unless clients in such cases have access to many other personal contacts with whom they talk about such knowledge, professional knowledge will in this case be limited to diffusion circles of rather limited scope – again, if compared to the mass media if these deal with such problems (as would be the case for problems with mortgage payments, which became a major international topic during the economic crisis that started in 2008) (see, e.g., Swan et al., 2003).

There seem to be few studies that examine such diffusion of professional knowledge in the public sphere of communities or societies at large (but see, e.g., Cranefield and Yoong, 2009; Knotek et al., 2009; Wilkinson et al., 2009). Compared to such top-down professional or scientific communication flows from professionals towards the general public, bottom-up flow from citizens to professionals and scientific knowledge is much slower, and usually carried out rather in large-scope experiments, for instance on patient groups or specialized opinion research and questionnaires.

Indeed, more frequently studied is the acquisition and diffusion of knowledge and expertise as well as other social beliefs (attitudes, ideologies, norms and values) among professionals and experts themselves (see, e.g., Apker and Eggly, 2004; Berkenkotter and Huckin, 1995; Buus, 2008; Feltham, 1996; Karseth and Nerland, 2007; Li *et al.*, 2007; Mertz, 1992; Tillema and Orland-Barak, 2006).

Professional interaction among colleagues is a general type of knowledge 'transfer' with a large number of more specific subtypes (for a general, philosophical analysis of knowledge transfer in communication, see, e.g., Graham, 2000). Again, knowledge transfer may be horizontal among colleagues with more or less the same professional knowledge or top-down and bottom-up between professionals with more or less professional knowledge. Thus, members of teams and other types of small groups may individually obtain new knowledge in individual tasks and communicate such knowledge to other team members, thus contributing to the joint knowledge of the team as a whole (for information and knowledge management in small groups, see, e.g., Nye and Brower, 1996; Thompson *et al.*, 1999).

Group experts or group leaders may communicate, top-down, their specialized professional knowledge to other members of groups or organizations, whether in face-to-face interaction, e-mail, talks or other forms of written communication. Actually, this is not only the case for knowledge but also for the transmission and reproduction of ideologies, for instance traditional medical ideologies from experts to residents in a hospital setting (Apker and Eggly, 2004). And vice versa, participants with less knowledge may inform, bottom-up, the experts with feedback about professional experiences (such as the application of professional knowledge in concrete situations), experiences that may be aggregated, generalized and abstracted by the experts – who in turn may inform other experts, for instance in professional publications.

The point of this brief review is to systematically examine the structures of communicative situations and their representation as context models and study the general types of knowledge 'flow.' This well-known flow-metaphor, defining knowledge or information as a liquid, as well as the spatial metaphors of top-down and bottom-up knowledge transfers, are obviously only conceptual shortcuts for very complex structures of text in context. For instance, depending on the situation, whether top-down or bottom-up, much (old) knowledge will be presupposed in the respective discourses. People on the job learn from experts only when they already have a minimum of professional knowledge of the job in question. Moreover, much learning is not verbal, but non-verbal when professionals show their special knowledge or skills in hands-on action and interaction.

In these forms of professional on-the-job interaction, knowledge transfer is also usually limited to the scope of the organization and the specialized knowledge of the profession – and hence usually of limited use outside the organization. It seems that these professional epistemic sites are not the preferred sites of the development of general commonsense knowledge throughout the whole epistemic community (society) at large.

The theoretical analysis of the role of knowledge in professional communication and interaction in terms of situation analysis, interaction and conversation structures and context models should be elaborated in more empirical terms on the basis of concrete research results. Thus, there are studies on such varied topics as the following:

- *Settings* are important conditions for exchange of professional knowledge, as has been shown for teachers informally talking about the job (their students) in the teachers' lounge (Mawhinney, 2010).
- The communication of knowledge (seeking feedback) among men and women in work groups not only depends on expertise but also on *gender* roles, in such a way that men seek less feedback from expert female colleagues if their traditional gender role is threatened (Miller and Karakowsky, 2005).
- Promoting *personal relationships* of employees in an organization for the communication of knowledge among them is an important goal of organizations (Kaše *et al.*, 2009).
- The relationship between knowledge 'donating' and 'collecting' is mediated by the willingness and eagerness to share knowledge as aspects of *team communication styles* as well as the role of the leader (De Vries *et al.*, 2006; De Vries *et al.*, 2010).
- *Social networks* in organizations are important for the sharing of knowledge (Cross *et al.*, 2001).
- Members of groups are influenced by *group consensus* and tend to ignore unshared information presented in a group discussion – group judgments are not more reliable than averages of the individual judgments (Gigone and Hastie, 1993).
- *Doctors'* collaborative communication style (e.g., explaining in more detail why and how to take medicine) has positive influence on patients' knowledge and medication use (Bultman and Svarstad, 2000).
- *Fear of negative evaluation* negatively influences information sharing in organizations, especially in interpersonal communication (Bordia *et al.*, 2006).
- Knowledge in an organization is transformed (enriched) during communication between different *occupation groups* and their local contexts (Bechky, 2003).

- There is more knowledge sharing at academic conferences in the *formal sessions* than in informal talk among colleagues (Reychav and Te'eni, 2009).

This small selection of topics and findings of research on interpersonal discourse and knowledge transfer among colleagues in organizational or institutional settings shows only some of the many parameters of communication situations that may influence what we may call the *epistemic dynamics* of groups and organizations: knowledge flows, transfer, transmission, interaction and so on. Most of this work takes places in communication and management studies. Despite sometimes complex designs ranging between classical attitude measurement (Likert scales, etc.) and ethnographical observation on the work floor, we hardly find sophisticated qualitative discourse analysis of such communication. Nor do such studies present theoretically explicit analysis of knowledge and how knowledge is actually expressed in, and reconstructed from, text or talk in such communication processes.

4.5.6   Mass communication and knowledge

Whereas as yet relatively little is known about interpersonal knowledge transfer, we know much more about the role of knowledge in public communication, for instance through the mass media and especially in education. Indeed, these are the preferred sites for the communication of socially shared knowledge, both about specific (news) events, as is the case of the news media, as well as of more generic knowledge, as is typically the case in educational situations.

Knowledge flow and transfer through the mass media is largely top-down, from a media organization to a (specific) public at large. Thus, within hours (as with the newspaper or Internet) or in minutes (as is the case for the radio or the Internet) thousands or millions of citizens may be informed about new public events, expressing the situation models of the journalists' interpretation or construction of such news events. Such communication, as we have seen in the previous chapter, will in turn be reconstructed or updated in the personal situation models of the recipients.

Unless of specific public importance – and due to many repetitions (as in the case of the 9/11 attacks) – most of these events remain rather episodic and hence will soon be forgotten (or at least no longer be accessible without a reminder cue)(see, e.g., Graber, 1984, 2001; Van Dijk, 1988a). Their contribution to the formation of social knowledge takes place indirectly by 'casual' learning, that is, by abstraction and generalization towards conceptual knowledge, e.g., about bomb attacks, about terrorism (see also Edgerton and Rollins, 2001; Robinson and Levy, 1986).

More direct and explicit knowledge transfer through the mass media is largely limited to various forms of *science popularization*, which no doubt is the form of knowledge transfer and diffusion most studied, and hence does not need much further analysis here (for reviews and analysis, see, e.g., Bell *et al.*, 2008; Bucchi and Trench, 2008; Gregory and Miller, 1998; Jacobi, 1986; Myers, 1990; Priest, 2010; Shinn and Whitley, 1985).

The usual structure of the communication situation in this case is that specialized (science, etc.) journalists recontextualize and transform scientific knowledge obtained through interviews or specialized publications by scientists as informative articles in the press (and sometimes on television). This three-step flow of knowledge from scientists to the public at large via mediating specialized journalists is especially interesting because of the ways specialized scientific knowledge and discourse is transformed into public discourse.

Such popularizing discourse needs to be based on general, common knowledge, occasionally enriched by a few technical terms (such as 'DNA' in news on genetic issues), and many other (multimodal) forms of reformulations of scientific notions, for instance with metaphors, definitions, explanations, schemas (see, e.g., Beacco, 1999; Calsamiglia and van Dijk, 2004; Jacobi, 1986; Myers, 1990, 2003). Unfortunately, the studies that focus on detailed discourse analysis of scientific communication usually fail to include an epistemic analysis of such text or talk or a more systematic account of the details of communicative situations and the influence on context models and the processes of recontextualization.

4.5.7   The communication of knowledge in education

Even better known than the diffusion of knowledge through the mass media is the production and reproduction of knowledge in educational situations – most of whose communicative events have new knowledge transfer as their main goal. Again, usually top-down, but more interactive than the mass media, communication events in schools and universities systematically involve *interaction* between double experts (experts as teachers and experts in some knowledge domain, such as a discipline) and novices (students) of various degrees of presumed ignorance (for detail, see, e.g., Anderson *et al.*, 1977; Cowie, 2000; Paechter, 2001; Salomon, 1993).

Knowledge acquisition in education – informally referred to as 'learning' – is a vast specialized field that cannot be reviewed here. Some of the properties of this kind of knowledge acquisition have been reviewed in the previous chapter, because schooling (rather than the media, for instance) is one of the few social interaction types and sites that are systematically studied in cognitive and educational psychology. We have found that such knowledge transfer depends on a complex set of variables, such a age, prior knowledge, interest, motivation, readability and other properties of learners as well as properties (lexicon, syntactic structures, coherence, global organization, images, etc.) of educational text and talk.

We also saw that active, interactional learning (with other learners or a computer) is generally more successful than more or less passive reception of new knowledge. It is at this point that a social psychological perspective on cooperation in interactive learning is most relevant. Such cooperation and the kinds of learning again depend on a number of relevant *context variables*, such as the overall goal of the learning event, the individual properties of the participants (as mentioned above), the specific tasks of each participant, as well as the properties, actions and discourse of the teacher.

Whether or not vast amounts of more or less specialized knowledge initially learned at school will soon be forgotten (after an exam), no doubt there remains a vast base of general 'world' knowledge students would not acquire at home, from peers, from television or the Internet. However, as yet we have little empirical insight into what current knowledge of average citizens is actually learned at school, especially since much relevant school knowledge is later confirmed or changed in other communication situations, especially by the mass media (see, e.g., Conway *et al.*, 1992; Custers, 2010; Naveh-Benjamin *et al.*, 1997; Phye, 1997; Semb *et al.*, 1993). Indeed, people 'learn' more (and possibly even more biased knowledge) about Iraq when 'we' wage war in that country than we learn about the country at school or from textbooks.

Specific school knowledge may be relevant first of all for the acquisition of knowledge outside of our everyday experiences, such as general geographical, social and historical knowledge about the whole country and the rest of the world and other peoples, needed especially to understand public discourse, for instance of the mass media.

Secondly, this slightly more advanced (high) school knowledge may pertain to the *understanding or explanation* of relevant personal experiences and commonsense facts, for instances of one's body, health and illness, interpersonal relationships, language, communication, societal organization, social groups, science and so on (see, e.g., Nagel, 1996; Normand, 2008; Yoon, 2008).

Besides the studies of interactional knowledge acquisition in the classroom, a major source of insights into such learning has been provided by systematic, and often critical, studies of **textbooks**. These studies often emphasize that such learning is closely associated with the acquisition of dominant ideologies and their legitimation, and hence also needs a more sociological analysis (Apple, 1979, 1982, 1986, 1993, 2012; Luke, 1988; Young, 1971).

The applicability of more or less specialized knowledge acquired at school makes such knowledge more or less relevant and hence more easily integrated into the general knowledge system. It is also at this point where semi-specialized knowledge must compete with commonsense knowledge (including stereotypes, etc.) as it is diffused among the population at large. Or vice versa, everyday experiences as well as knowledge acquired from other sources may conflict with stereotypical, prejudiced or racist beliefs learned from teachers or textbooks (see, e.g., Apfelbaum *et al.*, 2008; Kurtz-Costes *et al.*, 2008).

Obviously, as more people get specialized education, so the size and the specialization of general sociocultural knowledge will change – so that newspapers or television today are able to presuppose semi-specialized knowledge that would not have been common knowledge fifty years – or even ten years – ago.

Finally, and as transition to the next chapter, it must be emphasized that the knowledge acquired in educational situations in schools needs further sociological analysis, for instance as official knowledge, or in the special interests of specific groups, classes or organizations in society. The same is true for the general analysis of schools, universities, laboratories, academies and other institutions as sites for the (re)production of knowledge in society, topics that need to be dealt with in the next chapter.

4.6   Concluding remarks

Social psychology could be the central discipline for the study of knowledge and discourse, but we have seen that its dominant paradigms have barely studied either of these central phenomena of the everyday lives of group members. Yet, there are important social psychological notions that offer insight into these topics, beginning with the socially shared nature of beliefs such as attitudes or social representations.

It has been argued that a more general theory of social beliefs, dealing also with knowledge and ideologies, should go beyond a cognitive psychological account of their mental representations and investigate how they are formed, communicated, shared and changed in different communicative events and by participants of different groups and communities. We have seen that many traditional notions of social psychology, such as attitudes and social representations, need to be re-examined within a general theory of socially shared knowledge.

Finally, we reviewed how social beliefs in general, and knowledge in particular, are communicated in interpersonal, professional and other institutional communication. Much of this work has focused on general contents or topics, rather than on the details of the discursive structures of such communication.

On the other hand, detailed conversation analysis has been more interested in the structures and strategies of informal or institutional talk than in its contents or topics, or how social knowledge gets spread in groups or society at large, with the exception of educational interaction and learning in the classroom or the analysis of textbooks.

5 Discourse, knowledge and society

5.1 Introduction

On March 25, 2013, UK Prime Minister David Cameron informed the readers of the tabloid newspaper the *Sun* of his tough new policy on immigration, as follows:

01   IMMIGRATION has brought huge benefits to Britain: from Polish
02   heroes who fought for us during the war to West Indians who
03   helped us rebuild afterwards.
04   That's our island story – open, diverse and welcoming. I'm
05   immensely proud of it.
06   But we do this country's great history no favours unless we have a
07   sensible debate.
08   *Sun* readers know that immigration got out of control under
09   Labour.
10   Frankly, this country became a soft touch: 2.2 million more people
11   came in than went out.
12   Since Conservatives took office, we've worked hard to get things
13   more manageable.
14   And it's working: net migration is down by a third since the last
15   election.
16   But it's not just about numbers on a graph. It's also about mak-
17   ing sure that everyone who comes here pays their way and gives
18   something back.
19   Under Labour's immigration system, for example, it was legal for
20   those who overstayed visas to claim certain benefits.
21   That's not fair to people who already live here.
22   There's been a lot said about Bulgarians and Romanians coming
23   over next year.
24   We benefit from new countries joining the EU: they'll buy more
25   things from us and jobs will be created.
26   But as a Government we have to make sure people come here for
27   the right reasons.

28   That's why today I'm announcing a number of new measures on
29   immigration.
30   Currently there is no limit to how long European Economic Area
31   nationals can claim benefits while looking for a job.
32   From now on, if they don't have a job after six months their benefits
33   will end unless they have a genuine chance of finding work.
34   We're also going to sort out council housing. Right now, some
35   new migrants expect taxpayers to pay for them to have somewhere
36   to live.
37   We're going to bring new rules in. People shouldn't qualify for a
38   council house unless they've lived here for at least two years and can
39   show they're giving something back.
40   Currently, people from the EU can get free treatment on the NHS.
41   Under our plans, if you use our hospitals but don't pay our taxes we
42   will go after the costs in your home country.
43   Since I became Prime Minister, I've said that my Government will
44   back everyone who wants to get on in life.
45   And that's true whether your family have lived here for centuries
46   or you came last week.

Even prime ministers in the UK do not usually have direct, unmediated access to the press, but since the *Sun* could not agree more with this tougher immigration stand, and no doubt has been one of the populist forces behind Cameron's new policy, we here encounter a rather unique hybrid of political and media discourse: two institutions, a conservative government and an influential right-wing tabloid, in a joint public discourse informing the British citizens as well as immigrants about the new policy. Not surprisingly, *Sun* journalist K. Schofield introduces Cameron's statement in terms that are much less polished than those of Cameron, but essentially agreeing with him. Addressing the *Sun* readers explicitly, Cameron obviously is interested in winning votes he fears to lose to the right-wing anti-immigration party UKIP.

This example of media and political discourse is especially relevant for this chapter to provide insight not only into how public opinion on immigration is managed in the UK (and Europe) today but also into how knowledge is managed by social and political groups, institutions and organizations. Indeed, as we shall see in more detail below, Cameron not only formulates explicit opinions and policy intentions, but does so on the basis of what he presents for millions of *Sun* readers as the 'facts' of immigration and benefits for immigrants, as is implied by the use of explicit knowledge ascription in the sentence (line 8):

Sun readers know that immigration got out of control under Labour.

More generally, in this chapter we examine some topics in the sociology of knowledge and do so from a discourse analytical point of view. The classical approach in the field, e.g., as initiated by Marx, focused on the more or less deterministic influence of social class on knowledge and more generally on thought or ideas. Later developments focused on many other relations between society and social cognition, such as the role of groups, organizations and institutions involved in knowledge (re)production, for instance in science, or the role of knowledge as a power resource in society (for the history and later developments in the sociology of knowledge, see, e.g., Stehr and Meja, 2005; for further references, see below).

Most of this research takes place at a rather abstract, macrolevel of inquiry. On the one hand, there has been much less work on the role of the *microlevel of social interaction in the production of knowledge*. On the other hand, although the 'influence' of society on knowledge has been framed in many different terms, such as 'determination' or 'dependence,' the detailed sociocognitive nature of this kind of relationship has seldom been made explicit. Indeed, more generally, a sociological approach to knowledge was seldom concerned with the specifics of the *cognitive processes and representations* that define the societal influence on the formation and the structures of knowledge. Conversely, the same is true for the way knowledge controls social interaction, and hence, indirectly, the processes and structures of groups, organizations and institutions.

Relevant for our discussion, as has been repeatedly emphasized in earlier chapters, is especially the neglect of the fundamental role of *discourse* in the (re)production of knowledge in society. Whether in everyday conversation, classroom interaction, news reports, lectures or scientific books and articles, most knowledge beyond everyday experiences is acquired, expressed, communicated and socially distributed by multimodal text and talk. This chapter therefore shall focus more specifically on the role of one of these genres in the societal reproduction of knowledge, namely that of news in the press.

The previous chapters defined knowledge as beliefs shared by *epistemic communities* and their justification criteria. This chapter needs to make explicit this notion by examining some of the properties of such communities, such as their boundaries, membership and reproduction.

One of the topics of the classical sociology of knowledge was the relation between knowledge and 'distorted' or 'false' beliefs defined as *ideology*. On the basis of our earlier research into a more general theory of ideology (Van Dijk, 1998), we are now able to make explicit the relationship between knowledge and ideology, not only within a sociocognitive framework, but also from a more sociological perspective – adding to the more detailed discussion of ideology in the previous chapter.

The sociology of knowledge overlaps with more normative approaches in *social epistemology*, e.g., concerning the social nature of justification criteria and hence of truth, the nature of relativism and context, and many other topics. This chapter only marginally deals with these more philosophical aspects of the social nature of knowledge and truth, and will do so mainly through a more empirical account of the beliefs and practices of epistemic communities as the social basis of knowledge (see, e.g., Fuller, 2002; Goldman, 1999).

Given the large number of *historical studies of the sociology of knowledge*, this chapter will not repeat the account (and criticism) of the classical sociology of knowledge of, for example, Marx (e.g., Marx and Engels, 1947), Mannheim (1936, 1972), Scheler (1980), Durkheim (1915, 2002) and Merton (1983), or of the contemporary sociology of knowledge and science by Latour (e.g., Latour, 1987; Latour and Woolgar, 1986) and many others. Below, I shall only refer to these and other authors where relevant for our own approach (for readers and introductory and historical accounts of the sociology of knowledge, see, e.g., Abercrombie, 1980; Curtis and Petras, 1970; Hamilton, 1974; Hekman, 1986; Stark, 1958; Stehr and Meja, 2005).

5.2   Relating society and cognition

The sociology of knowledge deals with the relationships between society and cognition. Especially from a Marxist perspective, it does so traditionally from bottom to top, in the sense that social structures at the 'base' of society, such as class or group interests, are supposed to influence thought or ideas at the 'top' or 'superstructure' (for detail, see, e.g., Stark, 1958).

Within the framework of contemporary cognitive science, such a very general, abstract and vague description could and should be made more explicit so as to provide a more satisfactory basis for a sociological account of knowledge. Indeed, the relations between social groups and their structures or interests, on the one hand, and the cognitive production and discursive diffusion of knowledge, on the other, are very indirect and in need of a complex sociocognitive interface. Conversely, as we have seen before, cognitive science seldom deals with the social or cultural nature of knowledge and hence is in turn in need of a more explicit social component.

We shall analyze the society–cognition link as a mutual relationship – traditionally accounted for in terms of a 'dialectic.' Instead of the traditional macro approach we do so at the microlevel of society, that is, in terms of the cognition and interaction of social actors as members of epistemic communities taken as the 'basis' of the social order, and in terms of specific social and political practices such as the production and publication of news articles such as the one by Cameron and the journalist of the *Sun*.

Overall causal or rational relations between society and cognition are abstractions or correlations and need to be accounted for at the microlevel of individual experiences and interpretations as well as social interaction, communication and discourse. Since knowledge is a property of the mind-brain, and as such socially shared or distributed among members of communities, it is also through the actions and interactions of these members that we need to construe the society–cognition interface (for the social-interactional dimension of the brain, see also the discussion in Brothers, 1997).

5.2.1   Mental models and society

As we have seen in the previous chapters, mental models are the central theoretical construct of the sociocognitive interface. Represented in episodic memory, they represent the everyday subjective experiences of social actors as epistemic community members, including the perceptions of their situational environment and the planning and execution of social interaction (Gentner and Stevens, 1983; Johnson-Laird, 1983; Oakhill and Garnham, 1996; Van Dijk and Kintsch, 1983).

Relevant for this chapter is that mental models are not only personal and subjective, but have an intersubjective, social basis because they feature instantiations or applications of shared sociocultural knowledge (Dutke, 1996). This knowledge has been acquired by members during their epistemic socialization and development in the community, in parallel with their acquisition of language and increasingly through text and talk, as we have seen in the previous chapters. Indeed, to produce or understand discourse involves the expression, the formation or the update of socially based mental models of events talked about as well as the development of shared social knowledge.

This succinct summary of cognitive mental model theory already shows how individual experiences, perception and action are related to socially acquired and shared knowledge of an epistemic community, namely as processes of application or instantiation, on the one hand, and of generalization and abstraction, on the other, mutually relating personal experiences in episodic memory and social 'semantic' memory representing the knowledge system of the community.

In the previous chapter we have seen how interaction and communication, and hence discourse, are involved in the process by which personal experiences may be shared by the members of a community, as is the case in everyday storytelling in conversational interaction. For this chapter, Cameron's statement in the *Sun* is an example of how politicians and newspapers may join in the definition of the situation as they see it, namely whether immigrants disproportionally use and abuse social benefits in the UK. It is this specific belief, expressed with the authority of a prime minister, that readers of the *Sun* and other citizens may take as 'official knowledge' and hence as a presupposed basis for opinion formation. We shall therefore pay special attention in this chapter to the role of the news media in the reproduction of knowledge and belief.

Although much discourse and communication is model-based, that is, rooted in everyday experiences, generic sociocultural knowledge may also be acquired and shared more directly, typically so in expository discourse (Britton, 1984;

Nippold and Scott, 2010); in parent–child discourse (Papousek *et al.*, 1986), in textbooks (Britton *et al.*, 1993), classroom interaction (Cowie and van der Aalsvoort, 2000), popularization discourse (Myers, 1990; Shinn and Whitley, 1985) and other forms of educational discourse. The details of the strategies and structures of such discourse will be accounted for in Chapter 7. These discourses are typically related to social institutions such as families, schools, universities and libraries, and hence closely involved in a more sociological account of the acquisition, production, reproduction and diffusion of know-ledge in society, to be dealt with in this chapter.

We have recalled above that mental models of personal experience (perception, planning and interaction) are not limited to the representation of 'local' settings, participants, actions and goals. Through language and conceptual knowledge acquisition, they may also feature instances of a vast number of social structural concepts, such as social categories, groups or other collectivities (women, men, children, adults, professors, students, terrorists, etc.), classes (poor vs. rich), institutions (schools, prisons, etc.), social-political systems (democracies, dicta-torship), social events and rituals (marriages, birthday parties), power relations (oppression, manipulation) and so on (see, e.g., Bendix, 1988; Boster *et al.*, 1987; Flick, 1998; Garfinkel, 1962; see also the references on social cognition in the last chapter). Thus, in the example of Cameron's statement in the *Sun*, we see how readers may acquire further knowledge about immigrants and their alleged abuses of the British welfare system.

It is in this way, first of all, that social structure is represented in socially shared knowledge of epistemic communities, and then instantiated, as specific exemplars, in the mental models of specific experiences and action of their members. For instance, journalists researching or writing a story do so with a context model featuring instantiated knowledge about the profession of jour-nalist, about the institution of a newspaper, about the corporate media organ-ization they work for, or about the government or social groups they write about (Van Dijk, 1988a, 1988b, 1991, 2008a, 2009b). The same is true of a professor doing research or teaching a class with a context model featuring instances of their identity as professor and of the institution of a university or writing about the institution of the mass media.

Applied to the classical account of the influence of class interests on 'ideas,' this would require, first of all, shared experiences and hence consciousness of social actors as members of a class – e.g., the working class. However, knowledge or consciousness of such a class is not innate, nor does it emerge spontaneously from everyday class experiences, but it has to be learned as a concept, typically through the daily reproduction of various forms of political discourse – in turn possibly based on academic discourse (see, e.g., Aries and Seider, 2007; Burke, 1995; DeGenaro, 2007; Graetz, 1986; Kelsh *et al.*, 2010; Reay, 2005). Only then are experiences no longer purely individual, or merely intersubjectively shared (e.g., by storytelling) by others, but are represented as experiences of 'us' as class members, that is, in terms of shared knowledge of a social identity instantiated in mental models of daily experiences. A similar argument holds for the gender identity of women, or the sociopolitical identity of feminists (for the social psychological account of the formation and application of social identities, see, e.g., Abrams and Hogg, 1990, 1999; Brewer and Hewstone, 2003; Capozza and Brown, 2000; Tajfel, 1982).

In sum, the society–cognition interface is defined at the level of individual experiences of social actors as members of epistemic communities, and in terms of their mental models of discourse and other forms of interaction both forming and developing as well as instantiating and applying generally shared, sociocultural knowledge. It is also in this way, that is, through mental model theory, that we may update theories of social identity formation in social psychology. Hence, besides discourse and communication, bottom-up, personal and shared experiences form the 'base' of group formation and identity.

However, top-down, making sense of (interpreting) such experiences as experiences of a group member presupposes (usually discursively) acquired conceptual, socially shared knowledge about the group. Typically, such general knowledge about groups is construed by leaders, theorists or ideologues observing, generalizing and abstracting from the experiences of collectivities as social members, as we have seen for the example of David Cameron and the *Sun* and its journalists. Whereas the former aspect is an account of the social psychology of social identity formation, the latter aspect would typically belong to a sociological account of identity and group formation and the role of governments and mass media in this process.

This also shows that the cognition–society interface, although rooted and applied in daily experiences and action, essentially requires the top-down sociocognitive construction and discursive reproduction of group concepts that allow personal experiences and identities to be interpreted as social group experiences and identities.

5.2.2   The origins and reproduction of sociocultural knowledge

The account of the fundamental role of mental models as the interface between socially shared knowledge on the one hand and personal experiences, observations and actions, on the other, also highlights the fundamental role of knowledge as shared by the members of epistemic communities. Not quite trivially, experiences of social actors *as group members* presuppose knowledge of the very group of which they are members.

Not only cognitively, but also sociologically relevant and interesting is the question how this shared knowledge is acquired in the first place. Generally, as often stated above and explained in the previous chapters, such knowledge of individual members is largely acquired by text and talk, e.g., by daily conversations with parents, peers, friends or colleagues, through the mass media or through professional discourse, among many other genres or classes of genres. However, to avoid an infinite regress or a chicken–egg dilemma, we need to account for the fact that such discourses in turn presuppose the knowledge needed to generate them in the first place.

So, even if for most (new) members of groups or communities most knowledge is acquired, validated and especially described through text and talk, at the level of the group or community we would need to know about the 'origin' of such social knowledge. No doubt, ontogenetically, our knowledge is partly acquired by our sensory experiences, as emphasized since Locke (1690), De Condillac (1746), Hume (1750) and other philosophers, as well as by contemporary psychologists (e.g., Carpendale and Müller, 2004; Hood and Santos, 2009; Keil, 1979, 1998; Mandler, 2007; Spelke *et al.*, 1992). However, the sociocultural categorization of such knowledge as well as its later development and reproduction in the community is largely interactional and discursive (Cowie, 2000), though it presupposes the evolutionary development of elementary human knowledge structures, a topic that will not detain us here (see Bateson, 1972; Buskes, 1998; Callebaut and Pinxten, 1987; Plotkin, 2007; Rescher, 1990; Wuketits, 1990). It is this acquisition and development of 'collective' knowledge by whole communities that should be a central topic of the sociology and anthropology of knowledge.

As suggested above, for the social origins of *specific kinds of specialized, political or scientific knowledge* it is usually easier to trace the genealogy or archeology of specific concepts and terms to the work of specific leaders, writers, politicians, journalists or scholars, on the one hand, and their organizations or institutions, on the other (among a vast number of studies of the history of the social sciences and concepts, see, e.g., Black, 1996; Foucault, 1972; Galli and Nigro, 1990; Geary, 2005; Moscovici, 1961; Radnitzky and Bartley, 1987; Ritzer, 1994; Rüschemeyer and Skocpol, 1996).

Whether as a result of systematic observation or theoretical reflection, once formulated in public discourse, for instance through political, media or scientific discourse, such concepts and terms spread throughout the epistemic community. We here are dealing with the crucial processes of epistemic reproduction as they have been studied in the sociology of knowledge and popularization, although our account emphasizes and analytically explains in more detail the role of social cognition and discourse in these processes.

Although we have some insight into the spread and reproduction of scientific knowledge through various forms of public discourse, for instance through popularization by the mass media (see, e.g., Myers, 1990), we need more sociological insight into the conditions and consequences of the discursive reproduction of scientific knowledge and its popularization. Indeed, we need to know which scientific notions of which scholars, in which disciplines, in which institutions, in which languages and which countries tend to be popularized by which mass media, for which publics, and with what effects on the acquisition of new sociocultural knowledge in society.

There are many variables here, some related to power – such as the institution, language and country of scientific source discourse, as well as those of the mass media – whereas others depend on the social relevance or functions of such concepts and knowledge in the everyday life and experiences of the target audience (Bowler, 2009; Carayannis and Campbell, 2006; Guilhon, 2001; Jones and Miller, 2007; LaFollette, 2008). Perhaps the most striking modern example of scientific knowledge thus widely spread in society is that about computers, mobile phones, other digital instruments as well as the social networks used in such human–machine interaction.

5.3   Epistemic communities

Although informally defined above as collectivities of social actors sharing the same knowledge, the concept of *epistemic community* needs further sociological analysis. Thus, as suggested before, we would not typically categorize the passengers on a bus as an epistemic community. Similarly, although sharing specific knowledge, the notion would probably be only marginally useful to characterize the 'collectives' consisting of my partner and me, our family or the members of our university department. So, what defining/delimiting properties do we want to associate with the theoretical notion of an epistemic community that is empirically and conceptually useful (for detail, see also Beinhauer, 2004)?

5.3.1   Linguistic and interactional communities – communities of discourse

One way to begin to address the definition of epistemic communities is in terms of the very *functions* of shared knowledge: why, for what, do collectivities of people need shared knowledge in the first place? The reply to this question involves the relationship between linguistic (or discourse) communities, on the one hand, and communities of practice or interaction, on the other: socially shared knowledge fundamentally serves to communicate, to act and to interact successfully.

Thus, if linguistic communities are defined as groups of language users sharing the same (first) language – in practice also defined by a shared region or nation (if we want to exclude as members of the linguistic community of people in China knowing Spanish as a second language) – such linguistic knowledge obviously is part of their more general knowledge system (Gumperz, 1962). However, linguistic knowledge is not sufficient to engage in spoken or written discourse, for which vast amounts of "knowledge of the world" is also required, as studied in the previous and the next chapters. Besides general knowledge of the physical and biological environment, as shared by many linguistic communities within the same culture (to be dealt with later), engaging in private and public discourse also requires knowledge of the social and cultural environment of the language users. In order to understand many aspects of Spanish discourse, language users obviously need much knowledge about Spain or Latin American countries and societies.

In that sense, then, epistemic communities and linguistic communities are closely related and might be joined in the broader concept of *communities of discourse* (Cortese and Duszak, 2005; Cutting, 2000; Kennedy and Smith, 1994; Porter, 1992; Rodin and Steinberg, 2003; Ventola, 2000; Wuthnow, 1989). That is, first of all, socially shared knowledge is presupposed and hence needed to be able to engage in text or talk in a specific cultural community. Discourse is also the principal means knowledge of that community is acquired, spread and reproduced, e.g., especially through parent–child discourse in families, schools and the mass media. And conversely, first languages are typically acquired within the contexts of communities of discourse.

Knowledge is not only presupposed by language use, discourse or communication, but more generally by action and interaction (Bicchieri and Dalla Chiara, 1992). In order to be able to understand the actions and intentions of other social actors, to coordinate action and to plan collective action, specific knowledge of physical, biological, social and cultural environments is required. On the one hand, such knowledge is broader than the knowledge of a specific linguistic community, and more generally part of cultural knowledge shared by many linguistic communities or discourse communities. On the other hand, knowledge required for action and interaction may be more specific, for instance the knowledge necessary for professional practices – in turn related to the ability to participate in professional discourse.

Finally, the closely related notion of *communities of practice* requires, and is partly defined by, shared knowledge of specific groups of social actors regularly engaged in specific, joint interaction, and whose members share overall goals, as is the case for families, teams, clubs, university departments, shops and (small) business companies, among many others (Wenger, 1998). Again, as we saw more generally above, also in this case, the knowledge of epistemic communities is mutually relevant for the discourse of such communities: it is necessary to engage appropriately in such community discourse, and, on the other hand, such knowledge is acquired and validated through discourse and communication in the community – though usually based on more general social and cultural knowledge and broader discourse communities.

We see that the notion of epistemic community is closely related to, and in part presupposes, similar notions such as communities of discourse, interaction and social practice. In all these cases, such different forms of knowledge are required not only to actively participate *as competent members* of such communities, but also to do so *appropriately*, that is, by following specific rules and norms.

5.3.2 Membership

As is the case for all kinds of social or cultural communities, epistemic communities may also be further defined in terms of their members. Sociologically speaking, such membership may be relatively easy to define when social groups, collectives or organizations, as well as their access and membership, are regulated. One may become officially hired by a company or institution and thus by law or custom become a member. One may be admitted as an official member of a club, political party or other collective and such membership may be documented by a membership card, registration and so on.

Membership of linguistic communities is less well defined. Indeed, are small children or foreigners learning the language already members of such a community, or not yet? In specific situations, one may need to have so many years of schooling and official diplomas in order to count as a member – as is the case for the linguistic requirements for foreign students in many countries. And since linguistic and cultural communities are closely related, one may be competent grammatically speaking, but still lack many types of pragmatic knowledge required for appropriate discourse in a linguistic community, on the one hand, or speak with an accent, on the other. Hence, the very notion of linguistic community should be further analyzed in terms of different types and degrees of knowledge, competences and abilities.

The same is true for membership of epistemic communities. Children and foreigners may still lack the required social and cultural knowledge in order to engage in competent, appropriate action, interaction and discourse. Different types of socialization process define how such 'newcomers' of the community acquire 'epistemic literacy' through everyday informal interaction, on the one hand, or through formal schooling or other form of education on the other. Again, most countries or organizations require many years of official schooling, tests and diplomas before social actors are ratified as competent members, for instance in order to be able to vote, get a job or engage in higher-level, specialized schooling. Besides guaranteeing minimum levels of knowledge that allow competent action, interaction and discourse, such official requirements also contribute to social homogeneity and member identification with the community (Anderson *et al.*, 1977; Apple, 1979, 1993, 2012; Barnett, 1994; Bernstein, 1996; Frandji and Vitale, 2010; Gabbard, 2000; Mercer, 1987; Paechter, 2001; Sharp, 1980; Welch and Freebody, 1993; Young, 1971).

Despite official schooling, diplomas and other social institutions that epistemically socialize community members, there remain vast differences of knowledge among individual members, even among those with the same education and growing up and living in the same social environments (Furnham and Chamorro-Premuzic, 2006; Furnham *et al.*, 2007; Hambrick *et al.*, 2007). Variable personal interests are among the conditions that explain differences of media use, reading or joining different communities of practice, leading to considerable differences of knowledge. Thus, given our example of David Cameron's statement in the *Sun*, we may assume that *Sun* readers have a different knowledge set than the readers of, for instance, the *Guardian*, which critically comments on Cameron's intervention in an editorial significantly entitled *Facts and not Fiction*.

Later, and based on generally shared knowledge, members specialize, e.g., professionally (Eraut, 1994; Horvath and Sternberg, 1999). In this sense, social actors may become members of several, overlapping or hierarchically related epistemic communities. Whether formally or informally, membership for each community may thus be defined in terms of the (gradual) epistemic competence that is necessary in order to be able engage in (gradually) appropriate social interaction and discourse in various social contexts.

Given the vast knowledge differences of individual members of the 'same' epistemic community, not only formal education and tests but also the very communicative practices of the community may require minimum forms of competence. This is why in practice we may define epistemic communities also in terms of the knowledge presupposed by its various types of *public discourse*, as we have argued several times above (see also Gavin, 1998; Jansen, 2002; Wagner *et al.*, 2002).

Quite concretely, such may be the case in order to understand television news programs and (many) shows, to be able to read and understand most general news of a newspaper, and in order to be able to engage in appropriate conversation with colleagues on the job or with employees of public agencies. It is this kind of general, sociocultural knowledge as required for the appropriate participation in various situations and genres of public discourse that may serve as the basic Common Ground defining an epistemic community – even if there are members who know much more than this basic social knowledge.

Obviously, the set of people defined by such basic community knowledge is fuzzy. Not only are there members who know much more, but for several personal and social reasons, there are members who know much less – and hence will not be able to fully understand many types of public discourse, such as television news – beyond the knowledge level required for basic everyday interaction with family members, friends or colleagues on the job. We here enter the topic of the sociology of education, individual differences, social conditions of successful schooling and related topics – each of which also need a fundamental epistemic analysis in terms of the kinds of epistemic competences acquired by various social groups, categories or individuals.

5.3.3   Levels and types of epistemic communities

Epistemic communities come in many types and are analyzable at many levels, often also related to respective communities of discourse. Thus, first of all, epistemic communities are *spatiotemporally* variable. We now know much more – and different things – as a community than the 'same' community a hundred years ago, specifically so in the field of technological knowledge. That is, epistemic communities, just like individuals, gradually learn (and forget), and hence also require *historical epistemic analysis*. When new phenomena are being discovered, new material or symbolic objects being construed and lexically identified, this requires the kind of discursive strategies of description, characterization or definition to be further examined in Chapter 7.

The same is true for spatial or *regional* variation, often associated with different types of cultural knowledge, to be dealt with in the next chapter. Thus, the citizens of Spain may be defined as an epistemic community because of their shared specific knowledge about Spain as a country, society and culture – as shared, acquired and presupposed by the many types of public discourse in Spain, for instance in schooling and the mass media. But the same is true for communities of the citizens of Catalonia and Barcelona, as defined in terms of the specific local knowledge they have. But as citizens of Spain – and of Europe – they share in higher-level or broader epistemic communities, each again socially defined in terms of its special forms of public discourse, on the one hand, and by reference to such higher-level communities in more local discourse, on the other.

We see that the role of discursive presupposition is related to a hierarchical system of superposed epistemic communities. Citizens of Barcelona need to share general 'Spanish' knowledge with members of other cities or regions of Spain, but not necessarily vice versa: citizens of other parts of Spain have only limited knowledge, usually through the mass media, of relevant local knowledge in Barcelona (see, e.g., Butt *et al.*, 2008; Geertz, 1983; Mignolo, 1999).

The same argument applies at still higher, more abstract levels of societal and cultural knowledge, as is the case for the relations between Spain and the rest of Europe, or between Western Europe and South Asia, for example, as we shall further explore in the next chapter, especially so for intercultural discourse and communication.

Among the many types of epistemic communities defined by differential levels of education and schooling, social class, gender, occupation, organization, ideology or religion, perhaps most relevant here are the professional ones. Indeed, even more than most others, members of professional epistemic communities are selected, educated and hired with a specific focus on their knowledge and related competences and abilities (Connelly and Clandinin, 1999; Eraut, 1994; Freidson, 1986). They acquire such specialized knowledge in specific institutions, in specific educational forms of interaction, controlled by specific exams and other tests, and finally validated by competent participation in professional discourse and other forms of practice and interaction, as is the case for doctors, engineers, lawyers, sociologists and many other professionals.

As is the case for the hierarchical relations between regional and national knowledge, so professional knowledge is more specific and hence presupposes general sociocultural 'base' knowledge for its acquisition as well as for the non-technical aspects of their discourse, communication and interaction. This may also imply that what counts as general knowledge not only may need the specifics of specialized knowledge but also may be corrected or contradicted by specialized knowledge, and even rejected as mere popular belief or superstition.

It is one of the tasks of the discursive sociology of knowledge to detail the properties of, and the relationships between, these different epistemic communities, and to show how such communities may or must be characterized by the types of discourses underlying the acquisition and diffusion of knowledge with or across them (see also Keller, 2005).

5.4   Discourse and knowledge in context

The sociology of discourse and knowledge is not limited to a study of the (re) production of the contents and styles of different genres of public text and talk and the ways such discourse presupposes, expresses and conveys socially shared knowledge. We have emphasized the tremendous role of context as part of complex communicative events, as subjectively construed in special context models by language users (Van Dijk, 2008a, 2009a).

Thus, in our example from the *Sun*, it is not just the news text or Cameron's statement that (re)produces knowledge and other beliefs, but the fact that it is this newspaper, and this prime minister publishing these texts at this particular date, in the UK and with these specific aims, within the broader framework of the ongoing debate on immigration.

That is, readers not only represent the texts but also contexts when forming their knowledge and opinions. Within the framework of the sociology of knowledge and discourse, thus, we also need a systematic analysis of the social dimensions of the contextual constraints of communicative events. It is especially through the interpretation of such contexts that language users, e.g., as readers of newspapers, assess the *reliability* of discourse as a source of knowledge, and hence determine whether beliefs expressed by specific sources should be deemed to be knowledge in the first place.

In general, thus, the epistemic impact of context features obviously depends on (the speaker's model of the) identity, role and functions of the recipients (Tormala and Clarkson, 2008; for studies on the relation between knowledge, power, credibility and the organizational roles and identities of participants, see also, e.g., Aronowitz, 1988; Berkenkotter and Huckin, 1995; Bourdieu *et al.*, 1994; Coburn and Willis, 2000; Freidson, 1986; Gilles and Lucey, 2008; Goldman, 1999; Mumby, 1988; Thornborrow, 2002; Van Dijk, 2008b; Vine, 2004; Wodak, 1989a, 1989b).

The context analysis of Cameron's statement in the *Sun* is particularly interesting, because it blends those of the communicative domains of politics and mass media. No doubt Cameron is writing here as prime minister and not as journalist, but he is not addressing parliament or his party but specifically the readers of the *Sun*, as is the case for the journalist who introduces his statement. Also, the aims of the statement are defined for each social field – namely informing readers of a mass medium on the one hand, and influencing potential voters on the other. So, the communicative genre of this statement is a hybrid of a political and a media discourse. The text of this statement both indexes as well as adapts to this complex communicative situation.

Thus, we shall see below that the sociological analysis of knowledge as socially reproduced by the specific discourse genres of groups, institutions and organizations, such as the mass media, also needs a systematic analysis of their contexts, such as specific places (bedrooms, newsrooms, boardrooms, classrooms, courtrooms, etc.), times (such as to make the evening news or just before elections; see, e.g., Cook, 1989), participants (PMs, MPs, journalists, teachers, scientists, etc.) social or political actions or activities (informing, doing politics, legislating, educating, etc.), and specific aims (getting more votes, etc.)(for details of such context analysis, see Van Dijk, 2008a, 2009a).

Each of these context categories needs further analysis, as is the case for the internal organization, furniture and props of different places or spaces ('rooms,' see, e.g., McElroy *et al.*, 1983; Morrow and McElroy, 1981), the identities, roles and relations of the participants and the details, at various levels of generality, of social or political action. Thus, at a basic level of analysis, Cameron makes a statement in a tabloid newspaper, but *by doing this* he does many other things, such as addressing the readers of the *Sun*, making publicity for his party, trying to win votes, taking a position in a debate and so on (for such hierarchies of actions and action goals, see, e.g., Ellis, 1999). Indeed, this is a crucial feature of the micro–macro structure of the social order (Cicourel, 1981; Druckman, 2003; Mayes, 2005).

Similarly, we thus should examine the relations between mass media discourse, participants and timing (see, e.g., Tuchman, 1978) or between conversation and time (see, e.g., Auer *et al.*, 1999; Boden, 1997; Boltz, 2005; Greene and Cappella, 1986; Heldner and Edlund, 2010; Nevile, 2007).

Finally, systematic context analysis of the discursive reproduction of knowledge in society should focus on the *discourse genres* defined by such contexts: news reports, government statements, textbooks and many other genres are the discourse and activity types through which knowledge is expressed and communicated, each again with its own degrees of attributed reliability as a source (see Bazerman, 1988; Berkenkotter and Huckin, 1995).

Thus, a news article in the *Sun* no doubt has a lower credibility rating, even among its regular readers, than a news article in the *Guardian*. And a textbook on immigration usually will be found more credible and reliable than a political statement, even of the Prime Minister.

Within this broader theoretical framework, we shall examine below one of these genres more closely, news in the press, and see how it is involved in the social management of knowledge.

5.4.1   *Knowledge management in organizations*

Far beyond the sociology of knowledge, and involving cognitive and social psychology, communication studies, business administration and economics, is the vast current field of the study of knowledge management in organizations. Although many of the notions discussed in this book, especially in this and the previous chapter, of socially shared knowledge in interaction and epistemic communities also apply to organizations, there are many other dimensions that are beyond the scope of this book. Thus, knowledge, including practical knowledge and 'tacit' knowledge, is not just a sociocognitive phenomenon, but also a strategic symbolic resource or 'intellectual capital' that allows organizations to learn, innovate, to compete with others and to improve themselves. Research in the field, often closely related to practical implementation, focuses on the nature and the cognitive, social and economic conditions of the creating, sharing and dissemination of knowledge in the organization (for some recent general references among the vast number of books on this topic, see, e.g., Easterby-Smith and Lyles, 2011; Liebowitz, 2012; Rooney *et al.*, 2012; Schwartz and Te'eni, 2011; Wellman, 2013). Indeed, these studies are part of a larger field of studies on the "knowledge society" as the stage of social and socioeconomic development (Baert and Rubio, 2012; Sörlin and Vessuri, 2006), another topic beyond the scope of this book.

In the previous chapter we already reviewed some of the literature on the relation between discourse and knowledge in organizations, focusing especially on the role of knowledge in personal interaction situated in organizations. More broadly relevant for this chapter is the issue of the communication and dissemination of knowledge within and among organizations, as well as in society at large. On this topic, there are now many studies, especially in Organization Studies, whose review, however, is beyond the scope of this book (see, e.g., Canary and McPhee, 2010; Farrell, 2006; Kikoski and Kikoski, 2004; Liebowitz, 2012).

5.5   News reports

Most of what we know about the world beyond our daily experiences we learn through the mass media, specifically through news reports in the press or on the radio, television or the Internet. Compared to what we know about poems, novels, storytelling, advertising and many other discourse genres, the study of news as discourse was marginal at best, even in mass communication research and journalism. Before the 1970s, studies of news were either merely content analytical (the coverage of event X or country Z, etc.) or anecdotal.

In the 1970s appeared the first sociologically informed studies of the daily routines, beats and interactions of journalists, about the relationships between journalists and sources, or between newspapers as institutions or organizations and other organizations, for instance in terms of power (Gans, 1979; Tuchman, 1978). Only in the 1980s and later did the first more detailed, qualitative studies of news as a genre of text or talk appear, though as yet barely central in mass communication research until today (Bell, 1991; Bell and Garrett, 1997; Fowler, 1991; Montgomery, 2007; Richardson, 2007; Van Dijk, 1988a, 1988b).

Relevant for this chapter is especially the fact that news reports have hardly been studied from an *epistemic* point of view (see, e.g., Van Dijk, 2004a, 2005a). There has been psychological research on memory and knowledge updating in understanding news, as well as many studies on the effects of the news media on opinions and attitudes (see, e.g., Allen *et al.*, 1997; Baum, 2003; Blanc *et al.*, 2008; Graber, 1984; Kintsch and Franzke, 1995; Kraus, 1990; Larsen, 1981; Park, 2001; Perry, 1990; Van Dijk and Kintsch, 1983; Yaros, 2006).

Yet we need much more, and more detailed insights into such topics as the knowledge presupposed in news and by what kinds of recipients, what kinds of knowledge are expressed and conveyed about what issues, in what context and with what consequences. How do news reports manage the relationship between 'old' (already reported, but possibly forgotten) knowledge and new knowledge?

As a form of public discourse, communicating public knowledge about public affairs, news reports require more detailed analysis also from a discourse analytical point of view – further to be detailed in Chapter 7. In this chapter, a sociological account of news typically focuses on the parameters of the communicative situation as they are construed by journalists and readers, respectively. News is dialectically related to society in the sense that it varies with major public events in society, but at the same time, it construes and enhances such events as news events that require special attention. That is, news also defines society by defining our conception of society. Let us examine the relevant sociological aspects of news and news production and their relations with knowledge and discourse in somewhat more detail.

5.5.1   Setting (organization): the newspaper

Ignoring news on television, radio or the Internet (each of which requires its own contextual analysis), let us begin with some comments on the organizational setting of news production in the written press, namely the institution of the newspaper, possibly part of a large media organization (see, e.g., Cohen, 2005; Turow, 1984; Wolff, 2008). News is first of all produced as part of a commercial product, the daily newspaper, sold by subscription, in kiosks and on the street. In the daily paper, news is intertextually accompanied by news-related opinion articles, columns, editorials, reportages, interviews, weather reports, stock market information, human interest items and background articles, on the one hand, and advertisements on the other.

Together with these other newspaper genres, news must sell and make a profit. Hence, the contents and structures of news must be such that readers want to buy and read such news reports. Many traditional studies in mass communication have shown that, depending on context, some types of news, that is, news on specific topics, sell better than others – although the dialectics of cause (offer) and consequence (demand) are complicated issues: readers may want to read what is offered abundantly, and may not know what they are missing when it is hardly ever offered – again depending on the social and political context (for detail, see, e.g., Abel, 1981; Allan, 2010; Altschull, 1984; Cohen, 2005; Hulteng, 1979; MacKuen and Coombs, 1981; Nash and Kirby, 1989).

Most generally, according to studies of 'news values,' readers are more interested in what happens close by than far away, what is more relevant to their daily life and interests, what is consistent with their attitudes, ideologies and expectations, what is emotionally arousing (dramatic, threatening, sexual, unexpected) and features much human interest (personal lives, fame, scandal, etc.) (Bell, 1991; Da Costa, 1980; Fuller, 1996; Galtung and Ruge, 1965; Lee, 2009; Price and Tewksbury, 1997).

5.5.2   News production

Obviously, such preferences for news content as a commercial product have epistemic consequences. Readers learn more about topics or events that are frequently and prominently reported. Thus, we know much more about a prominent topic such as terrorism engaged in by Others than about little-reported racism, sexism and poverty in our own society – even when the numbers of real or potential victims of the latter conditions are vastly higher in the world than those of the former (of the large number of books on media and terrorism, see Alali and Eke, 1991; Alexander and Latter, 1990; Chomsky, 1987; Gerbner, 1988; Hachten and Scotton, 2002; Paletz, 1992; Schlesinger *et al.*, 1983; Schmid and de Graaf, 1982; on racism in the mass media, see, e.g., Downing and Husband, 2005; Hartmann and Husband, 1974; Jäger and Link, 1993; Van Dijk, 1991).

The end product of news reports on preferred, sellable stories requires special processes of production, as is the case for the various stages and forms of news gathering, daily beats, news conferences, news releases, the use of other media and so on. Also, to make sure that the newspaper receives a minimum amount of text and talk as material of sellable news stories, reporters need to follow a daily beat that includes the institutions and organizations that produce a steady amount of such material, such as the (national or local) government, parliament, the police, the courts, the universities, business corporations, sport organizations and so on. Such material may arrive as uninvited press releases, reports or other forms of text, or may be acquired in news conferences, interviews, telephone calls and so on (Gans, 1979; Machin and Niblock, 2006; Meyers, 1992; Tuchman, 1978; Van Hout and Jacobs, 2008).

Given the commercial requirements of the end product, news production itself must be geared towards news events, news actors and news sources that satisfy the criteria of newsworthiness mentioned above. This means that because of constraints of time and money, only some organizations or institutions will be routinely 'covered' during daily beats (e.g., government, political parties, large corporations, the police, major sport organizations, etc.), whereas others will only be covered incidentally (e.g., the unions when there is a strike), or hardly ever at all (organizations of immigrants, the poor, women, children, the handicapped and so on).

Whereas these constraints of newsmaking are still quite general and macrolevel, they influence and are influenced by the microstructure of daily interactions of editors, reporters and news sources. Thus, the daily editorial meeting (very little studied due to the lack of access for researchers) interactionally decides what stories on what topics will be covered in what way and where in the newspaper. Arguments in favor or against a news story may be expected again to be in terms of commercial relevance framed as readers' interests, followed by criteria of social, political and cultural relevance. *That is, it is in this meeting that one or a few editors decide what hundreds of thousands or millions of readers will know – or not – about the world.* A detailed study of the arguments, criteria, norms, values and goals of that professional interaction is obviously a crucial requirement to understand the role of the newspaper in the reproduction of knowledge in society. At the moment, our insight into that interaction is post hoc and inferential, that is, based on the analysis of what countries, events, actions or people do appear in the newspaper and which do not (see also the critical studies by the Glasgow University Media Group, 1976, 1980, 1982, 1985).

Besides dealing with incoming text (news releases, reports, other media, Internet, etc.), reporters interactively deal mostly with suppliers of reliable and relevant information, at the various sites mentioned above, more specifically with other symbolic elites who have access to and control over public discourse, e.g., in politics, business, science, the arts and sports – such as prominent politicians, party leaders, MPs – or their representatives – as well as directors of large organizations, leaders of important NGOs or other organizations, professors and so on (Ericson *et al.*, 1989; Manning, 2001; Soley, 1992; Strentz, 1989). It is for this reason that David Cameron had direct access to the *Sun* to make a statement for the readers on his new tough policy on benefits for immigrants.

The interaction in press conferences and interviews is again geared by the context model for such forms of communicative situations, namely the setting, the participants, the goals and the knowledge of the participants. Questioning and interrogation, thus, are aimed at updating or acquiring new knowledge and opinion on interesting, relevant and recent events that may form the content of sellable news stories (Clayman and Heritage, 2002). The discourse strategies of such interaction, as is the case for news interviews, will be dealt with in Chapter 7. Relevant here is the microsociological dimension of the ways news is produced through various kinds of interaction, and is geared to the acquisition and production of new, sellable knowledge.

The organizational complexity of news production, especially for large news organizations, with specialized sections and departments, a power hierarchy of editors and a vast array of daily interaction among journalists, among journalists and news sources, and the final processing of thousands of texts of which a few hundred are selected for publication, obviously also involves very complex epistemic structures and strategies. Indeed, what do journalists know about the knowledge and the interests of the readers (Boyd-Barrett and Braham, 1987; Tewksbury, 2003)? What knowledge of readers is presupposed in news stories? What do journalists know about the topics they write about? What knowledge do reporters assume news sources have, so that they may strategically organize their questions to get the most relevant or interesting knowledge? What epistemic criteria establish that information is true, and hence can be considered as knowledge of the epistemic community?

More generally, how is all this interaction, news gathering and news writing again a function of the social attitudes and ideologies of editors and reporters, and indirectly of their social class, education, gender, age and nationality, among other factors (Cooper and Johnson, 2009; Deuze, 2005; Ecarma, 2003; Fowler, 1991; Van Dijk, 1988a, 1988b; White, 2006)? That is, we here touch upon one of the crucial topics of the sociology of knowledge.

But instead of relating such social variables more or less directly or causally to the knowledge and opinions of journalists and hence to news production and news contents, we have emphasized that such a relationship first of all needs a more concrete, microlevel approach to daily newsmaking, and secondly requires the concept of context model that controls news gathering, interviews or news writing among many other discursive events that define news production. That is, it is not the 'objective' status or the power of news actors, news sources or news events that guides news gathering and news writing, but the way journalists represent these in their models of the communicative situation. The same is true for the representation of the reading public as recipients of the news reports.

This context model centrally features participants' current self-representation as journalists, as employees of a newspaper, as colleagues of other reporters, as subordinate to an editor and so on (Bohère, 1984). Again, it is this context model that dynamically controls all action and discourse at all stages, that is, in all subsequent communicative events and their genres, of the production of news. The knowledge device in this context model more specifically controls all talk and action that is aimed strategically at the acquisition of relevant new knowledge from the most knowledgeable, credible or famous sources.

5.5.3   News and knowledge

Most relevant for our discussion, obviously, is the relation between news and knowledge. So far we have studied some of the aspects of the relations between news as discourse and its organizational dimensions. But for this chapter and this section we more particularly need to establish a link between knowledge and its societal or organizational embedding in news production and news organizations (Van Dijk, 2004a, 2004b).

News is public discourse about recent events that newsmakers deem interesting or relevant for the readers. News presupposes but generally does not aim to 'teach' general facts. It tells about events such as wars, civil wars, revolutions, terrorist attacks, major accidents, economic or political crises or elections, among many other public events. In other words, the kind of knowledge we typically acquire from media news may also be called 'historical' or 'episodic': it is about relatively important events, and less about structure, systemic causes and consequences, regularities or generalities. Indeed, routine media news is often criticized for not providing insight into the structural conditions or background of social, political or economic events or problems such as poverty and inequality in the world (Rosenblum, 1981; Unesco, 1980).

Repeated communication of news about topics may, of course, contribute to inductive learning, e.g., by generalization, abstraction or decontextualization. Although we do not have empirical evidence to cite for this, it may be assumed that much general knowledge of the world beyond our experiences is thus learned inductively ('casually,' 'indirectly' or 'informally') from news in the press or on television (Gavin, 1998; Graber, 2001; Schwoch *et al.*, 1992).

Other media genres, however, such as commentary, editorials, opinion articles, background articles and popularization articles, related to important recent news, may formulate general knowledge about such events, for instance about historical or economic backgrounds or causes of revolutions and crises, or information about technical or medical aspects of diseases or new technologies (Harindranath, 2009; Wade and Schramm, 1969).

Cognitively, news is based on the situation models of journalists. These models are generally construed by journalists as a result of processing various source discourses (other media messages, eyewitness testimony, expert opinion, etc.), as explained above, and only seldom on direct observation of events (Van Dijk, 1988b). However, news discourse does not express situation models directly and completely, but only partially and relevantly to the current communicative situation, as represented by the context models of journalists.

This means, first of all, semantically, that situation models of events imply a vast amount of knowledge that may be presupposed because readers already have such knowledge or are able to infer it from their extant knowledge. Thus, a news report need not explain what countries, politicians, wars, bombs, unemployment or terrorists (and their properties) are – among hundreds of thousands of other concepts that have previously been learned during socialization, at school or through previous media usage. Indeed, news is called such because it expresses *new* information, and specifically new information about important, relevant or interesting recent events.

Secondly, situation models may feature knowledge that, although 'new' for the recipients, is not expressed in news discourse for other reasons, mostly because it is not considered sufficiently interesting or relevant by the journalist. Sometimes, new information may not be made public for a variety of normative reasons, e.g., because it was illegally obtained, because it is illegal to publish it (such as national secrets, etc.) or because it infringes privacy or libel laws (Barendt, 1997; Glasser, 2009; Wilkinson, 2009; Zelezny, 1993).

News production is not only based on situation models of public events, but also controlled by context models, as we have suggested above. That is, journalists represent themselves and write as journalists, as employees of a specific newspaper or other medium, with a specific public of recipients in mind, with a specific goal, etc. This explains why the 'same story' of the 'same event' may be reported quite differently in different newspapers and in different countries. Typical is the difference of news discourse about a given event in the quality or elite press, on the one hand, and the popular or tabloid press, on the other.

Thus, in our empirical study of 700 international news items in more than one hundred countries about the assassination of president-elect Bechir Gemayel of Lebanon in September 1982, we found that differences in type of newspaper were more significant than the assumed ideological differences between progressive vs. conservative newspapers in the world (Van Dijk, 1984b). One of the explanations of this ideological heterogeneity is that most of the news articles in the quality press more closely follow the style of the international news agencies on which most news reports were based.

Context models define the situational appropriateness of discourse. Thus the context models of journalists make sure that news items are written with different assumptions about the knowledge or interests of the readers. Highbrow quality newspapers, which typically may have highly educated readers, may presuppose more social or political knowledge than popular newspapers do for a larger audience (Frechie et al., 2005).

Besides knowledge about the knowledge of recipients, context models also feature the ideologies of the journalist and assumptions of such ideologies of the recipients, and thus may also adapt the expression of the new information (as represented in situation models) to such ideologies. This usually takes place through the application of the general strategy of the Ideological Square (Van Dijk, 1998), emphasizing Their bad things and Our good things, and de-emphasizing Their good things and Our bad things – thus expressing underlying polarization between ingroup and outgroup characteristics as represented in an ideology or its dependent socially shared attitudes. In the press, such ideologies quite typically are those of nationalism, eurocentrism, racism and sexism, among others (Brinks et al., 2006; Van Dijk, 1991; Wilson et al., 2003).

Both situation models of news events and context models of news production thus necessarily imply some kind of bias with respect to the events themselves. There is no such thing as a neutral or objective mental representation of such events. First of all, situation models are by definition incomplete: no direct observer is able to represent all (theoretically infinite) properties of events. That is, situation models are only a tiny fragment of selected aspects of an event. Secondly, situation models are selective for basic cognitive reasons: journalists focus on what is most salient, relevant or interesting personally (according to their own knowledge) or professionally (according to the assumed knowledge, interests of the recipients). Thirdly, situation models are ideologically biased in terms of the ideological group memberships of the journalists, processing event knowledge according to the strategy of the Ideological Square. Finally, most situation models are based on discourses that are already biased for the same reasons (Van Dijk, 2004a).

In other words, there are several, independent social and cognitive reasons why situation models of news events are necessarily incomplete, partial and ideologically biased. Context models about the current news production (e.g., knowing for what newspaper one is writing) may further enhance (and sometimes mitigate for professional reasons) such bias. The actual news report is the result of a biased underlying situation model as it is controlled by the application of the constraints of the context models that make sure that the news report is 'appropriate' for the current communicative situation (newspaper, public, etc.).

We see how the (re)production of social, economic and political knowledge in society as it is based on news reports and opinion articles in the mass media is a complex process mediated by (necessarily incomplete and biased) situation and context models of journalists, resulting in (biased) news report structures that are the 'input' of the similar models and processes of the recipients. This means that readers, given their own knowledge and ideologies, may in turn construe situation models of events that may be quite different from those of the journalists as (more or less persuasively) expressed in the news report. However, if recipients have no alternative personal experiences (mental models) of similar events, or no relevant general knowledge or ideologies about such events, they may well adopt the 'preferred' model suggested by the journalist, e.g., as we know it from racist reporting about minorities or immigrants.

Specifically relevant for this chapter is that the complex organizational processes and interactions involved in news production and the reproduction of episodic knowledge depend on the knowledge, interests and ideologies of journalists. These may again depend on their own professional education and experiences, nationality, ethnicity, social class or their gender, among other conditions, at a high level of analysis and description. The latter again need to be made explicit at more concrete lower-level processes and interaction, such as the teachers and textbooks in journalism school, media usage, personal experiences and so on. Again, we witness complex series of text or talk and concomitant complex series of social cognition, that is, of the formation of mental models (of experiences of reading about events), general knowledge, social attitudes and ideologies.

We see that what seems like a complex sociological process inevitably involves sociocognitive aspects. There is no direct (deterministic, causal, etc.) relationship between, for instance, the organization of a newspaper as an institution, interaction among journalists or among journalists and news sources, or the various social identities of journalists (occupation, gender, class, ethnicity, education, etc.), on the one hand, and the 'ideas' of journalists, such as their knowledge or ideologies, on the other. That is, the social 'basis' of journalists and newsmaking only influences the knowledge and opinions of journalists – and then news discourse – through the mediation of several layers, stages and strategies of understanding, interpretation and representation, such as mental models and socially shared representations such as the previous knowledge and ideologies of the social collectivities of which they are members. In more concrete terms: a black journalist does not automatically or necessarily write from a black or antiracist perspective, and a female journalist does not necessarily or always write as a woman, and even less as a feminist.

5.5.4   The power epistemics of Cameron's statement in the Sun

Some of the relevant context characteristics of the statement of David Cameron in the *Sun* have been summarized above, where we especially noted the interesting property of the communicative situation, namely of a prime minister directly writing in a newspaper, and addressing its readers.

Epistemically, this is interesting because millions of *Sun* readers thus get to know about (planned) immigration policy from the responsible prime minister (PM), rather than mediated through the news report of a journalist who gets to know about such policy through a spokesperson of the PM or through a press conference of the PM himself. The communication shortcut implied by the PM directly addressing *Sun* readers as citizens (and voters) thus also means that the information thus obtained is of utmost reliability, while not transformed by a sequence of intermediary discourses of spokespersons and journalists.

The information obtained directly from the PM, however, is only reliable where it pertains to what the PM is planning to do – as expressed in the last part of his statement: limiting benefits, housing and healthcare for immigrants. The reasons Cameron gives for such tougher policy are based on what he presents as knowledge about the uses or abuses of these services by immigrants, including:

- Immigration got out of control under Labour.
- 2.2 million more people came in than went out.
- Conservatives have worked hard to get things more manageable.
- (Therefore) net migration is down by a third since the last election.
- (Under Labour) it was legal for those who overstayed visas to claim certain benefits.

The semantic structure of these statements exhibits the usual polarization we know of the Ideological Square: positive self-presentation (of a Conservative government) and negative other-presentation (of a Labour administration). These statements, however, are presented and presupposed as facts, not as partisan assessments of a PM specifically addressing *Sun* readers, many of whose negative beliefs about the alleged abuse of benefits are consistent with those of the PM. Indeed, others, such as the *Guardian*, call these beliefs 'fiction' and not 'facts.' Hence, we here witness an ideological struggle of various institutions, namely newspapers and the Prime Minister, over the definition of the situation – namely the facts about whether immigrants cost (much) more to the country than what they contribute.

David Cameron knows that saying negative things about immigrants may be heard in the UK as an expression of xenophobia or of racist or ethnic prejudice. He therefore starts his speech with the usual disclaimer, emphasizing the (past) benefits of immigrants and especially stressing the great history and hospitality of the country (for detail about such disclaimers, see Van Dijk, 1991, 1993). Typical of such disclaimers (such as *I am not a racist, but ...*) is that their function is not merely to make a positive statement about both the outgroup and the ingroup, but to manage the impression of the following negative statement about the outgroup (here both Labour and immigrants).

We have seen in the previous chapters that it is difficult to make a clear distinction between (mere) beliefs or opinions, on the one hand, and knowledge as justified beliefs. Thus, whether immigration got out of control under Labour obviously depends of the point of view of the speaker and his ingroup. And since it is not a shared belief within the epistemic community of the UK, it is by that definition an opinion and not a fact. Yet, sociologically relevant here is that a PM makes such a statement and does so for a gullible public of *Sun* readers, many of whom share the same general attitude and ideology on immigration. This means that the statement is made in his powerful function as PM (as also represented in the context models of most of the readers), thus enhancing its credibility (the PM must have privileged access to such 'data'), and at the same time confirming broadly shared prejudices and stereotypes about what the *Sun* used to call "scrounging" immigrants (Van Dijk, 1991).

Moreover, of all the possible statements the PM could make about immigrants and the economy, he selects precisely those epistemic domains (unemployment benefits, healthcare and housing) that are immediately *relevant* in the daily lives of many *Sun* readers, as well as the general public. Obviously, he will not address the fact that most immigrants pay taxes and have created much work also for British citizens. Hence, we here witness again that the 'truth' is relative. Even if his statements were true, they do not convey the whole truth – as required from witnesses in courts in the USA.

Cameron's statement, thus, is part of a national debate on immigration that has raged, also in the UK, for decades. Especially relevant for this chapter is that the (re)production and management of knowledge is related to power, namely the power of prime ministers and tabloid newspapers. Secondly, the mass communication of opinions presented as knowledge and as stated by such powerful institutions provides ideologically biased information (about immigrants and benefits) that is used by the general public to create mental models and confirm attitudes against immigrants, and hence (re)produce the power of the dominant (British) majority. Finally, such biased representations at the same time contribute to the electoral advantages of the politicians and parties who claim to oppose alleged abuses of benefits by immigrants, as is the case for Cameron and the Conservative Party.

Hence, Cameron's statement in the *Sun* does not primarily aim to inform the readers about immigrants, benefits and his own policies, but to enhance his power and that of his party at the same time as enhancing the power of the British majority. We thus also see how xenophobia and racism are discursively (re)produced by the symbolic elites who have preferential access to public discourse, and how beliefs may be presented as knowledge in order to manipulate the public at large (for detail, see Van Dijk, 1993). We here find a crucial example of the interface of knowledge and discourse within the framework of a critical sociology.

5.6   Concluding remarks

The sociology of discourse and knowledge, and especially the sociological inquiry into their relationships, takes place at many levels between societal macrostructures and their manifestation, everyday production or implementation at the microlevel of text, talk and interaction and their detailed structures and strategies. The very theory relating all these levels is still in its infancy, and needs to go beyond the simplistic notions of the early sociology of knowledge and culture, for instance in terms of 'determination,' 'reflection,' 'basis' and 'superstructure,' and so on.

Microsociology of the last fifty years has shown that the social order at the macrolevel is daily produced in myriads of actions and interactions of social members, and at various levels of generality. Conversation Analysis has shown how such interactions are accomplished by the subtle structures and strategies of talk. Critical Discourse Analysis has similarly shown how societal structures of power, such as those of gender and ethnicity, are produced and reproduced by the many structures of discourse. Macrosociological accounts of social groups, organizations, institutions, social processes and relationships of power, domination and existence are thus 'grounded' in the everyday lives, interaction and discourses of social actors.

Conversely, local and microlevel aspects of social interaction and discourse need to be understood and analyzed not only in terms of their own norms and rules, but also as constituents of larger societal and political structures and processes. Indeed, the very 'local' discursive practices of Conversation Analysis itself as an approach in sociology as well as in discourse studies, can better be understood against the background of the large-scale developments of sociology and discourse studies as disciplines, the structures of university departments, the foundation of scholarly journals (e.g., in discourse studies) and so on.

Theoretically, such macro–micro relations, as well as relations of top-down and bottom-up influences, can be formulated in terms of the knowledge and opinions of scholars: their knowledge of the discipline and its history may constitute a motivation to engage in specific kinds of research, methods or topics. In other words, we again see that one of the ways social macro- and microstructures are related is through the minds of the social actors as participants – that is, through their specific mental models of scholarly activity and its relations to the structures of generic knowledge about the discipline, its theories and methods. This means that even a cognitive and social psychology of 'doing science' should be involved in the theory as well as the analysis.

It is within this multidisciplinary paradigm that we account more generally for the relations between discourse and knowledge in society. The logic of these relationships and its levels is obvious. Both discourse and knowledge are properties of individual human beings as social actors, and both mutually condition each other: knowledge is largely acquired by situated text and talk, and discourse itself can only be produced and understood with massive amounts of specific and generic knowledge. Both are conditions of interaction, as well as the consequences of such interaction in sharing and distributing knowledge in society. Language users are social actors and members of social categories and groups, women and men, old and young, black and white, rich and poor, and so on, and such relevant identities may become part of the definition of the communicative situation, that is, of the contexts of their talk and text. And so on for the higher levels of analysis, where language users as social actors are members of organizations and institutions, which as collectivities similarly may produce and be constituted by text and talk, as is essentially the case in politics, education, the mass media, the bureaucracy and other central domains of society and the polity.

At all levels, thus, both discourse and knowledge play a crucial role, by themselves as well as in combination. New knowledge is daily and socially produced in countless local interactions of the many epistemic organizations and institutions of society, most characteristically in schools, universities and laboratories, on the one hand, and the mass media and the Internet, on the other. Most of this production takes place in the text and talk of meetings, classes, experiments, analyses, papers, articles, reports, lectures and so on. And in all these local events of the global structures such discourse again presupposes old and generates new knowledge.

The example of Cameron's statement in the *Sun* about immigrants and benefits also has shown how powerful institutions such as prime ministers and tabloid newspapers are able to manage knowledge in order to create the anti-immigrant attitudes that will contribute to their own power as well as that of the dominant group of British citizens. We thus also see how the symbolic elites control, or have preferential access to, public discourse, how they manipulate the knowledge and beliefs of the public and thus reproduce the system of racism and xenophobia (Van Dijk, 1993, 2006a). It is the task of the sociology of discourse and knowledge of the future to study the details of these relationships.

6   Discourse, knowledge and culture

6.1   Introduction

A relativist conception of knowledge associates the justification of beliefs with the variable criteria of epistemic communities. In the previous chapter, we have seen that such is the case for different communities of society, for instance for scientific or professional communities. In this chapter, we extend that argument to cultural communities, especially also those in non-Western societies.

Epistemic criteria and authorities in Ancient Greece, the European Middle Ages and in most Western and non-Western cultures today, have changed continuously. Indeed, one of the many ways to define culture would be in terms of its epistemic standards. What is knowledge about spirits or angels, or the assumed influence of one or more gods or ancestors in everyday life, for the members of one (sub)culture may be seen as superstition or mere religious belief by those of other (sub)cultures, as was the case in traditional anthropology talking about the beliefs of "savages" (e.g., in Frazer, 1910).

Whereas today, in many cultures, knowledge is defined as such by scientists or other experts, before and elsewhere it may have been what was declared as justified true belief by priests, gurus or school boards, as we know from creationist ideas about evolution in the USA. In that sense, all knowledge is local, indigenous or folk knowledge. Despite important differences between everyday and scientific thinking, between *Our* knowledge and *Their* knowledge, especially as to their contents and methods, the fundamental processes involved are very similar (Kuhn, 1996: 280).

6.1.1   Towards an epistemic anthropology

Within this general relativist framework, this chapter explores some of the relations between knowledge, discourse and culture. It intends to contribute to what could be called the 'anthropology of knowledge' – if that were an established field in the discipline. There is an early *Annual Review* article about the "anthropology of knowledge" (Crick, 1982), but the author denies that there is such a field, and much of the review is barely about the cultural study of knowledge. Indeed, even contemporary monographs, readers or handbooks in anthropology seldom feature chapters specifically dedicated to knowledge and beliefs, and these concepts seldom appear in the subject indices. Yet, in the broader area of cultural anthropology and especially within cognitive anthropology, an *epistemic anthropology* or *epistemic ethnography* would today most certainly be a relevant field or method, to be linked with similar developments in other disciplines of the humanities and social sciences.

Anthropology has been in the forefront of the cultural study of language and discourse, as is the case for the ethnography of speaking, from the 1960s until linguistic anthropology today (relevant references will follow below). Similarly, cognitive anthropology, or, more generally, cultural anthropology, has been interested in the study of variable belief systems, worldviews or cosmologies for decades, for instance in the study of 'local' or 'indigenous' knowledge about kinship, color, plants, animals or the social and natural environment in general, as they have been studied in ethno-semantics and various 'ethnosciences.' Indeed, since the definition of Goodenough (1964) until today, for many anthropologists, culture has often been defined in terms of the knowledge members must possess in order to be able to function adequately in a community. More specifically, similar definitions have been given for linguistic knowledge as 'competence' in linguistic communities.

6.1.2   From the study of kinship to cultural models

The analysis of the structures, organization and function of knowledge in cognitive anthropology has changed over the last decades. Earlier approaches to kinship and the analysis of kinship terms adopted componential analysis from structural phonology in linguistics (Lounsbury, 1969; see also the other contributions in Spradley, 1972). The influence of the cognitive revolution in cognitive psychology since the 1970s introduced such notions as prototypes, scripts and in general schemas for the characterization of knowledge. Much of this research was later formulated in terms of 'cultural models,' that is, culturally shared mental representations about the world, to be distinguished from the notion of (personal) mental models as we use it in this book.

Interestingly, although anthropology has contributed so much to our insight into the cultural and empirical study of both discourse and knowledge, these different directions of research have seldom been combined. The widespread study of the cultural diversity of text and talk has barely explored their variable epistemic contexts, conditions and consequences. And conversely, although most data about local knowledges have been acquired by ethnographic interviews and the analysis of stories, myths and conversations with lay members and local experts, and members themselves have acquired much of their knowledge through verbal interaction with other members (parents, peers, teachers, etc.), this fundamental role of discourse in the reproduction of local knowledge has rather been neglected.

In this chapter we can only begin to chart the relations between discourse and knowledge in cultural contexts. We do so largely theoretically and by examining the current literature on local knowledge, with special interest in the role of discourse in the production and transmission of culture, as well as studies of discursive diversity within or across cultures possibly influenced by variable epistemic criteria. For instance, in many countries, especially in the USA, news in the press is assumed to be factual and separated from opinion, as expressed in editorials, columns or opinion articles. In Spain, France and Italy, however, no such strict separation exists, and news articles may feature commentary and interpretation by correspondents or reporters.

The study of the specific cultural relations between discourse and knowledge takes place against a more general background of the study of the relations between thought, language and culture that characterized anthropology since Boas and other founders of the discipline. One of the perennial debates in that tradition has been about the role of language in people's acquisition of knowledge of the world, stimulated by more or less strict interpretations of Sapir and Whorf's classical hypothesis.

Various directions of cognitive anthropology today advocate a more autonomous development of cultural knowledge, e.g., through observation, participation, interaction and non-verbal social practices. It is also widely assumed that such acquisition and development are also based on cognitive universals about how humans have learned – both ontogenetically and phylogenetically – to interact with their environment. Much cultural learning about our social and natural environment, thus, is non-verbal and implicit. This is a fortiori the case for the acquisition of the practical knowledge (as skills) required to be able to engage in the everyday action and interaction in the variable environments of different cultural contexts. Moreover, as we have seen in the previous chapters, except for explicit learning contexts, cultural knowledge is generally presupposed, and hence implicit even in discourse.

6.1.3   The crucial role of discourse in the cultural reproduction of knowledge

Despite this role of non-verbal learning, culture and cultural transmission without text or talk are impossible, first of all because many aspects of culture are not observable and hence need to be re-presented in discourse or other semiotic practices, and secondly because even observable social or natural environments are attributed meanings that only can be formulated in discourse. Hence, precisely the fundamental aspects of culture, namely the *meanings* attributed to objects, nature or conduct, essentially need 'language' to be acquired and transmitted.

Whereas many earlier studies of linguistic relativity thus deal with the fundamental role of language in the acquisition of cultural knowledge – in practice usually reduced to its lexicon and some aspects of morphology or syntax – we prefer to emphasize the role of *language use*, that is, *discourse*, in this process. Besides their learning from everyday non-verbal experiences and practices, new members do not learn about their environment or the world by the isolated application of lexical labels to things, but through complete multimodal discourse, such as parent–child interaction, peer conversation, stories, myths, news, TV programs, textbooks and explicit teaching by experts, among other genres.

Moreover, it is more likely that both grammar and the structures and rules of discourse are acquired also as a function of the fundamental relations between language users as social actors and their natural and social environment and as an integral part of social interaction. Indeed, in order to learn a language, one needs to learn the meanings of its expressions and such meanings are profoundly embedded in and hence presuppose our knowledge of the world. Although the complex issue of linguistic relativity, as well as decades of debate, cannot be reviewed in this chapter, we need to briefly summarize our sociocognitive and discourse analytical perspective on this issue below.

6.1.4   Cultural variations of presumptions of knowledge in talk

One of the aims of the integrated cultural study of discourse and knowledge, thus, is to examine how discourses may vary culturally in their ways of presupposing, implying, expressing and conveying knowledge in different communicative situations. For instance, in one culture, parents may assume that infants as yet have virtually no knowledge and may adapt parent–child discourse to this assumption by engaging in baby talk. In other cultures, parents may not adapt themselves to the lack of knowledge of infants, and will talk to them from the start more or less in the same way as to older children or adults (see, e.g., Ochs, 1982). Similarly, whereas reliable observation, credible sources and valid inference may be more or less general, if not universal, criteria for the justification of beliefs and hence as evidentials in much text and talk, the application of these criteria may not only vary for different discourse genres (e.g., for news vs. a historical study), but also for different cultures (for an anthropological approach to criteria of evidence in various settings and cultures, see, e.g., Engelke, 2009).

6.1.5   Knowledge, culture, relativism and contextualism

As discussed in previous chapters, our approach to the cultural study of knowledge is relativist in the sense that knowledge is not defined in absolute terms, as in traditional epistemology, namely as 'justified true beliefs,' but in terms of the criteria or standard of an epistemic community. Since we have no practical or empirical methods to establish what is universal truth, and knowledge in everyday life only functions by the criteria of a community, this is obviously also the way we must approach knowledge in a study of cultural variations in the definition and uses of knowledge.

Thus, Shanafelt (2002) discusses relativism, truth and falsity in ethnographic fieldwork in terms of different *domains of truth* (such as psychological, sociological observer-independent or transcendent truths). Hanson (1979) in his discussion of relativism in anthropology proposes calling this kind of relativity *contextualism*, in order to avoid the assumed problem that relativism implies the existence of different worlds in which a proposition would be true according to different communities. His definition of contextualism is, however, similar to ours of relativism: one world, but different knowledge (and hence different discourses) about this world because of different knowledge standards in different communities. Contextualism for us applies to different (especially communicative) *situations* in the same epistemic community, for instance when scholars in the university or an article apply different epistemic criteria than when they talk about some phenomenon in other situations (see, Van Dijk, 2008a; see also DeRose, 2009; Preyer and Peter, 2005).

6.1.6   Power

The relativist principles of contemporary anthropology and ethnography not only recognize and analyze different local and global knowledges and knowledge criteria, but also the fundamental role of *power* in the discursive production and reproduction of knowledge. This is true not only for a sociology of knowledge and discourse, but especially also in a critical anthropology examining how Western knowledge and criteria are increasingly dominating and excluding other knowledge and methods, and pretending to be universal, in a way that may be characterized as epistemic globalization, part of a more general cultural globalization. Hence, in our study of the cultural dimensions of the discursive reproduction of knowledge, we need to be aware of the many ways power is exercised – and resisted – in such local and global processes. It is also in this way that such a study is crucial within more general Critical Discourse Studies.

6.1.7   From knowledge and culture in context to constraints on discourse

Epistemic differences between communities and cultures may have consequences for the various levels of the structures of text and talk. For instance, in an analysis of illocution, the basic speech act of an assertion presupposes that the Speaker knows something the Hearer does not know. This is most likely a universal condition of communication. However, there are no doubt cultural differences in the specific application of this general appropriateness condition of assertions: *who* may make such an assertion, *to whom*, *when* and *how*?

The same is true for asking questions or any other speech act that has specific epistemic conditions, as well as for other pragmatic, semantic or formal properties of discourse. For instance, there may be cultures in which younger people or members of lower classes first need permission to make assertions of new knowledge to the elderly, teachers or members of a higher class. And if they do so, they may need to engage in special politeness or mitigation moves to save face to the recipients – so that these are not indexed as being ignorant. In other words, *we need a full contextual analysis of the communicative situation of discourse*, of which epistemic differences are only one appropriateness condition among several others. Hence, cultural diversity of the relation between discourse and knowledge is not only 'textual' but also contextual. This thesis continues our earlier research project on the nature of context (Van Dijk, 2008a, 2009a).

We see that there are many aspects to the combined cultural study of discourse and knowledge. Hence, this chapter will focus on the properties and the role of discourse in the acquisition and transmission of culturally shared knowledge, on the one hand, and on the role of variable cultural knowledge in the appropriate accomplishment of local text and talk, on the other. Before we focus on these topics, however, we need to clarify our views on a number of crucial theoretical concepts used in this chapter, such as the relations between culture and cognition.

6.2   Culture and cognition

The ethnographic and comparative study of knowledge and belief in different societies is part of a larger field of investigation that examines the relations between culture and cognition more generally. After earlier behavioristic and beside contemporary interactionist approaches to culture, the cognitive revolution of the 1960s also reached anthropology (see, among many other books, Bloch, 1998; D'Andrade, 1995; Holland and Quinn, 1987; Marchand, 2010; Quinn, 2005; Shore, 1996; for a surprisingly early collection of papers on culture and cognition, see Spradley, 1972).

Using theories and methods of the cognitive sciences, such as those of cognitive psychology and cognitive linguistics, such a cognitive approach to culture focuses on the variable ways different communities conceptualize, represent and talk about themselves and their social and natural environment and thus make sense of their everyday life (for detail see the recent handbook edited by Kronenfeld *et al.*, 2011).

In this chapter, we hope to contribute to cognitive anthropology with our theoretical study of the cultural diversity of knowledge and beliefs and the way these control (and are controlled by) culturally variable discourse. That is, whereas most earlier approaches to knowledge and culture focused more generally on the role of language, we emphasize the role of culturally situated text and talk in the acquisition and uses of cultural knowledge (as also advocated by anthropologists such as Sherzer, 1987).

As we have emphasized in the previous chapters and other work, a cognitive approach to the cultural diversity of the discourse–knowledge interface does not imply a reduction to cognition. In the same way as we do not reduce discourse to mere conduct, and assume that discursive interaction and other practices also have fundamental cognitive properties, a sociocognitive approach to knowledge cannot be reduced to a study of individual minds or memory either. Basic human knowledge structures have phylogenetically evolved as a condition and consequence of interaction and social life so as for humans to survive under variable environmental conditions (see the references in Chapter 2). Knowledge on the one hand is socially construed, transmitted, shared and changed by communities, and on the other hand it is socially acquired and used by its individual members, especially also in socially situated discourse. But this does not mean that knowledge is not at the same time mental, namely distributed, normalized and coordinated across the minds of individual members, who learn and variably apply as well change such cultural knowledge. We only need to continuously remind ourselves that even when focusing on cognition, we should not forget that we are talking about human cognition, and about beliefs acquired and shared by members of sociocultural communities. Such 'sociality' of cognition also presupposes social interaction and social relationships, e.g., those of power (Thomas, 2011).

Hence, it is the main tenet of our sociocognitive approach that a reduction to either a cognitive analysis or an interactionist analysis is inadequate for the study of discourse and knowledge, especially also in the broader framework of an analysis of cultures. Both discourse and knowledge belong to the cultural sphere of societies, and both have cognitive as well as embodied, social, practical or interactive levels and dimensions. Let us therefore examine their dialectical relationships in such cultural contexts.

6.2.1   Culture as cognition and action

As is the case for such general notions as language, discourse, communication, interaction, mind or cognition, we shall not even try to define the admittedly vague notion of 'culture' (for detail, see Kuper, 1999). Indeed, as early as 1952, Kroeber and Kluckhohn (1952) listed 164 definitions of culture. Interesting for the discussion in this chapter is that, since the definition of Goodenough (1964), many anthropologists subscribe to a definition of culture in terms of knowledge, namely the knowledge needed to function adequately in a community (see, e.g., Bloch, 1998; Keesing, 1979). If culture is something that needs to be learned by children and newcomers, shared by its members and transmitted across generations, such a cognitive conception of culture is of course attractive.

The same is true for other mental representations usually associated with culture, such as religious beliefs, social and political attitudes, ideologies, norms and values (Geertz, 1973). Other aspects of human societies usually defined as cultural, such as practices, rituals or ceremonies cannot, as such, be transmitted, only the knowledge and skills to produce or participate in them. Cultural artifacts of any kind, from utensils or pottery to paintings or other works of art, can of course be transmitted, but are rather studied as the *products* of the cultural practices, knowledge, skills and values of a culture – and shall not be further examined here, although they obviously are *material expressions of knowledge* and hence may be studied in an approach to knowledge in terms of situated cognition (see Chapter 3).

As recalled above, a sociocognitive approach to culture emphasizes the fundamental cognitive nature of culture, but does not *reduce* culture to cognition. In the same way as a language, as a crucial aspect of culture, is not only linguistic or discursive competence, but also performance, culture, too, has both aspects, namely shared knowledge and other beliefs on the one hand, and cultural *practices*, on the other (Bourdieu, 1977; Lave, 1988; see the review about the turn to the study of practice in anthropology by Ortner, 1984). In other words, culture is also defined by its actual manifestation or uses by concrete members in concrete social situations – as well as by its cultural products, such as artifacts, art, text and talk. It is this expression or enactment of culture that is experienced in everyday life, and is how culture can be learned and applied by individual members in the first place.

On the other hand, the inclusion of practices in a theory of culture does not mean either that we share theoretical approaches that *reduce* knowledge or culture to practices or interaction, as do many 'interactionist' schools of thought today, many of whose arguments about observability remind us of those of behaviorism many decades earlier. Human conduct always needs embodied but brain-mind controlled knowledge or skills, and can only be intended, engaged in and understood if associated with mental representations of some kind. In other words, actions or practices are to be defined as complex units of socially situated conduct and mental representations such as mental models, featuring individual or shared intentions, plans and goals, which are in turn based on general knowledge or other beliefs. Contemporary studies in the anthropology of knowledge propose integrated accounts of mind, body and environment (e.g., Marchand, 2010; see also the comments on the 'embodied knowledge' studies in that book by Cohen, 2010).

In other words, and by way of a first example from the relevant ethnographic literature, to define knowledge only in terms of 'situated practice,' as do Lauer and Aswani (2009) in their study of fishers' knowledge in the Western Solomon Islands, is to collapse the fundamental distinction between thought and action. In order to be able to fish and navigate, these fishers first need to acquire knowledge about fish, fishing, the sea, islands, directions, etc., as well as various skills or abilities (knowing how to fish, navigate). Not all of this knowledge may be explicit, let alone expressed in discourse. But it does not collapse with the practice of fishing or navigating itself, because such knowledge (e.g., about the geography) can and must also be used in other situations. Indeed, the fishers themselves showed this when they were able to *recognize* the geography of their environment on maps made by the researchers. In other words, and in quite plain terms, we need to repeat again, that knowledge as well as skills are not 'in' the practices – defined as conduct – but in the heads of these fishers. Obviously, this does not mean that we should not study these practices in detail – beginning with discourse – in order to study the knowledge presupposed by them.

The joint cognition–action approach to culture also implies that the distinction between cultural anthropology and social anthropology is artificial, as is the case for many disciplinary boundaries. Cultural practices take place in cultural situations and define social institutions and social structure, in the same way as the latter enable and constrain cultural practices (Giddens, 1986). Note, though, that the agency–structure interface itself must again be cognitive: social structures can only influence action or social practice through their shared representation, as social knowledge, in the minds of cultural members. The same is true for the role of social or cultural context and its influence on text or talk (Van Dijk, 2008a, 2009a).

This sociocognitive definition of culture as both situated cognition and practice, is obviously essential for the study of the relations between cultural knowledge, on the one hand, and discourse as cultural practice, on the other. They both need each other: without knowledge members cannot engage in discourse or any other cultural practice, and without discourse cultural knowledge can only be acquired very basically and marginally (for definitions of culture and the role of language, see also Duranti, 1997).

6.2.2   Cultural knowledge and beliefs

It is still quite common in the anthropological literature to find that *Their* knowledge is called *belief*. Virtually all (of *Our*) books or articles that use the notion of 'cultural beliefs' are about non-Western countries, communities, immigrants or minorities, or about 'our' (Western) past – that is, about *Others*.

As is the case for the distinction between knowledge and ideology, discussed in the previous chapters and my earlier books (see, e.g., Van Dijk, 1998), we see that there are still studies of culture that assert or presuppose that *We* have *knowledge*, whereas *They* have *beliefs*. This is not (just) because such studies use a more generic term to denote both knowledge and belief, but usually because these studies assert or imply that they are dealing with 'mere beliefs,' superstition, religion, myths and other 'irrational' beliefs that are inconsistent with 'our' (Western) knowledge criteria (Lloyd, 1990; Loewen, 2006; see also Bala and Joseph, 2007; Needham, 1972).

Indeed, in earlier studies in anthropology, references to such beliefs were still framed in terms of the thought of 'primitive' people or 'savages' – as in *pensée sauvage* by Lévi-Strauss (1962) – as was still the case for such prominent scholars as Boas (1911), Durkheim (1915), Frazer (1910), Tichenor (1921), Bartlett (1932), Malinowski (1926), Mead (1937) and many others. Many of them, however, also criticized the biased, Eurocentric definition of such 'primitive' beliefs and knowledge as irrational, as did Goldenweiser (1915) a hundred years ago in a brief article in *American Anthropologist* in which he emphasized the detailed knowledge of indigenous people, especially with respect to their environment (see also, e.g., Baker, 1998; Bickham, 2005; Jahoda, 1998).

Typically, cultural beliefs are found to pertain to such fundamental and hence universal aspects of human society as life and death, illness and health, sexuality, reproduction and child rearing, social interaction (e.g., cooperation, power, etc.), social structure (e.g., kinship), natural phenomena and the environment. These beliefs are often described so as to account for how *Their* everyday practices are different from *Ours*, for instance in interaction with *Our* doctors, scholars, politicians, journalists or, indeed, anthropologists (among many books, see the debates and criticism in, e.g., Briggs, 1989; Copney, 1998; De Mente, 2009; Edson, 2009; Englander, 1990; Finucane, 1995; Havens and Ashida, 1994; Latour, 1993; Little and Smith, 1988).

No doubt in many of the traditional studies of cultural beliefs the use of the concept of 'belief' may be correct if the belief is 'false' by dominant, 'global' epistemic standards, e.g., as based on current (Western) medical or other scientific knowledge. However, if the beliefs of the epistemic communities studied are generally taken to be true by their members and presupposed in local public discourse as well as in other forms of interaction, a relative and internal (emic) epistemology should of course deal with them as knowledge, e.g., in terms of *local knowledge* (Geertz, 1983).

However, the term 'local,' as well as others, such as 'indigenous' or 'folk,' as a qualifier of knowledge may also still be read as presupposing a fundamental distinction between local and other (global?) knowledge, whereas 'indigenous' is only used to talk about Others' knowledge, and not Ours. In this chapter, we'll review some of the literature on some types of knowledge in some non-Western communities, but do so within the relativist perspective that locally justified, shared and presupposed beliefs are also simply to be called *knowledge*.

No doubt, many of these 'other' communities also make a distinction between true and false beliefs, between fact and superstition, between knowledge and religion, or between news, history and myth. Thus, a cognitive anthropology that takes an emic perspective seriously by definition should use the term 'knowledge' when dealing with generally accepted, uncontested, presupposed beliefs of a community. Typically, then, 'given' cultural knowledge in that case is often implicit and taken for granted outside of situations of learning or conflict, or when new knowledge must be transmitted, for instance in the news. Knowledge "goes without speaking" in discourse and other social practices of all or most members of a community, whereas mere beliefs tend to be shared only by specific groups and are typically defended and made explicit in argument (see also Agar, 2005; Bicker *et al.*, 2004; Carayannis and Alexander, 2005; Haarmann, 2007; Monroe, 2003; Pike, 1993). We shall come back to this study of 'local' knowledge(s) below.

6.2.3   *Personal models vs. cultural models*

In the previous chapters, we have adopted and extensively applied the psychological notion of 'mental model' defined as a subjective representation of events or situations in episodic memory (Gentner and Stevens, 1983; Johnson-Laird, 1983; Van Dijk and Kintsch, 1983). In anthropology, the notion of a model, usually in terms of a *cultural model*, is rather used as a system of socio-culturally shared beliefs or social representations, that is, as a system of belief or a form of knowledge as defined earlier (D'Andrade, 1995; Haarmann, 2007; Holland and Quinn, 1987; Quinn, 2005; Shore, 1996; see below for a critical assessment of 'folk models' or 'cultural models,' see Keesing, 1987; for a recent update, see, e.g., Quinn, 2011).

To avoid confusion with the notion of personal, situation model as used in this book, I shall avoid using the notion of 'cultural model' in this chapter. Instead, I refer to them as (culturally variable) social systems of knowledge and beliefs, or as social representations about specific cultural domains (e.g., education or agriculture) or practices (such as teaching or sowing). This distinction is crucial if we want to account for the ways individual members of a culture not only use their general cultural knowledge and beliefs ('cultural models'), but contextually and subjectively may do so in unique ways depending on current personal settings, goals, identities and beliefs – and thus at the same time may initiate cultural change. This theoretical account of the relation between socially shared culture and its personal 'uses' makes explicit our position in the well-known anthropological debate about the relations between culture and its individual members (Benedict, 1935; Dumont, 1986; Malinowski, 1939; Morris, 1991; Triandis, 1995).

Methodologically, this implies that interviews with or observation of the conduct of members of other cultures do not provide direct access to their shared cultural knowledge, but only to individual usages or applications of such knowledge. Repeated observation, comparison, abstraction, decontextualization and generalization from personal intentions, interpretations or conduct may be necessary to arrive at the shared 'models' of a culture. In fact, Needham (1972) more generally warned against making inferences about people's belief from their utterances (see also the chapters in Moore and Sanders, 2006). Indeed, in our theoretical terms, this means that discourse is not only controlled by underlying situation models, but also by context models that in many way may transform underlying knowledge and beliefs so as to be more appropriate or efficient in the communicative situation, for instance because of politeness constraints (Van Dijk, 2008a, 2009a).

Moreover, although basic or base line knowledge may be shared by all competent members of a culture, there are significant differences not only between lay members and experts, but also among lay members themselves, e.g., as a consequence of personally or contextually variable experiences, hobbies or interests (see below). These differences especially have also been studied in psychology and Artificial Intelligence (AI), for instance in the study of expert systems.

Variable personal 'uses' or 'performances' of cultural systems by their members also allow for different types of deviation (Bucholtz, 1994; Denzin, 2003; Fine and Speer, 1992; Wirth, 2002). When shared by others, such breaches also explain the change and dynamics of cultural systems, and hence the ways communities may adapt to changing social, economic or environmental constraints and the experiences of their members. In other words, cultures are not always homogeneous and stable – even when most fundamental changes are typically very slow. It is this theoretical framework – linking shared sociocultural knowledge with members' models and members' discourse and interaction – that will also be adopted in our discussion in this chapter.

The notion of individual mental model as it is used here, should also not be confused with what are called personal epistemologies, especially in education, that is, personal opinions about the nature, standards or other properties of knowledge, usually collected by means of questionnaires (Hofer and Pintrich, 2002). This area of research has also led to cross-cultural studies of personal epistemologies, especially among student populations across the world (Khine, 2008), but is generally unrelated to the anthropology of knowledge we are discussing here.

Some of the comments made above on cultural models are also formulated in the detailed critical assessment by Keesing (1987) about the papers in the edited book by Holland and Quinn (1987) and on the notion of 'cultural models' (earlier called 'folk models' by the editors). One of the first points of his assessment is that the use of notions such as 'cultural models' or 'codes' suggests idealized rules shared by all members engaging as ideal speakers in appropriate talk and other interaction, and tends to neglect what speakers really do and say, that is, variation, deviation, negotiation, etc. Also, he says, a difference is often observed between 'folk' and 'expert' knowledge, a distinction that is problematic when representing a folk model of society. Keesing rightly asks exactly how cultural models are being defined, how they can be distinguished from other knowledge and how (and whether) they vary among cultures. He emphasizes the role of a social theory of knowledge, usually ignored in studies of cultural models, and proposes to distinguish between shared cultural models (I) and the personal (partial, alternative) versions of such models (II) invoked in everyday perception and interaction (Holland and Quinn, 1987 p. 377). Indeed, it is barely known exactly how members *use* folk models and account for the atypical, the marginal or the fuzzy (p. 380). It is also at this point where our distinction between socially shared knowledge systems and personal mental models of specific events is relevant – a distinction not made in theories of cultural models.

6.3   Sociocultural communities

In the previous chapter we adopted the concept of 'community' as the social basis of shared knowledge and belief. This notion already accounts for (sub) cultural differences within societies, as is the case for the different experiences and epistemic practices of scholars and journalists as well as the other, non-professional, members of society, e.g., between women and men, young and old, rich or poor.

Unlike the notion of a *social group* used to define ideologies (Van Dijk, 1998), the notion of *community* is fundamentally cultural. As we have seen before, an entire society/culture may have general, socioculturally shared knowledge (e.g., about immigration), whereas groups may be defined by their ideologies, ideological attitudes, goals and interests (e.g., prejudices about immigrants). Obviously, ideologies may vary culturally, and in that sense they are also part of culture (Asad, 1979; Geertz, 1973: Ch. 8), but as soon as ideologies are accepted and taken for granted as 'true' in a community, they function as knowledge within that community.

In sociology, the distinction between society (*Gesellschaft*) and community (*Gemeinschaft*) has been well known since Tönnies (1957/1887). In cultural anthropology, the distinction between societies and communities is often blurred, not only because ethnography is usually limited to the study of relatively small collectivities of people, but also because such study focuses on the cultural aspects of societies, such as a shared language, beliefs and feelings of identity, thereby defining them as communities. This is also why we speak of epistemic communities as collectivities of people that share knowledge.

Often small cultural communities are also speech communities (Gumperz, 1962; Morgan, 2004; Romaine, 1982). However, national communities may have different linguistic communities, as is the case in Spain, Switzerland or India, whereas linguistic communities may comprise various national communities, as is the case for English, French, German and Spanish.

As we have seen for the definition of culture above, cultural communities are not only defined by shared beliefs, knowledge or language, but also by 'ways of doing things,' that is, by their characteristic *practices* (see, among many references, e.g., Bourdieu, 1977; Lauer and Aswani, 2009; Lave, 1988; Martin, 1995). Especially relevant for us in this chapter is that, besides rituals and other habitual activities and encounters, it is especially 'ways of speaking,' that is discourse, that characterizes these practices – as typically studied in the ethnography of speaking (Gumperz and Hymes, 1972; Hymes, 1962, 1974; Saville-Troike, 1982).

We have also emphasized above that the study of cultural practices should not be reduced to practices defined as observable conduct. Against behaviorist or interactionist traditions in anthropology, Geertz (1973), and interpretive anthropology more generally, emphasized the fundamental role of the *meaning* attributed to conduct or other symbolic objects or activities. Hence cultural members themselves, as well as outsiders, need to engage in various kinds of *interpretation* in order to understand these practices (see also Marcus and Fischer, 1986). Since these notions of meaning and interpretation are ambiguous and vague, in our framework we define semantic interpretation in terms of mental situation models and pragmatic interpretation in terms of context models. Such (personal) models are in turn based on the shared knowledge and other beliefs of the community. As we saw in Chapter 4, in social psychology, such an approach to shared knowledge is formulated in terms of the social representations of a community (see, e.g., Jovchelovitch, 2007).

Note, though, that for Geertz (1973) and many other anthropologists, especially those of a traditional behaviorist bent, as well as many contemporary scholars in the study of conversation and interaction, such meanings are not to be found "in the head" of cultural members, with the argument that meanings are 'public' and 'social.' We have argued before, however, that it is an empiricist fallacy to reduce the public or social nature of meaning or interpretation to observable, non-mental properties of action or discourse. Cultural meanings or beliefs are *both* cognitive *and* social if they are represented in the minds of cultural members, as well as shared, that is distributed over the minds of these members – and if these members also know that other members share these beliefs (for discussion of Geertz's anti-cognitivist position, see, e.g., Shore, 1996: 50–52; Strauss and Quinn, 1997: Ch. 2; for a general discussion on culture and cognition, see also Ross and Medin, 2011).

In sum, we define cultural communities as collectivities of people who share integrated systems of social representations (knowledge, beliefs, norms, values, etc.) and systems of social practices (interactions, discourse, rituals, etc.). These are 'dialectically' related in the sense that the social representations control social practices, and social practices give rise to the formation, change, reproduction or transmission of social representations, especially through discourse and interaction more generally.

Many contemporary studies in cognitive anthropology emphasize that the notion of 'sharing' a culture, and hence sharing knowledge, is not without problems (Hazlehurst, 2011). As we shall also see below, there are not only significant differences, in any culture, between experts and lay members, but also many individual differences in any cultural community (Atran *et al.*, 2005; Ross and Medin, 2011).

Recall that in this book as well as in this chapter, we account for individual differences of knowledge in terms of mental models construing variable personal experiences depending on context (including personal autobiography). Despite this individual variation, there necessarily *needs* to be a minimum of *shared basic knowledge*, not only of language, discourse and communication, but also of the natural and social world. Without such knowledge, mutual understanding and social interaction would be impossible, even when such understanding may be partial and interaction sometimes problematic. Yet, for all practical purposes, most understanding and interaction is relatively successful and hence requires shared knowledge and abilities. It is with this shared knowledge as a fundamental cognitive resource that members are able to deal with variable contexts and problems, e.g., by adapting shared knowledge and rules to new situations, and hence (slowly) changing cultural knowledge itself. Hence, this *dynamic conception* of sharing does not preclude 'performance,' that is, individual uses, applications and variation, nor changes at the level of the community. It is an empirical question how much and what kind of knowledge is thus shared by what part of the community.

This conception of a cultural community is a macro-concept in the sense that, at the microlevel of individual members of a culture, we additionally need to account for their variable and situated personal discourse and other practices. We do this in terms of mental models, construed on the one hand on the basis of a unique personal history of experiences, personal knowledge, personal opinions as well as emotion and motivation, and on the other hand by the instantiation of socioculturally shared knowledge and beliefs.

6.4   Local knowledge(s)

For decades, anthropology has been specifically interested in the study of what is variously called 'cultural,' 'local,' 'indigenous' or 'folk' beliefs or knowledge(s) (Douglas, 1973; Geertz, 1983). As indicated above, we shall simply call beliefs (local) *knowledge* if they are generally shared, accepted, taken for granted and presupposed in the discourse and other social practices of a community. This usage is now common in many studies on knowledge in non-Western societies (among many books, see, e.g., Brøgger, 1986; Fardon, 1985, 1995; Harris, 2007; Lindström, 1990). Many of these studies of local knowledge focus on specialized knowledge of the natural environment, for instance within the framework of various forms of ethnoscience: ethnobiology, ethnobotany, etc. (Ellen, 2011; Kapoor and Shizha, 2010; Nazarea, 1999; see further references below). Indeed, many early cognitive studies of cultural knowledge were interested in the ethno-semantics or lexicography of natural taxonomies (see, e.g., Conklin, 1962; Michalove *et al.*, 1998; Sturtevant, 1964; VanPool and VanPool, 2009).

There has been extensive debate about the various terms used to describe the cultural diversity and specificity of knowledge (see, e.g., Barnard, 2006; Kuper, 2003; Lauer and Aswani, 2009; Pottier *et al.*, 2003; Sillitoe, 2007, 2010). Thus, Sillitoe makes the following comment with respect to the often contested term of 'indigenous knowledge' (IK):

[W]e find something akin to IK everywhere, whether in the New Guinea Highlands, the floodplains of Bangladesh, or the Durham dales of England. It is equivalent to assuming that all humans have subsistence regimes, technology, language, that they manoeuvre for power, acknowledge kinship relations, entertain supernatural ideas, and so on – namely the assumption of certain universal attributes, which also long underpinned any ethnographic inquiry. (Sillitoe, 2010: 13)

But the same author stresses that since the concept of IK itself, as well as notions such as 'economy' or 'kinship,' may be culturally variable, we should not only focus on the obvious varieties of the 'contents' of such knowledge, but what people call or use as 'knowledge' in the first place, that is, what constitutes, authorizes or validates their beliefs as knowledge. He stresses that such a study should not be limited – as is often the case – to the lexicon or grammar, but especially also be studied in "coherent utterances" (Sillitoe, 2010: 13, 25) – that is, in discourse, as we shall examine in more detail below. He does so for Wola speakers in the Southern Highlands of New Guinea, for whom, however, the 'mind' and its functions are not in the brain but in the chest. Whereas in

epistemology the basic epistemic criterion may be that of reliability (of observation, sources or inference), Sillitoe stresses the role of *trust* in statements as
a criterion of evidentiality. Such trust may be based on whether or not speakers, recipients or others have actually witnessed specific events or not, whether
knowledge is based on hearsay, inferred and so on. These epistemic criteria of
trust are similar to those of reliability or credibility in Western cultures e.g., in
evidence for trials or media reports, but in Wola they are even grammaticalized
in different verb forms.

6.4.1   Culture, knowledge and power

Uses of the term 'local knowledge' are known to clash with that of Western
(e.g., medical or development) professionals – as well as many epistemologists – who define knowledge only in terms of facts as established by (usually
Western or Northern) science, and who see local knowledge about health or the
environment as (mere) 'cultural beliefs' – which may even be seen to hamper
social or economic development. These studies and this debate have especially
focused on the management of the environment and healthcare (see the discussion in Apffel-Marglin and Marglin, 1996; Bala and Joseph, 2007; Brokensha
et al., 1980; Cunningham and Andrews, 1997; Good, 1994; Lauer and Aswani,
2009; Lindenbaum and Lock, 1993; Nygren, 1999; Pelto and Pelto, 1997).

The debate on the assumed superiority of Western knowledge is as old as
anthropology itself. Malinowski (1922) warned against preconceived ideas
about "savage" cultures, and emphasized the complexity of their organization,
kinship relations and knowledge. Boas (1911/1938), in his study of the mind
of what he called "primitive" man, argued against racist assumptions, which
he summarized as follows:

[W]e like to support our emotional attitude toward the so-called inferior races by reasoning. The superiority of our inventions, the extent of our scientific knowledge, the complexity of our social institutions, our attempts to promote the welfare of all members
of the social body, create the impression that we, the civilized people, have advanced
far beyond the stages on which other groups linger, and the assumption has arisen of
an innate superiority of the European nations and of their descendants. The basis of
our reasoning is obvious: the higher a civilization, the higher must be the aptitude for
civilization; and as aptitude presumably depends upon the perfection of the mechanism
of body and mind, we infer that the White race represents the highest type. The tacit
assumption is made that achievement depends solely, or at least primarily, upon innate
racial ability. Since the intellectual development of the White race is the highest, it is
assumed that its intellectuality is supreme and that its mind has the most subtle organization. (Boas, 1911/1938: 4–5)

Even today, at a more abstract sociopolitical level of analysis, a relativist *cultural* approach to the study of communities has been analyzed as opposed to
a universalist *liberal* approach advocating international norms and values for

which local knowledge may be seen as forms of ignorance or retardation (see, e.g., the study of the official policies with respect to Native Americans in the USA by Boggs, 2002; see also Marcus and Fischer, 1986: 32).

On the other hand, studies of traditional ecological knowledge (TEK) or local environmental knowledge (LEK) are increasingly emphasizing the relevance of such knowledge for sustainable management of local resources. Besides the increasing recognition of the relevance of local knowledge, especially of the environment, there are also voices that warn against an uncritical, romantic celebration of TEK without investigating its efficiency (for debate, see, e.g., Berkes, 1999; Dyer and McGoodwin, 1994; Ellen *et al.*, 2000; Hames, 2007; Williams and Baines, 1993).

Palmer and Wadley (2007) warn that much of this assumed local knowledge has been obtained in ethnographical research based on talk (interviews, stories, etc.), and that local environmental talk (LET) should not be confused with LEK. Indeed, in their study they found that residents in small fishing villages in Newfoundland appear to be quite skeptical about what other local residents say about the environment (below we come back to the study of knowledge and discourse).

This also suggests that the definition of knowledge as justified *shared* belief of a community always needs to be carefully tested, and obviously cannot be proven on the basis of interviews with a few informants. Hence, there are methodological studies that insist on an analysis of consensus (Romney *et al.*, 1986). Thus, Ayantunde *et al.* (2008), in a study of indigenous botanical knowledge in Niger, found that such knowledge varies as a function of age, gender, ethnicity, profession or religious beliefs. Today, more generally, cultural studies of knowledge emphasize intracultural variation, dynamic change or performance as opposed or complementary to more abstract, structuralist approaches that presuppose homogeneity of knowledge and culture.

6.4.2   Research on local knowledges

The knowledge systems of non-Western societies are often described in ethnographic studies of specific local practices, such as fishing or healthcare. These practices and their knowledge are methodologically assessed by participant observation, interviews, informal conversations and so on – and often based on the performance and formulation of local experts – whose identification is, of course, an important methodological problem (Davis and Wagner, 2003; see also Coffe and Geys, 2006).

Many studies have shown that in everyday action and decision making in many cultures, local knowledge and its concomitant practices are combined with cosmopolitan or universal ('Western') knowledge and practices, for instance in healthcare. Thus, on the one hand, obvious universal practices such as breastfeeding may have different meanings in different cultures, as Wright *et al.* (1993) show for traditional Navajo beliefs in the USA about which body fluids are considered sacred (blood, semen, milk), dangerous (menstrual blood) or mere by-products (sweat, tears and urine). On the other hand, these authors also found that among younger people, some core beliefs (e.g., about matrilineality) are usually combined with Anglo beliefs about the body or breastfeeding.

Similarly, Dahlberg and Trygger (2009) showed that lay knowledge of medicinal plants in rural South Africa is applied in the treatment of several minor illnesses, but that at the same time people have confidence in other knowledge systems by using 'Western' healthcare in local clinics for the treatment of more serious diseases.

In a study of the transmission of knowledge of South African traditional healers (*sangomas*), Thornton (2009) showed that such knowledge may integrate insights and experiences from several cultures (e.g., featuring divination and the control of ancestral spirits), and that *sangomas* see their craft as a profession and not a religion, and their practice as a result of rigorous training.

In a study of cultural beliefs about the risk factors of cervical cancer among Latinas in the USA, Chávez *et al.* (2001) examined how actual conduct, such as the use of Pap tests, depends on traditional beliefs, norms and values (such as those about sexual intercourse with various partners) and not only on socioeconomic conditions. They found that if their beliefs were closer to those of Anglo women, Latinas were more likely to have had a Pap test in the last two years – as is the case for Latinas who are older, speak more English, have a better education or who are married (see below for examples).

Several studies have shown that local knowledge and the practices based on it are remarkably consistent with the results of advanced technological observation techniques, such as geographic information systems, among others, as Lauer and Aswani (2009) showed for fishers in the Western Solomon Island and Robbins (2003) for herders and farmers in Rajastan, India.

Similarly, in a study of indigenous knowledge about the taxonomy and ecology of rock kangaroos in Australia, Telfer and Garde (2006) showed that such knowledge both complements and extends the (little) 'scientific' knowledge of such kangaroos. Such findings are used as a further argument against the polarization between scientific (or Western) and lay (or non-Western) knowledge, also criticized in the sociology of knowledge (Latour, 1987). Indeed, we see that many of the ethnographic studies show that local experts usually combine local knowledge with non-local knowledge (see also Johnson, 2012).

6.4.3   *Critical approaches to cultural knowledge*

In critical anthropology and area studies (e.g., in Latin American Studies) it is emphasized that all knowledge is local and hybrid, and that the binary opposition established between Western and non-Western knowledge systems is itself an ideological construct (Nygren, 1999). Moreover, as we have seen above, it is emphasized that local knowledge is also not homogeneous, and varies with gender, age, class or expertise.

Following earlier critical approaches in anthropology (e.g., Asad, 1973; Hymes, 1972), various 'postcolonial' approaches, especially in the study of literature, criticize the 'coloniality' of much current Western science and epistemology, and emphasize the need for autonomous approaches to the study of 'subaltern' knowledge (see, e.g., Escobar, 1997, 2007; Grosfoguel, 2007; Mignolo, 1999). Similar critical studies have highlighted the role of women in the production of cultural knowledge (Di Leonardo, 1991; Engelstad and Gerrard, 2005).

Among other critical contributions in the field of discourse and culture, we should finally also mention recent work on what is called Critical Intercultural Communication Studies (CICS) (Nakayama and Halualani, 2010). Scholars in this field, especially in the USA (the Nakayama and Halualani handbook has contributions from several ethnic groups, but only scholars working in the USA!), first of all are critical of traditional (uncritical) intercultural communication studies which ignored questions of power, domination and (neo)colonialism. They define culture primarily as ideological struggle and communication as "processes and practices of articulation" (Halualani and Nakayama, 2010: 6–7). The handbook features many position papers (some of which comment on earlier work of the authors) and many opinions on CICS, but no detailed empirical studies that show how CICS is done in practice. The notion of 'discourse' comes up, but there is no systematic discourse analysis of intercultural communication. Unlike other studies in culture and communication, the detailed index does feature several entries referring to knowledge, but apart from brief mentions, there is no detailed discussion of knowledge in any of the articles.

Summarizing a vast number of studies on knowledge and its postulated variation across cultures, many, if not most, authors conclude that the similarities between knowledge systems across the world are more pronounced than their differences.

6.5   The structures of (local) knowledge

Against this more general background of the history and the current state of affairs of the study of (local) knowledge in anthropology, we now need to focus on the analysis of its *structures*. Perhaps trivially, the *contents* of local knowledge are adapted to the local social and natural environment. Trivially, Wall Street brokers are ignorant about how to grow rice or about how to combat terrorism, among a vast amount of other types of local knowledges. And navigating with a small boat in the Pacific requires other (and more complex) geographical and embodied practical knowledge than riding a bicycle in Amsterdam.

It is therefore interesting to inquire into the fundamental organizational principles of different knowledge systems. No doubt, some of these are universal and defined by the basic structures of the human mind-brain as it has been adapted to the environment during its evolution. For instance, in all cultures people make a systematic difference between plants and animals. Even 'folk' taxonomies of living things are remarkably close to that of the scientific system that goes back to Linnaeus (which was also a folk taxonomy)(see, e.g., Atran, 1993, 1998; Berlin, 1992; VanPool and VanPool, 2009).

Unlike 'naturalist' theories such as those of Atran (1993, 1996, 1998), which emphasize the role of evolution and the cross-cultural unity of the human mind, Carey (1996) argues that 'folkbiology' is not innate, but an example of what she calls a *framework theory*, which children acquire in development around the age of six or seven, featuring a basic ontology (plants, animals) and phenomena (disease, reproduction, growth, death, etc.). Whereas these debates between naturalism or universalism and cultural relativism focus on the *contents* of knowledge, such as (innate or learned) knowledge about the natural environment, we of course also need to inquire into the possibility of *structural* differences between the knowledge systems of different cultures.

For several decades, cognitive approaches in anthropology have paid attention to the structures of knowledge and beliefs in various cultures. Starting with detailed studies of componential analysis of kinship as a major dimension of social structure in many societies (see, e.g., Lounsbury, 1969), and after ethnosemantic studies of local taxonomies of plants and animals (Berlin, 1992), many later studies tend to follow developments in cognitive psychology, and focus on categorization, prototypes, schemas and (cultural) models as representations of local knowledge (for detail see, e.g., D'Andrade, 1995; Holland and Quinn, 1987; Marchand, 2010; Quinn, 2005; Shore, 1996; Spradley, 1972).

Unfortunately, contemporary applications of notions such as 'schema' or 'model' in anthropology do not always provide us with detailed insights into the structures of cultural knowledge. They do go beyond mere taxonomies and deal with complex social phenomena, such as baseball as a national sport in the USA, aboriginal Dreamtime learning in Australia (Shore, 1996) or with marriage in the USA (Quinn, 1987). The analyses of these cultural models are qualitative, 'thick' descriptions of local ideas and practices, and hence offer more insight into cultural 'contents' than into culturally specific or variable *structures or organization* (see also Quinn, 2005; Strauss and Quinn, 1997). Quinn (2011) emphasizes the more specific methodological role of connectionist psychology, but such a conceptual paradigm has so far hardly been used to describe or explain the specifics of local knowledges.

Shore (1996) introduces a vast typology of different types of cultural models and distinguishes between personal and conventional models, and between cultural models and foundational schemas, but also between (mental) models and 'instituted' models – as systems of practice. He also includes several layers of linguistic models, including grammatical models and lexical models (such as taxonomies), on the one hand, and communication models such as persuasion on the other hand. With such a vast extension of the notion of model, however, it loses its specificity as a theoretical account of (mental) knowledge and collapses with such general notions as 'structure' or 'system.' Indeed, in the actual ethnography of various cultural phenomena, there is very little explicit description of cultural model structures – such as basic categories, relationships, rules. Cultural events may be described in detail, e.g., in lists, as is the case for Wawilak narrative and ceremonies in Australia, but hardly in terms of underlying abstract model structures.

Many of the theoretical concepts borrowed from cognitive psychology have been empirically tested only in the laboratory. Ethnography, as a qualitative method based on participant observation, interviews and the study of narrative, myths and everyday conversations, among other discourses, seldom engages in controlled experiments, however. Hence ethnographic fieldwork only indirectly yields access to the structures of local knowledge, usually through an (informal) analysis of local discourse and participant observation. Moreover, as was the case for the analysis of kinship terms and later for the ethno-semantic analysis of taxonomies and more generally the interest in ethnosciences, much ethnographic study is limited to isolated words and terms.

Hence, the study of (local) knowledge in cultural anthropology was usually combined with a study of the lexicon, and not a systematic analysis of discourse structures, as was also emphasized by Sherzer (1977, 1987). As we have seen above, and will further explore below, there is a long and rich tradition of discourse analysis in anthropology, but such studies generally do not focus on epistemic structures, whereas the studies of local knowledge hardly engage in discourse analysis, or are limited to the study of narrative (see below).

6.5.1   Keesing's study of Kwaio (Malaita, Solomon Islands)

Before further exploring the general question of the possible cultural variation of knowledge structures, let us briefly consider a concrete example from the literature, namely Keesing's classical study of the Kwaio of Malaita, Solomon Islands (Keesing, 1979, 1992). We have chosen this example because for Keesing the study of culture is fundamentally the study of knowledge and not a study of behavior or of a way of life. (Keesing, 1979: 15). This study is also especially interesting because the Kwaio knowledge system is expressed in different verb forms. Even in his 1979 article, Keesing argues against superficial interpretation of the Sapir–Whorf hypothesis, which postulates that our knowledge of the world depends on our linguistic knowledge.

In the theoretical introduction of his paper, Keesing holds that the differences between languages or cultures have often been exaggerated. He argues, though, that a more systematic and explicit study of knowledge may in turn explain specific aspects of language. Thus, a study of the lexical semantics of Kwaio shows that meanings crucially depend on symbolic structures (Keesing, 1979: 15). He does not believe, on the other hand, that the organization of the lexicon reveals the structure of the perceptual and conceptual world – although he thinks it trivial that the lexicon shows what (e.g., of the environment) is salient in a culture. Knowledge for him is located in the mind-brain of individuals, but broadly shared, transmitted within communities and hence learnable, although there are individual differences of such cultural knowledge (p. 16).

Keesing (1979) begins to show that some Kwaio verbs have a physical and a non-physical sense, as is also the case for many general metaphors in English (such as the verb *to pay* in the expression *to pay attention*, etc.). Thus in Kwaio, the verb *lafu-a* on the one hand means 'to lift (up),' and on the other hand 'to raise (or: give up) for sacrifice.' So, the second, non-concrete, meanings of many verbs refer to ritual, magic, spirits or ancestors. In this way, the Kwaio language reflects the belief that spirits of ancestors of one's own kin group control all events of everyday life – as is the case for the influence of God in the belief system of fundamentalist Christians, for instance in the USA.

Similarly, human efforts need the special spiritual potency (*mana*) of ancestors, which, however, requires ritual observances and offerings. It is especially important in Kwaio culture to respect the boundaries between the sacred, the mundane and the polluted – such that especially (the bodies of) women are seen to be polluted and polluting (e.g., with menstrual blood). Breaches of boundaries, e.g., by pollution, may lead to sickness, an explanation that is familiar in Western (and other) knowledge systems about the environment – although differences exist in what in each culture is seen as polluted.

It is this cosmology that is presupposed in the lexicon of Kwaio. In order to be able to go beyond a simple lexical or semantic analysis, Keesing thus devises more abstract categories and rules of the epistemic universe of Kwaio – although he also speaks of Kwaio *religion* (p. 23). In this belief system, a difference exists between different realms, e.g., between the *phenomenal* and the *noumenal*, that is between the physical, material world of everyday perception and experiences, on the one hand, and the world of invisible spirits and powers – such as those of the ancestors, on the other. Again, this distinction is also quite familiar from Christian conceptualizations (God, Holy Spirit, Heaven, etc.). All animate creatures have a 'shade' (*nununa*) in the noumenal realm – which is not subject to the physical-causal limitations of the phenomenal world. Secondly, as mentioned above, a distinction is made between the *sacred* (*abu*), *ordinary* (*mola*) and the *polluted* (*sua*). Thus, the sacred is associated with the ancestors, death, upward movements, shrines or men's houses, whereas the polluted with downwards movement or menstrual huts. Everyday life is usually 'ordinary.' Sacred states are usually closed and need to be 'opened up.' Thirdly, Kwaio distinguishes between magical and non-magical action.

Such symbolism is reminiscent of the epistemic and semantic structures of metaphors in English and other languages (among many other references, see Lakoff and Johnson, 1980). Thus, UP is not only morally or qualitatively good, but also spiritually, as is 'being in or going to heaven' (above), and also in the verb *to uplift* – whereas DOWN is first of all ordinary (as 'in down to earth') but especially also negative, as in 'going down,' the 'lower class' or 'the underworld.'

These and other basic distinctions and polarizations in the Kwaio belief system may be used in the metalanguage of the (lexical) semantics of Kwaio. Note, though, that this knowledge is not necessarily explicit and conscious, but – as is the case for much knowledge – merely tacitly presupposed.

A first theoretical question we need to address after this brief summary of some aspects of Kwaio cosmology and religion is whether, *and also in their own terms*, the beliefs in spirits and their influence are functioning as 'mere' beliefs, or as knowledge. Again, by our relativist definition and criteria of knowledge, if the beliefs are justified by local standards, generally shared and presupposed in discourse and interaction, then they are forms of knowledge, because they *function as knowledge*, and not as beliefs some people believe and other do not (or challenge).

Indeed, the same may be asked for a religion in many Western cultures: at the level of the whole culture, religious beliefs are just that, beliefs. However, within the religious cultures themselves, such beliefs may function as justified (revealed, etc.) knowledge – and be presupposed in the interpretation of the actions and events of everyday life, e.g., in the explanation of natural disasters.

It is not surprising that different cultural communities have different beliefs, and especially different religious beliefs. General binary oppositions, between the sacred and the profane, the ordinary and the magical, and metaphorical distinctions between UP and DOWN, are widespread, if not universal – and have been studied in anthropology and sociology for more than a century (among many other classical studies, see, e.g., Durkheim, 1915; Eliade, 1961; Geertz, 1973; Lévi-Strauss, 1958, 1962, 1974; Malinowski, 1954; Mauss, 1972; see also Greenwood, 2009; Stein and Stein, 2005).

Similarly, cosmology is not only about different realms and different categories of event and action but also about *explanation: why things happen*. Thus, cultures, but also communities within cultures (as is the case for Western cultures), may or may not distinguish between natural, biological or psychological causes or reasons of events or action. Such differences in their knowledge systems may control explanations of events. Note, though, that, as usual, epistemic issues may depend on local ontologies, as is the case for the presupposed existence of ancestors and their spirits in Kwaio cosmology.

We may provisionally conclude, and agree with Keesing, that although there are obvious epistemic, semantic and lexical differences between cultures (as well as their languages), the differences in the *system* of categories, taxonomies and social representations do not seem to be fundamental.

Indeed, the extant literature on local knowledge does not suggest that there are knowledge systems that are totally at variance with those of known Western cultures. Such a conclusion is consistent with the a priori position that because of the constraints of evolution and adaptation to the natural and social environment, as well as the conditions of human interaction and society, it is unlikely that humans in different cultures have radically different conceptions of the natural or social world. Given the constraints and affordances of nature, such differences are probably less marked in the representation of the natural environment (plants, animals, landscapes, etc.), more in the representation of social structures, given the possible difference of norms and values for human action and relationships, and most in religious or supernatural beliefs, which do not have to meet the constraints of the natural world – other than as postulated explanations of natural phenomena.

More generally, these assumptions characterize the classical and contemporary debate in anthropology about the assumed 'psychic unity' of humankind and the universality of mental structures (including linguistic universals), on the one hand, and the cultural diversity of communities and their beliefs, practices and languages, on the other (see, e.g., Shore, 1996: 15–41). There is no contradiction there but integration in complex systems of knowledge and other types of shared representations. The first studies of cognitive anthropology emphasize that whereas basic properties of perception and interaction may be universal and genetically preprogrammed, knowledge is socially construed, based on meanings and symbols that may be as variable as the language used to describe and experience them (Spradley, 1972).

6.6   Discourse, knowledge and culture

Against the background of the theory of the relations between knowledge and culture, in the rest of this chapter we need to address the question of how cultural variation in knowledge is related to similar variation and diversity of discourse.

Theory and empirical results in the cognitive psychology of discourse processing and AI tell us that all discourse presupposes vast amounts of knowledge. If this knowledge is culturally specific, the presuppositions based on it are also different. Thus, if Kwaio speak about 'the spirits of our ancestors' the use (in English) of the definite article *the* presupposes that such spirits exist for its speakers. Similarly, no doubt a local story about a local ritual will probably be fully understandable only by those participants who are able to form a mental model of such a ritual, for instance because they have personally experienced it.

In this sense, the relation between cultural knowledge or beliefs and discourse is straightforward: specific cultural knowledge is necessary to produce and fully understand the discourses of a community. Bartlett (1932), in his foundational study of the role of knowledge schemata in culture, showed that in order to understand an indigenous story of native North Americans ("The War of the Ghosts") one needs relevant indigenous knowledge. Without such knowledge, recipients of other cultures in their retelling typically transform the story so as to better fit their own cultural knowledge schemas.

Similarly, in a recent discourse analytical paper, Flowerdew and Leong (2010) showed that newspaper stories in Hong Kong presuppose knowledge about sociopolitical values and cultural identity, e.g., what it means to be a patriot, but that the epistemic strategies are flexibly adapted to the political context (pro-Beijing or pro-Western attitudes). These relationships between discourse, knowledge and culture already characterize the very acquisition of the language, which takes place at the same time as the acquisition of sociocultural knowledge (Ochs and Schieffelin, 2001).

What other culturally variable conditions define the relations between discourse and knowledge? For instance, if the justification criteria are different in different cultures, does this also mean that, for instance, moves of evidentiality are different (see, e.g., Nuckolls, 1993)? In the study by Keesing about Kwaio, summarized above, we have seen that specific knowledge structures may also affect the lexicon and the morphology, by assigning a 'literal' and a 'magical' metaphorical sense to specific verbs.

In the next chapter, we shall further examine these grammatical and other linguistic manifestations of asserted, recalled or presupposed knowledge in discourse and how different justification criteria may be at the basis of different evidentials and their expression in different languages.

In this chapter, we limit our discussion to specific contextual, pragmatic conditions of discourse related to knowledge and beliefs as these define the appropriateness of discourse in the cultural communicative situation. Since, as far as we know, there is hardly any literature on the cultural specificity and variation of epistemic conditions of discourse, a large part of our discussion needs to be theoretical, before giving some examples culled from existing cultural studies of discourse, and some data from our own earlier studies of discourse and racism (Van Dijk, 1984a, 1987, 1991, 1993).

6.6.1   Discourse as method

As is generally the case for the study of knowledge, we know about local knowledge only by inference from social practices, and especially from discourse. We routinely attribute knowledge to others because they are able to express this knowledge in text and talk, either explicitly or implicitly by presupposing knowledge already shared.

In everyday life, this empirical 'method' works just fine. In scholarly inquiry, and also in ethnography, we should be a bit more careful, of course, but again analyzing discourse is probably the most reliable and especially the most sensitive method of studying cultural knowledge and beliefs. Hence, the ample use of informal conversations, interviews, focus groups, diaries, life stories, gossip, rituals, formal meetings and sessions, think-aloud protocols or any other genre of text and talk, in ethnography (see, e.g., Chua *et al.*, 2008; Duranti, 1997, 2001b, 2004; Hanks, 1989; Moore and Sanders, 2006; Ochs and Capps, 1996).

Yet, there are well-known limitations of discourse as a source of knowledge about knowledge. First of all, and theoretically perhaps most important and yet often overlooked, discourse is not only produced on the basis of the general, shared sociocultural knowledge of an epistemic community, or personal as based on mental models of personal experience, that is, on semantic grounds, but is also subject to *pragmatic* constraints that make it appropriate in the communicative situation. This means that rules and strategies of interaction, such as those of politeness, may sometimes prevent the expression of what is known or, on the other hand, may stimulate the expression of what is not known. In fact, indigenous informants may be reluctant to divulge local knowledge, especially about sacred issues (see, e.g., Crick, 1982; Palmer and Wadley, 2007: 751).

Secondly, the contents and structures of discourse are not the same as those of underlying knowledge even if the pragmatic conditions are optimal for the formulation of knowledge. Such knowledge may be embedded as applied knowledge in the models of specific situations and events, and only part of such mental models are usually expressed and large parts presupposed – which requires special analysis of relevant inferences of discourse.

Thirdly, especially when knowledge pertains to earlier events, informants may have forgotten what we want to know or may have only partial knowledge about specific domains. Much knowledge is implicit or tacit: although it influences social practices, informants may not be able to formulate it, or may even be totally unaware of commonsense knowledge in the first place (for discussion on ethnographic interviews as a method, see, e.g., Agar and Hobbs, 1982; Hoffmann, 2007; Holstein and Gubrium, 1995; Paulson, 2011).

It is with these limitations, then, that we use text and talk as the most explicit means of accessing local knowledge, as is the case for interviews, accounts, descriptions, stories or myths, or the observation or active participation in everyday conversations, meetings, rituals or other forms of interaction – depending on the ethnographic context of inquiry. Below we examine how local knowledge has been obtained in various ethnographic studies and especially what kind of text or talk was engaged in and analyzed in such occasions.

6.6.2   Linguistic relativity and the discourse–cognition interface

It is beyond the scope of this chapter to review or even to summarize the complex debate, initiated by Boas, Sapir and Whorf, about the ways that language, and especially grammar, influence thought (see, e.g., Gumperz and Levinson, 1994; Lucy, 1992; Niemeier and Dirven, 1997) – usually referred to as the Sapir-Whorf hypothesis. In their *Annual Review* article for anthropologists about the topic, with the strange title (imposed by the editors) "Language and World View," Hill and Mannheim (1992) begin to emphasize that we should rather speak of an axiom, and not about a specific, testable hypothesis with dependent and independent variables. They also recall that the founding fathers of linguistic anthropology limit their observations about the dependency of thought on language to specific, highly habituated forms. So, they reformulate the basic axiom as follows:

In the narrower sense, however, a set of claims is being advanced that grammatical categories, to the extent that they are obligatory or habitual, and relatively inaccessible to the average speaker's consciousness, will form a privileged location for transmitting and reproducing cultural and social categories. (p. 387)

By way of example, they apply this principle in an analysis of English gendered pronouns, where unmarked *he* grammatically may be used to refer to both men and women, but its default interpretation is a reference to a man. In other words, a grammatical category, a specific 'masculine' pronoun, may bias a gendered interpretation of referents – and thus at the same time reproduces sociocultural structures of power: men, thus, are "the normative, unmarked category of a person" (p. 389). In this sense, thus, language appears to influence 'thought.'

Note, though, that a more complete analysis would need to mention that such biased interpretation of the English pronoun *he* only applies for its generic use. As a deictic or co-referential expression *he* cannot be used to refer to a specific woman, and hence is marked for reference to a (known) man only. The vast majority of uses of *he* are of this type, so that this 'habitual' use and interpretation also primes the interpretation of unmarked generic use as referring to a (non-specific) man. More generally, then, it hardly makes sense to study pronouns or any other grammatical category in isolation, instead of their actual use in text and context. We here find an important argument in favor of a more discursive approach to the study of linguistic relativity. Their final reference to the (meta)pragmatic work of Silverstein (1993) and the discourse-centered approach of Sherzer (1987) already suggests the necessity of such a broader framework.

One of the problems of the language–thought debate is that both terms are too general and too vague. First of all, the term *language* may refer to the language system or to actual language use. Secondly, it may traditionally refer to grammar, or even only the lexicon and syntax, or much more broadly to structures of text or talk – again, both generally, or in actual use in specific contexts. The same is true for *thought*, which may apply to mental processes (e.g., of interpretation) or to mental structures, and again more generally, e.g., to shared sociocultural knowledge or to specific contextual interpretations such as situation models.

Thus, it is likely that the pervasive sociocultural system of male domination, as it is also represented in the minds of its members, has influenced the development of the linguistic system, including its pronouns. Similarly, feminist challenges to male domination or traditional female roles, as expressed in the system of pronouns or the lexicon (*stewardess, nurse, fireman*, etc.) similarly have led linguistic adaptation. Indeed, it is easier to change a lexical convention than to change male domination in society – which also suggests that the language system and its uses appear to be the dependent variable of the relationship.

In sum, it appears that at the level of abstract linguistic and sociocultural knowledge, social structure influences language structure, and that given such language structures their uses may prime specific interpretations. However, interpretations in actual language use should be made explicit as situation models. These do not depend only on linguistic structure (and even less on grammar) but also on earlier personal experiences (old models) and general sociocultural knowledge of the epistemic community, as well as (e.g., gender) ideologies. This is why the use of generic *he* when referring to a man or a woman today is noted by many language users as pragmatically inappropriate and sexist.

For the discussion in this chapter, then, the issue of linguistic relativity is relevant especially when we deal with a much more focused relationship between specific discourse structures, on the one hand, and the structures of situation models and socially shared knowledge representations (scripts, etc.) on the other. Also, this relationship should be studied in both directions. Thus, structures of experience, as represented in mental models and as controlled by sociocultural knowledge and previous personal experiences, condition discourse structures at all levels, from semantic structures to their lexical and

morphosyntactic formulation. But they also follow the constraints of the grammar of the language and local rules of discourse (e.g., of conversation, storytelling or news reports) on the one hand, and of context models that control
options of variation on the other.

6.6.3   Discourse–cognition relationships

It is within such a paradigm that we need to evaluate earlier findings on the
relation between cognition and discourse. Thus, Slobin, (1990, 1991) in a
cross-cultural study shows that children speaking different languages encode
their experiences of the same pictures in a different way.

On the other hand, Chafe (1980), in the well-known "Pear Stories" experiments, using a brief film of a boy stealing some pears, asked children and
adults of different languages and cultures to retell the story of the film and
found remarkably few cultural differences. Californian subjects had more comments on film making, and people in other than English languages and cultures
more evaluative descriptions (about the stealing boy), but on the whole, the differences were more individual, or between oral (longer) and written (shorter)
storytelling. In general, the action sequence of the film was followed as well as
the usual narrative structure (which may of course partly be explained by the
near universal influence of Western movies and their canonical story structure).
Aksu-Koc (1996) applied the same method with Turkish subjects and found
that the structures of the retellings vary according to level of education and
more or less modern or traditional subcultures.

Among other questions, such results raise the question whether (i) the variation is only linguistic-discursive ('rhetorical' or 'narrative') or (ii) adults and
children in different cultures interpret the images or film in different situation
models, depending on (iii) different sociocultural knowledge about such scenes,
and finally depending on (iv) their pragmatic models of the communicative
(experimental) situation – each of which may influence the discourse structures.
A partial analysis of the experimental situation, and the cognitive structures and
conditions involved, will also give only partial insight into such complex depend-
encies. If the basic structures of experience, as reflected in model schema categories (Setting, Participants, etc.) are fundamental and partly even universal, and
grammar and some discourse structures more culturally variable and partly even
arbitrary, then we may indeed expect different discourse structures for the same
or similar experiences in different cultures with different languages. Indeed, also
within the same language, culture and epistemic community the same experience
(mental model) may variably be discursively expressed in many different ways,
depending on the current context model of the speaker.

Conversely, variable discourse structures in a given communicative situation
(e.g., newspaper reading) may express but also prime specific interpretations

as represented in mental models. Several studies in Critical Discourse Analysis (CDA) have shown that the use of passive verbs and nominalizations in English news reports (e.g., about riots) may de-emphasize the active negative role of ingroup members or institutions (such as the police)(Van Dijk, 1991). Such uses are controlled by biased mental models that in turn are controlled by underlying ideologies that tend to emphasize negative properties of outgroups, and de-emphasize negative properties of ingroups (Van Dijk, 1998).

In sum, discursive variation is controlled (and explained) by ideological group interests or by different pragmatic context models in the same culture. On the other hand, cultural diversity of discourse structures may be 'superficially' limited to the grammatical options of a given language or the discursive conventions ('ways of speaking') of a given culture (specific ways of engaging in conversation, telling stories or formulating news reports), or more fundamentally by different structures of experience (models) as based on different knowledge structures.

For instance, if in a (sub)culture all social events and human actions are understood by all or most members to be caused or controlled by ancestral spirits or God, such sociocultural knowledge will affect members' mental models of specific events, and thus explain one of the possible causes of culturally specific storytelling or explanations. On the other hand, narrative structures are merely linguistically variable for those storytellers who across cultures have more or less the same sociocultural knowledge and experiences (situation models) – say stockbrokers in Beijing and London. Systematic study of the cultural variation of discourse and its relation to cognition in general, and knowledge in particular, thus needs to make explicit different levels and components of the complex interface that controls the relationship.

6.6.4 *Epistemic conditions of different discourse genres and speech activities*

There are a vast number of discourse genres in the world, and many of these also vary across cultures. We have seen before that genres are not just defined by 'textual' ('verbal') characteristics, such as special style, register or topics, but especially also by properties of the context. We have studied this contextual basis of discourse genres in our studies of parliamentary debates, such as Tony Blair's speech about Iraq and Saddam Hussein in 2003, presenting a motion to go to war. As a genre, this speech is not (just) defined by its formal style, an occasional expression (*My honourable friend*, etc.) or its political topic, but especially by contextual parameters such as Setting (Time, Place, Circumstances), Participants (and their Identities, Roles and Relations), Action, Goals and Knowledge (for detail, see Van Dijk, 2000, 2008a, 2009a).

Relevant for the present discussion is the contextual knowledge condition of discourse genres in different cultures. Generally speaking, discourses pragmatically functioning as assertions, such as news or scholarly articles, are appropriate only if the speakers *know* what they are asserting (and assume the recipients do not) – where knowledge is implicitly presupposed to be based on such criteria as reliable observation, sources or inference, possibly varying depending on each community and context.

There are, however, discourse genres that pragmatically also make assertions but that do not necessarily presuppose that speakers or writers *know* what they are saying, at least not in the same way. Thus, stories, novels, myths, legends, sagas or fables, and fictional discourse more generally, are defined as such especially because what is being asserted is not (necessarily) true in the real world, or only partly true, or similar to the truth.

There is, however, considerable cultural as well as social variation in the relevance of this condition. Thus, it is well known that many viewers of soap operas (telenovelas) at least partly confuse the fictional world and events of these narratives with real ones – and not only in Brazil, where such telenovelas are a prominent part of everyday communicative experiences in many families.

Besides these social differences within the same culture or community (depending, for instance, on gender, age or education), people in many cultures may interpret myths or legends as fictional, but in others as truthful, e.g., about the history of a group, community or nation. Thus, such fictional genres may feature spirits, ghosts, living dead, unicorns or other fictional animals, with properties, abilities and engaging in actions that are impossible in the 'real' world – and depending on the culture, some or all recipients may more or less believe that what such discourse types refer to really existed or exists.

There are a vast number of studies, both in literary scholarship as well as in anthropology about these different fictional genres. In literary studies, the focus is generally on their narrative and other structures, and less on context – and only marginally on their epistemic aspects, apart from some theory on fiction in terms of possible worlds, among other approaches (among many studies, see, e.g., Gibson *et al.*, 2007; Ryan, 1991).

In ethnographic studies, besides analyses of structures of myths or folktales (Champagne, 1992; Lévi-Strauss, 1958; Propp, 1968), the contexts are also studied, for instance applying the categories of the well-known SPEAKING grid of Hymes (1972): Setting, Participants, etc. (Gubrium and Holstein, 2009; Hymes, 1996). Strangely, this grid does not feature Knowledge as a category, although obviously 'ways of speaking' crucially depend also on the knowledge of the participants, and specifically the knowledge of the speakers about the knowledge (or ignorance) of the recipients. Thus, it is relevant to know for a genre whether the speakers/authors are assumed to speak the truth or not, and whether or not the recipients are assumed to believe them (Bietenholz, 1994; Cassirer, 1955; Kirwen, 2005).

Of the many approaches to the study of myth, Holyoak and Thagard (1995) and Shelley and Thagard (1996) integrate earlier symbolic, structuralist and functionalist studies of myth and propose an analogical approach, similar to a metaphorical concept of discourse, in which elements of myths can be systematically related to aspects of the local culture. Atran (1996) emphasizes that a naturalistic approach to knowledge (based on innate folkbiology, etc.) stresses that for members of (practically all) cultures that believe in supernatural beings and phenomena these are not inconsistent with their natural knowledge of the environment and its laws of causality. Thus, myths and other narratives about supernatural beings and events are told or performed in special contexts, in which basic beliefs about the natural world are suspended – as is the case for reading novels or watching movies that feature events that defy everyday physics and biology

Despite the vast number of studies of 'indigenous' narrative, few ethnographic studies focus on the epistemic conditions of their contexts, such as the beliefs and knowledge of tellers and their communities. Albert (1986), in her classical study of discourse in Burundi, originally published in 1964, observes that "the distinction made in Rundi vocabulary between fact and fiction, knowledge and conjecture, truth, error, and falsehood, are close equivalents to those in Western culture." Similarly, there are lexical expressions for lies, errors, hypotheses without sufficient prior knowledge, etc., applying these specifically to the reliability of the speakers. But instead of breaching a rule of facticity, lying is interpreted as breaking a promise. Especially serious is calumny, speaking ill of other persons without good grounds. In fact, lying is no real problem if it has a legitimate function. Albert cites the proverb "The man who tells no lies cannot feed his children," and "Truth is good, but not all that is true is good to say," which is consistent with more general cultural rules of politeness and face.

6.6.4.1 Gossip and talk about others' minds

Cultural studies of gossip and rumor focus on the epistemic conditions and the social consequences of speaking (badly) about others. Gluckman (1963), in an influential article on gossip and scandal, cites Radin (1927) as saying "primitive people are indeed the most persistent and inveterate of gossips." But Gluckman offers a much broader analysis and explanation than Radin, highlighting the role of gossip in confirming community values, strengthening unity and autonomy with respect to other communities, especially in exclusive communities. He illustrates this with an analysis of a study by Colson (1953) of Makah Indians in the North-Western USA, where internal rivalry led to what Colson called "the art of verbal denigration" "brought to a high peak." Important, though, is the question of face: "The main moral norm is that you must scandalize about an opponent behind his back, if your allegations are at all open, to his face, you must be delicate and never give him ground to state that you have insulted him" (Gluckman, 1963: 313).

We see here how epistemic conditions of discourse are closely related to other contextual conditions, namely whether or not you speak about someone in her or his presence. Gluckman also applies this to other communities, such as the community of anthropologists. In a related study of Hopi gossip, Cox (1970) showed how gossip ("information management") characterized the power relations and interests of two political factions, the Traditionalists and Council supporters (Progressives).

Schieffelin (2008), in a more recent study of gossip in Bosavi (Papua New Guinea), focuses on an important contemporary theoretical issue, namely cultural variation of the theory of mind (ToM), and especially the speculative attribution of intentions, beliefs, wishes or other internal states of other people. One may cite what others have said, literally, but not talk about what they might have thought. Thoughts for the Bosavi are private. They are like personal possessions that may not be taken away by others. Prohibitions against gossip (*sa dabu*) thus extend to divulging what third parties may have thought, such as inferences of action.

Similarly, Ochs (1987) observes that in talk between caregivers and children in Western Samoa, the general tendency is that children are requested to explain themselves when their talk is unclear, because here caregivers also prefer not to guess what the children mean, as does frequently occur in talk between caregivers and children in the USA. Interestingly, Ochs explicitly refers to different *epistemological principles* in this case.

Obviously, the cultural rule not to speak about others' thoughts does not mean that the Bosavi are unable to attribute intentions to others or to make other mental inferences of action – which undoubtedly is a human universal (see, e.g., Tomasello and Carpenter, 2007). Interesting, though, is the difference with other (e.g., Western) cultures where talk on what others think or want is quite common, whether inferred from discourse, or from non-verbal action. Children learn to talk about their own thoughts – to express themselves well (Astington and Olson, 1990). Western children are not taught how *not* to talk about thoughts attributed to others, although as evidentials such attributions are obviously less reliable than being able to report what others have actually said.

There is evidence that mental state discourse facilitates ToM – that is, knowing or believing what others know or believe (see, e.g., Hughes and Dunn, 1998; Slaughter *et al.*, 2008). Interestingly, Bosavi culture does not seem to be an exception. Lu *et al.* (2008), in their study on talk and ToM among Chinese children, refer to cross-cultural studies that show that Chinese parents also refer less to mental states (see, e.g., Wang, 2001, 2003): "When describing people and making causal attributions, Chinese individuals tend to focus on external actions, social relationships, and contextual factors, as opposed to referring to internal states" (p. 1734). The authors wonder how Chinese children acquire ToM in such a situation, and show that more frequently referring to other people in telling about autobiographical experiences facilitates ToM (passing the false belief test, which implies that children understand that the beliefs of others about a situation may be different from their own).

Instead of talking about the internal states of others, however, it is important in Chinese culture to infer thoughts, wishes or desires in order to appropriately attend to others. This is also important because expressing such wishes or desires may be quite impolite in Chinese (as well as Japanese) culture: recipients are assumed to be able to infer such mental states. Interestingly, thus, inferring mental states is important not so much to talk about them, but rather to act upon them.

Hence, the sociocultural explanation of not talking about what others "have in mind" in this case is most likely to avoid others losing face by (having) to ask what they want, whereas in Bosavi culture the explanation is one of personhood and privacy – thoughts cannot be attributed because they are personal possessions, and only when they are expressed in discourse do they become public. The question may then be raised how Bosavi children learn to think about the thoughts of others, which they obviously need for appropriate and efficient interaction. Another explanation would be that talk about others' thought is not appropriate because it is epistemically unreliable – and one may thus make serious mistakes, for instance by accusing others of thoughts they may not have had.

6.6.4.2   Lies and lying

Of the many discursive practices studied in ethnographic and cross-cultural research and that have special epistemic conditions, lies and lying are an interesting example. Generally, lies may be defined as false assertions in the sense that the speaker knows or believes that what is being asserted is false. Moreover, lies usually also have a moral dimension in the sense that the speaker thus wants to deceive the recipients, by wanting the recipients to actually believe what is asserted and hence to believe what is false. As is the case for compliments, white lies, treason, interrogations by enemies, etc., such an intention may well be justified if knowing the truth may hurt the recipient or the relationship.

Sweetser (1987), commenting on a study of Coleman and Kay (1981), offers a sophisticated analysis of these various contextual conditions. First of all, she does not accept the philosophical definition of knowledge as true belief, but emphasizes that knowledge in cultural studies must deal with beliefs that *count as* knowledge – which is also the definition we use in this book. In what she calls the 'cultural model' of knowledge, she then formulates a number of rules, such as the norm (which she calls a rule) "Try to help, not harm," and if it is the case that "Knowledge is beneficial, helpful," then the rule is "Give knowledge (inform others); do not misinform," and "Say, what you believe, and do not say what you do not believe" (p. 47). In this framework, a lie is a false *statement* whose truth value is relevant (unlike in fiction, jokes or compliments), and where the speaker is fully informed (i.e., has adequate evidence, is not mistaken). Lying is morally wrong for various reasons, one of them being that speakers abuse their authority (as is the case for doctors about the health of their patients) of having access to the truth that recipients do not have. Further contextual analysis shows that lying is a fuzzy concept, depending on the kind of knowledge or belief, the speaker, the status of the speaker, the relations between participants, the goals of the speech act and so on. Since few kinds of knowledge are absolutely certain, and much knowledge is based on discourse of others and inferences, one would engage in many lies by making everyday assertions if such were an appropriate condition of assertions.

Different cultures may have the same cultural models of information and truth but evoke them under different circumstances (Sweetser, 1987: 61). Cultural studies of assertions, especially also in contexts of politeness, show that there are different contextual conditions of "telling the truth." Rules of interaction and politeness in some cultures may condition a 'wrong' answer to a question (e.g., about directions) rather than not answering or offering no help at all. Similarly, Ochs Keenan (1976) shows that in Malagasy conversation, specific knowledge may be treated as precious personal property that need not always be shared with strangers.

6.6.4.3   Questions

Not only discourse genres, but also speech acts may have culturally variable appropriateness conditions. Thus, direct questions as a speech act have as their most prominent function to get information from recipients. Hence they presuppose lack of knowledge of the speaker. As we shall see in detail in the next chapter, such lack of knowledge may pertain to just one category of an event (or rather, event model), such as the time (when), place (where), participants (who, whom), action or event (what) or its properties (how), on the one hand, or about a whole event or even a series of events (what happened?). No doubt, as is the case for assertions, questions are universal because knowledge is a universal condition of action and interaction, and hence in each culture missing knowledge may need to be acquired from others who are supposed to have it.

Yet, no doubt, as is the case for most speech acts, there are cultural differences in the ways they are actually performed, depending on various contextual parameters of appropriateness. First of all, the general condition of lack of knowledge on the part of the speaker and the assumed knowledge of the recipients is not satisfied in rhetorical and educational questions in many cultures. Thus, rhetorical questions of the type *Are you crazy?* are restricted to specific participants, because they perform speech acts that violate politeness conditions (Black, 1992; Ilie, 1994; Koshik, 2005). Similarly, teachers ask educational questions to test the knowledge of students, but not the other way around (Hargreaves, 1984; Lee, 2008; Mehan, 1978).

We have been unable to find systematic cross-cultural studies on the ways questions are asked, for instance in educational settings. But whereas speech acts such as greetings expressed as grammatical questions need not require an honest answer, e.g., *How are you?* in English, in other cultures they do function as real questions that require information, as is the case in Samoan *Where are you going?* (Duranti, 2001a).

6.6.5   The use of discourse in ethnographic studies of local knowledge

Whereas most of the ethnographic studies referred to above use various types of ethnographic interview, they seldom cite literally from these interviews and tend only to report the specific local knowledge searched for, for instance on conceptualization of the natural environment and the terms being used to describe it. Given the aim of ethnographic research, many of the interviews or conversations are merely paraphrased, summarized or analyzed by coding, and not by detailed qualitative discourse or conversation analysis of the actual talk of informants (Hopper, 1991; Maynard, 1989; Moerman, 1987). Hence, there are few data available of indigenous discourses that can be studied independently for the specific ways knowledge is being expressed or presupposed.

6.6.5.1   An example from South Africa

By way of illustration, here is a brief passage from an article by Thornton (2009) on traditional healing in South Africa. He cites one healer, Magodweni, describing non-material entities (but neither Christian spirits nor ancestors) *emandzawe*:

> (1) The origin of emandzau is from Maputo [Mozambique]. You will find that a Maputo man will come and settle in Swaziland [or South Africa]. Because of our Swazi tradition, a person is welcome. Maybe he eventually marries one of the daughters. Once they are integrated into the community, once he dies there, he is integrated into the community. Now the spirits of mandzawe, they connect to the spirit … to the family that he has been living with. This spirit is a go-between, as he is a spirit that has come to settle because he is not from this area; he comes from Maputo, and Beira [northern Mozambique]. (Thornton, 2009: 27)

This fragment expresses knowledge (about *emandzawe*) in various ways, namely that they are of foreign origin, and then in generic and gender terms (*a Maputo man*), explanation and presupposition of Swazi traditional hospitality (*a person is welcome*), also in generic terms, and the arrival of the (generic) man from Angola, possibly marrying one of the [Swazi] daughters – implying not only hospitality but also integration. Then the singular generic description (*a man*) changes to a plural when referring to *their* integration, that is, focusing on group integration. The crucial passage presupposes that *mandzawe* has or is spirit, and that this spirit can relate to the spirit of the family where he has lived – again presupposing that such families have spirits. Finally it is explained that this spirit can act as a go-between because it is a foreign spirit, but it is not clear from this passage between which entities this foreign spirit can be a go-between. After this passage, the author explains that the *ndzawe*, the foreign spirits, can teach and enable technology of healing, called *kufemba* ('to smell out') – a dramatic technique for identifying 'foreign bodies' in the body of a client.

Obviously, we would need more discourse and more detailed discourse analysis in order to make explicit the relation between discourse and knowledge in this talk. This small fragment, first of all, is part of an ethnographic interview, and hence contextually the speaker is probably responding to epistemic questions of the interviewer. This knowledge is mainly formulated in general and generic terms focused on a hypothetical man (it is not clear whether these foreign spirits – and healers – can also be women). Secondly, the concept of *ndzawe* is attributed special communicative powers, namely to be able to communicate with the spirits of the (local) family – also presupposed but not asserted here. Finally, this passage also formulates an explanation in terms of (presupposed) Swazi hospitality, an attribute of the group, and interactionally probably a move of positive self-presentation of the (Swazi) speaker, as a member. Notice that although the focus is on the description and explanation of *ndzawe*, the speaker thus also conveys knowledge about their own ethnic group, and presupposes other knowledge, for instance that foreigners can marry local girls and are integrated in their family.

6.6.5.2   An example from Latinas in California

The next examples are from an article from Chávez *et al.* (2001) about the perceived risks of cervical cancer among Latinas in the USA. Here are some examples from interviews with these women:

> (2) What I believe is that the delicate nature of the woman inside is also a cause. I heard a story in El Salvador about a woman who ... when she went for her exam they told her she had cancer. People said it was because

her husband ... was not careful when he had [sexual] relations with her. He
was very brusque with her, and he scratched her a lot. And so it grew worse
and she died. (California, 45-year-old Salvadoran immigrant, Chávez *et al.*,
2001: 1118)

This fragment is contextually relevant in an interview that has as its main
goal the elicitation of local knowledge about the causes and risks of cervical cancer (CC) among Latinas – especially in order to see whether their
beliefs influence their conduct: getting regular Pap tests. The first woman,
in example (2) attributes CC to the "delicate nature of the woman inside,"
that is, to an assumed bio-physiological property of women, consistent with
the general stereotype that women in general are more delicate than men.
To back up this belief, she tells a story about another Salvadoran woman,
who supposedly died of cancer because her husband "was not careful,"
"brusque" and as a consequence "scratched her a lot." Note, first of all, that
this is not a story of personal experience, or the experience of a friend, but
hearsay (*people said*) – a common move of evidentiality in many conversations. There is a clear line of actions and events that are described as a
full-scale explanation: he was rough, he scratched her, it got worse and she
died. Besides the stereotype of the delicacy of the women "inside," we also
find the main cause of the events: the man being (too) rough. In other words,
for this woman, CC may be caused by rough sex attributed to men, but it
is not clear whether she thinks this is the only or the main cause. Relevant,
though, is her presupposed knowledge that women can die as a consequence
of sexual violence or sexually transmitted disease, as we also see in talk
with another informant:

> (3) When men have relations with other women and come and do it with
> their wives, they are going to cause them to have a disease. Men give their
> wives diseases, but they do not analyze what they do, and unfortunately in
> this country we are in there is more prostitution. There are women who do
> it for nothing more than to pay the rent, that's all. But now even when the
> man does not fool around, now also the woman goes out with men other than
> her husband and they get infected and then they have children. (33-year-old
> Mexican immigrant, Chávez *et al.*, 2001: 1118)

In this example, too, sexual relations are blamed for CC, and the (main)
responsibility attributed to adulterous men who may transmit a disease to their
wives – so that it is the disease that is the immediate cause of CC. Notice
that no sources or evidence are mentioned, and that the K-statement is formulated in the generic plural (*men, women*, etc.). In a slightly different form, this
explanation of CC by attributing it to a disease caused by an adulterous man
is repeated in the next sentence. It is not quite clear what this woman means
by "but they do not analyze what they do" – unless she is referring to having,

for instance, an AIDS or STD test after having had sex with other women. The other women are moreover identified as prostitutes, with a further social explanation for the motives of these women (to pay the rent). Not only men are blamed, though. In the second part, women also are blamed because some of them go out with other men, and may thus become infected.

In sum, this small fragment seems to summarize in a few lines knowledge that may come from a sociology handbook on current sexual behavior in the USA as well as a study of risk of getting CC – or other diseases. Although in the second part of the fragment, women are also blamed, and prostitutes are said to infect men, in the whole passage the main cause is obviously the sexual conduct of men (who also are blamed for infecting women going out with them).

Apart from the complex chain of causes and effects, there is implicitly also a moral stance about women and men's sexual relations outside of marriage. In fact, these beliefs are consistent with those of interviewed doctors, who also blame (unprotected) sex with various partners as a major cause of CC. Here as elsewhere, it is not easy to distinguish between opinions (evaluative beliefs) and knowledge. The moral opinions of the interviewees obviously are personal opinions or conservative group attitudes. But although no evidence is cited, the other aspects of the supposed causes of CC, namely sexual conduct, are stated as facts. Finally, the authors emphasize that although "beliefs matter" – as the title of their paper suggests – in the decision of women to take a Pap test, much of the variance is socioeconomic, and also there is quite some variation in the knowledge and opinions of the various groups of Latinas. Crucial, apart from age, is number of years in the USA and speaking the language, which make it more likely that Latinas come to adapt attitudes like those of their Anglo peers. This shows that as a result of local and global changes of knowledge and beliefs, local or indigenous knowledge is permanently exposed to knowledge dominant in other groups or cultures.

6.6.5.3   An example from Native Americans
The next examples have been recorded by Wright *et al.* (1993) in their study of local knowledge about breastfeeding among Navaho women. Here are many examples of beliefs expressed about the benefits of breastfeeding:

> (4) [The elderly said] that breastfeeding was good. And [children] didn't get sick if you breastfed them too. They didn't really catch a cold or anything. After I got them off [the breast] it seemed like they all came down with colds and got sick all the time. (Wright *et al.*, 1993: 786)
> (5) If the nursing came from the mother then there was no identity problem. The young child would automatically feel that that's the mother and there is that closeness. The child is more secure and also the child is stronger mentally

for it, because of the attachment and the identification and the self-esteem for the child. [We] always felt that putting a child on a bottle was rather alien, not natural and we felt like you were rejecting your child by alienating it, by giving the child a bottle. There was no human comfort or the human stroking which was very beneficial to children. (Wright *et al.*, 1993: 786)

(6) Maybe it's the family environment Over there [where she had grown up] a family is a family. The environment was all right. May be that's what got me into doing it. Like over here, the family is not a family. Mostly broken families over here. Over there the families stay together and all that. (Wright *et al.*, 1993: 786).

(7) For me, breastfeeding was the time to sit and be with my babies, just talk to them and hold them. That was about the only time I really got the chance to be with my babies. So that was very important for me, that time to get really close to them and just be with them. For me, bottle feeding is like you're holding them way over there and … that's not really being close … I feel that you're showing them you love them when you're nursing them. (Wright *et al.*, 1993: 787)

(8) You see, if a baby is breastfed and partakes of the mother's bodily fluid, the child will be teachable. You see, when a baby doesn't partake of the mother's body fluid, it will have discipline problems. Babies that are bottle-fed have been fed the fluid of something other than the mother and [are] affected in this way. (Wright *et al.*, 1993: 787)

(9) I for one have spoken against it; this custom [bottlefeeding] was never given to be part of the Navajo way of life [*doo shíí nihaa deet' áada biniinaa at'é*]. You see, we as Navajos have done wrong by accepting this custom. Because of it our children have been affected, and [it has] disrupted their way of life. (Wright *et al.*, 1993:787)

(10) My sister used to prop up the bottle against the pillow and into the baby's mouth. She'll be doing other things like working and cooking, and the baby starts crying. She just puts the bottle into the baby's mouth. She doesn't pay attention, she just goes outside and the milk she just leaking. (Wright *et al.*, 1993: 788)

(11) The present generation are now bottle-fed, and it is not beneficial. You see, their teeth are affected and they are weakened by bottle-feeding … This custom was never given to be part of the Navajo way of life. (Wright *et al.*, 1993: 788)

(12) My sister, she just stuck the bottle into her kids' mouths. But then her kids, they got constipated they got sick a lot; they got ear infections. Almost the very time I saw them they had a cold. Something always sick. It seems like every little bit of draft got them sick. (Wright *et al.*, 1993: 788)

(13) At the time I was young and embarrassed to let anybody see it [her breast]. It seemed like I was shy at that time, and I was embarrassed I didn't want my husband to see it although he already knew, but it seems like he was going to make fun of me. (Wright *et al.*, 1993: 788)

An epistemic discourse analysis of these interview fragments may be summarized by the following observations about the local knowledge and beliefs about breastfeeding (BF):

- justification of K-statements in terms of (i) reliable authority (the elders in (4)), (ii) personal experiences, in (4), (5), (6), (7), (iii) inferences: reasoning back from positive and negative consequences, in (4) and (5)
- description of contextual explanation: the intact family environment stimulates it
- description of details of positive personal experience: example (7)
- generic statement about positive consequences of BF, and negative consequences of not-BF (8)
- relation of BF with (Navajo) way of life. It was wrong that we adopted bottlefeeding (9), (11)
- negative personal experience (via sister) (10)
- shame – about showing her breast to her husband during BF (13).

We see that in general these women derive knowledge about breastfeeding by combining personal or family (such as a sister) experiences with knowledge about the positive consequences of breastfeeding for their children – as well as negative consequences of not breastfeeding – with recommendations of the elderly as authority, as well as what the Navajo tradition recommends. They do so both in generic terms of general habits or rules, as well as in specific terms of personal experiences. Knowledge is especially also derived empirically by comparing positive and negative consequences of breastfeeding. Finally, there is a GOOD vs. BAD polarity between breastfeeding and bottlefeeding.

Besides these knowledge statements, the personal experiences are also mixed with moral statements, for instance about the sister in example (10), who is seen to neglect her baby by continuing to do her work. In other words, if it is known (from tradition, authority, other shared sociocultural knowledge or personal experience) that breastfeeding is good for children, then there is a basis for a moral argument that NOT breastfeeding is wrong – with the implied argument that one should always do what is best for the children.

More generally for our discussion, finally, is that knowledge and other beliefs – such as opinions – are sometimes hard to distinguish, as we have seen before. Thus, the statement "Breastfeeding is good for babies" is both a true statement of empirical (medical, experiential, etc.) fact, but also an opinion because of the evaluative term. The point is that it is not merely a *personal* opinion. It is not part of a personal mental model of members, but part of a general, socially shared attitude of a community – which features knowledge as well as general opinions. We also see that the kind of justifications for knowledge in these examples are quite similar to those that might be given in any culture – the authority of older people, tradition, personal and family experiences, and, more generally, reasoning in terms of empirical evidence about positive and negative consequences.

6.6.6   Knowledge about immigrants and ethnic minorities

Finally, let me examine some data of my own projects on discourse and racism in Europe and the Americas. The general aim of these projects was (i) to study how people in or from Europe talk and write about the Others, such as immigrants from the South, as well as resident minorities in the Americas (ii) to partly explain such text and talk in terms of underlying social representations such as shared ethnic prejudices and racist ideologies as well as the biased personal models derived from these representations, and (iii) to partly explain these data in terms of their role in society, such as the reproduction of (white) ethnic power in Europe and the Americas.

Parts of the project consisted of ethnographic fieldwork in various neighborhoods in Amsterdam, the Netherlands and San Diego, California, USA. Other data featured interviews with employers, radio programs, vast studies of media coverage, political debates in seven European countries and eight South American countries as well as the USA, and the study of textbooks in the Netherlands, Spain and various countries in Latin America. The results of the various sub-projects – carried out between 1981 and today – have been published in many books and articles (e.g., Van Dijk, 1984a, 1987, 1991, 1993, 1998, 2007, 2009b).

Given the aims of this mega-project of three decades, the focus of the study was on the influence of ethnic prejudice and racist ideologies on the structures of text and talk at many levels of analysis. However, this also required preliminary (re)formulation of theories of prejudice in a new sociocognitive framework, a proposal for a new theory of ideology, and the integration of the notion of semantic situation models and pragmatic context models as the crucial intermediary representations that link group attitudes (prejudices) and ideologies with specific discourse structures. Moreover, this sociocognitive framework was embedded in a sociological theory that explains the power of racist discourse in terms of the role of the symbolic elites in their reproduction in the dominant discourses in politics, media, education and business corporations.

Instead of repeating here the sociocognitive framework for the study of prejudice and ideology, partly already referred to in Chapters 3 and 4, the aim for this chapter is to get some more insight into what members of dominant ethnic groups actually (think they) know about immigrants and minorities. That is, whereas many ideologies and attitudes focus on Our good properties and Their bad ones, such evaluations in general need to be based on the kind of shared knowledge that is taken for granted, and not even disputed: what do local white people know about the Others in the first place, and how do they know it? Obviously, as argued before, it may well be that what is taken for granted as undisputed 'ethnic' knowledge may in fact be a prejudice. Since many prejudices are construed or confirmed as over-generalizations of isolated negative personal experiences, a more detailed look at some interview data from different countries and cultures may yield more detailed insight into the complex structures and strategies of social cognition, and how knowledge is related to, but different from attitudes and ideologies.

6.6.6.1   A Dutch story

Our first example is a story taken from an interview with a Dutch man (M) and a woman (W), recorded in 1983 in Amsterdam. The interviewees, who live in a neighborhood with immigrants from Turkey and Morocco, had been asked to talk about their experiences with the "foreigners" (*buitenlanders* in Dutch, the standard informal expression to refer to immigrants).

```
01              (14) (Van Dijk, 1984a: 86–97)
02    M: Since you are talking about that, it is a funny thing, well then I'll tell you some-
03       thing funny. You know that sheep slaughtering. It's one of those sad things. Well
04       then, alright, and there live around the corner, there lived a family, a Turk, and they
05       always had a pretty daughter. But one day, that lady who lives downstairs comes
06       over to me and says "Do you know where G. is?" And G., that was my mate, he
07       was the building supervisor [of a house across the road]. I said "Well, he is in the
08       shed." "Well," she says, "I've gotta talk to him for a minute." I say, "OK, come
09       with me," and we go over there together. I say: "G. eh," I say, "The neighbor got
10       to talk to you." And he says: "Well, what is it?" And then she says: "It stinks in the
11       staircase." I say: "Well, let's go have a look." "And the drain is clogged too, of the
12       sink." [imitates voice of neighbor] Well, also look at that. But by then we'd already
13       seen a sheep skin stashed away, hanging on the balcony.
14    ITER: Oh Gee!
15    M: You understand, they had slaughtered a sheep secretly in the shower.
16    W: Yes, 't was Ramadan.
17    M: You see, Ramadan. And everything that they couldn't get rid of, of that animal, they
18       had stuffed down that little pipe, you know
19    ITER: Of the drain
20    M: Of the drain
21    W: And that is the only story.
22    M: That whole thing was clogged. Opened up the thing. Police were there. Look, who
23       would DO a thing like that!
24    ITER: What, who, did those people ask the police? To interfere, or what, what
25       happened?
26    M: Yes, the police came
27    W: You are not alLOWED to slaughter sheep at home, don't you KNOW that!
28    M: And what it also means is, who is going to pay for it.
29    W: 'f course!
30    ITER: Yes
31    M: Because, you can't do anything against that.
```

32 w: Well, that's the only contact, that we once
33 m: And the funniest thing was, that was, so to speak not ... Who would do a thing like
34   that? You wouldn't slaughter a chicken in your room, would you, and
35 ITER: No, they do it a lot in the slaughterhouse now.
36 m: But that is the only thing.

For our epistemic analysis it is not directly relevant to provide a detailed narrative analysis (for detail, see Van Dijk, 1984a), but it can readily be seen
that the story follows the canonical narrative schema proposed by Labov and
Waletzky (1967): Preparation/Announcement of the Story, Summary, Setting,
Complication, Resolution, Evaluation and Coda, where several categories are
repeated, as is the case for the Complication (the pipe was clogged, they had
slaughtered a sheep) and the Evaluation (you cannot slaughter sheep). Also,
we shall here ignore the usual interactional dimensions of the conversations –
which would also require a much more detailed, professional transcript.

The story is about a well-known, stereotypical cultural event, sheep slaughtering by Muslims during Ramadan – which was sometimes done at home,
and which irritated Dutch neighbors, as is the case in this story, where the
Complication (lines 11–12) of the story is the surprising event that the drain of
the neighbor was clogged because of sheep remains.

Epistemically, the story is based on personal experience as represented in
the mental models of the man and the woman jointly telling the story – where
the man tells the main story and the woman provides further evaluations in
later turns. The story begins with a thematic connection with the previous part
of the conversation/interview ("Since you are talking about that," line 2) and a
prepositioned, repeated positive evaluation ("funny") so as to get the floor for
the story and motivate its telling in the first place.

Then the story focuses on the theme of sheep slaughtering, by way of the
usual initial summary – introduced by the Common Ground interactional
discourse marker "You know," which also invites recipients to draw their
own conclusions (Erman, 2001; Fox Tree and Schrock, 2002). The way this
theme is introduced implies that the speaker knows about sheep slaughtering
(by Muslims), and presupposes that the interviewer also knows about this –
both participating in a multicultural society with many Muslims. After the
announcement of the topic, there is an immediate negative evaluation ("one
of those sad things") of such slaughtering, consistent with quite general negative attitudes about some Muslim practices in the Netherlands. However, the
general evaluation of the event ("funny," "sad") is only moderately negative,
and in part also seen in terms of humor and empathy. As is the case for many
of the stories we collected in Amsterdam about immigrants in various neighborhoods, many of the complaints have to do with cultural differences, and
especially actions of "foreigners" that are inconsistent with prevalent Dutch
norms and values.

The man in line 4 then introduces most of the story, consisting of a Setting and a Complication, each with the relevant participants. The details of the event told, such as the reproduction of the relevant conversations of the participants are one of the ways the storyteller is able to enhance the credibility as well as the liveliness of the story. Such a credibility move pragmatically implicates that this is not (just) another racist tale about Muslims, but something that really happened. It is also in this way that events in a multicultural society are not only experienced but also told and reproduced, thus giving rise to shared opinions, possibly confirming existing stereotypes or prejudices – as is also the case here for the well-known stereotype of Muslims slaughtering sheep during Ramadan.

In line 15, the woman in fact does just that: she interprets and explains ("you understand") what happened in terms of a cultural event – Ramadan – repeated and confirmed by the man in the next turn, and thus shows that she is able to interpret a local event, an incident, in terms of general, socially shared knowledge about other ethnic groups and their customs. At the same time, there is a question of gender power enacted here when the contributions of the woman to the story are confirmed by the man, who is also the main storyteller.

This is not just a story showing general knowledge about cultural events and intercultural differences and conflict, but also has an important moral dimension, based on presupposed norms and values. Already the attribute "sad" in the beginning manifests a first evaluative dimension in the representation of the event (that is, in the storyteller's situation model of the event) and may be in the socially shared attitude about sheep slaughtering. At the end of line 22, and after briefly repeating the main events of the story, a rhetorical question with emphasis expresses this moral evaluation: "Look, who would DO a thing like that?" (Dutch: *Kijk, wie DOET dat nou?*) – a standard way to comment on any kind of moral deviation with a rhetorical question. This example also shows how generally shared knowledge about some aspects of the multicultural situation may be closely linked to the kind of evaluations that characterize social attitudes in general, and stereotypes and prejudices in particular – which presuppose knowledge of a norm.

The man repeats the rhetorical moral question in lines 33–34, but then adds a further argument to this moral judgment, by comparison with what we in 'our' culture would do or not – such as slaughtering a chicken at home, in one's room. He is using the ambiguous second person pronoun *you* (Dutch: *je*) which in this case could refer to the interviewer, but also, and more likely is a generic pronoun referring to anyone (like in "One doesn't do these things") – typical of normative statements.

Interestingly, the interviewer then adds that this kind of slaughtering is usually done at the slaughterhouse – most likely as a strategy to counter the force of the prejudice implied by the story – namely that Muslims do not usually do these kinds of things.

Finally, the storytellers add that this is the only (negative?) experience they have had and that they can tell about "But that is the only thing" – which may also be interpreted that in their view there is no reason to generalize from this story. Other storytellers often close their prejudiced stories by adding concluding narrative Codas such as: "This doesn't happen once, this doesn't happen twice, it happens all the time!"

Relevant for our discussion here is what kind of knowledge members have in multicultural societies about the customs of ethnic neighbors, and how their intercultural experiences with these neighbors are evaluated by comparison to ingroup norms and values – usually negatively – thus applying and confirming broadly shared stereotypes and prejudices. It is also for this reason that this type of story is often used as an extended argument in any conversation intended to make a negative point about the customs of the immigrants.

Not dealt with in our analysis here is the general sociocultural knowledge one needs to have about drains, pipes, clogging, slaughtering, sheep (and their skins) and so on – presupposed and taken for granted throughout. Such presuppositions may even be used to enhance the tension in the complication of the story, when the storyteller says: "But by then we'd already seen a sheep skin stashed away, hanging on the balcony," before adding later that a sheep had been slaughtered – something the recipients already could guess on the basis of the information about the sheep skin hanging out to dry.

6.6.6.2   A Californian story

Let us now have a look at a story recorded in San Diego, California, in 1985, during an interview with a Canadian couple, a man (M) and woman (W), who had migrated to the USA thirty years earlier. This story is also about immigrants:

01
02   (15) (A-TD-Ia,b)(Van Dijk, 1987: 75)
03
04   I: And the people who, who, do you have an idea about the people who do the burgla-
05   ries about here. I mean, what kind of people would they be?
06   W: Well, one day ... Yeah tell him about
07   M: A lot are Mexicans. I was home one time I had the flu, and uh I came out to the
08   kitchen to get myself a cup of tea, just in my pajamas, and I happen to look out of
09   the window, and I see them breaking in into the house next door. At first I thought
10   they were doing some work, that he had hired somebody to work at the windows
11   and then I realized they are breaking in. So I came to the garage door here, and I
12   got a real good description. I was terribly sick at the time, and I got a real good
13   description, at least one of them.

14 I: There were two?
15 M: There were three altogether.
16 I: Three!
17 M: And uh, people were in the yard there, and one was out here, and I got a good
18   description of him. He must have heard me, cause he took off, and I thought well,
19   uh I can grab that one, so I went out of the door, but he was so fast, he was gone,
20   he was down about there by the time I get out of the door, and he ran around the
21   block, and over the church right behind us. And uh, so anyway, I called the police
22   and gave them a description, and it wasn't ten minutes, they had a car in the area
23   apparently, he picked them up.
24 I: Really?
25 M: They were illegal aliens, Mexican.
26 W: They came over on the bus, didn't they?
27 M: Came over on the bus, and they had shopping bags, and they had uh I don't know
28   how many shopping bags stashed in the bushes.
29 W: They had twenty shopping bags stashed in the bushes.
30 M: Was it twenty?
31 W: Twenty.
32 M: In the church lot, near the church, behind the bushes. They had broken into how
33   many places was it?
34 W: I don't remember.
35 M: I think they said forty homes, up the hill and in the college area, uh the way down to
36   here, and they were working their way down here.
37 W: You wouldn't believe it.
38 M: And so they brought them back, and I identified them, this one feller, and uh the
39   police took him away, took him to jail and I was contacted by the police depart-
40   ment, by the attorney uh
41 W: prosecutor
42 M: prosecuting attorney, and he said that they were holding him for a trial, and they
43   would be, trial coming up such and such a date. Anyway, uh it wasn't long after
44   that, we got a letter, forget all about it, we sent him back to Mexico.
45 I: They wouldn't go through the hassle of doing, of trying him and uh
46 W: No
47 M: No
48 I: They just sent him back?
49 M: They just sent him back. Trying to (???) to the people, and just send them back
50   [laughs]. So this is what's done, they slap their wrist, and then "naughty, naughty,"
51   and "go home now."

Like the Dutch story, this Californian story is as prototypical as the event is stereotypically attributed to Mexicans. Again, such a story gives us an idea how personal knowledge about immigrants and minorities in Northern countries is produced and reproduced – and used as a basis for prejudiced overgeneralizations.

The amount of detail, the emphasis on one of the main truth criteria for knowledge, namely direct observation ("I got a good description of him," "I identified him," etc.), are not only narrative strategies to enhance credibility, but also an implicit argument against a charge of ethnic prejudice.

In other words, this and similar stories are being used not only by the story-tellers but also by others who no doubt have heard it as a "proof" that Mexicans are thieves. In fact, the story was told after a general question about the neighborhood, upon which the man replied that there were many burglaries and that many of these burglaries were committed by Mexicans (line 7) – a generalization that occasioned the story as personally experienced evidence for the generalization.

Actually, the man specifies (line 25) that the burglars were "illegal aliens," thus categorizing them not only negatively as thieves, but also as being "illegal" – and hence as people who had already broken the law. At the same time, this double categorization may work as an explanation: they were stealing *because* they were illegal.

When the story ends with an anti-climax (the Mexicans were sent back to Mexico), the moral Coda focuses especially on the criticism of the legal system, using the concrete metaphor of a "slap on the wrist" and the association of the crime with paternal discourse to children "naughty, naughty!" Notice that the concluding Coda, as is usual, does not merely apply to this event, but is an expression of a general attitude about the lenient treatment of criminals or "illegal aliens." Such attitudes and the underlying ideologies are obviously doxastic and not epistemic, so that the narrative point of this story is to provide evidence about 'facts' and a justification of the personal opinion as well of the general attitude.

6.6.6.3   Latin American discourse about minorities

Whereas Dutch and Californian stories about immigrants from the "South" are remarkably similar, what about storytelling and other discourse in Latin America about local minorities of African descent and about indigenous people? They may be seen as Others, from a 'white' Euro-Latin perspective, but not as immigrants. So, let us examine some fragments recorded or used by various scholars contributing to our edited book, translated from the Spanish as *Racism and Discourse in Latin America* (Van Dijk, 2009b).

Before we examine dominant discourse about minorities in Latin America, it is appropriate to cite a Guaraní woman, participating in a debate in a commission of the Senate of Argentina in 2002, by way of example of a voice of resistance against official dominant discourse. At the same time, this fragment may serve to highlight the local knowledge expressed and brought to bear as it is defined from a different perspective. The debate was about a "Bill on Indigenous People" which deals with the internal organization of the Instituto

Nacional de Asuntos Indígenas (National Institute of Indigenous Affairs), and especially the representation of indigenous people in the institute. In the debate, the Senators on the one hand praise indigenous language and culture, but on the other hand are dragging their feet to give real power to indigenous representatives, and even reject their criticism as breaching the harmony and love of the discussion. A woman from the representatives of the Guaraní then replies as follows:

> (16) Debate Argentine Senate (Van Dijk, 2009b: 27) (from: Corina Courtis, María Inés Pacecca, Diana Lenton, Carlos Belvedere, Sergio Caggiano, Diego Casaravilla, Gerardo Halpern, "Racism and Discourse: A Portrait of the Argentina Situation" (Van Dijk, 2009b: 13–55).
>
> *Quiero pedirle, señora, que no se enoje cuando preguntamos cosas. Nosotros también hemos tenido mucha paciencia, toda la paciencia del mundo, y aún la seguimos teniendo. Yo le pido que nos escuche porque nosotros la escuchamos con toda atención. Parecería como si fuéramos un Estado dentro de otro Estado, pero el Estado que conduce no se preocupa por estudiar, por entender, ni tan siquiera por escucharnos cuando tenemos la oportunidad de expresar nos. Usted está haciendo las cosas a su modo, desde su cultura, tratando de ayudarnos. Nosotros queremos que usted trabaje junto a nosotros. Lo primero que debemos lograr entre los pueblos originarios y los pueblos de cultura occidental es que, justamente, ustedes puedan entender todo lo que nosotros somos. No somos lo que va a decir el censo, que fue totalmente mal hecho. Tampoco se respeta el modo en que pedimos que se hiciera. Lo que pedimos es que, por sobre todas las cosas, cuando les planteamos dudas o les hacemos requerimientos concretos nos consideren como interesados directos, que es justamente lo que somos. Y sería importantísimo que ustedes, que como gobernantes no han podido sacar el hambre de Argentina, donde se están muriendo cien chicos por día de hambre y de desnutrición y muchas mujeres en los hospitales porque no hay comida, escucharan qué proponemos nosotros, los pueblos originarios. O sea, que nos escucharan y que nos dieran la posibilidad de tener territorios donde nosotros podamos repartir la riqueza que producimos y aplicar la cultura que tenemos. No pedimos más que eso: o sea, ayudarlos a ustedes, como pueblo occidental, a que no se les sigan muriendo chicos de hambre.*

I would like to ask you, madam, not to get angry when we ask questions. We have been very patient, we have had all the patience in the world, and we still do. I ask you to listen because we have given you our full attention. It seems as if we were a state within another state, but the leading state does not try to study, to understand, or even to listen when we have the opportunity to express ourselves. You are doing things your way, from your culture, attempting to help us. We want you to work together with us. The first thing we should achieve, between the native and the Western peoples, is precisely that you understand everything that we are. We are not what the census will say, which was not done properly. The way we asked it to be done was not respected either. What we are requesting is that, above all, when we raise doubts or put forward concrete demands, you consider us as directly interested parties, which is exactly what we are. And it would be very important for you, as leaders who have not been able to get rid of hunger in Argentina, where a hundred children die every day because of hunger and malnutrition, and many women in hospitals because there is no food, to hear what we, the native peoples, suggest. That is, that you listen to us and give us the possibility to have territories in which we can distribute the wealth we produce and apply the culture that we have. We ask no more than that; that is, to help you, as a Western people, to keep children from dying of hunger.

Besides the many political and other social functions of this speech, it also has several epistemic properties, presupposing and indirectly asserting forms of knowledge. Thus, first of all, it rejects the knowledge and knowledge criteria of the dominant state, viz., what the state pretends to know about the indigenous people, on the one hand, and by means of the census, on the other. Next, in an obviously critical as well as ironical move, this woman shows she knows about hunger in Argentina, implicitly blaming the Argentine leaders for this situation. Thirdly, she presupposes that the indigenous people may produce wealth and apply culture in the territories they need, and thus may contribute to fighting hunger. The political implicature (Van Dijk, 2005b, 2008a) of this assertion is also that apparently the state does not have the knowledge or the capacity to prevent hunger in the territory it controls. We see that political struggle not only implies a confrontation of dominant and dominated groups, and hence political and economic power, but also a vindication of indigenous knowledge.

Compare this strong voice with that of a 62-year-old (white) Argentine middle-class housewife, when she talks about immigrants in an interview:

(17) (Van Dijk, 2009b: 34) (from: Corina Courtis, María Inés Pacecca, Diana Lenton, Carlos Belvedere, Sergio Caggiano, Diego Casaravilla, Gerardo Halpern, "Racism and Discourse: A Portrait of the Argentina Situation" (Van Dijk, 2009b: 13–55).

El problema de esta gente es que se vienen a Buenos Aires y terminan amontonados en una villa. Para eso, mejor que se queden en su pueblo, que prosperen ahí. Hay que crear condiciones para que no se tengan que venir. Allá pueden hacer su quintita, tener gallinas. No les va a faltar de comer. En cambio acá no tienen trabajo, no saben qué hacer y se convierten en delincuentes. Además, no tienen trabajo porque quieren ganar demasiado. Si no, cualquiera los tomaría para trabajar en casas o para hacer changas. Pero son muy pretenciosos. Esos negritos, corno la criadita del tío Antonio, tienen muchas pretensiones. Y es esa gente la que trajo Perón, que no se conforman con nada.

The problem with these people is that they come to Buenos Aires and end up piled up in a shantytown. It would be better for them to stay in their village, for them to prosper there. We have to create the conditions for them not to have to come. There they can make their little country house, keep chickens. They won't go hungry. However, here they don't have jobs, they don't know what to do and they become criminals. And they don't have jobs because they want to earn too much. If not, anyone would take them to work in houses or to do odd jobs, but they are too pretentious. Those little black people, like Uncle Antonio's little maid, are too pretentious. And those are the people that Perón brought, who are never satisfied.

This racist and paternalistic passage also exhibits various kinds of knowledge, such as the miserable living conditions of the minorities as well as their lack of work, knowledge no doubt shared by the immigrants. It may even be the case that some of the immigrants become criminals. But the implied overgeneralization, that minorities without a job become criminals, is a racist prejudice. And that they demand (too) high salaries may be a justified belief shared among some sectors of the white middle class, but it will hardly be shared by the minorities themselves, thus making it a partisan belief based on an ideology of class.

The paternalistic recommendation "to stay in their village" in order to prosper is also based on assumed socioeconomic knowledge obviously not shared by the minorities – who no doubt do not leave their village because they are doing well there, or to live in miserable conditions in the *villas* of Buenos Aires or other big cities in Argentina.

In other words, this voice is the voice of domination, based on the biased ethnic and class beliefs of the white majority. Besides this assumed knowledge, however, the speaker also expresses shared social attitudes, for instance about minorities being too "pretentious" and never "satisfied."

The racism of this passage is perhaps most obvious in the series of diminutives associated with the minorities – as is also the case with their usual description as *cabecitas negras* (black little heads). Interestingly, in the discourses of politicians in Europe, the paternalistic argument against immigration, namely for immigrants "to stay in their own country and help develop it" is quite widespread – especially also because it appears to be formulated within the spirit of any recommendation "for their own good" (Van Dijk, 1993; Wodak and van Dijk, 2000).

The discourse of the Argentine woman is, of course, not surprising when even in parliament voices like the following by Mr. Scioli may be heard about immigrants:

(18) (Van Dijk, 2003)
Sr. Scioli: Señor presidente: quiero poner mucho énfasis en este punto que está describiendo el señor diputado Pichetto, porque nada tienen que ver las características de los inmigrantes que hoy están llegando a nuestro país, especialmente a nuestras grandes ciudades, con las de aquellos inmigrantes italianos y españoles que han hecho grande a nuestra patria, cuando vinieron a trabajar y a poner industrias.

Esto se ve claramente reflejado en el caso concreto de muchos delitos que están azotando la ciudad de Buenos Aires con tours de delincuentes que vienen de otros países, con tours sanitarios que vienen a ocupar nuestros hospitales, con delincuentes que vienen a usurpar casas y a ejercer la prostitución.

Argentina hoy vive al revés: estamos exportando ingenieros y científicos, y estamos importando delincuentes. Esto no significa ir contra la inmigración. Tenemos que tomar los ejemplos de otros países, como España, que ha producido un sinceramiento en la situación y protegido a los suyos.

Mr. Scioli: Mr. President, I want to emphasize the point that Mr. Deputy Pichetto is making, because the characteristics of the immigrants that today are arriving in our country, and especially in the large cities, have nothing to do with those of the Italian and Spanish immigrants who have made our country great, when they came to work and to found industries.

This is clearly reflected in the concrete case of the many crimes that are plaguing the city of Buenos Aires, with organized groups of criminals coming from other countries, and crowds of sick people filling our hospitals, with criminals occupying our houses and practicing prostitution.

Argentina now lives the other way round: we are exporting engineers and scientists, and we are importing criminals. This does not mean that I am against immigration. We have to take examples from other countries, like Spain, which takes the protection of its own seriously.

Also in this speech fragment, beliefs are displayed that are shared by Mr. Scioli and many other Argentines of European descent, and hence are taken for granted as knowledge, namely the difference between white Europeans and the indigenous immigrants arriving from Bolivia or Peru. He applies the usual polarized ideological strategy of emphasizing the positive characteristics of Our group and emphasizing the negative ones of the Others – a polarization that at the same time expresses the self-attribution of white superiority of underlying racist ideology. After a critical intervention of another *diputado*, Mr. Scioli categorically denies that his discourse is xenophobic – but only wants to protect Argentina against criminals.

The challenge to a critical analysis of these kinds of passages and argumentation, as is also relevant in political debates with racists in Europe, is that the knowledge they claim to have is hard to invalidate. No doubt it is true that there are differences between the immigrants then and now. No doubt it is true that many of the European immigrants built cities and industries. It is also true that many professionals have been leaving Argentina during the economic crisis of the 1990s. And probably at least some current immigrants are engaged in crime or occupy hospitals.

In this sense, this kind of knowledge is the common sense of the dominant group and persuasive for those who share its interests. The racist nature of this passage, hence, is based on the polarized nature of the underlying ideology that emphasizes the superiority of white Argentines of European descent, and the negative, criminal nature of non-white, indigenous people – by means of prejudiced overgeneralization.

The few examples we have examined here may be taken to be quite paradigmatic for Latin America, and the way dominant discourse among 'white' Latin Americans may disparage black and indigenous peoples – often legitimated by their partisan knowledge and in the interest of domination or exclusion. We find such discursive racism and biased beliefs in politics, in the media, in textbooks, in everyday conversations and many other dominant discourses. On the other hand, there are discourses of resistance, first of all by the black and indigenous peoples and their leaders, and secondly by those among the dominant population who are in solidarity with their resistance and who challenge racist discourse and practices, as also happened in Argentina's parliament (for detail and many other examples, see Van Dijk, 2009b).

6.7   Concluding remarks

The few examples we have shown here from Europe and the Americas show how knowledge is not simply justified true belief, but can be marshaled by different communities, or opposed social groups, in order to serve domination or resistance. Racist politicians do not always lie about immigration or the characteristics of minorities – but their half-truths may display underlying ideologies that function to sustain domination and exclusion through many other discourses and social practices. On the other hand, knowledge asserted by dominated groups may also be half-truths, but in that case used to resist and to obtain justice.

We have seen that the local knowledges of the world may not simply be justified shared beliefs that allow the members of communities to manage their everyday lives and their relationships with their social and natural environment. There is ample ethnographic evidence that local knowledge may be as sophisticated as much scientific 'global' knowledge. The basic criteria of functional knowledge – such as reliable observation, sources or inference – appear to be relevant in science as well as in everyday life, and in any community.

What some communities take for granted as knowledge, such as the existence of spirits or the influence of ancestors, others may deem to be superstitious beliefs – but the same applies for the religious beliefs in 'our own' (Western) community, which in many powerful Western countries, such as the USA, may even be dominant.

In other words, the epistemic divide is not between Western and non-Western, between local and global, between indigenous and universal or between scientific and everyday lay knowledge. The divide is not even between (justified) knowledge and (mere) belief, or between what is true or what is false, because we have seen that in their own interest groups will claim their own beliefs to be the truth and may apply them to dominate or to resist domination. Even the universal epistemic criteria of reliable observation, sources or inference, may be challenged in their concrete (more or less rigorous) application.

Consequent relativism, in the study of culture, too, appears to have no other (of course, relative and hence fundamentally dynamic) basic definition of knowledge than as the beliefs that are shared and defined as knowledge in each (local or global, etc.) community and hence presupposed in the concrete discourse and other social practices of its members. For a sociocognitive approach to knowledge this explains both the cognitive as well as the social dimensions of the cultural functions and reproduction of knowledge.

7   Language, discourse and knowledge

7.1   Introduction

After studying the relationships between discourse and knowledge in philosophy, psychology, sociology and anthropology in the previous chapters, this chapter focuses on the linguistic and discourse analytical study of these relationships.

Linguistics and discourse studies traditionally dealt only marginally with knowledge and focused especially on grammar and the study of the structures of discourse and conversation. Yet, some topics in linguistics, often at the boundary of discourse analysis, at least indirectly paid attention to 'information' and knowledge, as is the case for the study of topic and focus, evidentiality, epistemic modality and presupposition. In this chapter we shall only briefly summarize some of this research because there are now many studies about these topics. Rather, we shall take a broader, more discourse analytical and integrated approach of the epistemic structures of discourse (see, e.g., Chafe, 1972, for an early study of knowledge in linguistics).

In conversation analysis, still little given to cognitive studies, knowledge is now being studied in normative and moral terms of the epistemic access, primacy and responsibility of participants in interaction, such as who has rights to tell a story in a conversation, for instance because of more direct access to the events.

Beyond grammar, classical speech act theory formulated the appropriateness conditions of such speech acts as assertions and questions in terms of the (lack of) knowledge of the participants. We have already seen that such appropriateness conditions can more adequately be formulated in terms of context models controlling the production and comprehension of text and talk.

Finally, discourse and communication studies have paid attention to the way knowledge is spread in popularization discourse. In this chapter, we shall therefore focus also on the ways discourse structures beyond the sentence level are related to the expression and communication of knowledge.

In sum, both in linguistics and discourse studies there are a number of approaches that have dealt with epistemic structures of text and talk, but these

Table 7.1 *Schema of the knowledge–discourse interface in past and current research*

Knowledge	Discourse
a. **Types of knowledge**, such as personal experiences and generic knowledge	Discourse genres, such as personal stories, news reports or textbook lessons
b. **Sources of knowledge** and its justification: (i) multimodal personal experiences (vision, audition, touch, feeling), (ii) communication (hearsay, testimony, reliable sources) and (iii) inference	Evidentials
c. **Certainty** of the participants about their knowledge	Epistemic stance expressions
d. **Probability** of known events	Modalities
e. **Shared knowledge**, Common Ground	Implications, presuppositions, (in)definite expressions, etc.
f. **Old vs. new knowledge**	Topic, focus, information distribution, etc. Definitions, metaphors, organization of expository discourse, news reports, etc.

were barely related and hence in need of a coherent and more integrated theoretical framework (see also Pishwa, 2006). Table 7.1 summarizes some of the current approaches to the study of the role of knowledge in language use and discourse.

7.2 Triangulating discourse, cognition and society

Although this chapter focuses on the *epistemic structures* of discourse, it should be recalled that their analysis cannot be limited to the usual linguistic or discourse analytical categories. Rather it presupposes the kind of approaches summarized in the previous chapters, for instance in terms of situation models, context models, processing and representation in memory, epistemic communities and cultural variation and epistemic institutions and organizations, among many others. Hence the need for a triangulating analysis that links discourse structures with both cognitive and social structures.

For instance, as we shall see in more detail below, evidentials are (i) variable grammatical and discourse expressions that index (ii) more or less reliable sources of knowledge and thus implicate (iii) the rights and credibility and other moral properties of speakers in conversation and interaction. Similarly, a news report in the press has specific (i) discourse structures, such as a news schema and evidentials, (ii) expresses and conveys specific new knowledge about recent events, as represented in mental models of journalists, and (iii) as construed in interactional routines and criteria of news gathering and as published in a public medium of a corporate organization.

Crucial for nearly all epistemic phenomena discussed in this chapter is the sequential, discursive manifestation of the fundamental principle of dynamic knowledge management in interaction and communication, namely how new or otherwise salient knowledge is related to old or given knowledge of recipients as members of epistemic communities or as participants in communicative situations.

Thus, many of the very structures of discourse, such as those of coherence, implication, implicature, presupposition, topic–focus and common ground, cannot even be formulated in exclusively grammatical or linguistic terms, but need at least formulation in terms of abstract 'information' or in cognitive terms of mental models or knowledge representations. Similarly, the analysis of all discourse genres needs a discursive, a cognitive and a social approach.

7.2.1   The basic communicative function of language and discourse

Discourse has many cognitive and social functions, such as coordination, cooperation, affiliation, solidarity, domination, resistance and so on (among many books, see, e.g., Kärkkäinen, 2003; Levinson, 1983; Mayr, 2008; Mey, 1993; Stivers et al., 2011a; Van Dijk, 2008a; Wodak et al., 2011). Yet in this book and especially in this chapter we focus on the basic function of all text and talk: the communication of knowledge or information. It is plausible that the communicative functions of language have evolutionary advantage over other functions. Like other species, humans are able to communicate to conspecifics where to find food, to warn of predators or other dangers, convey emotions and so on. But only humans have non-indexical discourse that goes beyond the here and now, can tell stories about past personal experiences, account for them, engage in argumentation and communicate detailed plans for the future (Bickerton, 2009; Knight et al., 2000). Hence, it is not surprising that humans have developed sophisticated linguistic and discursive means to convey new knowledge and to relate it to old knowledge. Such communicative abilities in turn presuppose cognitive abilities (such as some kind of theory of mind) that allow language users to know what recipients surely or probably know, abilities that are also required for an explicit theory of Common Ground.

7.2.2   Types of knowledge

In epistemic approaches to language, discourse and conversation, the concepts of 'information' or 'knowledge' are used in a rather vague and general sense. For this chapter especially, however, we need to be more explicit, and make distinctions among different types of knowledge as they have been made in this book, and as summarized in Table 7.2, which also shows how and where this knowledge is mentally represented and how it is shared in what communicative situations.

Table 7.2 *Types of knowledge, representation and their social basis*

Type of knowledge	Mode of representation	Social basis
Generic knowledge	Semantic memory: concepts, prototypes, scripts, etc.	Largely socially shared and presupposed in epistemic communities
Knowledge of public events	Semantic memory? Public models	Partly socially shared and presupposed in epistemic communities
Interpersonal knowledge of events	Episodic memory: general models	Partly shared among individual persons (family, friends, colleagues, etc.) across situations
Interpersonal experiences	Episodic memory: experience models	Unique, partly shared among individuals, in one situation
Communicative experience	Episodic memory: context models	Unique, partly shared among interaction or communication participants
Personal knowledge	Episodic memory: general models	*Intra*personal, across situations
Personal experiences	Episodic memory: specific models	*Intra*personal, private and unique in one situation
Basic personal experiences	Episodic memory: fragments of mental models	Intrapersonal, private, unique in one situation, but with generic basis

The cognitive distinctions made above are not only based on various kinds of experimental evidence and cognitive psychological theorizing. In evolutionary, developmental and functional terms, such distinctions are also motivated by social perception, social interaction and especially also language use and discourse. Thus, as suggested above, different discourse genres correspond to different mental representations. Personal stories in conversation typically express mental models of (complex) personal experiences, whereas news in the media expresses public mental models of public events or the experiences of news actors. These personal and socially shared models are in turn based on personal and social generic knowledge, which may remain presupposed in (new) stories, but may sometimes also be explicitly formulated, especially when it is new generic knowledge, typically expressed in expository discourse genres.

Discourse genres and their structures, however, are defined not only by various underlying knowledge structures, but also by the structure of communicative situations as subjectively represented in the *context models* of participants, as we have seen in Chapter 3. It is not what recipients already know that controls topic–focus, indexical structures and presuppositions of sentences, but what speakers believe or know of such knowledge of recipients, as represented in the K-device of their context models. Similarly, a news report is based not merely on situation models of journalists about recent events, but crucially also on the context model representing writing for a newspaper and a general public – quite different from telling the 'same' story in a bar to a friend. Context models are also necessary as a basis for evidentials, namely when we report to others what we have heard or read before – one of the three major sources of knowledge – both in everyday conversation as well as in academic discourse such as the present book. This also suggests that, besides other textual or contextual properties, the type of source indexed by evidentials may be taken as a genre property, e.g., in order to distinguish between everyday conversations, scholarly articles, news reports or eyewitness testimony in court (see, e.g., Ainsworth, 1998; Loftus and Doyle, 1987; Walton, 2002, 2008). So, again and again in discourse we find a close integration of discourse structures, cognitive structures and social structures.

7.2.3   The K-device

As we have seen in Chapter 3, crucially relevant for this chapter is the K-device of context models, controlling the complex knowledge management of discourse and interaction: what recipients probably know already, may have forgotten, do not know as yet, might want to know, what has been communicated before and so on. All epistemic properties of text and talk discussed in this chapter are controlled by this fundamental device that also more generally controls all interaction:

- **Genres** – defined by types of knowledge (see Table 7.2)
- **Discourse topics** – the dynamic control of semantic macrostructures or topics that participants ongoingly find relevant to talk about
- **Lexicon** – language users ongoingly and sequentially adapt their discourse to the lexical competence of the recipients – as is the case in parent–child discourse, popularization discourse, etc.
- **Information structure of clauses** – for each clause the K-device keeps track of the *current state of the Common Ground* (CG) of the participants, and thus controls topic and focus parts of clauses and sentences
- **Epistemic stance** – the expression of knowledge may be modulated by the degree of certainty of the speaker
- **Evidentials** – indicating one of three major sources of knowledge: various kind of experience, discourse or inference
- **Implications** – new propositions derivable from explicit propositions + generic knowledge
- **Presupposition** – 'old' propositions that are part of the CG of the participants

- **Coherence** – both local and global coherence presuppose the activation of situation models and generic knowledge that establish relations between sequences of propositions.

Thus, the K-device is the control mechanism of the CG of the participants of text and talk underlying these and other structures of discourse. More generally, though, it embodies the very general principles of knowledge management in discourse, and hence ongoingly and dynamically needs to control the following:

- **Type of knowledge**: *what* do I know? (e.g., personal experience, public event, generic knowledge, etc.) as allowed or required by the discourse genre
- **Source of (or access to) knowledge**: *how* do I – did I come to – know?
- **Quality of knowledge** (certainty, confidence): how *well* do I know?
- **Target of knowledge**: what do he/she/they (need or want to) know now?
- **Entitlement of knowledge**: am I *entitled* to express, convey, spread this knowledge in this moment to this recipient? What is our epistemic relationship?

7.2.4   *Social context and interaction*

The triangular approach to discourse obviously not only involves a cognitive component representing and regulating knowledge and its communication, but also a social, interactional component. Indeed, not just any knowledge may be communicated to anyone, anywhere. As we shall see for the contemporary study of conversation, speakers may have different access, authority, entitlements, rights, obligations, prohibitions, responsibilities or accountability with respect to what they know and may or may not tell others.

As we saw in Chapter 5, language users are allowed or obliged to express and convey knowledge in a large number of personal and especially institutional situations, e.g., in classrooms, newsrooms or courtrooms – as subjectively represented in the context models of the participants. In the same chapter we saw what the complex *participation structures of communication situations* in the media may be, featuring reporters, correspondents, sources, editors, anchors and so on – all defined also in terms of the kind of expertise and knowledge they have and are expected or obliged to communicate.

Thus, the epistemic basis of all text and talk is ongoingly constrained by these social dimensions of the context model. *What* we know we may or must tell one friend and not another, a mother or priest and no one else, a teacher or a judge, and each communicative situation also requires *how* we may or must do so. Thus, we tend to imply and presuppose much more knowledge to people we know, and old information must be recalled more with some people or publics than others. Some discourse types, such as testimonies and scholarly papers are much stricter than others when it comes to indexing our sources of knowledge in various kinds of evidentials.

So, all structures mentioned above and below are systematically also controlled by the social dimensions of context models: the setting, the identity, roles and relations of participants, and the goals of the communicative event.

Contrary to current work on epistemics in conversation analysis, however, our theoretical approach does not integrate these social dimensions (access, authority, entitlements, etc.) directly in the analysis of talk, but in terms of the subjective context models of the participants. It does not matter whether or not speakers have the objective entitlement to convey specific knowledge in a conversation or an interrogation, but whether and how they dynamically and subjectively represent (are aware of) such an entitlement in the current communicative situation and at a particular moment of talk and how they act upon such representations. It is this subjective nature of the cognitively mediated social conditions of discourse that also explains why and how participants can produce epistemically inappropriate talk or text.

7.3   The epistemic structures of text and talk

With the cognitive and social framework construed so far, we are now ready to pay more specific attention to the discourse structures at various levels that are controlled by the K-device or otherwise associated with the knowledge of the participants. Below, we shall further develop the social and interactional framework needed to account for epistemic structures and strategies in text and talk.

Given the enormous literature on such phenomena as topic, focus, presupposition, evidentials and epistemic stance, we shall only be brief on these structures. Rather we focus on some epistemic structures, especially at the discourse level, that have been studied less often in linguistics – precisely because they require analysis beyond the sentence boundary of traditional grammars.

As is also the case for speaker strategies of discourse production, we shall start with the epistemic management of talk in interaction and then focus on the semantics of discourse, from higher-level discourse structures, such as overall genres and discourse topics, to the (better known) local structures of sentences.

Each of the epistemic structures and strategies in discourse discussed in this chapter would require extensive discourse examples and their analysis, an analysis that would no doubt double the already considerable length of this book. This means that this chapter will also be rather theoretical, refer to other studies and only give a few examples.

7.3.1   The epistemics of conversation and interaction

We have argued above that a sociocognitive approach to the study of epistemic structures in text and talk obviously cannot be limited to a theory of the cognitive basis of such structures, but also needs a social and interactional basis. Perhaps trivially, but importantly, we are dealing not only with minds and knowledge but with people and social members who think, know, talk, write and interact with others. We also need to inquire into the question who can say what to whom in a given communicative situation, who is entitled to express and convey knowledge, and how what kind of recipients may react to such information.

Such further social conditions of epistemic communication require an analysis of the relevant social situation in which knowledge is interactively expressed, conveyed and evaluated. As has been shown in our studies of context, social structure does not have a direct influence on discourse, but does so through the subjective definition of the communicative situation by the participants, as represented in their context models, as described above and in the previous chapters. Whereas before we focused on the knowledge component (the K-device) of such context models, we now need to be more specific about the participation structure or footing of communicative situations, such as the various identities, roles and relations of the participants as ongoingly activated or constructed by the participants (see, e.g., Erickson, 1988; Goffman, 1981; Levinson, 1988).

In institutional discourse, this may, for instance, involve such epistemic roles as experts and novices as well as the epistemic discrepancies or power involved in their relationships. In a different way, this also happens in everyday conversation: speakers telling a story about a personal experience usually know more about some event than the recipients. This is, indeed, what the fundamental communication function of language is all about.

In Chapter 5 on discourse, knowledge and society, we examined some of the macrosociological aspects of information and communication, for instance for discourse genres such as news reports. Within this broader macro-context, we now need to focus on the social, interactional micro-context of the communication of knowledge in text and talk. We need to know what normative and moral rules and norms apply in such epistemic contexts. Indeed, who may or should inform whom, and how (see, e.g., Stivers *et al.*, 2011a; see more detailed references below).

7.3.1.1   Epistemic primacy, entitlements and responsibilities: who may or must tell?

Not everyone has access to the press or television to inform the audience. Those who do need to satisfy many institutional and organizational conditions, such as being hired by a communication company, having professional qualifications, such as a having a journalism degree, having the role of reporter, correspondent or anchor, as well as epistemic conditions: they must know something the audience does not yet know (see, e.g., Freidson, 1986; Fröhlich and Holtz-Bacha, 2003; Gaunt, 1992).

We have earlier examined what daily routines journalists follow to get access to such new knowledge, called news, such as interviewing news sources, assisting at press conferences, reading press releases and other media, and (only sometimes) witnessing non-discursive news events themselves (Tuchman, 1978). Interestingly, most of these strategies are themselves discursive. The source of most news discourse is itself discourse. News reports are the result of a special form of 'text processing,' such as selection, summarization, paraphrasing, commenting, interpretation and so on (Van Dijk, 1988a).

In everyday conversation there are similar epistemic constraints on who can tell a story or inform about situations, events, actions or people recipients do not yet know about – or know less about. Thus, normatively, that is, by the epistemic criteria of our community, one can act as a source of knowledge for others only if one is a reliable source, that is, if one has direct or indirect access to such knowledge, for instance through one's own personal experiences, or as acquired from other (reliable) sources – the two major ways people acquire and justify knowledge. Thus speakers are only accountable for their own personal experiences or for citing correctly what others told them (but not for the content of what others told them)(Pomerantz, 1984). As we shall see below, after a more or less detailed story about a personal experience, speakers may next need to show various kinds of empathetic engagement or distance with respect to what has been told, whether or not they have had similar personal experiences, depending on the generality or specificity (granularity) of the story (Heritage, 2011).

Those who have epistemic access have the role of epistemic authority with respect to such knowledge and in relation to those participants who have no such access or only partial access. Epistemic authority entitles speakers to tell about such knowledge to others. One of the ways to index such authority is, for instance, through evidentials (Enfield, 2011; Fox, 2001; Heritage and Raymond, 2005).

More generally, conversation is organized by the relative epistemic status of participants, defined as a collection of entitlements and responsibilities as regards the knowledge of speakers (Enfield, 2011). Status also controls whether an utterance is heard as requesting or conveying information, even independent of intonation or morphosyntax, or what action is accomplished by the utterance (Heritage, 2012a). Hence, in different but related way to our postulation of a K-device as a central feature of context models, Heritage (2012b) speaks of an "epistemic engine" managing the (mutual) knowledge of speakers in conversation.

Conversation about previous interpersonal experiences or other events may involve several participants who all had access to such experiences. If such access was equal, then in principle all speakers are authorities over such shared knowledge. Yet, some of the participants may have had primary access to such knowledge, for instance because they knew first or because they know more about the events because they are experts. For instance, parents or grandparents may be assumed to know more about their (grand)children than others, so that social identities are also associated with specific territories of epistemic ownership and accountability (Heritage, 2011, 2012a; Raymond and Heritage, 2006). In general, those who have had primary access to knowledge also have conversational priority to tell about such knowledge. Sometimes speakers with less knowledge (K-) about a situation make a first assessment in the presence of a speaker with more knowledge (K+), in which case such an assessment may be challenged and downgraded in next turns (Heritage, 2011, 2012a, 2012b; Heritage and Raymond, 2005).

These various approaches to the study of knowledge in conversation are increasingly studied in a broader, interdisciplinary framework of conversational epistemics, in which notions of morality, such as affiliation and alignment in interaction and cooperation, are also dealt with (Stivers *et al.*, 2011a). Thus whereas alignment is a structural feature of talk, such as accepting presuppositions and matching the design preference of a turn, affiliation responses are more affective and pro-social and match the speaker's evaluative stance or display empathy with the prior action (Stivers *et al.*, 2011b; see also Enfield, 2011; see also below).

States of knowledge and epistemic discrepancies are not fixed in conversation and may dynamically change and be negotiated, upgraded and downgraded. Thus, initial expressions of ignorance by an expert as a reply to presupposed knowledge may require those who seek information to change their prior assumptions about the knowledge and ignorance of the expert (Mondada, 2011; on "not knowing" see also Keevallik, 2011).

According to our own theoretical framework, all these social and interactional structures and processes are only possible when speakers know about the general or specific knowledge of the other participants, that is, when they represent the other participants and their knowledge, as well as their access to such knowledge, as part of their context models. Having epistemic primacy does not as such control priority in talk, but what speakers subjectively construe as primacy in their context models. Since they may be mistaken, such primacy may also be challenged by recipients, as are the very sources and validity of their knowledge. Talk is not influenced by social facts, but by subjective definitions or constructions – models – of such facts.

Sometimes, context models are incomplete in the sense that speakers do not know exactly what recipients know. Before telling another person about new knowledge, therefore, they will typically engage in prefatory moves intended to elicit such knowledge and thus update the context model, as well as taking the floor to tell a story, e.g., with such questions as "Did I tell you about...?" (Jefferson, 1978).

As we shall further develop below for the description of assertive speech acts, speakers may express and convey their knowledge if they believe the recipients do not yet have such knowledge – the fundamental appropriate condition of assertions. But interaction has more constraints and principles, such as those of cooperation and politeness. Hence, if the communication of new knowledge would hurt or otherwise be against the best interests (face, reputation, health, feelings, etc.) of the speaker and/or the recipients, then assertions of new knowledge may also be interactionally or morally inadequate. Thus, epistemic authorities may have a license to tell, but not always the obligation to tell, and sometimes they may have a moral obligation not to tell – if the fundamental principle of social cooperation also implies not to hurt recipients, unless higher-order social norms (or a judge, etc.) require one to tell anyway.

Knowledge is a resource and possession that also imposes responsibility (Enfield, 2011). In some situations we are expected or even obliged to communicate our knowledge, such as is institutionally the case for students in exams, suspects or witnesses in court, reporters or correspondents of the media, professors in class or writing papers and so on. In everyday interaction, family members or close friends may be expected to tell about salient experiences, feelings or prior conversations or public messages.

7.3.1.2   Receiving knowledge in interaction

Recipients of knowledge in conversation first of all may have different participation roles. They may be explicit addressees of (prior turns) of talk, a letter or an e-mail, whether or not uniquely or as members of a collectivity of addressees. They may also be intentional or unintentional overhearers of talk or incidental readers of text – and thus acquire knowledge that was not addressed to them (Goffman, 1981).

As we have seen above, in Conversation Analysis the study of epistemics in this case focuses on the (next) actions of recipients of knowledge through prior turns at talk, for instance by examining in detail how recipients as next speakers align or affiliate themselves with previous speakers. In our own interdisciplinary framework it should be emphasized again that such an interaction sequence is not only an ordered sequence of turns or actions, but also involves thought in many ways. Thus, crucially, it is not (only) what previous speakers have actually said that influences, conditions or controls what a current speaker says, but the subjective representation of what has been said, that is a mental model of previous talk – as well as the plausible inferences of such talk. Thus, if we examine the conversational actions that follow a turn at talk, we should always bear in mind that next turns are conditioned by recipients' interpretations, constructions or definitions of what has been said before.

Recipients of new knowledge in conversation – or other forms of interaction and communication – can do many things. They may routinely accept such new knowledge if the communicative situation is controlled by a context model in which speakers are represented as sole reliable source. If knowledge is partly shared, complex questions of status, primacy and responsibility may influence how previous turns are accepted, challenged or corrected.

Acceptance cognitively involves the creation of a new situation model or updating an old one in case of a story about some recent events, or updating or changing generic knowledge in case of expository or pedagogical discourse.

Interactionally, such acceptance may be expressed by implicit acknowledgment, such as using the new knowledge as presupposition in further talk. Explicit acknowledgment may be expressed in many ways, by saying *Oh*, or *OK*, or *Yes*, or more explicitly *I didn't know (that)*. Such a preferred continuation of the conversation would be one of the ways participants align themselves with (the goals of) previous speakers, as one of the types of conversational cooperation (Enfield, 2011; Stivers *et al.*, 2011b).

However, recipients may do more than merely accept and acknowledge new information, and more explicitly or extensively affiliate with the previous speakers. They may do so by commenting positively on such new knowledge, by asking for details, or by contributing themselves related new knowledge, and so on – with the ultimate goal of enhancing or improving their image or the relationship itself.

7.3.1.2.1 Joint and distributed knowledge in storytelling

Affiliation typically may take place when two participants have shared personal experiences and thus cooperate in telling a story about it, as we have seen in the Californian burglary story examined in the previous chapter. See, for instance, in the following fragment of the interview, in which two senior citizens, a man (M) and a woman (W), husband and wife, tell about a burglary they have witnessed in the house next door:

(1) (A-TD-Ia,b)(Van Dijk, 1987: 75)

01   M: They were illegal aliens, Mexican.
02   W: They came over on the bus, didn't they?
03   M: Came over on the bus, and they had shopping bags, and they had uh I don't know
04   how many shopping bags stashed in the bushes.

05 w: They had twenty shopping bags stashed in the bushes.
06 m: Was it twenty?
07 w: Twenty.

Interesting here is that, in interaction with the interviewer as well as among themselves, the storytellers provide or confirm different aspects of their shared knowledge about the burglaries in the neighborhood. In this fragment, the man first concludes (line 1) from his knowledge of the arrest of the thieves that they were illegal aliens from Mexico – thus making the story relevant for the interview topic of immigrants in the neighborhood, and at the same time associating immigrants with crime, as is often the case in stories about immigrants. The woman then provides another detail of her knowledge about the burglars, but does so with a tag question, as if she has doubts about that information. However, interactionally, the tag question rather functions as a signal to her husband to confirm that knowledge and to continue the story, probably because he was the one who had primary access to that information. However, such access is not due to personal observation, but from hearsay (most likely from the police, referred to elsewhere in the same story) about how the burglars had arrived in the neighborhood or about the shopping bags they had hidden in the bushes. In line 3 the man first briefly confirms the knowledge tentatively expressed by his wife and immediately adds the information about the shopping bags. But then it is his turn to show lacking knowledge, namely about the number of shopping bags, information that is immediately supplied by the woman in the next turn (line 5) – which, however, is questioned by the man and then briefly confirmed by the woman (line 7). Obviously, the woman also does not have direct evidence of the number of bags, but shows better memory of what the police may have told her or her husband on earlier occasions. In this case the husband may well have had primary access to what the police had told him, but after previously having communicated that information to his wife, on a later occasion she may have better memory of a detail he may have forgotten. Hence, in conversational storytelling epistemic primacy is not just a question of direct access to information because of experience or hearsay, but also a question of better memory.

Of course, in this case, it may also be that the doubt about the number as expressed by the husband is a narrative and interactional move to attribute memory-primacy to his wife and give her a next turn in the storytelling, as she had done so before. So in this case, there is no clear evidence of primacy of access to the facts, no entitlement of authority displayed (even when the man may have heard about the facts of the burglaries from the police) but a narrative and interactional form of cooperation in joint storytelling with real or displayed difference of knowledge about the facts.

After the fragment cited above, the story continues as follows:

(2)

1 M: In the church lot, near the church, behind the bushes. They had broken into how
2   many places was it?
3 W: I don't remember.
4 M: I think they said forty homes, up the hill and in the college area, uh the way down to
5   here, and they were working their way down here.
6 W: You wouldn't believe it

Again the man signals lack of knowledge by an embedded question inviting his wife to supply that information, but when in line 3 she says she does not remember, the man in the next turn seems to have this information anyway. So, in the previous turn he could have mentioned that same insecure knowledge, but prefers to invite his wife to supply it. So, again we see that in joint storytelling speakers may cooperate by showing their shared knowledge but also display variable access and memory, which may well be different from what they really know or do not know. Similarly, again narratively, after the further (location) information of the burglaries supplied by the man in lines 1–2, the woman comments not by supplying more information or showing ignorance, but with a typical narrative evaluation turn in line 6, enhancing the interestingness of the facts just reported (*forty homes*) and hence their narratability, in terms of an epistemic qualification of the (in)credibility of the events.

Note also that in the story the source of the further information (most likely the police or other neighbors) about the burglaries is not mentioned. In the beginning of the story the man only stresses what he had witnessed himself. His visually based experience as a direct knowledge source and hence his narrative credibility is enhanced by repeating that he "had a good description" of one of the thieves.

7.3.1.2.2 Misalignment and disaffiliation

Next speakers may misalign or disaffiliate with previous speakers, for instance by not believing, not accepting, criticizing or otherwise failing to acknowledge the knowledge expressed in a previous turn. A speaker may have shared access to the facts, and discredit the rendering of it by the previous speaker in several ways, for instance by corrections, adding details or providing different interpretations or evaluations of the facts (Enfield, 2011; Stivers *et al.*, 2011b).

Given the general pragmatic norm that assertions require that only new knowledge should be conveyed, one of the standard ways of misaligning with previous speakers is to express or show that the information was not new – for instance by referring to a shared personal experience or the same knowledge source, or a previous conversation.

Similarly, the knowledge sources of the previous speaker may be discredited in many ways, basically by questioning their reliability – a criticism that itself may be backed up by personal experiences (e.g., previous unreliable activities of a source).

From this brief account we see that the epistemics of everyday interaction has many subtle norms and constraints for an adequate expression, communication or reception of knowledge. Participants may have different institutional identities (e.g., reporters), interactional roles (experts), communicative roles (addressees, readers) and relationships (professor–student, etc.). They may be entitled to express and communicate knowledge because they have (primacy of) access, but also be legally or morally required to provide knowledge, as is the case in court as well as in conversations among friends. Recipients may (mis)align or (dis)affiliate with previous speakers by (not) accepting their knowledge, or by elaborating or criticizing such knowledge or discrediting its sources as being unreliable. Thus, any kind of interactional 'operation' on (a source of) knowledge expressed in prior turns may thus be a next move in such epistemic sequences, such as acceptance, complete rejection, correction, elaboration, summarization, commentary or any other form of challenge. More generally, conversation analysis also shows the important nature of the sequentiality of the expression of knowledge in talk: who may or must express what information in talk first or second, and how earlier expressions of such knowledge influence later ones (for the linguistic implications of this dimension, see Clift, 2012).

7.3.1.3   Epistemic rights and duties in institutional interaction
These forms and strategies of epistemic interaction are not limited to informal everyday conversation but also may be observed in institutional interaction, such as interaction in the classroom or the courtroom, doctor–patient interaction, interviews and interrogations and many other genres. Besides the types, sources and quality of knowledge expressed in such situations, as discussed above, the settings, institutional identities, roles and relations of the speech participants, institutional goals, and rules, norms and laws may define the context models that control such talk (see, e.g., Peräkylä and Vehviläinen, 2003).

In many institutional situations the justification criteria of knowledge (the 'truth') may be stricter. This in turn may imply special constraints on the responsibility and reliability of participants in various roles, e.g., as victims, witnesses or experts. Witnesses in court are obliged to tell the truth because of their assumed primacy of access to the 'facts' as eyewitnesses, whereas experts are assumed to tell the truth because of their generic epistemic authority (expertise) or new current findings (by reliable methods)(Apter, 1996; Carroll and Seng, 2003; Cutler, 2009; Loftus and Doyle, 1987; Stygall, 2001; Winiecki, 2008).

Recipients in institutional interaction, depending again on their identity, role or relationship with speakers or writers, may expect or demand that speakers tell what they know, again as do judges in courtrooms, professors in classrooms or police officers in interrogation rooms. As in informal conversations, thus, recipients may (mis)align or (dis)affiliate with speakers by accepting, agreeing or confirming prior statements, but they may also challenge assertions, declarations or stories, require that (further) evidence be supplied, or elaborate, contradict, doubt previous statements (see, e.g., Heydon, 2005; Komter, 1995; Magnussen *et al.*, 2010; Maynard and Marlaire, 1992; Rabon, 1992; Shuy, 1998; Stokoe and Edwards, 2006; Thornborrow, 2002).

Relations of power and authority in most of these institutional interactions are enacted or confirmed by alignment and affiliation of less powerful with more powerful participants, whereas misalignment and disaffiliation may characterize responses of powerful speakers to statements of less powerful speakers (Haworth, 2006; Wodak, 1984).

7.3.2   *Discourse complexes and intertextuality*

The main argument in favor of discourse grammars several decades ago was that sentences in actual language use seldom come alone, and that they must be described in relation to preceding and following sentences and as part of sequences and whole discourses (Petöfi and Rieser, 1973; Van Dijk, 1972). It is therefore strange that in formal discourses studies the same argument has seldom been repeated at higher levels: discourses also seldom come alone, and they form complex sets with multiple, intertextual relationships, typically described in literary and communication studies, for instance, in terms of **intertextuality** (among many studies, see Meinhof and Smith, 2000; Plett, 1991).

Conversations with family members, friends or colleagues tend to presuppose and continue previous ones, and the same is true for news reports in the press, political or scholarly debates and so on. The very notions of 'old' and 'new' information, often used in studies of information structure, presuppose that functions of topic and focus depend on what has been said before. This typically holds for sentences or turns within text or talk, but in similar ways, and at a higher level, this also may be case for the relations between whole discourses, often studied in terms of intertextuality.

In other words, the specific knowledge to be expressed and presupposed in discourse at all levels, first of all may depend on the specific knowledge conveyed by previous discourses of the same or related participants in related communicative situations. Thus, a news report may repeat parts of what had been reported earlier, and maybe be prefaced by formulas such as *As we reported earlier* or by various presuppositional structures such as the use of definite articles or embedded clauses. Intertextually, this 'old' information thus may be assigned the function of a **global topic** and the new information of the current discourse the function of **global focus**. This functional division, however, does not structure clauses or sentences, as is the case for local topic–focus relationships, but is distributed all over text or talk – such that global focus function is assigned to all information not yet given in previous discourse or not yet supposed to be known to the recipients. In other words, Common Ground also requires intertextual information.

One way to see such a distinction is in titles and headlines that express the main macroproposition of the discourse, e.g., when a news report features a headline such as **OBAMA PLANS BIG EFFORT TO BUILD SUPPORT AMONG WOMEN** (*New York Times*, March 10, 2012). Here the initial noun phrase *Obama* has local topic function in the headline sentence, not only because of first position, but also because he is generally known, has been main news actor in many previous news stories, and because this specific article is one in a series on the Obama 2012 re-election campaign. Given the summarizing macro-functions of headlines (Van Dijk, 1988a), it is likely that Obama will also be a major actor in this news report, and given the series of previous *NYT* (and other media) articles, 'Obama' is also a global topic of this whole news report. But in this case, the (global) topic function is not limited to Obama, but includes the 'old' information that is relevant to understanding this news report, for instance about his re-election, information that is repeated and hence recalled for the readers of the *NYT* in the first, thematic lead sentence of the report:

> (3) WASHINGTON – President Obama's re-election campaign is beginning an intensified effort this week to build support among women, using the debate over the new health care law to amplify an appeal that already appears to be benefiting from partisan clashes over birth control and abortion. (*New York Times*, March 10, 2012)

Hence, to better understand the **new, global focus information** about Obama's plans to seek support among women, the readers are reminded of the ongoing debates (explicitly mentioned in this lead sentence) on birth control and abortion, as well as the new healthcare law. Hence, a global functional topic is not a noun phrase, nor an isolated concept or even a news actor, nor a set of propositions, but a complex information structure, as it has been accumulated in mental models until the present discourse. Such a complex information structure is part of the Common Ground of the journalist and the readers of the *NYT* – although the complete CG of this article is of course much more complex and features generic knowledge about (re-) election campaigns, US presidents, women, abortion, birth control and so on. Implied and presupposed but not spelled out in the lead sentence is that generally women are more likely to support Obama's (or democratic) ideas about birth control or abortion.

So, if journalists and readers have construed a **complex (macrolevel) mental situation model** of Obama's 2012 re-election campaign, then that mental model defines the **global topic** of this article – a model in turn based on large amounts of generic and specific (historical) knowledge about politics, elections and so on. All the information added to that model in this article then has **global focus** function.

It should be stressed that the technical *functional* notion of **discourse topic** should not be confused with the informal notion of 'topic' representing **semantic macropropositions**, that is, the most important information of a discourse – which represents both old and new information, as is also obvious in the headline sentence expressing the macroproposition (Van Dijk, 1980).

To avoid likely confusion between the two notions I shall use the technical expression **global functional topic** to refer to all the given or old information of a discourse, as represented by the old mental model of the (macro) event of which the current news report is an update, and continue to use the informal notion of **discourse topic** in order to refer to semantic macropropositions. Both are typical global notions, and have whole discourses as their scope, but the first is a functional notion, only defined in relation to a complementary concept, namely that of global functional focus, representing all the new information of text or talk.

7.3.3   Epistemic pragmatics

The theory of context models forms the sociocognitive basis of the pragmatics of discourse since it features, by definition, all relevant conditions for the appropriateness of text and talk (Van Dijk, 2008a, 2009a). This means that phenomena that have been studied in the large field of pragmatics in principle should be accounted for in terms of context models: speech acts, politeness, conversational postulates and so on.

In this book and this chapter, however, we focus only very briefly on the epistemic aspects of pragmatics, that is, those conditions that are based on the K-device regulating appropriate uses of knowledge in discourse. Hence we ignore those pragmatic phenomena that draw on other properties of communicative situations, such as power, status or kinship of participants, for instance as these influence the expression of politeness and deference, or speech acts such as commands. On the other hand, we do need to take into account some social properties of participants as they relate to knowledge, such as their epistemic expertise, authority, rights, primacy, responsibility and so on, as we have seen above for conversational interaction.

7.3.3.1   Epistemic speech acts

Epistemic speech acts are speech acts whose appropriateness depends on epistemic conditions, in the sense that speakers primarily want the recipients to know something they did not know, or ask something they do not know themselves – whatever other, direct or indirect illocutionary functions these speech acts may have (among the vast literature on speech acts and pragmatics, see Austin, 1962; Levinson, 1983; Searle, 1969). Thus, in threats, speakers also want the recipients to know something, but as a condition for the primary illocutionary function, namely that the recipients should act as desired by the speaker. Similarly, in promises, speakers also convey knowledge about their intentions of future actions, but as a condition for a commitment to future action. Since these aspects have been extensively dealt with in other studies, we only briefly summarize some of the epistemic conditions and some further properties of appropriate uses of these speech acts.

7.3.3.1.1   Assertions   The basic pragmatic and epistemic act is the assertion (Stalnaker, 1978). The normative appropriateness conditions of this speech act as traditionally formulated (Searle, 1969) are:

(i)   Speaker knows p
(ii) Speaker believes that Recipients do not know p
(iii) Speaker wants Recipients to know p
(iv) Speaker believes that the Recipients want or need to know p.

The belief in (ii) is based on the current CG in text or talk, which not only informs the speaker about what knowledge the recipients share, but by inference what they don't know as yet. Another source for condition (ii) is that the speaker is informing recipients about (a) a private experience or (b) recent discourse as a source of knowledge of an event to which the recipients have not (yet) had access. Condition (iv) may be inferred from a previous question in a Question–Answer adjacency pair in conversation, or more generally from implied ignorance in previous text and context.

Abstract, normative speech act theory ignores that in actual text and talk assertions are subject to more detailed, normative and moral social conditions – some of which are dealt with in the epistemic analysis of conversation. But there is more.

First of all, condition (i) should be further specified by requiring the 'normal condition' that if speakers do not know p or know that non-p, they should not assert that p – because in that case the assertion is inappropriate, and is in fact a pretension of knowledge where there is none, or a lie. Moreover, the very condition that a speaker knows p presupposes the usual epistemic conditions of reliable previous experiences or knowledge sources, as well as some obvious inferences. In other words, speakers who make assertions are entitled to make such assertions if their knowledge is valid, e.g., because they have access to knowledge. This may be the case for journalists who have access to reliable sources, or when people speak about private experiences, as in the following example of the burglary story cited above:

(4)

ɪ: And the people who, who, do you have an idea about the people who do the burglaries about here. I mean, what kind of people would they be?

w: Well, one day ... Yeah tell him about

ᴍ: A lot are Mexicans. I was home one time I had the flu, and uh I came out to the kitchen to get myself a cup of tea, just in my pajamas, and I happen to look out of the window, and I see them breaking in into the house next door.

Again, as before, the woman yields the floor to her husband in their joint storytelling, after starting to tell a story herself as a reply to the question with a typical Setting category (*one day*), in this case because her husband had first access to the events, because of what he had witnessed. So, the man continues the story by first answering the question of the interviewer about the identity of the burglars and then restarts the story with more specific Setting information. So, as we have seen before for conversational interaction, assertions are not limited to secondary information (what people have read in the paper or heard from the police), but they are especially credible when based on personal experience and observation. Hence the otherwise irrelevant detail (*I had the flu, get a cup of tea, in my pajamas*) has both narrative as well as epistemic functions: it makes stories more interesting and more credible. Cognitively, such details typically show in (re)telling based on personal experiences, that is, embodied situation models of memorable events. Hence, the basic pragmatic condition of assertions, namely that a speaker knows something recipients do not know is thus made explicit and relevant by the ways speakers explain *how* they knew and why such knowledge is credible. Knowledge sources (direct observation) may even be made more credible in conversation. Thus, the fact that the husband was at home during the day is made more credible by explaining that he had the flu and was in his pajamas, and that he could see the burglars is further made more credible by why he was in the kitchen. Hence, we see that in everyday conversation, storytellers may extensively be engaged in making their knowledge more credible by providing first- and second-level evidence about how they obtained such knowledge.

When drawing on generic specialized knowledge, such entitlement may be based on epistemic expertise, for instance in scholarly or legal discourse and communication. More generally, epistemic superiority in any kind of discourse, e.g., based on prior or privileged epistemic access, may imply authority over knowledge thus 'possessed' and voluntarily shared with the recipients.

There are situations, however, where the conditions of appropriate assertions are different, for instance when speakers have been requested to share
their knowledge, for instance in normal questions, or in commands to divulge
knowledge, for instance in interrogations. In this case, the other components –
such as Participant Roles – of the context model come into play, namely when
recipients are institutionally more powerful than speakers, when the law or
the recipient obliges speakers-knowers to divulge specific knowledge, as is
the case in police or courtroom interrogations (Kidwell, 2009; Komter, 1995,
1998).

Finally, there are further sociocultural constraints, also premised on the
properties of participants as subjectively represented (and hence possibly
misguided) in the context model of the speaker. For instance, if recipients are
generally more knowledgeable than the speaker, especially in the knowledge
domain at issue, and hence would normally have primacy access and authority
over such knowledge, then the presumption of condition (ii) that the recipients
do not know p, and condition (iv) that the recipients may want to know p, may
not be satisfied. And even if conditions (ii) and/or (iii) are satisfied, asserting p
may well threaten the face of the recipients, and hence be inappropriate or even
impolite in many situations and cultures. In that case, special discursive moves
and strategies may be needed in the actual formulation of the speech acts so as
to diminish the possible damage to the social face (reputation, honor, authority,
etc.) of the recipients, for instance by prefacing such assertions by expressions
such as "Of course you know that …" or "As you know…"

There may be other special conditions on assertions, for instance if the communication of knowledge somehow may hurt the speaker and/or the recipients.
Typical cases here are doctors who sometimes don't inform patients about
(details of) their illness, suspects in court who need not incriminate themselves, or withholding negative evaluations of recipients asking for an opinion
about themselves.

Given these various conditions of epistemic speech acts such as assertions,
we see that the general pragmatic condition of cooperation should be more
specifically formulated here in terms of *epistemic cooperation*, for instance in
terms of the epistemic entitlements and authority of speakers, the epistemic
status and relations of participants, the rights of recipients to know, or to be
protected against unwanted knowledge and so on.

In other words, the answer to the pragmatic meta-question *Who may assert
what to whom in what situation* requires an analytic effort that goes beyond
classical appropriateness conditions of speech acts. We need not only more
detail in the conditions, but also specific cognitive conditions on the kind of
knowledge that can be expressed and communicated, and social conditions, as
represented in context models about the normative and moral aspects of assertions, and the social positions and relations of the participants.

7.3.3.1.2 Questions The normative account of questions is of course closely related to that of assertions, because the implications of questions may be conditions of assertions. A question implies a lack of knowledge by speakers requested to be supplied by the recipients (see Chisholm, 1984; Searle, 1969; Tsui, 1992):

(i)   Speaker does not know p
(ii) Speaker believes Recipients know p
(iii) Speaker wants to know (whether) p
(iv) Speaker wants the Recipients to tell (whether) p.

Unlike assertions, questions have a directive nature, like requests: speakers want the recipients to do something, namely tell them something they do not know themselves. Again, condition (ii) is satisfied if speakers are justified about the knowledge of the recipients, for instance because of previously shown expertise in a knowledge domain or, more mundanely, because the speaker believes the recipients have had access to sources of knowledge (experiences, hearsay, etc.) the speaker does not have. Obviously, the conditions imply that in general a question is inappropriate if speakers ask something they already know – except in special institutional situations, such as exams or interrogations.

Again, further normative and moral conditions apply. Not anyone may ask anything from anyone else who is supposed to know something in any situation. Politicians may give speeches or press conferences and may not allow questions from reporters or may refuse or avoid replies to questions in interviews (Clayman and Heritage, 2002). Professors may give a class or a lecture and may not accept questions or only permit questions afterwards (Carlsen, 1997; Edwards and Davis, 1997).

There are a vast number of sociocultural constraints on what may be asked. If knowledge is a private possession it may not always be voluntarily shared with anyone who wants to know, as is the case for information about private affairs, such health conditions, feelings, sexual behavior, financial situation and so on (Borge, 2007).

Apart from contextual constraints on the mental models that may thus be communicated, we at the same time find other social constraints on the participants as represented in the context model. Thus, close friends may ask much more (and more private) information than strangers. Participants in specific roles, such as police officers, judges, lawyers or doctors may have the right to ask things other people may not ask, even if recipients do not want to share such information – as we know from the vast literature on professional interviews and interrogation (Boden and Zimmerman, 1991; Drew and Heritage, 1992; Kidwell, 2009; Millar *et al.*, 1992; Thornborrow, 2002; see also above).

Finally, asking questions may involve issues of face and other social relations of politeness, deference and power (Goody, 1978). Asking questions implies ignorance, and not all speakers in any situation want to display such ignorance for anyone, for instance if they themselves are authorities or have primary epistemic access to knowledge sources. In that case, asking questions may imply losing face or prestige in front of the recipients. On the other hand, if an expert asks a non-trivial question of a novice, such a question may be interpreted as recognizing the expertise of the recipient.

On the other hand, questions in interaction may presuppose knowledge. Thus Kidwell (2009) shows that a standard question of the police in some incident may be "What happened?" and this already presupposes that there was an incident in the first place, and also that the addressee is supposed to know the answer.

So, we see again that the context model controls the epistemic appropriateness of questions by specifying what kind of speakers may ask what kind of information from what kind of recipients, and in what kind of social/institutional situations.

Question–Answer adjacency pairs in conversation or in a media or classroom debate have many more – and more subtle – interactional features, as we have seen above and to which we shall return below. Participants may agree or disagree with assertions of the previous speaker, align themselves with assertions or questions, or they may protect themselves by not replying to questions, or ignore assertions of previous speakers. They may engage in elaborate preparatory moves in order to make sure recipients know (as in questions), or do not know (as in assertions), as well as about their expertise, entitlements, authority, privacy and so on, as discussed above. Thus, in a study of classroom interaction, Sert (2013) shows that after asking questions teachers engage in "Epistemic Status Checks" (e.g., "No idea?," "You don't know?") when students show with their body language they do not know the answer. Thus, we see again that in the actual performance of speech acts, language users use and update the K-device of their context models.

7.3.4   *Epistemic discourse semantics*

7.3.4.1   *Semantic macrostructures*

We have seen above that a distinction must be made between two sorts of 'discourse topic,' namely global functional topics that define what is old information in a discourse, on the one hand, and global meanings or topics that convey the most important information of text or talk, and that control local propositions, that is, local meanings of words, clauses and sentences, on the other hand.

Strangely ignored in much traditional formal linguistics and even in some approaches of discourse analysis, *semantic macrostructures* represent the overall meanings of text or talk, informally referred to as topics, themes, gist or upshot (Asher, 2004; Goutsos, 1997; Van Dijk, 1972, 1977, 1980).

These hierarchical structures define the overall, global coherence of discourse. They control top-down the local, sequential coherence of the propositions as they are expressed in discourse, as is typically (but not only) the case in discourse production. They are inductively derived from sequences of local propositions, as is typically the case in discourse comprehension and are usually best recalled in discourse reproduction (Louwerse and Graesser, 2006; Van Dijk and Kintsch, 1983).

As is generally the case for any meaning, semantic macrostructures may be only implicit in discourse. However, to facilitate production and especially comprehension, there are many discourse markers, moves, strategies or specific genre categories that express macropropositions, at various levels of generality: headlines and titles, leads and abstracts, thematic initial sentences and final concluding sentences or paragraphs. These macrosemantic markers typically occur at the beginning and are often highlighted, e.g., typographically (see below). Thus, the macropropositions they express may be used to interpret local words and sentences, and construe local, sequential coherence in talk and text – or sometimes at the end to make sure the recipient has not lost the general upshot after a large amount of more detailed, local information. See, for instance, the double headline of the news report in Chapter 1:

(5) **Taxpayer funding £100,000 a day for failed asylum seekers**
The taxpayer is spending more than £100,000 a day to house failed asylum seekers who have no right to be in the country.

We see, first of all, that headlines are sequentially independent: the second, more specific headline simply repeats the main headline with more detail, as would be the case for a hierarchical macrostructure of which each higher level summarizes the information at a lower level. We also see that macropropositions are subjective in the sense that journalists may express or signal aspects of a story they find interesting or more relevant for the readers, as is also the case here. A dry Home Office report on funding asylum seekers is thus made relevant and more memorable for readers if it is emphasized how much asylum seekers cost them (as taxpayers). Cognitively this may mean that the journalist is building a biased model of the Home Office information in the first place, or that such a mental model is ongoingly construed as displayed in the news article by emphasizing what is mostly relevant for the public. In the first case, headlines have mainly a semantic function (summarizing what is known), and in the second case they have a pragmatic function, by adapting to the audience and what they are supposed to be interested in.

Macropropositions are interpreted as the top-level information of (semantic) situation models in episodic memory, hierarchically dominating a possibly complex set of more detailed local information. When language users no longer have access to the details of discourse or the mental model that interprets it, they often still remember the main topics, as they are related to many details, and possibly repeated and hence strengthened in thought or talk (see Chapter 3).

The macropropositions in mental models and discourse need not always coincide. Indeed, as is the case in much political and media discourse, powerful speakers may want to hide the really important information, as represented in their models of an event or situation, by downgrading or even hiding such information in public discourse and emphasizing less important information in many ways, for instance by headlines, repetition and other devices.

Yet, at least normatively, the semantic macrostructures of discourse usually correspond with what for speakers is the most important information of a discourse, as this is represented in the top level of their mental model of an event. They define what and how knowledge as expressed in discourse may be variably important, relevant or interesting, thus allowing various strategies to emphasize or downgrade information in communication. Since all participants have their own situation model of discourse, they may of course have different interpretations, and hence different models, as well as different macrostructures (topics) – whatever the structures used by the speaker or writer strongly suggesting what their mental model and macrostructures are. Recipients may ignore such discourse markers and construe their own macrostructure, for instance because of previous experiences (mental models) or different general knowledge and ideologies.

Macrostructures not only are the major level for the expression on knowledge in discourse, and not only express (or construe, inductively) top levels of mental models of discourse, they also crucially involve generic knowledge. Language users need detailed generic knowledge of the world in order to be able to 'summarize' large, possibly incomplete or incoherent, sequences of local propositions in terms of more general, more abstract, global meanings. They may thus activate scripts of a voyage when reading about stations, airports or luggage, or conversely in discourse production, a general topic may activate or prime the detailed information by the general concept or macroproposition that dominates it in semantic or episodic memory. In this respect the hierarchical nature of macrostructures reflects the hierarchical structure of specific mental models of events and experiences, as well as much of the hierarchical structure of generic knowledge (Mani and Maybury, 1999; Marcu, 2000; Seidlhofer, 1995; Van Dijk, 1980).

In discourse comprehension language users tend to strategically infer and construe a macroproposition as soon as possible from the information in text, talk or context – typically with the help of initial macro-markers such as headlines and titles, but also by various prefaces in storytelling in talk ("Did I tell you about ...?"), announcements of items in news reports on TV and so on. As soon as recipients have a tentative macroproposition, this topic will help them to construe local coherence, to construe or (re)activate relevant mental models or model fragments, to activate generic knowledge and in general to activate and integrate all knowledge relevant for adequate understanding.

Experimental evidence shows that ambiguous discourse without initial macropropositions (e.g., in a title or headline) may be hard to understand (Bransford and Johnson, 1972; Kozminsky, 1977). Similarly, without the construction of macropropositions, discourse is more generally hard to produce or understand – while only processed locally – and very difficult to store, recall and summarize. Since macrostructures also define global coherence, their absence also makes local coherence production or comprehension very difficult and erratic – while missing an overall 'direction.'

Relevant for this chapter is especially the fact that without macropropositions in discourse, the knowledge represented in mental models of specific events is also disorganized and hence hard to use in later situations. For generic knowledge communication, as in expository discourse, the lack of macropropositions may index or cause such knowledge not to be hierarchically organized, for instance in schemas or scripts.

Since semantic macrostructures in discourse usually realize at least parts of the top-level structures of situation models, personal knowledge of specific events as defined by these models is not limited to its detailed, local structures but may also be more global and general. Since this is also the information that is best recalled from discourse, we may conclude that knowledge acquired from text and talk often is not the kind of knowledge that is literally expressed in discourse, but only the implicit gist, upshot or topic as construed by recipients and hence as top-level information in their own, possibly biased, situation model. This is a crucial aspect of the reproduction of knowledge in society – and especially relevant for oral discourse that has not been recorded for later inspection, as is the case for most everyday conversation, and in actual practice for most forms of communication in which recipients no longer have or seek access to the literal version of the discourse.

This is a fundamental sociocognitive aspect of the relation between knowledge and discourse and should be taken into account in all studies on the communication of knowledge in oral discourse: because of episodic memory limitations after longer delays, and hence also in longer talk, recipients no longer have complete access to the details of the knowledge that has been expressed before, but typically will remember only the current discourse topic plus some relevant (e.g., emotional) details.

7.3.4.2   Local, sequential coherence

More broadly studied, also in linguistics, are the cohesion and coherence relations between propositions, clauses, sentences or turns in local sequences of text or talk (among many other books, see, e.g., Bublitz *et al.*, 1999; Gernsbacher and Givón, 1995; Halliday and Hasan, 1976; Tomlin, 1987; Van Dijk, 1977). In our current theoretical framework this means that under control of the semantic macrostructures and hence the top level of situation models, local sentences express propositions that need to be connected for discourse to be locally, sequentially, coherent (Van Dijk and Kintsch, 1983). Unfortunately, given the limitations of sentence grammars that lack the level of macrostructure, traditional grammatical accounts of discourse topics and their relation to sequential or sentential topics as well as coherence are necessarily incomplete, because they have no way to define overall discursive 'aboutness' (see, e.g., the account of these notions in Kehler, 2004).

Local coherence is of two types: functional and referential. **Functional local coherence** is defined in terms of direct relations between propositions expressed in discourse, such as generalization, specification, elaboration, example, explanation and so on. Some of these relations have also been studied in terms of "rhetorical relations" in Rhetorical Structure Theory (Mann and Thompson, 1987, 1991) – which, however, does not distinguish between functional coherence relations and the referential ones we mention below, nor between hierarchical macrostructures and sequential microstructures of discourse.

Typical examples of (local) functional relations in discourse can be found in news reports. These tend to be organized by an increasing specification of earlier general propositions as they are typically expressed at the beginning of the text, for instance in headline and lead (Van Dijk, 1988a). See, for instance, the beginning of the news report cited in Chapter 1 and commented on above:

> (6) The Home Office spent almost £40 million last year supporting so-called "hard cases" – asylum seekers who have had their claims rejected but cannot leave for one reason or another.
> It is usually because of unsafe conditions in their home country, a medical condition or they have launched a judicial review on a legal point in their case.

Thus, the second sentence (*It is usually* ...) provides a specification of the very general and vague information of the previous sentence (*cannot leave for one reason or another*). Similarly, David Cameron in his *Sun* article analyzed in Chapter 5 similarly provides a specification of a general situation description and evaluation:

> (7) *Sun* readers know that immigration got out of control under Labour.
> Frankly, this country became a soft touch: 2.2 million more people came in than went out.

A later specification of a cause or reason of action often functions as an explanation. Such functional relations are in fact second-order relations because they presuppose a causal relation between the second fact and the previously mentioned fact (e.g., 'unsafe conditions in their home country are the cause of asylum seekers not going back there').

Whereas in news articles we typically see functional relations of specification and explanation, conclusions in scholarly articles may generalize what has just been reported in more specific detail in the 'body' of the text (Oldenburg, 1992; Swales, 2004; Teufel, 2010).

Referential local coherence, on the other hand, is indirect and based on the relations between the facts referred to by the discourse and those represented subjectively in the situation model of the discourse. In this case, we talk about relations between events, for instance those of temporality and causality, whole and part, close and near and so on. Thus, in his *Sun* article David Cameron causally relates his legislative policy to the immigration of people from Eastern Europe:

> (8) But as a Government we have to make sure people come here for the right reasons.
>
> That's why today I'm announcing a number of new measures on immigration (26–29).

Hence referential local coherence is defined in terms of the situation models of the participants – and hence also relative to the participants. Thus, discourses may be more or less coherent according to speakers and recipients or for different recipients (Albrecht and O'Brien, 1993; Goldman *et al.*, 1999; Lorch and O'Brien, 1995; Van Dijk, 1977; Van Dijk and Kintsch, 1983).

Again, we see that a crucial aspect of discourse, namely its coherence, should be defined not only in terms of semantic or conceptual relations between propositions, but (also) in terms of the underlying, subjective and intersubjective mental models of participants. Thus, in the asylum story of Chapter 1, the summarizing first part of the story, namely that asylum seekers often cannot go back to their home countries because of unsafe conditions – making the first and second sentence coherent – is followed by a specification of a consequence that is found to be especially relevant for the readers of the *Daily Telegraph*, thus also signaling the anti-immigration stance of this conservative newspaper:

> (9) But in the meantime the taxpayer must fund their accommodation and living allowances.

This also shows that in discourse we do not merely find an objective description or summarizing selection of major conditions and consequences of news events but an ideologically controlled selection of consequences that are construed as especially relevant for the readers, as is also obvious in David Cameron's construction of relating legislation to the arrival of immigrants from Eastern Europe. Indeed, instead of attributing the costs of asylum seekers to the government or the country, they are specifically attributed to the taxpayers, making the news report pragmatically more relevant for the readers. Such a strategy, making appeals to readers' fears, is typical of populist manipulation by the media or politicians (Van Dijk, 2006a).

Discourses are typically incomplete for the pragmatic reasons mentioned above: speakers do (need, should) not express the shared knowledge of the Common Ground, that is, information the recipients can easily infer by themselves, for instance from the previous text or context, earlier discourses or generic knowledge of the community. Hence, in order to establish local coherence, recipients must first of all construe a viable mental model of the discourse, and this construction of the mental model requires the activation of large amounts of generic knowledge that needs to be instantiated ('applied') in the construction of the details of a personal model of specific events.

In sum, global and local coherence of discourse crucially relies on the structures of subjective situation models of participants, as well as on the generic knowledge used in the construction of these models.

Relevant for more detailed cognitive analysis is the question *how much* generic knowledge needs to be – or usually is – activated to construe a situation model of the events referred to by a discourse. The more (and the deeper, more specific) knowledge is activated and instantiated, the more detailed the mental model. But, as we have seen in Chapter 3, such activation is contextually variable and depends on the participants (and their expertise), the time they have to hear or read the respective sentences, their goals or tasks (to understand globally or more locally, and in more detail), and so on. That is, as we shall see below, participants strategically adapt the level of specificity and the amount of detail in their situation model to the communicative situation.

Relevant for this chapter is the insight that a fundamental characteristic of discourse, namely its semantic coherence, cannot be limited to establishing relations among sequences of propositions expressed in text and talk, but crucially involves the more complete specific knowledge about a situation as construed in mental models, on the one hand, and the inferences in such models as they are derived from generic knowledge about such situations, on the other. Indeed, besides the activation of knowledge for the understanding of the meaning of words, clauses and sentences, this epistemic basis of the very production and comprehension of discourse coherence is no doubt among the most relevant aspects of the study of the relations between knowledge and discourse.

7.3.4.3   Sequencing and ordering

Besides their local coherence, sequences of propositions also have some *ordering constraints* related to mental models and more fundamental properties of perception and interaction, a property of discourse that is much less studied than, for instance, word order in sentences. Thus, in an account of events and actions, the *normal order* of propositions (and the clauses that express them) is conditioned by the temporal, causal and spatial order of the events referred to, and as represented in the situation model of the speaker. As soon as this order is reversed, e.g., by expressing consequences of an event before its causes or conditions, we no longer have normal order as defined by the mental model, but a functional relationship of explanation, as we have seen above for the asylum seeker news report. Similar constraints hold for the discursive linearization of spatial order (Briner *et al.*, 2012; Levelt, 1982; Morrow, 1986).

For other sequences, too, such as descriptions of situations, there are constraints on ordering based on fundamental properties of perception and perspective. Thus, we generally expect larger objects to be described or identified before smaller ones, wholes before parts, close scenes before faraway scenes, global before local, entities (persons, animals, objects, etc.) before their properties and so on. In a story or film there is a normal order in which we first find a representation of a city, neighborhood or landscape, then a street, then a house, a room in the house, the large contents of the room (e.g., a table) and finally the parts or smaller objects (like a book on the table, then a page in the book, etc.).

Functional relations of coherence, such as those of explanation, specification, generalization or example also show various systems of normal ordering, as is the case in the following example of the news item in the *Telegraph* on asylum seekers in Chapter 1 (lines 21–25):

> (10) Under what is known as Section 4 support, asylum seekers who have had their claim for shelter rejected but cannot currently return home are given accommodation and living support. In the 12 months up to September 2011, a total of 4,430 people were awarded such support – the equivalent of 12 a day.

Thus, the proposition that asylum seekers receive living support, expressed in the first sentence, is *specified* in the second sentence by making explicit how many asylum seekers received such support in a given period of time. Obviously, the order of presentation is generally fixed: it would be strange in this case to first say how many people received living support in the last year and then that these people are asylum seekers. Indeed, 'asylum seekers' as discourse and sentence topics have already been introduced, so the normal order for a news item is to present more detailed descriptions of their properties, actions or their roles in actions by others, e.g., in terms of quantification, time periods and so on.

Since situation models are multimodal and hence represent many types of experiences, this kind of mental visualization of scenes, events, actions, people, objects and their properties and relations, may also be expressed by special ordering constraints of sequences in text and talk. Deviations from such 'natural' ordering generally mean that they need special, strategic interpretations, such as highlighting, salience, etc.

Moreover, mental models are subjective and feature a central Self with respect to which events are seen, defined and evaluated. This also allows for a visual (or doxastic) perspective from which to observe or evaluate situations, events and actions. Self-centered discourse, such as much everyday storytelling, will thus define and order the events as seen by the speaker-Self. But various forms of fictional discourse, sometimes also in conversation, may locate the center of perspective with an actor, protagonist or even the recipients, as we know from much classical research on point of view and perspective in literary narrative and film (Bal, 1985, 2004; Branigan, 1984; Canisius, 1987; Genette, 1980; Lanser, 1981).

One of the conclusions of this work is that discourse order is on the one hand controlled by our knowledge about 'normal' order in everyday experiences of situations, as represented in mental models, and on the other hand by special discursive moves and strategies that have specific communicative functions, such as explanation, change of focus, salience, suspense enhancement and other narrative strategies.

7.3.4.4 Descriptions

Also little studied but an important aspect of sequential discourse meaning are the properties of *descriptions*, e.g., of situations, events, actions, actors, objects, landscapes, places and so on (Dale, 1992; Ehrich and Koster, 1983; Johnson-Laird and Garnham, 1980; Levelt, 1996; Tenbrink *et al.*, 2011).

In two influential studies, Van Leeuwen (1995, 1996) presented a systemic framework for the description of social actors and actions and their variable functions in discourse. For instance, social actors may be described as individuals or as members of social groups, be named or remain anonymous, they may be included or excluded (suppressed or backgrounded) in a story or news report, active or passive, identified by their role or function, with or without titles and so on.

We may describe entities at different levels, with more or fewer details, more or less precisely or vaguely, from different perspectives and so on (see below). Entities may be assigned different attributes, depending on their type. Thus, events and actions may be described in terms of time and causality, but not in terms of form, size or color, as is the case for objects, which in turn cannot be attributed intentions, as is the case for human beings. Relevant for discourse and conversation analysis is also the *order* of the sequences of propositions as they are expressed in subsequent sentences or turns, as we have seen above.

These and many other properties of descriptions, to be accounted for in discourse semantics, are not arbitrary, and again depend on our generic knowledge of the world and its situations and on the known structures of mental models of personal experiences. For instance, because of our general knowledge of temporal and causal relations of events or actions, we tend to describe sequences of events or actions in a chronological, 'natural' order, and not beginning with their consequences and then going back to their causal beginnings, as we have seen above.

Thus, in the *Wikipedia* article on racism used as an example in Chapter 3, we find a characteristic example of how generic scholarly knowledge about racism is expressed in discourse in terms of a whole article, beginning with the following initial definition:

> (11) Racism is usually defined as views, practices and actions reflecting the belief that humanity is divided into distinct biological groups called races and that members of a certain race share certain attributes which make that group as a whole less desirable, more desirable, inferior or superior.

Thus, racism as a social phenomenon or problem is defined in terms of more general notions such as 'views,' 'practices' or 'actions' of a specific kind, namely those which manifest a specific belief (that there are races and that some of these races have negative attributes). The concept of 'race' is itself defined in terms of specific biological groups, themselves defined as part of the concept of 'humanity.' Thus, generic knowledge is expressed in generic terms (e.g., as plurals such as 'practices,' 'groups,' 'views') and the definition is presented in a specific order, namely by an initial topical expression (*racism*) followed by a definition in more general terms, explicitly indexed by expressions such as *is usually defined as*, *called* and *divided into*.

In other words, what we need to account for here is what kind of conventional discourse norms are used to express models of personal experiences, for instance in stories, or generic knowledge structures, for instance in expository discourse. Since there is little detailed and integrated theoretical and empirical research on this issue, let us merely enumerate some of these properties of descriptions as controlled by underlying cognitive structures.

7.3.4.4.1 Levels of description   Situations, as well as the events, actions, people or objects contained in them, may be described at various *levels*, as we already have seen for the notion of semantic macrostructure (Van Dijk, 1977, 1980). We may describe an event in very general terms, as is typically the case in the headline or lead of a news report, or at much more specific levels, thus expressing the hierarchical structure of the situation model of the speaker or author. We may speak in general terms of events or actions such as a hold-up, a car accident or a terrorist attack, at a high level, but we may also describe the same event at more specific levels, such as the detailed causes of events, the preparations for such actions, the participants, the attributes of the participants and so on.

Within discourse, such levels of description may vary. In news reports, typically after headlines and leads, we expect increasingly more specific information about news events (Van Dijk, 1988a, 1988b). In a story, some global actions or events may be described in one sentence, whereas at other points, quite limited actions may be described with many sentences, signaling the importance of those actions. The same is true for the description of actors, objects or landscapes. Thus, Cameron in his *Sun* article describes his new immigration policy first in very general terms and then provides details, temporally comparing a previous (Labour) policy and a new future (Conservative) policy:

> (12) That's why today I'm announcing a number of new measures on immigration.
> Currently there is no limit to how long European Economic Area nationals can claim benefits while looking for a job.
> From now on, if they don't have a job after six months their benefits will end unless they have a genuine chance of finding work.

Similarly, variations in the level of description may depend on discourse genre and hence on context. We may describe a personal experience, for instance a theft in our house, in a different way when telling a conversational story to friends, being interrogated by the police or as a witness in court. Thus, we tend to describe our emotions at a more specific level to friends, but not to the police, whereas with the police or in court the focus may be on details of the theft that may lead to finding or sentencing the thieves.

We see that in addition to a cognitive account of descriptions in terms of underlying mental models, we need a specific discursive account in terms of variations of the level of description, to explain, for instance, how language users express and convey the importance or relevance of specific aspects of an event as represented in the model, or how specific aspects of an event are more or less interesting or relevant in different discourse genres and communicative situations.

Given the contextual constraints on discourse in general, and on levels of descriptions in particular, as well as the different functions that variations of these levels may have in interaction and communication, we already see that the third major dimension, that of social norms and social structure, also controls these variable discourse structures. Thus, personal details of a theft in a story to friends may be focused on to make the story emotionally and narratively more interesting for the recipients. But in interaction with the police or in court, there are social constraints on what should be told about, and what not, and at what level of specificity, namely as a functional part of the institutional, legal process.

The point of this observation is again that epistemic discourse structures, such as the variable levels of description, have a cognitive basis, such as the hierarchical structure of situation models that define what is more specific or more general. However, these underlying structures may be manipulated discursively in order to express and convey other interactional and communicative functions, such as the importance or salience of specific properties of situations. At the same time, the context model, representing the communicative situation and the genre, will apply specific social constraints on such discursive manifestations of underlying situation models, for instance as part of the aims of institutional actors and institutional processes.

This also shows again that there is no direct link between discourse structures and social structures: the latter can only influence discourse through the subjective definitions of the communicative situation by the participants as it is represented in their context models. In sum, although we deal with three dimensions, namely those of cognition, discourse and society, the control structures of actual text and talk as appropriate social action and interactions are cognitive, namely situation models and context models.

7.3.4.4.2 Granularity
Discourse may vary its levels of description, as described above, but also the amount of detail at each level, that is, its granularity (Marcu, 1999; Schegloff, 2000). If there are many details, the 'image' of an event, person or object is clearer, as we know from the number of pixels on a computer or TV screen. We may simply refer to a woman in a story or in a declaration for the police, but in both cases we may be expected to provide details, for instance about appearance or other attributes. In fact, in an attempt to be 'interesting,' as a form of positive self-presentation, we may want to 'do being extraordinary,' for instance embellishing a story when replying to a police officer asking "What happened" after an incident (Kidwell, 2009).

Again, such descriptions of detail, and their variation, are not arbitrary, but rooted in the structure of mental models and generic knowledge about situations, events, actions, actors or objects. In order to be able to identify objects or persons as such we may (need to) attend to a limited number of schematically organized identifying characteristics, such as size, form, color, parts and so on. We thus distinguish between head, limbs and trunk of human beings, and heads in terms of face, ears, eyes, hair, etc. – and so on for many things, partly also codified in the lexicon of the language. Thus, noses may be part of a face frame that is part of a human body frame, but not the hybrid 'entity' of half of the nose and half of the front of a person. Thus, we have person schemas and car schemas, among many others, that have a fundamental role in perception and interaction, as we know from classical schema theory in psychology (Anderson, 1980; Arbib *et al.*, 1987; Mandler, 1984; Markus and Smith, 1981).

Given these cognitive schema categories and the neurologically based structures of perception and memory, for instance, we may (need to and be able to) describe the color of the hair or the eyes of a suspect in the context of an interrogation, but hardly ever the size of the nose in millimeters or the top of the head in terms of number of hairs.

As is the case for levels of description, granularity may also vary within discourse, as well as across communicative situations. The more detailed a description the more important the thing described for the speaker and/or the recipients (Marcu, 1999). Some discourse genres and situations need very detailed description, as is the case in scientific and legal discourse, whereas other discourse genres, such as news reports or everyday conversations may allow very little detail. Again we see that the manifestation of underlying situation models in variable degrees of granularity depends on the constraints of discourse and its functions as represented in the context model.

On the other hand, when detail is given in popular genres such as news reports, it may have special functions, as is the case with the well-known 'number game' in news reports about immigration, for instance in the immigration article in the *Telegraph* discussed in Chapter 1:

> (13) Under what is known as Section 4 support, asylum seekers who have had their claim for shelter rejected but cannot currently return home are given accommodation and living support. In the 12 months up to September 2011, a total of 4,430 people were awarded such support – the equivalent of 12 a day.

Such quantitative precision in a news report has the rhetorical function of communicating exactness and hence reliability of news articles. At the same time, it implies 'how much' is spent on immigration, as is the case for the whole article, and hence how much 'the taxpayer' has to pay for immigration – a familiar number game move (see also below) in the strategy of the Conservative press and government to present immigration and immigrants in a negative way.

As anywhere in the expression of knowledge, the level or granularity of a description may also presuppose social information of the context model, such as the expertise of the speaker in scientific or forensic contexts. And again, there may be moral issues involved, for instance when great detail of text or talk hurts the social face or the emotions of recipients. For instance, 'doing delicacy' may also be required here when we communicate knowledge – such as details of a car accident or bodily harm – to loved ones.

7.3.4.4.3 Precision, vagueness and hedging Closely related to levels of description and degree of granularity is the variable *precision* with which situations, events, actions, people or objects are described (Ballmer and Pinkal, 1983; Bhatia, 2005; Drew, 2003; Gruber 1993; Jackson, 2002; Jucker *et al.*, 2003; Myers, 1996; Shapiro, 2008; Van Deemter, 2010).

There are many types of vagueness. One type of vagueness is lexical and terminological, e.g., due to the relativity of the description of attributes such as those of size, color, temperature: a small elephant is obviously much larger than a big mouse, and a body or weather temperature of forty degrees centigrade is quite high but is low when it comes to the temperature of boiling water or the temperature of a star. Also, names of categories are by definition fuzzy when it comes to delimiting sets of objects – there are many types of cups, some of which are borderline with glasses, beakers or mugs. Hence the proposal formulated by Rosch (1975, 1978) to define knowledge about such categories in terms of *prototypes* – which makes a robin a more typical bird than a penguin or an ostrich (among the now vast literature on prototypes, see also Cantor and Mischel, 1979; Kleiber, 1990; Taylor, 1989; Tsohatzidis, 1990).

Beyond the 'vague' knowledge of categories, such vagueness may also exist at the level of whole events or situations, as represented in mental models (Cantor, 1980; Semin, 1989). On the other hand, we may have a relatively precise mental model, but in specific genres and communicative situations choose to be quite vague in our description, for instance in order to avoid hurting the feelings of recipients, or to be polite to powerful people or to avoid incriminating oneself. Thus, political or media discourse may want to avoid describing racist prejudice and use the vague term 'popular discontent' – so as to avoid a negative description of the ingroup, a typical property of ideological text and talk (Van Dijk, 1991, 1993).

In other words, we should distinguish between linguistic or discursive vagueness and epistemic vagueness. In specific communicative situations we may be quite vague in our choice of words although our representation of an object or situation in a model may be very precise (e.g., refer to this particular cup or chair even when using a less appropriate lower-level denomination, e.g., for the type of cup or chair). The same is true for the description of an event, e.g., in the news: we may refer to a specific social or political conflict with the vague term 'conflict' although we concretely refer to a war, civil war, revolution, civil protest, ethnic conflict, etc. – sometimes to mitigate the discourse on ideological grounds (Van Dijk, 1998).

This also implies that the meanings of words and discourse and their associated situation models may vary *contextually*, that is, in different spatiotemporal settings, and when used for different aims, but also with different speakers and different audiences, that is, as controlled by context models (Van Dijk, 2008a, 2009a). Typically, events that black women describe with terms such as *discrimination* or *racism*, white participants or observers may not describe in such terms at all (Essed, 1991). Similarly, we also found in our own research on discourse on immigrants and minorities that racism is usually denied or mitigated (Van Dijk, 1992) or the term *racism* reserved to describe only the extreme right and not mainstream and more subtle racism (Van Dijk, 1984a, 1987, 1991, 1993).

See the following subtitle of the article on asylum seekers used as an example in Chapter 1:

> (14) **The taxpayer is spending more than £100,000 a day to house failed asylum seekers who have no right to be in the country.**

Although the quantitative expression in this news report, *more than £100,000 a day*, emphasized by its occurrence in both headline and sub-headline seems quite precise and in line with the usual number game of the press when dealing with immigrants (Van Dijk, 1991), the rest of the (sub-)headline is characteristically vague. Though the use of the generic *the taxpayer* refers to all taxpayers, it seems as if *each* taxpayer pays more than £100,000 a day, a way to address each reader as taxpayer in a different way than to say that these asylum seekers cost the state £40 million yearly. Similarly, the expression *failed asylum seeker* not only vaguely refers to the fact that they have had their claims rejected (as the article says in a passive voice, i.e., omitting who rejects these claims) but rather seems to suggest that they did something wrong or not good enough. Finally, the expression *who have no right to be in the country* is a vague and biased way to describe that they have had their claims rejected, that is, as a form of illegality. After all, when they cannot be sent back for humanitarian reasons or because their cases are still under review, they obviously have such a right by international law. Thus we see that vagueness can be used to attribute negative characteristics to outgroups or to represent the ingroup (such as the taxpayer) as a victim of the outgroup.

Among the related semantic phenomena of discourse, *hedging* in conversation and scholarly discourse has been extensively studied as a move to limit the commitment of the speaker or writer, or again as a means to avoid face threats, for instance in personal criticism. In scholarly discourse, hedging is the standard means to express uncertainty of scholarly results as well as limiting the possibly negative consequences of making mistakes, and hence it functions as a strategy of risk control (Hyland, 1998; Markkanen and Schröder, 1997). The account of hedging in discourse is relevant here because it is a discursive manifestation of the strategic expression of knowledge in text and talk. Even when beliefs, knowledge or opinions are quite certain, institutional, professional and interactional norms and constraints may require their expression to be hedged in many ways, e.g., by using modal expressions (*may*, *might*), adverbs (*perhaps*, *often*), diminutives and so on.

7.3.4.5 *Evidentiality*

Probably the epistemic property of language and knowledge most studied by linguists, after the study of topic and focus, is **evidentials**, especially also because in some languages they are coded in the very grammar, for instance by special morphemes or clitics (of the vast literature see, e.g., Aikhenvald, 2004; Chafe and Nichols, 1986; Diewald and Smirnova, 2010; Kamio, 1997; Mushin, 2001). Given the vast number of previous studies on this topic, we cannot possibly review let alone comment on even the most relevant ones, and we will mainly address this topic within our own framework.

Evidentials are usually defined in terms of linguistic expressions that indicate the *knowledge sources* speakers have for their assertions, such as sensory perception (vision, etc.), hearsay or inferences. They are mostly studied for languages that have special evidential morphology, such as Amerindian languages, some South-East European and Middle-Eastern languages and some languages in Asia and Australia. Western European languages express sources of knowledge more explicitly in lexical terms (e.g., *reportedly*), or in special evidential clauses (e.g., *I saw that, Mary told me that, I read in the paper that*, or *I conclude that*), as is typically the case in everyday conversations and news reports, as we have seen in the example on asylum seekers in Chapter 1:

> (15) Sir Andrew Green, chairman of Migration Watch UK, said: "This is a measure of the lengths to which people will go to stay in Britain.
>   "But in the end, if their cases fail they must leave or the credibility of the whole system is completely undermined."

Thus, the reporter of this news item explicitly attributes an opinion to a specific source (Sir Andrew Green), who is also identified (as chairman of Migration Watch UK) and hence as an expert on immigration, which suggests that the opinion is also well-founded on credible sources and evidence. Of course, the journalist does not tell us that Migration Watch UK is a conservative organization, whose headline on its website (www.migrationwatchuk.org) says it is "concerned about the present scale of immigration in the UK" but that it is "independent, voluntary and non political." Interestingly, the whole article is not attributed to any source at all, but reports events (Home Office spending) as if the reporter (identified in the byline as *Tom Whitehead, Home Affairs Editor*) is the primary sources of the facts, whereas it is likely that it is based on a Home Affairs press release or press briefing. This example shows that (explicit) evidentials not only identify sources of text and talk, but also may (fail to) convey the credibility of sources and the reliability of their information, and hence the credibility of the speaker (in this case the journalist) and the reliability of the news report.

Evidentials are often studied in close relationship (and sometimes even confused) with **epistemic stance or modality**, e.g., as expressed by auxiliary verbs and modal adverbs in English (*may, must, perhaps, maybe*, etc.), because such stance may be influenced by the perceived reliability of the sources of one's knowledge or beliefs (Cornillie, 2009). But since epistemic evidentials and modalities are independent phenomena of discourse, we will deal with them separately. We will come back to epistemic modality below.

Relevant for this chapter and this book is *a theory of evidentials that combines the three essential components recalled above: a social, cognitive and discursive component.* The social dimension of evidentials has to do with some of the aspects mentioned above and below for the epistemics of conversation, such as authority, responsibility and entitlement, as well as the credibility of the speaker. Although relevant for the very ways knowledge and beliefs are acquired in the first place, the cognitive dimension is usually quite limited in studies of evidentials, so we'll focus on that dimension. Finally, the linguistic and discursive dimension of the theory mainly deals with the expression of evidentiality in the grammars of various languages, on the one hand, or in conversation structures, such as order and sequentiality, on the other.

7.3.4.5.1 The cognitive conditions of evidentiality: mental models

Most of the studies mentioned above categorize and summarize the sources of information indexed by indexicals in terms of *direct* (as is the case for visual or other sensory information) and *indirect* (hearsay or inferences) (see also Plungian, 2001). However, such a categorization of sources needs a more explicit analysis in terms of the mental models of the speakers. They can only differentiate and hence differentially express or index different sources if they have represented them mentally.

Thus, to understand the very conditions that make the expression of evidentiality possible in the first place, we must briefly recall its cognitive basis. In order to be able to make an assertion about a current or past event, language users need to have a *mental model*, stored in their autobiographical memory, in which they may themselves be represented as agents, patients, observers or another role.

Any implicit or explicit reference to 'sources' of belief or knowledge, such as various modes of sensory perception (vision, etc.), must be based on a multimodal model of experience as described in Chapter 3. Thus, in order to describe a past event and provide an account of how they knew about an aspect of that event, speakers first need to activate the relevant multimodal information of such a mental model acquired in a perceptual event. It is important to stress this more complex basis of speaker knowledge. In the literature, examples in the form of brief isolated examples with expressions of evidentiality seem to suggest that such isolated information is available as such to language users.

Thus, the visually acquired information that it is raining outside (a standard example in this kind of study) is part of a more complex model of experience featuring my Self, and in my role as observer (at home or in the street), wet streets, the sky and so on.

A similar mental model then also provides the information 'that it has rained last night' if I observe that the street is still wet, namely through an *inference* based on general knowledge relating rain and wet streets. In the literature, such inferences are mentioned as a second 'source' of knowledge acquisition, but it is important to show how – from what kind of knowledge – they are derived in the first place. Such an inference may have been derived at the moment of the formation of the mental model, or later, during the ongoing communicative event, for instance when we need that information for current purposes (see the psychological literature on epistemic inferences reviewed in Chapter 3). Such inferences may thus be based on consequences, parts, manifestations or other properties related to an event as represented in a mental model, such as rain falling from a cloudy sky, causing streets and people to get wet and so on, and as represented in generic knowledge about rain applied to a specific situation, that is, a specific mental model.

Incidentally, the generally used concept of knowledge 'source' is hardly appropriate when referring to multimodal perception and inferences. Rather, more generally, we should rather be referring to various *methods* of acquiring information or to the 'basis' (Bednarek, 2006) of our knowledge.

Thirdly, knowledge may be derived from what is traditionally called 'hearsay,' and which more appropriately should simply be called discourse, text or talk. Again, such knowledge is first represented in semantic situation models (the information expressed in such discourse) and pragmatic context models (the episodic representation of the communicative event). It is this more complex information of two types of mental model that is the basis for currently indexing a statement as expressing information acquired from other sources/ methods, such as the weather report or a phone call of a friend.

Ignoring in this chapter the detailed processes involved in this search, activation and analysis of old discourse models, it is relevant to mention that each of these models may be separately accessible. Thus, we may still remember having read or heard about some event by discursive 'mediation' (Plungian, 2001), but we may have forgotten when, how and from whom we acquired that information. Or conversely, we may remember having read the paper, or talked to a friend, that is, have access to the relevant context model in episodic memory, but no longer to the (semantic) information represented in the situation model of that encounter: we no longer recall what was in the paper this morning or what we talked about with a friend last week. Again, these communication models (as we may call both of them together) may also be the basis of relevant inferences, as is the case for the experience models based on perception.

In sum, virtually all knowledge or belief as signaled to be acquired by perception, inference or discourse is derived from activated 'old' mental models.

In some (few) situations, language users may express and index knowledge *now* being acquired in the current communicative situation, that is, as represented in the semantic and pragmatic mental models now under construction, for instance in online commentary (like sports programs on the radio or TV). More generally, this may be the case in explicit meta-commentary (*Do you understand what I am saying?*) or discourse markers (*You know*) or comments on the ongoing environment (*I see you are wearing a new shirt*, or the plausible inference, *I see you bought a new shirt*).

Despite such ongoing commentary based on current mental models, most evidentials are based on older mental models of previous (communicative or other) events. It is not surprising that they typically are expressed in stories and accounts (see also Mushin, 2001).

Relevant analysis of these old models also provides other information that is relevant for the expression of evidentiality. First of all, they show the role of current speaker, as the Self of the old models, possibly in different *roles*, such as an experiencer, agent, patient or mere observer of the events. Secondly, the models show whether or not there were other participants, also in different roles, thus allowing for inferences about who had *access* to the 'same' information (though differently represented in their respective personal mental models of the event) and whether the information is purely *subjective* or possibly *intersubjective*. Thus, we may witness other participants not only as engaging in specific action, but also as possible perceivers of the events or discourse, and hence as joint sources of knowledge about the event (*We saw ... John saw ...* or *Do you remember we saw ...*). Since intersubjectively shared knowledge is usually considered to be more reliable, it may be crucial to index such a property of our experience or communication models.

Representation of events in mental models obviously also provides a more explicit way to compare events across situations, to generalize and to abstract and to establish whether or not a current experience is normal or extraordinary, as may be expressed in 'mirative' evidentials such as *surprisingly*. That is, instead of simply describing the event itself in terms of what is out of the ordinary, we need to relate such an experience or judgment to the current speaker, and hence as represented in a mental model construed by the speaker. And secondly, it is this mental model that allows comparison with other mental models of other experiences – or predictions of mental models as inferentially derived from general knowledge about such events. Again, all forms of understanding and judgment of events, and hence the conditions defining evidentiality of all types, are necessarily based on mental models.

Similarly, we may rely not only on old communication models, but also on models of *future events* or *plans of action*, and these may also be described and 'evidentially' indexed in terms of the wishes, wants or hopes of the current speaker.

Finally, *the actual expression of evidentiality is controlled by the current context model of the ongoing communicative event*, featuring not only the current knowledge of the speaker but also of the recipients, that is, the dynamically changing Common Ground. This and other information of the ongoing context model regulates what kind of information about the sources or methods of current knowledge must be indexed as relevant for the communicative event in general and the recipients in particular. It is this current context model which specifies the very *functions* of evidential expression, such as those related to reliability, credibility and other conditions of persuasion, geared towards the preferred mental models of the recipients: that they believe what we say, that they think we are a reliable source, etc. (Marín-Arrese, 2009, 2011a, 2011b).

The context model also specifies what information must now be sought in the old models in view of communication, e.g., in a story or news report, and how such information should be marked epistemically so as to enhance the credibility of the speaker and the validity of the information. Thus, it may be more relevant to show that I witnessed an event 'with my own eyes,' than that I (also) heard or read about it in the paper. Similarly, it may be more relevant, and more reliable, to mention that there were other participants witnessing an event, and thus express that '*we* saw it,' and not only that '*I* saw it,' or that I read an expert about it rather than heard it from just anybody.

In sum, the context model controls evidentiality, first of all by establishing what information is now relevant to be communicated (on the basis of our beliefs about the current knowledge and interests of the recipients), secondly by searching the relevant information in old situation and context models, thirdly by marking how such knowledge was acquired so as to index the reliability of its sources or methods, and thus the validity of the information thus acquired, and finally by indexing the credibility of the current speaker, and hence in turn their reliability as a source of knowledge.

Lazard (2001: 362), in a study of the grammaticalization of evidentials in South-Eastern Europe and the Middle East, metaphorically refers to speakers "as split in two": the one who is now speaking and the one who earlier saw or heard. In our theoretical terms, we refer to one current speaker whose talk or text is being controlled by (old) experience or context models which are activated and made relevant by the current context model representing the ongoing communicative situation.

The mental model theory of evidentiality should also account for new empirical research that needs to be carried out on the use of evidential expressions in different genres and contexts of discourse in different languages. Episodic models of experiences, in general, and of communication, in particular, tend to be only partly accessible after longer delays (see Chapter 3 for references). After a few days, weeks and especially months, we no longer remember most of our experiences and of a few very salient experiences only a few relevant details (e.g., their macrostructures). Most earlier communicative events are forgotten and we may only remember some elements what we have 'learned' from them (their situation model). This means that most of the information available for the expression of evidentiality is no longer accessible after some delay, or only very vaguely so. It is therefore likely that the use of evidentials is limited to the description of ongoing, recent or salient past events, as is the case, more generally, for storytelling and its cognitive basis (see also Chafe, 1980; DeConcini, 1990; Herman, 2003; King, 2000; Mushin, 2001; Neisser and Fivush, 1994).

We see that a slightly more detailed cognitive analysis of discourse production in terms of different kinds of mental models provides us with a more coherent theory of the management of evidentiality. In the literature on evidentials, these processes and representation are usually ignored or taken for granted, but they are crucial to explain how and why evidentiality is relevant in the first place. At the same time, such a theory offers a more solid semantic and pragmatic basis for the grammar of evidentiality.

The mental model theory of the sources or methods of the acquisition of information as indexed by morphological, lexical or other discourse structures yields a very rich framework for further theoretical analysis, observation and linguistic typology:

- It shows how perceptual *sources* – or rather *methods* – of knowledge acquisition are not merely instances of isolated vision (hearing, touch, smell, etc.) but part of a more *complex multimodal event* as represented in a mental model.
- This same more complex event provides the data for drawing *inferences* about unknown (non-perceived) aspects of an event.
- The model offers a rich array of other evidence that may be needed for display in talk or text, such as the presence of other *participants or observers*, and hence provide an account of types of shared *access* and *intersubjectivity*.
- Both semantic and pragmatic models of previous communication provide the evidence attributed to other sources ('hearsay'). The situation models of such discourse (of the event we heard or read about) may be similar to our own mental models of our own experiences and hence can be compared to our model and judged for their plausibility and hence their validity.
- This information represented in our old situation and context models is itself activated, selected, *made relevant in the ongoing, dynamic context* model that controls the current discourse and hence its evidential expressions.
- Part of this ongoing context model, namely the representation of the *social epistemic relations* of primacy, authority, expertise, etc. of the participants, also controls who may or should express what information, when, to whom, in a conversation, as we have seen above. In other words, the mental model

theory of evidentiality at the same time provides a cognitive basis of the *epistemics of conversation* and interaction in general.

With these general principles in mind, we still need to account for exactly how evidentiality is managed in context models. So far, we have only a rather simple context model, centrally featuring a K-device managing the knowledge of discourse or interaction, involving, for instance, the specification of a possibly complex Common Ground, so as to be able to decide what (new) knowledge may or should now be communicated. The cognitive model-theoretic analysis of evidentiality suggests that this K-device should be further enriched by specifying language users' (possibly implicit) awareness of where any 'new' information now being communicated in the current discourse comes from.

This means that the K-device of the context models must have pointers to the models of experience (including old context models), stored in episodic memory, where such new information was stored, and represented as seen or otherwise directly perceived, as inferred from other information in the model, or as communicated in previous text or talk. It is this *semantic* basis of knowledge represented in given mental models that provides the necessary information for the *pragmatic functions* of the context model.

Such a context model controls not only who, in what identity, and what role (expert, authority), may express what kind of knowledge and where they may do so in the discourse or interaction, *but also what type of information in given models of experience must be selected as being most relevant and persuasive*, for instance as acquired through the most reliable methods. Although such methods are often irrelevant or obvious from text or context, and may remain implicit, it often makes sense to explicitly describe them in explicit evidentials so as to show how the speaker knows, whether the source or method of knowledge acquisition was or is reliable, and especially how these are made relevant in the current communicative situation and the current recipient.

Next, epistemic methods may be more or less reliable and yield more or less valid beliefs and this also needs to be expressed, so as to make sure the speaker does not make claims that are too strong or too weak, and that recipients do not draw wrong conclusions from the evidence as presented. Hence the difference between saying that scholars have *discovered, proven, claimed* or merely *suggested* a finding, as we know from work on hedging in academic discourse (see above) – and similar differences in everyday conversation (I *saw, read* or merely *thought* or *guessed* something). Generally, thus, one may distinguish between *strong, medium* and *weak* evidentials as levels of the way the speaker evaluates the reliability of the source or method (see, e.g., Marín-Arrese, 2011a). These levels may be read off the structure of the information sources as represented in the K-device controlling the knowledge management in the current communicative event, as represented in the schema of Figure 7.1.

The basic idea of that schema is that there are only three basic methods of knowledge acquisition, namely inference, perception and discourse or communication. Each of these methods, however, is recursive. Thus, perception as well as discourse may be the input for new knowledge arrived at by inference, and discourse may again be an evidential method for the speakers or discourses cited in a discourse. The higher and more to the left of the schema, the more direct is the method or source of knowledge acquisition. This also shows that inference is not always indirect, but only when based on perception or other discourses. Information directly derived from given Common Ground knowledge is immediately available – while not in need of any external knowledge acquisition (perception or discourse) in the first place. Indeed, it is information recipients could derive themselves in the first place from shared CG knowledge (generic or historical knowledge, earlier common experiences, previous encounters or discourse, the current situation or what has just been said).

With this general mental model theory of evidentiality as a basis, we may proceed to a more general, multidisciplinary theory of evidentiality, discourse and society and apply the theory to special genres and situations.

Thus, in court, hearsay is usually not admitted as evidence (Kurzon, 1988; Shuy, 1998), whereas inferences may be rejected as 'calls for speculation' – and only specific forms of direct (e.g., visual) perception may be admitted (Cutler, 2002, 2009). Moreover, any skeptical counterargument even of such evidence may have to be prevented by emphasizing that 'all normal conditions' obtain, in the sense that witnesses were not in any way prevented from 'normal' vision (failing eyesight, enough light, perspective, closeness, etc.). This practice also shows that a socially based theory of evidentiality needs further constraints on what kinds of mental model and what properties of such mental models are required as valid information.

Scientific discourse, obviously, has its own norms of evidence, defined by the usual methods of observation, the use of instruments, experiments, argumentation or who or what publications count as having authority in a specific discipline or on a specific topic.

It is customary in the literature on evidentials to distinguish between *direct* and *indirect* sources of knowledge, where perception is usually categorized as direct, and discourse (hearsay, testimony) and inference as indirect, at least in relation to the state of affairs current text or talk is about. Note, though, that if the state of affairs is itself a discourse, a claim about what others have said or written could be direct, as is the case in literal quotation of speakers in the media.

Also, as we shall see below, direct and indirect evidence does not always correspond to different degrees of reliability. The direct perception of a novice may count less than the reported one of an expert, and visual perception in

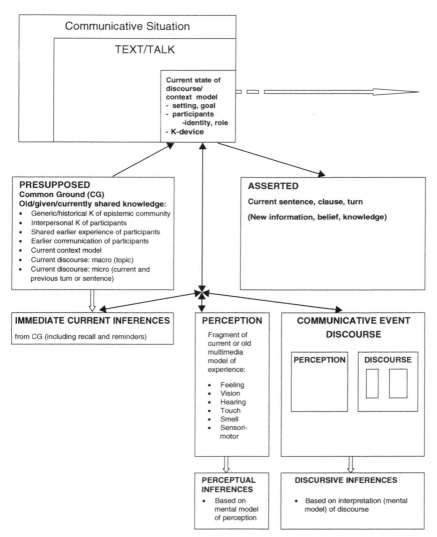

Figure 7.1 Schema of the structure of the information sources controlling knowledge management in the current communicative event

difficult circumstances may be found to be less reliable than a persuasive argument based on impeccable inferences.

More generally, as we shall see below, different types of epistemic source or method do not always correspond to degrees of reliability or validity as attributed by speakers or recipients, nor to their certainty about states of affairs, e.g., as expressed in epistemic modalities. As is the case for all observations of evidentiality and modality, they should be made with respect to current text, talk and/or context.

7.3.4.5.2 Discourse as evidence   Especially relevant for this book and this chapter is the role of testimony or hearsay, that is, discourse as a basis or method of belief. There can be no doubt, as often repeated before, that in most contexts of life, as from the first years of school and then in most professional (white-collar) situations, text or talk is the major source of knowledge and belief. Usually, in the analysis of evidentials, discursive evidence is characterized as 'indirect' and hence as less reliable than direct observation. But such is only the case for discourse about personal experiences of others when compared to our own personal experiences, for instance in storytelling, and it also depends on the credibility of the other speaker. In many other situations, our *only* source is discursive, as is the case for nearly all academic discourse and much political discourse, as well as educational discourse. Depending on the knowledgeability of the authors and represented sources, the reliability of the methods used and represented in the discourse, discursive evidence may not only be the only source but also a highly credible source.

Davis (2002), in a more philosophical study, examines in which respects conversation may be treated as a reliable source of knowledge. Given the assumption that, by Grice's conversational postulates, people usually tell the truth, there is prima facie evidence that we may believe what they tell us. However, most of the things we know about the world, we undoubtedly once learned from text or talk, but we no longer remember when and where and from whom (as we also know from the psychology of episodic memories). Davis argues that such should not be reason to reject such beliefs as unfounded. Indeed, if we were to be so skeptical most of the shared knowledge of a community and society would have to be rejected.

From this and other, socially oriented, studies of discourse and knowledge in this chapter and book, we see again that knowledge is not only an epistemic but also a moral issue, in the sense that we are supposed to tell the truth, that we may generally believe what others tell is, unless we have reasons to believe that this is not the case. In other words, true discourse is the default and hence is a reliable source of evidence. A much more general systematic study of discourse and source or method of knowledge and belief as part of argumentation, legitimation and persuasion obviously needs to formulate the details of such a general rule (see also Goldman, 1999).

7.3.4.5.3 The interactional and social functions of evidentiality
We see that the conditions of the very use of evidentiality in discourse must be formulated in terms of the situation and context models of the participants as

these subjectively represent their relevant and ongoing states of knowledge and belief. Another issue is what the *interactional and communicative functions* are of marking expressions with indicators or explicit references to sources or methods of knowledge acquisition: *why* do language users have recourse to evidentials in the first place? *Why* is it conversationally or discursively relevant to show how they know what they assert?

We have seen that one of the 'indirect' sources of knowledge is text or talk. *This very condition reflexively also applies to the current discourse itself.* This means that in order to be able to function as a reliable source of knowledge for recipients, speakers must make sure that their own discourse is based on reliable sources, modes or methods of knowledge acquisition and that such be made persuasively obvious to recipients.

Marín-Arrese (2011a: 790) emphasizes these persuasive functions of the expression of evidentiality in order to enhance the perceived validity information and source credibility and the legitimation of assertions and actions, as we also have seen above in the example of the news report on asylum seekers. She does so within a broader framework in terms of the 'force dynamic' dimension of epistemic modals, whose processes of logic, evidence and common sense may 'force' recipients to believe the speaker (see, e.g., Langacker, 2009; Sweetser, 1990; Talmy, 1985).

Speakers or writers may have recourse to a series of credibility-enhancing moves and strategies such as evidentials and other structures of text and talk. Thus, they may not only mention vision, discourse or inference as a source for their knowledge, but also engage in detailed arguments as to why their visual or auditory perception was impeccable, why their specific discourse sources are specifically knowledgeable or why their reasons or arguments are valid. In other words, evidentials do not always come alone but may be part of complex evidential strategies or (in)formal proof.

One way to enhance the credibility of perception, for instance, is to mention many *details* of an event that could not have been invented – as happens in everyday storytelling, as well as in news reports, testimony in court or scholarly discourse (Van Dijk, 1984a, 1988a, 1988b).

When using other discourses as a source, this may be shown by quoting such sources literally – thus not only enhancing the credibility of the current speaker or writer, but also possibly distancing themselves from the source when their own opinions are different from those of the source, or when doubts about the reliability or the opinions of the source are in order, as is routinely the case in news reports (Van Dijk, 1988a, 1991) or to mark distance with respect to one's own earlier discourse (see Lazard: 2001: 362).

More generally, then, evidentials of different kinds as well as other epistemic strategies are used in order to establish, confirm or enhance the credibility of speakers, their reliability as a source of knowledge and as an authority who has or had access to the events reported or to a reliable source who did have such access.

Haviland (1987) stresses that, among their many functions, evidentials may also be used interactionally as 'fighting words,' when participants in conversation fight 'with' the truth, and that they may encode not only what speakers or addressees know, or how they know it, but *morally* also what they *should* know.

We see that, whereas mental models offer the very information needed to be able to engage in evidential expressions and strategies in the first place, and hence *how* they do so, the type of communicative event and genre explains *why* speakers have recourse to such strategies in the first place. As we have seen for the analysis of speech acts and conversations, and will see below, notions such as credibility, responsibility, authority and entitlement play a role in the epistemic structures of text and talk (Fox, 2001; Stivers *et al.*, 2011a).

More generally, such criteria emphasize the necessity of studying evidentials and their functions in text and talk, and not as expressed in isolated sample sentences, as is still the dominant practice in many linguistic studies of evidentials, and not only as individual expressions of knowledge sources, but as part of dynamic interactions and as part of communicative situations (Clift, 2006; Hill and Irvine, 1993; see also the references to conversation analytical studies of knowledge referred to above).

Thus, Fox (2001), in a paper that reviews and emphasizes the need for an interactional approach to evidentiality, shows that the same speaker may use different evidential strategies for the same statement directed to different recipients, once marked as hearsay (with the adverb *apparently*) and in another context as own knowledge – unmarked by an evidential or by a zero-evidential (as knowledge derived from other sources). In our theoretical framework, this means that the speaker activates the same (old) context model representing the source of the information, but that it depends on the *current* context model, and hence the representation of the recipients and their probable interests or criteria, whether or not that information is presented as own knowledge or as knowledge derived from other sources. In other words, the use of evidentials depends on a detailed assessment by the speaker of the relevant dimensions of the communicative situation, including the recipients, and especially what impression a current discourse or discourse fragment will have on them.

The relevance of (con)text and position in conversation for the interpretation of evidentials has been observed by various authors (see, e.g., Heritage and Raymond, 2005). Thus, Clift (2006) shows that reference to earlier discourse of a speaker (*I said ...*) may take place in assessment situations in which a speaker not only may show agreement with an assessment of the previous speaker but also claims priority of the assessment by showing to have explicitly talked and commented on an issue before. In other words, in conversation, reported own speech may function as a form of evidence and hence as *interactional evidentials* that claim or establish the *authority* of the speaker (Clift, 2006: 583).

Incidentally, contrary to the opinion of Schegloff (2003), cited by the same author (Clift, 2006: 586), who rejects the intentions of speakers as a source of a conversational turn while emphasizing the role of previous actions in a conversation, it should be recalled, again, *that previous actions in conversation can only condition actions of next speakers indirectly, namely after being interpreted*. Reduction of text and talk to interaction is unable to explain how next speakers may have many ways to understand, interpret and represent previous turns and actions, and may hence 'react' in many different ways *not to the previous actions themselves but to their representation of them in their ongoing mental models* (e.g., establishing if something was a promise or a threat). We always need an analysis at three levels, (i) a cognitive, mediating, basis, (ii) social and communicative context, and (iii) the dynamics of sequential organization of text and talk.

Fox (2001) stresses that evidentials may not only convey the credibility and responsibility of speakers for their claims. They may also, as we suggested above, be used to distance the speaker from a source or an organization as responsible for some information. Indeed, as is generally the case for scholarly articles, and indeed for Fox's own paper, citing others is, on the one hand, a way of showing who is recognized as expert or to which research paradigm one belongs. On the other hand, citing critically may function as marking distance from the opinions of others. In the same paper, she shows that the use of evidential marker *I see* may be relevant in a situation where a speaker as a visitor to a family does not want to take the responsibility and entitlement the mother of a child would have when commenting on that child's negative action. Indeed, without such a marker, her statement may be heard as inappropriate criticism and not as a mere statement of a fact that has already been observed by others anyway.

Kamio (1997), in a study of grammatical markers in Japanese, stresses another social aspect of the use of evidentials, namely the 'territory of information' to which a statement belongs. Thus, a speaker who is not familiar with, or has no access to such a territory as a participant or expert, is normatively expected to mark any statement about such a territory not as own knowledge but as derived from the discourse of competent others.

Scholarly discourse uses evidentials in many ways as obligatory moves of accounting for the source(s) of ideas or statements, as when referring to previous studies. Such evidentials have several functions. Firstly, such references acknowledge the originality and hence the epistemic primacy of other scholars. Secondly, such references also emphasize the credibility of a study by providing a (reliable) source. At the same time, thirdly, scholars my distance themselves from an idea by attributing it to other scholars. We have seen in the *Wikipedia* article on racism that such references may be quite vague:

(16)
- (i)   Racism is usually defined as views (...)
- (ii)   The exact definition of racism is controversial (...)
- (iii)   There is little scholarly agreement about (...)
- (iv)   Critics argue that (...)
- (v)   Some definitions would have it that (...)
- (vi)   Other definitions only include
- (vii)   Among the questions about how to define ...
- (viii) Racism and racial discrimination are often used to describe discrimination (...)
- (ix)   According to the United Nations convention (...)
- (x)   In politics, racism is commonly located on the far right (...)
- (xi)   Practices and ideologies of racism are universally condemned by the United Nations in the Declaration of Human Rights.

Although the article gives references at the end, the views attributed within the article are vaguely attributed to 'usual' or 'common' definitions. Only the United Nations is mentioned as a specific source in the text.

7.3.4.5.4   The linguistic expression of evidentiality   With the cognitive conditions of evidentially as well as their (also cognitively represented, and hence subjective or intersubjective) social functions and uses in communicative situations, evidentiality may be variably marked or expressed in the structures of text and talk in different languages. Thus, as indicated above, most linguistic studies focus on, and compare, the specific explicit morphology of evidentials in specific (e.g., Amerindian) languages. Such morphological structures, usually associated with the verb, may index that the knowledge expressed in a sentence was directly acquired by vision, hearing or other sensory information, or indirectly by previous discourse ('hearsay') or inference. Western European languages do not have such morphological markers of evidentiality, but express sources/methods of knowledge acquisition with lexical means or whole clauses (e.g., '*I saw that ...*,' '*I read that ...*,' '*Mary said that ...*,' etc.) (for general introduction and survey, see especially Aikhenvald, 2004; Chafe and Nichols, 1986; Diewald and Smirnova, 2010; Givón, 1989; Mushin, 2001).

Not all linguists agree on the way to describe evidentials. Thus, Boye and Harder (2009) distinguish between authors who describe evidentials as (i) *grammatical markers* of information source, which may be different in different languages (such as Aikhenvald, 2004), (ii) more broadly, as a *semantic phenomenon* which may be expressed in many other than grammatical structures – also as epistemic modals (such as Chafe and Nichols, 1986) or (iii) a cognitive, communicative-functional or pragmatic phenomenon, independent of grammatical or other linguistic structures (represented by the authors themselves). Within a cognitive linguistic paradigm, they define evidentiality as a 'substance domain' of language, as is the case for time, aspectuality, modality or person, and which may be codified in many ways in different languages.

We have seen above that a discursive and interactional approach to evidentiality is not limited to a study of evidential markers of words or sentences, but more broadly examines the expression and the functions of referring to sources or methods of knowledge and belief acquisition in communicative situations, examining also the social meanings of their use or non-use, such as authority, affiliation or distance with respect to knowledge sources (Fox, 2001) or whole knowledge territories (Kamio, 1997).

Many linguistic studies, however, only examine the formal properties of evidentials. Thus, several studies observe the close relationships between evidentials and epistemic modals, in the sense that, for instance, the same expression (such as *must* or *it is obvious* in English) may index strong inferential evidentiality, on the one hand, and certainty of the speaker, on the other (Aijmer, 2009; Cornillie, 2009). Below, we shall come back to the study of epistemic modals related to evidentiality.

Simons (2007), in a study relating evidentiality and presupposition after embedding verbs, shows that such verbs (such as in *Mary said/believes/suggests … that John has been fired*) not only mark mediating (hearsay) evidentiality but at the same time the reliability of the source. She especially stresses that the embedded clause of such verbs often expresses the *main point* of the utterance, whereas the main clause rather has a discourse function, namely to mark the source of the information expressed in the embedded clause. Although the notion of 'main point' is hard to define, interactionally it may be defined in terms of the kind of information a recipient wants to know, such as what was asked in a question (e.g., what happened to John, in the example). Of course, if the question in the same example is about Mary (e.g., what bothers her), then the main clause expresses the main point.

McCready and Ogata (2007) show for Japanese that evidentials should rather be analyzed as epistemic modals and as part of propositions, e.g., given their behavior under scope, when embedded in conditionals and their relation to other modal operators and anaphors. More generally, they observe that inferential evidentials may well also feature an assessment of possibility and hence dominate a modality (see also Chafe and Nichols, 1986).

Despite the close relation between evidentiality and epistemic modality, most authors emphasize that these two different dimensions of language should be distinguished: evidentials only index the source or method of belief or information acquisition, whereas modality indicates the way information, of whatever source, is evaluated as being more or less valid and as a reason for more or less commitment of speakers to their statements or their certainty about states of affairs (see, e.g., Aikhenvald, 2004; Faller, 2006).

In a broader text-based study of evidentiality in news discourse, Bednarek (2006) combines an analysis of evidentiality and epistemic modality or stance in terms of what she calls *epistemological positioning*. She proposes her own detailed framework, in which she distinguishes between *sources* of information in the strict sense (usually Self, and sometimes Other, see also Squartini, 2008), on the one hand, and the various types of evidence or the external or internal *basis* of knowledge (which Squartini (2008) calls *modes* and I have called *methods* above), such as perception, general knowledge, proof, obviousness, unspecified, hearsay or 'mindsay' (thoughts attributed to others), on the other hand. Bednarek applies her framework in a detailed analysis of evidentially marked fragments from the British press in terms of schemas for dominant and embedded clauses of complex sentences in news reports. Thus, a sentence in a news report may be based on hearsay (as a basis) by a source (an Other) and such information may again feature events defined in terms of perception – where each of the information units may be marked as expressing strong or weak certainty of the participants – thus combining evidentiality and modality. Also, inferences are made more explicit by relations to general knowledge or by argumentative backings (e.g., as expressed by *'this means that ...'*). Important in this more detailed empirical study of the sometimes very complex sentences in the news is not only how complex epistemic positioning (evidentiality and modality) may be intertwined, but also how in complex structures the *conditions may be recursive*: thus, what holds for the evidentials and modalities of a text may again apply to those of a text cited in such a text (a cited text is more reliable and credible if it is in turn based on reliable perception of its author, on reliable inferences and citation of reliable and credible authors, e.g., experts).

With these few comments we see that it makes sense to take a broad sociocognitive view of evidentiality and not limit it to a comparative typological study of morphological markers of information sources. Rather, different languages have different ways to express how language users display how they have acquired the knowledge that serves as evidence for their discourse in assertive contexts.

We have seen that even lexical or clausal expressions of knowledge sources or methods should be studied in a broader discourse and conversation analytical framework. Evidentials may thus be studied as part of more elaborate discursive and interactional strategies of persuasively showing the sources, methods, reasons or arguments that show the validity of information and the reliability of speakers.

A more conversational approach, moreover, shows how evidentiality is part of the broader interactional management of the expression of knowledge, its position in talk, and the access, primacy, authority and entitlement of the participants expressing knowledge or reacting to such displays of knowledge.

Given the complexity of the issues involved, we have pleaded for a theoretical framework that makes explicit the sources or methods of knowledge in terms of mental models, social and interactional meanings and constraints and complex discourse structures.

7.3.4.6 Epistemic modality: degrees of certainty

Closely related to evidentiality, and in a sense a linguistic consequence of its epistemic grounds, we now briefly need to focus on *epistemic stance* or *modality*, that is, the expression of the *(un)certainty* of the speaker about, or the perceived probability of, a state of affairs, typically expressed by modal verbs *(seem, appear)*, modal auxiliaries *(may, might, could, must*, etc.) and adverbs *(perhaps, likely)* in English (see, e.g., Bybee and Fleischmann, 1995; Egan, 2007; Kärkkäinen, 2003; Marín-Arrese, 2006, 2011a; Nuyts, 2001a, 2001b; Simon-Vandenbergen, 2008).

First of all, a remark about the very label of this kind of epistemic discourse structure. Though widely used in academic English, there is no clear equivalent of *stance* in other European languages, which typically translate the term with notions that come closer to the meaning of *attitude* – such as *houding* in Dutch, *Haltung* in German, *actitud* or *postura* in Spanish and so on. In Chapter 4, we have defined attitudes as specific, ideologically based, socially shared, mental representations, such as attitudes about immigration or abortion. For this reason, we will speak rather of expressions of epistemic modality – and not about stance as personal 'attitude.'

In addition, some authors use the notion of *epistemic positioning* in order to combine evidentiality and modality, two dimensions for the expression of the sources/methods of knowledge acquisition and of the evaluation of these sources/methods as well as the information derived from them (see, e.g., Bednarek, 2006; Hart, 2011; Marín-Arrese, 2011a).

Also, it is relevant to avoid other terminological confusions sometimes found in the literature on evidentials and modalities. Hence, we distinguish the following dimensions and their relevant properties:

- sources (language users, social agents): knowledgeability
- methods (perception, communication): reliability
- beliefs, knowledge, information: validity
- personal evaluation of information or beliefs: (un)certainty
- social consequence of evaluation: commitment.

Obviously, these levels are mutually related in the sense that more knowledge-able sources are assumed to use more reliable methods, which enhance the validity of the beliefs acquired with these methods, which in turn may rationally (though need not) produce more certainty in the current speaker, which on this basis may feel socially committed with such a belief in social situations and interactions.

7.3.4.6.1   Mental model theory of epistemic modalities   Given the mental model-theoretic framework presented above for evidentials, it is obvious that the theory of epistemic modalities should also at least partly be formulated in such a framework. Since modalities are usually interpreted as expressing the *(un)certainty* of language users about propositions or states of affairs (depending on the theory), it makes sense to model such obvious examples of mental states. Speakers who index or explicitly express (un)certainty are assumed to be more or less aware of their own internal state, as they are studied in the philosophy of self-knowledge (see Chapter 2) or the psychology of metacognition (see Chapter 3). That is, speakers not only represent states of events they talk about in terms of situation models, but also in terms of models of themselves, as current speakers and thinkers, e.g., in experience and context models, as well as the relations between themselves (and their beliefs) and the relation to reality, that is as *relational meta-models*.

These meta-models may thus represent the degree of certainty about a belief, for instance in terms of the subjective probability of events, as currently derived from evidentially expressed or implied sources/methods: perception, discourse or inference, as explained above. Thus, as indicated, more know-ledgeable sources and (using) more reliable methods are in principle seen as leading to more valid beliefs and possibly to making language users more certain, unless other reasons or emotions (e.g., desires, fear) intervene. All this takes place cognitively, and hence we need a (more detailed) cognitive theory of how these different levels and stages of knowledge acquisition and evaluation can be made explicit.

7.3.4.6.2   Subjectivity, intersubjectivity and objectivity   Lyons (1977) already made a distinction between *subjective* and *objective* modalities. Thus, we may express our subjective belief or impression that it will soon start to rain (e.g., looking at the sky, etc.) or objectively predict this on the basis of external expert evidence such as the weather report, and express both with the ambiguous modality *may: It may rain later today*. Each of these may be used as a basis of more or less certainty, e.g., as expressed by *must, certainly, definitely, surely, no doubt*. Hence, both subjective and objective modalities are graded.

One way of accounting for the difference between these modalities is to define subjective modality in terms of the personal state of mind, namely *(un)certainty* of language users, and objective modality as (degrees) of *probability*, independently of the speaker, and based on external evidence, such as statistical probabilities, scientific research and so on. *Subjective epistemic modality*, in our terms, would be represented in terms of personal meta-models that language users have of their own state of mind with regard to events. On the other hand, *objective alethic modalities* (possibility, necessity) are directly attributed to the events in reality, and not as dependent on a personal evaluation, that is, represented as part of the first-order event model itself.

Nuyts (2001b), in a study of probability expressions in German and Dutch, examines this distinction between subjective and objective modalities more closely, and shows that objectivity may often be construed as evidential *intersubjectivity* (see also Nuyts, 2012). Thus subjectivity not only means that evidence may be weak, but especially that it pertains to (personal) events to which only the speaker has *access*, whereas objectivity may be construed as facts to which others (e.g., a scientific community) have access. Hence, the author suggests that (inter)subjectivity is in the evidential domain (how knowledge is acquired) rather than in the epistemic domain, although these domains interact (Nuyts (2001b) p. 386). Cornillie (2007) also differentiates between source-evidentiality and (inter)subjectivity.

Sanders and Spooren (1996), in an experimental study of Dutch epistemic modifiers (*moeten* 'must' and *blijken* 'obviously be'), first of all define these and other epistemic modifiers in terms of the *degrees of certainty* of the speaker (see also Marín-Arrese, 2011a). Such certainty is not based on the factuality of the evidence as such, but on its *causal relation* to the focal event the speaker is (un)certain about. However, besides certainty, they show that the epistemic modifiers may also express *degrees of subjectivity*, depending on whether the evidence is observational or knowledge-based (inferential). Thus, *non-subjective* modifiers express that the validity of the information given as evidence can be shared by speaker and recipient (and others), as is the case for *observational* evidence (*it looks like*, etc.). Other modifiers, such as *may* and *must* are called *semi-subjective* because they depend on the *reasoning* of the speaker (not necessarily accepted by the recipients). *Subjective* are clausal expressions such as *I think that ...* or *I believe that ...*, which tend to be used on the basis of knowledge-based evidence.

As is the case for many studies of modal expressions, we see that in this study, too, variations (in different languages) not only depend on the state of mind (certainty) of the speaker, but also on evidentiality (based on observation or inference). Contrary to the distinction by Lyons (1977) between subjective and objective, related to the factuality of events, the authors argue that epistemic modals rather express a commitment to what is said, and in that case they are all *subjective–performative*. Hence modal verbs only function as such in the present tense because they express the *current* stance about past or present states of affairs. Interestingly, however, their experiments showed that there is a tendency among language users to "cautiously" use subjective modifiers even when stronger, non-subjective modifiers could be used.

These findings show again that the use of epistemic modalities should not only be accounted for in purely cognitive terms, but also in *interactional* and *social terms*, involving the identity, role and relationships of the participants, such as positive self-presentation (appearing too sure may create a negative image), establishing or affirming authority or primacy over specific knowledge, possibly contested by other participants and so on, as summarized above for evidentials.

The same is true for the use of many types of *hedging* in academic discourse, where caution may avoid commitments that might have negative professional consequences should they turn out to be false (see above). Similarly, in news reports and other institutional texts there is a complex array of ways of marking the degree of certainty about reported events (Jaworski *et al.*, 2003; Rubin, 2010). It need not be repeated again that language users are only able to engage in such conversational strategies if they represent these social identities, relations or roles in their mental models.

The notions of subjectivity, intersubjectivity and non-subjectivity used in several studies of epistemic modalities may have a more explicit formulation in terms of mental model theory. It is generally observed that intersubjectivity enhances reliability of methods, validity of beliefs and certainty of speakers: *We observed, concluded* or *read that…* is usually stronger as evidence than saying that I do or did so. However, intersubjectivity has more complex roots in the minds of language users.

First of all, intersubjectivity may be represented at the highest level of discourse representation, that is, in the very *context model* of the communicative situation, that is, when a *discourse has several authors*, typically so in scholarly or other institutional discourse. The use of plural authorial *we* in this case not only suggests various writers but also various experts who are knowledgeable, who may apply reliable methods, control each other and so on. The shared context model of these authors thus controls cooperation at all levels of text preparation and production. No doubt such discourse is also most prestigious epistemically, precisely for this reason – apart from the technical and other organizational conditions that make such discourse more credible – unless the group or organization has a bad reputation, collectively. As always for evidentials and modalities, all depends on the context.

On the other hand, for text or talk of one author, *we* may be used in the academic or political sense to diminish the impression of subjectivity, but only one author is responsible for the discourse – as represented in the context model (Harwood, 2005, 2007). Yet, speakers and writers are not only represented in the context model in their communicative roles, but also in social identities and roles, e.g., as professors or experts, and hence as members of collectivities or prestigious institutions. Hence, even when speaking or writing alone, as representatives of a larger and prestigious group, organization or community, their subjectivity is so to speak *upgraded to a higher degree of intersubjectivity*, and hence credibility.

Epistemically, this means that authors are not only a knowledgeable source, as such, but also a more knowledgeable participant in the experiences they report, using more reliable methods of observation as the perceptual grounds of their discourse, or more reliable forms of inference from given general (e.g., scholarly) knowledge, observed events or from other discourses (which again may be prestigious in their own right).

In other words, at all levels of the communicative event and its claims, and hence also in the underlying mental models of experiences or discourses of others, and the inferences derived from them, knowledgeable or otherwise expert protagonists contribute to the perceived validity of their claims.

7.3.4.6.3 Grammatical complexities Although most studies maintain that epistemic modality is independent of evidentiality, they at the same time show that the use of modal expressions is closely related to types of evidence, the way language users evaluate sources or methods of reliability, the validity of the propositions or the probability of states of affairs. Some formal studies, such as McCready and Ogata (2007) on Japanese evidentials, in fact define the evidentials in terms of modalities – given the fact they can be embedded under conditionals and modals – while expressing a "degree of conviction toward the proposition in their scope" (p. 180).

This and other studies examine the nature of epistemic expressions in terms of their functions in different grammatical contexts. Thus, Papafragou (2006), who deals with the truth conditions of epistemic modalities – which are often denied because of their ungrammaticality in conditionals or questions – is critical to exclude even subjective modalities from the propositional contents of utterances. With other studies she agrees that subjective modalities are like performatives and *indexical* in the sense of possible worlds in the conversational background of the current speaker at the time of the utterance (also expressed in "For all I know..."), whereas objective modalities are related to what is generally known in some community, that is, what is known as "publicly available evidence." (p. 1695). She therefore also stresses the importance of the *contexts* of the utterance – here defined in terms of the knowledge of speakers or communities.

The subtlety of the differences between different expressions of epistemic modality is also dealt with by Simon-Vandenbergen (2008) examining the differences between *certainly* and *definitely* in different grammatical collocations. Thus, although both words express speaker certainty, and although both expressions may be used with *most* and *almost*, an experiment among native speakers suggests that it is more common to say *most definitely* but *almost certainly*. Among the many pragmatic and other differences she found (e.g., different uses in formal and informal speech, differences of age, use as a marker of intensity, etc.) *certainly* is used as a totality word, and *almost certainly* as a marker of careful academic assessment (avoiding extreme formulations), whereas *definitely* is scalar and *most definitely* expresses a high degree of speaker involvement.

We see, again, that subtle and changing differences of meaning between modal expressions – even when both express certainty of speakers – also need a description in terms of various kinds of pragmatic concepts and context properties (such as identity and role of speakers, relations between participants, types of communicative situations, genres). Indeed, although often used to refer to the same mental state of speakers when defining epistemic modalities, *certainty* and *involvement* seem to be different notions – as is the case for *commitment* – all used to describe mental states expressed by epistemic modalities.

As we saw above, Cornillie (2009) also stresses the "close relationship" but a non-overlapping difference between evidentiality and epistemic modalities: "Evidentiality refers to the reasoning processes that lead to a proposition, and epistemic modality evaluates the likelihood that this proposition is true" (p. 47). He stresses that speaker commitment does not depend on the value or mode of information but rather on speakers' interpretation of the source of information, and that their evaluation of the reliability of such a source does not necessarily imply a specific commitment: even strong (e.g., observational) evidence may lead to a low degree of epistemic commitment.

It should be stressed that notions such as *certainty, conviction, stance, attitude, involvement, commitment* and others, as used in the studies of modal expressions are all cognitively quite vague or ambiguous. Moreover, the same is true for the intentional object of these 'states of mind': are speakers (un)certain about (committed to, think about, feel about, etc.) what they say (an expression, an utterance, a discourse), what their utterance or discourse expresses (a meaning, a proposition), a mental representation (a mental model of a state of affairs), a state of affairs in the world, the evidence they have for such a state of affairs or the reliability of the source or method of establishing such evidence?

7.3.4.7   Implication

One of the most straightforward epistemic aspects of discourse is the crucial property of *implication and implicitness* (Bertuccelli-Papi, 2000; Sticha, 1996). Though pervasive as a semantic phenomenon, it is little studied in linguistics, precisely because implications are by definition not expressed, but remain 'implicit.' For non-cognitive approaches to discourse this is a serious problem precisely because they are not directly 'observable.' They are only indirectly inferable when next speakers in conversation comment on implications of a previous turn. This shows that participants not only assign meaning to explicit expressions, but also derive inferences from what has been explicitly said, as is the point of the difference between discourse meaning and underlying mental models (Graesser and Bower, 1990; Rickheit and Strohner, 1985; Van de Velde, 1984).

Implicit discourse meaning is sometimes also studied in terms of *tacit knowledge*. Thus Zappavigna (2013), inspired by ideas of Polanyi (1966) about 'tacit' knowledge as non-expressible knowledge and working within a Functional Systemic framework, studies grammatical structures of interviews with computer experts by 'unpacking' the 'under-representation' of meaning in nominalizations, generalizations, agency and modalities. Note, though, that since the empiricist Functional Systemic framework explicitly does not have a cognitive dimension (Van Dijk, 2008a), the analysis is presented in terms of *meaning* 'shortcuts' as allowed by the grammar of English, not really in terms of tacit or implicit *knowledge* as it is usually dealt with in philosophy or psychology (see previous chapters).

Our theoretical framework allows a simple and elegant definition of implication, namely as any information that is part of the situation model of a discourse but that is not expressed in the discourse itself. In comprehension, such an implicit meaning is inferred from the meanings (propositions, etc.) explicitly expressed in discourse, an inference that is based on the generic knowledge about a situation or its properties or other information in the mental model of an event. In more formal terms, this would, for instance, involve the inference of implicit proposition q, given the explicitly expressed proposition p, and the general knowledge that p entails q, as in logical modus ponens, or a more inductive kind of inference (such as inferring that someone is dead after falling from a high building, etc.). Indeed, this is also the way local coherence is usually established – because speakers know that recipients can infer 'missing' propositions from their own knowledge, as we have seen above for the definition of discourse coherence.

In contrast with a logical or formal semantic approach to inferences, implications are not just any proposition implied by another proposition – which would include a vast number of possible implications a speaker would not ever entertain and a recipient would not and could not derive because they are irrelevant. Hence, the discursive implications are only those propositions that a speaker and/or recipient construe as such in their situation model interpreting a discourse, for instance in order to better understand other parts of the discourse or because they are otherwise relevant for the interaction or communication.

This also means that implications should not be defined as propositions that are derived from propositions but as mental representations derived from the current state of a discourse during understanding. This may mean that, given a sequence of propositions in a discourse, realizing a fragment of the situation model of the discourse, language users may further 'develop' such a model simply by applying relevant, socially shared generic knowledge.

Thus, if we hear a story about someone having dinner in a restaurant, a dinner and restaurant script (Schank and Abelson, 1977) may be activated and transform generic knowledge into the instantiated knowledge that can be used to complete a mental model without the speaker having to be explicit about such information (Van Dijk and Kintsch, 1983). Indeed, as we shall see below, such implicit knowledge may later in the discourse be *presupposed*, e.g., when referring to *the* waitress or *the* menu with a definite expression without explicitly having introduced these script elements before.

Note that implications by definition are subjective, as is also the case for the mental models of which they are part. They may be part of the model of the speaker, but not be construed as such by the recipient and vice versa. Yet, although subjective, the interpretation of implicit meanings of discourse is not arbitrary but is constrained by sociocognitive norms that regulate plausible inferences and expectations. In a story about a woman being hungry and being described as going to eat in a restaurant, the plausible expectation is, for instance, that she sat at a table, ordered food, ate the food, paid for it and left. If one of these implications is not true, then the speaker will be expected to explicitly deny it and say things such as "But, she got nothing to eat because the kitchen was closed" (or "the waiters were on strike" or "she felt sick and did not eat anything after all," etc.).

In other words, our generic knowledge of the world provides the norms for the specific structures of mental models as well as the 'normative' ways people talk about their experiences or the ways news reports tell about news events. Indeed, it is from such mental models that such knowledge is derived as a generalization in the first place.

This is a fortiori the case not only for this kind of empirical knowledge of the world, but also for the very conceptual structure of knowledge, which allows language users to infer that someone was using a means of public transport when described as taking a train. Such conceptual implications may again be presupposed in next sentences of a discourse.

Notice that implications are not limited to single propositions or sentences. Contrary to a sentence-based semantics, discourse semantics of course allows that implications are derived, and hence construed in a model, on the basis of a longer description of a situation. In a novel we may read about many things a protagonist does and says, and after many pages infer that he is depressed, aggressive or a conservative or that the sequence thus described globally means that he was robbing a bank. Of course, such inferences may be treated as more or less plausible hypotheses, as is the case for all strategic discourse processing, which, however, can be confirmed when later in a discourse one of these inferences is expressed as a presupposition (see Goldman *et al.*, 1999; Trabasso, 2005; Van den Broek *et al.*, 1997; Van Dijk and Kintsch, 1983).

That implications, as well as implicatures (see below), may be ideologically based by presupposing partisan mental models of speakers is obvious in much political discourse. Thus, David Cameron in his *Sun* article claims the following about immigration policies after denouncing that immigration "got out of control" under Labour:

> (17) Since Conservatives took office, we've worked hard to get things more manageable.
> And it's working: net migration is down by a third since the last election.

By making this statement about his immigration policy as 'working' Cameron is implying that 'net immigration is down by a third' *due to* his policy. Literally, he may well be right that immigration is down by a third since the elections, although there may be many other causes of such a change. We see that implications have the important political function of *deniability*: if challenged, Cameron could always argue that he never actually *said* that immigration is down due to his policies, even when all readers would have made that inference. Racist propaganda of political parties today often uses such implications instead of making literal racist statements (Daniels, 2009; Jäger, 1989; Wodak *et al.*, 2013; Van Dijk, 1993).

7.3.4.8 *Implicature*

Implicatures, as most notably introduced by Grice (1975, 1989), are usually defined as pragmatic implications (Atlas, 2000; Davis, 1998; Gazdar, 1977; Potts, 2005). They are not only derived, as is the case for (semantic) implications, from the knowledge of the world of the participants, but from the knowledge of the communicative situation as represented by the participants, that is, from their context models. Thus, if Tony Blair, in his speech in parliament in March 2003, describes Saddam Hussein as a tyrant, the pragmatic – and in this case the political – implicature may be that Britain should remove Saddam Hussein, go to war and so on, depending on the detailed pragmatic and political properties of the parliamentary debate (see Van Dijk, 2008a, 2009a). In similar ways, sudden changes of topic may implicate that a speaker is bored or for other reasons does not want to speak about the current topic of conversation or stating that a valuable object is missing, may implicate an accusation of the recipient.

Whereas these examples are characteristic of implicatures, their detailed theoretical account is less straightforward. If they are a kind of implication, that is, implicit meanings derived from text or talk, they must be represented somewhere, typically in a mental model. But the relevant inference cannot simply be derived from the knowledge of the world. Indeed, describing a president as a tyrant does not generally imply that a country goes (or should go) to war against him. But when Saddam Hussein is described as such by Tony Blair, as Prime Minister, and as part of a motion defended in parliament, and given the current international political situation in 2003, then such a political implicature may be derived from his speech – and it is precisely in this way that Members of Parliament understand his speech, as is obvious from their interventions in the debate. If that is so, then such a meaning should be represented in the situation model of Blair's speech, as construed by himself as well as his recipients. In that respect, an implicature is no different from other (semantic) implications.

So what makes implicatures *pragmatic* implications? Given our framework, in which pragmatics is based on context models, the obvious answer would be that the implication is derived and can be derived only in the present communicative situation. Indeed, Tony Blair and other leaders have negatively described Saddam Hussein on other occasions, without implicating any desire to go to war against him. Hence, the current implicature must be based on generic knowledge of the world, for instance about the usual causes or arguments for war, on the one hand, and on the details of the current communicative situation, on the other. Indeed, decisions to go to war can only be taken (in the UK) by governments and backed up by parliaments, and Tony Blair *now* speaks as Prime Minister, and addresses the MPs in parliament, and the intention of his speech is to get the support of parliament for his belligerent policy. Mentioning in such a situation that Saddam Hussein has weapons of mass destruction, and that hence he represents a threat to world peace, would be possible *casus belli*, the political implication of which is obvious. Although such an implicature may be obvious for Blair, Bush, Aznar and others, it was not obvious to all those who opposed the war, and hence did not consider the reasons given as sufficient, or sufficiently reliable, as a motive to go to war.

In other words, implicatures as context-based implications require the construction of a situation model that is not only based on explicit discourse plus inferences from generic world knowledge, as is the case for semantic implications. Rather, they also need sometimes subtle inferences based on an analysis of the – by definition implicit – context model of the participants: current time, place, speaker identities roles and relations, current social or political acts accomplished by discourse, its aims and purposes and the now relevant knowledge of the participants, as just described for Blair's speech. Implications and implicatures, thus, largely take place 'below' the level of 'observable' text or talk, namely in the minds of the participants – including what they think about the thoughts of other participants (for details on the nature of context-based implicatures, see Van Dijk, 2008a, 2009a).

The same is true for the *Sun* article of David Cameron on immigration we examined earlier. Besides the many knowledge-based semantic implications of that article (see above), the political implicatures are even more important, and are to be explained in terms of the context model of Cameron representing himself as Prime Minister and the recipients as readers of the *Sun*, and the goal to thus legitimate his new, restrictive immigration policy. Thus, when he starts by saying that immigration has brought immense benefits to Britain, and the country is open, diverse and welcoming, he pragmatically implicates, and emphasizes by adding that he is proud of this, that he has a positive view of immigration. This again politically implicates that he and his party cannot be accused of being against immigration or xenophobic – a characteristic move of positive self-presentation initiating the second part of a disclaimer, which indeed follows: "But we do this country's great history no favours unless we have a sensible debate."

7.3.4.9 Presupposition

Whereas implications have been little studied in linguistics and discourse analysis, *presuppositions* have been in the forefront of studies of linguistics and the philosophy of language. This is probably the case because linguistic presuppositions often have 'observable' manifestations in text and talk, for instance in definite expressions, clause position, topic–focus distribution, factive verbs, special adverbs and other presupposition 'triggers' (Beaver, 2001; Cooper, 1974; Deemter and Kibble, 2002; Gazdar, 1979; Kempson, 1975; Petöfi and Franck, 1973; Van der Auwera, 1975).

Whereas the systematic observation of such expressions, traces or triggers of presupposition is a frequent topic in the study of text and talk, the theoretical framework defining presupposition is often more muddled.

Most explicit is the classical **logical definition** of presupposition in terms of a proposition that is implied by another proposition and its negation. Thus, the proposition "The French did not support Blair's plans to go to war against Iraq" is a presupposition of the sentence *Blair regretted that the French did not support his plan to go to war against Iraq*, as well as of its negation *Blair did not regret ...* – because of the use of the factive verb *to regret*.

Such a formal definition does not tell us much about the underlying cognitive structures of presuppositions or about their variable discursive manifestations. Probably this formal definition applies especially to the propositions expressed in subordinate clauses of factive verbs (like *to regret, to stop, to continue*, etc.) but not by other presupposition triggers, e.g., depending on the *scope* of the expression. For instance, the sentence *Even the French supported the war* presupposes that the French were not expected to support the war, but that presupposition is not implied by the negated sentence *Even the French did not support the war*, which presupposes, on the contrary, that the French were expected to support the war. Similarly, the same sentences beginning with *Also*, presuppose that others did (or did not) support the war. In sum, a more sophisticated account is called for.

Another, more **social psychological account** is to define presupposition in terms of shared knowledge, and as part of the Common Ground of participants in a communicative situation. This is relatively straightforward, but still much too vague, because it does not tell us much about where and how such 'shared knowledge' is represented. In our theoretical framework, such an account would be formulated in terms of shared situation models as controlled by context models.

However, although such would be a correct general basis for an account of presuppositions, it is still not specific enough. It is true that understanding a sentence of discourse happens in relation to the situation model construed so far, as well as other knowledge of the communicative situation as represented in the current state of the context model. But this is a lot of knowledge, and *presuppositions of words or sentences* are more specific meanings (propositions, etc.) among all this knowledge. To understand the sentences about Blair's regret about the French not supporting the war against Iraq, one needs vast amounts of knowledge about Blair, prime ministers, wars, politics, the French and so on. Blair's sentence is meaningful and can be appropriately understood only with at least some of this general and specific knowledge. In a general sense, we may say that such knowledge is 'presupposed' by this sentence – or rather by the discourse in which this sentence appears. But in this case, 'presuppose' means rather 'is a condition for the interpretation of.'

In the specific sentence mentioned above it is only the embedded proposition that is a *linguistic presupposition* of the sentence, because it is the proposition as expressed in the subordinate clause that is presupposed. Thus, the use of the definite description *the war* implies that the speaker presupposes that the recipients know what war he is referring to – since it is part of the CG defined by the whole discourse and the communicative situation, as represented in current situation and context models.

Such an account is most obvious in a discourse-based approach to language, because in that case any proposition that has been asserted before and which is implied by a following sentence automatically becomes a presupposition. This is at least an advance over sentence-based approaches that only account for 'preceding' discourse in terms of invented prior sentences or questions.

Earlier treatments of presupposition have dealt with what is often called **accommodation**, that is, expressions that suggest presuppositions but that do not imply knowledge shared by the recipients – while also not earlier expressed by the speaker. Typical examples would be *My sister teaches mathematics*, in a conversation in which the speaker has never mentioned having a sister. In this way a recipient may infer that the speaker has a sister but such information is not asserted but formally presupposed. In fact, we may speak of a form of *oblique* or *indirect assertions* in this case.

Again, in a cognitively based discourse approach there is nothing special about these cases, because they are the usual ways of presupposing knowledge-based inferences, not much different from referring to *the* waiter in a restaurant story without having mentioned him before (see especially the critical account of the notion of accommodation by Werth, 1993). Referring to one's sister, brother, parents, wife or even car or bicycle or parts of one's body without first introducing such entities is a normal form of 'presupposition' based on inferences derived from general knowledge about speakers as human beings in our society. This means that – under specific further constraints – CG is not only formed by generic sociocultural knowledge, as well as the current state of situation, context and text models, but also by its most plausible or accessible inferences (e.g., people have fathers and mothers, and often brothers and sisters; restaurants have waiters, etc.). It is then a question of definition whether or not such inferences are counted as presuppositions or as part of what we called indirect or implicit assertions.

Such notions activate conceptual knowledge that is inserted in the mental model of recipients as old, socioculturally 'given' information, at the same time as the 'new' information of such sentences. That such presuppositions only hold for commonly shared knowledge is shown by the fact that a speaker in London and living in a flat will hardly be able to speak about 'my crocodile' to someone who does not know her well without first telling that person that she has such a pet.

The only difference between this and many other presuppositions is that this kind of 'accommodated' information was not yet an explicit part of the previous discourse and hence may not yet have been inserted in the current situation model. But it was in a sense part of the CG, because context information is always added to the CG, and hence general knowledge about speakers, including that many speakers have sisters is available. If this information is not taken for granted in conversation (as in "Oh, I did not know you have a sister!") the recipient rejects the supposition of CG, but rather interprets it an indirect form of assertion, that is, as *new* information, although such knowledge is not focused on as in normal assertions, as in "*I have this sister who ...*"

From this very succinct account of the role of presupposition, knowledge and discourse, we may conclude that much of the traditional literature on presupposition in linguistics and philosophy was premised on a very reduced conception of language use in terms of isolated, invented sentences, instead of naturally occurring discourse, as well as ignoring the cognitive mental models that play a role in discourse production and understanding.

Our theoretical framework, thus, allows various conceptions of presupposition. First, in very general terms, if CG is defined as before, a presupposition of a sentence S in a discourse D is a proposition p of CG that is implied by S. In that sense, p is a condition of meaningfulness for S. In other words, this definition in terms of shared propositions between CG and a sentence in discourse establishes the semantic 'overlap' between what is already known by the participants and a new sentence in discourse. Since CG is defined in terms of the (shared) *knowledge* of the participants (and not in terms of propositions expressed in sentences) this definition is pragmatic rather than semantic if the proposition expressed by S is assumed to be known by the speaker, that is, part of the situation model of the speaker.

So, it may be more correct to define presuppositions in this general sense in terms of the overlap of the current state of the situation model of the speaker with the CG shared by the participants. This also leaves open the question whether the structures of the model are to be defined in terms of propositions or not. For instance, the current situation model may just share a discourse participant with CG (e.g., speaking about a person the recipient knows). We may simply call this kind of knowledge-based pragmatic presupposition the *epistemic presupposition* of a sentence in discourse (this concept of presupposition is, of course, close to the pragmatic definition provided by Stalnaker in his discussion of Common Ground, 1974, 2002).

Yet, *linguistic presuppositions* are usually defined more strictly in the sense that they must be 'triggered' by *specific grammatical structures* of a sentence S of discourse D, as is the case for factive verbs (such as *discover*, *regret*, etc.), definite articles, initial *that*-clauses, cleft-sentence structures, some adverbs (such as *even* and *also*) and so on. Yet, the precise meaning of the conceptual metaphor of 'triggering' is not clear. It may mean that 'triggers' are specific grammatical expressions of specific (propositional) meaning relations, e.g., between an expression and its semantic implications, on the one hand, or signals of, or pointers to, specific knowledge elements (e.g., about objects, persons, events, actions, etc.) of the CG, on the other.

Since the presuppositional implications of grammatical expressions depend on text and context, it seems more plausible to construe them in a more pragmatic–epistemic way rather than in terms of (abstract) meanings or propositions. Indeed, as we see in such examples as editorial decisions to authors of journal articles, writing *I regret that your article cannot be published*, the depended *that*-clause expresses a proposition that obviously was (not yet) shared with the recipient, and hence is not part of the CG, and hence not a presupposition of this sentence, despite the use of the 'factive' verb *to regret* – which in this case seems more like an emotional modal operator, as is the use of *regrettably*. More generally, e.g., in newspaper discourse, dependent *that*-clauses seem to trigger presuppositions, but in fact express new information (see, e.g., Abbott, 2008). Instead of changing the fundamental nature of pragmatic presupposition and CG, we thus might want to change the linguistic assumption about *that*-clauses as presupposition triggers – especially if they occur in last (focus) position. Simons (2007) shows that embedded *that*-clauses are often 'main points' of factive evidentials (e.g., '*Mary discovered that ...*') and hence convey new information that is not part of CG.

More generally, thus, the CG-based definition of presupposition does not imply that in many contexts speakers or writers have to assert totally 'new' information. People often repeat themselves, may assert what many people know or comment on a shared context (e.g., a 'nice day') and so on (Abbott, 2008). Again, instead of changing the general definition of presupposition, it thus seems more appropriate to modify the conditions of assertions (and Grice's conversational postulates) and allow speakers to 'assert' (repeat, emphasize, etc.) known or given information – as we all do in everyday conversations as well as in pedagogical situations – given specific rhetorical contexts and constraints (indeed, we would not usually deem a newspaper article appropriate if it consisted of a large number of the same sentences).

Similarly, as we have seen for some 'accommodative' uses of presupposition triggers such as definite articles and possessive adjectives (as in *the waiter* and *my sister*), they may signal knowledge that is not yet explicitly part of the CG but should now be added to the CG, as in an implicit or indirect assertion, on the basis of an inference from generic knowledge (as also proposed by the 'dynamic' account of CG-expansion proposed by Stalnaker, 1974, 2002; see also the critical comments on such a 'dynamic' approach by Schlenker, 2008). Indeed, this also suggests that CG is not 'closed' in the sense that participants explicitly 'know' all the logical or empirical implications of what they know, but need to engage in explicit processes of inference, indeed as 'triggered' by specific expressions. The *my crocodile* counterexample shows, again, that the interpretation of such 'triggers' depends on text and context in that some expressions are interpretable only if discourse referents have explicitly been introduced before, and hence are explicitly part of the CG before an assertion.

In sum, grammatical structures may be seen as formalized or 'codified' indicators of interpretations, but actual interpretations, including inferences of presupposed knowledge, depend on text and context and hence on the dynamic development of the Common Ground in discursive interaction – defined in

290 Language, discourse and knowledge

terms of mental models. We shall come back to presuppositions in our discussion of topic and focus below.

Examine the Cameron *Sun* article for some characteristic examples of relevant political and ideological presuppositions, exhibiting nationalist self-glorification and the well-known bipolar ideological emphasis on the positive aspects of *Us* (Our Conservative party) and the negative ones of *Them* (the Labour party):

(18)
- But we do this country's great history no favours unless we have a sensible debate.
  - » Our country has a great history (of immigration)
  - » There has not been a sensible debate before (on immigration)
- *Sun* readers know that immigration got out of control under Labour.
  - » Immigration got out of control under Labour
- Since Conservatives took office, we've worked hard to get things more manageable.
  - » Things (immigration) were not manageable before (under Labour)

7.3.4.10 Elaboration

Crucially, discourse expresses how new information is related to old or given information, both at the level of sentence structure, as is the case for topic and focus (see below), as well as at the level of whole text or talk. We already assumed, at a global level, that all the old information of a discourse has the function of global functional topic, whereas all the new information has the function of global functional focus.

Also at the local, sequential level we need to examine in more detail how new knowledge is introduced in discourse, beyond the focus parts of clauses or sentences. Given a sentence or discourse topic, adding new information in discourse may be called expansion, development, amplification or *elaboration*. We shall provisionally use the latter term because it is often informally used to describe a property of discourse.

A related notion of elaboration is used in Rhetorical Structure Theory (Mann and Thompson, 1988) as one of the functional relations between propositions of discourse. Our notion is different in the sense that it is a more general discursive strategy that needs further theoretical and empirical analysis and not an unanalyzed interpropositional or intersentential rhetorical relation (see also Knott *et al.*, 2001).

Hobbs (1985) provides a formal definition of elaboration in terms of implication: subsequent propositions in discourse are elaborations of an earlier proposition if they jointly imply that earlier proposition. This is also one of the ways we defined macropropositions (Van Dijk, 1980) – as these are implied by all propositions of a discourse: all propositions of a story with details on my vacation obviously are an elaboration of the topical proposition 'I was on vacation.'

At first sight, it seems there are hardly any rules or strategies for meaningful or appropriate elaboration, as long as the continuation is locally and globally coherent, as specified above. This means, first of all, that elaborations need to be constrained by the overall discourse topic – or else introduce a change of topic. Secondly, each next sentence must be locally coherent following the functional and referential conditions of local semantic coherence, discussed above.

The general constraints of local and global coherence, however, still leave much freedom to the speakers, and it remains to be seen whether there are any further constraints. Thus, if we write about Tony Blair, as a sentence topic, and his current decision to invade Iraq as a discourse topic, can we then sequentially select any aspect of Blair or this decision as long as the elaboration is locally or globally coherent? And if so, are there no other rules or norms for meaningful or appropriate elaborations? Similarly, if Cameron as Prime Minister (PM) addresses *Sun* readers by announcing a tougher immigration policy, can he just say anything on such a policy?

Some of these constraints we have discussed before in terms of **linearization** and **sequencing**. Thus, generally, there tends to be a linear 'natural order' of descriptions, for instance based on temporality (begin–end), causality (cause–consequences), size (big–small), containment (outside–inside), attributes (entity–properties) and so on. Some of these relationships are derived from the 'natural' structure of the situation models defining the interpretation of discourse, in which, for instance, causes of events are usually represented as preceding these events. But a hierarchical representation of a situation in a model does not specify what aspects of an event, action, actor or scene need to be mentioned first, and then in what order. The rules of discursive linearization thus provide a constraint for the projection of mental models onto text and talk. Hence, elaboration should be globally and locally coherent as well as sequentially ordered, which may be partly based on fundamental cognitive principles of perception and the planning of actions.

Whatever the rules of sequencing, discourse is very flexible and there are strategies that may break the rules in order to realize different functions. For instance, causal ordering may be reversed and causes mentioned after the event in order to give explanations – one of the functional relations of coherence. Identities of actors may be revealed only much later in discourse, for instance in order to create tension, as is the case in classical detective novels (whodunits). We may first mention a small object or a person and then the environment (place, etc.) if such an object or person is specifically focused on, for instance after a search as reported in a story or news report, e.g., "The lost child was finally found in ..." Finally, news reports, unlike most stories, are not ordered by time or causality of the events reported, but hierarchically and linearly by importance, relevance or recency, that is, with the most important information first, in headline and lead, and details towards the end (Van Dijk, 1988a).

Natural ordering in mental models as well as in the discourse expressing them is partly based on generic knowledge, for instance about time, causality, the structures of events, actions, persons, objects, landscapes. Models of stereotypical events and actions are generally instantiations of generic scripts, as is the case for a story about going to the movies or eating in a restaurant. Actors in stories tend to be described first in terms of their relevant identities (gender, age, appearance, etc.) and only then their actions and attributes. We do not first say of a non-identified person that she wore a long dress, and only then that she was a woman or a girl. Further empirical study of many discourse genres will be necessary to find more detailed norms of discursive elaboration.

Since elaboration presupposes local and global coherence, changing topics may involve a lack of elaboration. Thus, Horowitz *et al.* (1993) introduce the notion of *dyselaboration* in the description of psychotherapeutic interviews, as a move or strategy of clients who avoid continuing to speak about a painful topic or who want to correct or deny something they have said before.

Kidwell and Martinez (2010) show that in interrogations, law-enforcement officers may engage in a 'soft accusation' method of elaboration and turn expansion that aligns a subject's talk and admission of guilt as a smooth continuation of long "telling about oneself" turns of officers. Interesting for this chapter is the fact that in this case the interrogator, rather than the subject, has primary epistemic rights of disclosure. More generally in conversation, interruptions or long turns of powerful participants, whether in informal or in institutional settings, are among the many interactional means that hamper or prevent elaboration of co-participants.

Finally, given the constraints of local and global coherence, sequential elaboration should follow the contextual constraints of *genre*, and the kinds of information conveyed in such genres. Thus, a news report on Tony Blair and the Iraq war is supposed to remain within the *epistemic domain* of Britain, Blair, policies, Iraq, wars and so on. Hence information of a more personal kind, such as quarrel with his wife or having a cold, would not be an appropriate local elaboration even if locally and globally coherent for most newspapers. Tabloids may well also breach such a convention – because they define different contexts.

Similarly, when David Cameron writes about his new immigration policy, he is not only contextually constrained by the hybrid genre of a political speech published in a newspaper, implying limits of space and specifically addressing readers of the *Sun*. If he elaborates on his immigration policy, such details should specifically interest the readers of the *Sun* as citizens and voters, such that immigration is down, allegedly because of Conservative policies, that benefits for immigrants will be limited and so on – and emphasizing that such was not the case under Labour. In other words, the elaboration is not only controlled by a specification of the mental models Cameron has of the past and current immigration situation and his own policies, it is also pragmatically controlled by the context model representing what is relevant and interesting for the readers, while at the same time politically implicating the good things of his own party and the bad things of Labour.

7.3.4.11 *Definitions*

Prominent, especially in scientific, expository or pedagogical discourse, **definitions** may be seen as the expressed and linearized manifestation of underlying generic knowledge, but always adapted to the communicative situation as construed by the participants. Traditionally, definitions were characterized in terms of a superordinate genus (e.g., 'car is a sort of vehicle') and a specification of its properties as different (e.g., 'having four wheels') from others members of the superordinate set (e.g., vehicles, Cormack, 1998).

The cognitive presupposition of such definitions is that recipients know the superordinate category and understand the description of the specific differences. Yet, often more specific middle-range categories (such as that of 'car') are better known and used more often than more abstract, higher-level categories (such as 'vehicle,' Rosch, 1978). Hence, useful definitions in pedagogical discourse would need to presuppose such middle-level categories in order to define more specific lower-level categories, such as that of a 'berlina' as a type of car.

As we have seen in Chapter 3, concepts may not be defined in terms of such 'static definitions' but rather require context-dependent representations (Barsalou and Medin, 1986) – which, however, we would account for in terms of mental models of personal experiences.

Cognitively, expository or pedagogical discourse is organized by generic, conceptual knowledge structures rather than by mental models such as those underlying everyday stories and news reports – although the latter may typically be used as examples. We have seen that such generic knowledge structures may be hierarchical and hence need to be linearized in semantically coherent sequences – and stylistically (lexically, syntactically, etc.) adapted to the participants specified in the context model, such as university students or children. The epistemic constraint is that the knowledge expressed in the definition is formulated in terms that are known to the recipients. Since generic knowledge may be fairly abstract, metaphor is one of the ways definitions may be associated with more concrete experiences (see below).

Both cognitively and discursively interesting is that many if not all definitions feature a limited number (about seven) of dimensions, such as size, weight, form, appearance, composition, density and function for material objects – probably related to the major neural aspects of multimodal experiences with such objects (Calsamiglia and van Dijk, 2004). Similarly, event types – as is also the case for communicative events – may be organized, and hence defined, in terms of Setting (Space, Time), Participants (Identities, Roles, Relations), Actions/Events, Goals or Causes and Knowledge of the participants or Affordances of objects (Van Dijk, 2008a, 2009a; Zacks et al., 2001). The question then is how for different communicative situations and genres such dimensions are sequentially ordered in discourse.

Interesting for our discussion are not only the structures of epistemic discourse, but also its cognitive and social foundations. Thus, socially speaking, definitions vary especially by the context of communication, and more specifically by the identities and relations of the participants (professors and students; mothers and children), the aims of the activity (explanation, instruction, etc.), the knowledge differential between the participants and the institutional settings (classroom, family, etc.). Often definitions embody ideologically based summaries of social representations and hence express social struggle of power and power abuse, as are the different definitions of the concept of 'marriage' (McConnell-Ginet, 2006), 'gender' (Fagot et al., 1997) or 'schizophrenia' (First and Pincus, 1999).

We may conclude that definitions are properties of the semantics of discourse that provide contextually variable expressions of generic knowledge of speakers or writers intended for specific recipients, and with different communicative and interactional aims, such as explanation and teaching, on the one hand, or defending or contesting dominant concepts or social structures. In that sense, they are the most direct discourse mappings of underlying knowledge structures, often closely related to underlying ideologies, but always controlled by the constraints of the context as represented by the participants.

7.3.4.12   Metaphor

Since metaphors, as expressions of knowledge, have received extensive attention in the literature, we need not detail these findings here. New studies of metaphor have emphasized that metaphor is not primarily a rhetorical figure or an embellishment of discourse but rather a fundamental way of thinking, for instance by relating more abstract concepts to more concrete, experienced ones (among a vast number of books, see e.g., Kövecses, 2005; Lakoff, 1987; Lakoff and Johnson, 1980, 1999; Musolff and Zinken, 2008; Stern, 2000).

This approach ties in with studies of knowledge in psychology that emphasize the multimodal, grounded nature of knowledge (see, e.g., Barsalou,

2008) – which we have associated primarily with mental models as representations of experiences.

Already this brief summary shows that metaphor as one of the important aspects of discourse meaning has a cognitive and maybe even a neural basis. Relevant for this chapter is that metaphors are not only forms of thought exhibiting abstract knowledge structures and relations between generic knowledge and concrete models of experiences, they also organize discourse meanings. For instance, the well-known metaphor of a 'code' used to describe the genetic information (DNA) of chromosomes is typically continued and detailed in large fragments of discourse, thus using other metaphors (such as 'letters' for amino acids and 'transcription') in a complex of description and explanation (Calsamiglia and Van Dijk, 2004; Condit, 1999; Knudsen, 2005; Pramling and Saljö, 2007).

As is the case for all discourse expressions of knowledge, and as we have just emphasized for definitions, the metaphor–knowledge interface is also *context-dependent*: different speakers use different metaphors for different recipients in different communication contexts and engaging in different social acts, presupposing different knowledge and ideologies among the recipients (Ashton, 1994; Bosch, 1984; Camp, 2006; Gibbs and Gerrig, 1989; Givón, 2005; Kövecses, 2009; Shinjo and Myers, 1987; Stern 2000). Obviously, in our framework, it is not the social context itself that defines the production and understanding of metaphors, but the way the participants define these context parameters in their context models (Van Dijk, 2008a).

7.3.4.13 *Information structure: topic and focus*
The distinction between 'old' and 'new' information (and related distinctions) that characterizes so many semantic discourse structures examined above also organizes the semantic, syntactic and phonological structure of clauses and sentences at the local level of discourse. Here too we shall be very brief about this classical distinction, because it has been dealt with in a huge literature on *information structure* for more than fifty years, (see e.g., Chafe, 1974, 1994; Dahl, 1974; Erteschik-Shir, 2007; Geluykens, 1984; Hajičová *et al.*, 1996; Kniffka, 2008; Lambrecht 1994; Partee and Sgall, 1996; Sgall *et al.*, 1973; Steube, 2004; Van Dijk, 1977).

Note that most studies on information structure are limited to sentence grammars and thus ignore the fundamental discourse dependence of the distinction as well as its underlying mental models. Hence we shall limit our discussion to the ways the topic–focus articulation may be dealt with in terms of the distribution of knowledge or information defined in terms of text models, situation models and context models. Sentence grammars typically discuss information structure in terms of a (construed) previous sentence or question, and thus indirectly recognize the fundamental discursive nature of information structure, namely as the distribution of various kinds of knowledge (old, new, etc.) over different levels and scopes of discourse structure (whole discourses, sequences, sentences, clauses, phrases, words, morphemes).

For non-cognitive sentence grammars the very notion of 'information structure' may be relatively obscure, since obviously it is not definable merely in grammatical (syntactic, phonological or semantic) terms or separate levels of representation (see, e.g., Fanselow, 2008; Vallduvi, 1992). On the other hand, a much broader sociocognitive theory of discourse and communication more naturally is able to define the relevant notions (such as topic, focus and presupposition) in terms of a combination of sentence and discourse structures and their relationship with underlying text models, situation models and context models, as they also define the dynamic K-device of Common Ground (CG).

Roughly speaking, in English and many other languages, the unstressed (often first) part of sentences typically expresses the information that has *topic* (or theme) function, and the stressed (often last) part the information that has *focus* (comment, rheme) function. Topic in this case often corresponds with *old* or *given* information, and focus with *new* or *salient* information, where old and new information are to be defined with respect to the CG of the participants (Karttunen, 1974; Stalnaker, 1974; for related notions, such as Background-Presupposition, see e.g., Geurts and van der Sandt, 2004).

Since CG is a complex epistemic function of the K-device of context models, it should be analyzed in terms of the kind of knowledge(s) it has activated at the beginning of a sentence or turn, as also mentioned above:

(i) relevant given **generic knowledge** of the epistemic community
(ii) previous **shared experiences** (shared old experience models)
(iii) knowledge about the current communicative situation (the **context model**)
(iv) what has actually been said in the discourse so far, e.g., the current **discourse topic** (the fragmentary **text model**)
(v) information derived from the previous part of the current discourse, that is, the partial **situation model** construed so far
(vi) information expressed in the **previous sentence or turn** as well as its function (sequential or sentential topic or focus).

In a more explicit sociocognitive theory of epistemic discourse structures, in general, and of the information structure (topic, focus, etc.) of sentences, in particular, notions such as 'old' and 'new' are too vague. For instance, components of the current communicative situation, represented in the context model, such as participants and their identities, roles and relations, are hardly 'old' information, but present, immediately accessible information.

Hence, expressions referring to the participant with the current speaker role (expressed by the pronouns *I* or *me*) or the current recipient role (expressed by the pronoun *you*) usually have topic function, except when marking a distinction or contrast with other participants in the situation or context model, as expressed by focus stress (e.g., *She gave the book to ME, and not to my brother!*). This is also usually the case for expressions referring to referents that have been mentioned before in the current discourse and hence have been introduced as participants in the current situation model. The same is true for referents whose existence has been inferred from the current situation model together with generic knowledge applied to the model, such as the topical reference to *the waiter* in a restaurant story or *my father* in a story about the family – traditionally dealt with as accommodating presuppositions, as we have seen above.

Just like focus elements, topics may be stressed, for instance in cases of contrast, selection or parallelism, with respect to other elements of a group mentioned, as in *John and Mary were planning to go to the movies. JOHN wanted to go to a Hitchcock movie, but MARY preferred Billie Wilder.*

Although definite initial noun phrases (NP) often signal textually or contextually given or inferred discourse referents and hence are assigned topic function, there are examples of 'new topics' where the referent of such initial NPs has not been mentioned or inferred before, typically so in news reports (e.g., *The Prime Minister, in London, today*) but such examples may also be explained in terms of uniqueness (there is only one Prime Minister) or in contextual deictic terms (the PM of our country, as is the case for *today*). In this example, if the expression of new or unknown information is assigned focus function, then the whole sentence would need to be assigned focus function. If, on the other hand, topic function is defined in terms of *aboutness*, and the sentence is obviously about the (more or less 'given' as the *one and only* and *our*) Prime Minister, we see that the delimitation of topic and comment is quite problematic, because the expression *The Prime Minister* would be assigned topic function by aboutness criteria and focus function because it refers to a newly introduced discourse referent.

We must conclude that the concept of aboutness is quite vague, because the sentence about the Prime Minister is no less about the things he or she did today, collapsing aboutness and reference to any property of a situation, or rather its subjective representation in the mental situation model (Van Dijk, 1977). Aboutness is often valid as an intuitive criterion for standard sentence structures in discourse where initial NPs co-refer to current global or sequential discourse referents and hence are assigned topic function because the sentence or the story is *about* me, or John, as discourse actors introduced before. Aboutness topicality may be defined for (usually left-dislocated) indefinite expressions that introduce new discourse referents (see, e.g., Endriss and Hinterwimmer, 2008; Reinhart, 1981).

More generally, the notion of (sentence) topic is not very precise, because notions such as 'old,' 'given,' 'available,' 'activated' information (see e.g.,

Prince, 1981) are vague or ambiguous, since the relevant notion of CG itself is a combination of various sources, as we have seen above for the kinds of knowledge or information as it is 'given' or 'known' at the beginning of each sentence or turn (or of a whole discourse or conversation), whether or not in short-term memory (STM), or already introduced in a situation model, actually mentioned earlier in the discourse and so on.

7.3.4.13.1 Topic Hence Prince (1981), after examining earlier proposals (as expressed by such notions as 'given,' 'new,' 'predictability,' 'recoverability,' 'salience' and 'shared knowledge') prefers the notion of relative *assumed familiarity* of discourse referents in a discourse model. She thus construes a hierarchical familiarity schema ranging from *new* ((*anchored* or *unanchored*), (*brand new* or *unused*)), *inferable* (*containing* or *non-containing*), to *evoked* (*textually* or *situationally*), which also defines a *familiarity scale*, ranging from *evoked* to *brand new*. As is the case for all notions of topic and focus, these and similar distinctions should not be associated with the knowledge of the speaker, but with the beliefs of the speaker about the (assumed) knowledge of the recipients (Chafe, 1976), which in our terms are defined by the K-device of the context model.

This means that recipients must apply fast, practical but imperfect strategies to identify discourse or sentence referents in text models, situation models and context models (Van Dijk and Kintsch, 1983). In many languages, thus, the unstressed initial position of NPs, recent mention, sequential topicality and co-referential identity of a discourse referent as well as the identity of current participants of the communicative situation, may jointly be used by a strategy that provisionally assigns topic function to an NP.

Although a full functional analysis of topic structure of a longer discourse is impossible in this short section, a few examples from David Cameron's *Sun* article may show the complexity of such analysis and the need for a new framework. Thus, take the very first sentence of the article:

> (19) IMMIGRATION has brought huge benefits to Britain: from Polish heroes who fought for us during the war to West Indians who helped us rebuild afterwards.

Since there are no previous sentences except for the headline, there is no discursively explicit given or old information to define topicality. Indeed, the very *discourse* topic, namely 'immigration,' is new and hence in this case the first noun phrase of this sentence seems to have focus rather than topic function – as does the rest of the sentence. Contextually and hence pragmatically 'known' is, of course, the information about Britain when the PM speaks about it. Indeed, in a sense, 'Britain' would in this case be 'old' or 'given' in what the PM talks about and what is relevant for the readers of the *Sun*.

Indeed, quite a common reformulation of this sentence structure would be something like "Britain has hugely benefited from immigration." The first position of 'immigration' in this sentence thus, although expressing 'new' information and hence having focus function, at the same time introduces (at least part of) the *discourse topic* of this whole article – as is often the case in initial 'thematic' sentences.

The second part of this sentence functionally specifies the information about the huge benefits in the first part. Again, for many, if not most, readers, this is all new information and hence should be assigned focus function. The complex prepositional phrase (*from* ... *to* ...) usually indexes such focus information. Yet, again, there are 'known' or 'given' elements in these phrases. Thus, again contextually and hence pragmatically, the expression *us*, occurring twice, as expressed by the PM obviously refers to us in the UK, and hence to a given or known collectivity, of which the recipients, the readers of the *Sun*, are a part – the new information is that embodied in the expressions on what others (Polish heroes and West Indians) did for us. Hence, if such pragmatically 'given' information has topic function, we see that it may be deeply embedded in a sentence, and not necessarily appear in an initial NP. The same is true for focus information, which when new in discourse may appear in an initial NP, especially at the beginning of text or talk and thus introducing (parts of) discourse topics.

Interestingly, lines 5–6 of this article:

(20) *Sun* readers know that immigration got out of control under Labour.

seem to start with an NP that has obvious topic function, not only because it is *about Sun* readers, but actually addresses them, and hence is a deictic expression because it refers to a relevant aspect of the communicative situation (as represented in the context model of the Prime Minister). So, the information on the *Sun* readers is contextually 'given,' 'old' or 'salient.' However, this is, strictly speaking, also true of the rest of the sentence – which we already analyzed above in terms of a presupposition of the factive verb *know*. Thus, if Cameron knows what the *Sun* readers know, such information is obviously also known to the *Sun* readers themselves as is the fact that they know this information. Hence, if the information expressed in the whole sentence is known to the participants and hence part of the CG, it should be assigned topic function – indeed, it does not tell the readers anything they did not know. Of course, from a pragmatic and communicative point of view, this is no problem. As is also the case in this discourse, language users often repeat or remind recipients of what they know already. So, we see that definitions in terms of 'old' and 'new' information, as defined in situation and context models, may be at variance with the *structural* organization of sentences. Indeed, syntactically, in this sentence, the first NP "*Sun* readers" obviously has topic function in this sentence (the sentence is also *about* them), and the rest of the sentence expresses focus information, namely attributing something to the readers – although the readers, purportedly, already know what is attributed to them. On the other hand, this attribution of knowledge to recipients is a well-known strategic move to presuppose knowledge that may not be common knowledge at all, but is in fact an oblique assertion of a partisan opinion, as is the case here when Cameron blames Labour. And in that sense, the information of the last part of the sentence *is* new information, and pragmatically an accusation of Labour.

We see in the example of two sentences in an article that the assignment of topic function, as we shall also see below for the notion of focus, is far from straightforward and depends on whether we (only) examine syntactic sentence structure (word order, etc.), semantic structures, pragmatic information (who is speaking to whom with what goal and what speech act) and the information in situation and context models. Thus, whole first sentences may appear to have epistemic focus information and later sentences may semantically express only topic information, although their structure does not reflect this, but on pragmatic grounds the information is 'new' anyway (namely when Cameron quasi-presupposes and hence obliquely accuses Labour). Only by explicitly separating these different discourse levels and dimensions are we able to deal with different aspects of topicality in sentences.

7.3.4.13.2   Focus   The notion of *focus* is hardly more precise. Most straightforward would be to define it as any 'new' information in the sentence that neither has been activated and instantiated before by the CG, and hence is new in the situation or context model, nor is inferable from them.

Sentence elements in focus typically receive relative stress and occur towards the end of the clause or sentence in English, or at the beginning with a stressed cleft-sentence form: *It is JOHN who ...*; *SKATING is what they did* .... The same is the case for expressions or parts of expressions that need to be emphasized or contrasted in relation to what has been referred to or actually mentioned before: *MARY didn't flunk the exam, JOHN did*, where 'someone flunked the exam' is known, presupposed information, and hence topic, and the identity of the persons who flunked or did not flunk the exam is new information. This may also apply to fragments of words, as in *This merchandise is for EXport, not IMport*, which Kniffka (2008) defines as 'expression focus' as distinct from 'denotation focus,' as defined in terms of the elements discourse is about, and which we define in terms of situation and context models (for contrastive focus, see, e.g., Zimmermann, 2008).

In other words, if a propositional function is known from the (con)text, e.g., '[someone] killed the postman,' then identifying the argument in the empty slot also makes such an expression have focus function. This is also conveyed by traditional sentence-grammatical approaches that construe (previous) text or context in terms of implicit questions (e.g., *Who killed the postman?*) presupposing a proposition (*someone killed the postman*) added to the CG, so that the reply to the question defines new information with focus function (Van Kuppevelt, 1995). In a theory of discourse, such a formal, artificial construct would not be necessary, since it is the previous text or context model that defines CG and hence the information recipients already have and may be expecting, also without (invented or real) questions.

Kniffka (2008) classifies focus as defined in terms of answers to questions, contrast, etc. as *pragmatic*, while mainly defined in terms of the communicative goals of the speaker, and focus-sensitive expressions such as *only* and *even*, as *semantic*, involving selections from alternatives (although possibly based on pragmatic uses). Indeed, if focus is defined in terms of dynamically adapted speaker beliefs about the ongoingly changing knowledge (that is, situation models of an event) of recipients, that is, in terms of a context dimension, the definition is pragmatic.

Another (formal) way to account for focus is in terms of Alternative Semantics (Rooth, 1992, 2008), such that the focused element of a sentence is one of a set of alternatives of which the other elements are 'false.' This seems a plausible interpretation for contrastive or selective focus, but hardly for many other forms of focus that merely index new discourse referents or their properties without an implication of excluding other options (as in *This morning I talked to the postman and ...*).

Dryer (1996), in a detailed discussion of topic, focus and presupposition, proposes a more cognitive definition of the old–new polarization in terms of degrees of *activation* of information (both information about discourse referents as well as whole propositions). He relevantly also emphasizes that not all (non)represented or (non)active propositions are actually *believed*, so that definition in terms of CG and (true, believed, assumed, shared) presuppositions would be inadequate. So he makes a distinction between three types of propositions: those that are activated and believed, those that are believed but not activated and those that are activated but not believed.

From this very brief and hence very incomplete treatment of one of the classical notions of knowledge management in language, namely the expression of information structures in sentences, we see that all aspects of the distinction between topic and focus require formulation in terms of underlying situation and context models (the cognitive dimension of knowledge) as well as in terms of their expression in whole discourses, sequences of sentences and sentences, respectively. The crucial issue is how the situation model now under construction is expanded by each sentence – with focus information not present in the model or in the previous discourse, and with topic information

302   Language, discourse and knowledge

linking the new information with the current state of the situation model and text model.

Depending on the natural language, these different epistemic functions of sentence constituents may variably be expressed or signaled by sentence order-ing (initial, final), special constructions (cleft sentences), particles (as Japanese *wa* and *ga*, signaling topic and focus, respectively), morphemes, definite and indefinite articles and various forms of phonological prominence (pitch accent or boundary tones), often in combination. We shall not deal with these gram-matical (syntactic and phonological) aspects of topic and focus, because they only indirectly relate to the pragmatic functions of topic and focus as the sen-tential means of expanding current models with new information. Whereas focus functions generally map towards the latter and/or stressed part of sen-tences, such structures may be ambiguous while also expressing other than epistemic functions, such as contrast, correction, reactivation, selection, call-ing attention to, etc., as shown in some of the examples above, and defined in our theory as new, distinct, contrasted or different in relation to known, given or present information in text models, situation models or context mod-els. Thus, in English, special (left-dislocated) ordering of focus elements, e.g., at the beginning of the sentence, then needs to be marked by special phono-logical emphasis (for such grammatical analysis, see, e.g., Fanselow, 2008; Gussenhoven, 2008).

Crucial for our discussion is that given their mental models as described, language users may use these polarized *discourse* expressions of information structure (topic and focus functions) to code, communicate and understand different types of epistemic functions, e.g., as old, given, active, present, earl-ier expressed, presupposed, on the one hand, or as new, reactivated, asserted or interesting information, on the other. Obviously, as often repeated above, isolated sentence analysis, even enriched with some background knowledge or presuppositions, is unable to account for the complex expression of infor-mation structure or knowledge distribution in natural text and talk (see also Jacobs, 2004).

Relevant for this chapter and this book is that the complex distinction between topic and focus, representing the 'information structure' of clauses or sentences, tends to be variously defined in terms of the linguistic expres-sions strategically influencing the ways recipients manage their knowledge, essentially establishing complex, often gradual, relations between more or less 'given' (old, inferable, etc.) and more or less 'new' knowledge. As suggested, these are not about the knowledge of speakers or recipients, but rather about the (possibly misguided – and hence often interactionally corrected) beliefs of the speaker about the dynamically changing knowledge of the recipients, as represented in the K-device in the context model of the speaker. As is the case for presupposition, such an analysis will usually involve making explicit the

CG of the participants, defined here in terms of elements (participants, events, etc.) of various types of mental models. These models or model fragments of recipients may be assumed by the speaker to be

   (i) already active (and hence part of STM or some control memory), as is the case for context models, e.g., defining setting, participants and goals of the ongoing communicative situation, or for situation models defining current discourse topic and previously introduced discourse referents
  (ii) activated, e.g., by various kinds of inference
 (iii) construed, in relation to activated text, situation or context models.

We see that a more cognitive approach tends to prefer a formulation in terms of grades of *activation* of information, rather than as 'old' or 'given' (see also Dryer, 1996).

In other words, despite the complexity of the many linguistic possibilities of expressing such information functions as 'old' and 'new' knowledge, their general 'communicative' function, as is the case for many other properties of discourse, is to offer recipients strategic linguistic clues about how to dynamically and ongoingly expand or change their knowledge.

7.3.4.14   Summary of epistemic discourse semantics

Given this brief summary of some of the discourse structures expressing or presupposing discourse, we may further organize our analysis in the Table 7.3.

According to our theoretical framework, all epistemic structures of discourse are based on situation models, context models and generic knowledge, and involve a few cognitive strategies, such as specification, selection and inference. The overarching and basic strategy of discursive communication is how 'new' knowledge is related to 'old' knowledge, at all levels of discourse. Here old knowledge is defined by various CG sources, such as current text, current context, previous contexts and old situation models, as well as generic knowledge and their plausible and relevant inferences.

Although many semantic structures have been briefly dealt with above, no doubt there are other aspects of discourse meaning that require epistemic analysis. Moreover, those that have been briefly dealt with would (and did) each require book-length treatment of special cases, surface structure expression and variations for different languages.

Thus, there are many ways persons, objects, places or their properties can be described in discourse, depending on context, and hence on genre, goals, style, etc., for instance by a proper name (first and/or last), a definite description of a locally unique characteristic, by their membership of a group or category and so on.

Despite the constraints of global and local coherence, there are many ways a discourse can be elaborated, by focusing on the details of an action, the

Table 7.3 *Epistemic structures in discourse semantics*

Semantic structure	Epistemic basis	Epistemic process	Comments/explanations
Global functional topic and comment	Context and situation models of previous discourses; intertextual Common Ground (CG)	Global comparison of intertextual old–new information	Global information shared with previous discourses (= part of CG) in a discourse complex (e.g., a debate, etc.) is global functional topic, and new global information in current discourse is global functional focus
Macrostructure (discourse topic)	Situation model: top levels	Inference from generic knowledge (GK)	Relevance constraints by context model (only socioculturally appropriate topics are selected)
Global coherence			
Extensional/ referential	Situation model	GK-based inferences about "missing link" propositions	Due to constraints of context model, speakers do not express propositions to establish (referential) local coherence if the recipients can infer these from the situation model on the basis of generic knowledge
Local/sequential coherence			
Sequencing and linearization	Situation model Normal order	Projection hierarchical situation model on linear sequence of propositions of discourse	Propositions in discourse sequences are 'normally' ordered by general, perceptual, experiential, embodied and other cognitive principle: Global>Local, Whole>Part, Cause>Consequence, Before>After, Object>Properties, etc. Deviations have special functions
Elaboration	Situation model Generic knowledge	Selection, specification	Development of situation model on the basis of conceptual GK, e.g., persons>attributes of persons, etc.
Description	Generic knowledge	Selection	E.g., conceptual options to describe actions or actors (individual, group member, named, anonymous, identity, role, etc.)
Level of description	Situation model: top to bottom	Generalization vs. specification	Semantic discourse structure may vary between very general (as in macrostructures) to very specific. More specific structures get special attention
Definition	Generic knowledge	Specification	Conceptual relations between superordinate category and its differentiating attributes, e.g., *a car is a vehicle that …*
Granularity: degree of detail	Situation model: each level	Selection	At each level of a model more or fewer details may be selected for realization – depending on their relevance, importance, etc.

Precision	Situation model Context model	Focus	Properties of situations may be described in more or less precise or vague terms (i.e., with more or less sharp focus), depending on context constraints (e.g., politeness)
Certainty/stance	Situation model	Meta-model	Situation models may be part of meta-models representing the beliefs of language users (*I know, believe, guess, hope, etc. that M*)
Probability/ necessity	Situation model	Alethic evaluation of all events of model	Different from epistemic stance of representations/models of events, these may themselves be attributed various levels of probability, from barely possible to necessity (as in *might, may, probably, must, necessarily*)
Implication	Situation model Generic knowledge	Inference	Proposition implied by an explicit (= expressed in discourse) proposition, part of the situation model, but not expressed in discourse, inferred on the basis of GK
Implicature	Situation model Context model	Inference	Proposition implied by explicit proposition on the basis of information of the context model
Presupposition	Current state of: situation model, (con) text model, (CG)	Inference	Proposition implied by any explicit proposition that is part of CG (GK, current state of situation model, text model, context model, etc.): previously shared information at each moment of ongoing text or talk, etc.
Metaphor	Situation model Generic knowledge	Concretization	Concretization of more abstract concepts in terms of more embodied (sensorial, emotional) experiences, e.g., immigration = WAVE
Evidentials	Situation model Context model Generic knowledge	Activation	Sources of knowledge: (i) personal experiences (= old situation models), (ii) discourse (hearsay, testimony)(= old context models), (iii) GK – all plus inferences
Topic and focus	Current state of: situation model (con) text model (CG)	Selection	Topic: 'old' (part of) proposition: part of CG + inferences (e.g., *My father* ...); (i) focus: 'new' (part of) proposition: not in CG, or (ii) 'old' (part of) proposition selected/contrasted with other 'old' propositions (as in *JOHN didn't do it, MARY did*, etc.).

appearance of a person, her thoughts, the consequences of the actions and so on. Some of these have been mentioned above – such as order, level and granularity of descriptions. Many others no doubt need to be further explored. Given the theoretical framework proposed, as it was applied to a dozen or more discourse structures, it seems plausible that these other semantic structures can also be accounted for in the same terms, such as the ways mental models control discourse meaning and reference, together with inferences from generic knowledge.

7.3.5   Surface structure realization of epistemics

Since they have received ample attention in linguistics, we shall not deal with the many 'surface structure' manifestations of epistemic structures in discourse, of which some have already been mentioned before. Thus, model-based local coherence may be signaled by various cohesion markers, such as definite articles, pronouns, lexical repetition and so on. Evidentials in some languages are expressed in special verb morphology or by special clitics, where most other (Western) languages use explicit references to experiences and discursive sources of knowledge. Epistemic stance, expressing certainty or other attitudes towards knowledge, is typically expressed in English by modal expressions such as *may* and *might*, adverbs such as *maybe* and *perhaps* or by verb morphology (e.g., the use of subjunctives, counterfactuals) in other languages. Information structure, mapping old/given and new information on sentence functions such as topic and focus, may be expressed by word order, stress and special grammatical operations (topicalization, etc.).

The main communicative function of these various grammatical structures in discourse is to provide recipients with strategic markers that may be used to construe meaningful and locally and globally coherent semantic representations as the input for mental models that interpret discourse and discourse fragments and their context. Note, though, that these surface structure expressions of underlying semantic and epistemic structures are neither necessary nor sufficient for discourse understanding.

Most of the cognitive 'work' is done by the semantics and pragmatics of discourse, which is crucial in the construction of situation models and context models.

And vice versa, discourse meaning is strategically construed on the basis of socially shared generic knowledge and its application in the construction of situation models of events talked or written about.

The information in these models is much more detailed than the information actually expressed in text and talk or sentence structures. Recipients need little grammatical structure and only fragmentary semantic information in order to be able to construe their underlying models. As a general rule, old or given knowledge in discourse tends to be implicit, presupposed, reduced (as in pronouns) and unstressed (as in initial sentence topics). And even much of the new knowledge conveyed by discourse need not be expressed but may be inferred from generic knowledge or old mental models in the construction of a current situation model that defines the subjective interpretation of recipients.

Thus, indeed, the metaphor of the iceberg is quite apt to describe the rather limited role of 'visible' or 'hearable' grammatical expressions of knowledge in discourse: most of the old and even the new knowledge involved in text and talk remains invisible and implicit. Discourse production and comprehension is a vastly complex mental process, in which underlying epistemic processing relating new knowledge with old knowledge is a basic dimension, which in turn is a condition for the other interactional and social functions of language and discourse.

7.4   Concluding remarks

Many of the epistemic properties of discourse mentioned in this chapter have received (more) detailed attention in many books and articles. Obviously, it cannot be the task of one chapter to offer new insights into so many different aspects of language use and discourse. Yet, precisely because of this specialization, and its sometimes highly technical nature, these many studies have seldom been integrated into a large framework, as we have tried to do, namely to deal with them as examples of the general way knowledge is expressed, conveyed, presupposed, elaborated and used in text and talk.

Thus, we have shown first of all how all epistemic phenomena of discourse need a cognitive basis in terms of underlying situation models and context models specifying the knowledge of the participants about the events they talk or write about, as well as the communicative situation they are participating in. If the fundamental function of discourse is to convey new knowledge, and also as a basis of the many other functions of language use, then we obviously need a theoretical framework within which such old and new knowledge can be explicitly described in the first place.

Similarly, this expression and communication of knowledge is constrained by interactional and other social constraints, defined by the identities, roles and relations among the participants and their goals. Normative and moral rules thus limit who can tell (inform, etc.) what to whom, when and how – as defined by access, expertise, entitlement and other epistemic properties of participants.

Within this broad theoretical framework, starting with intertextual and global information structures and relations, we thus summarized how each discourse in a sequence, and within discourse from top to bottom, and from sentence or turn to the next, old or otherwise given knowledge is presupposed as a basis for the construction of new knowledge

- in whole discourses
- as new topics or semantic macrostructures
- as focus information in sentences
- as definitions of new concepts through old concepts
- as elaboration of given knowledge.

We have also seen that, again depending on context and natural language, this may take place in many variable ways, e.g., in terms of more or less explicit or implicit discourse, with more or less details, at different levels, and respecting again many social constraints, such as those of politeness and tact, or under institutional constraints of authority and power.

We already know many details of the expression and presupposition of knowledge in discourse and their conditions summarized as Common Ground, especially on topic and focus, epistemic modalities, evidentials and presuppositions. Yet, there are many more semantic, pragmatic and stylistic aspects of discourse that need to be accounted for in an integrated, sociocognitive epistemics of text and talk.

Most studies in this area have taken place in linguistic theories limited to sentence grammars, and have ignored the obvious necessity of studying epistemic structures in the complex, hierarchical and sequential structures of text and talk. Indeed, old or presupposed knowledge, as well as Common Ground, should not be studied for isolated example sentences and assumed previous sentences or propositions, but as an inherent part of theories and analysis of discourse structures. Here the relation between 'old' or 'given' knowledge as related to 'new' knowledge is most naturally shown in the very structures of text and talk.

Hence, these well-known topics of research all need reformulation and integration in a coherent theoretical framework that combines (i) cognitive analysis, e.g., in terms of mental models, (ii) social analysis of the interaction and the communicative situation, e.g., in terms of the goals, epistemic authority and entitlements of the participants and (iii) discourse analysis of the complex structures of text and talk at all levels and for any scope.

Moreover, many other epistemic properties of discourse that have received much less attention in linguistics, mostly because they could not be accounted for in the grammar of isolated sentences, need to be focused on. Thus, we need much more detailed insight into how knowledge is developed, that is, expressed and presupposed as distributed across whole discourses and not just locally, within sentences. We need to know how different kinds of knowledge, such as personal or public models or generic knowledge structures, are expressed and constructed by different discourse genres, as is the case in everyday conversational stories, news reports or expository discourse in educational contexts. In that sense, the study of knowledge in discourse is still in its infancy.

8   Conclusions

This multidisciplinary study examines the complex relationships between two fundamental notions of the humanities and social sciences: discourse and knowledge. It accounts in detail for the general insight that in order to be able to produce and understand discourse, language users need vast amounts of knowledge of the world, and that most of this very knowledge is precisely acquired by discourse.

These symbiotic relationships between discourse and knowledge have partly been studied in nearly all disciplines of the humanities and social sciences, but until now a general integrative monograph dealing with the discourse–knowledge interface was lacking. This book for the first time offers such an integrated approach by systematically examining the myriad of related aspects of discourse and knowledge as they have been studied in epistemology, cognitive and social psychology, sociology, anthropology and linguistics.

Details of these aspects have been accounted for in many thousands of works on knowledge since Antiquity, and many hundreds if not thousands of books (and even more articles) on language and discourse published since the 1960s. This book cannot possibly come even close to studying the technical details of these earlier works. On the contrary, its aim is precisely to offer a broad, multidisciplinary perspective lacking in the more detailed earlier studies. In this final chapter, we summarize some general findings of our general, integrated approach.

8.1   Epistemology: the nature of knowledge

The empirical study of knowledge in psychology and the social sciences generally ignores the more abstract reflection on the nature of knowledge as it is studied in epistemology and much (though not all) of epistemology in turn tends to disregard the results of more empirical research. Although this monograph is generally oriented towards a more empirical approach to knowledge and its relations to discourse, it also needs to reflect, from the outset, upon the very nature of knowledge, and at least briefly introduce and comment on the basic ideas in contemporary epistemology.

Especially relevant for this book is the first critical observation on the study of knowledge in epistemology, namely the virtual absence of the realization of the basic fact that much, if not most, of human knowledge is acquired by discourse and communication. Knowledge is usually said to be acquired in three basic ways, namely by observation and experience, by discourse and communication and by reasoning and inference. Yet, the crucial discourse dimension of knowledge acquisition in epistemology tends to be reduced to a study of the (lacking) reliability of 'hearsay' or 'testimony,' as if knowledge acquisition were mainly a question of evidence in court instead of the very basis of all human society. Indeed, in this sense, the epistemology of the role of discourse in the acquisition, reproduction and diffusion of knowledge is still in its infancy, if it has even been born yet.

Secondly, by its very philosophical nature, epistemology tends to study knowledge in abstract, conceptual terms, and not primarily as real knowledge of real human beings, real social actors and real epistemic communities. Even when allowing for the usual distribution of scholarly tasks, and hence leaving much of such a study of 'natural' knowledge to psychology and the social sciences, even epistemology itself has benefited from a more cognitive and social orientation in the last decades.

Thus, it has become clear that the way beliefs are presupposed, considered, treated or used as knowledge depends on the social and cultural variability of epistemic standards or criteria in different epistemic communities. Epistemic relativism, however, is not exactly a popular position in epistemology, where truth is seen as absolute, given the traditional definition of knowledge as justified true beliefs. The problem is that in the everyday life of human societies no such absolute truth is a realistic and practical criterion.

In linguistics, there has been a tendency in the twentieth century to start with the study of smaller units (phonemes, words, sentences) and work towards an account of larger and more complex units of analysis, such as text and talk. Similarly, whereas earlier studies were usually more formal and context-free, later studies focused on real, naturalistic discourse of real language users in real interaction and communication.

Similarly, we may observe a tendency in epistemology towards a more naturalistic, relativistic and contextualist account of knowledge as cognitive representations, on the one hand, and as socially situated, on the other. Thus, we more modestly define *natural knowledge* in terms of the (historically changing) epistemic criteria available in the community, which is usually good enough for all practical purposes. Indeed, within the community this means that knowledge and truth are perfectly combined as the basis of all human perception, interaction and discourse. Hence, relativism is itself also relative, as it should be: *within* an epistemic community, knowledge is indeed defined as *true* belief. But what is knowledge and truth in one community may be seen as false belief, error or superstition from the perspective of another. What a theory of natural knowledge should account for is how knowledge and knowledge criteria are established, acquired, changed, presupposed and used within epistemic communities.

Even within the same community such variation may be observed across different contexts, as is the case for knowledge and discourse in scientific, political or everyday contexts. Indeed, by the strictest criteria of scientific or legal evidence, the newspaper or we ourselves in our everyday storytelling most likely seldom speak the 'whole truth,' as is required in the formula for swearing in witnesses in US courts. Indeed, as is the case for variability, contextualization is a very general phenomenon that applies widely beyond epistemology in all the sciences as a necessary correction of empirically unwarranted generalization. Hence, real knowledge and empirical truth are not monolithic but relative, variable and contextual.

Within this more naturalistic approach to knowledge, even when avoiding relativism or contextualism, our own definition of knowledge combines cognitive and social psychological dimensions, and fundamentally takes knowledge as belief justified by the epistemic criteria of a community (and as 'true' belief within the community, although we prefer to reserve the notion of truth for discourse and use 'correctness' for beliefs). More specifically but crucially, social knowledge in such an approach requires that such beliefs are shared in the community, and thus may act as the basis of the acquisition or development of personal and new beliefs by its members. From our discourse analytical perspective, this allows us to define (social, generic, etc.) knowledge as the beliefs generally presupposed, at each moment, in the public discourses of the community. We thus have a first fundamental relationship between discourse and knowledge.

Next, the adequacy of the usual 'unit' or 'content' of knowledge, namely the *proposition*, is also challenged and replaced by the more articulate notion of *mental model*, borrowed from contemporary cognitive psychology, correctly or incorrectly representing real or fictitious states of affairs. *Propositional attitudes* such as hoping or wishing in that case are primarily about mental states, and only secondarily about states of affairs, and hence may be represented as higher-order mental models (featuring *Self*) representing the relations between mental models and states of affairs.

Given the role of perception and experience as the most direct source of (personal) knowledge, and a primitive condition of adaptation to the natural and social environment of organisms and species, it is assumed that *experience models* and their elementary structures are the prototypes of all mental models, featuring a Setting (Time, Place), Participants (and their identities, roles and relationships), Action/Event and Goals. Hierarchically organized experience models segment continuous everyday life into discrete micro- and macro-events at various levels and control all perception and interaction. A specific type of experience model, the *context model*, subjectively represents communicative situations and defines pragmatic appropriateness and indexicality, whereas *situation models* represent what discourses such as stories are about and hence their meaningfulness, coherence, etc. In other words, all knowledge and knowledge sources can be unified in terms of mental model theory, including the inferences based on mental models.

More specific for humans and their obvious comparative advantage over other primates, is that they not only are able to form adequate mental models of their environment, but also are able to communicate about them by natural language. Even more specifically, and beyond forms of animal communication about the environment, such natural language, in the form of discourse, is able to communicate past experiences, tell stories and talk about future events, as plans, as well as alternative, possible, counterfactual or fictional events (Byrne, 2002; Gerrig and Prentice, 1991; Roese, 1997). We thus not only arrive at a first, simple conception of knowledge as representation and experience efficiently and relevantly represented in mental models, but also of its relation to discourse as a fundamental source of knowledge beyond direct, empirical experience: we also learn about the environment through talk and communication with conspecifics.

Next, beyond the mental models of individual experience and as communicated by stories, human beings also developed the mechanism to generalize, abstract from and decontextualize these mental models of experience, and form *generic knowledge* structures about the world that could be efficiently applied in future experiences and interactions, by 'reverse' instantiation and application in the formation of new or adapted models.

Moreover, such generic knowledge is not only developed by each individual, and on the basis of personal experiences, but can also be expressed and communicated as such, in many forms of pedagogical or expository discourse for children and newcomers in the community. Hence, both specific and generic knowledge can be interpersonally shared and reproduced in the community, as is the case for the sociocultural criteria that define beliefs as knowledge in the first place. Indeed, relevant knowledge is not only *context independent* but also *socially shared*.

It is within this very simple but basic conception of knowledge that we need to develop a philosophy of knowledge that is specifically adapted to its relations with talk and text. Indeed, the very notion of a mental model, and its generic basis, already accounts for both our correct ('true') representation of the environment, as well as for the cognitive basis of storytelling or other 'accounts,' which at the same time function as a secondary but crucial source for the knowledge of others.

And since communicative situations themselves are a central part of the social environments of human beings, their discourses must also be appropriate and efficient with respect to those situations. Hence, language users also construe special mental models, *context models*, of such situations. We thus have a cognitive basis of both the *semantics* as well as the *pragmatics* of discourse.

Many fundamental notions of epistemology thus find their place in such a framework. Thus, if beliefs are the fundamental cognitive building blocks of knowledge, namely as representations of real or possible events or situations, they count as knowledge if they satisfy the justification criteria of the epistemic community, such as reliable observation, reliable discourse and reliable inference as sources of knowledge. It is in this sense that knowledge is 'true' if its representation 'corresponds' with reality by such socially and culturally variable criteria.

Empirically, such justification criteria for each community can be inferred from the very forms of mundane or scientific discourses of justification, for instance in accounts and argumentations. Again, we see that, more than in traditional epistemology, a more natural approach to knowledge also seems to constantly require a much more explicit relation between knowledge and discourse. Thus, discourse is much more than a crucial source of knowledge. It also offers insights into the structures, the social nature and the very criteria of the acceptance of beliefs as knowledge in society.

8.2   Knowledge, discourse and cognition

As has been recalled above, cognitive psychology and cognitive science more generally have been at the forefront of the study of the relations between discourse and knowledge during the last forty years. Many of its notions, and especially that of a *mental model*, have even served us in the formulation of the epistemological foundation of our study.

Usually ignoring epistemology, cognitive science first of all contributed to our insight into the mental nature and organization of *generic knowledge* as represented in semantic memory, for instance in terms of conceptual relations, prototypes, exemplars, schemas and scripts of various kinds. Despite decades of cognitive approaches to the study of the representation of knowledge, these proposals hardly seem to have progressed much when it comes to a detailed description of the organization of the vast and complex knowledge system in mind/memory and brain. We even have no idea how *much* an average adult person knows about the historical events and the general properties and the structure of the social and natural world.

More recently, and inspired by advances in neuropsychology and by our insights into the specialization of specific brain regions, the definition of knowledge also has received a more 'embodied' variant. In our perspective, such multimodal knowledge defines personal experience models rather than generic knowledge. Generic knowledge is necessarily more abstract and decontextualized, so that it can be applied and instantiated (as mental models) in interaction and communication among persons with different personal experiences and hence in sharing knowledge in epistemic communities.

The second major contribution, both in cognitive psychology and Artificial Intelligence (AI), has been the *empirical study and simulation of the representations and processes involved in discourse production and comprehension.* From the start, especially in AI, it was emphasized that such processes require vast amounts of knowledge of the world even for the understanding of simple stories. For pragmatic reasons, discourse is structurally incomplete because speakers/writers assume that recipients are able to infer implicit propositions from their more generic knowledge, for instance in order to be able to *construe local and global coherence* of discourse. Hence, relevant fragments of generic knowledge are ongoingly activated and instantiated and inferences drawn from it so as to construe the local and global meanings of discourse.

Only in the early 1980s was it then proposed that the processing of discourse is not limited to construing coherent sequences of propositions representing meaning, but should be based on subjective *mental models*, stored in episodic memory and representing the events or situations the discourse is about, that is, its referential basis. Indeed, much of the coherence of discourse is thus not meaning-based (intensional) but referent-based (extensional), as is the case for temporal and causal relations between events. Such subjective mental models represent not only events or states of affairs but also personal opinions and emotions about such events. Indeed, language users each have their own unique interpretation (model) of a discourse and its meaning. Mental models are multimodal because they involve all possible, embodied, experiences of participants – vision, hearing, sensorimotor, emotions and so on.

Much later we then proposed that such a cognitive theory of discourse processing is still incomplete because it lacks a pragmatic component defined in terms of, equally subjective, *context models* representing communicative situations and accounting for the appropriateness of discourse. We have seen above that such context models are a special type of more general *experience models* that regulate (control, define, plan, recall) the events and actions of our everyday life.

Discourse production, thus, consists in the partial, strategic expression of a ('semantic') situation model under the control of a dynamic *context model*. The context model ongoingly regulates which information of the situation model (e.g., of an experience, an event) is relevant to be expressed at each moment, which information is already known by the recipients or which can be easily inferred, and hence need not be expressed, which is interesting or less so, polite and so on. This also explains why the explicit meaning of a discourse is much less elaborate than the underlying situation models of speakers and recipients.

At the same time, we thus have an elegant definition of implicit information: all information in the situation model (and hence intended or understood) that is not expressed in the discourse.

Unfortunately, experimental studies demonstrating the empirical nature of context models are still lacking because even the theory has not yet been accepted in prevailing theories of discourse processing – no doubt because experiments are conducted in standard laboratory contexts and seldom in real communicative situations outside the lab.

Context models must feature a central and crucial *knowledge device (K-device)* that ongoingly monitors the epistemic states of the participants: speakers at all times must believe or know what recipients know and adapt their discourse to such (assumed) knowledge, as it is also studied in terms of *Common Ground*. Hence, the concept of Common Ground is thus fully integrated in the pragmatic component (the context model) of the theory, as it should be, because it is about an epistemic property of the participants as well as their epistemic relations.

Within this new and more complete theoretical framework of discourse processing, we reviewed *experimental studies about the role of knowledge in discourse processing*, not only at the level of clauses and sentences expressing simple mental models, but also of complex sequences of sentences and their local and global coherence, as well as other structures (such as schematic formats or superstructures). One major area of empirical research that is relevant for this book is the role of *prior knowledge* in the comprehension of discourse. As may be expected, many studies show that more detailed prior knowledge or expertise generally benefits discourse comprehension and recall, especially at higher levels and of implicit texts that activate their superior knowledge. However, more knowledgeable subjects may also make less of an effort or pay less attention and hence may sometimes recall less (details) than other subjects who read a text more carefully. Within this paradigm, many different studies may focus on the role of discourse in the correction of incorrect prior knowledge.

Crucial for a cognitive theory of the relations between discourse and knowledge is not only the study of the role of established generic or specific knowledge in discourse production and comprehension, but also *how new knowledge is acquired or changed by discourse*. This is what learning is all about. Despite extensive studies in the vast field of educational psychology and classroom experiments, however, the cognitive details of these epistemic processes are less well known.

Experimental studies tend to be short-range, and hence focus on discourse recall rather than on more stable, long-term knowledge formation and integration, which is much harder to study in the laboratory. Hence, most studies focus on the variable experimental *context conditions* of text processing and their effect on recall, such as reading and study time, different subjects (differing by age, gender, prior knowledge, goals, interest and motivation, reading abilities and so on).

Special experimental attention is paid to the many types of *experimental activities and strategies* of discourse processing and learning, such as explanation, extrapolation, generating topics and headers or problem solving.

For decades, the experimental literature has reported the influence of several *text properties* on "learning from text," such as the presence of images or schemas, written or spoken presentation, variable syntax or lexicon, local and global coherence, more or less explicit or elaborated text, hierarchical structure, metaphor and many more. As may be expected, more variable structures, especially those that facilitate mental model building or conceptual organization, positively influence the acquisition of knowledge – especially among subjects who are less knowledgeable and hence in need of extra text structure for comprehension and hence for learning.

Text processing and knowledge acquisition are placed in the framework of a discussion on various kinds of memory, such as the role of working memory and its different tasks and capacity, episodic memory and its Self-centered multimodal mental models of situations and contexts, as well as semantic memory and its conceptual structures. It is also in this framework that the very point of text processing is defined, namely to construe mental models of the world or the communicative situation – and not to construe phonological, morphological, syntactic or semantic structures. It is therefore crucial to elaborate theories of working memory that explain in detail how short-term processing of text details is related to the construction of mental models in episodic memory or conceptual knowledge in semantic memory.

Crucial for this book is whether and how we should distinguish between personal *knowledge* and *remembering* events or persons as represented in episodic/autobiographical memory, especially since the experience and context models controlling information processing are soon largely forgotten, except in very salient (e.g., traumatic or otherwise emotionally laden) communicative events. Similarly, it is not yet clear exactly how episodic knowledge and generic knowledge should be distinguished, especially if socially shared knowledge, e.g., of memorable public events, has the *structure* of mental models but the *functions* of shared conceptual knowledge presupposed in discourse and interaction.

Due to the impressive successes of the cognitive psychology of discourse since the 1970s, we today have fairly detailed insight into the details of text processing, as well as the role of mental models and general knowledge. Yet there are many issues and problems that still remain obscure, beginning with the details of the very overall and local organization of the knowledge system in the mind-brain.

We still know very little of the internal organization of episodic memory as the site of mental models, or about the difference between personal knowledge on the one hand and specific autobiographical memories.

We know that working memory is by definition limited, so it is still unclear where all the controls are represented and operative in the extremely complex production or comprehension of text and talk, involving for instance:

- Language users should speak grammatically, and hence have a grammar and lexicon actively working at all moments.
- They should speak meaningfully, so need to have a mental model of the situation or event they talk about, if only to be able to speak coherently.
- Both for the comprehension of sentence meanings and for the construction of mental models of events and situations, language users ongoingly activate and de-activate vast regions of generic and historical knowledge.
- But at the same time they need to speak appropriately in each communicative situation, so they need to dynamically construe and update a context model.
- More specifically, and most relevant for this book, is that with each word and sentence and at all levels of discourse, language users should take into account the current beliefs and knowledge of the recipient, and thus a Common Ground.
- More specifically, they should respect the contextual or textual constraints of a discourse genre, such as a conversation, a story, a news report, a scientific article or a speech in parliament.
- They not only need to attend to and control their own text or talk, but in interaction need to permanently attend to, understand, represent and react to what others have just said in conversation.
- They may speak as members of one or more ideological groups, and hence not only need to activate their generic knowledge for the construction of specific mental situation and context models, but also the underlying attitudes and ideologies of their group(s).

All this, and much more, goes on in parallel, at the same time, sometimes in fractions of seconds. We are still very far removed from an explanation of how all these processes can be adequately controlled in working memory, or some kind of intermediary control memory that organizes the relations between episodic memory and other aspects of long-term memory, with the immediate and short-range processes of working memory.

We still need to know, especially also for the issues discussed in this book, when exactly, and how, and how much and what kind of knowledge is activated (and de-activated) at each point of the production or comprehension of text or talk. So, despite the progress of the field, on some fundamental issues we still know very little.

8.3   Discourse, knowledge and social cognition

As I have observed in many earlier studies, the ideal disciplinary field for the study of the relations between discourse and knowledge is social psychology. It is therefore striking that precisely this discipline has generally ignored both, and rather focused on 'behavior' on the one hand and 'attitude,' 'attribution' and 'identity' on the other.

Indeed, of the few approaches to (commonsense) knowledge in social psychology, that on *social representations* by Moscovici and others has been most consistent, but hardly integrated in the international literature on cognition, memory or discourse processing. Also, the theory of the very internal structure or organization of these social representations hardly goes beyond rather vague proposals about central and peripheral knowledge. Crucial for this book is that we have no insight into the detailed cognitive ways such representations are acquired from discourse – or how discourse is produced on their basis. Interestingly, social representations seem to overlap with what are being called attitudes in the traditional literature, as is the case for social representations on immigration, poverty or abortion, involving socially shared and norm- or value-based opinions.

Despite the lack in social psychology of a general theory of knowledge and the role of discourse in knowledge acquisition and distribution in epistemic communities and society at large, it remains the only discipline that requires and allows an integrated account of various *kinds of social belief*, of which sociocultural knowledge is central or basic (depending on the nature of the organization of social cognition).

Among the socially shared beliefs whose relation to knowledge needs to be explored in social psychology is that of *ideology*, defined as the basic self-schema of social groups, their interests and their relations to other groups. Contrary to more individualistic approaches in terms of personality characteristics (e.g., as conservative vs. progressive people), we present a broader social approach in terms of group relations, such as those of competition or power and the shared cognitive representations of group members. Ideologies are expressed in specific ideological practices, and especially also by discourse. They are also largely acquired by text and talk. Since individuals are members of several ideological groups, their practices and hence their discourses may be complex manifestations of different and even contradictory goals, norms or values. Thus, as a feminist or antiracist, a woman may be progressive, but as a neoliberal in economic issues, she may adhere to more conservative values.

Ideologies are derived from discourse and then control more specific socially shared *attitudes* – which should not be confused by personal opinions as represented in mental models of specific events – in general, or prejudices in particular, often also organized in a polarized way (Us vs. Them). Our detailed discussion of *social representations* suggests that they are not crucially different from attitudes, although they also embody commonsense knowledge about socially relevant issues and not just socially shared opinions. Whereas ideologies are socially rooted in *groups*, knowledge is defined for (epistemic) *communities* – and languages for linguistic communities.

Fundamental for discourse and interaction in general is that knowledge is shared by participants in various ways, namely as *Common Ground*, which may be composed of socioculturally shared knowledge of a community, specific knowledge of the current communicative situation or knowledge derived from previous parts of the same discourse. In Chapter 7 we deal with the linguistic and discursive aspects of Common Ground (CG). Theoretically, in our framework, CG is dynamically and ongoingly construed by the K-device of the context model that controls interaction.

The social psychology of knowledge deals with the ways social beliefs are communicated and shared among individual persons, within groups or across groups in epistemic communities. Empirical research focuses, among other things, on the kind of topics being talked about by what kind of participants in what kinds of communicative situations – and finds that nearly half of the contents of conversation can be predicted (e.g., as related to the current circumstances, needs, problems, wishes or plans of participants). Hence, topics vary by gender, age or profession of participants and always depend on the context. In institutional text and talk, topics and hence knowledge distribution varies with the usual categories of the context, such as the identities, roles and relations of the participants and their current social actions and goals.

The mass media are the major institution and source for the dissemination of event knowledge, based on journalistic situation models, and of the 'casual' learning of generic knowledge about the world by generalization and abstraction of mental models. The school (through classroom interaction and textbooks) is the prime site for the direct acquisition of generic world knowledge, e.g., about geography, history, society and the sciences – knowledge hardly acquired in other communicative situations of many citizens – even when most of such generic knowledge is later forgotten.

8.4   Discourse, knowledge and society

Whereas the classical sociology of knowledge since Marx and Engels has focused on deterministic relations between an economic base at the 'basis' and 'ideas' defined as the 'superstructure' of society, contemporary approaches more ethnographically and empirically study the daily production of science and knowledge, for instance in the everyday practices of laboratories. Within this latter perspective, a more interactional and discursive conception of knowledge production, as advocated in this book, finds its natural context, so as to complete the triangular relations between discourse, cognition and society that defines our general multidisciplinary framework.

Missing both in the classical as well as the contemporary sociology of knowledge, however, is the *cognitive interface* between social structures and individual experiences, interaction and discourse. Continuing the theoretical framework sketched in the previous chapters, therefore, we again emphasize the central role of *mental models* that organize the daily experiences, interaction and discourses of individual people as members of groups, communities and organizations. Hence mental models are at present the only theoretical construct that links the personal with the social, and hence discourse with society. Groups, communities and organizations can only function as such if their members share social representations such as knowledge, ideologies, norms and values. Such social cognition on the one hand emerges 'bottom-up' from the daily experiences of members as represented in their mental models, and on the other hand makes sense 'top-down' of such daily experiences as mental models. It is this complex sociocognitive theoretical framework that accounts for such traditional concepts as class consciousness, and which equally applies to the formation of the shared representations of members of ideological groups or epistemic communities.

Another fundamental dimension of the classical and modern sociology of knowledge is its neglect of the *predominantly discursive nature of knowledge acquisition and diffusion of knowledge in society*. The central *epistemic institutions* of society, such as the mass media, schools, universities, laboratories and business organizations, are at the same time *discursive institutions*. Even when new knowledge may be based on observation and experiment, and implemented in technologies and products, its very development and reproduction are largely interactional and discursive between their members. This is at the same time the only way knowledge acquisition of individual scientists or other knowledge workers can be communicated in the scientific community and society at large, and hence be spread, tested and accepted as collective knowledge.

The sociology of the mass media, universities, laboratories, journals and scientific organizations obviously should also deal with such dimensions as organization, membership or power, among many others, but the sociology of knowledge more specifically needs both a sociocognitive and a discursive foundation.

Presupposed but not detailed as the social basis of shared knowledge in the previous chapters, the concept of the *epistemic community* is one of the central notions of the sociology of knowledge. As is the case for linguistic communities and communities of practice, epistemic communities may also first be characterized by their *functions*, namely as the social structures that allow the organized acquisition and diffusion of knowledge necessary for the communication and interaction of their members.

Epistemic communities are also defined by their *members* and *access*. Yet, we have seen that shared knowledge of a collectivity is essentially fuzzy since epistemically competent members may vary considerably in their amount and type of knowledge – as is the case for children, immigrants or other newcomers, and the differences between experts and lay members. Indeed, how many years of schooling or diplomas or which competences (reading the newspaper, or writing a letter, etc.) are required in each society in order to become a ratified member of this epistemic community? Whatever these differences and hence the fuzziness of the notion of epistemic communities, the ability to engage in conversation with family members, friends or colleagues on the job, as well as the passive participation in public discourse presupposes and requires a type of 'general knowledge' that may be considered the epistemic basis of the community. That is, each member may presuppose and be presupposed to share such knowledge in the common practices of everyday life in that community – which obviously are different at the New Stock Exchange, a French secondary school or an indigenous village in the Brazilian jungle.

Besides such 'common knowledge,' each community also has a possibly large variety of *specialized knowledges*, acquired and expressed in specialized discourses, institutions and practices. Thus, one of the main sociological dimensions of knowledge as it also appears in other chapters of this book is the distinction between *lay and expert knowledge*, which is not only a fundamental cognitive difference, but also associated with many other social dimensions of the epistemic community, such as specialized education, organizations, roles, occupations, media, power relations, legitimacies and so on. Indeed, as we see, large parts of the very organization and practices of modern societies are epistemically based.

Discourse is most succinctly defined as text or talk (language use, etc.) in *context*. Defined as the mental model of the communicative situation as it is dynamically construed by the participants, the parameters of such contexts of course have a social foundation as they define the different discursive practices we call genres. Thus spatiotemporal settings, social identities, roles and relations of participants, the currently accomplished social action and its goals, as well as the shared knowledge of the participants are all typical social dimensions as they condition the very pragmatic appropriateness of text and talk in each situation. It is their sociocognitive representation in mental models that thus provides the interface between the social dimensions of the communicative situation and the structures of discourse.

Within this general framework, we examined the epistemic aspects of a major source of knowledge in society: *news in the press*. On the basis of earlier research, we summarized a complex theoretical framework that relates news production with the elements of situation and context models of journalists on the one hand and news structures on the other. Virtually all social aspects of news production thus appear to have epistemic conditions and consequences. We thus obtain insight into the cognitive and interactional aspects of the production of public knowledge of the world.

8.5   Discourse, knowledge and culture

Knowledge as defined in this book is relative because epistemic criteria vary from community to community. Such relativity is especially obvious from a cultural perspective, namely when studying beliefs in different societies. Traditionally, such variation was conceptualized in Western anthropology in the usual polarized manner of all ideologies: *Ours* is knowledge, and *Theirs* is mere belief, or even superstition, etc. – thus expressing and enacting racist, ethnicist or Eurocentric domination.

Today, ethnographical research recognizes a variety of *knowledges* in the world, with variable criteria, and also variable attitudes about types of belief. Indeed, not only traditional but also 'modern' societies tend to mix official or scientific knowledge with traditional methods and concepts. Hence the slogan that *all* knowledge is local, and hence 'folk' knowledge.

Relevant in an anthropological approach to knowledge is therefore that cultures have often been defined in epistemic terms, that is, in terms of the knowledge individuals must possess in order to be able to function adequately as competent members of a society. In fact, this is one of the definitions of an epistemic community. Yet, it is emphasized that cultures can no more be reduced to cognition than they can be defined and reduced to action, interaction and social practices. Hence, also in this chapter our approach is an integrated sociocognitive one.

Relevant in the ethnographic study of knowledge is the difference between personal knowledge (or personal variants of community knowledge), on the one hand, and shared sociocultural knowledge on the other, as well as the difference between lay and expert knowledges. The methodological consequence of this distinction is that interviews with a few informants should not always be taken as reliable evidence of shared sociocultural knowledge but may very well be personal variants of such knowledge. Indeed, the discourse of informants is not epistemically transparent as a method of direct access to (personal or social) knowledge, but is also always controlled by context models representing the subjective interpretation of the communicative situation (such as the goals of an interview, or the identity, role or relations of the participants).

Much research in cognitive anthropology thus focuses on various structures of knowledge and belief – from early componential analysis of kinship terms and the ethno-semantics of plants and animals to contemporary cognitive schemata about more complex sociocultural phenomena, such as marriage, among many other examples. One of the interesting conclusions from this research is that at the level of everyday experiences and the environment (e.g., knowledge of plants and animals) knowledge is not fundamentally different between cultures, or between 'Western' ('modern') and 'indigenous' knowledge. Differences appear rather at the mid-level of knowledge about social structures, such as those of kinship, and especially those of metaphysical entities, such as gods, spirits and ancestors. It is also at these higher levels that people of all cultures seek *explanations* of everyday events. Also within modern Western societies these three levels give rise to relatively undisputed knowledge of nature or the environment, on the one hand, and ideological or normative differences about social structure (e.g., about divorce) and conduct and religious beliefs, on the other. It is not surprising that many anthropologists emphasize the similarities between different knowledge systems – and hence the cognitive unity of human beings – rather than the (more superficial) differences.

Although discourse studies in anthropology are usually not focused on epistemic characteristics but rather on formal properties and social functions, obviously different knowledges also influence different discourse structures, at least at the level of contents – for instance as part of the explanation of actions in storytelling. Thus, even at the basic level of the lexicon we may find morphological differences between 'literal' and 'magical' meanings of words.

Intercultural experiments with the interpretation and retelling of images or film seem to confirm that whereas in different cultures subjects may focus in their retelling on different aspects of a movie, generally the evidence shows that their understanding of the movie, that is, their situation model, and hence the sociocultural knowledge on which such interpretations are based, is not fundamentally different. Again, it is the context models, namely what the subjects think is required of them in the experimental situation, that may be variable for subjects in different cultures or of different ages.

One of the more interesting results of ethnographic studies relating discourse, knowledge and culture is the different conditions in which language users may make assertions, to whom, about what topics, when and whom they may question or when lies or gossip are (in)appropriate. Thus, it is shown that in some cultures it is not appropriate to make assertions about the ('private') thoughts or intentions of others, but that only literal talk can be reported – which apart from moral criteria also show different criteria for evidentials (where empirical observation is superior to inference). Similarly, myths and similar discourse genres require special (ritual) contexts in which epistemic criteria may be different from those of everyday conversations. In other words, most cultures do seem to make a difference between fact and fiction.

Finally, some brief analyses of some concrete examples of discourses in different cultures suggest how personal and shared knowledge is used as a resource for storytelling, explanation of cultural differences or as arguments in racist talk about immigrants. This analysis also shows that a difference between knowledge and opinion in storytelling is very hard to make. Indeed, both are implicated in the same mental models of an event or situation. Similarly, these examples also show that discourse in many cultures is based on a hybrid of more traditional local beliefs and 'modern' non-local (or dominant, Western) beliefs, for instance in the realm of health.

8.6   Language, discourse and knowledge

Based on the epistemological, cognitive, social psychological, sociological and anthropological studies of knowledge and its relationships with discourse, Chapter 7 finally offers a systematic description of the ways knowledge is expressed, presupposed or otherwise indexed by discourse structures of various levels.

Classical studies of topic and focus, evidentials, epistemic modals and presupposition all show how in the expression of knowledge there is a systematic polarized distinction between given, old or non-salient or non-activated knowledge and new, salient or activated information. Thus, at the level of phonology newer or more salient information tends to be stressed, while at the level of syntax it is placed in a later position. Obviously, this distinction reflects the very *communicative functions* of much language use, namely to contribute to the new knowledge of recipients. The same is true for such semantic structures as between explicit and implicit information, assertion and presupposition and the conditions of speech acts.

Secondly, as shown in the study of evidentials, discourse may lexically (as in English) or morphologically signal the (reliability of the) source of knowledge, and hence the validity of reported information and the credibility of the speakers. Hence such information about sources and the reliability of the 'method' of obtaining knowledge (vision, hearsay, inference, etc.) may also be used as basis for the epistemic evaluation of the beliefs thus obtained and hence for inferences about whether events are true or false, or more or less likely, as expressed in many modal expressions.

Whereas such epistemic approaches to language and language use show how grammar in different languages may structurally index the nature (old vs. new, salient vs. non-salient) of knowledge and its validity, a more cognitive approach frames such differences in terms of Common Ground, that is, as various kinds of shared knowledge among the participants, such as sociocultural knowledge of an epistemic community, previous discourse, previous part of the same discourse or information about the current communicative situation.

Such an approach is made more explicit in terms of mental situation and context models in our own theoretical framework.

It is finally shown that the epistemic basis of talk and text is not limited to phonological salience, pronouns, definite articles, sentence ordering, epistemic modalities or evidentials, among other epistemically relevant expressions, but is pervasive at all levels of discourse.

Thus recent Conversation Analysis has shown how access, entitlement or primacy of telling about known events organizes many aspects of talk and also has a moral dimension. Speech act analysis may be carried out within a more specific epistemic perspective by examining the conditions on the (shared or non-shared) nature of knowledge among participants.

Besides the well-known account of knowledge or information in the study of topic, focus, evidentials and modality, usually still within sentence-grammatical frameworks that ignore discourse structures, there are many other knowledge-based phenomena of text and talk. Thus, we have seen in Chapter 3 how local and global discourse coherence is essentially based on mental situation models which supply the usual inferences or 'missing links' between sentences, and how such mental models themselves are construed on the basis of shared sociocultural knowledge. Situation models thus also explain how and where and under what conditions implicit information of discourse needs to be represented.

Similarly, settings, objects, persons, actions or events may be described at various levels of generality or specificity, with more or less detail, precision or granularity. Thus, there are many other semantic properties of discourse that show how knowledge as represented in mental models or generic knowledge systems manifests itself in discourse. From the start, we have taken cognitive mental model theory as the basic notion of knowledge representation about the situations, events and actions of our natural and social environment. Modified by dynamic and situationally variable context models, the structures of such models, and hence of our knowledge of the world, in many ways influence the production and comprehension of talk, for instance in storytelling, argumentation, expository discourse, the level and specificity of description, metaphor and many more. Although text and talk have many social functions, including those of cooperation and affiliation, the basic function is the communication of new knowledge. Thus, at all levels of discourse, from intonation, the functional articulation of word order in terms of topic and focus, evidentials, modalities and the many other semantic phenomena just mentioned, we find a fundamental *expression of epistemic processing*, namely how new information or knowledge is combined with the prior knowledge of recipients.

These and many other structures of discourse show how many aspects of the specific or general knowledge of speakers, and especially as represented in their situation models, may variably be expressed, presupposed or indexed at various levels of text and talk. It should, however, be stressed that such a 'semantic' base of discourse, that is, the expression of various aspects of situations talked about, is only one fundamental condition of discourse. What is also needed is the 'pragmatic' base of discourse, as made explicit in context models, which show how the semantics may be modified by variations of setting, participant identities, roles and relations, the social act being accomplished, as well as the intentions and goals of the speakers and writers.

It is also in this context model that we need to locate the knowledge device that dynamically controls how the (assumed) knowledge of the participants should be appropriately expressed or otherwise signaled in discourse.

8.7   Concluding remarks

It is customary at the end of even voluminous monographs that authors modestly or honestly claim they have only 'scratched the surface' of a problem studied. This study is no exception. After many years of exploring much of the relevant literature on knowledge in several disciplines, as well as their relations to discourse, the impression remains that we have done no more than chart the domain of what now may be called the multidisciplinary field of *discourse epistemics*.

We have found that there are vast areas of epistemics where scholars of different disciplines ignore each other. We have found that whole domains are excluded for ideological reasons, as is the case for anti-cognitive approaches in many interactionist studies, for instance in Conversation Analysis and Discursive Psychology. The same is true for the generally asocial and apolitical approach or the limited experimental methods in much of the cognitive sciences.

Indeed, whereas epistemology may be sophisticated in its armchair reflections on knowledge and belief, only more recently has it included a more cognitive or sociological empirical approach, but this still largely ignores that most knowledge is acquired and validated by discourse.

On the other hand, cognitive psychology has dealt extensively with knowledge, knowledge representations and their role in discourse production and comprehension, but will seldom search and cite an epistemological study of knowledge or sociological research on knowledge distribution, groups or institutions. Social psychology should offer the core of the study of knowledge and discourse, but its dominant paradigms have ignored both.

The sociology of knowledge, despite its long tradition in Marxism, has ignored both the cognitive and the discursive aspects of the reproduction of knowledge in society. Anthropology has been the cradle of contemporary discourse analysis, and has also extensively studied knowledge and beliefs in different cultures, but seldom established a link between the two. And, finally, linguistics has focused on some grammatical expressions of knowledge, such as topic–focus, pronouns, evidentials, modalities or presuppositions, typically of isolated sentences, but has largely ignored the complex underlying cognitive framework defining Common Ground, as well as the many semantic discourse structures that require epistemic analysis.

Each of these disciplines and approaches, and each of the phenomena studied, require – and sometimes have produced – detailed monographs. Because of the complexity of the phenomena, these studies have been carried out within the rather limited theories, methods or perspectives of each discipline or region. In this monograph we have shown, necessarily at a higher and hence more superficial level, that the study of knowledge should be carried out in a deeply integrated way, as had already been shown, in recent decades, for the study of discourse. We have now shown that these two fundamental phenomena of the mind, interaction and society should also be studied together, and in all disciplines. Text and talk cannot be understood without detailed and explicit epistemic analysis. Knowledge can only be partly examined explicitly and empirically without a systematic analysis of how it is expressed, presupposed, indexed, acquired, reproduced, confirmed or challenged by discourse. We have shown that a multidisciplinary, sociocognitive approach is able to provide integrated insight into both knowledge and discourse, and especially their fundamental relationships.

References

Abbott, B. (2008). Presuppositions and common ground. *Linguistics and Philosophy*, 31(5), 523–538.

Abel, E. (ed.) (1981). *What's news: the media in American society*. San Francisco, CA: Institute for Contemporary Studies.

Abel, R. R., and Kulhavy, R. W. (1986). Maps, mode of text presentation, and children's prose learning. *American Educational Research Journal*, 23(2), 263–274.

Abelson, R. P. (1973). The structure of belief systems. In R. C. Schank, and K. M. Colby (eds.), *Computer models of thought and language* (pp. 287–340). San Francisco: Freeman.

    (1976). Script processing in attitude formation and decision making. In J. S. Carroll, and J. W. Payne (eds.), *Cognition and social behavior* (pp. 33–46). Hillsdale, NJ: Erlbaum.

    (1994). A personal perspective on social cognition. In P. G. Devine, D. L. Hamilton, and T. M. Ostrom (eds.), *Social cognition: impact on social psychology* (pp. 15–37). San Diego, CA: Academic Press.

Abercrombie, N. (1980). *Class, structure, and knowledge: problems in the sociology of knowledge*. New York University Press.

Abercrombie, N., Hill, S., and Turner, B. S. (eds.) (1990). *Dominant ideologies*. London/Boston: Unwin/Hyman.

Aboud, F. E. (1988). *Children and prejudice*. Oxford: Blackwell.

Abrams, D., and Hogg, M. A. (eds.) (1990). *Social identity theory: constructive and critical advances*. New York: Harvester-Wheatsheaf.

Abrams, D., and Hogg, M. A. (1999). *Social identity and social cognition*. Oxford: Blackwell.

Abric, J. C. (1994). *Pratiques sociales et représentation*. Paris: Presses universitaires de France.

Abu-Akel, A. (2002). The psychological and social dynamics of topic performance in family dinnertime conversation. *Journal of Pragmatics*, 34(12), 1787–1806.

Ackermann, D., and Tauber, M. J. (eds.) (1990). *Mental models and human-computer interaction*, vol. 1. Amsterdam/New York: North-Holland.

Adler, J. E. (1996). Transmitting knowledge. *Nous*, 30(1), 99–111.

Adorno, T. W. (1950). *The authoritarian personality*. New York: Harper.

Aebischer, V., Deconchy, J. P., and Lipiansky, E. M. (1992). *Idéologies et représentations sociales*. Fribourg: Delval.

Agar, M. (2005). Local discourse and global research: the role of local knowledge. *Language in Society*, 34(1), 1–22.

Agar, M., and Hobbs, J. R. (1982). Interpreting discourse: coherence and the analysis of ethnographic interviews. *Discourse Processes*, 5(1), 1–32.

Agnone, J. (2007). Amplifying public opinion: the policy impact of the US environmental movement. *Social Forces*, 85(4), 1593–1620.

Aijmer, K. (2009). Seem and evidentiality. *Functions of Language*, 16(1), 63–88.

Aikhenvald, A. Y. (2004). *Evidentiality*. Oxford University Press.

Ainsworth, P. B. (1998). *Psychology, law, and eyewitness testimony*. Chichester/New York: Wiley.

Ainsworth, S., and Burcham, S. (2007). The impact of text coherence on learning by self-explanation. *Learning and Instruction*, 17(3), 286–303.

Ainsworth, S., and Loizou, A. T. (2003). The effects of self-explaining when learning with text or diagrams. *Cognitive Science: A Multidisciplinary Journal*, 27(4), 669–681.

Aksu-Koc, A. (1996). Frames of mind through narrative discourse. In D. I. Slobin, J. Gerhardt, A. Kyratzis, and J. Guo (eds.), *Social interaction, social context, and language: essays in honor of Susan Ervin-Tripp* (pp. 309–328). Hillsdale, NJ: Lawrence Erlbaum.

Alali, A. O., and Eke, K. K. (1991). *Media coverage of terrorism: methods of diffusion*. Newbury Park, CA: Sage.

Albert, E. (1986). Culture patterning of speech behavior in Burundi. In J. Gumperz, and D. Hymes (eds.), *Directions in sociolinguistics: the ethnography of communication* (pp. 72–105). New York: Blackwell.

Albrecht, J. E., and O'Brien, E. J. (1993). Updating a mental model: maintaining both local and global coherence. *Journal of Experimental Psychology: Learning, Memory, and Cognition*, 19(5), 1061–1070.

Alexander, P. A., and Jetton, T. L. (2003). Learning from traditional and alternative texts: New conceptualizations for the information age. In Graesser, Gernsbacher, and Goldman (eds.), (pp. 199–241).

Alexander, Y., and Latter, R. (eds.) (1990). *Terrorism and the media: dilemmas for government, journalists and the public*. Washington, DC: Brassey's (US).

Allan, S. (ed.) (2010). *The Routledge companion to news and journalism*. New York: Routledge.

Allen, C., and Bekoff, M. (1997). *Species of mind: the philosophy and biology of cognitive ethology*. Cambridge, MA: MIT Press.

Allen, G. L., Kirasic, K. C., and Spilich, G. J. (1997). Children's political knowledge and memory for political news stories. *Child Study Journal*, 27(3), 163–177.

Alston, W. P. (1993). *The reliability of sense perception*. Ithaca, NY: Cornell University Press.

   (1996). *A realist conception of truth*. Ithaca, NY: Cornell University Press.

   (2005). *Beyond "justification": dimensions of epistemic evaluation*. Ithaca, NY: Cornell University Press.

Altschull, J. H. (1984). *Agents of power: the role of the news media in human affairs*. New York: Longman.

Alvermann, D. E., and Hague, S. A. (1989). Comprehension of counterintuitive science text: effects of prior knowledge and text structure. *Journal of Educational Research*, 82(4), 197–202.

Alvermann, D. E., and Hynd, C. R. (1989). Effects of prior knowledge activation modes and text structure on nonscience majors' comprehension of physics. *Journal of Educational Research*, 83(2), 97–102.

Alvermann, D. E., Hynd, C. E., and Qian, G. (1995). Effects of interactive discussion and text type on learning counterintuitive science concepts. *Journal of Educational Research*, 88(3), 146–154.

Ammon, U., Dittmar, N., Mattheier, K., and Trudgill, P. (2006). *Sociolinguistics: an international handbook of the science of language and society*, 2nd edn. Berlin/New York: de Gruyter.

Anderson, C. A., and Owens, J. (eds.) (1990). *Propositional attitudes: the role of content in logic, language, and mind*. Stanford, CA: Center for the Study of Language and Information.

Anderson, J. R. (1980). *Concepts, propositions, and schemata: what are the cognitive units?* Nebraska Symposium on Motivation. Lincoln, NE: University of Nebraska Press.

Anderson, R. C. (1973). Learning principles from text. *Journal of Educational Psychology*, 64(1), 26–30.

Anderson, R. C., Spiro, R. J., and Montague, W. E. (eds.) (1977). *Schooling and the acquisition of knowledge*. Hillsdale, NJ: Lawrence Erlbaum.

Anmarkrud, Ø., and Bråten, I. (2009). Motivation for reading comprehension. *Learning and Individual Differences*, 19(2), 252–256.

Antonietti, A., Liverta Sempio, O., and Marchetti, A. (eds.) (2006). *Theory of mind and language in developmental contexts*. New York: Springer.

Antos, G., Ventola, E., and Weber, T. (eds.) (2008). *Handbook of interpersonal communication*. Berlin: De Gruyter Mouton.

Apfelbaum, E. P., Pauker, K., Ambady, N., Sommers, S. R., and Norton, M. I. (2008). Learning (not) to talk about race: when older children underperform in social categorization. *Developmental Psychology*, 44(5), 1513–1518.

Apffel-Marglin, F., and Marglin, S. A. (eds.) (1996). *Decolonizing knowledge: from development to dialogue*. Oxford/New York: Clarendon Press/Oxford University Press.

Apker, J., and Eggly, S. (2004). Communicating professional identity in medical socialization: considering the ideological discourse of morning report. *Qualitative Health Research*, 14(3), 411–429.

Apple, M. W. (1979). *Ideology and curriculum*. Boston, MA: Routledge & Kegan Paul.
    (1982). *Education and power*. Boston, MA: Routledge & Kegan Paul.
    (1986). *Teachers and texts: a political economy of class and gender relations in education*. New York: Routledge & Kegan Paul.
    (1993). *Official knowledge: democratic education in a conservative age*. London: Routledge.
    (2012). *Knowledge, power, and education: the selected works of Michael W. Apple*. New York: Routledge.

Apter, T. (1996). Expert witness: who controls the psychologist's narrative? In R. Josselson (ed.), *Ethics and process in the narrative study of lives* (pp. 22–44). Thousand Oaks, CA: Sage.

Arbib, M. A. (ed.) (2006). *Action to language via the mirror neuron system*. Cambridge University Press.

Arbib, M. A., Conklin, E. J., and Hill, J. A. C. (1987). *From schema theory to language*. New York: Oxford University Press.

Argyle, M., Trimboli, L., and Forgas, J. (1988). The bank manager/doctor effect: disclosure profiles in different relationships. *The Journal of Social Psychology*, 128(1), 117–124.

Aries, E. J., and Johnson, F. L. (1983). Close friendship in adulthood: conversational content between same-sex friends. *Sex Roles*, 9(12), 1183–1196.

Aries, E. J., and Seider, M. (2007). The role of social class in the formation of identity: a study of public and elite private college students. *Journal of Social Psychology*, 147(2), 137–157.

Armand, F. (2001). Learning from expository texts: effects of the interaction of prior knowledge and text structure on responses to different question types. *European Journal of Psychology of Education*, 16(1), 67–86.

Armbruster, B. B., Anderson, T. H., and Ostertag, J. (1987). Does text structure/summarization instruction facilitate learning from expository text? *Reading Research Quarterly*. 1987, Sum, 22(3), 331–346.

Arminen, I. (2005). *Institutional interaction: studies of talk at work*. Aldershot, Hants/Burlington, VT: Ashgate.

Armstrong, D. M. (1973). *Belief, truth and knowledge*. Cambridge University Press.
    (1997). *A world of states of affairs*. Cambridge University Press.
    (2004). *Truth and truthmakers*. Cambridge University Press.

Aronowitz, S. (1988). *Science as power: discourse and ideology in modern society*. Minneapolis, MN: University of Minnesota Press.

Arvaja, M., Häkkinen, P., Eteläpelto, A., and Rasku-Puttonen, H. (2000). Collaborative processes during report writing of science learning project: the nature of discourse as a function of task requirements. *European Journal of Psychology of Education*, 15(4), 455–466.

Asad, T. (ed.) (1973). *Anthropology and the colonial encounter*. New York: Humanities Press.

Asad, T. (1979). Anthropology and the analysis of ideology. *Man*, 14(4), 624–627.

Asher, N. (2004). Discourse topic. *Theoretical Linguistics*, 30(2–3), 163–201.

Ashton, E. (1994). Metaphor in context: an examination of the significance of metaphor for reflection and communication. *Educational Studies*, 20(3), 357–366.

Asp, E. D., and de Villiers, J. (2010). *When language breaks down: analysing discourse in clinical contexts*. New York: Cambridge University Press.

Astington, J. W., and Olson, D. R. (1990). Metacognitive and metalinguistic language: learning to talk about thought. *Applied Psychology*, 39(1), 77–87.

Atkinson, J. M. (1992). A comparative analysis of formal and informal courtroom interaction. In Drew, and Heritage (eds.).

Atlas, J. D. (2000). *Logic, meaning, and conversation: semantical underdeterminacy, implicature, and the semantics/pragmatics interface*. New York: Oxford University Press.

Atran, S. (1993). *Cognitive foundations of natural history: towards an anthropology of science*. Cambridge University Press, Éditions de la Maison des Sciences de l'Homme.
    (1996). Modes of thinking of living kinds. In D. R. Olson, and N. Torrance (eds.), *Modes of thought: explorations in culture and cognition* (pp. 216–260). Cambridge University Press.
    (1998). Folk biology and the anthropology of science: cognitive universals and cultural particulars. *Behavioral and Brain Sciences*, 21, 547–609.

Atran, S., Medin, D. L., and Ross, N. O. (2005). The cultural mind: environmental decision making and cultural modeling within and across populations. *Psychological Review*, 112(4), 744–776.

Audi, R. (1997). The place of testimony in the fabric of knowledge and justification. *American Philosophical Quarterly*, 34(4), 405–422.

(2010). *Epistemology: a contemporary introduction to the theory of knowledge*, 3rd edn. New York: Routledge.

Auer, P., Couper-Kuhlen, E., and Müller, F. (1999). *Language in time. The rhythm and tempo of spoken interaction*. New York: Oxford University Press.

Augoustinos, M. (1995). Social representations and ideology: towards the study of ideological representations. In U. Flick, and S. Moscovici (eds.), *The psychology of the social: language and social knowledge in social psychology* (pp. 200–217). Reinbek: Ro.

Augoustinos, M., and Every, D. (2007). The language of "race" and prejudice: a discourse of denial, reason, and liberal-practical politics. *Journal of Language and Social Psychology*, 26(2), 123–141.

Augoustinos, M., and Reynolds, K. J. (eds.) (2001). *Understanding prejudice, racism, and social conflict*. Thousand Oaks, CA: Sage.

Augoustinos, M., LeCouteur, A., and Soyland, J. (2002). Self-sufficient arguments in political rhetoric: constructing reconciliation and apologizing to the Stolen Generations. *Discourse and Society*, 13(1), 105–142.

Augoustinos, N., Walker, I., and Donaghue, N. (2006). *Social cognition: an integrated introduction*, 2nd edn. London: Sage.

Austin, J. L. (1950). Truth. *Aristotelian Society*, Suppl. vol. 24, 111–129.

(1962). *How to do things with words*. Cambridge, MA: Harvard University Press.

Ayantunde, A., Briejer, M., Hiernaux, P., Udo, H., and Tabo, R. (2008). Botanical knowledge and its differentiation by age, gender and ethnicity in Southwestern Niger. *Human Ecology*, 36(6), 881–889.

Azevedo, R., and Jacobson, M. J. (2008). Advances in scaffolding learning with hypertext and hypermedia: a summary and critical analysis. *Educational Technology Research and Development*, 56(1), 93–100.

Back, A. (ed.) (2005). *Getting real about knowledge networks: unlocking corporate knowledge assets*. New York: Palgrave Macmillan.

Baddeley, A. D. (1986). *Working memory*. Oxford/New York: Clarendon Press/Oxford University Press.

(1994). The magical number 7: still magic after all these years. *Psychological Review*, 101(2), 353–356.

(2007). *Working memory, thought, and action*. Oxford University Press.

Baddeley, A. D., and Hitch, G. J. (1974). Working memory. In G. H. Bower (ed.), *The psychology of learning and motivation*, vol. 8 (pp. 47–89). New York: Academic Press.

Baddeley, A. D., Conway, M., and Aggleton, J. (eds.) (2002). *Episodic memory: new directions in research*. Oxford University Press.

Baert, P., and Rubio, F. D. (eds.) (2012). *The politics of knowledge*. London/New York: Routledge.

Bahrick, H. P. (1984). Semantic memory content in permastore: fifty years of memory for Spanish learned in school. *Journal of Experimental Psychology: General*, 113, 1–29.

Bahrick, H. P., and Hall, L. K. (1991). Lifetime maintenance of high-school mathematics content. *Journal of Experimental Psychology: General*, 120(1), 20–33.

Baker, L. D. (1998). *From savage to Negro: anthropology and the construction of race, 1896–1954*. Berkeley, CA: University of California Press.

Bal, M. (1985). *Narratology: introduction to the theory of narrative*. University of Toronto Press.

Bal, M. (ed.) (2004). *Narrative theory: critical concepts in literary and cultural studies*. London/New York: Routledge.

Bala, A., and Joseph, G. G. (2007). Indigenous knowledge and western science: the possibility of dialogue. *Race and Class*, 49(1), 39–61.

Ballmer, T. T., and Pinkal, M. (eds.) (1983). *Approaching vagueness*. Amsterdam/New York: North-Holland.

Barclay, C. R. (1993). Remembering ourselves. In G. M. Davies, and R. H. Logie (eds.), *Memory in everyday life*. Advances in Psychology, vol. 100 (pp. 285–309). Amsterdam: North Holland.

Barendt, E. M. (1997). *Libel and the media: the chilling effect*. Oxford/New York: Clarendon Press/Oxford University Press.

Barkan, E. (1992). *Retreat of scientific racism: changing concepts of race in Britain and the United States between the world wars*. Cambridge University Press.

Barnard, F. M. (2006). *Reason and self-enactment in history and politics: themes and voices of modernity*. Montreal/Ithaca, NY: McGill-Queen's University Press.

Barnett, R. (1994). *The limits of competence: knowledge, higher education, and society*. Buckingham: Open University Press.

Barsalou, L. W. (2003). Abstraction in perceptual symbol systems. *Philosophical Transactions of the Royal Society of London: Biological Sciences*, 358, 1177–1187.

(2008). Grounded cognition. *Annual Review of Psychology*, 59, 617–645.

Barsalou, L. W., and Medin, D. L. (1986). Concepts: static definitions or context-dependent representations? *Cahiers de Psychologie Cognitive*, 6, 187–202.

Bar-Tal, D., Graumann, C. F., Kruglanski, A. W., & Stroebe, W. (Eds.). (1989). *Stereotyping and prejudice: changing conceptions*. New York: Springer.

Bar-Tal, D. (1990). *Group beliefs: a conception for analyzing group structure, processes and behavior*. New York: Springer-Verlag.

(1998). Group beliefs as an expression of social identity. In S. Worchel, J. F. Morales, D. Paez, and J. C. Deschamps (eds.), *Social identity: international perspectives* (pp. 93–113). Thousand Oaks, CA: Sage.

(2000). *Shared beliefs in a society: social psychological analysis*. Thousand Oaks, CA: Sage.

Bar-Tal, D., and Kruglanski, A. (eds.) (1988). *The social psychology of knowledge*. Cambridge University Press.

Bartels-Tobin, L. R., and Hinckley, J. J. (2005). Cognition and discourse production in right hemisphere disorder. *Journal of Neurolinguistics*, 18(6), 461–477.

Bartholomé, T., and Bromme, R. (2009). Coherence formation when learning from text and pictures: what kind of support for whom? *Journal of Educational Psychology*, 101(2), 282–293.

Bartlett, F. (1932). *Remembering*. Cambridge University Press.

Barwise, J., and Perry, J. (1999). *Situations and attitudes*. Stanford, CA: CSLI Publications.

Bateson, G. (1972). *Steps to an ecology of mind: collected essays in anthropology, psychiatry, evolution, and epistemology*. San Francisco, CA: Chandler Co.

Bauer, P. J. (2007). *Remembering the times of our lives: memory in infancy and beyond.* Mahwah, NJ: Lawrence Erlbaum.

Baum, M. (2003). *Soft news goes to war: public opinion and American foreign policy in the new media age.* Princeton University Press.

Bazerman, C. (1988). *Shaping written knowledge: the genre and activity of the experimental article in science.* Madison, WI: University of Wisconsin Press.

Beacco, J. C. (1999). *L'astronomie dans les médias: analyses linguistiques de discours de vulgarisation.* Paris: Presses de la Sorbonne Nouvelle.

Beaver, D. I. (2001). *Presupposition and assertion in dynamic semantics.* Stanford, CA. CSLI Publications.

Bechky, B. A. (2003). Sharing meaning across occupational communities: the transformation of understanding on a production floor. *Organization Science*, 14(3), 312–330.

Beck, I. L., McKeown, M. G., and Gromoll, E. W. (1989). Learning from social studies texts. *Cognition and Instruction*, 6(2), 99–158.

Bednarek, N. (2006). Epistemological positioning and evidentiality in English news discourse: a text-driven approach. *Text and Talk*, 26(6), 635–660.

Beeman, M., and Chiarello, C. E. (eds.) (1997). *Right hemisphere language comprehension: perspectives from cognitive neuroscience.* Mahwah, NJ: Lawrence Erlbaum.

Beghtol, C. (1998). Knowledge domains: multidisciplinarity and bibliographic classification systems. *Knowledge Organization*, 25(1–2), 1–12.

Beinhauer, M. (2004). *Knowledge communities.* Lohmar: Eul.

Bell, A. (1991). *The language of news media.* Oxford/Cambridge, MA: Blackwell.

Bell, A., and Garrett, P. (eds.) (1997). *Approaches to media discourse.* Oxford/Malden, MA: Blackwell.

Bell, A. R., Davies, A. R., and Mellor, F. (2008). *Science and its publics.* Cambridge University Press.

Bendix, R. (1988). *Embattled reason: essays on social knowledge.* New Brunswick: Transaction Books.

Benedict, R. (1935). *Patterns of culture.* London: Routledge.

Bennett, J., Hogarth, S., Lubben, F., Campbell, B., and Robinson, A. (2010). Talking science: the research evidence on the use of small group discussions in science teaching. *International Journal of Science Education*, 32(1), 69–95.

Benoit, W. L., and Benoit, P. J. (2008). *Persuasive messages: the process of influence.* Malden, MA: Blackwell.

Benson, S., and Standing, C. (2001). Effective knowledge management: knowledge, thinking and the personal–corporate knowledge nexus problem. *Information Systems Frontiers*, 3(2), 227–238.

Berkenkotter, C., and Huckin, T. N. (1995). *Genre knowledge in disciplinary communication.* Hillsdale, NJ: Lawrence Erlbaum.

Berkes, F. (1999). *Sacred ecology.* New York: Routledge.

Berlin, B. (1992). *Ethnobiological classification: principles of categorization of plants and animals in traditional societies.* Princeton University Press.

Bernecker, S., and Dretske, F. I. (eds.) (2000). *Knowledge: readings in contemporary epistemology.* Oxford University Press.

Bernstein, B. B. (1996). *Pedagogy, symbolic control, and identity: theory, research, critique.* London/Washington, DC: Taylor & Francis.

Berntsen, D., and Jacobsen, A. S. (2008). Involuntary (spontaneous) mental time travel into the past and future. *Consciousness and Cognition*, 17(4), 1093–1104.

Bertuccelli-Papi, M. (2000). *Implicitness in text and discourse*. Pisa: ETS.

Bezuidenhout, A., and Cutting, J. C. (2002). Literal meaning, minimal propositions, and pragmatic processing. *Journal of Pragmatics*, 34(4), 433–456.

Bhatia, V. K. (1993). *Analyzing genre: language use in professional settings*. London: Longman.

(2005). *Vagueness in normative texts*. Bern/New York: P. Lang.

Bicchieri, C., and Dalla Chiara, M. L. (eds.) (1992). *Knowledge, belief, and strategic interaction*. Cambridge University Press.

Bicker, A., Sillitoe, P., and Pottier, J. (eds.) (2004). *Development and local knowledge: new approaches to issues in natural resources management, conservation and agriculture*. London/New York: Routledge.

Bickerton, D. (1995). *Language and human behavior*. Seattle: University of Washington Press.

(2009). *Adam's tongue: how humans made language, how language made humans*. New York: Hill & Wang.

Bickham, T. O. (2005). *Savages within the empire: representations of American Indians in eighteenth-century Britain*. Oxford University Press.

Bietenholz, P. G. (1994). *Historia and fabula: myths and legends in historical thought from antiquity to the modern age*. Leiden: Brill.

Billig, M. (1982). *Ideology and social psychology: extremism, moderation, and contradiction*. New York: St. Martin's Press.

(1989). *Arguing and thinking: a rhetorical approach to social psychology*. Paris: Éditions de la Maison des Sciences de l'Homme.

(ed.) (1976). *Social psychology and intergroup relations*. London: Academic Press.

Billig, M., Condor, S., Edwards, D., Gane, M., Middleton, D., and Radley, A.R. (1988). *Ideological dilemmas: a social psychology of everyday thinking*. London: Sage.

Bischoping, K. (1993). Gender differences in conversation topics, 1922–1990. *Sex Roles*, 28(1–2), 1–18.

Black, A. (1996). *Evolution and politics: how can the history of political thought educate us?* University of Dundee, Dept. of Political Science and Social Policy.

Black, E. (1992). *Rhetorical questions: studies of public discourse*. University of Chicago Press.

Blackburn, P., van Benthem, J., and Wolter, F. (eds.) (2006), *Handbook of modal logic*. Amsterdam: North-Holland.

Blackburn, S. (1985). *Knowledge, truth and reliability*. Oxford University Press.

Blackburn, S., and Simmons, K. (eds.) (1999). *Truth*. Oxford University Press.

Blanc, N., Kendeou, P., van den Broek, P., and Brouillet, D. (2008). Updating situation models during reading of news articles: evidence from empirical data and simulations. *Discourse Processes*, 45, 103–121.

Bloch, M. (1998). *How we think they think: anthropological approaches to cognition, memory, and literacy*. Boulder, CO: Westview Press.

Blome-Tillmann, M. (2008). The indexicality of 'knowledge.' *Philosophical Studies*, 138(1), 29–53.

Bluck, S. (ed.) (2003). *Autobiographical memory: exploring its functions in everyday life*. Hove: Psychology Press.

Boas, F. (1911). *The mind of primitive man*. New York: Macmillan.

Boden, D. (1994). *The business of talk: organizations in action*. London/Cambridge, MA: Polity Press.

    (1997). Temporal frames: time and talk in organizations. *Time and Society*, 6(1), 5–33.

Boden, D., and Bielby, D. D. (1986). The way it was: topical organization in elderly conversation. *Language and Communication*, 6(1–2), 73–89.

Boden, D., and Zimmerman, D. H. (eds.) (1991). *Talk and social structure: studies in ethnomethodology and conversation analysis*. Berkeley, CA: University of California Press.

Bodner, G. E., and Lindsay, D. S. (2003). Remembering and knowing in context. *Journal of Memory and Language*, 48(3), 563–580.

Boggs, J. P. (2002). Anthropological knowledge and native American cultural practice in the liberal polity. *American Anthropologist*, 104(2), 599–610.

Bohère, G. (1984). *Profession, journalist: a study on the working conditions of journalists*. Geneva: International Labour Office.

Boisvert, D., and Ludwig, K. (2006). Semantics for nondeclaratives. In Lepore, E., and Smith, B. C. (eds.), *The Oxford handbook of philosophy of language* (pp. 864–892). Oxford University Press.

Boltz, M. G. (2005). Temporal dimensions of conversational interaction: the role of response latencies and pauses in social impression formation. *Journal of Language and Social Psychology*, 24(2), 103–138.

Bordia, P., Irmer, B. E., and Abusah, D. (2006). Differences in sharing knowledge interpersonally and via databases: the role of evaluation apprehension and perceived benefits. *European Journal of Work and Organizational Psychology*, 15(3), 262–280.

Borge, S. (2007). Unwarranted questions and conversation. *Journal of Pragmatics*, 39(10), 1689–1701.

Bosch, P. (1984). *Lexical learning, context dependence, and metaphor*. Bloomington, IN: Indiana University Linguistics Club.

Boscolo, P., and Mason, L. (2003). Topic knowledge, text coherence, and interest: how they interact in learning from instructional texts. *Journal of Experimental Education*, 71(2), 126–148.

Boster, J. S., Johnson, J. C., and Weller, S. C. (1987). Social position and shared knowledge: actors' perceptions of status, role, and social structure. *Social Networks*, 9(4), 375–387.

Botzung, A., Denkova, E., and Manning, L. (2008). Experiencing past and future personal events: functional neuroimaging evidence on the neural bases of mental time travel. *Brain and Cognition*, 66(2), 202–212.

Bourdieu, P. (1977). *Outline of a theory of practice*. Cambridge University Press.

Bourdieu, P., Passeron, J. C., and Saint-Martin, M. (1994). *Academic discourse: linguistic misunderstanding and professorial power*. Cambridge: Polity Press.

Bowler, P. J. (2009). *Science for all: the popularization of science in early twentieth-century Britain*. University of Chicago Press.

Boyd, F. B., and Thompson, M. K. (2008). Multimodality and literacy learning: using multiple texts to enhance content-area learning. In K. A. Hinchman, and H. K. Sheridan-Thomas (eds.), *Best practices in adolescent literacy instruction* (pp. 151–163). New York: Guilford.

338   References

Boyd-Barrett, O., and Braham, P. (eds.) (1987). *Media, knowledge, and power: a reader*. London/Wolfeboro, NH: Croom Helm in association with the Open University.

Boye, K., and Harder, P. (2009). Evidentiality: linguistic categories and grammatical-ization. *Functions of Language*, 16(1), 9–43.

Brandom, R. B. (1994). *Making it explicit: reasoning, representing, and discursive commitment*. Cambridge, MA: Harvard University Press.

Branigan, E. (1984). *Point of view in the cinema: a theory of narration and subjectivity in classical film*. Berlin/New York: Mouton.

Bransford, J. D., and Johnson, M. K. (1972). Contextual prerequisites for understanding: some investigations of comprehension and recall. *Journal of Verbal Learning and Verbal Behavior*, 11, 717–726.

Bråten, I. (2008). Personal epistemology, understanding of multiple texts, and learning within internet technologies. In Khine (ed.), (pp. 351–376).

Bråten, I., Amundsen, A., and Samuelstuen, M. S. (2010). Poor readers – good learners: a study of dyslexic readers learning with and without text. *Reading and Writing Quarterly: Overcoming Learning Difficulties*, 26(2), 166–187.

Breakwell, G. M., and Canter, D. V. (eds.) (1993). *Empirical approaches to social representations*. Oxford/New York: Clarendon Press/Oxford University Press.

Brewer, M. B. (2003). *Intergroup relations*. Philadelphia, PA: Open University Press.

Brewer, M. B., and Hewstone, M. (eds.) (2003). *Self and social identity*. Malden, MA: Blackwell.

Briggs, R. (1989). *Communities of belief: cultural and social tension in early modern France*. Oxford: Clarendon Press.

Briley, D. A., and Aaker, J. L. (2006). When does culture matter? Effects of personal knowledge on the correction of culture-based judgments. *Journal of Marketing Research*, 43(3), 395–408.

Briner, S. W., Virtue, S., and Kurby, C. A. (2012). Processing causality in narrative events: temporal order matters. *Discourse Processes*, 49(1), 61–77.

Brinks, J. H., Timms, E., and Rock, S. (eds.) (2006). *Nationalist myths and modern media: contested identities in the age of globalization*. London/New York: Tauris Academic Studies.

Britt, M. A., Perfetti, C. A., Sandak, R., and Rouet, J. F. (1999). Content integration and source separation in learning from multiple texts. In Goldman, Graesser, and van den Broek (eds.) (pp. 209–233).

Britt, M. A., Rouet, J. F., Georgi, M. C., and Perfetti, C. A. (1994). Learning from history texts: from causal analysis to argument models. In G. Leinhardt, I. L. Beck, and C. Stainton (eds.), *Teaching and learning in history* (pp. 47–84). Hillsdale, NJ: Lawrence Erlbaum.

Britton, B. K. (ed.) (1984). *Understanding expository text: a theoretical and practical handbook for analyzing explanatory text*. Hillsdale, NJ: Lawrence Erlbaum.

Britton, B. K., and Black, J. B. (eds.) (1985). *Understanding expository text: a theoretical and practical handbook for analyzing explanatory text*. Hillsdale, NJ: Lawrence Erlbaum.

Britton, B. K., Woodward, A., and Binkley, M. R. (eds.) (1993). *Learning from textbooks: theory and practice*. Hillsdale, NJ: Lawrence Erlbaum.

Britton, B. K., Stimson, M., Stennett, B., and Gülgöz, S. (1998). Learning from instructional text: test of an individual-differences model. *Journal of Educational Psychology*, 90(3), 476–491.

Brøgger, J. (1986). *Belief and experience among the Sidano: a case study towards an anthropology of knowledge*. Oslo: Norwegian University Press.

Brokensha, D., Warren, D. M., and Werner, O. (eds.) (1980). *Indigenous knowledge systems and development*. Washington, DC: University Press of America.

Brothers, L. (1997). *Friday's footprint: how society shapes the human mind*. New York: Oxford University Press.

Brown, J., and Gerken, M. (eds.) (2012). *Knowledge ascriptions*. Oxford University Press.

Brown, J. W. (1991). *Self and process: brain states and the conscious present*. New York: Springer-Verlag.

Brown, R. (ed.) (2001). *Intergroup processes*. Malden, MA: Blackwell.

Brown, R., and Gilman, A. (1960). The pronouns of power and solidarity. In T. A. Sebeok (ed.), *Style in language* (pp. 253–277). Cambridge, MA: MIT Press.

Brownell, H., and Friedman, O. (2001). Discourse ability in patients with unilateral left and right hemisphere brain damage. In R. S. Berndt (ed.), *Handbook of neuro-psychology*, 2nd edn., vol. 3: Language and aphasia (pp. 189–203). Amsterdam: Elsevier Science Publishers.

Brownell, H., and Joanette, Y. (1990). *Discourse ability and brain damage: theoretical and empirical perspectives*. New York: Springer-Verlag.

Brueckner, A., and Ebbs, G. (2012). *Debating self-knowledge*. New York: Cambridge University Press.

Bruner, J. (2002). *Making stories: law, literature, life*. New York: Farrar, Straus and Giroux.

Bublitz, W., Lenk, U., and Ventola, E. (1999). *Coherence in spoken and written discourse: how to create it and how to describe it*, selected papers from the International Workshop on Coherence, Augsburg, April 24–27, 1997. Amsterdam: John Benjamins.

Bucchi, M., and Trench, B. (eds.) (2008). *Handbook of public communication of science and technology*. New York: Routledge.

Bucholtz, M. (ed.) (1994). *Cultural performances*. Proceedings of the third Berkeley Women and Language Conference, April 8, 9, and 10, 1994. Berkeley, CA: Berkeley Women and Language Group.

Bukobza, G. (2008). The development of knowledge structures in adulthood. In A. M. Columbus (ed.), *Advances in psychology research*, vol. 54 (pp. 199–228). Hauppauge, NY: Nova Science Publishers.

Bultman, D. C., and Svarstad, B. L. (2000). Effects of physician communication style on client medication beliefs and adherence with antidepressant treatment. *Patient Education and Counseling*, 40(2), 173–185.

Burke, T. E. (1995). *Questions of belief*. Aldershot: Avebury.

Burnstein, E., and Sentis, K. (1981). Attitude polarization in groups, In R. E. Petty, T. M. Ostrom, and T. C. Brock (eds.), *Cognitive responses in persuasion*. Hillsdale, NJ: Lawrence Erlbaum.

Buskes, C. (1998). *The genealogy of knowledge: a Darwinian approach to epistemology and philosophy of science*. Tilburg University Press.

Butcher, K. R. (2006). Learning from text with diagrams: promoting mental model development and inference generation. *Journal of Educational Psychology*, 98(1), 182–197.

Butcher, K. R., and Kintsch, W. (2003). Text comprehension and discourse processing. In A. F. Healy, and R. W. Proctor (eds.), *Handbook of psychology: experimental psychology*, vol. 4 (pp. 575–595). Hoboken, NJ: John Wiley and Sons.

Butt, D., Bywater, J., and Paul, N. (eds.) (2008). *Place: local knowledge and new media practice*. Newcastle, UK: Cambridge Scholars.

Buus, N. (2008). Negotiating clinical knowledge: a field study of psychiatric nurses' everyday communication. *Nursing Inquiry*, 15(3), 189–198.

Bybee, J., and Fleischman, S. (eds.) (1995). *Modality in grammar and discourse*. Amsterdam: John Benjamins.

Byrne, R. M. J. (2002). Mental models and counterfactual thoughts about what might have been. *Trends in Cognitive Sciences*, 6(10), 426–431.

Caillies, S., and Tapiero, I. (1997). Text structures and prior knowledge. *L'Année Psychologique*, 97(4), 611–639.

Caillies, S., Denhière, G., and Kintsch, W. (2002). The effect of prior knowledge on understanding from text: evidence from primed recognition. *European Journal of Cognitive Psychology*, 14(2), 267–286.

Calisir, F., and Gurel, Z. (2003). Influence of text structure and prior knowledge of the learner on reading-comprehension, browsing and perceived control. *Computers in Human Behavior*, 19(2), 135–145.

Calisir, F., Eryazici, M., and Lehto, M. R. (2008). The effects of text structure and prior knowledge of the learner on computer-based learning. *Computers in Human Behavior*, 24(2), 439–450.

Callahan, D., and Drum, P. A. (1984). Reading ability and prior knowledge as predictors of eleven and twelve year olds' text comprehension. *Reading Psychology*, 5(1–2), 145–154.

Callebaut, W., and Pinxten, R. (eds.) (1987). *Evolutionary epistemology: a multiparadigm program*. Dordrecht: D. Reidel.

Calsamiglia, H., and van Dijk, T. A. (2004). Popularization discourse and knowledge about the genome. *Discourse and Society*, 15(4), 369–389.

Cameron, D. (1997). Performing gender identity: young men's talk and the construction of heterosexual masculinity. In S. A. Johnson, and U. H. Meinhof (eds.), *Masculinity and language* (pp. 47–64). Oxford: Blackwell.

Camp, E. (2006). Contextualism, metaphor, and what is said. *Mind and Language*, 21(3), 280–309.

Canary, H. E., and McPhee, R. (eds.) (2010). *Communication and organizational knowledge: contemporary issues for theory and practice*. New York: Routledge.

Canisius, P. (1987). *Perspektivität in Sprache und Text*. Bochum: N. Brockmeyer.

Cantor, N. (1980). Perceptions of situations: situation prototypes and person-situation prototypes. In D. Magnusson (ed.), *The situation: an interactional perspective*. Hillsdale, NJ: Lawrence Erlbaum.

Cantor, N., and Mischel, W. (1979). Prototypes in person perception. *Advances in Experimental Social Psychology*, 12, 4–47.

Capozza, D., and Brown, R. (eds.) (2000). *Social identity processes: trends in theory and research*. Thousand Oaks, CA: Sage.

Cappelen, H., and Lepore, E. (2005). *Insensitive semantics: a defense of semantic minimalism and speech act pluralism*. Malden, MA: Blackwell.

Caramazza, A., and Mahon, B. Z. (2003). The organization of conceptual knowledge: the evidence from category-specific semantic deficits. *Trends in Cognitive Sciences*, 7(8), 354–361.

Carayannis, E. G., and Alexander, J. M. (2005). *Global and local knowledge: glocal transatlantic public–private partnerships for research and technological development*. New York: Palgrave Macmillan.

Carayannis, E. G., and Campbell, D. F. J. (eds.) (2006). *Knowledge creation, diffusion, and use in innovation networks and knowledge clusters: a comparative systems approach across the United States, Europe, and Asia*. Westport, CT: Praeger.

Carey, S. (1996). Cognitive domains as modes of thought. In D. R. Olson, and N. Torrance (eds.), *Modes of thought: explorations in culture and cognition* (pp. 187–215). Cambridge University Press.

Carlsen, W. S. (1997). Never ask a question if you don't know the answer: the tension in teaching between modeling scientific argument and maintaining law and order. *Journal of Classroom Interaction*, 32(2), 14–23.

Carnap, R. (1956). *Meaning and necessity: a study in semantics and modal logic*. University of Chicago Press.

Carney, R. N., and Levin, J. R. (2002). Pictorial illustrations still improve students' learning from text. *Educational Psychology Review*, 14(1), 5–26.

Carpendale, J. I. M. E., and Müller, U. E. (2004). *Social interaction and the development of knowledge*. Mahwah, NJ: Lawrence Erlbaum.

Carr, M., Mizelle, N. B., and Charak, D. (1998). Motivation to read and learn from text. In Steven A. Stahl, and Cynthia R. Hynd, (eds.), *Learning from text across conceptual domains* (pp. 45–70). Mahwah, NJ: Lawrence Erlbaum.

Carroll, W., and Seng, M. (2003). *Eyewitness testimony: strategies and tactics*. Eagan, MN: Thomson West.

Carruthers, P. (2009). How do we know our own minds: the relationship between mindreading and metacognition. *Behavioral and Brain Sciences*, 32, 121–182.

Carston, R., and Uchida, S. (eds.) (1998). *Relevance theory: applications and implications*. Amsterdam: John Benjamins.

Caspari, I., and Parkinson, S. R. (2000). Effects of memory impairment on discourse. *Journal of Neurolinguistics*, 13(1), 15–36.

Cassell, E. J. (1985). *Talking with patients*. Cambridge, MA: MIT Press.

Cassirer, E. (1955). *Mythical thought*. New Haven, NY: Yale University Press.

Castañeda, S., Lopez, M., and Romero, M. (1987). The role of five induced-learning strategies in scientific text comprehension. *Journal of Experimental Education*, 55(3), 125–130.

Catt, I. E., and Eicher-Catt, D. (eds.) (2010). *Communicology: the new science of embodied discourse*. Madison, NJ: Fairleight Dickinson University Press.

Caughlin, J. P., and Afifi, T. D. (2004). When is topic avoidance unsatisfying? Examining moderators of the association between avoidance and dissatisfaction. *Human Communication Research*, 30(4), 479–513.

Caughlin, J. P., and Golish, T. D. (2002). An analysis of the association between topic avoidance and dissatisfaction: comparing perceptual and interpersonal explanations. *Communication Monographs*, 69(4), 275–295.

Caughlin, J. P., and Petronio, S. (2004). Privacy in families. In A. L. Vangelisti (ed.), *Handbook of family communication* (pp. 379–412). Mahwah, NJ: Lawrence Erlbaum.

Chafe, W. L. (1972). Discourse structure and human knowledge. In R. O. Freedle, and J. B. Carroll (eds.), *Language comprehension and the acquisition of knowledge* (pp. 41–70). New York: Winston.

(1974). Language and consciousness. *Language* 50, 111–133.

(1976). Givenness, contrastiveness, definiteness, subjects, topics and point of view. In C. Li (ed.), *Subject and topic* (pp. 27–55). New York: Academic Press.

Chafe, W. L. (ed.) (1980). *The Pear Stories: cognitive, cultural, and linguistic aspects of narrative production*. Norwood, NJ: Ablex.

Chafe, W. L. (1994). *Discourse, consciousness, and time: the flow and displacement of conscious experience in speaking and writing*. University of Chicago Press.

Chafe, W. L., and Nichols, J. (eds.) (1986). *Evidentiality: the linguistic coding of epistemology*. Norwood, NJ: Ablex Corp.

Chambers, S. K., and André, T. (1997). Gender, prior knowledge, interest, and experience in electricity and conceptual change text manipulations in learning about direct-current. *Journal of Research in Science Teaching*, 34(2), 107–123.

Champagne, R. A. (1992). *The structuralists on myth: an introduction*. New York: Garland.

Chan, C. K. (2001). Peer collaboration and discourse patterns in learning from incompatible information. *Instructional Science*, 29(6), 443–479.

Chan, C. K., Burtis, P. J., Scardamalia, M., and Bereiter, C. (1992). Constructive activity in learning from text. *American Educational Research Journal*, 29(1), 97–118.

Chang, C. C., and Keisler, H. J. (1973). *Model theory*. Amsterdam/New York: North-Holland/American Elsevier.

Chapman, S. B., Highley, A. P., and Thompson, J. L. (1998). Discourse in fluent aphasia and Alzheimer's disease: linguistic and pragmatic considerations. *Journal of Neurolinguistics*, 11(1–2), 55–78.

Chávez, L. R., McMullin, J. M., Mishra, S. I., and Hubbell, F. A. (2001). Beliefs matter: cultural beliefs and the use of cervical cancer-screening tests. *American Anthropologist*, 103(4), 1114–1129.

Chemero, A. (2009). *Radical embodied cognitive science*. Cambridge, MA: MIT Press.

Chen, W. L., and Looi, C. K. (2007). Incorporating online discussion in face to face classroom learning: a new blended learning approach. *Australasian Journal of Educational Technology*, 23(3), 307–326.

Chenail, R. J., and Morris, G. H. (eds.) (1995). *The talk of the clinic: explorations in the analysis of medical and therapeutic discourse*. Hillsdale, NJ: Lawrence Erlbaum.

Chinn, C. A., O'Donnell, A. M., and Jinks, T. S. (2000). The structure of discourse in collaborative learning. *Journal of Experimental Education*, 69(1), 77–97.

Chisholm, W. (ed.) (1984). *Interrogativity: a colloquium on the grammar, typology, and pragmatics of questions in seven diverse languages*, Cleveland, Ohio, October 5th, 1981-May 3rd, 1982. Amsterdam: Benjamins.

Chomsky, N. (1987). *On power and ideology: the Managua lectures*. Boston, MA: South End Press.

Christiansen, M. H., and Kirby, S. (eds.) (2003). *Language evolution*. Oxford University Press.

Chua, L., High, C., and Lau, T. (eds.) (2008). *How do we know? Evidence, ethnography, and the making of anthropological knowledge*. Newcastle: Cambridge Scholars.

Cicourel, A. V. (1981). Notes on the Integration of micro- and macro-levels of analysis. In K. Knorr Cetina, and A. V. Cicourel (eds.) *Advances in social theory and methodology* (pp. 51–80). Boston, MA: Routledge & Kegan Paul.

Clancey, W. J. (1997). *Situated cognition: on human knowledge and computer representations.* Cambridge University Press.

Clariana, R. B., and Marker, A. W. (2007). Generating topic headings during reading of screen-based text facilitates learning of structural knowledge and impairs learning of lower-level knowledge. *Journal of Educational Computing Research,* 37(2), 173–191.

Clark, C. (ed.) (1988). *Social interaction: readings in sociology.* New York: St. Martin's Press.

Clark, H. H. (1996). *Using language.* Cambridge University Press.

Clark, H. H., and Marshall, C. R. (1981). Definite reference and mutual knowledge. In A. K. Joshi, B. Webber, and I. Sag (eds.), *Elements of discourse understanding* (pp. 10–63). Cambridge University Press.

Clayman, S. E., and Heritage, J. (2002). Questioning presidents: journalistic deference and adversarialness in the press-conferences of US presidents Eisenhower and Reagan. *Journal of Communication,* 52(4), 749–775.

Clift, R. (2006). Indexing stance: reported speech as an interactional evidential. *Journal of Sociolinguistics,* 10(5), 569–595.

   (2012). Who Knew? A view from linguistics. *Research on Language and Social Interaction,* 45(1), 69–95.

Coady, C. A. J. (1992). *Testimony: a philosophical study.* Oxford/New York: Clarendon Press/Oxford University Press.

Coburn, D., and Willis, E. (2000). The medical profession: knowledge, power, and autonomy. In G. L. Albrecht, R. Fitzpatrick, and S. C. Scrimshaw (eds.), *The handbook of social studies in health and medicine* (pp. 377–393). Thousand Oaks, CA: Sage.

Coffe, H., and Geys, B. (2006). Community heterogeneity: a burden for the creation of social capital? *Social Science Quarterly,* 87(5), 1053–1072.

Cohen, E. (2010). Anthropology of knowledge. In Marchand (ed.) (pp. 183–192).

Cohen, E. D. (ed.) (2005). *News incorporated: corporate media ownership and its threat to democracy.* Amherst, NY: Prometheus Books.

Cohen, L. J. (1992). *An essay on belief and acceptance.* Oxford: Clarendon Press.

Cohen, R. S., and Wartofsky, M. W. (eds.) (1983). *Epistemology, methodology, and the social sciences.* Dordrecht: Reidel.

Cohen, S. (1987). Knowledge, context, and social standards. *Synthese,* 73, 3–26.

Coleman, E. B., Brown, A. L., and Rivkin, I. D. (1997). The effect of instructional explanations on learning from scientific texts. *Journal of the Learning Sciences,* 6(4), 347–365.

Coleman, L., and Kay, P. (1981). Prototype semantics: the English verb 'lie.' *Language,* 57(1), 26–44.

Coliva, A. (ed.) (2012). *The self and self-knowledge.* Oxford University Press.

Collins, A. M., and Quillian, M. R. (1972). Experiments on semantic memory and language comprehension. In L. W. Gregg (ed.), *Cognition in learning and memory.* New York: Wiley.

Colson, E. (1953). *The Makah Indians: a study of an Indian tribe in modern American society.* Minneapolis, MN: University of Minnesota Press.

Condit, C. M. (1999). How the public understands genetics: nondeterministic and non-discriminatory interpretations of the blueprint metaphor. *Public Understanding of Science*, 8(3), 169–180.

Conklin, H. C. (1962). Lexicographical treatment of folk taxonomies. In F. W. Household, and S. Saporta (eds.), *Problems in Lexicography*. Bloomington, IN: Indiana University Research Center in Anthropology, Folklore, and Linguistics.

Connelly, F. M., and Clandinin, D. J. (1999). *Shaping a professional identity: stories of educational practice*. New York: Teachers College Press.

Converse, P. E. (1964). The nature of belief systems in mass publics. In D. E. Apter (ed.), *Ideology and discontent* (pp. 206–261). New York: Free Press.

Conway, A. R. A. (ed.) (2007). *Variation in working memory*. Oxford University Press.

Conway, M. A. (1990). *Autobiographical memory: an introduction*. Buckingham: Open University Press.

Conway, M. A. (ed.) (1997). *Cognitive models of memory*. Cambridge, MA: MIT Press.

Conway, M. A., Cohen, G., and Stanhope, N. (1992). Very long-term memory for knowledge acquired at school and university. *Applied Cognitive Psychology*, 6(6), 467–482.

Cook, T. E. (1989). *Making laws and making news: media strategies in the US House of Representatives*. Washington, DC: Brookings Institution.

Cooper, C. A., and Johnson, M. (2009). Representative reporters? Examining journalists' ideology in context. *Social Science Quarterly*, 90(2), 387–406.

Cooper, D. E. (1974). *Presupposition*. The Hague: Mouton.

Copney, C. V. (1998). *Jamaican culture and international folklore, superstitions, beliefs, dreams, proverbs, and remedies*. Raleigh, NC: Pentland Press.

Corlett, J. A. (1996). *Analyzing social knowledge*. Lanham, MD: Rowman & Littlefield.

Cormack, A. (1998). *Definitions: implications for syntax, semantics, and the language of thought*. New York: Garland.

Cornillie, B. (2007). *Evidentiality and epistemic modality in Spanish (semi-) auxiliaries: a cognitive-functional approach*. Berlin: De Gruyter Mouton.

   (2009). Evidentiality and epistemic modality: on the close relationship between two different categories. *Functions of Language*, 16(1), 44–62.

Cortese, G., and Duszak, A. (2005). *Identity, community, discourse: English in intercultural settings*. Bern/New York: Peter Lang.

Coulmas, F. (1998). *The handbook of sociolinguistics*. Oxford, UK/Cambridge, MA: Blackwell.

Cowie, H. (ed.) (2000). *Social interaction in learning and instruction the meaning of discourse for the construction of knowledge*. Oxford/New York: Pergamon.

Cowie, H., and van der Aalsvoort, G. (eds.) (2000). *Social interaction in learning and instruction: the meaning of discourse for the construction of knowledge*. Amsterdam: Pergamon/Elsevier Science.

Cox, O. C. (1970). *Caste, class, and race: a study in social dynamics*. New York/London: Monthly Review Press.

Crane, T. (2009). Intentionalism. In B. P. McLaughlin, A. Beckermann, S. Walter (eds.), *The Oxford handbook of philosophy of mind* (pp. 474–493). Oxford/New York: Clarendon Press/Oxford University Press.

Cranefield, J., and Yoong, P. (2009). Crossings: embedding personal professional knowledge in a complex online community environment. *Online Information Review*, 33(2), 257–275.

Cresswell, M. J. (1985). *Structured meanings: the semantics of propositional attitudes*. Cambridge, MA: MIT Press.

Crick, M. R. (1982). Anthropology of knowledge. *Annual Review of Anthropology*, 11, 287–313.

Crimmins, M. (1992). *Talk about beliefs*. Cambridge, MA: MIT Press.

Cross, R., Parker, A., Prusak, A., and Borgatti, S. P. (2001). Knowing what we know: supporting knowledge creation and sharing in social networks. *Organizational Dynamics*, 30(2), 100–120.

Cunningham, A., and Andrews, B. (1997). *Western medicine as contested knowledge*. New York: Manchester University Press, distributed exclusively in the USA by St. Martin's Press.

Curtis, J. E., and Petras, J. W. (eds.) (1970). *The sociology of knowledge: a reader*. London: Duckworth.

Custers, E. J. F. M. (2010). Long-term retention of basic science knowledge: a review study. *Advances in Health Sciences Education*, 15(1), 109–128.

Cutica, I., and Bucciarelli, M. (2008). The deep versus the shallow: effects of co-speech gestures in learning from discourse. *Cognitive Science*, 32(5), 921–935.

Cutler, B. L. (2002). *Eyewitness testimony: challenging your opponent's witness*. Notre Dame: National Institute for Trial Advocacy, Notre Dame Law School.

Cutler, B. L. (ed.) (2009). *Expert testimony on the psychology of eyewitness identification*. New York: Oxford University Press.

Cutting, J. (2000). *Analysing the language of discourse communities*. Amsterdam: Elsevier.

D'Andrade, R. G. (1995). *The development of cognitive anthropology*. Cambridge University Press.

Da Costa, A. L. (1980). *News values and principles of cross-cultural communication*. Paris: Unesco.

Dahl, Ö. (1974). *Topic and comment, contextual boundness and focus*. Hamburg: Buske.

Dahlberg, A. C., and Trygger, S. B. (2009). Indigenous medicine and primary health care: the importance of lay knowledge and use of medicinal plants in rural South Africa. *Human Ecology*, 37(1), 79–94.

Dailey, R. M., and Palomares, N. A. (2004). Strategic topic avoidance: an investigation of topic avoidance frequency, strategies used, and relational correlates. *Communication Monographs*, 71(4), 471–496.

Dale, R. (1992). *Generating referring expressions: constructing descriptions in a domain of objects and processes*. Cambridge, MA: MIT Press.

Daniels, J. (2009). Cloaked websites: propaganda, cyber-racism and epistemology in the digital era. *New Media and Society*, 11(5), 659–683.

Davidson, B. (2002). A model for the construction of conversational common ground in interpreted discourse. *Journal of Pragmatics*, 34(9), 1273–1300.

Davidson, D. (1984). *Inquiries into truth and interpretation*. Oxford University Press (Clarendon).

(1996). The folly of trying to define truth. *Journal of Philosophy*, 93(6), 263–278.

(2005), *Truth and predication*. Cambridge, MA: Belknap Press.

Davis, A., and Wagner, J. R. (2003). Who knows? On the importance of identifying "experts" when researching local ecological knowledge. *Human Ecology*, 31(3), 463–489.

Davis, O. L. J., Hicks, L. C., and Bowers, N. D. (1966). The usefulness of time lines in learning chronological relationships in text materials. *Journal of Experimental Education*, 34(3), 22–25.

Davis, S. (2002). Conversation, epistemology and norms. *Mind and Language*, 17(5), 513–537.

Davis, S., and Gillon, B. S. (eds.) (2004). *Semantics: a reader*. Oxford University Press.

Davis, W. A. (1998). *Implicature: intention, convention, and principle in the failure of Gricean theory*. Cambridge University Press.

 (2004). Are knowledge claims indexical? (David Lewis, Stewart Cohen, and Keith DeRose). *Erkenntnis*, 61(2–3), 257–281.

Dawson, M. A. (1937). Children's preferences for conversational topics. *The Elementary School Journal*, 37, 429–437.

De Beaugrande, R. (1984). *Text production: toward a science of composition*. Norwood, NJ: Ablex.

De Condillac, B. (1746). *Essai sur l'origine des connoissances humaines. Ouvrage où l'on réduit a un seul principe tout ce qui concerne l'entendement human: première partie*. Amsterdam: Chez Pierre Mortier.

De Mente, B. (2009). *The Chinese mind: understanding traditional Chinese beliefs and their influence on contemporary culture*. North Clarendon, VT: Tuttle.

De Vries, R. E., Bakker-Pieper, A., and Oostenveld, W. (2010). Leadership = communication? The relations of leaders' communication styles with leadership styles, knowledge sharing and leadership outcomes. *Journal of Business and Psychology*, 25(3), 367–380.

De Vries, R. E., van den Hooff, B., and de Ridder, J. A. (2006). Explaining knowledge sharing: the role of team communication styles, job satisfaction, and performance beliefs. *Communication Research*, 33(2), 115–135.

Deacon, T. W. (1997). *The symbolic species: the co-evolution of language and the brain*. New York: Norton.

Deaux, K., and Philogène, G. (eds.) (2001). *Representations of the social: bridging theoretical traditions*. Oxford: Blackwell.

DeConcini, B. (1990). *Narrative remembering*. Lanham, MD: University Press of America.

Dee-Lucas, D., and di Vesta, F. J. (1980). Learner-generated organizational aids: effects on learning from text. *Journal of Educational Psychology*, 72(3), 304–311.

Dee-Lucas, D., and Larkin, J. H. (1995). Learning from electronic texts: effects of interactive overviews for information access. *Cognition and Instruction*, 13(3), 431–468.

Deemter, K., and Kibble, R. (2002). *Information sharing: reference and presupposition in language generation and interpretation*. Stanford, CA: CSLI.

DeGenaro, W. (ed.) (2007). *Who says? Working-class rhetoric, class consciousness, and community*. University of Pittsburgh Press.

Dennett, D. C. (1987). *The intentional stance*. Cambridge, MA: MIT Press.

Denzin, N. K. (2003). *Performance ethnography: critical pedagogy and the politics of culture*. Thousand Oaks, CA: Sage.

DeRose, K. (2009). *The case for contextualism*. Oxford University Press.

Deuze, M. (2005). Popular journalism and professional ideology: tabloid reporters and editors speak out. *Media Culture and Society*, 27(6), 861–882.

Devine, P. G. (1989). Stereotypes and prejudice: their automatic and controlled components. *Journal of Personality and Social Psychology*, 56(1), 5–18.

Devine, D. J. (1999). Effects of cognitive ability, task knowledge, information sharing, and conflict on group decision-making effectiveness. *Small Group Research*, 30(5), 608–634.

Di Leonardo, M. (ed.) (1991). *Gender at the crossroads of knowledge: feminist anthropology in the postmodern era.* Berkeley, CA: University of California Press.

Diakidoy, I. A. N., Kendeou, P., and Ioannides, C. (2003). Reading about energy: the effects of text structure in science learning and conceptual change. *Contemporary Educational Psychology*, 28(3), 335–356.

Diewald, G., and Smirnova, E. (2010). *Linguistic realization of evidentiality in European languages.* Berlin: De Gruyter Mouton.

Dijkstra, K., Bourgeois, M. S., Allen, R. S., and Burgio, L. D. (2004). Conversational coherence: discourse analysis of older adults with and without dementia. *Journal of Neurolinguistics*, 17(4), 263–283.

Douglas, M. (1973). *Rules and meaning: the anthropology of everyday knowledge.* London: Penguin.

Dovidio, J. F., and Gaertner, S. L. (eds.) (1986). *Prejudice, discrimination, and racism.* New York: Academic Press.

Dovidio, J. F., Glick, P., and Rudman, L. A. (eds). (2005). *On the nature of prejudice: fifty years after Allport.* Malden, MA: Blackwell.

Downing, J. D. H., and Husband, C. (2005). *Representing race: racisms, ethnicities and media.* London: Sage.

Dretske, F. I. (1981). *Knowledge and the flow of information.* Cambridge, MA: MIT Press.

(2000). *Perception, knowledge, and belief. Selected essays.* Cambridge University Press.

Drew, P. (2003). Precision and exaggeration in interaction. *American Sociological Review*, 68(6), 917–938.

Drew, P., and Heritage, J. (eds.) (1992), *Talk at work: interaction in institutional settings.* Cambridge University Press.

Druckman, D. (2003). Linking micro and macro-level processes: interaction analysis in context. *International Journal of Conflict Management*, 14(3), 177–190.

Dryer, M. S. (1996). Focus, pragmatic presupposition, and activated propositions. *Journal of Pragmatics*, 26(4), 475–523.

Duek, J. E. (2000). Whose group is it anyway? Equity of student discourse in problem-based learning (PBL). In C. E. Hmelo, and D. H. Evensen, *Problem-based learning, a research perspective on learning interactions* (pp. 75–107). London: Lawrence Erlbaum.

Duell, O. K. (1984). The effects of test expectations based upon goals on the free recall of learning from text. *Contemporary Educational Psychology*, 9(2), 162–170.

Duff, M. C., Hengst, J. A., Tranel, D., and Cohen, N. J. (2008). Collaborative discourse facilitates efficient communication and new learning in amnesia. *Brain and Language*, 106(1), 41–54.

348   References

Dummett, M. A. E. (1978). *Truth and other enigmas.* Cambridge, MA: Harvard University Press.

Dumont, L. (1986). *Essays on individualism: modern ideology in anthropological perspective.* University of Chicago Press.

Dunbar, R. I. M., Marriott, A., and Duncan, N. D. C. (1997). Human conversational behavior. *Human Nature*, 8(3), 231–246.

Duranti, A. (1997). *Linguistic anthropology.* Cambridge University Press.

(2001a). Properties of greetings. In A. Duranti (ed.), *Linguistic anthropology: a reader* (pp. 208–238). Malden, MA: Blackwell.

Duranti, A. (ed.) (2001b). *Key terms in language and culture.* Malden, MA: Blackwell.

Duranti, A. (ed.) (2004). *A companion to linguistic anthropology.* Oxford: Blackwell.

Durkheim, E. (1915). *The elementary forms of religious life.* London: George Allen & Unwin.

(2002[2010]). *Le problème sociologique de la connaissance.* Chicoutimi: J.-M. Tremblay.

Dutke, S. (1996). Generic and generative knowledge: memory schemata in the construction of mental models. In W. Battmann, and S. Dutke (eds.), *Processes of the molar regulation of behavior* (pp. 35–54). Lengerich, Germany: Pabst Science Publishers.

Dyer, C. L., and McGoodwin, J. R. (1994). *Folk management in the world's fisheries: lessons for modern fisheries management.* Niwiot, CO: University Press of Colorado.

Dymock, S. J. (1999). Learning about text structure. In G. B. Thompson, and T. Nicholson (eds.), *Learning to read: beyond phonics and whole language* (pp. 174–192). Newark, DE: International Reading Association.

Eagleton, T. (1991). *Ideology: an introduction.* London: Verso.

Eagly, A. H., and Chaiken, S. (1993). *The psychology of attitudes.* Fort Worth, TX: Harcourt Brace Jovanovich.

Easterby-Smith, M., and Lyles, M. A. (eds.) (2011). *Handbook of organizational learning and knowledge management.* Chichester, West Sussex/Hoboken, NJ: Wiley.

Ecarma, R. E. (2003). *Beyond ideology: a case of egalitarian bias in the news?* Lanham, MD: University Press of America.

Echterhoff, G., Higgins, E. T., and Levine, J. M. (2009). Shared reality: experiencing commonality with other's inner states about the world. *Perspective on Psychological Science*, 4(5), 496–521.

Edgerton, G. R., and Rollins, P. C. (eds.) (2001). *Television histories: shaping collective memory in the media age.* Lexington, KY: University Press of Kentucky.

Edson, G. (2009). *Shamanism: a cross-cultural study of beliefs and practices.* Jefferson, NC: McFarland and Co.

Edwards, B., and Davis, B. (1997). Learning from classroom questions and answers: teachers' uncertainties about children's language. *Journal of Literacy Research*, 29(4), 471–505.

Edwards, D., and Potter, J. (1992). *Discursive psychology.* London: Sage.

Egan, A. (2007). Epistemic modals, relativism and assertion. *Philosophical Studies*, 133(1), 1–22.

Eggins, S., and Slade, D. (1997). *Analysing casual conversation*. London/New York: Cassell.

Ehrich, V., and Koster, C. (1983). Discourse organization and sentence form: the structure of room descriptions in Dutch. *Discourse Processes*, 6(2), 169–195.

Ehrlich, M. F., Tardieu, H., and Cavazza, M. (1993). *Les modèles mentaux: approche cognitive de représentations*. Paris: Masson.

Eiser, J. R., Claessen, M. J. A., and Loose, J. J. (1998). Attitudes, beliefs, and other minds: shared representations in self-organizing systems. In Stephen J. Read, and Lynn C. Miller (eds.), *Connectionist models of social reasoning and social behavior*. Mahwah, NJ: Lawrence Erlbaum.

Eliade, M. (1961). *The sacred and the profane: the nature of religion*. New York: Harper & Row (Harper Torchbooks/The Cloister Library).

Ellen, R. (2011). "Indigenous knowledge" and the understanding of cultural cognition: the contribution of studies of environmental knowledge systems. In Kronenfeld, Bennardo, de Munck, and Fischer (eds.) (pp. 290–313).

Ellen, R., Parkes, P., and Bicker, A. (eds.) (2000). *Indigenous environmental knowledge and its transformations*. Amsterdam: Harwood Academic Publishers.

Ellis, C. (1989). *Expert knowledge and explanation: the knowledge–language interface*. Chichester, UK/New York: E. Horwood/Halsted Press.

Ellis, D. G. (1999). Research on social-interaction and the micro–macro issue. *Research on Language and Social Interaction*, 32(1–2), 31–40.

Endriss, C., and Hinterwimmer, S. (2008). Direct and indirect aboutness topics. *Acta Linguistica Hungarica*, 55(3–4), 297–307.

Enfield, N. J. (2011). Sources of asymmetry in human interaction: enchrony, status, knowledge and agency. In Stivers, Mondada, and Steensig (eds.) (2011b) (pp. 285–312).

Engelke, M. E. (ed.) (2009). *The objects of evidence: anthropological approaches to the production of knowledge*. Chichester, UK/Malden, MA: Wiley-Blackwell.

Engelstad, E., and Gerrard, S. (2005). *Challenging situatedness: gender, culture and the production of knowledge*. Delft: Eburon.

Englander, D. (ed.) (1990). *Culture and belief in Europe, 1450–1600: an anthology of sources*. Oxford: Blackwell.

Englebretsen, G. (2006). *Bare facts and truth: an essay on the correspondence theory of truth*. Aldershot: Ashgate.

Eraut, M. (1994). *Developing professional knowledge and competence*. London/Washington, DC: Falmer Press.

Erickson, F. (1988). Discourse coherence, participation structure, and personal display in a family dinner table conversation. *Working Papers in Educational Linguistics*, 4, 1–26.

Ericson, R. V., Baranek, P. M., and Chan, J. B. L. (1989). *Negotiating control: a study of news sources*. University of Toronto Press.

Ericsson, K. A., and Kintsch, W. (1995). Long-term working memory. *Psychological Review*, 102, 211–245.

Erman, B. (2001). Pragmatic markers revisited with a focus on *you know* in adult and adolescent talk. *Journal of Pragmatics*, 33(9), 1337–1359.

Erteschik-Shir, N. (2007). *Information structure: the syntax-discourse interface*. Oxford University Press.

Escobar, A. (1997). Anthropology and development. *International Social Science Journal*, 49(4), 497–515.

(2007). Worlds and knowledges otherwise: the Latin American modernity/coloniality research program. *Cultural Studies*, 21(2–3), 179–210.

Essed, P. (1991). *Understanding everyday racism: an interdisciplinary theory*. Newbury Park, CA: Sage.

Eveland, W. R., Marton, K., and Seo, M. Y. (2004). Moving beyond "just the facts": the influence of online news on the content and structure of public affairs knowledge. *Communication Research*, 31(1), 82–108.

Fagot, B. I., Leinbach, M. D., Hort, B. E., and Strayer, J. (1997). Qualities underlying the definitions of gender. *Sex Roles*, 37(1–2), 1–18.

Faller, M. (2006). *Evidentiality and epistemic modality at the semantics/pragmatics interface*. Paper presented at the 2006 Workshop on Philosophy and Linguistics, University of Michigan.

Fals-Borda, O. (1991). *Knowledge and social movements*. Santa Cruz, CA: Merrill.

Fanselow, G. (2008). In need of mediation: the relation between syntax and information structure. *Acta Linguistica Hungarica*, 55(3–4), 397–413.

Fardon, R. (1985). *Power and knowledge: anthropological and sociological approaches*. Proceedings of a conference held at the University of St. Andrews in December 1982. Edinburgh: Scottish Academic Press.

Fardon, R. (ed.) (1995). *Counterworks: managing the diversity of knowledge*. London/ New York: Routledge.

Farr, R. M., and Moscovici, S. (eds.) (1984). *Social representations*. Cambridge University Press.

Farrell, L. (2006). *Making knowledge common: literacy and knowledge at work*. New York: Peter Lang.

Feltham, C. (1996). Beyond denial, myth and superstition in the counselling profession. In R. Bayne, and I. Horton (eds.), *New directions in counselling* (pp. 297–308). London: Routledge.

Ferguson, H. J., and Sanford, A. J. (2008). Anomalies in real and counterfactual worlds: an eye-movement investigation. *Journal of Memory and Language*, 58(3), 609–626.

Festinger, L. (1957). *A theory of cognitive dissonance*. Stanford University Press.

Fetzer, J. S. (2000). *Public attitudes toward immigration in the United States, France, and Germany*. Cambridge University Press.

Fillmore, C. J. (1968). The case for case. In E. Bach, and R. T. Harms (eds.), *Universals in linguistic theory* (pp. 1–88). New York: Holt, Rinehart and Winston.

Fincher-Kiefer, R. (1992). The role of prior knowledge in inferential processing. *Journal of Research in Reading*, 15(1), 12–27.

Fine, E. C., and Speer, J. H. (eds.) (1992). *Performance, culture, and identity*. New York: Praeger.

Finucane, R. C. (1995). *Miracles and pilgrims: popular beliefs in medieval England*. New York: St. Martin's Press.

First, M. B., and Pincus, H. A. (1999). Definitions of schizophrenia. *British Journal of Psychiatry*, 174, 273.

Fisher, S., and Todd, A. (eds.) (1983). *The social organization of doctor–patient communication*. Washington, DC: Center for Applied Linguistics. Distributed by Ablex Publishing Corporation, Norwood, NJ.

Fiske, S. T., and Taylor, S. E. (2007). *Social cognition: from brain to culture*, 3rd edn. New York: McGraw-Hill.

Fivush, R., and Hudson, J. A. (eds.) (1990). *Knowing and remembering in young children*. Cambridge University Press.

Flick, U. (1998). Everyday knowledge in social psychology. In U. Flick (ed.), *The psychology of the social* (pp. 41–59). New York: Cambridge University Press.

Flowerdew, J., and Leong, S. (2010). Presumed knowledge in the discursive construction of socio-political and cultural identity. *Journal of Pragmatics*, 42(8), 2240–2252.

Foucault, M. (1972). *The archeology of knowledge*. London: Tavistock.

Fowler, R. (1991). *Language in the news: discourse and ideology in the press*. London/New York: Routledge.

Fox, B. A. (2001). Evidentiality: authority, responsibility, and entitlement in English conversation. *Journal of Linguistic Anthropology*, 11(2), 167–192.

Fox, E. (2009). The role of reader characteristics in processing and learning from informational text. *Review of Educational Research*, 79(1), 197–261.

Fox Tree, J. E., and Schrock, J. C. (2002). Basic meanings of *you know* and *I mean*. *Journal of Pragmatics* 34, 727–747.

Frandji, D., and Vitale, P. (eds.) (2010). *Knowledge, pedagogy, and society: international perspectives on Basil Bernstein's sociology of education*. Abingdon, Oxon/New York: Routledge.

Franks, J. J., Vye, N. J., Auble, P. M., Mezynski, K. J., Perfetto, G. A., Bransford, J. D., Stein, B. S., and Littlefield, J. (1982). Learning from explicit versus implicit texts. *Journal of Experimental Psychology: General*, 111(4), 414–422.

Fraser, C., and Gaskell, G. (eds.) (1990). *The social psychological study of widespread beliefs*. Oxford/New York: Clarendon Press/Oxford University Press.

Frazer, J. G. (1910). *Questions on the customs, beliefs, and languages of savages*. Cambridge University Press.

Frechie, S., Halbert, H. W., and McCormick, C. (2005). *The newspaper reader*. New Jersey: Pearson–Prentice Hall.

Frederiksen, C. H. (1999). Learning to reason through discourse in a problem-based learning group. *Discourse Processes*, 27(2), 135–160.

Freeden, M. (1996). *Ideologies and political theory: a conceptual approach*. Oxford/New York: Clarendon Press/Oxford University Press.

Freeden, M. (ed.) (2013). *The Oxford handbook of political ideologies*. Oxford University Press.

Freedle, R. O. (1977). *Discourse production and comprehension*. Norwood, NJ: Ablex.

Freidson, E. (1986). *Professional powers: a study of the institutionalization of formal knowledge*. University of Chicago Press.

Fricker, E. (2006). Second-hand knowledge. *Philosophy and Phenomenological Research*, 73(3), 592–618.

Friedman, W. J. (2007). The role of reminding in long-term memory for temporal order. *Memory and Cognition*, 35(1), 66–72.

Fröhlich, R., and Holtz-Bacha, C. (eds.) (2003). *Journalism education in Europe and North America: an international comparison*. Cresskill, NJ: Hampton Press.

Fuller, J. (1996). *News values: ideas for an information age*. University of Chicago Press.

Fuller, S. (1988). *Social epistemology*. Bloomington IN: Indiana University Press.
(2002). *Social epistemology*, 2nd edn. Bloomington, IN: Indiana University Press.
Furnham, A., and Chamorro-Premuzic, T. (2006). Personality, intelligence and general knowledge. *Learning and Individual Differences*, 16(1), 79–90.
Furnham, A., Christopher, A. N., Garwood, J., and Martin, G. N. (2007). Approaches to learning and the acquisition of general knowledge. *Personality and Individual Differences*, 43(6), 1563–1571.
Gabbard, D. (ed.) (2000). *Knowledge and power in the global economy: politics and the rhetoric of school reform*. Mahwah, NJ: Lawrence Erlbaum.
Gagné, E. D., and Rothkopf, E. Z. (1975). Text organization and learning goals. *Journal of Educational Psychology*, 67(3), 445–450.
Galli, I., and Nigro, G. (1990). Les représentations sociales: la question de la genèse. *Revue Internationale de Psychologie Sociale*, 3(3), 429–450.
Gallini, J. K., Seaman, M. A., and Terry, S. (1995). Metaphors and learning new text. *Journal of Reading Behavior*, 27(2), 187–199.
Gallini, J. K., Spires, H. A., Terry, S., and Gleaton, J. (1993). The influence of macro and micro-level cognitive strategies training on text learning. *Journal of Research and Development in Education*, 26(3), 164–178.
Gallistel, C. R. (ed.) (1992). *Animal cognition*. Cambridge, MA: MIT Press.
Galtung, J., and Ruge, M. H. (1965). The structure of foreign news. *Journal of Peace Research* 2, 64–91.
Gans, H. J. (1979). *Deciding what's news: a study of CBS evening news, NBC nightly news, Newsweek, and Time*. New York: Pantheon Books.
García-Carpintero, M., and Kölbel, M. (eds.) (2008). *Relative truth*. Oxford University Press.
Garfinkel, H. (1962). Common sense knowledge of social structures: the documentary method of lay/professional fact finding. In J. M. Scher (ed.), *Theories of the mind* (pp. 689–712). New York: Free Press.
Garner, R., Gillingham, M. G., and White, C. S. (1989). Effects of "seductive details" on macroprocessing and microprocessing in adults and children. *Cognition and Instruction*, 6(1), 41–57.
Garnham, A. (1987). *Mental models as representations of discourse and text*. Chichester, West Sussex, England/New York: E. Horwood Halsted Press.
Gaskell, G., and Fraser, C. (1990). The social psychological study of widespread beliefs. In C. Fraser, and G. Gaskell (eds.), *The social psychological study of widespread beliefs* (pp. 3–24). Oxford: Clarendon Press.
Gaunt, P. (1992). *Making the newsmakers: international handbook on journalism training*. Westport, CT: Greenwood Press.
Gavin, H. (1998). *The essence of cognitive psychology*. London: Prentice Hall.
Gazdar, G. (1977). *Implicature, presupposition and logical form*. Bloomington, IN: Indiana University Linguistics Club.
(1979). *Pragmatics: implicature, presupposition and logical form*. New York: Academic Press.
Gazzaniga, M. S. (1998). *The mind's past*. Berkeley, CA: University of California Press.
Geary, D. C. (2005). Folk knowledge and academic learning. In B. J. Ellis, and D. F. Bjorklund (eds.), *Origins of the social mind: evolutionary psychology and child development* (pp. 493–519). New York: Guilford Press.

Gee, J. P., and Handford, M. (eds.) (2012). *The Routledge handbook of discourse analysis*. London: Routledge.

Geertz, C. (1973). *The interpretation of cultures: selected essays*. New York: Basic Books.

(1983). *Local knowledge: further essays in interpretative anthropology*. New York: Basic Books.

Geluykens, R. (1984). *Focus phenomena in English: an empirical investigation into cleft and pseudo-cleft sentences*. Wilrijk, Belgium: Universitaire Instelling Antwerpen, Departement Germaanse, Afdeling Lingüistiek.

Genette, G. (1980). *Narrative discourse: an essay in method*. Ithaca, NY: Cornell University Press.

Gentner, D., and Stevens, A. L. (eds.) (1983). *Mental models*. Hillsdale, NJ: Lawrence Erlbaum.

Gerbner, G. (1988). *Violence and terror in the mass media*. Paris, France/Lanham, MD: Unesco/UNIPUB.

Gernsbacher, M. A., and Givón, T. (eds.) (1995). *Coherence in spontaneous text*. Amsterdam: John Benjamins.

Gernsbacher, M. A., and Robertson, D. A. (2005). Watching the brain comprehend discourse. In A. F. Healy (ed.), *Experimental cognitive psychology and its applications* (pp. 157–167). Washington, DC: American Psychological Association.

Gerrig, R. J. (1987). Relevance theory, mutual knowledge, and accidental irrelevance. *Behavioral and Brain Sciences*, 10(4), 717–718.

Gerrig, R. J., and Prentice, D. A. (1991). The representation of fictional information. *Psychological Science*, 2, 336–340.

Gertler, B. (ed.) (2003). *Privileged access: philosophical accounts of self-knowledge*. Aldershot: Ashgate.

Geurts, B., and van der Sandt, R. (2004). Interpreting focus. *Theoretical Linguistics*, 30(1), 1–44.

Gibbs, R. W. (1987). Mutual knowledge and the psychology of conversational inference. *Journal of Pragmatics*, 11(5), 561–588.

Gibbs, R. W., and Gerrig, R. J. (1989). How context makes metaphor comprehension seem "special." Special Issue: Context and metaphor comprehension. *Metaphor and Symbolic Activity*, 4(3), 145–158.

Gibson, J. J. (1986). The theory of affordances. In J. J. Gibson (ed.), *The ecological approach to visual perception* (pp. 127–143). Hillsdale, NJ: Lawrence Erlbaum.

Gibson, J., Huemer, W., and Pocci, L. (eds.) (2007). *Fiction, narrative, and knowledge: a sense of world*. London/New York: Routledge.

Giddens, A. (1986). *The constitution of society: outline of the theory of structuration*. Berkeley, CA: University of California Press.

Gigone, D., and Hastie, R. (1993). The common knowledge effect: information sharing and group judgment. *Journal of Personality and Social Psychology*, 65(5), 959–974.

Gilles, V. E., and Lucey, H. E. (2008). *Power, knowledge and the academy: the institutional is political*. New York: Palgrave Macmillan.

Gillett, G. (2003). Form and content: the role of discourse in mental disorder. In K. W. M. B. Fulford, K. Morris, J. Z. Sadler, and G. Stanghellini (eds.), *Nature and narrative: an introduction to the new philosophy of psychiatry* (pp. 139–153). New York: Oxford University Press.

Givón, T. (1989). *Mind, code, and context: essays in Pragmatics.* Hillsdale, NJ: Lawrence Erlbaum.

(2005). *Context as other minds: the pragmatics of sociality, cognition and communication.* Amsterdam: John Benjamins.

Givry, D., and Roth, W. M. (2006). Toward a new conception of conceptions: interplay of talk, gestures, and structures in the setting. *Journal of Research in Science Teaching*, 43(10), 1086–1109.

Glasgow University Media Group (1976). *Bad news.* London: Routledge & Kegan Paul.

(1980). *More bad news.* London: Routledge & Kegan Paul.

(1982). *Really bad news.* London: Writers & Readers.

(1985). *War and peace news.* Milton Keynes: Open University Press.

Glasser, C. J. (ed.) (2009). *International libel and privacy handbook: a global reference for journalists, publishers, webmasters, and lawyers.* New York: Bloomberg Press.

Glenberg, A. (1999). Why mental models must be embodied. In Rickheit, and Habel (eds.) (pp. 77–90).

Gluckman, M. (1963). Gossip and scandal. *Current Anthropology*, 4(3), 307–316.

Glynn, S. M., and Takahashi, T. (1998). Learning from analogy-enhanced science text. *Journal of Research in Science Teaching*, 35(10), 1129–1149.

Goffman, E. (1981). *Forms of talk.* University of Pennsylvania Press.

Goldenweiser, A. A. (1915). The knowledge of primitive man. *American Anthropologist*, New Series, 17(2), 240–244.

Goldman, A. I. (1986). *Epistemology and cognition.* Cambridge, MA: Harvard University Press.

(1992). *Liaisons: philosophy meets the cognitive and social sciences.* Cambridge, MA: MIT Press.

(1993). *Philosophical applications of cognitive science.* Boulder, CO: Westview Press.

(1999). *Knowledge in a social world.* Oxford, UK/New York: Clarendon Press/Oxford University Press.

(2002). *Pathways to knowledge: private and public.* Oxford University Press.

(2006). *Simulating minds: the philosophy, psychology, and neuroscience of mindreading.* Oxford University Press.

Goldman, S. R. (1997). Learning from text: reflections on the past and suggestions for the future. *Discourse Processes*, 23(3), 357–398.

Goldman, S. R., and Bisanz, G. L. (2002). Toward a functional analysis of scientific genres: implications for understanding and learning processes. In Jose A. Leon, and Jose Otero (eds.), *The psychology of science text comprehension* (pp. 19–50). Mahwah, NJ: Lawrence Erlbaum.

Goldman, S. R., and Rakestraw, J. A. J. (2000). Structural aspects of constructing meaning from text. In Michael L. Kamil, and Peter B. Mosenthal (eds.), *Handbook of reading research*, vol. 3 (pp. 311–335). Mahwah, NJ: Lawrence Erlbaum.

Goldman, S. R., and Varma, S. (1995). CAPping the construction-integration model of discourse comprehension. In C. Weaver, S. Mannes, and C. Fletcher (eds.), *Discourse comprehension: essays in honor of Walter Kintsch* (pp. 337–358). Hillsdale, NJ: Lawrence Erlbaum.

References   355

Goldman, S. R., Graesser, A. C., and van den Broek, P. (eds.) (1999). *Narrative comprehension, causality, and coherence: essays in honor of Tom Trabasso.* Mahwah, NJ: Lawrence Erlbaum.

Good, B. (1994). *Medicine, rationality, and experience: an anthropological perspective.* Cambridge University Press.

Goodenough, W. H. (1964). Cultural anthropology and linguistics. In D. Hymes (ed.), *Reader in Linguistics and Anthropology* (pp. 36–39). New York: Harper & Row.

Goody, E. N. (ed.) (1978). *Questions and politeness: strategies in social interaction.* Cambridge University Press.

Goodyear, P., and Zenios, M. (2007). Discussion, collaborative knowledge work and epistemic fluency. *British Journal of Educational Studies,* 55(4), 351–368.

Goutsos, D. (1997). *Modeling discourse topic: sequential relations and strategies in expository text.* Norwood, NJ: Ablex.

Graber, D. A. (1984). *Processing the news: how people tame the information tide.* New York: Longman.

(2001). *Processing politics: learning from television in the Internet age.* University of Chicago Press.

Graesser, A. C., and Bower, G. H. (eds.) (1990). *Inferences and text comprehension: the psychology of learning and motivation,* vol. 25. New York: Academic Press.

Graesser, A. C., Gernsbacher, M. A., and Goldman, S. R. (eds.) (2003). *Handbook of discourse processes.* Mahwah, NJ: Lawrence Erlbaum.

Graetz, B. (1986). Social structure and class consciousness: facts, fictions and fantasies. *Australian and New Zealand Journal of Sociology,* 22(1), 46–64.

Graham, P. J. (2000). Transferring knowledge. *Nous,* 34(1), 131–152.

Greco, J. (2010). *Achieving knowledge: a virtue-theoretic account of epistemic normativity.* New York: Cambridge University Press.

Greco, J., and Sosa, E. (eds.) (1999). *The Blackwell guide to epistemology.* Malden, MA: Blackwell.

Greenberg, G., and Tobach, E. (eds.) (1990). *Theories of the evolution of knowing.* Hillsdale, NJ: Lawrence Erlbaum.

Greene, J. O., and Cappella, J. N. (1986). Cognition and talk: the relationship of semantic units to temporal patterns of fluency in spontaneous speech. *Language and Speech,* 29(2), 141–157.

Greenwood, S. (2009). *The anthropology of magic.* Oxford/New York: Berg.

Gregory, J., and Miller, S. (1998). *Science in public: communication, culture and credibility.* New York: Plenum.

Grice, H. P. (1975). Logic and conversation. In P. Cole, and J. Morgan (eds.), *Syntax and semantics,* vol. 3: Speech acts (pp. 68–134). New York: Academic Press.

(1989). *Studies in the way of words.* Cambridge, MA: Harvard University Press.

Groenendijk, J. A. G., de Jongh, D., and Stokhof, M. B. J. (1987). *Studies in discourse representation theory and the theory of generalized quantifiers.* Dordrecht: Foris.

Grosfoguel, R. (2007). The epistemic decolonial turn: beyond political-economy paradigms. *Cultural Studies,* 21(2–3), 211–223.

Gruber, H. (1993). Political language and textual vagueness. *Pragmatics,* 3(1), 1–29.

Gubrium, J. F., and Holstein, J. A. (2009). *Analyzing narrative reality.* Thousand Oaks, CA: Sage.

Guéraud, S., Harmon, M. E., and Peracchi, K. A. (2005). Updating situation models: the memory-based contribution. *Discourse Processes,* 39(2–3), 243–263.

Guilhon, B. (ed.) (2001). *Technology and markets for knowledge: knowledge creation, diffusion, and exchange within a growing economy.* Boston, MA: Kluwer Academic.

Gumperz, J. J. (1962). Types of linguistic community. *Anthropological Linguistics* 4, 28–40.

(1982a). *Discourse strategies.* Cambridge University Press.

Gumperz, J. J. (ed.) (1982b). *Language and social identity.* Cambridge University Press.

Gumperz, J. J., and Hymes, D. (eds.) (1972). *Directions in sociolinguistics: the ethnography of communication.* New York: Holt, Rinehart and Winston.

Gumperz, J. J., and Levinson, S. C. (eds.) (1994). *Rethinking linguistic relativity.* Cambridge University Press.

Guri-Rozenblit, S. (1988). The interrelations between diagrammatic representations and verbal explanations in learning from social science texts. *Instructional Science,* 17(3), 219–234.

Gussenhoven, C. (2008). Notions and subnotions in information structure. *Acta Linguistica Hungarica,* 55(3–4), 381–395.

Guzzetti, B. J. (2001). Texts and talk: the role of gender in learning physics. In E. B. Moje, and D. G. O'Brien (eds.), *Constructions of literacy: studies of teaching and learning in and out of secondary schools* (pp. 125–146). Mahwah, NJ: Lawrence Erlbaum.

Haarmann, H. (2007). *Foundations of culture: knowledge-construction, belief systems and worldview in their dynamic interplay.* Frankfurt am Main: Peter Lang.

Haas, A., and Sherman, M. A. (1982). Conversational topic as a function of role and gender. *Psychological Reports,* 51(2), 453–454.

Haas, P. (1992). Introduction: epistemic communities and international policy coordination. *International Organization,* 46(1), 1–35.

Hachten, W. A., and Scotton, J. F. (2002). *The world news prism: global media in an era of terrorism.* Ames, IA: Iowa State Press.

Haddock, A., Millar, A., and Pritchard, D. (eds.) (2010). *Social epistemology.* Oxford University Press.

Haenggi, D., and Perfetti, C. A. (1992). Individual differences in reprocessing of text. *Journal of Educational Psychology,* 84(2), 182–192.

Hagemann, T. A., and Grinstein, J. (1997). The mythology of aggregate corporate knowledge: a deconstruction. *George Washington Law Review,* 65(2), 210–247.

Haghighat, C. (1988). *Le racisme "scientifique": offensive contre l'égalité sociale.* Paris: L'Harmattan.

Hahlweg, K., and Hooker, C. A. (eds.) (1989). *Issues in evolutionary epistemology.* Albany, NY: State University of New York Press.

Hajičová, E., Partee, B. H., and Sgall, P. (eds.) (1996). *Discourse and meaning. Papers in honor of Eva Hajičová.* Amsterdam: John Benjamins.

Halliday, M. A. K., and Hasan, R. (1976). *Cohesion in English.* London: Longman.

Halualani, R. T., and Nakayama, T. K. (2010). Critical intercultural communication studies: at a crossroads. In Nakayama and Halualani (eds.), (pp. 1–16).

Hambrick, D. Z., Meinz, E. J., and Oswald, F. L. (2007). Individual differences in current events knowledge: contributions of ability, personality, and interests. *Memory and Cognition,* 35(2), 304–316.

Hames, R. (2007). The ecologically noble savage debate. *Annual Review of Anthropology,* 36, 177–190.

Hamilton, P. (1974). *Knowledge and social structure: an introduction to the classical argument in the sociology of knowledge*. London: Routledge & Kegan Paul.

Hamilton, R. J. (1997). Effects of three types of elaboration on learning concepts from text. *Contemporary Educational Psychology*, 22(3), 299–318.

Hanks, P. (2011). Structured propositions as types. *Mind*, 120, 11–52.

Hanks, W. F. (1989). Text and textuality. *Annual Review of Anthropology*, 18, 95–127.

Hanson, F. A. (1979). Does God have a body? Truth, reality and cultural relativism. *Man*, 14(3), 515–529.

Hargreaves, D. H. (1984). Teachers' questions: open, closed and half-open. *Educational Research*, 26(1), 46–51.

Harindranath, R. (2009). *Audience–citizens: the media, public knowledge and interpretive practice*. Thousand Oaks, CA: Sage.

Harp, S. F., and Mayer, R. E. (1997). The role of interest in learning from scientific text and illustrations: on the distinction between emotional interest and cognitive interest. *Journal of Educational Psychology*, 89(1), 92–102.

Harris, M. (ed.) (2007). *Ways of knowing: anthropological approaches to crafting experience and knowledge*. New York: Berghahn Books.

Hart, C. (2011). Legitimizing assertions and the logico-rhetorical module: evidence and epistemic vigilance in media discourse on immigration. *Discourse Studies*, 13(6), 751–769.

Hartmann, P. G., and Husband, C. (1974). *Racism and the mass media: a study of the role of the mass media in the formation of white beliefs and attitudes in Britain*. Totowa, NJ: Rowman & Littlefield.

Harwood, N. (2005). 'We do not seem to have a theory... The theory I present here attempts to fill this gap': inclusive and exclusive pronouns in academic writing. *Applied Linguistics*, 26(3), 343–375.

(2007). Political scientists on the functions of personal pronouns in their writing: an interview-based study of 'I' and 'we.' *Text and Talk*, 27(1), 27–54.

Hastie, R., Park, B., and Weber, R. (1984). Social memory. In Wyer, and Srull (eds.), vol. 2 (pp. 151–212).

Haugeland, J. (1998). *Having thought: essays in the metaphysics of mind*. Cambridge, MA: Harvard University Press.

Havens, N., and Ashida, T. (1994). *Folk beliefs in modern Japan*. Tokyo: Institute for Japanese Culture and Classics, Kokugakuin University.

Haviland, J. (1987). *Fighting words: evidential particles, affect and argument*. Proceedings of the Thirteenth Annual Meeting of the Berkeley Linguistics Society. Berkeley, CA: Berkeley Linguistics Society.

Haworth, K. (2006). The dynamics of power and resistance in police interview discourse. *Discourse and Society*, 17(6), 739–759.

Hazlehurst, B. (2011). The distributed cognition model of mind. In Kronenfeld, Bennardo, de Munck, and Fischer (eds.) (pp. 471–488).

Hazlett, A. (2009). Knowledge and conversation. *Philosophy and Phenomenological Research*, 78(3), 591–620.

Heider, F. (1946). Attitudes and cognitive organization. *Journal of Psychology*, 21, 107–112.

(1958). *The psychology of interpersonal relations*. New York: Wiley.

Hekman, S. J. (1986). *Hermeneutics and the sociology of knowledge*. University of Notre Dame Press.

Heldner, M., and Edlund, J. (2010). Pauses, gaps and overlaps in conversations. *Journal of Phonetics*, 38(4), 555–568.

Heritage, J. (2011). Territories of knowledge, territories of experience: empathic moments in interaction. In Stivers, Mondada and Steensig (eds.) (2011b) (pp. 42–68).

(2012a). Epistemics in action: action formation and territories of knowledge. *Research on Language and Social Interaction*, 45(1), 1–29.

(2012b). The epistemic engine: sequence organization and territories of knowledge. *Research on Language and Social Interaction*, 45(1), 30–52.

Heritage, J., and Raymond, G. (2005). The terms of agreement: indexing epistemic authority and subordination in assessment sequences. *Social Psychology Quarterly*, 68(1), 15–38.

Herman, D. (ed.) (2003). *Narrative theory and the cognitive sciences*. Stanford, CA: CSLI.

Hewstone, M., Stroebe, W., and Jonas, K. (eds.) (2008). *Introduction to social psychology*. Malden, MA: Blackwell.

Heydon, G. (2005). *The language of police interviewing: a critical analysis*. Houndsmill: Palgrave.

Hidi, S. E. (1995). A reexamination of the role of attention in learning from text. *Educational Psychology Review*, 7(4), 323–350.

Hijzen, D., Boekaerts, M., and Vedder, P. (2006). The relationship between the quality of cooperative learning, students' goal preferences, and perceptions of contextual factors in the classroom. *Scandinavian Journal of Psychology*, 47(1), 9–21.

Hill, J. H., and Irvine, J. T. (eds.) (1993). *Responsibility and evidence in oral discourse*. Cambridge University Press.

Hill, J. H., and Mannheim, B. (1992). Language and world view. *Annual Review of Anthropology* 21, 381–406.

Himmelweit, H. T. (1990). Societal psychology: implications and scope. In Himmelweit, and Gaskell (eds.) (pp. 17–45).

Himmelweit, H. T., and Gaskell, G. (eds.) (1990). *Societal psychology*. London: Sage.

Hobbs, J. R. (1985). *On the coherence and structure of discourse*. Report No. CSLI-85–37, Center for the Study of Language and Information, Stanford University.

Hofer, B. K., and Pintrich, P. R. (eds.) (2002). *Personal epistemology: the psychology of beliefs about knowledge and knowing*. Mahwah, NJ: Lawrence Erlbaum.

Hoffmann, G. A. (2007). The semantic theory of truth: Field's incompleteness objection. *Philosophia*, 35(2), 161–170.

Hogg, M. A., and Abrams, D. (eds.) (2001). *Intergroup relations: essential readings*. Philadelphia, PA: Psychology Press.

Holland, D., and Quinn, N. (eds.) (1987). *Cultural models in language and thought*. New York: Cambridge University Press.

Holmes, J. (1995). *Women, men and politeness*. New York: Longman.

Holstein, J. A., and Gubrium, J. F. (1995). *The active interview*. Thousand Oaks, CA: Sage.

Holyoak, K. J., and Gordon, P. C. (1984). Information processing and social cognition. In Wyer, and Srull (eds.), vol. 1.

Holyoak, K. J., and Thagard, P. (1995). *Mental leaps: analogy in creative thought*. Cambridge, MA: MIT Press.

Hood, B. M., and Santos, L. (eds.) (2009). *The origins of object knowledge*. Oxford University Press.

Hopper, R. (ed.) (1991). Ethnography and conversation analysis after Talking Culture. *Research on Language and Social Interaction* 24, 161–387.

Horowitz, M. H., Milbrath, C., Reidbord, S., and Stinson, C. (1993). Elaboration and dyselaboration: measures of expression and defense in discourse. *Psychotherapy Research*, 3(4), 278–293.

Horton, W. S., and Gerrig, R. J. (2005). The impact of memory demands on audience design during language production. *Cognition*, 96(2), 127–142.

Horton, W. S., and Keysar, B. (1996). When do speakers take into account common ground? *Cognition*, 59(1), 91–117.

Horvath, J. A., and Sternberg, R. J. (eds.) (1999). *Tacit knowledge in professional practice: researcher and practitioner perspectives*. Mahwah, NJ: Lawrence Erlbaum.

Horwich, P. (1990). *Truth*. Oxford University Press.

Hosseini, S. A. H. (2010). *Alternative globalizations: an integrative approach to studying dissident knowledge in the global justice movement*. London: Routledge.

Hotter, M., and Tancred, P. (eds.) (1993). *Engendering knowledge: the impact of feminism on the academy*. Montreal: McGill Centre for Research and Teaching on Women.

Hudson, J. A., and Nelson, K. (1986). Repeated encounters of a similar kind – effects of familiarity on children's autobiographical memory. *Cognitive Development*, 3, 253–271.

Hughes, C., and Dunn, J. (1998). Understanding mind and emotion: longitudinal associations with mental-state talk between young friends. *Developmental Psychology*, 34(5), 1026–1037.

Hughes, G., and Cresswell, M. (1968). *An introduction to modal logic*. London: Methuen.

Hulteng, J. L. (1979). *The news media: what makes them tick?*. Englewood Cliffs, NJ: Prentice Hall.

Hultman, G., and Horberg, C. R. (1998). Knowledge competition and personal ambition: a theoretical framework for knowledge utilization and action in context. *Science Communication*, 19(4), 328–348.

Hume, D. (1750). Philosophical essays concerning human understanding. London: A. Millar.

Hutchins, E. (1995). *Cognition in the wild*. Cambridge, MA: MIT Press.

Hyland, K. (1998). *Hedging in scientific research articles*. Amsterdam: John Benjamins.

Hymes, D. (1962). The ethnography of speaking. In T. Gladwin, and W. C. Sturtevant (eds.), *Anthropology and Human Behavior* (pp. 13–53). Washington, DC: Anthropological Society of Washington.

Hymes, D. (ed.) (1972). *Reinventing anthropology*. New York: Vintage Books.

Hymes, D. (1974). Ways of speaking. In R. Bauman, and J. Sherzer (eds.), *Explorations in the ethnography of speaking* (pp. 433–451). Cambridge University Press.

(1996). *Ethnography, Linguistics, narrative inequality: toward an understanding of voice*. London: Taylor & Francis.

Ichikawa, J., and Jarvis, B. (2012). Rational imagination and modal knowledge. *Nous*, 46(1), 127–158.

Iding, M. K. (1997). How analogies foster learning from science texts. *Instructional Science*, 25(4), 233–253.

Ilie, C. (1994). *What else can I tell you? A pragmatic study of English rhetorical questions as discursive and argumentative acts*. Stockholm: Almqvist and Wiksell.

Ismael, J. T. (2007). *The situated self*. Oxford University Press.

Jackendoff, R. (2003). *Foundations of language: brain, meaning, grammar, evolution*. Oxford University Press.

Jackson, F. (2002). Language, thought and the epistemic theory of vagueness. *Language and Communication*, 22(3), 269–279.

Jacobi, D. (1986). *Diffusion et vulgarisation: Itinéraires du texte scientifique*. Paris: Les Belles Lettres.

Jacobs, J. (2004). Focus, presuppositions, and discourse restrictions. *Theoretical Linguistics*, 30(1), 99–110.

Jacobson, N. (2007). Social epistemology: theory for the "Fourth wave" of knowledge transfer and exchange research. *Science Communication*, 29(1), 116–127.

Jäger, S. (1989). Rechtsextreme Propaganda heute. In K. Ehlich (ed.), *Sprache im Faschismus* (pp. 289–322). Frankfurt: Suhrkamp.

Jäger, S., and Link, J. (1993). *Die vierte Gewalt. Rassismus und die Medien*. (The Fourth Power. Racism and the Media). Duisburg: DISS.

Jahoda, G. (1998). *Images of savages: ancient roots of modern prejudice in Western culture*. London/New York: Routledge.

Jansen, S. C. (2002). *Critical communication theory new media, science, technology, and gender*. Lanham, MD: Rowman & Littlefield.

Jaspars, J. M. F., and Fraser, C. (1984). Attitudes and social representations. In Farr, and Moscovici (eds.) (pp. 101–124).

Jaworski, A., Fitzgerald, R., and Morris, D. (2003). Certainty and speculation in news reporting of the future: the execution of Timothy McVeigh. *Discourse Studies*, 5(1), 33–49.

Jefferson, G. (1978). Sequential aspects of storytelling in conversation. In J. Schenkein (ed.), *Studies in the organization of conversational interaction* (pp. 219–248). New York: Academic Press.

Jeong, A., and Lee, J. M. (2008). The effects of active versus reflective learning style on the processes of critical discourse in computer-supported collaborative argumentation. *British Journal of Educational Technology*, 39(4), 651–665.

Jeong, H., and Chi, M. T. H. (1997). Construction of shared knowledge during collaborative learning. In Rogers Hall, Naomi Miyake & Noel Enyedy (eds), *Proceedings of the 2nd International Conference on Computer Support for Collaborative Learning*. International Society of the Learning Sciences.

(2007). Knowledge convergence and collaborative learning. *Instructional Science*, 35(4), 287–315.

Jodelet, D. (ed.) (1989). *Les représentations sociales*. Paris: Presses Universitaires de France.

Jodelet, D. (2008). Social representations: the beautiful invention. *Journal for the Theory of Social Behaviour*, 38(4), 411–430.

Johnson, J. C., and Griffith, D. C. (1996). Pollution, food safety, and the distribution of knowledge. *Human Ecology*, 24(1), 87–108.

Johnson, M. K. (2007). Memory and reality. *American Psychologist*, November, 760–771.

Johnson, M. K., and Raye, C. L. (2000). Cognitive and brain mechanisms of false memories and beliefs. In Schacter, and Scarry (eds.) (pp. 35–86).

Johnson, S. (2012). *Indigenous knowledge*. Cambridge, UK: White Horse Press.

Johnson-Laird, P. N. (1983). *Mental models: towards a cognitive science of language, inference, and consciousness*. Cambridge, MA: Harvard University Press.

Johnson-Laird, P. N., and Garnham, A. (1980). Descriptions and discourse models. *Linguistics and Philosophy*, 3(3), 371–393.

Johnson-Laird, P. N., Oakhill, J., and Garnham, A. (eds.) (1996). *Mental models in cognitive science. Essays in honour of Phil Johnson-Laird*. Hove: Psychology Press.

Jones, B., and Miller, B. (2007). *Innovation diffusion in the new economy: the tacit component*. New York: Routledge.

Joshi, S. T. (ed.) (2006). *In her place: a documentary history of prejudice against women*. Amherst, NY: Prometheus Books.

Jost, J. T. (2006). The end of the end of ideology. *American Psychologist*, 61(7), 651–670.

(2009). "Elective affinities": on the psychological bases of left-right differences. *Psychological Inquiry*, 20(2–3), 129–141.

Jost, J. T., and Banaji, M. R. (1994). The role of stereotyping in system-justification and the production of false consciousness. Special Issue: Stereotypes: Structure, function and process. *British Journal of Social Psychology*, 33(1), 1–27.

Jost, J. T., and Major, B. (eds.) (2001). *The psychology of legitimacy: emerging perspectives on ideology, justice, and intergroup relations*. New York: Cambridge University Press.

Jost, J. T., Nosek, B. A., and Gosling, S. D. (2008). Ideology: its resurgence in social, personality, and political psychology. *Perspectives on Psychological Science*, 3(2), 126–136.

Jovchelovitch, S. (2007). *Knowledge in context: representations, community and culture*. New York: Routledge/Taylor & Francis Group.

Jucker, A. H., Smith, S. W., and Ludge, T. (2003). Interactive aspects of vagueness in conversation. *Journal of Pragmatics*, 35(12), 1737–1769.

Kadmon, N. (2001). *Formal pragmatics: semantics, pragmatics, presupposition, and focus*. Oxford: Blackwell.

Kalyuga, S., Chandler, P., and Sweller, J. (2004). When redundant on-screen text in multimedia technical instruction clan interfere with learning. *Human Factors*, 46(3), 567–581.

Kamalski, J., Sanders, T., and Lentz, L. (2008). Coherence marking, prior knowledge, and comprehension of informative and persuasive texts: sorting things out. *Discourse Processes*, 45(4–5), 323–345.

Kamio, A. (1997). *Territory of information*. Amsterdam: John Benjamins.

Kamp, H., and Partee, B. H. (eds.) (2004). *Context-dependence in the analysis of linguistic meaning*. Amsterdam/Boston: Elsevier.

Kamp, H., and Reyle, U. (1993). *From discourse to logic: introduction to model-theoretic semantics of natural language, formal logic and discourse representation theory*. Dordrecht: Kluwer Academic.

Kanuka, H. (2005). An exploration into facilitating higher levels of learning in a text-based internet learning environment using diverse instructional strategies. *Journal of Computer-Mediated Communication*, 10(3), online.

Kapoor, D., and Shizha, E. (eds.) (2010). *Indigenous knowledge and learning in Asia/ Pacific and Africa: perspectives on development, education, and culture.* New York: Palgrave Macmillan.

Kärkkäinen, E. (2003). *Epistemic stance in English conversation: a description of its interactional functions, with a focus on I think.* Amsterdam: John Benjamins.

Karseth, B., and Nerland, M. (2007). Building professionalism in a knowledge society: examining discourses of knowledge in four professional associations. *Journal of Education and Work,* 20(4), 335–355.

Karttunen, L. (1974). Presuppositions and linguistic context. *Theoretical Linguistics,* 1, 181–194.

Kaše, R., Paauwe, J., and Zupan, N. (2009). HR practices, interpersonal relations, and intrafirm knowledge transfer in knowledge-intensive firms: a social network perspective. *Human Resource Management,* 48(4), 615–639.

Kausler, D. H., and Hakami, M. K. (1983). Memory for topics of conversation: adult age differences and intentionality. *Experimental Aging Research,* 9(3), 153–157.

Keesing, R. M. (1979). Linguistic knowledge and cultural knowledge: some doubts and speculations. *American Anthropologist,* 81(1), 14–36.

(1987). Models, "folk" and "cultural": paradigms regained? In Holland, and Quinn (eds.) (pp. 369–393).

(1992). *Custom and confrontation: the Kwaio struggle for cultural autonomy.* University of Chicago Press.

Keevallik, L. (2011). The terms of not knowing. In Stivers, Mondada and Steensig (eds.) (2011b) (pp. 184–206).

Kehler, A. (2004). Discourse topics, sentence topics, and coherence. *Theoretical Linguistics,* 30(2–3), 227–240.

Keil, F. C. (1979). *Semantic and conceptual development: an ontological perspective.* Cambridge, MA: Harvard University Press.

(1998). Cognitive science and the origins of thought and knowledge. In W. Damon, and R. M. Lerner (eds.), *Handbook of child psychology,* vol. 1: Theorectical models of human development, 5th edn., (pp. 341–413). Hoboken, NJ: John Wiley & Sons.

Keller, R. (2005). *Die diskursive Konstruktion von Wirklichkeit. Zum Verhältnis von Wissenssoziologie und Diskursforschung.* Konstanz: UVK.

Kellermann, K. (1987). Information exchange in social interaction. In M. E. Roloff, and G. R. Miller (eds.), *Interpersonal processes: new directions in communication research. Sage annual reviews of communication research,* vol. 14 (pp. 188–219). Newbury Park, CA: Sage.

Kellermann, K., and Palomares, N. A. (2004). Topical profiling: emergent, co-occurring, and relationally defining topics in talk. *Journal of Language and Social Psychology,* 23(3), 308–337.

Kelsh, D., Hill, D., and Macrine, S. L. (eds.) (2010). *Class in education: knowledge, pedagogy, subjectivity.* New York: Routledge.

Kempson, R. M. (1975). *Presupposition and the delimitation of semantics.* Cambridge University Press.

Kendeou, P., and van den Broek, P. (2007). The effects of prior knowledge and text structure on comprehension processes during reading of scientific texts. *Memory and Cognition,* 35(7), 1567–1577.

Kennedy, M. L., and Smith, H. M. (1994). *Reading and writing in the academic community*. Englewood Cliffs, NJ: Prentice Hall.

Kerlinger, F. N. (1984). *Liberalism and conservatism: the nature and structure of social attitudes*. Hillsdale, NJ: Lawrence Erlbaum.

Keysar, B. (1997). Unconfounding common ground. *Discourse Processes*, 24(2–3), 253–270.

Keysar, B., and Horton, S. W. (1998). Speaking with common ground: from principles to processes in pragmatics. A reply to Polichak and Gerrig. *Cognition*, 66, 191–198.

Keysar, B., Barr, D. J., Balin, J. A., and Brauner, J. S. (2000). Taking perspective in conversation: the role of mutual knowledge in comprehension. *Psychological Sciences*, 11, 32–38.

Keysar, B., Barr, D. J., Balin, J. A., and Paek, T. S. (1998). Definite reference and mutual knowledge: process models of common ground in comprehension. *Journal of Memory and Language*, 39(1), 1–20.

Khine, M. S. E. (2008). *Knowing, knowledge and beliefs: epistemological studies across diverse cultures*. New York: Springer Science + Business Media.

Kidwell, M. (2009). What happened? An epistemics of before and after in at-the-scene police questioning. *Research on Language and Social Interaction*, 42(1), 20–41.

Kidwell, M., and Martinez, E. G. (2010). 'Let me tell you about myself': a method for suppressing subject talk in a 'soft accusation' interrogation. *Discourse Studies*, 12(1), 65–89.

Kikoski, C. K., and Kikoski, J. F. (2004). *The inquiring organization: tacit knowledge, conversation, and knowledge creation: skills for 21st-century organizations*. Westport, CT: Praeger.

Kim, S. I., and van Dusen, L. M. (1998). The role of prior knowledge and elaboration in text comprehension and memory: a comparison of self-generated elaboration and text-provided elaboration. *The American Journal of Psychology*, 111(3), 353–378.

King, D. J. (1973). Influence of exposure interval and interitem interval on the learning of connected discourse. *Journal of Experimental Psychology*, 97(2), 258–260.

King, J. C. (2007). *The nature and structure of content*. Oxford University Press.

King, N. A. (2000). *Memory, narrative, identity: remembering the self*. Edinburgh University Press.

Kintsch, W. (1974). *The representation of meaning in memory*. Hillsdale, NJ: Lawrence Erlbaum.

  (1980). Learning from a text, levels of comprehension, or: why anyone would read a story anyway. *Poetics*, 9, 87–98.

  (1988). The role of knowledge in discourse comprehension: a construction–integration model. *Psychological Review*, 95(2), 163–182.

  (1994). The psychology of discourse processing. In M. A. Gernsbacher (ed.), *Handbook of psycholinguistics* (pp. 721–739). San Diego, CA: Academic Press.

  (1998). *Comprehension: a paradigm for cognition*. New York: Cambridge University Press.

Kintsch, W., and Franzke, M. (1995). The role of background knowledge in the recall of a news story. In Lorch, and O'Brien (eds.) (pp. 321–333).

Kintsch, W., and van Dijk, T. A. (1978). Toward a model of text comprehension and production. *Psychological Review*, 85(5), 363–394.

Kintsch, W., McNamara, D. S., Dennis, S., and Landauer, T. K. (2007). LSA and meaning: in theory and application. In T. Landauer, D. S. McNamara, S. Dennis, and W. Kintsch (eds.), *Handbook of latent semantic analysis* (pp. 467–479). Mahwah, NJ: Lawrence Erlbaum.

Kirk, R. (1999). *Relativism and reality: a contemporary introduction*. London: Routledge.

Kirkham, R. L. (1992). *Theories of truth: a critical introduction*. Cambridge, MA: MIT Press.

Kirwen, M. C. (ed.) (2005). *African cultural knowledge: themes and embedded beliefs*. Nairobi: MIAS Books.

Klandermans, B. (1997). *The social psychology of protest*. Oxford: Blackwell.

Kleiber, G. (1990). *La sémantique du prototype: catégories et sens lexical*. Paris: Presses universitaires de France.

Kniffka, H. (2008). Basic notions of information structure. *Acta Linguistica Hungarica*. 55(3–4), 243–276.

Knight, C., Studdert-Kennedy, M., and Hurford, J. R. (eds.) (2000). *The evolutionary emergence of language: social function and the origins of linguistic form*. Cambridge University Press.

Knorr Cetina, K. (1999). *Epistemic cultures: how the sciences make knowledge*. Cambridge, MA: Harvard University Press.

Knotek, S., Sauer-Lee, A., and Lowe-Greenlee, B. (2009). Consultee-centered consultation as a vehicle for knowledge diffusion and utilization. In S. Rosenfield, and V. Berninger (eds.), *Implementing evidence-based academic interventions in school settings* (pp. 233–252). New York: Oxford University Press.

Knott, A., Oberlander, J., O'Donnell, M., and Mellish, C. (2001). Beyond elaboration: the interaction of relations and focus in coherent text. In T. Sanders, J. Schilperoord, and W. Spooren (eds.), *Text representation: linguistic and psycholinguistic aspects* (pp. 181–196). Amsterdam: John Benjamins.

Knowlton, B. J. (1998). The relationship between remembering and knowing: a cognitive neuroscience perspective. *Acta Psychologica*, 98(2–3), 253–265.

Knudsen, S. (2005). Communicating novel and conventional scientific metaphors: a study of the development of the metaphor of genetic code. *Public Understanding of Science*, 14(4), 373–392.

Kobayashi, K. (2009). The influence of topic knowledge, external strategy use, and college experience on students' comprehension of controversial texts. *Learning and Individual Differences*, 19(1), 130–134.

Kockelman, P. (2006). Representations of the world: memories, perceptions, beliefs, intentions and plans. *Semiotica*, 162(1/4), 73–125.

Kompus, K., Olsson, C. J., Larsson, A., and Nyberg, L. (2009). Dynamic switching between semantic and episodic memory systems. *Neuropsychologia*, 47, 2252–2260.

Komter, M. L. (1995). The distribution of knowledge in courtroom interaction. In P. Ten Have, and G. Psathas (eds), *Situated order: studies in the social organization of talk and embodied activities* (pp. 107–128). Washington, DC: University Press of America.

(1998). *Dilemmas in the courtroom: a study of trials of violent crime in the Netherlands*. Mahwah, NJ: Lawrence Erlbaum.

Kopperman, R. (1972). *Model theory and its applications*. Boston, MA: Allyn & Bacon.

Koriat, A., and Goldsmith, M. (1994). Memory in naturalistic and laboratory contexts: distinguishing the accuracy-oriented and quantity-oriented approaches to memory assessment. *Journal of Experimental Psychology: General*, 123(3), 297–315.

Kornblith, H. (1993). *Inductive inference and its natural ground: an essay in naturalistic epistemology*. Cambridge, MA: MIT Press.

Kornblith, H. (ed.) (1994). *Naturalizing epistemology*. Cambridge, MA: MIT Press.

Kornblith, H. (2002). *Knowledge and its place in nature*. Oxford/Toronto: Clarendon Press/Oxford University Press.

Koshik, I. (2005). *Beyond rhetorical questions: assertive questions in everyday interaction*. Amsterdam: John Benjamins.

Kövecses, Z. (2005). *Metaphor in culture: universality and variation*. Cambridge University Press.

(2009). The effect of context on the use of metaphor in discourse. *Iberica*, 17, 11–23.

Koven, M. (2009). Managing relationships and identities through forms of address: what French–Portuguese bilinguals call their parents in each language. *Language and Communication*, 29(4), 343–365.

Kozminsky, E. (1977). Altering comprehension: the effect of biasing titles on text comprehension. *Memory and Cognition*, 5(4), 482–490.

Kraus, S. (ed.) (1990). *Mass communication and political information processing*. Hillsdale, NJ: Lawrence Erlbaum.

Krauss, R. M., and Fussell, S. R. (1990). Mutual knowledge and communicative effectiveness. In J. Galegher, R. E. Kraut, and C. Egido (eds.), *Intellectual teamwork: social and technological foundations of cooperative work* (pp. 111–145). Hillsdale, NJ: Lawrence Erlbaum.

Kraut, R. E., and Higgins, E. T. (1984). Communication and social cognition. In Wyer, and Srull (eds.) vol. 3.

Kroeber, A. L., and Kluckhohn, C. (1952). *Culture: a critical review of concepts and definitions*. Cambridge, MA: Papers of the Peabody Museum, Harvard University, vol. 47, no. 1.

Kronenfeld, D. B., Bennardo, G., de Munck, V. C., and Fischer, M. D. (eds.) (2011). *A companion to cognitive anthropology*. Chichester: Wiley.

Kruglanski, A. W. (1989). *Lay epistemics and human knowledge: cognitive and motivational bases*. New York: Plenum Press.

Kuhn, D. (1996). Is good thinking scientific thinking? In D. R. Olson, and N. Torrance (eds.), *Modes of thought: explorations in culture and cognition* (pp. 261–281). Cambridge University Press.

Kuper, A. (1999). *Culture: the anthropologists' account*. Cambridge, MA: Harvard University Press.

(2003). The return of the native. *Current Anthropology*, 44(3), 389–402.

Kurtz-Costes, B., Rowley, S. J., Harris-Britt, A., and Woods, T. A. (2008). Gender stereotypes about mathematics and science and self-perceptions of ability in late childhood and early adolescence. *Merrill-Palmer Quarterly: Journal of Developmental Psychology*, 54, 386–410.

Kurzon, D. (1988). Prolegomena to a speech act approach to hearsay evidence. *International Journal for the Semiotics of Law/Revue Internationale de Semiotique Juridique*, 1(3), 263–273.

Labov, W. (1972a). *Language in the inner city: studies in the Black English Vernacular*. University of Pennsylvania Press.

(1972b). *Sociolinguistic patterns*. University of Pennsylvania Press.

Labov, W., and Waletzky, J. (1967). Narrative analysis: oral versions of personal experience. In J. Helm (ed.), *Essays on the verbal and visual arts* (pp. 12–44). University of Washington Press.

Lackey, J. (1999). Testimonial knowledge and transmission (considerations on the epistemology of testimony and cognition). *Philosophical Quarterly*, 49(197), 471–490.

LaFollette, M. C. (2008). *Science on the air: popularizers and personalities on radio and early television*. University of Chicago Press.

Lakoff, G. (1987). *Women, fire and dangerous things: what categories reveal about the mind*. University of Chicago Press.

(2004). *Don't think of an elephant! Know your values and frame the debate: the essential guide for progressives*. White River Junction, VT: Chelsea Green.

(2008). *The political mind: why you can't understand 21st-century politics with an 18th-century brain*. New York: Viking.

Lakoff, G., and Johnson, M. (1980). *Metaphors we live by*. University of Chicago Press.

(1999). *Philosophy in the flesh: the embodied mind and its challenge to Western thought*. New York: Basic Books.

Lambrecht, K. (1994). *Information structure and sentence form: topic, focus and the mental representations of discourse referents*. Cambridge University Press.

Langacker, R. W. (2009). *Investigations in cognitive grammar*. Berlin: De Gruyter Mouton.

Lanser, S. S. (1981). *The narrative act: point of view in prose fiction*. Princeton University Press.

Larraín, J. (1979). *The concept of ideology*. Athens: University of Georgia Press.

Larsen, S. F. (1981). *Knowledge updating: three papers on news memory, background knowledge, and text processing*. Aarhus, Denmark: Institute of Psychology, University of Aarhus.

Latour, B. (1987). *Science in action: how to follow scientists and engineers through society*. Cambridge, MA: Harvard University Press.

(1993). *We have never been modern*. London: Harvester-Wheatsheaf.

Latour, B., and Woolgar, S. (1986). *Laboratory life: the construction of scientific facts*. Princeton University Press.

Lau, R. R., and Sears, D. O. (eds.) (1986). *Political cognition*. Hillsdale, NJ: Lawrence Erlbaum.

Lauer, M., and Aswani, S. (2009). Indigenous ecological knowledge as situated practices: understanding fishers' knowledge in the Western Solomon Islands. *American Anthropologist*, 111(3), 317–329.

Lave, J. (1988). *Cognition in practice: mind, mathematics and culture in everyday life*. Cambridge University Press.

Lave, J., and Wenger, E. (1991). *Situated learning: legitimate peripheral participation*. Cambridge University Press.

Lazard, G. (2001). On the grammaticalization of evidentiality. *Journal of Pragmatics*, 33(3), 359–367.

Lee, B. P. H. (2001). Mutual knowledge, background knowledge and shared beliefs: their roles in establishing common ground. *Journal of Pragmatics*, 33(1), 21–44.

Lee, C. W. (2007). Is there a place for private conversation in public dialogue? Comparing stakeholder assessments of informal communication in collaborative regional planning. *American Journal of Sociology*, 113(1), 41–96.

Lee, I. (2008). Student reactions to teacher feedback in two Hong Kong secondary classrooms. *Journal of Second Language Writing*, 17(3), 144–164.

Lee, J. H. (2009). News values, media coverage, and audience attention: an analysis of direct and mediated causal relationships. *Journalism and Mass Communication Quarterly*, 86(1), 175–190.

Lehrer, K. (1990). *Theory of knowledge*. Boulder, CO: Westview Press.

(2000). Discursive knowledge. *Philosophy and Phenomenological Research*, 60(3), 637–653.

Leonard, B., de Partz, M. P., Grandin, C., and Pillon, A. (2009). Domain-specific reorganization of semantic processing after extensive damage to the left temporal lobe. *Neuroimage*, 45(2), 572–586.

Lerner, D. (1960). *Evidence and inference*. Chicago, IL: Free Press of Glencoe.

Levelt, W. J. M. (1982). Linearization in describing spatial networks. In S. Peters, and E. Saarinen, (eds.) *Processes, beliefs and questions*. Dordrecht: Reidel.

(1989). *Speaking: from intention to articulation*. Cambridge, MA: MIT Press.

(1996). Perspective taking and ellipsis in spatial descriptions. In P. Bloom, and M. A. Peterson (eds.), *Language and space* (pp. 77–107). Cambridge, MA: MIT Press.

Levelt, W. J. M., and Barnas, A. (2008). *Formal grammars in linguistics and psycholinguistics*. Amsterdam/Philadelphia: John Benjamins.

Levinson, S. C. (1983). *Pragmatics*. Cambridge University Press.

(1988). Putting linguistics on a proper footing: explorations in Goffman's concepts of participation. In P. Drew, and A. Wootton (eds.), *Erving Goffman: exploring the interaction order* (pp. 161–227). Boston, MA: Northeastern University Press.

Lévi-Strauss, C. (1958). *Anthropologie structurale*. Paris: Plon.

(1962). *La pensée sauvage*. Paris: Plon.

(1974). *Tristes tropiques*. New York: Atheneum.

Lewis, K., Belliveau, M., Herndon, B., and Keller, J. (2007). Group cognition, membership change, and performance: investigating the benefits and detriments of collective knowledge. *Organizational Behavior and Human Decision Processes*, 103(2), 159–178.

Leydesdorff, L. A. (2001). *A sociological theory of communication: the self-organization of the knowledge-based society*. New York: Universal Publishers.

Li, L., Cao, H. J., Wu, Z. Y., Wu, S., and Xiao, L. (2007). Diffusion of positive AIDS care messages among service providers in China. *Aids Education and Prevention*, 19(6), 511–518.

Lieberman, P. (1987). *On the origins of language: an introduction to the evolution of human speech.* Washington, DC: University Press of America.

Liebowitz, J. (ed.) (2012). *Knowledge management handbook: collaboration and social networking.* Boca Raton, FL: CRC Press.

Lin, T. J., and Anderson, R. C. (2008). Reflections on collaborative discourse, argumentation, and learning. *Contemporary Educational Psychology*, 33(3), 443–448.

Lindenbaum, S., and Lock, M. M. (eds.) (1993). *Knowledge, power, and practice: the anthropolgy of medicine and everyday life.* Berkeley, CA: University of California Press.

Lindström, L. (1990). *Knowledge and power in a South Pacific society.* Washington, DC: Smithsonian Institution Press.

Lipson, M. Y. (1982). Learning new information from text: the role of prior knowledge and reading ability. *Journal of Reading Behavior*, 14(3), 243–261.

Little, R., and Smith, S. M. (eds.) (1988). *Belief systems and international relations.* Oxford: Blackwell.

Lloyd, C. V. (1990). The elaboration of concepts in three biology textbooks: facilitating student learning. *Journal of Research in Science Teaching*, 27(10), 1019–1032.

Locke, J. (1690). *An essay concerning humane understanding: In 4 books.* London: Printed by E. Holt, for T. Basset.

Loewen, G. V. (2006). *How can we explain the persistence of irrational beliefs? Essays in social anthropology.* Lewiston, NY: Edwin Mellen Press.

Loftus, E. F. (1996). *Eyewitness testimony.* Cambridge, MA: Harvard University Press.

Loftus, E. F., and Doyle, J. M. (1987). *Eyewitness testimony: civil and criminal.* New York: Kluwer Law.

Lorch, R. F. (1989). Text signaling devices and their effects on reading and memory processes. In *Educational psychology review*, 1, 209–234. NY: Plenum.

Lorch, R. F., and O'Brien, E. J. E. (eds.) (1995). *Sources of coherence in reading.* Hillsdale, NJ: Lawrence Erlbaum.

Lounsbury, F. G. (1969). The structural analysis of kinship semantics. In S. A. Tyler (ed.), *Cognitive anthropology* (pp. 193–212). New York: Holt, Rinehart and Winston.

Louwerse, M. M., and Graesser, A. C. (2006). Macrostructure. In K. Brown (ed.), *Encyclopedia of language and linguistics*, 2nd edn. Oxford: Elsevier.

Louwerse, M., and van Peer, W. (eds.) (2002). *Thematics: interdisciplinary studies.* Amsterdam: John Benjamins.

Lu, H. J., Su, Y. J., and Wang, Q. (2008). Talking about others facilitates theory of mind in Chinese preschoolers. *Developmental Psychology*, 44(6), 1726–1736.

Lucy, J. A. (1992). *Language diversity and cognitive development: a reformulation of the linguistic relativity hypothesis.* Cambridge University Press.

Luke, A. (1988). *Literacy, textbooks, and ideology: postwar literacy instruction and the mythology of Dick and Jane.* London/New York: Falmer Press.

Lynch, A. (1996). *Thought contagion: how belief spreads through society.* New York: Basic Books.

Lyons, J. (1977). *Semantics* (2 vols). Cambridge University Press.

Macaulay, R. K. S. (2004). *Talk that counts: age, gender, and social class differences in discourse.* New York: Oxford University Press.

(2005). *Extremely common eloquence: constructing Scottish identity through narrative*. Amsterdam/New York: Rodopi.

Machin, D., and Niblock, S. (2006). *News production: theory and practice*. Abingdon, England: Routledge.

Mackie, D. M., and Cooper, J. (1983). Attitude polarization: effects of group membership. *Journal of Personality and Social Psychology* 46, 575–585.

MacKuen, M., and Coombs, S. L. (1981). *More than news: media power in public affairs*. Beverly Hills, CA: Sage.

Magnussen, S., Melinder, A., Stridbeck, U., and Raja, A. Q. (2010). Beliefs about factors affecting the reliability of eyewitness testimony: a comparison of judges, jurors and the general public. *Applied Cognitive Psychology*, 24(1), 122–133.

Malinowski, B. (1922). *Argonauts of the Western Pacific*. London: Routledge.

(1926). *Crime and custom in savage society*. London: Kegan Paul, Trench, Trubner.

(1939). The group and the individual in functional analysis. *The American Journal of Sociology*, 44(6), 948–962.

(1954). *Magic, science and religion: and other essays*, with an introduction by R. Redfield. Garden City, NY: Doubleday.

Mandler, J. M. (1984). *Stories, scripts, and scenes: aspects of schema theory*. Hillsdale, NJ: Lawrence Erlbaum.

(2007). On the origins of the conceptual system. *American Psychologist*, 62(8), 741–751.

Manfredi, P. A. (1993). Tacit beliefs and other doxastic attitudes. *Philosophia*, 22(1–2), 95–117.

Mani, I., and Maybury, M. T. (eds.) (1999). *Advances in automatic text summarization*. Cambridge, MA: MIT Press.

Mann, W. C., and Thompson, S. A. (1987). *Rhetorical structure theory: a theory of text organization*. Marina del Rey, CA: Information Sciences Institute, University of Southern California.

(1988). Rhetorical structure theory: towards a functional theory of text organization. *Text*, 8, 243–281.

(1991). *Discourse description*. Amsterdam: John Benjamins.

Mannes, S., and St. George, M. (1996). Effects of prior knowledge on text comprehension: a simple modeling approach. In B. K. Britton and A. C. Graesser (eds.), *Models of understanding text* (pp. 115–139). Hillsdale, NJ: Lawrence Erlbaum.

Mannheim, K. (1936). *Ideology and utopia: an introduction to the sociology of knowledge*. London/New York: Kegan. Paul, Trench, Trubner & Co./Harcourt, Brace & Co.

(1972). *Essays on the sociology of knowledge*, edited by Paul Kecskemeti. London: Routledge & Kegan Paul.

Manning, P. (2001). *News and news sources: a critical introduction*. Thousand Oaks, CA: Sage.

Marchand, T. H. J. (ed.) (2010). *Making knowledge: explorations of the indissoluble relation between mind, body and environment*. Malden, MA: Wiley-Blackwell.

Marcu, D. (1999). Discourse trees are good indicators of importance in text. In Mani, and Maybury (pp. 123–135).

370   References

(2000). *The theory and practice of discourse parsing and summarization.* Cambridge, MA: MIT Press.

Marcus, G. E., and Fischer, M. M. J. (1986). *Anthropology as cultural critique: an experimental moment in the human sciences.* University of Chicago Press.

Maria, K., and MacGinitie, W. (1987). Learning from texts that refute the reader's prior knowledge. *Reading Research and Instruction,* 26(4), 222–238.

Marín-Arrese, J. I. (2006). Epistemic stance and commitment in the discourse of fact and opinion in English and Spanish: a comparable corpus study. In A. M. Hornero, M. J. Luzón, and S. Murillo (eds.), *Corpus linguistics: applications for the study of English* (pp. 141–157). Berlin: Peter Lang.

(2009). Effective vs. epistemic stance, and subjectivity/intersubjectivity in political discourse: a case study. In A. Tsangalidis, and R Facchinetti (eds.), *Studies on English Modality. In Honour of Frank R. Palmer* (pp. 23–52). Berlin: Peter Lang.

(2011a). Effective vs. epistemic stance, and subjectivity in political discourse: legitimising strategies and mystification of responsibility. In C. Hart (ed.), *Critical discourse studies in context and cognition* (pp. 193–223). Amsterdam: John Benjamins.

(2011b). Epistemic legitimizing strategies, commitment and accountability in discourse. *Discourse Studies,* 13(6), 789–797.

Markkanen, R., and Schröder, H. (eds.) (1997). *Hedging and discourse: approaches to the analysis of a pragmatic phenomenon in academic texts.* Berlin/New York: Walter de Gruyter.

Markman, A. B. (1999). *Knowledge representation.* Mahwah, NJ: Lawrence Erlbaum.

Markus, H., and Smith, J. (1981). The influence of self-schemata on the perception of others. In N. Cantor, and J. Kihlstrom (eds.), *Personality, cognition, and social interaction* (pp. 233–262). Hillsdale, NJ: Lawrence Erlbaum.

Martin, J. R., and White, P. R. R. (2005). *The language of evaluation: appraisal in English.* New York: Palgrave Macmillan.

Martin, L. M. W. (ed.) (1995). *Sociocultural psychology theory and practice of doing and knowing.* Cambridge University Press.

Martín Rojo, L., and Gómez Esteban, C. (2005). The gender of power: the female style of labour organizations. In M. M. Lazar (ed.), *Feminist critical discourse analysis: gender, power, and ideology in discourse* (pp. 61–89). Houndmills/New York: Palgrave Macmillan.

Marx, K., and Engels, F. (1846/1947). *The German ideology.* New York: International Publishers.

Mason, R. A., and Just, M. A. (2004). How the brain processes causal inferences in text: a theoretical account of generation and integration component processes utilizing both cerebral hemispheres. *Psychological Science,* 15(1), 1–7.

Matilal, B. K., and Chakrabarti, A. (eds.) (1994). *Knowing from words: Western and Indian philosophical analysis of understanding and testimony.* Dordrecht: Kluwer Academic.

Mauss, M. (1972). *A general theory of magic.* New York: W. W. Norton (Norton Library).

Mawhinney, L. (2010). Let's lunch and learn: professional knowledge sharing in teachers' lounges and other congregational spaces. *Teaching and Teacher Education,* 26(4), 972–978.

Mayer, R. E. (2002). Using illustrations to promote constructivist learning from science text. In Otero, León, and Graesser (eds.) (pp. 333–356).

Mayes, P. (2005). Linking micro and macro social structure through genre analysis. *Research on Language and Social Interaction*, 38(3), 331–370.

Maynard, D. W. (1989). On the ethnography and the analysis of talk in institutional settings. In J. Holstein, and G. Miller (eds.), *New perspectives on social problems* (pp. 127–164). Greenwich, CT: JAI Press.

Maynard, D. W., and Marlaire, C. L. (1992). Good reasons for bad testing performance: the interactional substrate of educational exams. *Qualitative Sociology*, 15, 177–202.

Mayr, A. (2008). *Language and power: an introduction to institutional discourse.* London/New York: Continuum.

McConnell-Ginet, S. (2006). Why defining is seldom "just semantics": marriage and "marriage." In B. J. Birner, and G. L. Ward (eds.), *Drawing the boundaries of meaning: neo-Gricean studies in pragmatics and semantics in honor of Lawrence R. Horn* (pp. 217–240). Amsterdam: John Benjamins

McCready, E., and Ogata, N. (2007). Evidentiality, modality and probability. *Linguistics and Philosophy*, 30(2), 147–206.

McCrudden, M. T., and Schraw, G. (2007). Relevance and goal-focusing in text processing. *Educational Psychology Review*, 19(2), 113–139.

McCrudden, M. T., Schraw, G., Lehman, S., and Poliquin, A. (2007). The effect of causal diagrams on text learning. *Contemporary Educational Psychology*, 32(3), 367–388.

McElroy, J. C., Morrow, P. C., and Wall, L. C. (1983). Generalizing impact of object language to other audiences: peer response to office design. *Psychological Reports*, 53, 315–322.

McGinn, C. (2009). Imagination. In B. P. McLaughlin, A. Beckermann, and S. Walter (eds.). *The Oxford handbook of philosophy of mind* (pp. 595–606). Oxford/New York: Clarendon Press/Oxford University Press.

McGuire, W. J. (1986). The vicissitudes of attitudes and similar representations in twentieth century psychology. *European Journal of Social Psychology*, 16(2), 89–130.

(1989). The structure of individual attitudes and attitude systems. In A. R. Pratkanis, S. J. Breckler, and A. G. Greenwald (eds.), *Attitude structure and function* (pp. 37–70). Hillsdale, NJ: Lawrence Erlbaum.

McHoul, A. W. (ed.) (2001). *How to analyse talk in institutional settings: a casebook of methods.* New York: Continuum.

McHugh, P. (1968). *Defining the situation: the organization of meaning in social interaction.* Indianapolis, IN: Bobbs-Merrill.

McNamara, D. S. (2001). Reading both high and low coherence texts: effects of text sequence and prior knowledge. *Canadian Journal of Experimental Psychology*, 55, 51–62.

McNamara, D. S., and Kintsch, W. (1996). Learning from text: effects of prior knowledge and text coherence. *Discourse Processes*, 22, 247–287.

McNamara, D. S., and Magliano, J. (2009). Toward a comprehensive model of comprehension. *Psychology of Learning and Motivation*, 51, 297–384.

McNamara, D. S., and O'Reilly, T. (2002). Learning: knowledge acquisition, representation, and organization. In J. W. Guthrie et al. (eds.), *The encyclopedia of education.* New York: Macmillan Reference.

McNamara, D. S., Kintsch, E., Songer, N. B., and Kintsch, W. (1996). Are good texts always better? Text coherence, background knowledge, and levels of understanding in learning from text. *Cognition and Instruction*, 14, 1–43.

Mead, M. (ed.) (1937). *Cooperation and competition among primitive peoples*. New York: McGraw-Hill.

Mehan, H. (1978). Structuring school structure. *Harvard Educational Review*, 48(1), 32–64.

Meinhof, U. H., and Smith, J. (eds.) (2000). *Intertextuality and the media: from genre to everyday life*. Manchester University Press.

Menon, V., Boyett-Anderson, J. M., Schatzberg, A. F., and Reiss, A. L. (2002). Relating semantic and episodic memory systems. *Cognitive Brain Research*, 13(2), 261–265.

Mény, Y., and Lavau, G. E. (1991). *Idéologies, partis politiques et groupes sociaux*. Paris: Presses de la Fondation nationale des sciences politiques.

Mercer, N. (ed.) (1987). *Common knowledge: the development of understanding in the classroom*. London/New York: Methuen.

Merton, R. K. (eds.) (1983). *The sociology of science: theoretical and empirical investigations*. University of Chicago Press.

Mertz, E. (1992). Steps toward a social semiotic of selves (article review of the contributions to semiotics-self-and-society). *Semiotica*, 90(3–4), 295–309.

Metusalem, R., Kutas, M., Urbach, T. P., Hare, M., McRae, K., and Elman, J. L. (2012). Generalized event knowledge activation during online sentence comprehension. *Journal of Memory and Language*, 66(4), 545–567.

Mey, J. L. (1993). *Pragmatics: an introduction*. Oxford: Blackwell.

Meyer, B. J. F. (1975). *The organization of prose and its effects on memory*. Amsterdam: North-Holland.

Meyerhoff, M., and Schleef, E. (2010). *The Routledge sociolinguistics reader*. London: Routledge.

Meyers, M. (1992). Reporters and beats: the making of oppositional news. *Critical Studies in Mass Communication*, 9(1), 75–90.

Michalove, P. A., Georg, S., and Ramer, A. M. (1998). Current issues in linguistic taxonomy. *Annual Review of Anthropology*, 27, 451–472.

Mignolo, W. (1999). *Local histories/global designs: coloniality, subaltern knowledges, and border thinking*. Princeton University Press.

Millar, R., Crute, V., and Hargie, O. (1992). *Professional interviewing*. London/New York: Routledge.

Miller, D. L., and Karakowsky, L. (2005). Gender influences as an impediment to knowledge sharing: when men and women fail to seek peer feedback. *Journal of Psychology*, 139(2), 101–118.

Miller, G. A. (1956). The magical number seven, plus or minus two: some limits on our capacity for processing information. *Psychological Review*, 63, 81–97.

Miller, H. T., and Fox, C. J. (2001). The epistemic community. *Administration and Society*, 32(6), 668–685.

Minsky, M. (1975). A framework for representing knowledge. In P. Winston (ed.), *The psychology of computer vision*. New York: McGraw-Hill.

Miyake, A., and Shah, P. (eds.) (1999). *Models of working memory: mechanisms of active maintenance and executive control*. Cambridge University Press.

Moerman, M. (1987). *Talking culture: ethnographic and conversational analysis.* University of Pennsylvania Press.

Mondada, L. (2011). Management of knowledge discrepancies. In Stivers, Mondada, and Steensig (eds.) (2011b) (pp. 27–57).

Monroe, J. (ed.) (2003). *Local knowledges, local practices: writing in the disciplines at Cornell.* University of Pittsburgh Press.

Montgomery, M. (2007). *The discourse of broadcast news.* New York: Routledge.

Moore, H. L., and Sanders, T. (eds.) (2006). *Anthropology in theory: issues in epistemology.* Malden, MA: Blackwell.

Morgan, M. (2004). Speech community. In Duranti (ed.), (pp. 3–22).

Morris, B. (1991). *Western conceptions of the individual.* New York: Berg.

Morrow, D. G. (1986). Places as referents in discourse. *Journal of Memory and Language*, 25(6), 676–690.

Morrow, D. G., Bower, G. H., and Greenspan, S. L. (1989). Updating situation models during narrative comprehension. *Journal of Memory and Language*, 28(3), 292–312.

Morrow, P. C., and McElroy, J. C. (1981). Interior office design and visitor response. *Journal of Applied Psychology*, 66, 630–646.

Moscovici, S. (1961). *La Psychoanalyse, son image et son public.* Paris: Presses Universitaires de France.

   (1981). On social representations. In J. P. Forgas (ed.), *Social cognition* (pp. 181–209). London: Academic Press.

   (2000). *Social representations: studies in social psychology.* Cambridge: Polity Press.

Moscovici, S., Mucchi-Faina, A., and Maass, A. (eds.) (1994). *Minority influence.* Chicago, IL: Nelson-Hall.

Mumby, D. K. (1988). *Communication and power in organizations: discourse, ideology, and domination.* Norwood, NJ: Ablex.

Munz, P. (1993). *Philosophical Darwinism: on the origin of knowledge by means of natural selection.* London/New York: Routledge.

Musgrave, A. (1993). *Common sense, science, and scepticism: a historical introduction to the theory of knowledge.* Cambridge University Press.

Mushin, I. (2001). *Evidentiality and epistemological stance: narrative retelling.* Amsterdam: John Benjamins.

Musolff, A., and Zinken, J. (eds.) (2008). *Metaphor and discourse.* New York: Palgrave Macmillan.

Myers, G. (1990). *Writing biology: texts in the social construction of scientific knowledge.* Madison, WI: University of Wisconsin Press.

   (1996). Strategic vagueness in academic writing. In E. Ventola, and A. Mauranen (eds.), *Academic writing: intercultural and textual issues* (pp. 3–18). Amsterdam: John Benjamins.

   (2003). Discourse studies of scientific popularization: questioning the boundaries. *Discourse Studies*, 5(2), 265–279.

Naceur, A., and Schiefele, U. (2005). Motivation and learning – the role of interest in construction of representation of text and longterm retention: inter- and intraindividual analyses. *European Journal of Psychology of Education*, 20(2), 155–170.

Nagel, N. G. (1996). *Learning through real-world problem solving: the power of integrative teaching.* Thousand Oaks, CA: Corwin Press.

Nakayama, T. K., and Halualani, R. T. (eds.) (2010). *The handbook of critical intercultural communication.* Malden, MA: Wiley-Blackwell.

Nash, C., and Kirby, B. (1989). *Whose news? Ownership and control of the news media (with simulation game).* Manchester Development Education Project.

Natti, S., Halinen, A., and Hanttu, N. (2006). Customer knowledge transfer and key account management in professional service organizations. *International Journal of Service Industry Management*, 17(3–4), 304–319.

Naveh-Benjamin, M., Lavi, H., McKeachie, W. J., and Lin, Y. G. (1997). Individual-differences in students' retention of knowledge and conceptual structures learned in university and high-school courses: the case of test anxiety. *Applied Cognitive Psychology*, 11, 507–526.

Nazarea, V. D. (1999). *Ethnoecology: situated knowledge/local lives.* Tucson, AZ: University of Arizona Press.

Needham, R. (1972). *Belief, language and experience.* Oxford: Blackwell.

Neisser, U. (1978). Memory: what are the important questions? In M. M. Gruneberg, P. E. Morris, and R. N. Sykes (eds.), *Practical aspects of memory* (pp. 3–24). London: Academic Press.

Neisser, U. (ed.) (1982). *Memory observed: remembering in natural contexts.* San Francisco: Freeman.

(1993). *The perceived self: ecological and interpersonal sources of self-knowledge.* Cambridge University Press.

(1997). *The conceptual self in context culture, experience, self-understanding.* New York: Cambridge University Press.

Neisser, U., and Fivush, R. (eds.) (1994). *The remembering self: construction and accuracy in the self-narrative.* Cambridge University Press.

Neisser, U., and Hyman, I. E. (2000). *Memory observed: remembering in natural contexts.* New York: Worth Publishers.

Nevile, M. (2007). Action in time: ensuring timeliness for collaborative work in the airline cockpit. *Language in Society*, 36(2), 233–257.

Newtson, D. A., and Engquist, G. (1976). The perceptual organization of ongoing behavior. *Journal of Experimental Social Psychology*, 12, 436–450.

Nichols, S., and Stich, S. P. (2003). *Mindreading: an integrated account of pretence, self-awareness, and understanding other minds.* Oxford/New York: Clarendon/Oxford University Press.

Niemeier, S., and Dirven, R. (eds.) (1997). *The language of emotions: conceptualization, expression, and theoretical foundation.* Amsterdam: John Benjamins.

Nieuwland, M. S. (2013). "If a lion could speak…": online sensitivity to propositional truth-value of unrealistic counterfactual sentences. *Journal of Memory and Language*, 68(1), 54–67.

Nieuwland, M. S., and Martin, A. E. (2012). If the real world were irrelevant, so to speak: the role of propositional truth-value in counterfactual sentence comprehension. *Cognition*, 122(1), 102–109.

Nippold, M. A., and Scott, C. M. (eds.) (2010). *Expository discourse in children, adolescents, and adults: development and disorders.* New York: Psychology Press.

Normand, R. (2008). School effectiveness or the horizon of the world as a laboratory. *British Journal of Sociology of Education*, 29(6), 665–676.

Nuchelmans, G. (1973). *Theories of the proposition: ancient and medieval conceptions of the bearers of truth and falsity.* Amsterdam: North-Holland.

Nuckolls, J. B. (1993). The semantics of certainty in Quechua and its implications for a cultural epistemology. *Language in Society,* 22(2), 235–255.

Nussbaum, E. M. (2008). Collaborative discourse, argumentation, and learning: preface and literature review. *Contemporary Educational Psychology,* 33(3), 345–359.

Nuyts, J. (2001a). *Epistemic modality, language, and conceptualization: a cognitive-pragmatic perspective.* Amsterdam: John Benjamins.

(2001b). Subjectivity as an evidential dimension in epistemic modal expressions. *Journal of Pragmatics,* 33(3), 383–400.

(2012). Notions of (inter)subjectivity. *English Text Construction,* 5(1), 53–76.

Nye, J. L., and Brower, A. M. (eds.) (1996). *What's social about social cognition? Research on socially shared cognition in small groups.* Thousand Oaks, CA: Sage.

Nygren, A. (1999). Local knowledge in the environment–development: discourse from dichotomies to situated knowledges. *Critique of Anthropology,* 19(3), 267–288.

O'Keefe, D. J. (2002). *Persuasion: theory and research.* Thousand Oaks, CA: Sage.

O'Reilly, T., and McNamara, D. S. (2007). Reversing the reverse cohesion effect: good texts can be better for strategic, high-knowledge readers. *Discourse Processes,* 43(2), 121–152.

Oakhill, J., and Garnham, A. (eds.) (1996). *Mental models in cognitive science: essays in honour of Phil Johnson-Laird.* Hove: Psychology Press.

Oberschall, A. (1993). *Social movements: ideologies, interests, and identities.* New Brunswick, NJ: Transaction.

Ochs Keenan, E. (1976). The universality of conversational implicatures. *Language in Society,* 5, 67–80.

Ochs, E. (1982). Talking to children in Western Samoa. *Language in Society* 11: 77–104.

(1987). The impact of stratification and socialization on men's and women's speech in Western Samoa. In S. Steele, and S. U. Philips (eds.), *Language, gender, and sex in comparative perspective* (pp. 50–70). New York: Cambridge University Press.

Ochs, E., and Capps, L. (1996). Narrating the self. *Annual Review of Anthropology,* 25, 19–43.

(2001). *Living narrative: creating lives in everyday storytelling.* Cambridge, MA: Harvard University Press.

Ochs, E., and Schieffelin, B.B. (2001). Language acquisition and socialization. In A. Duranti (ed.), *Linguistic anthropology: a reader* (pp. 263–301). Oxford: Blackwell.

Oldenburg, H. (1992). *Angewandte Fachtextlinguistik: "conclusions" und Zusammenfassungen.* Tübingen: Gunter Narr.

Operario, D., and Fiske, S. T. (1999). Integrating social identity and social cognition: a framework for bridging diverse perspectives. In Abrams, and Hogg (eds.), (pp. 26–54).

Ortner, S. B. (1984). Theory in anthropology since the sixties. *Comparative Studies in Society and History,* 26, 126–166.

Ostrom, T. M., Skowronski, J. J., and Nowak, A. (1994). The cognitive foundation of attitudes: it's a wonderful construct. In P. G. Devine, D. L Hamilton, and T. M. Ostrom (eds.), *Social cognition: impact on social psychology* (pp. 195–258) San Diego, CA: Academic Press.

Otero, J., León, J. A., and Graesser, A. C. (eds.) (2002). *The psychology of science text comprehension*. Mahwah, NJ: Lawrence Erlbaum.

Ozuru, Y., Dempsey, K., and McNamara, D. S. (2009). Prior knowledge, reading skill, and text cohesion in the comprehension of science texts. *Learning and Instruction*, 19(3), 228–242.

Paechter, C. F. (eds.) (2001). *Knowledge, power, and learning*. Thousand Oaks, CA: Sage.

Paletz, D. L. (ed.) (1992). *Terrorism and the media*. Newbury Park, CA: Sage.

Palmer, C. T., and Wadley, R. L. (2007). Local environmental knowledge, talk, and skepticism: using 'LES' to distinguish 'LEK' from 'LET' in Newfoundland. *Human Ecology*, 35(6), 749–760.

Panda, N., and Mohanty, A. K. (1981). Effects of adjunct questions on learning from connected discourse. *Psychological Studies*, 26(2), 117–123.

Papafragou, A. (2006). Epistemic modality and truth conditions. *Lingua*, 116(10), 1688–1702.

Papousek, H., Papousek, M., and Koester, L. S. (1986). Sharing emotionality and sharing knowledge: a microanalytic approach to parent–infant communication. In P. B. Read, and Carroll E. Izard (eds.), *Measuring emotions in infants and children*, vol. 2 (pp. 93–123). New York: Cambridge University Press.

Park, C. Y. (2001). News media exposure and self-perceived knowledge: the illusion of knowing. *International Journal of Public Opinion Research*, 13(4), 419–425.

Partee, B. H., and Sgall, P. (eds.) (1996). *Discourse and meaning: Papers in Honor of Eva Hajičová*. Amsterdam: John Benjamins.

Paulson, S. (2011). The use of ethnography and narrative interviews in a study of 'cultures of dance.' *Journal of Health Psychology*, 16(1), 148–157.

Peeck, J. (1993). Increasing picture effects in learning from illustrated text. *Learning and Instruction*, 3(3), 227–238.

Pelto, P. J., and Pelto, G. H. (1997). Studying knowledge, culture, and behavior in applied medical anthropology. *Medical Anthropology Quarterly*, 11(2), 147–163.

Peräkylä, A., and Vehviläinen, S. (2003). Conversation analysis and the professional stocks of interactional knowledge. *Discourse and Society*, 14(6), 727–750.

Perloff, R. M. (2003). *The dynamics of persuasion: communication and attitudes in the 21st century*. Mahwah, NJ: Lawrence Erlbaum.

Perner, J. (1991). *Understanding the representational mind*. Cambridge, MA: MIT Press.

Perry, D. K. (1990). News reading, knowledge about, and attitudes toward foreign-countries. *Journalism Quarterly*, 67(2), 353–358.

Perry, J. (1993). *The problem of the essential indexical and other essays*. Oxford University Press.

Petöfi, J. S., and Franck, D. M. L. (eds.) (1973). *Presuppositions in linguistics and philosophy*. Frankfurt: Athenaeum.

Petöfi, J. S., and Rieser, H. (eds.) (1973). *Studies in text grammar*. Dordrecht: Reidel.

Petty, R. E., and Cacioppo, J. T. (1981). *Attitudes and persuasion: classic and contemporary approaches.* Dubuque, IA: W.C. Brown.

   (1986). *Communication and persuasion: central and peripheral routes to attitude change.* New York: Springer-Verlag.

Pfister, H. R., and Oehl, M. (2009). The impact of goal focus, task type and group size on synchronous net-based collaborative learning discourses. *Journal of Computer Assisted Learning,* 25(2), 161–176.

Phye, G. D. (1997). Learning and remembering: the basis for personal knowledge construction. In G. D. Phye (ed.), *Handbook of academic learning: construction of knowledge* (pp. 47–64). San Diego, CA: Academic Press.

Pickering, M. (2001). *Stereotyping: the politics of representation.* Houndmills: Palgrave.

Pike, K. L. (1993). *Talk, thought, and thing: the emic road toward conscious knowledge.* Dallas, TX: Summer Institute of Linguistics.

Pishwa, H. (ed.) (2006). *Language and memory: aspects of knowledge representation.* Berlin/New York: De Gruyter Mouton.

Planalp, S., and Garvin-Doxas, K. (1994). Using mutual knowledge in conversation: friends as experts on each other. In S. Duck (ed.), *Dynamics of relationships* (pp. 1–26). Thousand Oaks, CA: Sage.

Platchias, D. (2011). *Phenomenal consciousness: understanding the relation between experience and neural processes in the brain.* Durham, UK: Acumen.

Plett, H. F. (ed.) (1991). *Intertextuality.* Berlin/New York: W. de Gruyter.

Plotkin, H. C. (1993). *Darwin machines and the nature of knowledge.* Cambridge, MA: Harvard University Press.

   (1997). *Evolution in mind: an introduction to evolutionary psychology.* London: Penguin.

   (2007). *Necessary knowledge.* Oxford University Press.

Plungian, V. A. (2001). The place of evidentiality within the universal grammatical space. *Journal of Pragmatics,* 33(3), 349–357.

Polanyi, L. (1981). Telling the same story twice. *Text,* 1(4), 315–336.

Polanyi, M. (1966). *The tacit dimension.* Garden City, NY: Doubleday.

Pomerantz, A. (1984). Agreeing and disagreeing with assessments: some features of preferred/dispreferred turn shapes. In J. M. Atkinson, and J. Heritage (eds.), *Structures of social action* (pp. 57–101). Cambridge University Press.

Pontecorvo, C. (1987). Discussing for reasoning: the role of argument in knowledge construction. In Erik de Corte, Hans Lodewijks, and Roger Parmentier (eds.), *Learning and instruction: European research in an international context,* vol. 1 (pp. 71–82). Elmsford, NY: Pergamon Press.

Popper, K. R. (1972). *Objective knowledge: an evolutionary approach.* Oxford: Clarendon Press.

Porter, J. E. (1992). *Audience and rhetoric: an archaeological composition of the discourse community.* Englewood Cliffs, NJ: Prentice Hall.

Potter, J. (1996). *Representing reality: discourse, rhetoric and social construction.* London/Thousand Oaks, CA: Sage.

Pottier, J., Bicker, A., and Sillitoe, P. (eds.) (2003). *Negotiating local knowledge: power and identity in development.* London: Pluto Press.

Potts, C. (2005). *The logic of conventional implicatures.* Oxford University Press.

Pramling, N., and Saljö, R. (2007). Scientific knowledge, popularisation, and the use of metaphors: modern genetics in popular science magazines. *Scandinavian Journal of Educational Research*, 51(3), 275–295.

Pratkanis, A. R., Breckler, S. J., and Greenwald, A. G. (eds.) (1989). *Attitude structure and function*. Hillsdale, NJ: Lawrence Erlbaum.

Preyer, G., and Peter, G. (eds.) (2005). *Contextualism in philosophy: knowledge, meaning, and truth*. Oxford/New York: Clarendon Press/Oxford University Press.

(2007). *Context-sensitivity and semantic minimalism: new essays on semantics and pragmatics*. Oxford University Press.

Price, H. H. (1969). *Belief*. London: Allen & Unwin.

Price, V., and Tewksbury, D. (1997). News values and public opinion: a theoretical account of media priming and framing. In G. Barnett, and F. J. Foster (eds.), *Progress in communication sciences* (pp. 173–212). Greenwich, CT: Ablex.

Priest, S. H. (ed.) (2010). *Encyclopedia of science and technology communication*. Thousand Oaks, CA: Sage.

Prince, E. F. (1981). Toward a taxonomy of given/new information. In P. Cole, (ed.), *Radical pragmatics* (pp. 223–256). New York: Academic Press.

Propp, V. (1968). *The morphology of the folktale*, 2nd edn. (trans. T. Scott). Austin, TX: University of Texas Press.

Prosser, H., and Walley, T. (2006). New drug prescribing by hospital doctors: the nature and meaning of knowledge. *Social Science and Medicine*, 62(7), 1565–1578.

Purkhardt, S. C. (1993). *Transforming social representations: a social psychology of common sense and science*. London/New York: Routledge.

Putnam, H. (1975). *Mind, language and reality*. Cambridge University Press.

Quine, W. V. O. (1960). *Word and object*. Cambridge, MA: MIT Press.

(1969). Epistemology naturalized. In *Ontological relativity and other essays* (pp. 69–90). New York: Columbia University Press.

Quinn, N. (1987). Convergent evidence for a cultural model of American marriage. In Holland, and Quinn (eds.), (pp. 173–192).

Quinn, N. (ed.) (2005). *Finding culture in talk: a collection of methods*. New York: Palgrave Macmillan.

Quinn, N. (2011). The history of the Cultural Models school reconsidered: a paradigm shift in cognitive anthropology. In Kronenfeld, Bennardo, de Munck, and Fischer (eds.), (pp. 30–46).

Quintana, S. M., and McKown, C. (eds.) (2008). *Handbook of race, racism, and the developing child*. Hoboken, NJ: John Wiley & Sons.

Rabon, D. (1992). *Interviewing and interrogation*. Durham, NC: Carolina Academic Press.

Radin, P. (1927). *Primitive man as philosopher*. New York: Appleton.

Radnitzky, G., and Bartley, W. W. I. (eds.) (1987). *Evolutionary epistemology, rationality, and the sociology of knowledge*. LaSalle, IL: Open Court Press.

Radvansky, G. A., and Zacks, J. M. (2011). Event perception. *Wiley Interdisciplinary Reviews: Cognitive Science*, 2(6), 608–620.

Raftopoulos, A. (2009). *Cognition and perception*. Cambridge: MA: MIT Press.

Rajaram, S. (1993). Remembering and knowing: two means of access to the personal past. *Memory and Cognition*, 21(1), 89–102.

Raymond, G., and Heritage, J. (2006). The epistemics of social relations: owning grandchildren. *Language in Society*, 35, 677–705.

Razmerita, L., Kirchner, K., and Sudzina, F. (2009). Personal knowledge management: the role of Web 2.0 tools for managing knowledge at individual and organisational levels. *Online Information Review*, 33(6), 1021–1039.

Reay, D. (2005). Beyond consciousness? The psychic landscape of social class. *Sociology: The Journal of the British Sociological Association*, 39(5), 911–928.

Reid, D. J., and Beveridge, M. (1986). Effects of text illustration on children's learning of a school science topic. *British Journal of Educational Psychology*, 56(3), 294–303.

Reinhart, T. (1981). Pragmatics and linguistics: an analysis of sentence topics. *Philosophica* 27, 53–94.

Renninger, K. A., Hidi, S., and Krapp, A. (eds.) (1992). *The role of interest in learning and development*. Hillsdale, NJ: Lawrence Erlbaum.

Rescher, N. (ed.) (1990). *Evolution, cognition, and realism: studies in evolutionary epistemology*. Lanham, MD: University Press of America.

Resnick, L. B., Levine, J. M., and Teasley, S. D. (eds.) (1991). *Perspectives on socially shared cognition*. Washington, DC: American Psychological Association.

Reychav, I., and Te'eni, D. (2009). Knowledge exchange in the shrines of knowledge: the "how's" and "where's" of knowledge sharing processes. *Computers and Education*, 53(4), 1266–1277.

Reynolds, S. L. (2002). Testimony, knowledge, and epistemic goals. *Philosophical Studies*, 110(2), 139–161.

Richard, M. (1990). *Propositional attitudes: an essay on thoughts and how we ascribe them*. Cambridge University Press.

Richardson, J. E. (2007). *Analysing newspapers: an approach from critical discourse analysis*. New York: Palgrave Macmillan.

Rickheit, G., and Habel, C. (eds.) (1999). *Mental models in discourse processing and reasoning*. Amsterdam/New York: North-Holland.

Rickheit, G., and Strohner, H. (eds.) (1985). *Inferences in text processing*. Amsterdam: Elsevier.

Riley, S. C. E. (2003). The management of the traditional male-role: a discourse analysis of the constructions and functions of provision. *Journal of Gender Studies*, 12(2), 99–113.

Rinck, M., and Bower, G. H. (2004). Goal-based accessibility of entities within situation models. In B. H. Ross (ed.), *The psychology of learning and motivation: advances in research and theory*, vol. 44 (pp. 1–33). New York: Elsevier Science.

Ritzer, G. (1994). *Sociological beginnings: on the origins of key ideas in sociology*. New York: McGraw-Hill.

Robbins, P. (2003). Beyond ground truth: GIS and the environmental knowledge of herders, professional foresters, and other traditional communities. *Human Ecology*, 31(2), 233–253.

Robinson, J. P., and Levy, M. R. (1986). *The main source: learning from television news*. Beverly Hills, CA: Sage.

Rodin, J., and Steinberg, S. P. (eds.) (2003). *Public discourse in America: conversation and community in the twenty-first century*. Philadelphia, PA: University of Pennsylvania Press.

Roese, N. J. (1997). Counterfactual thinking. *Psychological Bulletin*, 121, 133–148.

Rolin, K. (2008). Science as collective knowledge. *Cognitive Systems Research*, 9(1–2), 115–124.

Romaine, S. (ed.) (1982). *Sociolinguistic variation in speech communities*. London: Edward Arnold.

Romney, A. K., Batchelder, W. H., and Weller, S. C. (1986). Culture as consensus: a theory of culture and informant accuracy. *American Anthropologist*, 88(2), 313–338.

Rooney, D., Hearn, G., and Kastelle, T. (eds.) (2012). *Handbook on the knowledge economy*. Cheltenham: Edward Elgar.

Rooth, M. (1992). A theory of focus interpretation. *Natural Language Semantics*, 1, 75–116.

    (2008). Notions of focus anaphoricity. *Acta Linguistica Hungarica*, 55(3–4), 277–285.

Rorty, R. (1991). *Objectivity, relativism, and truth*. Cambridge University Press.

Rosch, E. (1975). *Basic objects in natural categories*. Berkeley, CA: University of California, Language Behavior Research Laboratory.

    (1978). Principles of categorization. In Rosch, and Lloyd (eds.).

Rosch, E., and Lloyd, B. B. (eds.) (1978). *Cognition and categorization*. Hillsdale, NJ: Lawrence Erlbaum (pp. 27–48).

Rosenberg, M. J., and Hovland, C. I. (1960). Cognitive, affective, and behavioral components of attitudes. In C. I. Hovland, and M. J. Rosenberg (eds.), *Attitude organization and change* (pp. 1–14). New Haven, CT: Yale University Press.

Rosenblum, M. (1981). *Coups and earthquakes: reporting the world to America*. New York: Harper & Row.

Roskos, K., Boehlen, S., and Walker, B. J. (2000). Learning the art of instructional conversation: the influence of self-assessment on teachers' instructional discourse in a reading clinic. *The Elementary School Journal*, 100(3), 229–252.

Ross, N., and Medin, D. L. (2011). Culture and cognition: the role of cognitive anthropology in anthropology and the cognitive sciences. In Kronenfeld, Bennardo, de Munck, and Fischer (eds.) (pp. 357–375).

Roth, C., and Bourgine, P. (2005). Epistemic communities: description and hierarchic categorization. *Mathematical population studies*, 12(2), 107–130.

Roth, W. M. (2005). *Talking science: language and learning in science classrooms*. Lanham, MD: Rowman & Littlefield.

Rouchota, V., and Jucker, A. H. (eds.) (1998). *Current issues in relevance theory*. Amsterdam: John Benjamins.

Rouet, J. F., Levonen, J. J., Dillon, A., and Spiro, R. J. (eds.) (1996). *Hypertext and cognition*. Mahwah, NJ: Lawrence Erlbaum.

Rubin, D. S. (ed.) (1986). *Autobiographical memory*. New York: Cambridge University Press.

Rubin, V. L. (2010). Epistemic modality: from uncertainty to certainty in the context of information seeking as interactions with texts. *Information Processing and Management*, 46(5), 533–540.

Rüschemeyer, D., and Skocpol, T. (eds.) (1996). *States, social knowledge, and the origins of modern social policies*. Princeton University Press Russell Sage Foundation.

Ruse, M. (1986). *Taking Darwin seriously: a naturalistic approach to philosophy*. Oxford: Blackwell.

Ryan, M. L. (1991). *Possible worlds, artificial intelligence, and narrative theory.* Bloomington, IN: Indiana University Press.

Ryle, G. (1949). *The concept of mind.* London: Hutchinson.

(1971). *Collected papers,* vol. II: Collected essays, 1929–1968. London: Hutchinson.

Sadoski, M. (2001). Resolving the effects of concreteness on interest, comprehension, and learning important ideas from text. *Educational Psychology Review,* 13(3), 263–281.

Salili, F., Chiu, C., and Hong, Y. (eds.) (2001). *Student motivation: the culture and context of learning.* Dordrecht: Kluwer Academic.

Salmon, N. U., and Soames, S. (eds.) (1988). *Propositions and attitudes.* Oxford University Press.

Salomon, G. (ed.) (1993). *Distributed cognitions: psychological and educational considerations.* Cambridge University Press.

Salomon, G. (1997). Of mind and media: how culture's symbolic forms affect learning and thinking. *Phi Delta Kappan,* 78(5), 375–380.

Samuelstuen, M. S., and Bråten, I. (2005). Decoding, knowledge, and strategies in comprehension of expository text. *Scandinavian Journal of Psychology,* 46(2), 107–117.

Sanders, J., and Spooren, W. (1996). Subjectivity and certainty in epistemic modality: a study of Dutch epistemic modifiers. *Cognitive Linguistics,* 7(3), 241–264.

Sarangi, S., and Roberts, C. (eds.) (1999). *Talk, work, and institutional order: discourse in medical, mediation, and management settings.* Berlin/New York: De Gruyter Mouton.

Saville-Troike, M. (1982). *The ethnography of communication: an introduction.* Oxford: Blackwell.

Sayre, K. M. (1997). *Belief and knowledge: mapping the cognitive landscape.* Lanham, MD: Rowman & Littlefield.

Scarbrough, E. (1984). *Political ideology and voting: an exploratory study.* Oxford/New York: Clarendon Press/Oxford University Press.

(1990). Attitudes, social representations, and ideology. In Fraser, and Gaskell (eds.), (pp. 99–117).

Scevak, J. J., and Moore, P. J. (1998). Levels of processing effects on learning from texts with maps. *Educational Psychology,* 18(2), 133–155.

Schacter, D. L. (ed.) (1999). *The cognitive neuropsychology of false memories.* Hove: Psychology Press.

Schacter, D. L., and Scarry, E. E. (2000). *Memory, brain, and belief.* Cambridge, MA: Harvard University Press.

Schacter, D. L., Addis, D. R., and Buckner, R. L. (2007). Remembering the past to imagine the future: the prospective brain. *Nature Reviews – Neuroscience,* 8, 657–661.

Schank, R. C., and Abelson, R. P. (1977). *Scripts, plans, goals and understandings: an inquiry into human knowledge structures.* Hillsdale, NJ: Lawrence Erlbaum.

(1995). Knowledge and memory: the real story. In Wyer (ed.), vol. 8 (pp. 1–85).

Schegloff, E. A. (1992). On talk and its institutional occasions. In Drew, and Heritage (eds.), (pp. 101–34).

(2000). On granularity. *Annual Review of Sociology* 26, 715–720.

(2003). On conversation analysis: an interview with Emanuel E. Schegloff with Svetla Cmejrková and Carlo L. Prevignano. In C. L. Prevignano, and P. J. Thibault (eds.), *Discussing conversation analysis, the work of Emmanuel E. Schegloff.* (pp. 11–55). Amsterdam: John Benjamins.

Schegloff, E. A., and Sacks, H. (1973). Opening up closings. *Semiotica* 8, 289–327.

Scheler, M. (1980). *Problems of a sociology of knowledge.* London: Routledge & Kegan Paul.

Schiefele, U. (1999). Interest and learning from text. *Scientific Studies of Reading*, 3(3), 257–279.

Schieffelin, B. B. (2008). Speaking only your own mind: reflections on talk, gossip and intentionality in Bosavi (PNG). *Anthropological Quarterly*, 81(2), 431–441.

Schiffrin, D., Tannen, D., and Hamilton, H. E. (eds.) (2013). *The handbook of discourse analysis*, 2nd edn. Malden, MA.: Blackwell.

Schlenker, P. (2008). Be articulate: a pragmatic theory of presupposition projection. *Theoretical Linguistics*, 34(3), 157–212.

Schlesinger, P., Murdock, G., and Elliott, P. (1983). *Televising 'terrorism': political violence in popular culture.* London: Comedia.

Schmid, A. P., and de Graaf, J. (1982). *Violence as communication: insurgent terrorism and the Western news media.* Beverly Hills: Sage.

Schmitt, F. F. (ed.) (1994). *Socializing epistemology: the social dimensions of knowledge.* Lanham, MD: Rowman & Littlefield.

Schnotz, W. (1993). Adaptive construction of mental representations in understanding expository texts. *Contemporary Educational Psychology*, 18(1), 114–120.

(2002). Towards an integrated view of learning from text and visual displays. *Educational Psychology Review*, 14, 101–120.

Schutz, A. (1962). *Collected papers.* The Hague: M. Nijhoff.

Schwartz, D. G., and Te'eni, D. (2011). *Encyclopedia of knowledge management.* Hershey, PA: Information Science Reference.

Schwarz, M. N. K., and Flammer, A. (1981). Text structure and title-effects on comprehension and recall. *Journal of Verbal Learning and Verbal Behavior*, 20, 61–66.

Schwoch, J., White, M., and Reilly, S. (1992). *Media knowledge: readings in popular culture, pedagogy and critical citizenship.* Albany, NY: SUNY Press.

Searle, J. R. (1969). *Speech acts: an essay in the philosophy of language.* Cambridge University Press.

(1971). *The philosophy of language.* Oxford University Press.

(1983). *Intentionality: an essay in the philosophy of mind.* Cambridge University Press.

(1992). *The rediscovery of the mind.* Cambridge, MA: MIT Press.

(1993). The problem of consciousness. *Social Research*, 60(1), 3–16.

(1995). *The construction of social reality.* New York: Free Press.

(1998). *Mind, language, and society: philosophy in the real world.* New York: Basic Books.

(2002). *Consciousness and language.* Cambridge University Press.

Seidlhofer, B. (1995). *Approaches to summarization: discourse analysis and language education.* Tübingen: G. Narr.

Semb, G. B., Ellis, J. A., and Araujo, J. (1993). Long-term-memory for knowledge learned in school. *Journal of Educational Psychology*, 85(2), 305–316.

Semin, G. R. (1989). Prototypes and social representations. In Jodelet (ed.), (pp. 239–251).

Semin, G. R., and Smith, E. R. (2008). *Embodied grounding: social, cognitive, affective, and neuroscientific approaches.* Cambridge University Press.

Sert, O. (2013). 'Epistemic status check' as an interactional phenomenon in instructed learning settings. *Journal of Pragmatics*, 45(1), 13–28.

Sgall, P., Hajičová, E., and Benešová, E. (1973). *Topic, focus and generative semantics.* Kronberg: Taunus.

Shanafelt, R. (2002). Idols of our tribes? Relativism, truth and falsity in ethnographic fieldwork and cross-cultural interaction. *Critique of Anthropology*, 22(1), 7–29.

Shapiro, L. A. (2010). *Embodied cognition.* New York: Routledge.

Shapiro, S. (2008). *Vagueness in context.* Oxford/New York: Clarendon Press/Oxford University Press.

Sharp, R. (1980). *Knowledge, ideology and the politics of schooling.* London: Routledge & Kegan Paul.

Shears, C., Hawkins, A., Varner, A., Lewis, L., Heatley, J., and Twachtmann, L. (2008). Knowledge-based inferences across the hemispheres: domain makes a difference. *Neuropsychologia*, 46(10), 2563–2568.

Shelley, C., and Thagard, P. (1996). Mythology and analogy. In D. R. Olson, and N. Torrance (eds.), *Modes of thought: explorations in culture and cognition* (pp. 152–183). Cambridge University Press.

Sherratt, S. (2007). Right brain damage and the verbal expression of emotion: a preliminary investigation. *Aphasiology*, 21(3–4), 320–339.

Sherzer, J. (1977). The ethnography of speaking: a critical appraisal. In M. Saville-Troike (ed.), *Linguistics and Anthropology* (pp. 43–58). Washington, DC: Georgetown University Press.

(1987). A discourse-centered approach to language and culture. *American Anthropologist*, 89(2), 295–309.

Shinjo, M., and Myers, J. L. (1987). The role of context in metaphor comprehension. *Journal of Memory and Language*, 26(2), 226–241.

Shinn, T., and Whitley, R. (eds.) (1985). *Expository science: forms and functions of popularisation.* Dordrecht/Boston, MA.: Reidel.

Shipley, T. F., and Zacks, J. M. (eds.) (2008). *Understanding events: from perception to action.* Oxford University Press.

Shore, B. (1996). *Culture in mind: cognition, culture, and the problem of meaning.* New York: Oxford University Press.

Short, K. (1992). Researching intertextuality within classroom learning environments. *Linguistics and Education*, 4(3–4), 313–334.

Shuy, R. W. (1998). *The language of confession, interrogation, and deception.* Thousand Oaks, CA: Sage.

Sidanius, J., and Pratto, F. (1999). *Social dominance: an intergroup theory of social hierarchy and oppression.* New York: Cambridge University Press.

Sillitoe, P. (ed.) (2007). *Local science vs. global science: approaches to indigenous knowledge in international development.* New York: Berghahn Books.

Sillitoe, P. (2010). Trust in development: some implications of knowing in indigenous knowledge. *Journal of the Royal Anthropological Institute*, 16(1), 12–30.

Silverstein, M. (1993). Metapragmatic discourse and metapragmatic function. In J. Lucy (ed.), *Reflexive Language: Reported Speech and Metapragmatics* (pp. 33–58). Cambridge University Press.

Simons, M. (2007). Observations on embedding verbs, evidentiality and presupposition. *Lingua*, 117, 1034–1056.

Simon-Vandenbergen, A. M. (2008). Almost certainly and most definitely: degree modifiers and epistemic stance. *Journal of Pragmatics*, 40(9), 1521–1542.

Slaughter, V., Peterson, C. C., and Carpenter, M. (2008). Maternal talk about mental states and the emergence of joint visual attention. *Infancy*, 13(6), 640–659.

Slobin, D. I. (1990). The development from child speaker to native speaker. In J. W. Stigler, R. A. Shweder, and G. Herdt (eds.), *Cultural psychology: essays on comparative human development* (pp. 233–256). New York: Cambridge University Press.

(1991). Learning to think for speaking: native language, cognition, and rhetorical style. *Pragmatics*, 1, 7–26.

Slotte, V., Lonka, K., and Lindblom-Ylänne, S. (2001). Study-strategy use in learning from text: does gender make any difference. *Instructional Science*, 29(3), 255–272.

Smith, E. R., and Queller, S. (2004). Mental representations. In M. B. Brewer, and M. Hewstone (eds.), *Social cognition* (pp. 5–27). Oxford: Blackwell.

Smith, N. V. (1982). *Mutual knowledge*. London/New York: Academic Press.

Soames, S. (2010). *What is meaning?* Oxford University Press.

Soler, S. (2004). *Discurso y género en historias de vida. Una investigación de relatos de hombres y mujeres en Bogotá*. Bogota: Caro y Cuervo.

Soley, L. C. (1992). *The news shapers: the sources who explain the news*. New York: Praeger.

Sörlin, S., and Vessuri, H. M. C. (eds.) (2006). *Knowledge society vs. knowledge economy: knowledge, power, and politics*. New York: Palgrave Macmillan.

Sosa, E. (ed.) (1994). *Knowledge and justification*. Aldershot, England/Brookfield, VT: Dartmouth.

Sosa, E., Kim, J., Fantl, J., and McGrath, M. (eds.) (2008). *Epistemology: an anthology*, 2nd edn. Oxford: Blackwell.

Sowa, J. F. (2000). *Knowledge representation: logical, philosophical, and computational foundations*. Pacific Grove, CA: Brooks/Cole.

Spelke, E. S., Breinlinger, K., Macomber, J., and Jacobson, K. (1992). Origins of knowledge. *Psychological Review*, 99(4), 605–632.

Sperber, D. (1990). The epidemiology of beliefs. In Fraser, and Gaskell (eds.), (pp. 25–44).

Sperber, D., and Wilson, D. (1990). Spontaneous deduction and mutual knowledge. *Behavioral and Brain Sciences*, 13(1), 179–184.

(1995). *Relevance: communication and cognition*. Cambridge, MA: Blackwell Publishers.

Spires, H. A., and Donley, J. (1998). Prior knowledge activation: inducing engagement with informational texts. *Journal of Educational Psychology*, 90(2), 249–260.

Spradley, J. P. (1972). *Culture and cognition: rules, maps, and plans*. San Francisco, CA: Chandler.

Squartini, M. (2008). Lexical vs. grammatical evidentiality in French and Italian. *Linguistics*, 46(5), 917–947.

Stahl, S. A., Hynd, C. R., Glynn, S. M., and Carr, M. (1996). Beyond reading to learn: developing content and disciplinary knowledge through texts. In L. Baker, P. Afflerbach, and D. Reinking (eds.), *Developing engaged readers in school and home communities* (pp. 136–146). Mahwah, NJ: Lawrence Erlbaum.

Stalnaker, R. C. (1974). Pragmatic presuppositions. In M. Munitz, and P. Unger (eds.), *Semantics and philosophy* (pp. 197–214). New York University Press.

(1978). Assertion. In P. Cole (ed.), *Syntax and semantics*, vol. 9: Pragmatics (pp. 315–332). New York: Academic Press.

(1999). *Context and content: essays on intentionality in speech and thought*. Oxford University Press.

(2002). Common ground. *Linguistics and Philosophy*, 25(5–6), 701–721.

(2008). *Our knowledge of the internal world*. Oxford: Clarendon Press.

Stark, W. (1958). *The sociology of knowledge: an essay in aid of a deeper understanding of the history of ideas*. London: Routledge & Kegan Paul.

Stehr, N., and Meja, V. (eds.) (2005). *Society and knowledge: contemporary perspectives in the sociology of knowledge and science*. New Brunswick, NJ: Transaction.

Stein, R. L., and Stein, P. L. (2005). *The anthropology of religion, magic, and witchcraft*. Boston: Pearson – Allyn & Bacon.

Stemmer, B. (1999). Discourse studies in neurologically impaired populations: a quest for action. *Brain and Language*, 68(3), 402–418.

Stephan, W. G., and Stephan, C. W. (1996). *Intergroup relations*. Dubuque, IA: Brown & Benchmark.

Stern, J. (2000). *Metaphor in context*. Cambridge, MA: MIT Press.

Steube, A. (ed.) (2004). *Information structure: theoretical and empirical aspects*. Berlin: Walter de Gruyter.

Steup, M. (ed.) (2001). *Knowledge, truth, and duty: essays on epistemic justification, responsibility, and virtue*. Oxford University Press.

Steup, M., and Sosa, E. (eds.) (2005). *Contemporary debates in epistemology*. Malden, MA: Blackwell.

Sticha, F. (1996). On implicitness in language and discourse: a contrastive view. In E. Hajičová, O. Leska, P. Sgall, and Z. Skoumalova (eds.), *Prague Linguistic Circle Papers*, vol. 2 (pp. 331–346). Amsterdam: John Benjamins.

Stivers, T., Mondada, M., and Steensig, J. (2011a). Knowledge, morality and affiliation in social interaction. In Stivers, Mondada, and Steensig (eds), (pp. 3–24).

Stivers, T., Mondada, M., and Steensig, J. (eds.) (2011b). *The morality of knowledge in conversation*. Cambridge University Press.

Stokoe, E., and Edwards, D. (2006). Story formulations in talk-in-interaction. *Narrative Inquiry*, 16(1), 56–65.

Strauss, C., and Quinn, N. (1997). *A cognitive theory of cultural meaning*. Cambridge University Press.

Strawson, P. F. (1950). Truth. *Aristotelian Society*, suppl, vol. 24, 139–156.

Strentz, H. (1989). *News reporters and news sources: accomplices in shaping and mis-shaping the news*. Ames, IA: Iowa State University Press.

Stroebe, W., Kruglanski, A., Bar-Tal, D., and Hewstone, M. (eds) (1988). *The social psychology of intergroup conflict*. New York: Springer-Verlag.

Strømsø, H. I., Bråten, I., and Samuelstuen, M. S. (2008). Dimensions of topic-specific epistemological beliefs as predictors of multiple text understanding. *Learning and Instruction*, 18(6), 513–527.

Sturtevant, W. C. (1964). Studies in ethnoscience. *American Anthropologist*, 66(2), 99–131.

Stygall, G. (2001). A different class of witnesses: experts in the courtroom. *Discourse Studies*, 3(3), 327–349.

Sunderlin, W. D. (2002). *Ideology, social theory, and the environment*. Lanham, MD: Rowman & Littlefield.

Swales, J. (2004). *Research genres: explorations and applications*. New York: Cambridge University Press.

Swan, J., Scarbrough, H., and Robertson, M. (2003). Linking knowledge, networking and innovation processes: a conceptual model. In L. V. Shavinina (ed.), *The international handbook on innovation* (pp. 680–694). New York: Elsevier Science.

Sweetser, E. (1987). The definition of LIE. In Holland and Quinn (eds.) (pp. 43–66).
    (1990). *From etymology to pragmatics: metaphorical and cultural aspects of semantic stucture*. Cambridge University Press.

Tajfel, H. (ed.) (1978). *Differentiation between social groups: studies in the social psychology of intergroup relations*. London: Academic Press.

Tajfel, H. (1981). *Human groups and social categories: studies in social psychology*. Cambridge University Press.

Tajfel, H. (ed.) (1982). *Social identity and intergroup relations*. Cambridge University Press.

Talmy, L. (1985). Force dynamics in language and thought. *Papers of the Chicago Linguistic Society*, 21(1), 293–337.

Tanesini, A. (1999). *An introduction to feminist epistemologies*. Malden, MA: Blackwell.

Tannen, D. (1994a). *Gender and discourse*. New York: Oxford University Press.
    (1994b). *Talking from 9 to 5: how women's and men's conversational styles affect who gets heard, who gets credit, and what gets done at work*. New York: Morrow.

Tannen, D., Kendall, S., and Gordon, C. (eds.) (2007). *Family talk: discourse and identity in four American families*. Oxford University Press.

Taylor, E. L. (1989). Language and the study of shared cultural knowledge. In D. T. Helm, W. T. Anderson, A. J. Meehan, and A. W. Rawls (eds.) *The interactional order: new directions in the study of social order* (pp. 215–230). New York: Irvington.

Tedeschi, J. T. (ed.) (1981). *Impression management theory and social psychological research*. New York: Academic Press.

Telfer, W. R., and Garde, M. J. (2006). Indigenous knowledge of rock kangaroo ecology in western Arnhem Land, Australia. *Human Ecology*, 34(3), 379–406.

Ten Have, P. (2007). *Doing conversation analysis: a practical guide*, 2nd edn. London: Sage.

Tenbrink, T., Coventry, K. R., and Andonova, E. (2011). Spatial strategies in the description of complex configurations. *Discourse Processes*, 48(4), 237–266.

Tetlock, P. E. (1989). Structure and function in political belief systems. In Pratkanis, Breckler, and Greenwald (eds.), (pp. 129–151).

Teufel, S. (2010). *The structure of scientific articles: applications to citation indexing and summarization*. Stanford, CA: Center for the Study of Language and Information.

Tewksbury, D. (2003). What do Americans really want to know? Tracking the behavior of news readers on the internet. *Journal of Communication*, 53(4), 694–710.

Thiede, K. W., Anderson, M. C. M., and Therriault, D. (2003). Accuracy of metacognitive monitoring affects learning of texts. *Journal of Educational Psychology*, 95(1), 66–73.

Thomas, L. (2011). Sociality in cognitive and sociocultural anthropologies: the relationships aren't just additive. In Kronenfeld, Bennardo, de Munck, and Fischer (eds.), (pp. 413–429).

Thomas, W. I. (1928/1966). Situational analysis: the behavior pattern and the situation. (1928). In M. Janovitz (ed.), *W. I. Thomas on social organization and social personality*. University of Chicago Press.

Thompson, C. P. (ed.) (1998a). *Autobiographical memory: theoretical and applied perspectives*. Mahwah, NJ: Lawrence Erlbaum.

(1998b). *Eyewitness memory: theoretical and applied perspectives*. Mahwah, NJ: Lawrence Erlbaum.

Thompson, J. B. (1984). *Studies in the theory of ideology*. Berkeley, CA: University of California Press.

Thompson, L. L., Levine, J. M., and Messick, D. M. (eds.) (1999). *Shared cognition in organizations: the management of knowledge*. Mahwah, NJ: Lawrence Erlbaum.

Thornborrow, J. (2002). *Power talk: language ad interaction in institutional discourse*. London: Longman.

Thorndyke, P. W. (1979). Knowledge acquisition from newspaper stories. *Discourse Processes*, 2(2), 95–112.

Thornton, R. (2009). The transmission of knowledge in South African traditional healing. *Africa*, 79(1), 17–34.

Tichenor, H. M. (1921). *Primitive beliefs*. Girard, KS: Haldeman-Julius.

Tillema, H., and Orland-Barak, L. (2006). Constructing knowledge in professional conversations: the role of beliefs on knowledge and knowing. *Learning and Instruction*, 16(6), 592–608.

Tomasello, M. (1998). *The new psychology of language: cognitive and functional approaches to language structure*. Mahwah, NJ: Lawrence Erlbaum.

(2008). *Origins of human communication*. Cambridge: MA: MIT Press.

Tomasello, M., and Carpenter, M. (2007). Shared intentionality. *Developmental Science*, 10(1), 121–125.

Tomlin, R. S. (ed.) (1987). *Coherence and grounding in discourse: outcome of a symposium, Eugene, Oregon, June 1984*. Amsterdam: John Benjamins.

Tönnies, F. (1957). *Community and society (Gemeinschaft und Gesellschaft)*. East Lansing, MI: Michigan State University Press.

Tormala, Z. L., and Clarkson, J. J. (2008). Source trustworthiness and information processing in multiple message situations: a contextual analysis. *Social Cognition*, 26(3), 357–367.

Trabasso, T. (2005). Goal plans of action and inferences during comprehension of narratives. *Discourse Processes*, 39(2–3), 129–164.

Trabasso, T., and van den Broek, P. (1985). Causal thinking and the representation of narrative events. *Journal of Memory and Language*, 24(5), 612–630.

Triandis, H. C. (1995). *Individualism and collectivism*. Boulder, CO: Westview Press.

388   References

Tsohatzidis, S. L. (ed.) (1990). *Meanings and prototypes: studies in linguistic categorization*. London/New York: Routledge.

Tsui, A. B. M. (1992). A functional description of questions. In M. Coulthard (ed.), *Advances in spoken discourse analysis* (pp. 89–110). London: Routledge.

Tuchman, G. (1978). *Making news: a study in the construction of reality*. New York: Free Press.

Tulving, E. (1972). Episodic and semantic memory. In E. T. Tulving, and W. Donaldson (eds.), *Organization of memory*. New York: Academic Press.

  (1983). *Elements of episodic memory*. Oxford/New York: Clarendon Press/Oxford University Press.

  (2002). Episodic memory: from mind to brain. *Annual Review of Psychology*, 53(1), 1–25.

Turner, J. C., and Giles, H. (eds.) (1981). *Intergroup behaviour*. Oxford: Blackwell.

Turow, J. (1984). *Media industries: the production of news and entertainment*. New York: Longman.

Tversky, B., Zacks, J. M., Hard, B. M. (2008). The structure of experience. In Shipley, and Zacks (eds.), (pp. 436–464).

Unesco (1980). *Many voices, one world*. Report by the International Commission for the Study of Communication Problems (chaired by Sean Mac Bride). Paris: Unesco/London: Kogan Page.

Valencia, S. W., and Stallman, A. C. (1989). Multiple measures of prior knowledge: comparative predictive validity. *National Reading Conference Yearbook*, 38, 427–436.

Vallduví, E. (1992). *The informational component*. New York: Garland.

Van Ausdale, D., and Feagin, J. R. (2001). *The first R: how children learn race and racism*. Lanham, MD: Rowman & Littlefield.

Van Benthem, J. F. A. K. (2011). *Logical dynamics of information and interaction*. Cambridge University Press.

Van de Velde, R. G. (1984). *Prolegomena to inferential discourse processing*. Amsterdam: John Benjamins.

Van Deemter, K. (2010). *Not exactly: in praise of vagueness*. Oxford University Press.

Van den Broek, P. W., Bauer, P. J., and Bourg, T. (eds.) (1997). *Developmental spans in event comprehension and representation: bridging fictional and actual events*. Mahwah, NJ: Lawrence Erlbaum.

Van der Auwera, J. (1975). *Semantic and pragmatic presupposition*. Wilrijk: Universiteit Antwerpen.

Van Dijk, T. A. (1972). *Some aspects of text grammars: a study in theoretical linguistics and poetics*. The Hague: Mouton.

  (1977). *Text and context: explorations in the semantics and pragmatics of discourse*. London/New York: Longman.

  (1980). *Macrostructures: an interdisciplinary study of global structures in discourse, interaction, and cognition*. Hillsdale, NJ: Lawrence Erlbaum.

  (1984a). *Prejudice in discourse: an analysis of ethnic prejudice in cognition and conversation*. Amsterdam: John Benjamins.

  (1984b). *Structures of international news*. Report to UNESCO. University of Amsterdam, Dept. of General Literary Studies, Section of Discourse Studies, Unpublished ms. (summarized in Van Dijk, 1988b).

Van Dijk, T. A. (ed.) (1985). *Handbook of discourse analysis*, 4 vols. London: Academic Press.

Van Dijk, T. A. (1987). *Communicating racism: ethnic prejudice in thought and talk.* Newbury Park, CA: Sage.

(1988a). *News analysis: case studies of international and national news in the press.* Hillsdale, NJ: Lawrence Erlbaum.

(1988b). *News as discourse.* Hillsdale, NJ: Lawrence Erlbaum.

(1989). Race, riots and the press: an analysis of editorials in the British press about the 1985 disorders. *Gazette*, 43, 229–253.

(1991). *Racism and the press.* London/New York: Routledge.

(1992). Discourse and the denial of racism. *Discourse and Society*, 3(1), 87–118.

(1993). *Elite discourse and racism.* Thousand Oaks, CA: Sage.

(1998). *Ideology: a multidisciplinary approach.* London: Sage.

(2000). Parliamentary debates. In Wodak, and van Dijk (eds.), (pp. 45–78).

(2003). Knowledge in parliamentary debates. *Journal of Language and Politics*, 2(1), 93–129.

(2004a). Discourse, knowledge and ideology. In M. Pütz, J. Neff, and T. A. van Dijk (eds.), *Communicating ideologies: multidisciplinary perspectives on language, discourse and social practice* (pp. 5–38). Frankfurt am Main: Peter Lang.

(2004b). Knowledge and news. *Revista Canaria e Estudios Ingleses* 49, 71–86.

(2004c). Text and context of parliamentary debates. In P. Bayley (ed.), *Cross-cultural perspectives on parliamentary discourse* (pp. 339–372). Amsterdam: John Benjamins.

(2005a). Contextual knowledge management in discourse production. A CDA perspective. In R. Wodak and P. Chilton (eds.), *A New Agenda in (Critical) Discourse Analysis* (pp. 71–100) Amsterdam: John Benjamins.

(2005b). War rhetoric of a little ally: political implicatures of Aznar's legitimization of the war in Iraq. *Journal of Language and Politics*, 4(1), 65–92.

(2006a). Discourse and manipulation. *Discourse and Society*, 17(3), 359–383.

Van Dijk, T. A. (ed.) (2006b). Discourse, interaction and cognition. Special issue of *Discourse Studies* 8(1), 5–7.

(2007). *Discourse studies*, 5 vols. Sage Benchmarks in Discourse Studies. London: Sage.

Van Dijk, T. A. (2008a). *Discourse and context: a socio-cognitive approach.* Cambridge University Press.

(2008b). *Discourse and power.* Houndmills: Palgrave Macmillan.

(2009a). *Society and discourse: how social contexts influence text and talk.* Cambridge University Press.

(2009b). *Racism and discourse in Latin America.* Lanham, MD: Lexington Books.

Van Dijk, T. A. (2011a). Discourse, knowledge, power and politics. Towards Critical Epistemic Discourse Analysis. In C. Hart (ed.), *Critical Discourse Studies in Context and Cognition* (pp. 27–63). Amsterdam: John Benjamins.

Van Dijk, T. A. (ed.) (2011b). *Discourse studies: a multidisciplinary introduction*, one-volume edition. London: Sage.

Van Dijk, T. A. (2012). Knowledge, discourse and domination. In M. Meeuwis and J.-O. Östman (eds.), *Pragmaticizing understanding: studies for Jef Verschueren* (pp. 151–196). Amsterdam: John Benjamins.

Van Dijk, T. A., and Kintsch, W. (1983). *Strategies of discourse comprehension*. New York/Toronto: Academic Press.

Van Harmelen, F., Lifschitz, V., and Porter, B. (eds.) (2008). *Handbook of knowledge representation*. Amsterdam: Elsevier.

Van Hout, T., and Jacobs, G. (2008). News production theory and practice: fieldwork notes on power, interaction and agency. *Pragmatics*, 18(1), 59–85.

Van Kuppevelt, J. (1995). Discourse structure, topicality and questioning. *Journal of Linguistics*, 31(1), 109–147.

Van Leeuwen, T. J. (1995). Representing social action. *Discourse and Society*, 6(1), 81–106.

(1996). The representation of social actors. In C.R. Caldas-Coulthard, and M. Coulthard (eds.), *Texts and practices: readings in critical discourse analysis* (pp. 32–70). London: Routledge.

(2005). *Introducing social semiotics*. London: Routledge.

Van Oostendorp, H. (1996). Updating situation models derived from newspaper articles. *Zeitschrift für Medienpsychologie*, 8(1), 21–33.

Van Oostendorp, H., and Goldman, S. R. (eds.) (1999). *The construction of mental representations during reading*. Mahwah, NJ: Lawrence Erlbaum.

Van Oostendorp, H., and Zwaan, R. A. (eds.) (1994). *Naturalistic text comprehension*. Advances in Discourse Processing, vol. LIII. Norwood, NJ: Ablex.

Van Voorst, J. (1988). *Event structure*. Amsterdam: John Benjamins.

VanPool, C. S., and VanPool, T. L. (2009). The semantics of local knowledge: using ethnosemantics to study folk taxonomies represented in the archaeological record. *Journal of Anthropological Research*, 65(4), 529–554.

Varela, F. J., Thompson, E., and Rosch, E. (1991). *The embodied mind: cognitive science and human experience*. Cambridge, MA: MIT Press.

Velmans, M., and Schneider, S. (eds.) (2007). *The Blackwell companion to consciousness*. Oxford: Blackwell.

Ventola, E. (2000). *Discourse and community: doing functional linguistics*. Tübingen: Narr.

Verdi, M. P., and Kulhavy, R. (2002). Learning with maps and texts: an overview. *Educational Psychology Review*, 14(1), 27–46.

Veroff, J., Douvan, E., and Kulka, R. A. (1981). *The inner American*. New York: Basic Books.

Verschueren, J., Östman, J. O., and Blommaert, J. (1994). *Handbook of pragmatics*. Amsterdam: John Benjamins.

Vezin, L. (1980). Text organisation: supplied or constructed during learning, and acquired skills. *International Journal of Psycholinguistics*, 7(3), 63–80.

Vine, B. (2004). *Getting things done at work: the discourse of power in workplace interaction*. Amsterdam: John Benjamins.

Voithofer, R. (2006). Studying intertextuality, discourse and narratives to conceptualize and contextualize online learning environments. *International Journal of Qualitative Studies in Education*, 19(2), 201–219.

Von Cranach, M., Doise, W., and Mugny, G. (1992). *Social representations and the social bases of knowledge*. Lewiston, NY: Hogrefe & Huber.

Wade, S. E. (1992). How interest affects learning from text. In Renninger, Hidi, and A. Krapp (eds.), (pp. 255–277).

Wade, S., and Schramm, W. (1969). The mass media as sources of public affairs, science and health knowledge. *Public Opinion Quarterly* 33, 197–209.

Waern, Y. (1977). On the relationship between knowledge of the world and comprehension of texts: assimilation and accommodation effects related to belief structure. *Scandinavian Journal of Psychology*, 18(2), 130–139.

Wagner, W., Kronberger, N., and Seifert, F. (2002). Collective symbolic coping with new technology: knowledge, images, and public discourse. *British Journal of Social Psychology*, 41, 323–343.

Wake, D. G. (2009). Teaching expository text structures: using digital storytelling techniques to make learning explicit. In F. Falk-Ross, S. Szabo, M. B. Sampson, and M. M. Foote (eds.), *Literacy issues during changing times: a call to action* (pp. 164–188). Pittsburg, KS: College Reading Association.

Walton, D. N. (2002). *Legal argumentation and evidence.* Pennsylvania State University Press.

(2008). *Witness testimony evidence: argumentation, artificial intelligence, and law.* Cambridge University Press.

Wang, Q. (2001). Did you have fun: American and Chinese mother–child conversations about shared emotional experiences. *Cognitive Development*, 16(2), 693–715.

(2003). Emotion situation knowledge in American and Chinese preschool-children and adults. *Cognition and Emotion*, 17(5), 725–746.

Wegener, D. T., and Petty, R. E. (1998). The naive scientist revisited: naive theories and social judgment. *Social Cognition*, 16(1), 1–7.

Wegner, D. M., and Vallacher, R. R. (1981). Common-sense psychology. In J. Forgas (ed.), *Social cognition: perspectives on everyday understanding.* New York: Academic Press.

Welch, A. R., and Freebody, P. (eds.) (1993). *Knowledge, culture, and power: international perspectives on literacy as policy and practice.* London/Washington, DC: Falmer Press.

Wellman, J. L. (2013). *Organizational learning: how companies and institutions manage and apply knowledge.* Basingstoke: Palgrave Macmillan.

Wenger, E. (1998). *Communities of practice: learning, meaning and identity.* Cambridge University Press.

Werth, P. (1993). Accommodation and the myth of presupposition: the view from discourse. *Lingua*, 89(1), 39–95.

West, C. (1984). *Routine complications: troubles with talk between doctors and patients.* Bloomington, IN: Indiana University Press.

White, P. R. R. (2006). Evaluative semantics and ideological positioning in journalistic discourse: a new framework for analysis. In I. Lassen, J. Strunck, and T. Vestergaard (eds.), *Mediating ideology in text and image: ten critical studies* (pp. 37–67). Amsterdam: John Benjamins.

Wilen, W. W. (ed.) (1990). *Teaching and learning through discussion: the theory, research and practice of the discussion method.* Springfield, IL: Charles C Thomas.

Wilkinson, A., Papaioannou, D., Keen, C., and Booth, A. (2009). The role of the information specialist in supporting knowledge transfer: a public health information case study. *Health Information and Libraries Journal*, 26(2), 118–125.

Wilkinson, N. (2009). *Secrecy and the media: the official history of the United Kingdom's D-notice system*. London/New York: Routledge.

Williams, H. L., Conway, M. A., and Cohen, G. (2008). Autobiographical memory. In G. Cohen, and M. A. Conway (eds.), *Memory in the real world*, 3rd edn. (pp. 21–90). Hove and New York: Psychology Press.

Williams, J. P. (1991). Comprehension by learning-disabled and nondisabled adolescents of personal/social problems presented in text. *The American Journal of Psychology*, 104(4), 563–586.

Williams, N. M., and Baines, G. (eds.) (1993). *Traditional ecological knowledge: wisdom for sustainable development*. Canberra: Centre for Resource and Environmental Studies, Australian National University.

Williams, T. (2000). *Knowledge and its limits*. Oxford University Press.

Wilson, C. C., Gutiérrez, F., and Chao, L. M. (2003). *Racism, sexism, and the media: the rise of class communication in multicultural America*. Thousand Oaks, CA: Sage.

Winiecki, D. (2008). The expert witnesses and courtroom discourse: applying micro and macro forms of discourse analysis to study process and the 'doings of doings' for individuals and for society. *Discourse and Society*, 19(6), 765–781.

Wirth, U. (2002). *Performanz. Zwischen Sprachphilosophie und Kulturwissenschaft*. Frankfurt: Suhrkamp.

Wodak, R. (1984). Determination of guilt: discourses in the courtroom. In C. Kramarae, M. Schulz, and W. M. O'Barr (eds.), *Language and power* (pp. 89–100). Beverly Hills, CA: Sage.

 (1989a). *Sprache und Macht – Sprache und Politik*. Vienna: Österreichischer Bundesverlag.

Wodak, R. (ed.) (1989b). *Language, power, and ideology: studies in political discourse*. Amsterdam: John Benjamins.

Wodak, R., and van Dijk, T. A. (eds.) (2000). *Racism at the top: parliamentary discourses on ethnic issues in six European states*. Klagenfurt, Austria: Drava Verlag.

Wodak, R., Johnstone, B., and Kerswill, P. (eds.) (2011). *The Sage handbook of sociolinguistics*. London: Sage.

Wodak, R., Khosravinik, M., and Mral, B. (eds.) (2013). *Right-wing populism in Europe*. London: Bloomsbury.

Wolfe, M. B. W., and Mienko, J. A. (2007). Learning and memory of factual content from narrative and expository text. *British Journal of Educational Psychology*, 77(3), 541–564.

Wolff, M. (2008). *The man who owns the news: inside the secret world of Rupert Murdoch*. New York: Broadway Books.

Wosnitza, M., and Volet, S. (2009). A framework for personal goals in collaborative learning contexts. In M. Wosnitza, S. A. Karabenick, A. Efklides, and P. Nenniger (eds.), *Contemporary motivation research: from global to local perspectives* (pp. 49–67). Ashland, OH: Hogrefe and Huber.

Wright, A. L., Bauer, M., Clark, C., Morgan, F., and Begishe, K. (1993). Cultural interpretations and intracultural variability in Navajo beliefs about breast-feeding. *American Ethnologist*, 20(4), 781–796.

Wright, C. (1993). *Realism, meaning, and truth*. Oxford, UK/Cambridge, MA: Blackwell.

Wuketits, F. M. (1990). *Evolutionary epistemology and its implications for humankind.* State University of New York Press.

Wuthnow, R. (1989). *Communities of discourse: ideology and social structure in the Reformation, the Enlightenment, and European socialism.* Cambridge, MA: Harvard University Press.

Wyer, R. S. (ed.) (1995). *Knowledge and memory: the real story.* Hillsdale, NJ: Lawrence Erlbaum.

(1996). *Ruminative thoughts.* Mahwah, NJ: Lawrence Erlbaum.

Wyer, R. S. (2004). The cognitive organization and use of general knowledge. In J. T. Jost, M. R. Banaji, and D. A. Prentice (eds.), *Perspectivism in social psychology: the yin and yang of scientific progress* (pp. 97–112). Washington, DC: American Psychological Association.

Wyer, R. S., and Srull, T. K. (eds.) (1984). *Handbook of social cognition.* Hillsdale, NJ: Lawrence Erlbaum.

Yaros, R. A. (2006). Is it the medium or the message? Structuring complex news to enhance engagement and situational understanding by nonexperts. *Communication Research*, 33(4), 285–309.

Yearley, S. (1992). Green ambivalence about science: legal-rational authority and the scientific legitimation of a social movement. *British Journal of Sociology*, 43(4), 511–532.

Yoon, S. A. (2008). An evolutionary approach to harnessing complex systems thinking in the science and technology classroom. *International Journal of Science Education*, 30(1), 1–32.

Young, M. F. D. (ed.) (1971). *Knowledge and control: new directions for the sociology of education.* London: Collier-Macmillan.

Zacks, J. M., and Sargent, J. Q. (2009). Event perception: a theory and its application to clinical neuroscience. In B. H. Ross (ed.), *Psychology of learning and motivation*, vol. 53 (pp. 253–299). Burlington: Elsevier.

Zacks, J. M., and Swallow, K. M. (2007). Event segmentation. *Current Directions in Psychological Science*, 16(2), 80–84.

Zacks, J. M., Tversky, B., and Iyer, G. (2001). Perceiving, remembering, and communicating structure in events. *Journal of Experimental Psychology: General*, 130(1), 29–58.

Zagzebski, L. T. (1996). *Virtues of the mind: an inquiry into the nature of virtue and the ethical foundations of knowledge.* Cambridge University Press.

Zammuner, V. L. (1981). *Speech production: strategies in discourse planning: a theoretical and empirical enquiry.* Hamburg: H. Buske.

Zanna, M. P., and Olson, J. M. (eds.) (1994). *The psychology of prejudice: the Ontario Symposium*, vol. 7. Hillsdale, NJ: Lawrence Erlbaum.

Zappavigna, M. (2013). *Tacit knowledge and spoken discourse.* London/New York: Bloomsbury Academic.

Zelezny, J. D. (1993). *Cases in communications law.* Belmont, CA: Wadsworth.

Ziman, J. M. (1991). *Reliable knowledge: an exploration of the grounds for belief in science.* Cambridge University Press.

Zimmermann, M. (2008). Contrastive focus and emphasis. *Acta Linguistica Hungarica*, 55(3–4), 347–360.

Zwaan, R. A. (1994). Effect of genre expectations on text comprehension. *Journal of Experimental Psychology: Learning, Memory, and Cognition*, 20, 920–933.

(1999). Situation models: the mental leap into imagined worlds. *Current Directions in Psychological Science*, 8(1), 15–18.

(2009). Mental simulation in language comprehension and social cognition. *European Journal of Social Psychology*, 39(7), 1142–1150.

Zwaan, R. A., and Radvansky, G. A. (1998). Situation models in language comprehension and memory. *Psychological Bulletin*, 123(2), 162–185.

Zwaan, R. A., and Taylor, L. J. (2006). Seeing, acting, understanding: motor resonance in language comprehension. *Journal of Experimental Psychology: General*, 135(1), 1–11.

Index

aboutness, 297
accommodation and presupposition, 287
activation
   of information, 301, 303
affiliation, 229–237
affordances, 54
age
   and topics of talk, 128
alignment, 229–237
Alternative Semantics, 301
anthropology, 5
   epistemic, 167
   and knowledge, 168
appropriateness, 55
Artificial Intelligence, 6, 65
assertions, 240
   indirect, 287
   oblique, 287
assimilation, 66
asylum seekers, 1, 2, 3, 4, 7
attitudes, 8, 91, 100–101
autobiographical experiences, 83
autobiographical memory, 51
Aznar, J. M., 14, 284, 389

behaviorism, 92
belief states, 36
belief systems, 31, 63
beliefs, 28–31, 63
   acceptance of, 31
   context of, 31
   cultural, 175–177
   implicit vs. explicit, 31
   social, 93, 94–111
   specific vs. generic, 31
   strength of, 31
   types vs. tokens, 30
   variable, 31
   widespread, 94
Blair, T., 14, 15, 16, 17, 18, 19, 20, 21, 22, 23, 26, 27, 31, 36, 37, 38, 197, 284, 285, 286, 291, 292

bridging inferences, 52
Bush, G. W., 14, 284

Cameron, D., 127, 139, 140, 142, 143, 144, 145, 150, 152, 153, 158, 163, 164, 165, 166, 249, 250, 254, 283, 285, 290, 291, 292, 298, 299, 300, 340
categories, 63
certainty, 275
classroom, 77
cognition
   and culture, 172–179
   distributed, 116–117
   and knowledge, 62–64, 314–318
   shared, 93
   and society, 147
cognitive psychology, 4, 6–7, 11
coherence, 4, 52, 58
   global, 245
   local, 248–250
coherentism, 28
cohesion, 248
Common Ground, 5, 23, 27, 47, 54, 87, 117–120, 224, 238, 250, 263, 286, 288, 289, 296, 298, 300
common sense, 114
communication of knowledge, 120–137
   interpersonal, 122
communication studies, 9
communicative situation, 54
communities, 94, 111–113
   definition of, 112
   of discourse, 147–149
   linguistic, 147
   of practice, 112, 148
   sociocultural, 179–182
concepts, 63
context, 22–23, 47
   knowledge in, 152–154
   of learning from text, 72
context models, 22, 47, 54–58, 120, 159, 225
   and appropriateness, 55

context models (*cont.*)
  dynamic, 54
  of journalists, 160
  multimodality of, 54
  and pragmatics, 55
  pre-planned, 55
contextualism, 23, 170
conversation, 8
  epistemic structures of, 229–237
Conversation Analysis, 10
conversational epistemics, 231
conversations
  dinner time, 125
cooperation
  epistemic, 242
correctness, 32
correspondence, 30
co-text, 37
counterfactuals, 32, 41, 49
credibility, 3
critical anthropology, 171
critical approaches to cultural knowledge,
    185–186
Critical Discourse Analysis, 197
Critical Discourse Studies, 11, 171
Critical Intercultural Communication
    Studies, 186
cultural knowledge and beliefs, 175–177
cultural models, 177–179
culture, 5, 8
  and cognition, 172–179
  as cognition and action, 173–175
  and discourse and knowledge, 191–220
  and knowledge, 167–221, 323–325
  and power, 184

Daily Telegraph, 1, 2, 3, 5, 7, 9, 249, 251, 256
definitions, 293–294
deictic expressions, 22, 57
deniability, 283
descriptions, 252
  levels of, 253
discourse
  coherence, 52, 58
  communicative function of, 224
  communities of, 147–149
  definitions in, 293–294
  and elaboration, 290–293
  epistemic structures of, 228
  as evidence, 268
  expository, 27, 59
  focus in, 300–303
  genres, 48, 197, 225
  implications in, 281–283
  implicatures in, 283–285
  information structure in, 295–303

and knowledge, 325–327
and mental models, 25–26, 193
metaphors in, 295
modality, 275–280
multimodal, 47
natural, 47
ordering of, 251
reliability, 153
schematic structure, 58
semantics, 244–306
sequencing of, 251
the study of, 10–12
surface structures of, 307
Discourse–Cognition–Society framework, 12
discourse epistemics, 5, 11
discourse processing, 47–49
  and knowledge, 64–69
  and prior knowledge, 65–68
discourse structures
  and learning, 80
Discourse Studies, 9–10
discourse topic, 52, 58
discursive psychology, 93
distributed cognition, 116–117
  ecological, 116
domain
  epistemic, 292
dynamic knowledge management, 224
dynamic logic, 37

editorials, 91
elaboration, 290–293
Episodic Memory, 24, 50, 52, 63, 83–85
epistemic 5
  anthropology, 167
  cooperation, 242
  discourse semantics, 244–306
  domain, 292
  dynamics, 134
  engine, 231
  interaction management, 113
  literacy, 149
  modality, 275
  organizations, 4
  positioning, 275
  pragmatics, 239–244
  presupposition, 288
  professions, 8
  recursion, 120
  speech acts, 240
  stance, 259, 275
  standards, 167
epistemic communities, 6, 8, 16, 28, 92, 141,
    147–152
  membership of, 149–151
  types of, 151–152

epistemic structures, 223
    of conversation, 229–237
epistemics, 228
epistemological positioning, 274
epistemology, 14–44, 310–314
    discourse analytical perspective, 16
    role of knowledge in, 22
ethnography, 5
    of speaking, 10
ethnomethodology, 10
events, 49
    complex, 50
    real vs. fictional, 42
    sequences, 50
evidence
    discourse as, 268
evidential strategies, 269
evidentiality, 259–268
    and interaction, 270
    linguistic expressions of, 272
    social functions of, 268
evolution
    of language, 224
evolutionary psychology, 48
experience models, 49
experiences, 49, 84
experimental subjects, 73
expert knowledge, 106
expert systems, 64
expertise, 67
expository discourse, 59

facts, 37–39
fiction, 41
fictional events, 41
focus, 295–303
footing, 229
force dynamic, 269
functional local coherence, 248

gender
    and topics of talk, 126–128
genealogy
    of knowledge, 146
generic knowledge, 7, 62, 85–88
genre, 10
    of discourse, 48, 225
global coherence, 245
global focus, 238
Global Functional Focus, 239, 290, 304
Global Functional Topic, 239, 244, 290
global topic, 238
goals, 75
gossip, 199
grammar
    and information structure, 302

and modality, 279
granularity, 255
group knowledge, 106
groups, 94
    definition of, 112
    epistemic, 113
    ideological, 112
    types of, 112
Guardian, 150, 154, 163

hearsay, 22
hedging, 257, 278

ideological groups, 98
ideological schema, 99
Ideological Square, 161, 163
ideology, 3, 8, 95–100, 141, 161
    and groups, 112
    as personal ideological choice, 97
    schemas of, 99
    social vs. personal, 97
immigrants, 209
    knowledge about, 209–220
immigration, 140, 285, 298
implication, 281–283
    pragmatic, 284
implicature, 283–285
implicitness, 281
indexical expression, 22
indexicality, 31
indexicals, 57, 279
inferences, 27
information, see also knowledge
    activation of, 301, 303
information structure, 295–303
    and grammar, 302
institutional interaction, 236
intentionality, 17, 30
interactional evidentials, 271
interest, 76
intergroup relations, 93
intersubjectivity, 277
intertextuality, 237

journalist, 3
    context models of, 160
justification, 33–34
justified true beliefs, 6

K-device, 23, 47, 54, 57, 66, 84, 226–227,
    228, 230, 239, 244, 265, 296, 298,
    302, 316
knowledge
    access to, 30
    acquisition, 68–82, see also knowledge
        acquisition

knowledge (*cont.*)
  anthropology and, 168
  assimilation of, 66
  autobiographical, 84
  categorial organization of, 63
  and cognition, 45–89, 314–318
  cognitive theory of, 62–64
  commmunication of, 120–137
  in context, 152–154
  contextual, 16, 22–23
  criteria, 21
  cultural, 175–177
  and culture, 167–221, 323–325
  declarative, 18
  definition of, 21, 28
  device, 55
  and discourse processing, 64–69
  and discourse structures, 325–327
  discursive, 28
  domains, 86
  engineering, 64
  expert, 67, 106
  functions of, 18–21
  genealogy of, 146
  generic, 7, 27, 46, 49, 51, 59, 85–88
  group, 106
  about immigrants, 209–220
  joint, 113
  knowledge of, 18
  knowledge vs. opinion, 3
  and language, 325–327
  learning of, 68–82
  levels of, 67
  local, 182–186
  management, 226, *see also* knowledge
    management
  material expressions of, 174
  media, 135
  and memory, 82–88
  as mental model, 24–25
  mutual, 120
  natural, 6, 28–43
  new, 3
  and the news, 3, 155–163
  objective vs. subjective, 39
  old, 3
  old vs. new, 302
  personal, 7, 21, 83
  personal vs. generic, 27
  personal vs. social, 94–95
  and power, 171
  pragmatic approach to, 33
  prior, 65, 68, 74
  propositional vs. operational, 18
  about racism, 59

  relative, 16
  relativity of, 6
  representations, 65
  reproduction of, 53
  schemas, 61
  self-, 30
  and semantic macrostructures, 244–247
  and social beliefs, 106–111
  and social cognition, 90–138, 319–320
  society, 154
  and society, 139–167, 320–323
  sociocultural, 145–147
  sources, 259
  specialized group, 106
  structures of local, 186–191
  the study of, 6–10
  subjective, 62
  of subjects, 67
  surface structures of, 307
  tacit, 281
  theory of natural, 21–28
  topic, 67
  traditional local, 184
  types of, 224
  updating, 3
  versions of, 95
  and Working Memory, 82–83
  of the world, 2, 46
knowledge acquisition, 64
  cooperation, 77
  methods of, 261
knowledge in education, 137
knowledge management, 9, 226
  dynamic, 224
  in organizations, 130–134, 154–155
Kwaio, 188, 189, 190, 191, 192, 362

language, 325–327
  evolution of, 224
language use, *see* discourse
learning, 68–82
  collaborative, 77
  context of, 72
  and cooperation, 77
  and discourse structures, 80
  and gender, 75
  and motivation, 76
  and reading ability, 75
  strategies, 79
  from text, 69–72
levels of description, 253
lies, 201
linearization, 291
linguistic communities, 147
linguistic presupposition, 286, 288

linguistic relativity, 194
linguistic structures
    and knowledge, 325–327
linguistics, 5, 9–10, 222
local coherence, 248–250, 281
    functional, 248
    referential, 249
local knowledge, 182–186
long term memory, 24, 63

macrosemantic markers, 245
manipulation, 250
media
    knowledge, 135
memory, 7, 24
    autobiographical, 84
    working, 82–83
mental models, 7, 49–53
    abstraction of, 51
    counterfactual, 49
    and discourse, 25–26
    of experience, 49
    generalization of, 51
    as knowledge, 24–25
    multimodality of, 49
    and reproduction of knowledge, 53
    and society, 143–145
    structures of, 50–53
    uniqueness of, 51
mental representations, 4, 6, 17, 29
    vs. discourse meaning, 35
meta-models, 29, 41, 276
metaphor, 294–295
methods
    of knowledge acquisition, 261
mirror neurons, 83, 120
misconceptions, 66
modal expressions, 35
modal logic, 41
modality, 259, 275–280
    and grammar, 279
    subjective vs. objective, 276
models, see mental models
    cultural, 177–179
motivation, 76
multimodal discourse, 47
multimodality, 49, 54
mutual knowledge, 120
myth, 199

narrative, 199
natural knowledge, 14
    properties of, 28–43
neural networks, 63
neuropsychology, 7, 48

New York Times, 90, 107
news
    and knowledge, 159–163
news production, 156–159
news reports, 1, 2, 3, 4, 7, 51, 155–163, 223,
    226, 245, 248, 256, 269, 278, 292
normalization of social beliefs, 115

Obama, B., 90, 91, 94, 97, 109, 238, 239
objectivity, 3
ontology, 40–41
opinion, 3, 22, 29, 91
    opinion vs. knowledge, 3
ordering
    of discourse, 251
organization studies, 9
organizations
    knowledge management in, 130–134,
        154–155
Other Minds, 83

participation structure, 53, 227
personal epistemologies, 178
personal knowledge, 7, 94–95
popularization
    of science, 135
possible worlds, 35, 41
power
    and knowledge, 171
practices, 174, 180
pragmatics, 55
    epistemic, 239–244
precision, 257
predicate logic, 37
prejudices, 3, 8, 103–104
presupposition, 285–290
    and accommodation, 287
    epistemic, 288
    linguistic, 286, 288
    logical definition of, 285
    psychological account of, 286
prior knowledge, 68, 74
proposition, 29
propositional attitude, 29, 35
propositions, 35–37
prototypes, 63, 86
psycholinguistics, 57, 58
psychology of discourse processing, 57
public opinion, 101–103

questions, 202, 243

racism, 45, 59, 258
racist propaganda, 283
readers, 2, 3, 4, 6, 7

reading ability, 75
reality monitoring, 42
reasoning, 27
referential local coherence, 249
relativism, 33, 170
relativity
    of knowledge, 6
relevance, 54
reliability, 3, 33–34
    of discourse, 153
religion, 189
Rhetorical Structure Theory, 290

Saddam Hussein, 17, 20, 26, 38, 197, 284
schemas, 63
schematic structure, 58
science popularization, 135
Self, 51, 83, 84
self-knowledge, 30
semantic macrostructures, 52, 244–247
Semantic Memory, 62, 85–88
semantics, 35
    discourse, 244–306
    minimalist, 31
semiotics, 9
sequencing, 291
    of discourse, 251
shared cognition, 93
sharing social beliefs, 114–120
situated practice, 175
situation
    communicative, 54
situation models, 51–53, 239
situations, 40, 49
social beliefs, 93, 94–111
    and knowledge, 106–111
    normalization of, 115
    sharing, 114–120
social cognition, 8, 90–138
    and knowledge, 319–320
    the system of, 95
social context, 227
social epistemology, 141
social groups, 111–113
social identity theory, 93
social psychology, 7–8, 90–138
social representations, 93, 104–106
societal psychology, 92
society
    and cognition, 147
    and knowledge, 139–167, 320–323
    and mental models, 143–145
sociocultural knowledge, 145–147
sociolinguistics, 57

sociology, 8
sociology of knowledge, 4, 8, 27, 122, 140,
    141, 142, 146, 152, 154, 159, 165, 171,
    185, 320, 321, 327, 329, 357, 358, 369,
    378, 382, 385
sources
    of knowledge, 259
speaker meaning, 52
speech acts
    epistemic, 240
stance
    epistemic, 259, 275
statements, 35
stereotypes, 3, 8, 103–104
storytelling, 51, 233
strategies of learning, 79
structures of local knowledge, 186–191
subjectivity, 275–280
subjects, experimental, 73
Sun, 139, 140, 142, 143, 144, 145, 150,
    152, 153, 154, 158, 163, 164, 165,
    166, 249, 254, 283, 285, 290, 291,
    293, 299
surface structure
    of knowledge, 306–307

tacit knowledge, 281
territory of information, 271
testimony, 22
text grammar, 10
textbooks, 136
Theory of Mind, 120, 200, 224
topic, 295–303
topic knowledge, 67
topics
    discourse, 244–247
topics of talk
    and age, 128
    constraints on, 130
    gender differences, 126–128
    and knowledge acquisition, 126
    Traditional Ecological Knowledge, 184
triangulating discourse, cognition and
    society, 223
truth, 6, 12, 30, 32

utopias, 97

vagueness, 257

widespread beliefs, 94
Wikipedia, 45, 59
Working Memory, 63, 82–83
    Long-Term, 83